Psychology and Crime

Crime is an expensive aspect of society, and each year huge amounts of public money are spent on the courts, police, probation services and prisons, while the human cost in terms of pain, fear and loss is incalculable.

Psychology and Crime comprehensively covers the vital role of psychological theories and methods in understanding and managing criminal behaviour. It analyses in depth the application of psychological findings to a range of serious crimes such as arson, violent crime and sexual crime. It examines the use of psychology by the police and the courts and discusses the role of psychology in crime reduction strategies.

Written by a leading authority on the subject and informed by over twenty years of teaching experience, the new edition of this successful text has been thoroughly revised and updated to take account of the most recent research in the field. New features also include:

- expansive coverage of the development of criminal behaviour
- chapter summaries and end-of-chapter discussion points
- text boxes throughout highlighting key issues, debates and brief histories
- supplementary online resources at www.routledge.com/cw/hollin.

Psychology and Crime is an essential introduction and reference for undergraduate and postgraduate students in psychology, criminology, sociology and related subjects. It also represents an invaluable resource for professional training courses and anyone planning a career in the criminal justice system.

Clive R. Hollin is Professor of Criminological Psychology in the School of Psychology at the University of Leicester, UK. Alongside his various university appointments, he has worked as a psychologist in prisons, the Youth Treatment Service, special hospitals and regional secure units. In 1998, he received the Senior Award for Distinguished Contribution to the Field of Legal, Criminological and Forensic Psychology from the British Psychological Society.

Psychology and Crime

An introduction to criminological psychology

Second edition

Clive R. Hollin

Routledge
Taylor & Francis Group

LONDON AND NEW YORK

Second edition published 2013
by Routledge
27 Church Road, Hove, East Sussex BN3 2FA

Simultaneously published in the USA and Canada
by Routledge
711 Third Avenue, New York, NY 10017

Routledge is an imprint of the Taylor & Francis Group, an informa business

First edition published by Routledge 1989

British Library Cataloguing in Publication Data
A catalogue record for this book is available from the British Library

Library of Congress Cataloging in Publication Data
Hollin, Clive R.
  Psychology and Crime : An Introduction to Criminological Psychology /
Clive R. Hollin. — Second Edition.
    pages cm
  First published 1989 by Routledge.
  Includes bibliographical references and index.
  ISBN 978-0-415-49703-9 (hbk.) — ISBN 978-0-415-49702-2 (pbk.) —
ISBN 978-0-203-07428-2 (ebk.) (print) 1. Criminal psychology. I. Title.
  HV6080.H64 2013
  364.3—dc23   2012026857

ISBN: 978-0-415-49703-9 (hbk)
ISBN: 978-0-415-49702-2 (pbk)
ISBN: 978-0-203-07428-2 (ebk)

Typeset in Times New Roman
by Cenveo Publisher Services

MIX
Paper from
responsible sources
FSC® C013604

Printed and bound by CPI Group (UK) Ltd, Croydon, CR0 4YY

For Gregory, again

Contents

Preface

It has been a distinctly odd experience writing this book. The first edition of *Psychology and Crime*, published in 1989 and written during 1987–8, was my first single-authored book published near the start of my academic career. (It's hard to believe now but I actually wrote the first draft by hand: I still have the seven A4 pads, one per chapter.) The first edition was primarily written because there were no suitable books available for my undergraduate course on criminal behaviour. *Psychology and Crime* was more successful than I might have dared hope: it remains in print after 23 years, has been reprinted 15 times, and has sold more than 16,000 copies. As the years ticked by, I resisted several requests from the publishers for a new edition because, I reckoned, if it continues to sell then why change it? However, as I drew close to the end of my career, I increasingly felt that a rewrite of my first book would be an appropriate closing of the circle. A contract was signed and I set to work.

As I began work on this second edition several revelations hit home. First, it was not going to be as straightforward a task as I'd envisaged in simply updating the original text. In the original Preface I made the comment that 'During the writing it quickly became apparent that it was impossible to cover everything that might justifiably be called criminological psychology'. Well, the exponential growth in 'everything' since the 1980s is staggering: as well as several general texts from both sides of the Atlantic on the topic of psychology, crime and law, there has been an explosion in the number of specialist books and journals on the market. Yet further, the Internet provides an impossible amount of information: I have just typed 'psychology and crime' in Google Scholar and have been informed that there are 'about 860,000 hits'! As my son would say at this point, 'good luck with that'.

The second revelation, which came as a genuine surprise, was that my writing style had changed significantly over the years. I don't know whether a change in style over time is common among writers but I was taken aback at how even the basics of my writing, such as the way sentences were structured, had changed significantly. I spent (read: lost) a great deal of time trying to rework the original text but in the end admitted defeat and accepted that I'd have to start again as if writing a brand new book. There were some passages from the original that I could work with but basically this is a new book. Indeed, the content and structure of the book has changed. In the original I left out for reasons of space material on the development of criminal behaviour. Although I later wrote another book published in 1992, *Criminal Behaviour: A Psychological Explanation to Explanation and Prevention*, that covered the material omitted from *Psychology and Crime*, I always felt the two books were really one. Well, now they are.

My thinking about what the book was trying to achieve has also shifted. Given the impossible amount of available material, I came to see the rewrite as a resource that would provide information but also direct readers to other useful and informative sources. In order to be resourceful, I have included a large number of academic references, suggested further reading, and listed various websites. The references cited were all available at the end of 2011, which is my cut-off point for new material: there are several 2012 references cited but these are papers which were available electronically at the pre-publication stage before the end of 2011 so the full 2012 reference is given for the sake of completeness. The addresses of various Internet sites are also given: I've tried to include official government sites and those from large organisations as not only do they contain masses of information, they will probably be long-lived. In the ephemeral world of the Internet, sites will come and go but it's not hard to find more! I also found myself becoming aware that I was using material from a range of countries, partly to inform the text in terms of international comparisons, partly because I was drawing on reports written from a local perspective which it made sense to identify, and partly because some empirical findings made better sense when placed in a geographical context. Thus, there's lots of 'a study conducted in Sweden' and 'an American survey', and so on. I've also tried (and probably failed) to be precise about divisions within the UK as they affect the text. Finally, I've imported a quirk I introduced into my teaching a little while ago. One of the problems with academic psychology, and there are many, is that the subject matter can ironically seem rather divorced from real life. To help students regain that connection I've used 'The Lighter Side' to suggest films and novels that I know well and illustrate a theme relevant to the chapter. I appreciate that others will have their own favourites but these are mine! In the same vein, I've also included some discussions of famous cases and controversial issues such as capital punishment.

There have been several strong influences on my academic thinking over the years. The most enduring figure, although he won't know it, is John Radford who was one of my PhD supervisors many moons ago. John would return copies of my draft PhD chapters with the kindest of comments but basically suggesting that I needed to sort out my writing. I recall that it dawned on me at the time that writing has to be taken very seriously: I don't mean that it has necessarily to be serious but that it has to be, well, readable. What makes good writing is highly subjective but, for me, it should use plain English, follow the rules of grammar, and be comprehensible to the intended readership. I try, John, I really do try.

The two people who had the most effect on my academic thinking, Arnie Goldstein and Don Andrews, are both no longer with us. They say you should never meet your heroes but I did meet both of them several times and came to know them quite well. Arnie was an absolute role model for an applied psychologist: he knew exactly what he was trying to achieve (read his books) and had the ability to draw together the right people to make things happen. He wrote like a dream (read his books!) and with his faded New York accent he was an outstanding and humorous speaker, whether to a conference with hundreds in the audience or to a small workshop with a dozen people present, he was always engaging and informative.

Don Andrews will, I think, be looked back upon as one of the group of Canadian psychologists who had a profound effect on the way rehabilitative services for offenders are designed and implemented. A prolific researcher, he mixed empirical academic papers with commentary papers, reviews, and text books, his applied edge is seen in his development of the Level of Service Inventory, a much used measure of risk and need to inform practice with offenders. He was learned and forthright in demolishing any opposition to his views: I once heard his text with James Bonta, *The Psychology of Criminal Conduct*, described as a 'book with an attitude'. I think Don would have quite liked that description. Like Arnie, Don was always good value as a conference speaker: I heard him speak, always the bushy beard and faded denim jacket, several times and always came away feeling that what he said was important – we can reduce reoffending if we do the right things!

I have been fortunate over the years in working with several outstanding colleagues (and several less so but we'll brush over that one). I collaborated over a long period with Kevin Howells to produce a string of books and papers, Mary McMurran was a partner in crime for longer, I suspect, than we both care to remember, and James McGuire is quite simply an exceptional psychologist. In The Leicester Group, as we fondly call ourselves, Emma Palmer and Ruth Hatcher are close colleagues (as was Charlotte Bilby before she moved north to a better place) who occasionally prove that the whole can be greater than the sum of the parts. It is something of a cliché to say one learns from one's students but nonetheless I have had the pleasure of working with and learning from some excellent doctoral students. They each have their own special memories for me but for various reasons I particularly prize having worked with: Rebecca Horn who has gone on to do some wonderful applied work, Clive Long who still just keeps publishing and publishing, Ruth Mann who remained undaunted by every demand a PhD threw at her, Adam Carter who refused to be beaten by anything, and Glen Thomas who triumphantly battled every page of the way.

Finally, there's my family who provide the base from which everything is possible. My partner in life, Felicity Schofield, is the same as in the Preface first time around: she deserves special mention for listening patiently as I repeatedly explained at length that I was never going to write another (*expletive deleted*) book again once this (*expletive deleted*) one was finished. In the last Preface I also mentioned that our second child, Kate, had just arrived as I finished writing. Well, no more children to report and the two we have are now big people with their own lives and careers. Among many parental high spots are publishing* with my son, Gregory, and seeing Kate, who has the talent to be anything she wants to be in life, first act on stage and then go on to make such a success of her teaching career.

So now it's done and here it is, the second edition. I hope it's useful and encourages at least a few readers to want to take up the study of crime. As for me, well that's all folks as I look forward to spending more time in the garden. Although, having said that, I've had a really good idea for another, shorter, book. Just one more time, perhaps?

Clive R. Hollin
Leicester, 2012

---

*Hollin, G. J. S., & Hollin, C. R. (2009). Psychology in its place: Personal reflections on the state we're in. *Psychology Teaching Review, 15*, 55–60.

1 Psychology and crime

One of the more enjoyable aspects of studying crime is that it entails reading and understanding theory and research from a wide range of disciplines. This academic range is exemplified by the membership of the Forensic Research Centre at the University of Leicester, which includes a range of university departments including archaeology, chemistry, criminology, economics, engineering, geography, geology, health sciences, law, pathology, psychiatry, and psychology. This list could reasonably be augmented by genetics, economics, philosophy, and sociology; doubtless there are other specialities that could also be added. Given this list of interested parties, it should be clear already that psychology alone is not going to explain crime in its many forms and guises. It follows that psychology is not going to provide all the answers to the question of how to manage and reduce crime. Nonetheless, given that a great deal of crime does involve people, then it can be argued that an understanding of crime should include at least some reference to psychology.

An attempt to formulate an understanding of crime is not an empty academic exercise, there are many important real-life considerations to take into account. For example, reported crimes need to be investigated, those accused of committing crimes are prosecuted and tried, victims may need support, and legal sanctions are delivered to the guilty. In these and many other crime-related matters, psychological theory and research can be applied to make a contribution to managing the realities of crime and the criminal justice system. Thus, the emphasis in this book will be on the *contribution* that psychology can make to the study of crime and, importantly, to its management. However, before moving to the various topics encompassed within the study of psychology and crime, there are three basic issues to consider, in order to set the scene for what follows. What is psychology? What is crime and criminology? What is the relationship between psychology, criminology, and crime?

What is psychology?

The *Oxford Dictionary of Psychology* (Colman, 2003) offers the following definition of psychology: 'The study of the nature, functions, and phenomena of behaviour and mental experience'. As the *Oxford Dictionary* acknowledges, this deceptively simple definition masks a tangle of complexity. Introductory psychology texts, such as Eysenck (2000), illustrate the range and scope of contemporary psychology, including such diverse topics as child development, occupational selection, social interaction, brain functioning, learning, psychotherapy, and the list goes on. Overall, it is reasonable to conclude that psychology is the study of people (although some psychologists study animals).

The study of people can be approached from two broad perspectives: first, how do we each function as an individual? And second, how do we interact with each other? The psychology of the individual may be concerned with cognitive functioning, such as perception, memory, thinking, and learning; or with the development of qualities such as intelligence, creativity, and personality; or with the relationship between biological and psychological functioning. The study of interactions between people, generally referred to as social psychology, may encompass groupings such as families or people at work, or teams that play sport; the formation of friendships; and cross-cultural differences in social functioning. Of course, individual and social functioning can go awry, leading some psychologists to study abnormal psychology (or *psychopathology*), which may include conditions such as schizophrenia and depression, or childhood problems, or personality disorder.

There are several specialist areas of applied psychology, mostly developed from the mainstream areas of enquiry and generally studied at postgraduate level before leading to professional practice. Alongside criminological psychology, educational and child psychology is concerned with psychological aspects of teaching, children's learning, and the educational system. Occupational and organisational psychology are concerned with the application of psychological theory and expertise to the recruitment and training of staff, organisational structures and systems, leadership and management, and so forth. There are a cluster of specialities to do with improving psychological (clinical psychology and counselling psychology) and physical (health psychology) well-being, as well as sports psychology that, unsurprisingly, is concerned with exercise and sport.

Psychological theory

Psychology is rich in theories. A broad theoretical distinction is neatly illustrated by the titles of two texts, *Psychology: The Study of Mental Life* (Miller, 1969), as opposed to *Science and Human Behaviour* (Skinner, 1953). Is psychology concerned with our 'interior' world or should it focus on what we do? In other words, do we emphasise mind or behaviour? The notion of 'mind' and the associated philosophical 'mind-body problem' (Gregory, 1987) is central to theories of psychology and, as will be seen, is important in how we understand and, as a society, respond to criminal behaviour.

In classical Cartesian dualism, as expounded by René Descartes (1596–1650), the mind and body are separate both in substance and in operation. In contrast to this *mentalist* tradition, with many shades between the two, there are *materialistic* views of the mind. One materialistic position, which Gregory refers to as the *peripheralist* view – often associated with behaviourism, itself a complex web (O'Donohue & Kitchner, 1999) – holds that internal or 'private' events are to be understood as elements of behaviour and not afforded any causal status over our actions. Another materialistic stance, which Gregory calls the *centralist* view, takes mental activity to be identified with biological processes in the central nervous system. In psychology, the centralist view is currently fashionable, as can be seen, for example, with cognitive neuroscience.

The history of psychology shows the rise and fall of variations of mentalist and materialistic theories (Richards, 1996). At the turn of the 20th century, Sigmund Freud (1856–1939) devised an elaborate mentalist theory, which gave rise to psychoanalysis, involving psychic energies, or *psychodynamic* forces, driving our actions at both the conscious and unconscious level (Kline, 1984; Storr, 1989). On the other hand, the American John B. Watson (1878–1958) argued that behaviour should be the focus of psychological enquiry. The advent of behaviourism – to be followed by social learning theory (Bandura, 1977) – as a mainstream approach within psychology can be directly traced to Watson's influence. The cognitive revolution in psychology (Baars, 1967) saw psychologists turn to the study of attention, memory, reasoning, and so on. The search for the biological correlates of cognition has more recently seen the emergence of cognitive neuroscience.

The psychodynamic tradition

The greatest figure associated with this approach is, of course, Sigmund Freud who, although medically trained, had a profound influence on the nascent psychology of his day. Indeed, Freud's theory and its subsequent growth remains a major force in some areas of contemporary psychology and psychiatry. Freud was a prolific writer. The (translated) standard edition of his complete works runs to 24 volumes as compiled over several years by Strachey, Strachey and Tyson; and there are two museums given to Freud's memory (see Box 1.1).

Freud's theory is concerned with the structure of the mind, placing it squarely in the mentalist tradition. In particular, Freud sought to explain different levels of consciousness. Freud suggested that there are three levels of consciousness: first, the *conscious* level that includes the mental events which we are aware of experiencing at a given time; second, the *preconscious* level that concerns what we could bring to mind if we were prompted; third, the *unconscious*, which is the part of the mind that we are unaware of and unable to access at will. The *unconscious* is where we keep all those nasty and unpleasant memories and desires that, should they enter consciousness (as they sometimes do in dreams), would cause us extreme anxiety.

In his later work, Freud introduced the notion of three distinct mental structures, the *id*, the *ego*, and the *superego*. The id is the source of mental energy, striving to release energy into the mental system. The id seeks to maximise pleasure and to avoid pain and so is said to operate according to the *pleasure principle*. The superego strives for perfection in meeting the moral standards we seek to maintain. The ego seeks to perform a balancing act between the id and superego: operating according to the *reality principle*, the ego seeks to curb the urges (including sexual urges) for instant gratification demanded by the id, and to moderate the restrictions and constraints of the perfection-seeking superego. Influenced, perhaps, by the physical and engineering sciences of his day, Freud offered a view of the mind that is analogous to a closed mechanical system in which energy is moved from one part of the system to another, with the safety valves of defence mechanisms along the way, to maintain a steady functioning equilibrium.

Box 1.1   The Freud museums

There are two Freud museums, one in London and one in Vienna. The London museum is at 20 Maresfield Gardens, London NW3 5SX, which became the home of Sigmund Freud and his family in 1938 when they escaped the Nazi occupation of Austria. As can see seen from the museum's website (www.freud.org.uk), which has a fantastic archive of photographs of Freud and his relatives and of great figures from the history of psychoanalysis, there is a wealth of material on show at the museum.

The Freud museum at Berggasse 19, Vienna 1090 (www.freud-museum.at/cms) is situated in Freud's apartment and office where he both worked and lived with his family for 47 years until fleeing from the Nazis in 1938. The museum has an exhibition documenting Freud's life and work including the original furnishings, articles that Freud used on a daily basis and pieces from Freud's collection gathered over the years. I can say that when I visited it was an unexpectedly moving experience: being so close to the history of one's field was rather humbling.

Freud's complex ideas inspired some of the most famous names in the history of psychology including, among others, post-Freudians such as Carl Jung (1875–1961), Alfred Adler (1870–1937), Erik Erikson (1902–94), Karen Horney (1885–1952), Harry Stack Sullivan (1892–1949), and Freud's daughter, Anna Freud (1895–1982). The ideas and theories that flowed from Freud's theory (Brown, 1961) have been and continue to be highly influential in mainstream psychology and other disciplines. Psychoanalysis specifically and psychodynamic therapies generally are practised by many practitioners all over the world from a range of professional backgrounds. Indeed, Freud's ideas have permeated the art, drama, literature and cinema of Western culture. There are many, many examples but Freud's influence is perhaps at its most obvious in Hitchcock's *Spellbound* (1945). Freud also makes a guest appearance alongside Sherlock Holmes in *The Seven-Per-Cent Solution*, a novel by Nicholas Meyer published 1974, which became a film in 1976, written in the style of a Sherlock Holmes adventure. Freud's guest appearances in novels continued when in 2006 he was a character in *The Interpretation of Murder* by Jed Rubenfeld.

The behavioural tradition

The materialistic approach advocated by Watson, strongly influenced by the work of the physiologist and Nobel Prize winner Ivan Pavlov (1849–1936), is best seen in his paper *Psychology as the Behaviorist Views It*, published in 1913. This paper presents Watson's manifesto for the discipline (see Morris & Todd, 1999) and set in train a line of thinking and empirical research that includes contributions from major figures such as Edward Thorndike (1874–1949), Edward Tolman (1886–1959) and Clark Hull (1884–1952). The culmination of this behavioural endeavour is to be found in the work of Burrhus F. Skinner (1904–90), often referred to as *radical behaviourism* (Bjork, 1993; Ringen, 1999; Skinner, 1953, 1974, 1985).

The emphasis in Skinner's behaviourism is on understanding the role of environmental, rather than internal or 'private', events in bringing about behaviour (Skinner, 1974, 1985). This is not to say that Skinner and other behaviourists deny the existence of private events, rather such phenomena are not afforded a causal status in explaining behaviour.

Theoretical developments, as exemplified by the work of Albert Bandura, saw behaviourism evolve into social learning theory (Bandura, 1977, 1986), then into social cognitive theory (Bandura, 2001). The particular contribution of social learning theory was to attempt to make explicit the place of thought and emotion within a behavioural position. As research into cognition grew in scope so mentalist accounts of human action became more sophisticated and an explicit *cognitive* psychology emerged.

Cognitive psychology

If behaviourism was concerned with observable behaviour, what is the focus of cognitive psychology? Well, cognition obviously, but how can we be more precise? The dictionary definition for *cognition* is: 'The mental activities involved in acquiring and processing information' (Colman, 2003: 140). This definition is in sympathy with M. W. Eysenck's view that 'The fundamental assumption [of the cognitive approach] is that human cognition depends on an information-processing system' (Eysenck, 2000: 31). The constituents of such an information-processing system are held to have their basis in both biological and psychological functioning.

At a biological level, the autonomic and central nervous system play a part in cognitive processes such as attention, memory, language, and reasoning. The search for a connection between biological, particularly neurological, and psychological functioning is an enterprise that stretches some way back in time.

The practice of *phrenology*, developed in the 19th century from the theories of the Viennese physician Franz Joseph Gall (1758–1828), held that an individual's personality traits could be determined by 'reading' the contours of their skull. The basis of Gall's theory was that the brain is the organ of the mind that, in turn, is composed of many distinct faculties. Each of the mind's faculties occupies a different place in the brain so that, as the shape of the skull is (supposedly) determined by the shape of the brain, the surface of the skull may be 'read' to give a picture of an individual's psychological capacity. While popular for some time (e.g., Stocker, 1904), it is now clear that there is no scientific basis to the claims of phrenology. However, the basic principle underlying Gall's theories – that psychological functioning could be related to brain activity and, indeed, to localised areas of activity within the brain – was perceptive and is now widely accepted.

The term *cognitive neuroscience* describes the amalgam of neuroscience, neurology, and cognitive science that is Gall's modern-day descendant. The fast pace of technological advance, as seen with the advent of magnetic resonance imaging (MRI), has allowed this field to advance rapidly (e.g., Gazzaniga, Ivry, & Mangun, 2002). As seen in the subtitle of Gazzaniga et al.'s text, cognitive neuroscience's stance as 'the biology of the mind' places it squarely within a mentalist tradition.

In addition to aspects of cognition such as perception and memory, there is also *social* cognition, which refers to how we think about ourselves and other people. Social cognition incorporates psychological processes such as attribution, social stereotypes, prejudice, schemas, and affect and cognition (Fiske & Taylor, 1991). Neuroscience has expanded its boundaries in this direction with the emergence of social neuroscience and social cognitive neuroscience. However, as Vul, Harris, Winkielman, and Pashler (in press) argue, the way in which researchers make associations between social behaviour and brain activity is less than straightforward. As Vul et al. explain, studies frequently rely on correlations between measures of brain activation, generally gathered using functional magnetic resonance imaging (fMRI), a specialised form of MRI scanning, and behavioural and self-reported measures of personality or emotion. The way in which these correlations are calculated and reported can introduce a methodological bias that inflates the magnitude of the relationship between brain activity and social functioning. In an emerging field, such debates about appropriate research strategies are part of the process of the development of theory.

If psychodynamic, behavioural, and cognitive psychology are three of the mainstream theoretical strands within mainstream psychology, then personality theory is the fourth.

Personality theory

Some texts adopt a wide definition of the term 'personality', including all the main psychological approaches – psychodynamic, behavioural, social learning – under the broad umbrella of personality (e.g., Pervin, Cervone, & John, 2005). A more narrow approach, important in the context of theories of criminal behaviour, is to consider personality within the specific context of *trait* theory. Trait theory owes much to figures such as Gordon W. Allport (1897–1967), Raymond B. Cattell (1905–98), and Hans J. Eysenck (1916–97).

A trait may be thought of as an individual's disposition to think and behave in a consistent manner across different settings. Thus, a person who displays a domineering personality trait may well be domineering at work, in their family life, with their friends, and so on. Eysenck's theory suggests that there are two main personality traits, themselves products of genetic influence and environmental conditioning, namely *extraversion* and *neuroticism* (Eysenck, 1970). In Eysenck's theory, a trait is conceived of as a continuum ranging from high to low, thereby giving extraversion-introversion and unstable (high) neuroticism-stable (low) neuroticism. In Eysenck's theory, these main traits are actually higher order factors, themselves composed of other traits and arranged in a hierarchical fashion. For example, extraversion is composed of several linked traits such as being highly active, sociable, and sensation-seeking; the introverted person would exhibit low levels of these traits. At a basic level, traits such as being sociable are composed of habitual responses, such as enjoying meeting people, which in turn are composed of specific responses.

All theories have their day and as thinking and research progresses so new theories are formed. An emerging theoretical approach within Psychology has its roots in Charles Darwin's (1809–82) theory of evolution.

Evolutionary psychology

The emergence of evolutionary explanations of human social behaviour can be traced the influential work of the American biologist Edward O. Wilson. Wilson's starting point is clearly stated in the Preface to the 2nd edition of *Sociobiology* (Wilson, 1975):

> Where cognitive neuroscience aims to explain *how* the brains of animals and humans work, and genetics how heredity works, evolutionary biology aims to explain *why* brains work, or more precisely, in light of natural selection theory, what adaptations if any led to the assembly of their respective parts and processes.
>
> (Wilson, 2000: vii)

The crux of Wilson's argument is that in same way that evolution shapes the physical characteristics of a species, so those same evolutionary forces account for social behaviour. Wilson's starting point in the development of his theories was his work on the social behaviour and social organisation of ants, remarkable insects that are eminently successful in controlling and colonising their environment (Wilson, 1971). The success of ants, Wilson argued, could be explained through the evolution of social structures that allow them to adapt efficiently to their environment. From this principle, Wilson proposed that through a blend of our understanding of population biology and social behaviour, a new area of biological enquiry could emerge. This new area Wilson called *sociobiology* (Wilson, 1975).

Wilson's next step was to apply the ideas developed from his study of ants to social organisation in other species, including humans. Thus, the starting point for sociobiology lies in the proposition that human social behaviour, as with other species, has a large hereditary component (Wilson, 1978). Further, Wilson maintained, human social behaviour, like other characteristics of a species, is subject to the laws of evolution. If these two propositions are accurate, then applying the laws of evolution to human social behaviour will produce a new understanding of our society and what it is to be human.

The ideas underpinning sociobiology in the application of evolutionary theory to understanding social structures and processes has led to a great deal of public and academic debate (Brown, 1999; Dawkins, 1976, 2006; Dennett, 1995; McGarr & Rose, 2006). In the public domain, this debate is evident, for example, in the implications of evolutionary theory for topics such as how we understand religious belief and how religion is taught in schools.

The application of Darwin's theory of evolution to human social behaviour attempts to blend evolutionary and psychological theory. Now, the idea that some aspects of human functioning are innate is not remarkable: for example, (Chomsky, 1975) advocated that the propensity for language acquisition is innate, enabling the child rapidly to acquire language and to communicate with others in its immediate environment. Similarly, Seligman (1971) advanced the concept of *preparedness* to explain why some phobias are more easily acquired and hence more frequently found than others. Seligman suggested that some phobias – several associated with animals, such as spiders (arachnophobia) and snakes (ophidiophobia), and some associated with personal survival, as with fear of heights (acrophobia) and loud noises (phonophobia or ligyrophobia) – are learned more readily than phobias that involve a less 'natural' feature of the environment. While it is not difficult to see why it makes sense to be prepared to be afraid of snakes, the same cannot be said of fear of numbers, as seen with the fear of the number 13 (triskaidekaphobia) and of 666 (hexakosioihexekontahexaphobia), or fear of mirrors and seeing one's own reflection (eisoptrophobia). Seligman suggests that our evolutionary history has prepared us to learn to fear environmental threats as an adaptive human trait in order to survive and so reproduce. In other cases, as with numbers, clearly some other level of explanation is necessary. This next level of explanation for the acquisition and maintenance of phobias may involve learning, personality or cognition.

If some human behaviours are innate then it is a short step to ask how did that innate propensity arise? A ready answer to that question, following E. O. Wilson, is 'through the process of evolution'.

The publication of *The Adapted Mind: Evolutionary Psychology and the Generation of Culture* (Barkow, Cosmides, & Tooby, 1992) is a landmark text that draws together evolutionary and psychological theory and research to produce an account of various human activities including social cooperation, sexual attraction, and language. Thus, evolutionary psychologists began to move towards the position that evolution has resulted in humans acquiring specific cognitive mechanisms that have the function of solving the problems we faced in adapting to the environment. This approach can be applied to broad areas of psychology, as with evolutionary social psychology and evolutionary developmental psychology, or to more specific topics such as fear and gender roles.

The development of evolutionary psychology led Buss (1995) to declare that it is a new paradigm for psychology, a new way of approaching the study of humans and understanding our place in the world. There is now a range of texts on the topic of evolutionary psychology as it enters the mainstream of psychological theory (Buss, 1999, 2005, 2008; Dunbar & Barrett, 2007; Dunbar, Barrett, & Lycett, 2005).

Evolutionary psychology has attracted criticisms both from within psychology (Panksepp & Panksepp, 2000) and from cognate disciplines such as sociology (Jackson & Rees, 2007). As Conway and Schaller (2002: 152) note: 'Novel perspectives almost always meet some sort of skeptical resistance, and even the most useful theoretical ideas must sometimes – like new kids in school – endure harsh challenges and critical rebukes before they are eventually accepted on the intellectual playground'. Conway and Schaller's point is true but it is also the case that there may be struggles between disciplines in grasping the basic concepts and shared understandings of another discipline.

In the context of the interactions between social scientists and biologists, Dingwall, Nerlich, and Hillyard (2003: 641) make some basic points: with regard to biologists they comment that 'Biologists must recognize that objects in the natural and social world are fundamentally different. The realism that they take as a self-evident part of molecular biology cannot be sustained in sociological research'. They continue: 'It is equally important for social scientists to take biology more seriously. The dismissive fashion in which social scientists have treated it since World War II does not do justice to the scale and subtlety of the body of work involved' (641).

Applying theory

The theoretical positions outlined above, mentalist and materialistic alike, can be applied to produce an account of criminal behaviour. It is self-evident that different theories will produce different accounts of criminal behaviour. Is a crime committed because the individual acts rationally of their own free will? Does a crime take place because environmental influences, such as parents or peer group, determined that the behaviour would be inevitable? What role, if any, do biological factors play in criminal behaviour? The application of theory leads to practice: if a criminal act is seen to be a purposeful act of free will, then the way society responds to crime may be different if the same act is understood as one that is determined by biological or environmental factors.

The application of psychological theories to explaining criminal behaviour, along with their implications for policy and practice, will be discussed in due course. However, in considering the application of psychology to the phenomenon of crime, we now move to a brief overview of crime and criminology. We begin with the most basic question of all: 'what is crime?'

What is crime?

The straightforward answer, which has much to recommend it, to the question 'what is crime?' has been provided by Williams (1955: 21): 'A crime is an act that is capable of being followed by criminal proceedings, having one of the types of outcome (punishment, etc.) known to follow these proceedings'. There are three essential points to draw from Williams' statement: (1) a crime is an act that is deemed to be 'criminal' in law; (2) there are criminal proceedings that may follow the act to determine if there has been a breach of criminal law and to identify those who are guilty of the crime; and (3) there is a formal outcome following those proceedings.

The development of a code of law and a system to maintain and enforce that law is a substantial task: in contemporary society, the arrangement that serves this purpose is called the *criminal justice system*. The study of the theory, philosophy, and nature of law, legal systems, and legal institutions is called *jurisprudence* and is a speciality in its own right (Bix, 2006). The issues of concern to jurisprudence have been discussed for centuries: they were as evident in ancient Greece as they are today and are seen across cultures in the work of Western academics and Islamic scholars. It is also the case that some of the questions raised by jurisprudence – such as the relationship between morality and law, and the use of punishment – spill into social science and psychology as will be seen in due course.

However, to return to the three elements within Hall's definition of a crime, the first point to note is that a crime is an act. This apparently simple statement masks a web of complexity!

A crime is an act

For legal purposes, an act may generally take one of three forms: (1) an act of commission; (2) an act of omission; or (3) an act of possession.

Commission: Acts of commission are acts in which some definite action is taken: examples of this type of criminal act include taking someone's property, hitting another person, or planting a bomb.

Omission: Not to act when expected to can be criminal. A failure to act is seen, for example, when those with a duty of care fail to take action when it is required. A failure in a duty to care may be evident when parents neglect to take care of their children, or when health professionals fail in their professional obligations. Similarly, a failure to enact a safety procedure, so endangering others, when legally required can be a criminal offence.

Possession: The possession of certain items can, in law, constitute an unlawful act. This type of crime is most frequently seen in cases of possession of prohibited drugs and possession of firearms.

The act of committing a crime, the 'guilty act' or *actus reus*, can be thought of as the 'outer' element of a crime. However, for most crimes the outer element must be go together with an 'inner' element in that the guilty act, the *actus reus*, must be accompanied by the intent of a guilty mind, the *mens rea*. In common law, the combination of *actus reus* and *mens rea* produces criminal liability. The principle that applies here is '*Actus non facit reum nisi mens sit rea*', that is, 'an act does not make a person guilty unless (their) mind is also guilty'. In order for an individual to be liable for a crime they must have committed an act forbidden by law – an act cannot be a crime unless specifically and explicitly prohibited by law – and they must have intended to do so. Therefore, to establish an individual's guilt for a specific crime, it is necessary to provide proof of fault, responsibility, or blameworthiness for both the behaviour and the intent of the accused.

However, as is often the case in the complexities of law, there are exceptions to this rule as with crimes, called *crimes of strict-liability*, where ignorance of the law is not a defence. Strict liability can be seen in the law relating to some traffic offences: if a person is charged with speeding it is irrelevant for the purposes of law whether or not they knew they were exceeding the speed limit, it is only necessary to prove that the person who is charged with speeding was driving the vehicle at a speed in excess of the speed limit. Outside of criminal law, liability may also be found in health and safety regulations where, for example, it is the responsibility of employers to safeguard the well-being of their employees and the public. To be unaware of health and safety responsibilities is not a defence should an incident occur.

Crimes of strict liability apart, there are instances in law when *mens rea* does not apply. In other words, there are circumstances when the law takes the view that the individual does not have the mental capacity to act with intent and so be deemed to be responsible for their actions. There are three instances in which an individual's actions might be defended on the basis that they were not acting with intent: these are *infancy*, *insanity*, and *automatism*.

Infancy: Can a child commit a crime? It is, of course, the case that children can carry out acts, sometimes serious acts, that are forbidden by law, but can it be said a child acted with criminal intent? This question is highly relevant to psychology. At what age do children

---

Box 1.2 International variations in the age of criminal responsibility

In England and Wales and Northern Ireland the age of responsibility is 10 years but in Scotland it is 8 years.
- In the Netherlands it is 12 years.
- In the Nordic countries of Demark, Finland, Norway and Sweden it is 15 years.
- In Belgium it is 18 years.
- In the USA, the age varies across different states, most commonly between 16 and 18 years (Maher, 2005).

have the intellectual capacity to become responsible for their actions? Is there a specific age at which *mens rea* can be said to be applicable? Further, as children do not have the same levels of cognitive functioning as adults, is it fair to apply criminal law in the same way to adults and children? Should children be punished in the same way as adults?

In most jurisdictions, a distinction is made in law between children and adults through the concept of an *age of criminal responsibility*. There is no agreement across different legal systems as to the age at which a child should be held legally responsible for their actions (see Box 1.2).

Insanity: If a person above the age of criminal responsibility has acted in a way that is criminal but he or she genuinely has no sense of responsibility for their actions then *mens rea* is absent. In circumstances where the individual cannot be said to have guilty intent with respect to their actions, a criminal trial that may result in punishment is not warranted. Thus, the state may accept that the individual is in need of psychiatric and medical care and so rather than enforcing criminal law the case is subject to mental health law. An individual who is subject to mental health law may be ordered by the court to undertake compulsory treatment, sometimes in conditions of high security. Not all regions of the world have mental health legislation, and there is some variability in the law among those who do.

Automatism: Automatic behaviour is an infrequently found type of human action in which the individual in not conscious of their actions (Arboleda-Flórez, 2002). This type of behaviour is seen in sleepwalking, hypnosis, involuntary reflex responses, or in neurological disorders such as epilepsy. If it can be shown that an individual accused of a crime committed the act in a condition of automatism then *mens rea* would be absent.

Hall's second point raised the spectre of criminal proceedings that follow the crime.

Criminal proceedings

If a society is to have a criminal justice system, then there has to be agreement within that society on what constitutes a crime. As a society codifies the way it defines and responds to crime, so its rules or laws are written down. These laws formally state what is and what is not acceptable and specify the penalties for behaviour that is judged to be criminal. The responsibility for the administration of the law becomes enforceable by the state, as does the administration of the penalties for breaking the law. Blackburn (1993) notes that the earliest known written legal system, inscribed on steel and now held in the Louvre, is the Code of Hammurabi, King of Babylon, which has been dated at around 2200 BC.

The passage of time has seen several types of legal system evolve in different countries and cultures that are variously based on *common law, civil law, religious law* or combinations of the three. In a system based on common law, the law is made by judges who use their learning, knowledge, and understanding of precedent to make a judgment on the evidence and facts presented in court in a given case. In contrast, civil law (sometimes referred to as *Romano-Germanic law*) uses a given set of rules, the *code of law*, which judges apply to the cases that come before them. Thus, in common law, the court's decision for a given case, having considered the evidence, is based on the precedent set by specific cases; in civil law a set of rules is applied to a given case, in light of the evidence, to reach a verdict.

Finally, religious law, as the name implies, is based on religious principles: the Jewish Halaka, the Islamic Sharia, and Christian Canon Law are examples of religious law. Unlike common law and civil law, religious law may be wide-ranging in their concern for how believers are to live their lives generally, rather than being solely concerned with criminal acts.

The interplay of the various arrangements that inform the development of a legal system is evident even within the confines of a small unitary state such as the United Kingdom. The United Kingdom consists of four countries, England, Northern Ireland, Scotland, and Wales, and the relative influences of civil and common law are evident across these countries where is no single legal system. As employed in both England and Wales, English law is based mainly on common law; in Scotland the system is influenced by both common law and Roman law; while common law applies in Northern Ireland but with some differences from English law. A review of the criminal justice system in Northern Ireland was conducted at the turn of the century, making various recommendations for change (Criminal Review Group, 2000).

In England and Wales, the courts are headed by the Supreme Court of Judicature that, for criminal cases, is made up of the Court of Appeal and the Crown Court. The Appellate Committee of The House of Lords is the highest court (for criminal and civil cases) in England, Wales, and Northern Ireland. The status of highest court means that any decision made by the House of Lords is binding on all courts in those jurisdictions.

Legal decision-making

If someone is accused of breaking the law and they deny having done so, then how can their guilt or innocence be established? One way to determine guilt or innocence is to introduce a *trial*, a means by which right can prevail over wrong. There are several forms of trial that have been used over time.

Trial by ordeal is an ancient system that entails the person accused of crime being subjected to some form of highly painful test in order to determine their guilt or innocence. The reasoning behind such a test is that God would miraculously intercede on behalf of the innocent – called *judicium Dei*, a judgment by God in favour of the innocent – so that the blameless would emerge from the trial uninjured, or their injuries would quickly heal, while God would allow the guilty to suffer or to die. The European tradition was for the accused to be tested against fire or water. In ordeal by fire, the accused was required to grasp a red-hot iron or to walk a set distance, usually about nine feet, over red-hot metal. Ordeal by water could entail the accused having to remove a stone from a pot of boiling water (or some other liquid such as boiling oil), drink poisoned water or be submerged in water. The latter type of ordeal, submersion, is perhaps most associated with the witch hunts of the 16th and 17th centuries, where women accused of being witches were securely bound and submerged. Those women innocent of the practice of witchcraft would sink (and probably drown), the guilty women would float and face the consequences. As with trial by ordeal, *trial by combat* was prevalent in medieval Europe in the Middle Ages until about the 16th century. Trial by combat worked on the same principle, *judicium Dei*, as trial by ordeal: those involved in the dispute physically fought each other until one was dead or disabled and the victor won the dispute.

As time passed, so European societies progressed and changed: trial by ordeal and trial by combat fell away and a new process, *trial by jury*, came into use. The idea underpinning trial by jury is that in a given case the facts are heard by members of the community, the *jurors*, so that their values as citizens become part of the trial, diluting the power of state in the legal process. The introduction into English law of a jury drawn from the community was not a new idea, a similar process had existed in ancient Greece, while in England there was precedent in the jury of accusation as found in Anglo-Saxon law. In common law, the jury is responsible for finding the facts: this task entails listening to details of the case, evaluating the evidence, settling on the facts, and arriving at a guilty or not guilty decision in keeping with both the law and the jury instructions as given by the judge. The jury has the task of reaching a verdict of guilty or not guilty; for those found guilty, the sentence is the responsibility of the judge.

Formal outcome

If the outcome of a trial is that the accused is guilty, then the third part of Hall's definition comes into play. There will be a formal outcome, a *sentence*, determined in accordance with the law of the land, to which the guilty person will be subjected. As will be seen in Chapter 8, a sentence can be intended to serve several different purposes, however, the most common purpose is to inflict punishment on the defendant. There are two basic ways to administer punishment (which can occur simultaneously): (1) take away something the individual values and/or (2) impose conditions that the individual dislikes. There are several variations on 'taking away': there may be confiscation of assets, mainly property and money (and arguably children and intangibles such as status); the loss of various degrees of personal freedom ranging from community sanctions, as with probation, to a period of imprisonment; or the ultimate punishment of loss of life through the death penalty. Similarly, there are variations on the theme of 'imposition': the defendant's life can be made unpleasant, to varying degrees, through the curtailment of their liberty using means such as curfew and electronic tagging; or punishment may be delivered through institutional regimes such as 'short, sharp shocks' and boot camps; finally, at the extreme, there are cruel and unusual forms of punishment such as long periods of solitary confinement, corporal punishment (in its various forms), and hard labour.

The myriad of issues and questions raised by Hall's seemingly straightforward definition of crime is now apparent. However, matters become even more complicated when we ask, who decides what constitutes a crime and on what basis and for whose benefit do they decide? What are the justifications for the administration of penalties to law-breakers? To begin to answer these questions we turn to the study of crime.

Crime and criminology

There were, of course, attempts to explain and understand crime long before criminology became established as a discipline in its own right. Just as psychology grew from a heritage of philosophy, physiology, and medicine, so the emergent criminology also had its roots in other disciplines. Indeed, as Hayward (2005: 110) observes: 'Psychology and criminology emerged as distinct disciplines at a very similar historic moment – the latter half of the nineteenth century'. It is interesting to look at how crime was understood before the advent of contemporary criminology.

Early explanations for crime

The earliest explanation of crime, evident across many countries and cultures, lay in seeing the wrongdoer as possessed by spirits and demons of evil intent. If the criminal was possessed, then it followed that casting out the demons was the way to deal with the situation. The consequence of a belief in demonic possession, as discussed above, was to be found in the principle of *judicium Dei* and the practice of trial by ordeal.

Spiritual explanations for crime have fallen by the academic wayside, however another longstanding approach to understanding crime, the reverberations of which are still evident today, stems from philosophy. This approach to understanding crime, known as the *classical* school of thought, can be traced to Immanuel Kant (1724–1804) and the Enlightenment philosophers. The trademark of Enlightenment philosophy was a view of human action as the product of reason and free will. The two figures credited with taking the tenets of Enlightenment philosophy and applying them to crime are the Italian mathematician and economist Cesare Bonesana Marchese de Beccaria (1738–94) and the English philosopher and jurist Jeremy Bentham (1748–1832).

Classical theory holds central the notion of free will in explaining why a person commits a crime. Simply, when the opportunity for crime arises, classical theory holds that the individual has a free, rational choice between criminal and non-criminal behaviour in deciding which action they will take. The accompanying assumption to rational choice, as Roshier (1989: 14–5) states, is that 'The goal of our rationality is personal satisfaction; rational self-interest is the key motivational characteristic that governs our relationship with crime and conformity'. Lilley, Cullen, and Ball (2002) dubbed the view of the criminal as someone who totals the gains and losses of crime as the 'criminal as calculator'.

The contribution that Beccaria made to the development of criminal justice is generally credited to a single book, published in 1764, *Dei Delitti e Delle Pene* (*On Crimes and Punishments*, English translation 2008). Lilley et al. (2002) outline 11 points that summarize Beccaria's position (see Box 1.3).

The points made by Beccaria are familiar to us today: we take it for granted that the punishment should fit the crime, that extreme punitive measures are not acceptable and that, with due allowance for age and mental disorder, criminals are responsible for their actions.

At the same time as Beccaria's work was published, Jeremy Bentham similarly argued that a rational calculation of the balance between profit and pain guided the individual's free

---

Box 1.3 Beccaria's position on criminal justice (after Lilley et al., 2002)

1. To ensure peace we surrender some individual freedoms for the overall good of society. We might think of this mutual agreement as a social contract.
2. As criminal law restricts the freedom of the individual so the laws should be limited in scope.
3. An individual accused of a crime should be presumed innocent until proved otherwise.
4. The criminal law, defining all crimes and punishments, should exist in written form and be available to all.
5. The purpose of punishment for committing a crime is the delivery of retribution.
6. The severity of punishment should be proportionate to what is required for the purposes of preventing crime and for deterrence.
7. The punishment should fit the crime not the criminal.
8. Punishment should be certain and immediate.
9. The purpose of punishment is *not* to make an example of the criminal or to change or reform the criminal.
10. It is understood that the criminal acts in a rational manner in committing the crime.
11. The overriding goal of a criminal justice system should be crime prevention.

choice of whether or not to commit a criminal act. Bentham's main concern was with social reform, including reform of the criminal law, for which he advocated a *utilitarian* approach. The basis of utilitarianism is that we decide on the moral value of an action by the contribution it makes to the overall good so that, in essence, the ends justify the means. Thus, like Beccaria, Bentham came to the view that the administration of punishment should be regulated in order that it may prevent further crime.

The advent of classical thought heralds the emergence of the notion of using punishment as a deterrent, a means to prevent crime for the greater good. Again, we now commonly accept this principle as an integral function of the criminal justice system: it is through punishment that criminals are deterred from committing more crimes, while the avoidance of punishment keeps the rest of us on the right side of the law. The issue of the effectiveness of punishment as a deterrent is discussed in Chapter 11.

We may wish to ask some questions about the classical view of criminal behaviour. The statement that a criminal is an individual who, of their own free will, rationally decides to break the law for personal gain is a hypothesis rather than an explanation. We are left asking where does free will come from? Do all people have free will in equal amounts? Why do some people make decisions to commit criminal acts and not others? Is it the case that we obey the law just because we fear punishment?

Roshier (1989: 72) addresses the question of aetiology: 'If human action expresses motives and purposes, a question that arises is where the motives for *criminal* action come from … The classical answer is simply that they are there; they are taken as given. They are part of a conception of human rationality which … is one of the starting assumptions of classical criminology'.

Classical theory was the dominant force in Europe and America in the late 18th and the 19th centuries, guiding both judicial philosophers and criminal justice system of the time. With the advent of positivist theories (see below), the classical school waned in popularity and influence throughout the 20th century. However, as will be discussed, the 1970s, 1980s, and 1990s have seen a renewed interest in classical criminology.

Criminal anthropology

The writings of the Italian psychiatrist and scholar Cesare Lombroso (1835–1909) are often taken as a defining point at which the discipline of criminology began to take shape. As is the case for all scholars, Lombroso was influenced by the science of the times. Traces of Gall's phrenology can be seen in his work, along with influences from the growing knowledge of evolution through Darwin's books, and from the proposed relationship between genetic inheritance and mental functioning, as seen in the writings on intelligence by Sir Francis Galton (1822–1911).

In his early work, Lombroso drew on research methods from anthropology – hence the description of Lombroso's work as criminal anthropology – in gathering data on the physical appearance of convicted criminals. Informed by his empirical work, in 1876 Lombroso published a book, *L'Uomo Delinquente* (*The Criminal Man*), in which he advanced the thesis that the physical appearance of some criminals resembled the atavistic characteristics of the first, primitive humans. These characteristics could be seen in the abnormal size and shape of the skull, face, and other parts of the criminal's body. The criminal had ears like a chimpanzee, a twisted nose, eye defects, and a receding chin.

An alternative explanation for Lombroso's findings other than the criminal as a genetic throwback may be found in the sample he studied. At the time when Lombroso conducted his research, prisons were typically used as repositories for a range of unfortunate individuals (Long & Midgley, 1992). The prison population would have included those at the edges of society such as the destitute, the infirm, the homeless, the physically diseased, and the mentally disordered. It is likely that some of these prisoners would have physical deformities, possibly as a result of congenital conditions.

While Lombroso's descriptions of the criminal classes were much loved by the caricaturists of the time, they also attracted academic debate. Lombroso's own student, Enrico Ferri (1856–1929), disagreed with Lombroso's theories, suggesting that social and psychological factors were of greater importance in understanding criminal behaviour. Charles Buckman Goring (1870–1919), an English physician, conducted a similar study to Lombroso's comparing the physical characteristics of thousands of prisoners in English jails with those of soldiers in the Royal Engineers. Goring's finding, published in 1913 in the book *The English Convict*, revealed no differences between the two groups and he concluded that Lombroso's theories were not correct (Goring, 1972).

Lombroso did not, however, claim that all criminal were genetic throwbacks: he estimated that 'the born criminal' accounted for about one-third of all criminals. In his later work, such as *Le Crime, Causes et Remèdes* (*Crime, Its Causes and Remedies*, 1899), Lombroso modified his theories to take into account the influence of social and economic factors in understanding criminal behaviour. However, as is inevitably the case in discussing crime, there is also a political aspect to consider. As Gould (2007: 396) notes in his discussion of criminal anthropology: 'The major figures in the Italian school were socialists who viewed their theory as the spearhead for a rational, scientific society based on human realities'.

The practical reality of criminal anthropology is that if some individuals are genetically determined to be criminal then, by definition, nothing can be done to change the inevitable. It follows that those individuals born to be criminal must be removed or isolated from the rest of society. There is always a strong possibility that any discussion about the removal of a part of the gene pool to eliminate certain individuals such as criminals leads to unpalatable 'solutions' such as eugenics. History tells us that attempts to isolate a section of the population on the basis of their genetic inheritance produces a bitter, segregated society.

In hindsight, as an empiricist using both statistical analysis and theory from a range of disciplines to formulate an understanding of a real-world issue, Lombroso anticipated much of what was to follow. Indeed, as the academic debate unfolded he was, like all good empiricists, prepared to adjust and change his theories. Nonetheless, it is Lombroso's fate to be remembered for his early work as depicted in cartoons of simian criminals.

The social origins of crime: the Chicago School

The beginnings of the move away from the individual and towards social factors in explaining crime may be seen in the work of Clifford R. Shaw (1895–1957) and Henry D. McKay (1899–1980). Shaw and McKay were researchers based at the University of Chicago and their view of crime was shaped by the writings of Robert E. Park (1864–1944) – described by Lilley et al. (2002: 33) as 'a newspaper reporter-turned-sociologist', although he did hold a degree in philosophy and psychology – and the theories of the sociologist Ernest W. Burgess (1886–1966).

Burgess and Park were interested in the way in which cities grew and expand in size: they developed the view that the way cities grow is not random but that urban growth follows a sequence of rings or zones (Park, Burgess, & McKenzie, 1925). Thus, at the centre of a city is the business district, typically non-residential but with banks, shops, a good transport system, and so on. As one moves away from the centre, so one progresses through zones characterised by factories and poor quality housing until, some distance from the centre, eventually reaching better quality housing with transport links into the centre. This zonal arrangement is not static, zones can expand and contact as the economy and population of a city changes over time: this urban change produces what Park and Burgess called *zones in transition*. A zone of transition is that part of the city where there is pressure for resources: in such a zone there may be a competition for space for housing and business, a high concentration of people who cannot afford to move out, impoverished people seeking accommodation, a shortage of good quality housing, schools, and so on. In zones of transition, Park and Burgess argued, there are high levels of *social disorganisation* that act to weaken family and community relationships and networks.

In terms of crime, Shaw and McKay, along with other researchers in the Chicago School, set forth the hypothesis that the net effect of social disorganisation is to lower a community's control over the criminal behaviour of some of its constituents. It follows that one of the characteristics of a zone of transition will be high levels of crime, particularly juvenile crime, as social control of the actions of young people is weakened. When social control is at its weakest, these disorganised areas of the city may engender organised groups or gangs that perpetuate a cycle of criminal activity.

Shaw and McKay (1972) were able to gather data, primarily from court records but also from individual case studies, that supported their hypothesis about the criminogenic effect of weakened social bonds in zones of social disorganization. While there are criticisms of this work – such as its overreliance on official statistics, and its concentration on street crime – Shaw and McKay's contribution is important for two reasons. First, the development of the concept of *social control* to explain crime set in motion a line of criminological theorising that led to a succession of new theories based around the notion of control. Some of these control theories – such as naturalisation and drift theory (Sykes & Matza, 1957), containment theory (Reckless, 1961), and social bond theory (Hirschi, 1969) – contain elements of psychology but are clearly sociological in emphasis. However, as will be discussed in Chapter 3, other theories incorporating social factors, such as differential association theory (Sutherland, 1947), differential reinforcement theory (Jeffery, 1965), and social learning theory (Akers, 1977), have much more of a leaning towards psychology.

Second, the Chicago School brought together the discipline of sociology and the study of crime in a systematic way. As in America, the interplay between sociology and the study of crime has a long history in Britain (see Rock, 2007). A sociological approach to the study of crime is evident in contemporary criminology where sociology is probably the discipline with the greatest influence in terms of research and theory. Indeed, Carrabine, Iganski, Lee, Plummer, and South (2004: 5) state: 'Crime is a truly sociological concept'.

A different sociological approach to control theory, with its beginnings in a school of thought within sociology called *symbolic interactionism* (Blumer, 1969), began to emerge in the 1960s.

The interactionist position

The questions that engaged the social interactionist were primarily concerned with the interplay between social context, language and meaning. Thus, acts that we call 'criminal' are criminal not because of their inherent qualities but because, within a given social context, we elect to give them the label 'criminal' (Becker, 1963). An act is therefore socially constructed as a 'criminal act', which serves to label the person who committed the act as a 'criminal'. Once the label of 'criminal' is given to an individual, then a new set of assumptions about that person come into play, alongside enactment of the consequences that society deems to be suitable for a criminal.

The interactionist position rests on several theoretical premises. It is taken that each individual's behaviour is informed by their personal interpretation of reality and the meanings they give to events in their social world. The meanings we ascribe to social events are learned, particularly through our interactions with other people. Finally, the self-evaluations we make of our own behaviour are, in turn, influenced by the meanings we have learned from other people.

Labelling theory

If crime is socially constructed and the label 'criminal' is bestowed on those who act in a way we call criminal, what effect does it have on the individual to be labelled a criminal? As the proverb says, 'Give a dog an ill name and hang him' (Smith, 1970): those individuals who are labelled criminals will be perceived by society as being of a criminal type, with all the attendant personal characteristics of a criminal. The term *stigma* is used to refer to the public attitude of condemnation of the criminal. A consequence of the label 'criminal' is the exclusion of the labelled individual from some sections of society, along with the associated view that they as criminals deserve whatever retribution society sees fit to hand out. The sociologist Howard Becker gives an account the social phenomenon of labelling in his book *Outsiders*, published in 1963, illustrating how the criminal is popularly described as a person different from others and shunned as such.

It is highly debatable whether the stereotypes of a criminal and their future behaviour are likely to be correct, but the stereotypes persist. Indeed, stereotypes of the characteristics of criminals may even be particular to certain types of crime: for example, Hollin and Howells (1987) showed that attributions of the characteristics of those committing crimes of acquisition were couched in terms of failings in socialisation but that the acts of sex offenders were explained by the offender's mental instability.

The insidious effect of labelling may come about through the process of a *self-fulfilling prophecy*. If a young person is labelled a criminal, there are social forces that can lead them to modify their self-image to become the person described by the label. When a young person attracts the label criminal, the label becomes a role, a way of life, so that they are treated differently by those around them, and their life changes so that they become that role. Thus, the person's identity changes to that of a 'criminal' with all its associated values, attitudes, and beliefs: the young person is no longer a school pupil or an employee, they are a criminal with all the associated undesirable character traits. To complete the circle, the young person becomes someone to be avoided and treated with suspicion: they are now different to the rest of us and deserve to be treated as such. The criminal will find either overtly or covertly that they are barred from certain types of employment; the young offender may find that their school, their family, or their peer group is unwilling to offer a welcome; 'known offenders' may attract an undue amount of attention from the police. As the process unfolds, so the young person's initial anti-social behaviour graduates to criminal behaviour as they become increasingly involved in a criminal lifestyle. The developing offender may well spend a period in custody with other criminals, they are more likely to be arrested, their education and their job prospects suffer, they may have family problems, and their peer group changes to others playing the same delinquent role.

Conflict theory

The application of a view of society as composed of conflicting groups to explain crime came into force in the late 1960s and early 1970s. An approach to understanding crime based on conflict is associated with criminologists such as Dahrendorf (1959), Turk (1969), Quinney (1970), and Chambliss and Seidman (1971). Conflict theory advanced significantly with the adoption of Marxist theory by criminologist Willem Bonger. Bonger (1969 [1916]) began to formulate a Marxist critique of crime but the seminal expression of this theoretical approach, sometimes referred to as radical criminology, is credited to the British sociologists Ian Taylor, Paul Walton, and Jock Young, and in particular to their book *The New Criminology* published in 1973. Giddens makes the following observation:

> The publication of *The New Criminology* by Taylor, Walton and Young in 1973 marked an important break with earlier theories of deviance. Its authors drew on elements of Marxist thought to argue that deviance is deliberately chosen and often political in nature. They rejected the idea that deviance is 'determined' by factors such as biology, personality, anomie, social disorganization or labels.
>
> (Giddens, 2006: 803)

In contrast to the consensus view, conflict theory holds that an act in itself is not naturally immoral or criminal, rather what we call criminal is *socially* defined or constructed. The emphasis on social construction runs counter to theories that rely on genetic, biological, or psychological variables to explain crime. The new criminology saw crime in the context of a Marxist analysis of a class-based capitalist system. Crime was not viewed as the sole province of any particular class within society; rather the type of crime is seen as a function of the political system.

In a capitalist society, there is an unequal distribution of wealth and power, some people are poor, dissatisfied, and without a voice, others are wealthy and hold huge social influence. The inequality of the distribution of wealth and power creates a social climate based on conflict that, it is argued, promotes crime. In order to gain access to the material goods enjoyed by others, the poor and powerless lower classes commit the types of crime, such as car crime, theft, and burglary that are within their limited scope. The affluent middle classes commit 'white-collar' crimes such as tax evasion and theft from employers for personal gain. The wealthy and powerful upper class indulge in activities, sometimes not accorded the status of crime, such as exploitation, profiteering, and environmental pollution in order to increase their wealth and power.

In its rejection of individual factors as being of primary importance in an analysis of crime, the advent of the new criminology signalled the beginnings of a schism between psychology and criminology. The shifting relationship between criminology and psychology is discussed below.

Conflict theory has attracted various criticisms. There are obvious queries, such as why do some people, regardless of their wealth or power, *not* commit crimes? There have been criticisms of the theory for its neglect of race, along with feminist criticisms of the Marxist focus on class and a lack of gender-awareness (see Carrabine et al., 2004). In part as a response to these criticisms and in part as the natural refinement of any theory, the new criminology evolved into *left realism* (Lea & Young, 1984). The main thrust of left realist criminology lies in a greater emphasis on the effects of crime on victims, many of whom are without wealth or power. The advent of *cultural criminology* is a further stage in the evolution of new criminology (Ferrell, Hayward, & Young, 2004).

As noted, among the many questions raised by Hall's apparently clear-cut definition of crime, there is the issue of who decides what constitutes a crime and on what basis and for whose benefit do they decide? The application of criminological theory, itself heavily influenced by sociological theory, allows answers to be formed to the question of just who makes the decisions and for what purpose.

Applying theory to the definition of crime

Following Giddens (2006), we can distinguish several broad sociological approaches to explaining crime including *functionalist* theories, *interactionist* theories, *conflict* theories, and *control* theories.

Functionalist theories: a society built on consensus

As Hayward and Morrison (2005: 68) explain: 'Functionalist theories see society as an integrated whole, where ultimately all parts of the subsystems operate in an integrated ("organic") and coordinated way'. Thus, a society's stability depends upon the agreement, or consensus, across society about the norms, rules, and values that members of society should respect and follow. These mutually agreed values become the rules by which we are socialised as we grow up. Thus, a society's legal system may be understood as a consensual statement of the behaviour that will and will not be tolerated by that society as acceptable conduct. A crime is therefore an act which meets with the disapproval of the majority: in this light, a distinction can be made between two types of act.

Statutory crimes (*malum prohibitum*) refer to those acts that are deemed to be criminal for the greater good. In the UK, for example, we all drive on the left-hand side of the road, in other countries people drive on the right. There is no great expression here of a society's moral values, one side of the road is pretty much the same as the other, but travelling by road is infinitely better for everyone if we all drive on the same side. To drive on the wrong side of the road is not inherently bad but it is dangerous and it is illegal.

In contrast to *malum prohibitum* crimes, there are other acts, collectively termed *mala in se,* which all right-thinking members of society agree are wrong. An act of this type is one that we agree to be *wrong or evil in itself.* The very nature of such acts, regardless of their status in law, offends the values that we all hold to be important. In this light, criminal law can be seen as a reflection of the *moral values* prevalent within society at a given point in its history. For example, the murder of one human being by another is universally held to be wrong, regardless of whether a law prohibiting murder exists, and so it is clearly *malum in se.* There are various acts that fall under the rubric of *mala in se*: these acts include inflicting harm on another person, as with, for example, assault and rape; or transgressions against another's property, as with burglary, malicious damage, and trespass.

The formation of distinctions between different types of crime can be of practical use in informing judgements about appropriate levels of punishment. The more serious, morally dubious, offences such as theft, fraud, and violence against the person (referred to as *indictable* or *notifiable* offences) attract stiff penalties. The less serious offences, such as minor traffic offences and petty damage to property (*non-indictable* or *summary* offences) attract more lenient penalties. (In practice, some crimes are 'trial-able either way' with punishments to match.)

However, there are occasions when a society may be morally divided, or when there is a moral consensus on a particular matter that is not reflected in the law. Thus, a discrepancy can arise between what to some people, sometimes even the majority of people, is *morally* objectionable (or justifiable), as opposed to *legally* wrong. For example, blood sports are morally intolerable to some members of society, while others defend the freedom to hunt, shoot, and so on. The objections to blood sports in the UK led to the Hunting Act 2004, which prohibited some, not all, types of hunting. The changes in law brought about by this Act meant that for some people, although not for others, law and morality are in agreement on blood sport. The example of hunting, alongside other issues such as euthanasia, racism, sexism, and animal experimentation, illustrates how moral debate can challenge criminal law and how criminal law must have the flexibility to accommodate shifting societal mores. Advances in technology can also present challenges to the law-makers: activities such as copying DVDs and computer fraud and hacking are contemporary issues that criminal law seeks to address.

So acts once not punishable by law can become *criminalized*. In the USA, it was perfectly legal to own and sell marijuana until the federal law was amended in 1937. In the UK, there have been legislative changes regarding the sale of solvents to certain age groups, and changes with respect to rape in marriage. To return to hunting, it is possible that a change of government will lead to a repeal of the laws banning some blood sports. The changing nature of the law is illustrated by Sutherland and Cressey (1960) who note that at various times in the past, activities such as printing a book, having gold in one's house, or driving with reins have all been criminal acts. In modern times, acts such as abortion, suicide, and consenting homosexual behaviour in adults over the age of 21 years have all been removed from criminal law (or *decriminalized*). As Walker (1965) points out, as well as ensuring the maintenance of society's moral values and protecting the individual's person and property, criminal law seeks to protect and preserve a stable society through laws that exist for the defence of the realm and that prevent public acts that might shock, corrupt, or deprave. Legally imposed punishment serves to express society's disapproval of the individual's actions and to maintain social solidarity in its moral judgements.

Conflict theories: the political view

The basic tenets of a conflict view of crime are the opposite to those inherent within the consensus view. Thus, rather than seeing society as a system functioning as an integrated unit, society is viewed as a diverse collection of competing groups, engaged in a perpetual struggle. These competing groups, evident throughout society, may be formally constituted with their own administrative structures and rules, as seen with employer organisations, trade unions, and different religious groups. The formation of some groups may be based on a range of factors including age, lifestyle, wealth, and social status.

Some groups may develop formal rules about dress and their members' conduct, as perhaps most clearly seen in the uniforms of public schools and delinquent gangs. There are groups that oppose each other politically, as with the recognised political parties, Conservative, Labour, and so on, which stand for election and seek to govern the country. There are other groups that are political in the sense that they seek to bring social change through direct action or by lobbying for legislative change. These pressure groups may have a specific focus such as banning abortion or pornography, or campaigning for the rights of a minority group; alternatively they may have wider aims, such as opposing capitalism and globalisation or advancing green issues. These groups may generate conflict, sometimes violent conflict, as they seek to bring about change.

Within a framework of conflict, criminal law is seen as designed to suit the purposes of the dominant class. The way in which crime is defined is a statement of the preferences and interests of those in positions of power who are able to impose their preferred views on the formation and running of the law. As conflict theory has its basis in politics and economics, so the criminal justice system is viewed in the same way. Criminal law is held to exist for the purpose of protecting the rich and powerful from the rest of society and preserving their interests. As those with wealth and power control the regulation of crime, so the legal system will discriminate against the poor and the powerless. The function of the 'justice' system is therefore the preservation and protection of capitalist interests, and to maintain the status quo with respect to the unequal distribution of wealth and power.

The protectionist function of the criminal justice system is seen in the inequalities within society. While the poor, the proletariat, may commit crime with similar frequency to the wealthy bourgeoisie, they are arrested and punished much more often. Further inequalities are evident in the penalties for different types of crime, with harsher penalties for offences against property rather than against people. Indeed, following an interactionist perspective, context and meaning can be used to move away from a consensual moral stance of 'right' and 'wrong'. Taking the life of another person, be it murder or manslaughter, is a criminal act however, this is not always a question of right or wrong. Is it a crime if one person kills another in an act of self-defence, or to defend their family, or in battle during war? Is the execution of a convicted criminal as endorsed by the state through the application of the death penalty a crime? If we take the meaning and context into account, are these crimes or examples of 'legitimate' killings? An individual becomes a criminal when the people who hold power – judges, parents, police, teachers, etc. – decide to confer the label 'criminal'. Thus, what constitutes criminal behaviour is a judgement, made on social, moral, and political grounds, by certain sections of society towards certain classes of behaviour. This argument does not, of course, apply only to criminal behaviour: the same reasoning has been used to explain the creation of groups variously labelled 'alcoholic', 'mentally ill', 'sexually deviant', and so on.

What is criminological psychology?

The interface between psychology and crime has been given a number of titles including *forensic psychology*, *legal psychology*, and *criminological psychology*. It used to be the case that the British Psychological Society had a division called the Division of Criminological and Legal Psychology (DCLP), reflecting the twin specialisations within psychology of the study of criminal behaviour and the study of the legal system. However, in the 1990s the name of the DCLP was changed to the Division of Forensic Psychology (DFP), although the division's academic journal remains *Legal and Criminological Psychology*. The choice of the term 'forensic' to describe the range of topics previously gathered under the rubric of criminological and legal psychology is at best limiting and at worst misleading if not incorrect. Blackburn (1996) has discussed the indiscriminate use by psychologists of the term 'forensic': he suggests that forensic psychology is the use of psychological knowledge to aid legal decision-making, not a particular form of psychological expertise. As Blackburn (1996: 5) states: 'This is not a pedantic argument about dictionary definitions … forensic psychological practices are not simply those which a vaguely connected with the law. They are activities undertaken *for* the law'. The indiscriminate redefining of the term forensic by a BPS Committee is reminiscent of Lewis Carroll's *Through the Looking Glass*: '"When I use a word", Humpty Dumpty said, in rather a scornful tone, "it means just what I choose it to mean"'.

In considering the subtitle for this 2nd edition, I chose to stick with *criminological* as the most suitable for my purpose. Criminological is suitably all encompassing: if the term refers to matters related to crime then it includes legal matters while justifiably allowing other material to be included. Therefore, *criminological psychology*, as the term is used here, refers to psychological knowledge applied to the study of criminal behaviour and the various agencies charged with its management.

In a broader sense, criminological psychology also refers to the point of contact between the disciplines of criminology and psychology. The relationship between these two disciplines has not always been cordial, although each has something to learn from the other. Hayward (2005) gives a criminologist's view on the interface between criminology and psychology, Hollin (2007) gives the opposite perspective. In the chapters that follow, the overlap between the two disciplines will become even clearer.

Chapter summary

- The study of crime engages a range of academic disciplines of which psychology is but one among many.
- Psychology has a long history, dating back to Sigmund Freud and psychoanalytic theory, of concern with criminal behaviour.
- A precise definition of 'crime' is hard to find. An appreciation of the concept of crime relies on how a society, which constructs its own rules and criminal justice system, is understood. We now take it that a crime has two elements: *actus reus*, the guilty act; and *mens rea*, the guilty mind.
- The exceptions to the *mens rea* requirement are to be found in the age of criminal responsibility, a child below the age at which we become responsible for our actions cannot commit a crime; and in mental health law when a disturbance of the mind casts doubt over the individual's fitness to stand trial.
- The methods using to determine the guilt or innocence of a person accused of crime have varied over the centuries, including trial by ordeal and trial by combat, and invariably harsh punishments were bestowed on the guilty. We are now more familiar with a trial by jury and a legal system in which the punishment fits the crime.

Points for discussion

- Explanations of criminal behaviour have changed as theories have been developed, from psychodynamic, through operant learning and personality, to accounts based on social learning theory and neuropsychological development. What form will psychological explanations for crime take 10 years from now?
- The administration of law relies on the notion of free will, that we can rationally choose to obey or to break the law. However, some psychological theories suggest that our actions are shaped and determined by our experiences, including our upbringing, relationships, education, and so on. Is it possible to reconcile these two positions?
- If our inherited genetic constitution plays a part in shaping our actions, what implication does this have for the criminal justice system?

Essential reading

Eysenck, M. W. (2000). *Psychology: A Student's Handbook*. Hove, East Sussex: Psychology Press. An excellent introductory textbook for the newcomer to psychology.

Hollin, C. R. (2007). Criminological psychology. In M. Maguire, R. Morgan, & R. Reiner (Eds.), *The Oxford Handbook of Criminology* (4th ed.) (pp. 43–77). Oxford: Oxford University Press.
A brief history of the fluctuating relationship between criminology and psychology.

Lilley, R. J., Cullen, F. T., & Ball, R. A. (2007). *Criminological Theory: Context and Consequences* (4th ed.). Thousand Oaks, CA: Sage.
There are many criminology textbooks to choose from, I like this one for its highly readable style.

Maguire, M., Morgan, R., & Reiner R. (Eds.) (2007). *The Oxford Handbook of Criminology* (4th ed.). Oxford: Oxford University Press.
State-of-the-art chapters on many matters criminological.

Newburn, T. (Ed.) (2009). *Key Readings in Criminology*. Cullompton, Devon: Willan Publishing.
A crash course in everything you would ever need to know about criminology.

The lighter side

Rubenfeld, J. (2006). *The Interpretation of Murder*. London: Headline Review.
It's 1909 and Sigmund Freud arrives in Manhattan, but before long there's a murder to solve!

References

Akers, R. L. (1977). *Deviant Behavior: A Social Learning Approach* (2nd ed.). Belmont, CA: Wadsworth.
Arboleda-Flórez, J. (2002). On automatism. *Current Opinion in Psychiatry, 15,* 569–576.
Bandura, A. (1977). *Social Learning Theory*. New York, NY: Prentice-Hall.
—— (1986). *Social Foundations of Thought and Actions: A Social Cognitive Theory*. Englewood Cliffs, NJ: Prentice-Hall.
—— (2001). Social cognitive theory: An agentic perspective. *Annual Review of Psychology, 52,* 1–26.
Barkow, J. H., Cosmides, L., & Tooby, J. (1992). *The Adapted Mind: Evolutionary Psychology and the Generation of Culture*. New York, NY: Oxford University Press.
Baars, B. J. (1967). *The Cognitive Revolution in Psychology*. New York, NY: Guildford Press.
Beccaria, C. (2008[1794]). *On Crimes and Punishments and Other Writings*. A. Thomas (Ed.), (Trans. by A. Thomas & J. Parzen). Toronto: University of Toronto Press.
Becker, H. (1963). *Outsiders: Studies in the Sociology of Deviance*. New York, NY: Free Press.
Bix, B. (2006). *Jurisprudence: Theory and Context (*4th ed.). London: Sweet & Maxwell.
Bjork, D. W. (1993). *B. F. Skinner: A Life*. New York, NY: Basic Books.
Blackburn, R. (1993). *The Psychology of Criminal Conduct: Theory, Research and Practice*. Chichester, Sussex: John Wiley & Sons.
—— (1996). What *is* forensic psychology? *Legal and Criminological Psychology, 1,* 3–16.
Blumer, H. (1969). *Symbolic Interactionism*. Engelwood Cliffs, NJ: Prentice-Hall.
Bonger, W. (1969, orig. 1916). *Criminality and Economic Conditions*. Bloomington, IN: Indiana University Press.
Brown, A. (1999). *The Darwin Wars: The Scientific Battle for the Soul of Man*. London: Simon & Schuster.
Brown, W. C. (1961). *Freud and the Post-Freudians*. Harmondsworth: Penguin.
Buss, D. M. (1995). Evolutionary psychology: A new paradigm for psychological science. *Psychological Inquiry, 6,* 1–30.
—— (1999). *Evolutionary Psychology: The New Science of Mind*. Boston, MA: Allyn & Bacon.
—— (ed.) (2005). *The Handbook of Evolutionary Psychology*. New York, NY: Wiley.

—— (2008). *Evolutionary Psychology: The New Science of the Mind* (3rd ed.). Boston, MA: Allyn & Bacon.

Carrabine, E., Iganski, P., Lee, M., Plummer, K., & South, N. (2004). *Criminology: A Sociological Introduction*. London: Routledge.

Chambliss, W. & Seidman, R. (1971). *Law, Order and Power*. Reading, MA: Addison-Wesley.

Chomsky, N. (1975). *Reflections on Language*. New York, NY: Pantheon Books.

Colman, A. (2003). *Oxford Dictionary of Psychology*. Oxford: Oxford University Press.

Conway, L. G. III & Schaller, M. (2002). On the verifiability of evolutionary psychological theories: An analysis of the psychology of scientific persuasion. *Personality and Social Psychology Review, 6*, 152–166.

Criminal Review Group (2000). *Review of the Criminal Justice System in Northern Ireland*. Norwich: HMSO.

Dahrendorf, R. (1959). *Class and Class Conflict in Industrial Society*. Stanford, CN: Stanford University Press.

Dawkins, R. (1976). *The Selfish Gene*. Oxford: Oxford University Press.

—— (2006). *The God Delusion*. New York, NY: Bantam Books.

Dennett, D. (1995). *Darwin's Dangerous Idea: Evolution and the Meanings of Life*. London: Allen Lane.

Dingwall, R., Nerlich, B., & Hillyard, S. (2003). Biological determinism and symbolic interaction: Heredity streams and cultural roads. *Symbolic Interaction, 26*, 631–644.

Dunbar, R. & Barrett, L. (Eds.) (2007). *Oxford Handbook of Evolutionary Psychology*. Oxford: Oxford University Press.

Dunbar, R., Barrett, L., & Lycett, J. (2005). *Evolutionary Psychology: A Beginner's Guide: Human Behaviour, Evolution and the Mind*. Oxford: Oneworld Publications.

Eysenck, H. J. (1970). *The Structure of Personality* (3rd ed.). London: Methuen.

Eysenck, M. W. (2000). *Psychology: A Student's Handbook*. Hove, East Sussex: Psychology Press.

Ferrell, J., Hayward, K., & Young, J. (2004). *Cultural Criminology: An Invitation*. London: Sage.

Fiske, S. T. & Taylor, S. E. (1991). *Social Cognition* (2nd ed.). New York, NY: McGraw-Hill.

Gazzaniga, M. S., Ivry, R. B., & Mangun, G. R. (2002). *Cognitive Neuroscience: The Biology of the Mind* (2nd ed.). London: W. W. Norton.

Giddens, A. (2006). *Sociology* (5th ed.). Cambridge: Polity Press.

Goring, C. (1972, orig. 1913). *The English Convict: A Statistical Study*. Montclair, NJ: Patterson Smith.

Gould, S. J. (2007). *The Richness of Life: The Essential Stephen Jay Gould*. London: Vintage Books.

Gregory, R. L. (Ed.) (1987). *The Oxford Companion to the Mind*. Oxford: Oxford University Press.

Harmon-Jones, E. & Winkielman, P. (2007). *Social Neuroscience: Integrating Biological and Psychological Explanations of Social Behavior*. New York, NY: Guilford Press.

Hayward, K. (2005). Psychology and crime: Understanding the interface. In C. Hale, K. Hayward, A. Wahidin, & E. Wincup (Eds.), *Criminology* (pp. 109–137). Oxford: Oxford University Press.

Hayward, K. & Morrison, W. (2005). Theoretical criminology: A starting point. In C. Hale, K. Hayward, A. Wahidin, & E. Wincup (Eds.), *Criminology* (pp. 61–88). Oxford: Oxford University Press.

Hirschi, T. (1969). *Causes of Delinquency*. Berkeley, CA: University of California Press.

Hollin, C. R. (2007). Criminological psychology. In M. Maguire, R. Morgan, & R. Reiner (Eds.), *The Oxford Handbook of Criminology* (4th ed.) (pp. 43–77). Oxford: Oxford University Press.

Hollin, C. R. & Howells, K. (1987). Lay explanations of delinquency: Global or offence-specific? *British Journal of Social Psychology, 26*, 203–210.

Jackson, S. & Rees, A. (2007). The appalling appeal of nature: The popular influence of evolutionary psychology as a problem for sociology. *Sociology, 41*, 917–930.

Jeffery, C. R. (1965). Criminal behaviour and learning theory. *Journal of Criminal Law, Criminology and Police Science, 56*, 294–300.

Klinef, P. (1984). *Psychology and Freudian Theory*. London: Methuen.

Lea, J. & Young, J. (1984). *What is to be Done about Law and Order?* Harmondsworth, Middlesex: Penguin Books.

Lilley, R. J., Cullen, F. T., & Ball, R. A. (2002). *Criminological Theory: Context and Consequences* (3rd ed.). Thousand Oaks, CA: Sage.

Lombroso, C. (1876). *L'Uomo Delinquente*. Milan: Hoepli.

—— (1895). *L'Homme Criminel* (vols. 1 and 2). Felix: Alcan.

—— (1899). *Le Crime, Causes et Remèdes*. Paris: Scleicher Frères Editeurs.

Long, C. G. & Midgley, M. (1992). On the closeness of the concepts of the criminal and the mentally ill in the nineteenth century: Yesterday's professional and public opinions reflected today. *Journal of Forensic Psychiatry, 3,* 63–79.

McGarr, P. & Rose, S. (Eds.) (2006). *Stephen J. Gould: The Richness of Life: The Essential Stephen J. Gould*. London: Vintage.

Maher, G. (2005). Age and criminal responsibility. *Ohio State Journal of Criminal Law, 2,* 493–512.

Miller, G. (1969). *Psychology: The Study of Mental Life*. Harmondsworth, Middlesex: Penguin Books.

Morris, E. K. & Todd, J. T. (1999). Watsonian behaviorism. In W. O'Donohue & R. Kitchener (Eds.), *Handbook of Behaviorism* (pp. 15–69). San Diego, CA: Academic Press.

O'Donohue, W. & Kitchner, R. (Eds.) (1999). *Handbook of Behaviorism*. San Diego, CA: Academic Press.

Panksepp, J. & Panksepp, J. B. (2000). The seven sins of evolutionary psychology. *Evolution and Cognition, 6,* 108–131.

Park, R., Burgess, E. W., & McKenzie, R. D. (1925). *The City*. Chicago, IL: University of Chicago Press.

Pervin, L. A., Cervone, D., & John, O. P. (2005). *Personality: Theory and Research* (9th ed.). Hodoken, NJ: John Wiley & Sons.

Quinney, R. (1970). *The Social Reality of Crime*. Boston, MA: Little, Brown.

Reckless, W. C. (1961). *The Crime Problem* (3rd ed.). New York, NY: Appleton-Century-Crofts.

Richards, G. (1996). *Putting Psychology in its Place: An Introduction from a Critical Historical Perspective*. London: Routledge.

Ringen, J. (1999). Radical behaviorism: B. F. Skinner's philosophy of science. In W. O'Donohue & R. Kitchener (Eds.), *Handbook of Behaviorism* (pp. 159–178). San Diego, CA: Academic Press.

Rock, P. (2007). Sociological theories of crime. In M. Maguire, R. Morgan, & R. Reiner (Eds.), *The Oxford Handbook of Criminology* (4th ed.) (pp. 51–82). Oxford: Oxford University Press.

Roshier, B. (1989). *Controlling Crime: The Classical Perspective in Criminology*. Milton Keynes: Open University Press.

Seligman, M. E. P. (1971). Phobias and preparedness. *Behavior Therapy, 2,* 307–321.

Shaw, C. R. & McKay, H. D. (1972). *Juvenile Delinquency and Urban Areas*. Chicago, IL: University of Chicago Press.

Skinner, B. F. (1953). *Science and Human Behavior*. New York, NY: Macmillan.

—— (1974). *About Behaviorism*. London: Jonathan Cape.

—— (1985). Cognitive science and behaviourism. *British Journal of Psychology, 76,* 291–301.

Smith, W. G. (1970). *The Oxford Dictionary of English Proverbs* (3rd ed.). Oxford: Oxford University Press.

Stocker, R. D. (1904). *The ABC of Phrenology*. London: Henry J. Drane.

Storr, A. (1989). *Freud: A Very Short Introduction*. Oxford: Oxford University Press.

Strachey, J., Strachey, A., & Tyson, A. (Eds.) (1953–1974). *The Standard Edition of the Complete Psychological Works of Sigmund Freud* (24 volumes). London: Hogarth Press.

Sutherland, E. H. (1947). *Principles of Criminology* (4th ed.). Philadelphia, PA: Lippincott.

Sutherland, E. H. & Cressey, D. R. (1960). *Principles of Criminology* (6th ed.). Philadelphia, PA: Lippincott.

Sykes, G. & Matza, D. (1957). Techniques of neutralization: A theory of delinquency. *American Sociological Review, 22,* 664–673.

Taylor, I., Walton, P., & Young, J. (1973). *The New Criminology: For a Social Theory of Deviance*. London: Routledge & Kegan Paul.

Turk, A. (1969). *Criminality and Legal Order*. Chicago, IL: Rand McNally.

Vul, E., Harris, C., Winkielman, P., & Pashler, H. (2009). Puzzlingly high correlations in fMRI studies of emotion, personality, and social cognition. *Perspectives on Psychological Science, 4,* 274–290.

Walker, N. (1965). *Crime and Punishment in Great Britain.* Edinburgh: Edinburgh University Press.

Watson, J. (1913). Psychology as the behaviorist views it. *Psychological Review, 20,* 158–177.

Williams, G. (1955). The definition of crime. In J. Smith & B. Hogan (Eds.), *Criminal Law* (2nd ed.) (pp. 364–394). London: Butterworths.

Wilson, E. O. (1971). *The Insect Societies.* Cambridge, MA: Harvard University Press.

—— (1975). *Sociobiology: The New Synthesis.* Cambridge, MA: The Belknap Press of Harvard University Press.

—— (1978). *On Human Nature.* Cambridge, MA: Harvard University Press.

—— (2000). *Sociobiology: The New Synthesis, 25th Anniversary Edition.* Cambridge, MA: The Belknap Press of Harvard University Press.

2   Crime

The basics

Crime is a truly egalitarian phenomenon: it pays no heed to the victim's age, class, race, social status, or even to their previous victimisation; its occurrence does not depend on time of day, day of the week, or month of the year; it pays no attention to international boundaries or cultural divides; it has no respect for social rules and moral values. Crime can arrive in many forms: there are violent crimes, sexual crimes, crimes against property, victimless crimes, and white-collar crimes; there are terrorist offences, crimes perpetrated against the state, and crimes perpetrated by the state; there are crimes that cause deep distress and crimes that go unnoticed; and there are crimes that are solved and crimes that remain unsolved.

Crime is ubiquitous in our everyday lives. We may personally experience crime by becoming a victim and we all know someone who has been a victim of crime. Pick up any newspaper, local, national, or international, and there will be a story about crime; switch on the radio or television and the news will include a crime-related story. We are appalled by some crimes and on occasions crimes can stir strong emotions across a country, as seen when a child goes missing or is murdered (see Box 2.1); on the other hand some crimes, such as shoplifting and car theft, attract little in the way of widespread consternation. Some crimes catch the public attention and, for a brief period, become part of our everyday lives as we wait for the criminal to strike again or for the police to announce that they made an arrest.

Crime is also a source of entertainment. Most bookshops have shelves filled with crime novels, some of them telling tales involving characters that we all know well. The familiar crime fiction *dramatis personae* include Sherlock Holmes, Dr Watson and Moriarty, Hercule Poirot, Maigret, Miss Marple, Sam Spade, Dick Tracy, Hannibal Lecter, Tom Ripley, Philip Marlowe, Inspector Morse (not to neglect Sergeant Lewis), Inspector Rebus and Adam Dalgliesh; Lord Peter Wimsey represents the nobility; Cadfael and Father Brown guarantee that the church is not left out; and The Famous Five make sure that children don't miss out on the fun of solving crime. There are similarly famous characters in the cinema and on television (including some who have made the move from the printed page to the screen), including Dixon of Dock Green, Perry Mason, Starsky and Hutch, Goldfinger, The Joker, Horatio Caine (a personal favourite!) and not forgetting that Scooby-Doo has a good clear-up rate in the highly specialist field of solving cartoon crime, although he has not as yet pitted his wits against Sideshow Bob!

The cost of crime

Crime is a big and very expensive business. Aside from the human costs, the economic reality is that crime soaks up a great deal of hard cash from the public purse. We have to pay,

---

Box 2.1 Crimes that caught the public's attention

James Bulger: The murder of a child invariably touches people's emotions, the rare event of the murder of a child by one or more other children hits the headlines. On 12 February 1993, the 2-year-old James Bulger was abducted from a shopping centre near Liverpool while with his mother. CCTV images showed him being led by the hand away from the shopping centre. He was then tortured, suffering horrendous injuries, then murdered by his abductors, two 10-year-old boys. His mutilated body was discovered, over two miles away on a railway line, 2 days after his murder. The two 10-year-olds, Robert Thompson and Jon Venables, were charged with Bulger's abduction and murder and found guilty on 24 November 1993: they are the youngest convicted murderers in recent English history.

Genette Tate: Genette Tate was a 13-year-old newspaper delivery girl who went missing close to her home village of Aylesbeare, east Devon, in August 1978. She was seen by friends who minutes later found her bicycle and the newspapers lying in a country lane. A large search of the area failed to find her and her body was never found.

Suzy Lamplugh: Susannah Lamplugh was a 25-year-old estate agent reported missing on 28 July 1986 in Fulham, South West London. A tantalising clue was found in her list of appointments in which she was to meet a 'Mr. Kipper' for a house showing. Mr. Kipper was never found. The police unsuccessfully carried out DNA testing on more than 800 unidentified bodies and skeletal remains but her body was never found. In 1986, Suzy's mother, Diana Lamplugh, set up The Suzy Lamplugh Trust with the aim of helping people to avoid violent victimisation and of offering assistance to relatives and friends of missing people. The trust also encouraged research into violence and organised conferences for professionals working in the field of crime prevention. (I was pleased once to contribute a talk on workplace violence to one such conference.)

---

through our taxes, for a police force to catch criminals, for a court system to ensure that justice is done, for a prison and probation service to watch over convicted criminals, and for the costs of compensation for victims.

We pay insurance premiums that reflect the risks of car crime and of burglary. There are the hidden financial costs of white-collar crimes such as fraud, tax evasion, and embezzlement. There are financial costs to the health service in caring, both physically and psychologically,

---

Box 2.2 The cost of crime: prisons

We can begin to appreciate the financial cost of the criminal justice system just by considering the number of prisons in England and Wales. (Scotland and Northern Ireland have their own prisons.) It should be remembered that each of the prisons will have costs for maintenance and upkeep, running costs for heat, electricity, and so on, salary costs for the staff, both prison service and civilian, who work in the prison, prisoner costs as in food, medical, and dental services, psychological services, and so on.

There are 130 prisons in England and Wales to hold a prison population of 85,374 (June 2011 figure from the Ministry of Justice website). These prisons cater for young and adult, male and female, offenders: the largest prison is Wandsworth, London with a capacity of 1,665 prisoners; the smallest is East Sutton Park, Kent with 100 prisoners. To illustrate the sums, East Sutton park has an annual budget for 2011–2 in excess of £2.5 million.

---

for those injured in the commission of crime. The fire service bears the some of the financial costs of arson; while those who travel by air must stand the costs of airport security. There are financial costs associated with shoplifting, credit card theft, and internet scams. If an injured or distressed employee does not turn up for work after being victim to a crime, then their employer may have to bear a loss in productivity, turnover, and profit.

There are society-wide financial costs associated with trying to prevent crime, including the purchase and maintenance of hardware such as burglar alarms, CCTV cameras, and safety lighting; in addition, there are the costs of security staff for car parks, public houses, and so on. There are other, perhaps more subtle, losses to take into account. A murder victim may, for example, represent a loss in public investment: if a doctor is murdered then the outlay for their education and training is wasted and the contribution they might have made to the well-being of others and good of society is lost.

As Cohen (2005) shows, society can spend a great deal of its resources, financial and otherwise, on crime. We all meet the costs of crime through our national and local taxes, through our insurance premiums, and in the prices we pay for the goods that we purchase. Crime soaks up public wealth, deflecting money away from being spent for the public good on healthcare, schools, or public transport.

If for no other reason than to give a better understanding of the harsh economics involved, it makes sense that we have a reliable estimate of the crime rate. An accurate knowledge of the numbers of crimes in the system is important from both theoretical and practical perspectives. If a certain crime occurs at a low frequency then perhaps this tells us something particular about the perpetrators or the circumstances in which the offence takes place. A crime that occurs at a low frequency, especially if it is unpredictable, may well be difficult or costly to prevent. For example, the theft of a major work of art is comparatively rare and it is extremely difficult, if not impossible, to predict when and where the next theft will take place. On the other hand, if a crime occurs at a high frequency, it follows that large numbers of people are involved. If we take the example of drunk and disorderly behaviour, it is not difficult to think where and when you would go to observe large numbers of drunk and disorderly people. High-frequency crimes are easier to detect, and possibly easier to reduce, than low-frequency crimes, although there will still be costs involved.

It is not difficult to see why crime is always a political hot issue. While we all want to be safe in our beds, most of us do not want to have to pay increased taxes in order to sleep peacefully. The dilemma for any government lies in controlling a rising crime rate while at the same time reducing costs in an area of public expenditure that is not, frankly, a real vote-winner: 'Crime rates down at reduced cost!' is not a familiar headline.

An accurate numerical estimate of the amount of crime at any one time in a particular area has a range of uses. At a local level, knowledge of rates of crime can inform people of their personal risks and what precautions it may be prudent for them to take to avoid crime. At a national level, if the crime data show that crime is increasing, then it may follow that the forces of law and order will require more of the public purse simply to maintain the status quo, or an increased need for victim support, or that changes are needed to reduce crime. The collection of accurate crime figures also has the advantage of helping the evaluation of initiatives to reduce crime by setting a baseline against which to look for change.

Criminal statistics

It generally falls to government departments to produce the criminal statistics for their jurisdiction. In England and Wales, the annual publication of *The Criminal Statistics* presents the details (e.g., Ministry of Justice, 2008). The introduction to the 2008 report notes that 'The statistics in this volume relate to offenders dealt with by formal police cautions, reprimands or warnings, or criminal court proceedings in England and Wales' (Ministry of Justice, 2008: ii). The content covers a wide array of material: there are, among others, chapters on court proceedings, offenders found guilty, and motoring offences. As well as presenting the most recent figures, the regular collation of the crime statistics allows year-on-year comparisons to be made.

There is much to be learned from the statistics in the 2008 report (the figures in the 2008 report are for 2007 and make comparisons with 2006). We see, for example, that the number of offenders who were either convicted or cautioned during 2007 increased from the previous year by just over half of 1 per cent to 1.78 million: however, for more serious indictable offences the number of offenders convicted or cautioned rose to 518,400, a 2 per cent increase against 2006. The largest increases by type of crime were for drug offences (14 per cent) and fraud and forgery (9 per cent). The good news was a *decrease* in the number of offenders convicted or cautioned for violence against the person (down by 5 per cent) and for indictable motoring offences (down by 10 per cent). The total number of offenders found guilty in 2007 was 1.42 million, down by less than 1 per cent on the previous year, although 313,300 offenders were found guilty of indictable offences, an annual increase of 3 per cent.

As shown by reviews of the way in which the crime statistics are compiled (e.g., Smith, 2006), there are a range of shifting issues in collecting reliable criminal statistics. The way in which a given crime is defined may change: for example, the law was amended in 1994 to expand the definition of rape to include rape within marriage. In addition, new crimes can be defined within law. In England and Wales, the Sexual Offences Act 2003 introduced new offences relating to sexual activity with a child less than 16 years of age (see Chapter 7). There may be, as discussed below, variations in police recording practices that can skew the figures: however, this is less of an issue following the introduction in 2002 of the national crime recording standards (Simmons, Legg, & Hosking, 2003).

Given the issues with changes in the law and definitions of specific offences, the main practical problem lies in collecting the figures at source. As in many matters statistical, the reliability of the measurement of the frequency and types of crime prevalent across society relies on the quality of the raw data. Where do the data to measure the amount of crime come from?

Measuring crime

In the late 18th century, the custom started in England and Wales of systematically gathering information about court proceedings and the numbers of convictions with the purpose of gauging the moral health of the country. The practice of gathering and collating information from courts, published as the *Judicial Statistics*, remained in place for about 50 years. A significant change to the recording practice occurred in 1857, when the court figures were augmented by the numbers of crimes reported to and recorded by the police. The figures from the combination of police-recorded crime and crime that passed through the courts were presented annually – the 'official statistics' – by the Home Office in the publication *Criminal Statistics* (now *Criminal Statistics, England and Wales*). The work of the courts is now presented by the Ministry of Justice in the report *Judicial and Court Statistics* (published as *Judicial Statistics* until 2005).

Many countries have similar recording systems for collating their national crime statistics: for example, the Scottish government publishes an annual *Statistical Bulletin*, in

America the *Uniform Crime Reports* are collected annually by the FBI, and in Australia the *Crime and Criminal Justice Statistics* are available from the Australian Institute of Criminology.

Official statistics

The *Criminal Statistics* for England and Wales is the main source of crime data for those two countries. These official statistics, published annually by the Home Office, present a record of the number and types of crime recorded each year by the police in England and Wales. As detailed in Box 2.3 , there are a range of UK government publications that give details about specific areas of the criminal justice system. The publications noted in Box 2.3 are the tip of a wealth of statistics and research available on the Home Office and Ministry of Justice websites.

When reading the criminal statistics there are a number of terms that are used: the specific meanings of these terms is shown in Box 2.4.

A distinction can be drawn between the *incidence* and *prevalence* of crime: incidence is the average frequency over the whole population; prevalence is the percentage of the population who actually experience crime. If we take the example of robbery, Kershaw, Nicholas, and Walker (2008) note that in 2007–8 across England and Wales, the crime of robbery accounted for just 2 per cent of all crimes recorded by the police. It is not unreasonable therefore to conclude that during that those years the national incidence of robbery was comparatively low. However, Kershaw et al. (2008) also note that for England and Wales in the same period, 62 per cent of robberies were recorded by just three police forces: these were Metropolitan, Greater Manchester, and West Midlands. Thus, in these three areas of the country the prevalence of robbery is a disproportionately long way ahead of the national average.

Changes over time

If matters such as the definitions of crime and the means of recording crime remain constant over time (or can be adjusted for accurately when they change), then it is possible to detect changes in crime over relatively long periods of time. As Maguire (2007) shows, since the mid-1930s, there has been a steady growth in the total number of offences recorded by

---

Box 2.3   Official statistics: publications

Criminal Statistics concerns offenders dealt with by formal police cautions, reprimands, or warnings, or criminal court proceedings in England and Wales.

Judicial and Court Statistics presents a comprehensive set of statistics on judicial and court activity, across all types of court, regarding number of cases, outcomes, and so on.

Offender Management Caseload Statistics provide details about those offenders under the supervision of the probation service. The information includes the main characteristics of offenders, work relating to pre- and post-release supervision, and details of breaches of community sentences. The figures also provide information about offenders in prison including length of sentences, numbers of receptions and releases, types of crime, demographic details, and trends in the size of the prison population.

Box 2.4   Statistical terminology

Count: This term refers to the raw numbers, the actual quantity of a specific offence. For example, Kershaw et al. (2008) note that in 2007–8 (rounded to the nearest hundred) the police recorded 292,300 burglaries in England and Wales.
Frequency: This term refers to how the numbers of crime are distributed across the population.
Rate: The way in which the numbers are seen in terms of some characteristic of the population from which the numbers were taken. For example, 100 burglaries per year in a small village with a population of 5,000 people is a markedly different crime rate to the same number of annual burglaries in a town with a population of 50,000.

---

the police. The numbers of crimes recorded by the police remained remarkably constant from the late 1800s until the early 1930s, but in the mid-1930s, the numbers of crimes recorded by the police grew markedly and, with the exception of one or two blips in the curve, has continued to rise each year since. In recent times, the recorded crime rate has risen rapidly with each passing decade, from approximately 500,000 in the 1950s, to 1,000,000 in the mid-1960s, 2,000,000 by the mid-1970s, 3,000,000 in the early 1980s, 5,000,000 in the 1990s, and around 6,000,000 in the mid-2000s.

From the raw figures it may seem reasonable to conclude that, even after adjusting for population growth, we live in a society in which crime is perpetually increasing. We could even take this view a step further and suggest that the methods of controlling crime are not working and that policy changes are urgently needed. (A call for a change in criminal justice policy seems inevitably to translate into arguments about the need for longer prison sentences and the reinstatement of capital punishment.) However, before making the leap from official statistics to criminal justice policy, we should ask about the reliability of the official figures. Just how accurate are the official figures as an estimate of the true quantity of crime? To try to answer this question researchers have turned to the three main groups involved in crime – the police, the offenders, and the victims – to investigate the frequency of crime from these three different perspectives.

Police recording of crime

The process that leads to the police to record a crime is straightforward: a person becomes aware of a crime, most probably as a witness or a victim, and then reports it to the police; the police then take whatever action, including investigation of the reported crime, they judge to be correct in the circumstances. In addition, a police officer may in the course of their duties, through observation or by admissions from suspects, become aware of a crime and exercise discretion as to its formal recording. Thus, police recording of crime relies, in large part, upon members of the public deciding to report an incident.

There are various factors that can influence the public's willingness to contact the police. For example, ease of communication may influence both the quality and quantity of crimes reported to the police. The ready availability of telephones makes it far easier to telephone the police at 2 am than to take the unlikely option of walking to the police station. Further, if a mobile telephone is to hand then it can be used immediately to report a crime, rather than waiting until later and then deciding that it is not worth contacting the police.

Social changes can also influence the public's readiness to report crimes. As I write, I have a leaflet from our local Neighbourhood Watch on my desk that asks local members to do 'As we requested and report [to the police] every incident that they are aware of ... report all crimes no matter how small so that the statistics can be more accurate'. If we all did this, then it is a fair bet that our local crime figures would increase!

If we accept that some crimes will not be reported to the police (see below), when a crime is reported does this guarantee that it will be counted in the official statistics? Maguire (2007: 258) notes: 'Despite rules to limit it, the police inevitably retain considerable discretion as to which of the incidents observed by or reported to them and deemed to be crimes and recorded as such. How this discretion is exercised may be influenced by a wide variety of social, political, and institutional factors, and may change over time'.

Factors influencing police recording

If a crime is reported to the police or if the police discover a crime then why would they not record it? Coleman and Moynihan (1996) suggest that there are various contexts – social and political, organisational, and situational – within which to understand police decision-making regarding the recording of crime. Similarly, Maguire (2007) comments that police discretion about recording can be influenced by political, social, and institutional factors that may change over time.

Social, political, and organisational factors

The police are a large and highly complex organisation. The Home Office website states that there are 43 police forces in England and Wales. These 43 police forces employ a large number of people in a variety of roles, as demostrated by Mulchandani and Sigurdsson (2009: 1): 'As at 31 March 2009, there were 243,126 full-time equivalent (FTE) staff working in the 43 police forces of England and Wales. Police officers accounted for 59.1 per cent of this total, police community support officers 6.8 per cent, traffic wardens 0.2 per cent, designated officers 1.3 per cent ... and other police staff 32.6 per cent'. On the basis of these figures alone, it is reasonable to say that by most standards, the police force is a large and complex organization.

The managerial structures necessary for effective governance of such a large organization as the police, alongside the necessary financial and accounting arrangements, are complex with several levels of responsibility and accountability both nationally and locally. The Home Office states on its website that it works with chief police officers and police authorities to manage police forces. There are three levels of responsibility for the running of the country's police forces: (1) the Home Office, which provides funding and takes overall responsibility for coordination of the police; (2) the chief police officers, who take responsibility for the regional forces; and (3) the local police authorities, composed of local magistrates, elected city or county councillors and independent community representatives, whose task is to make sure that local forces operate effectively and with efficiency. In addition to all of the above, HM Inspectorate of Constabulary has the task of monitoring and inspecting each police force in England and Wales in order to ensure that their performance reaches agreed standards and that year-on-year performance is improved.

The behavioural principle of reinforcement states that the frequency of a given behaviour will be maintained or increased when it is rewarded. If the police are rewarded for recording crime then there is every reason to be sure that their 'recording crime behaviour' will stay steady or increase over time. As Coleman and Moynihan (1996) suggest, if the financial resources made available to the police are dependent upon the level of crime they record, then it is clearly in the police's interests to maintain a high level of recorded crime. Given such a context, it is entirely understandable and predictable that police recording of crime will increase (i.e., be reinforced). On the other hand, if it is not the number of crimes *reported* but the number of crimes *cleared up* – itself a difficult statistic to tie down (see Bottomley and Pease, 1986) – on which resources depend, then there is every reason for the police *not* to record those crimes that they know are difficult or impossible to resolve.

There may be political (with a small 'p') factors that influence police recording of crime at either a local or a national level. If there is local concern regarding a particular type of offence in a part of a town or city, say drug crime or prostitution (drugs and sex can usually be counted on when it comes to the public's concerns about crime), then a crackdown on drugs or prostitution in that locality can produce figures that show an apparent rise in drug use or prostitution. The same phenomenon can occur at a national level, as seen with the publicity around reducing crime related to binge-drinking.

The net result of local fluctuations in police activity may be to produce figures that indicate an apparent *increase* in crime. This increase in the figures does not, of course, necessarily have to mean that there has been a *real* increase in that type of crime. It may be the case that, to use statistical terminology, improved sampling (through increased police activity and more accurate recording) has given a better estimate of the true population. In other words, the recorded figure has edged a little closer to reality.

A much discussed real-life example of how local variations in the way reported crime is recorded by the police lies, as Maguire (2007) states, in 'The strange case of Nottinghamshire'. Nottinghamshire has attracted interest because it provides a good case study of the complexities of unravelling the recorded crime statistics.

The county of Nottinghamshire is in the Midlands and does not contain large cities on the scale of London, Birmingham, or Manchester, which are generally associated with high levels of crime. However, Nottinghamshire has consistently been associated with a high crime rate when compared with similar English counties. This anomaly was noted by Farrington and Dowds (1985) and is still evident in the recorded crime figures (Walker, Kershaw, & Nicholas, 2006). In their study of police crime recording practices in Nottinghamshire, Farrington and Dowds suggested several reasons for the apparent irregularity in the figures. They commented that, compared with two other Midlands police forces, Nottinghamshire police recorded a greater amount of crimes involving property of low value, and they also recorded a greater number of crimes following admissions by known offenders. In addition, Farrington and Dowds suggested that Nottinghamshire may also have an underlying higher crime rate than its neighbours, the magnitude of which is magnified by recording practice.

Situational factors

As Hough and Mayhew (1983) note, the police may, with justification, judge that a reported 'crime' is a mistake, or that there is a lack of evidence to support investigation of the reported crime. In other instances, an informal caution may be given to those involved in the reported crime, in which case the offence will not appear in the official figures. In a similar vein, an incident may be satisfactorily resolved by the appearance of a police officer: family disputes and arguments in public houses are typical examples of a situation in which a crime is reported but goes unrecorded. It is also possible that the person who reported the crime will later ask for their report to be dropped. In such cases, the incident becomes 'no crime' and does not appear in the criminal statistics. Sparks, Genn, and Dodd (1977), in a survey of three London areas, reported that instances of 'no crime' accounted for between 18 and 28 per cent of recorded crimes.

The time lapse between the when the crime was committed and when it was reported to the police may also be important. Those reported crimes that are judged to be too 'stale' to merit investigation may fail to be recorded (Farrington and Bennett, 1981). Of course, one of the issues associated with unrecorded crime, by definition, lies in knowing the numbers of crimes are reported to the police but not recorded. While the true numbers of unrecorded crimes can never be known exactly, as discussed below, surveys of the general public do allow estimates to be made.

The difference between the number of crimes actually committed and the number in the official statistics is often referred to as the *Dark Figure*. The Dark Figure is, by definition, difficult to quantify. However, as will be seen there are ways by which estimates of this quantity of 'unknown crime' can be produced.

If the issues surrounding police recording of crime are writ large on a national scale, what happen when we move to police recording of crime on an international scale? The European Commission has begun to collate the figures on police recorded crime across the European Union (Taveres & Thomas, 2009). In a piece of research of Herculean proportions, Taveres and Thomas collated police recorded crimes from 1998 to 2007 for 29 European Union (EU) member states as well as 3 EU candidate countries, 2 EU potential candidate countries, and 4 EFTA/EEA countries.

The resulting report is packed with statistics and quickly becomes compulsive reading – which country has had the greatest increase in crime? Which country's capital city has the highest murder rate? – and Taveres and Thomas draw some broad conclusions. Where comparisons are possible, trends in total crime figures for 1998–2007 across the EU are that crime rose from 1999, peaked in 2002, and the fell consistently in the 5 years to 2007. In terms of specific types of crime, violent crime rose by 3 per cent, and drug trafficking and robbery both increased by 1 per cent from 1998 to 2007. The good news is that over the same period, the theft of motor vehicles fell by 7 per cent and domestic burglary was down by 3 per cent.

Taveres and Thomas note that the annual rate for homicides in the period 2005–7 was approximately 1.4 per 100,000 of the population, rising to about 1.9 per 100,000 in capital cities. The homicide figures are perhaps a reflection of social and political upheaval, with the capitals of Estonia (Tallinn) and Lithuania (Vilnius) recording the highest rates. It will be recalled that around the early 1990s, both these countries – that, along with Latvia, form the Baltic States – regained their independence from the Soviet Union. In the major European capitals, the lowest homicide rates were found in Lisbon and Berlin; across all the capital cities the lowest possible rate of zero was recorded for Vaduz and Valletta.

In terms of the criminal justice system, Taveres and Thomas note that while there was only a minimal change in the number of police officers in EU member states, the prison population rose steadily, by about 1 per cent a year, so that the average rate for 2005–7 is 123 prisoners per 100,000 of the population.

The collection of crime statistics on the scale presented by Taveres and Thomas allows a diverse range of observations to be made and highlights trends over time. Nonetheless, the figures are based on police recording, with all the associated caveats, and can therefore say nothing of the Dark Figure of unrecorded crime. In attempting to shed light on the magnitude of the Dark Figure and so help understand the intricacies of the processes that lead some crimes to be left unreported, researchers have turned their attention both to those individuals who commit crime and those who are its victims.

Self-report surveys

An obvious way to find out more about criminal behaviour is to ask the people who commit crimes. There is a long tradition of self-report studies in which offenders are asked to give details about the crimes they have committed (Hood & Sparks, 1970). In a typical self-report study, a sample of people are selected, say on the basis of their age, and asked, generally either by questionnaire or interview, about any crimes they might have committed. There are several self-report questionnaires designed for this type of research (Elliot & Ageton, 1980; Hindelang, Hirschi, & Weis, 1981), which have been put to use with various populations including children of school age (e.g., Belson, 1975), university students (e.g., Furnham, 1991) and young offenders (e.g., Palmer & Hollin, 2001a). Self-reported offending is often of interest in the context of studying its association with some other variable such as personality (Furnham, 1991) or moral reasoning (Palmer & Hollin, 2001b), although self-report can also be used to give an insight into the 'real' extent of criminals' offending.

Groth, Longo, and McFadin (1982) used a self-report methodology with men convicted of sexual offences against both women and children. The sex offenders, given assurances that confidentiality would be respected, were asked about their history of sexual offending. When asked about the number of offences for which they had not been caught, the men said that they had on average committed five undetected sexual crimes. The range of undetected crimes the sexual offenders declared was substantial, from low numbers to more than 200 offences.

When we see claims to such large numbers of undetected crimes we pause to ask if the offenders who make such claims are telling the truth. Do the respondents in self-report studies always tell the truth: are some crimes invented or exaggerated? Of course, it can work the other way: offenders may withhold some crimes perhaps because of their seriousness or because they feel ashamed of what they have done.

There have been several attempts to cross-check the validity of offenders' self-report. A longstanding verification technique is to compare self-reports with police records. Studies using this method have recorded high levels of agreement between the official and self-report accounts (Blackmore, 1974; Farrington, 1989). There are other methods used to verify the accuracy of offenders' self-report including cross-checking with peers, using test-retest to see if the offenders' accounts remain constant, and incorporating checks for social desirability and lie questions into the study as a check on honesty in responding. Hindelang, Hirschi, and Weis (1981) concluded from their review of self-report methodology that there is a good level of correspondence between self-reported offending and official records.

A study by Farrall (2005) looked at the self-reported offending of 141 convicted offenders serving a period of supervision by the probation service in England and Wales. The offenders' self-reports were considered in light of the degree of correspondence to subsequent convictions and to their probation officer's knowledge of their offending. Farrall found that about half of the sample had committed an offence, mainly property offences, while on probation. In the main, the probation officers were aware of the offending and the association was close between self-report and conviction. In summarising the findings on self-report and conviction, Farrall (2005: 129) concludes: 'There is indeed a strong relationship between these two sources of information on individuals' criminal careers'.

Kroner, Mills, and Morgan (2007) investigated the self-reported offending of a sample of Canadian prisoners serving sentences for violent crimes. In keeping with Farrall's findings, Kroner et al. reported only a minimal loss of information through self-report. When loss occurred, it was most probably explicable by memory attrition given the long time gaps, up to 10 years, between some offences and the time of the study. It seems likely that, even for serious offences, offenders' self-reporting of their criminal activity is reliable.

Self-report studies can also be used to look at crimes committed by different age groups, taking a close look at types of crime, the frequency with which crimes are committed, and so on. A good example of such a fine-grained approach is provided by a Swedish report on youth and crime (Swedish National Council for Crime Prevention, 2007). As well as recording the national picture, this report also considers variations in youth crime across 25 Swedish counties. Through a national school survey, asking pupils about their involvement in criminal activities, data were gathered from a cross-section of classes and schools. This type of large-scale survey with several thousand respondents invariably produces a wealth of information.

When a survey is repeated several times, as was the case with the Swedish survey, trends in the data can be looked for to see if crime generally or specific types of crime are changing in frequency. The researchers were able to say, 'During the period between 1995 and 2005, 57.6 percent of Sweden's year nine youth reported having committed a theft offence over the course of a year, while 36.4 percent reported having committed an act of vandalism and 18.1 percent some form of violent act' (Swedish National Council for Crime Prevention, 2007: 8). It is not unexpected that less serious crimes, such as vandalism, are far more frequently reported than serious, violent crimes.

Offending, Crime and Justice Survey

In England and Wales, the *Offending, Crime and Justice Survey* (OCJS; Roe & Ashe, 2008) uses self-reports to elicit the views, attitudes, and experiences of young people about crime. The survey samples a randomly selected group of young people, living in private households, on a national basis. The content of the survey is concerned with 20 'core offences', with each offence categorised as being a *property-related offence* (e.g., burglary, vehicle theft), a *violent offence* (e.g., robbery, assault), or *drug selling* (Class A or other drugs).

The survey started in 2003 (Budd, Sharp, & and Mayhew, 2005) with a sample of more than 10,000 people aged from 10 to 65 years. The later surveys conducted between 2004 and 2006 focused on young people aged from 10 to 25 years. In the later surveys, some of the young people who had been interviewed previously agreed to participate in a further interview. In addition to the young people taking part for a second time, new respondents aged from 10 to 25 years were added to maintain the total annual sample at around 5,000 young people. The repeated use of the same respondents adds a longitudinal dimension to the survey, allowing changes and trends over time to emerge.

Surveys such as the OCJS provide substantial amounts of information on patterns of offending among young people. Thus, Roe and Ashe reported that during the previous year, more than 75 per cent of young people had not committed any of the survey's 20 core offences. The immediate conclusion therefore is that most young people are good, law abiding citizens. Where offences had been committed they were mainly occasional and trivial in nature, with only a small percentage of young people (6 per cent) committing an offence six or more times in the past year. The most common offences were assault (12 per cent of the respondents) and thefts (10 per cent); the least common were criminal damage (4 per cent), drug-selling offences (3 per cent), vehicle-related thefts (2 per cent), and burglary and robbery (less than 1 per cent). There were very few young people (3 per cent) who said that they had carried a knife. The 2005 survey showed no significant change in levels of offending compared with the first survey in 2003. The peak age range at which offending took place was 14–17 years, with males were more likely than females to have committed an offence.

The distinction between being a victim of crime and being a criminal is not always as clear-cut as may be imagined. The survey found that many of the young people who committed crimes had also been the victim of a crime. Indeed, more than half of those young people who said they had committed an offence in the last year said that they personally had also been the victim of a crime during the same period. The victimisation rate of half among those who said they committed a crime compares to a rate of about one-fifth among those young people who had not committed a crime. The younger respondents, aged from 10 to 15 years, were more likely than the older respondent to report that they had been victim of a crime. These crimes typically occurred at school or college and were not usually reported to the police. The younger victims were more likely that the older victims to know the person who committed the crime against them. Fellow school pupils or friends were the most common perpetrators of assault against the 10- to 15-year age group. For the 16- to 25-year age group, the criminal incidents were generally most likely to take place in a pub, bar or nightclub, or in the street. With this older age group, the most frequent perpetrators were friends or someone who the young person said they had seen around the places they frequented.

Alongside criminal offences, the OCJS also asked about anti-social behaviour. The broad term 'anti-social behaviour' is often used to refer to *both* criminal and non-criminal activities that cause concern and give offence to other people. The OCJS asked about four specific types of anti-social behaviour: (1) being noisy or rude in a public place so that people complained or the individual got into trouble with the police; (2) behaviour that resulted in a neighbour complaining; (3) making graffiti in a public place; and (4) threatening or insulting behaviour to another person directed at their race or religion. The most commonly reported types of anti-social behaviour were being noisy or rude in public (13 per cent) and behaviour that led a neighbour to complain (11 per cent); graffiti (4 per cent) and personal abuse based on race and religion (2 per cent) were least common. The peak age for committing anti-social behaviour in the previous 12 months was 14–15 years.

The OCJS is based upon interview but rather than the traditional paper-and-pencil format, the OCJS uses computer-assisted personal interviewing (CAPI) and computer-assisted self-interviewing (CASI). With CAPI, the interviewer reads the questions from a laptop computer and enters the respondent's answers into the appropriate text boxes. The interview generally lasts for approximately one hour. Where CASI is used, the respondent reads the questions, again on a laptop, and types in their answers. A variation in the methodology is the use of Audio-CASI where the respondent listens to the questions using headphones before entering their answer onti the computer. The advantage of CASI is that it removes the potential embarrassment of biased responding that may result from being asked about sensitive topics.

In self-report studies, there are a range of methodological issues in the design of the study that can influence an individual's account of their misdemeanours. The traditional way to conduct self-report studies is either through a questionnaire or through interview. In pencil-and-paper questionnaire studies the person is given the questionnaire and completes it, generally anonymously, either alone or in a group. Box 2.5 shows items used in a self-report study of delinquent behaviour carried out with university students.

In face-to-face interview studies, the researcher will talk through the questions, usually following a structured or semi-structured interview format, to gain information from the offender. This method has the advantage that it allows the interviewer to follow up on points

---

Box 2.5 Self-reported delinquency

The items below are taken from a 46-item self-report delinquency measure originally devised by Elliot and Ageton (1980) and used, in a slightly modified form, with UK students (Hollin, Marsh, & Bloxsom, 2011; Palmer & Hollin, 1998). The scale measures crimes against the person, crimes against property, status crimes, illegal service crimes, public disorder crimes, and hard drug abuse. The response to each item is a rating from 1 to 8: *1 = never; 2 = 2–3 times a year; 3 = once a month; 4 = 2–3 times a month; 5 = once a week; 6 = 2–3 times a week; 7 = once a day; 8 = 2–3 times a day.* Respondents were asked how often they had:

- Purposely damaged or destroyed other property that did not belong to you (not counting family or school property)?
- Stolen (or tried to steal) a motor vehicle such as a car or motorcycle?
- Attacked someone with the idea of seriously hurting or killing them?
- Been loud, rowdy, or unruly in a public place (disorderly conduct)?
- Sold hard drugs such as heroin, cocaine, and LSD?
- Avoided paying for things such as films, bus or train rides, or food?

---

that require clarification or are of particular interest. An interview also reduces the chances of missing data: anyone who has carried out research with questionnaires will know about the difficulties that unanswered questions pose for analysis! The main methodological issues with interviews stem from the interactive nature of the process: it is likely that the characteristics – age, sex, socioeconomic status, and race – of the interviewer and interviewee will influence the quality of information. In addition, the location may be important, with variations in answers likely for a home setting, particularly if a parent is in earshot while drug use is being discussed, compared with a school-based interview where peers are present.

The growth in the availability and use of computers has allowed the development of internet-based questionnaires. The methodology is basically the same as with a paper-and-pencil questionnaire but with a change in the means of administration. The advantages of internet-based questionnaires are that, perhaps particularly for younger people, they are quick to complete and the data can be automatically collated as questionnaires are completed. The time saved by automated data collation, alongside the increase in accuracy of recording, makes this approach very attractive to researchers. Lucia, Herrmann, and Killias (2007) compared the results of paper-and-pencil and internet-based questionnaires on self-report of delinquency in a sample of students in Swiss schools. They found that there was little difference in the quality of data produced by the two methods of questionnaire administration. However, students answering the internet-based questionnaire were more motivated to respond, completed the questionnaire more quickly, and felt more confident in the confidentiality of their answers.

In addition to the issues posed by the style of administration, there are other methodological issues to consider in self-report studies. As in any research, the sample-taking part of the study is critically important. If a self-report study is carried out at a school, for example, then it will miss those pupils who are absent or playing truant (the data from the truants may be the most interesting!). There can be issues in defining the reference point for the respondents and the specificity of responding. If the questionnaire has a 12-month reference point, then it may be relatively easy for the respondents to remember their actions. If the questionnaire asks recall over a 24-month period then the task changes. In a similar way, if the questionnaire asks 'Have you ever...' as opposed to 'How many times and when...', then the demands on the respondent's memory are increased.

The general picture that emerges from the self-report studies is that the official statistics are an underestimate the true extent of crime, especially among the young. It seems that delinquency, mainly of the less serious type, is so common among young people as to be the norm rather than a deviant activity. As will be seen in Chapter 4, investigation of the nature and extent of offending among young people has led to some significant advances in understanding the aetiology of criminal behaviour.

Advocates of self-report studies, while acknowledging the various methodological issues, point to the advantages of this approach, saying that it gives a picture of offences both involving victims and 'victimless' crimes such as drug abuse and vandalism. Nonetheless, the trend in survey research has moved away from the offender to the victim.

Victim surveys

The first victim surveys appeared in the late 1960s in the form of government reports from the USA (e.g., Biederman, Johnson, McIntyre, & Weir, 1967; Ennis, 1967) that had been conducted to augment the official crime figures published in the *Uniform Crime Reports*. These surveys began to shed a little illumination on the Dark Figure, revealing more of the true nature and extent of criminal activity. At the level of national government, it was increasingly felt that if policies were to be put in place to reduce crime, then a fuller understanding of hidden crime, as provided by victim surveys, was necessary. As described by Coleman and Moynihan (1996), the first national victim survey, the National Crime Survey (NCR), was carried out in the USA in 1972. In spite of its various methodological limitations, the force of the NCR was to suggest that victims were reporting a crime rate up to five times greater than indicated by the official statistics. However, it also became apparent that victim surveys could provide a great deal more than bare figures. Victim surveys could be used to gain information about which crimes were reported and which were left unreported and could provide qualitative details such as the public's attitudes to crime and punishment and fear of crime.

Victim surveys became increasingly popular and, for example, were conducted in Australia (Congalton & Najman, 1974) and the Scandinavian countries (Aromaa, 1974). In England and Wales, the first national victim survey, *The British Crime Survey*, was published in 1983 (Hough & Mayhew, 1983).

The British Crime Survey

In Britain, as elsewhere in the world, small-scale victim surveys had been carried out in different parts of the country: for example, in England, victim surveys had been conducted in London (Jones, MacLean, & Young, 1986; Sparks, Genn, & Dodd, 1970) and on Merseyside (Kinsey, 1984). However, the decision was made in the early 1980s that the Home Office would conduct a national survey, *The British Crime Survey* (BCS), initially covering England, Scotland, and Wales. Scotland has produced its own crime survey since the early 1990s (see Anderson & Leitch, 1993) and Northern Ireland has developed its own crime survey based on the BCS (see Freel & French, 2008).

Jansson (no date) provides a succinct history of the first 25 years of the BCS, noting that the original aim was an improved understanding of victimisation across the whole country. The BCS, Jansson continues, was essentially a research tool that provided three outcomes: (1) an improved count of crime, including crimes that had not been reported to or recorded by the police); (2) identification of the risk factors associated with criminal victimisation; and (3) details of the public's worries about crime and their experiences of contact with the police. As time passed, the BCS provided information regarding patterns and trends in crime.

The methodology for the first BCS (Hough & Mayhew, 1983) was a *household survey* in which 16,000 households were selected (80 per cent of which participated) from the Electoral Register, with the aim of interviewing one person aged 16 years or older from each household. The interview asked respondents if they had experienced being a victim of crime and, if so, for details of the crime and whether they had reported it to the police. The interview also included questions on attitudes towards crime.

The first point to make from the first BCS is that most people do not experience crime: indeed, as Sparks (1981: 17) commented: 'Criminal victimization is an extremely rare event ... crimes of violence are extremely uncommon'. Further, when crimes do occur, it is the trivial types of crime, such as theft from a motor vehicle, which are the most common. The more serious offences, such as assault and robbery, occur at a very low rate. Thus, for example, Hough and Mayhew (1983) estimate that the 'statistically average' person over the age of 16 years can anticipated being burgled once every 40 years and being robbed once every 500 years.

Given the low probability of victimisation, the first BCS gave a pointer as to the magnitude of the Dark Figure. At a time when the number of crimes recorded by the police in England and Wales was around 3,000,000, the BCS estimate was almost four times greater at approximately 11,000,000 crimes. Why was there such a gap between people's experience and the official record? The findings from the BCS offered some insights into the choices victims of crime made about dealing with what had happened. Victims were selective about which crimes they reported to the police: for example, there was a high rate of reporting of theft of a motor vehicle (for insurance purposes) but a low reporting rate for theft in a dwelling (theft in a dwelling, as distinct from burglary, is when who is in the victim's home legitimately, such as a workman or party guest, takes the stolen goods).

The first BCS also examined the reasons why victims did not reporting a crime. The main reasons given by victims were the view that the crime was too trivial, or that they thought that there was nothing the police could do, or that they dealt with the matter personally. Parenthetically, there are several other reasons why a victim (or witness) may not report a crime. The victim may not realise an act is criminal: for example, physical violence may be seen as bullying rather than assault and therefore not something to report to the police. In crimes such as fraud or theft from an employer, the victim might be unaware that the crime has taken place and so cannot report it. The individual may be a 'willing victim' in the crime as with, for example, some homosexual behaviour and drug-dealing. Finally there are 'victimless crimes': if a telephone kiosk is vandalised or a false income tax return submitted, who is the victim to report the crime?

After the first survey, the BCS was repeated in 1984, 1988, 1992, 1994, 1996, 1998, 2000, and 2001, since when it has been conducted with continuous interviewing. The BCS now interviews more than 51,000 people aged 16 or over annually: in 2009 it was extended to include 4,000 interviews with children aged between 10 and 15 years. Thus, the stage has now been reached where there are quarterly BCS updates available from the Home Office (e.g., Home Office, 2009) along with the traditional annual reports (e.g., Walker, Flatley, Kershaw, & Moon, 2009).

As would be expected with any research project that is repeated, the passage of time has seen a number of methodological changes in the way the survey is conducted. Indeed, the survey is now subject to annual review in order to revise and improve the existing questions, and to introduce questions about new topics. The technical details on the survey, from briefing of interviewers to content of the SPSS data files, are available (Bolling, Grant, & Donovan, no date).

A major change in the BCS can be seen with respect to sampling: the sample size has increased from 11,000 respondents in 1982 to more than 47,000 in 2005/6. A growth in size on this scale invariably means that there will be a trade-off with the response rate. The very high response rate achieved in the earlier surveys with smaller samples, as seen with an 81 per cent response rate in 1982, has not been maintained in the later surveys, with 75 per cent in 2005/6. However, there are adjustments that can be made for non-response to maintain the quality of the survey. In addition, the BCS now includes 'booster' samples of young people and people from black and ethnic minority backgrounds in order to be confident that there are sufficient data from these groups to provide reliable information.

The BCS has also taken advantage of technological developments. As with the *Offending, Crime and Justice Survey*, the BCS interviews are now conducted with the aid of a laptop computer rather than pen and paper. The data monitoring systems to ensure the data integrity at all stages from questionnaire design, to interviewing, and then data entry and analysis – including checks for and correcting any bias caused by non-responses – have become more sophisticated. The work of the Home Office statisticians has been augmented by independent advice and reviews of the whole enterprise (Smith, 2006).

It is apparent that the BCS now is a refined piece of (expensive) large-scale social research. The key question, of course, is what have we learned from all of these data?

Key findings from the BCS: types of crime

The BCS shows that the relative proportions of the different types of crime reported by those taking part in the survey have not changed significantly since 1981. It remains the case that property crimes, particularly vandalism and theft, account for the majority people's experiences of crime. Violent crime is relatively uncommon: in the 1981 survey, one-fifth of BCS crimes were violent crimes, a proportion which has remained stable over time.

Key findings from the BCS: crime and the Dark Figure

The exact magnitude of the Dark Figure is impossible to know, there will always be crimes that remain hidden from view for a variety of reasons (see below). However, the BCS has shown that there is probably a fluctuating relationship between the number of crimes recorded in the survey and numbers recorded by the police. Jansson (no date) observes that the BCS estimates of crime showed an increase throughout the 1980s, reaching a high point in 1995 of 19,000,000 crimes, before decreasing and remaining stable at around 11,000,000, the same level as was evident in the early 1980s. However, over the same period, the numbers of crimes recorded by the police rose from about 3,000,000 to 5,000,000: however, some of this growth in police recorded crime may well be due changes in the counting rules for crime along with changes in public reporting and in police recording practices.

Table 2.1 gives details of the differences between BCS and police figures for different types of crime.

The figures in Table 2.1 perfectly illustrate the points made earlier in this chapter regarding police recording of crime. First, the official figures are considerably lower than survey

Table 2.1 Crime-specific variation in police and BCS recorded crime: 2007–8 compared with 2008–9 (after Walker et al., 2009)

BCS crime
- All BCS crime: stable (10.7 million crimes in 2008/9)
- Violent crime: stable
- Violent crime with injury: stable
- Domestic burglary: stable
- Vehicle-related theft: stable
- Theft from the person: up 25 per cent
- Vandalism: stable

Police-recorded crime
- All police recorded crime: down (by 5 per cent to 4.7 million crimes)
- Violence crime: down 6 per cent
- Violence crime with injury: down 7 per cent
- Domestic burglary: up 1 per cent
- Offences against vehicles: down 10 per cent
- Theft from the person: down 12 per cent
- Criminal damage: down 10 per cent

---

figures (giving an indication of the magnitude of the Dark Figure). Second, there is much more fluctuation in the official figures than in the survey figures which remain reasonably constant over time.

Key findings from the BCS: trends in types of crime

Given its history spanning three decades, the BCS provides an estimate of the frequency with which different types of crime are experienced in England and Wales. If we begin with violent crime, there were approximately 2,200,000 violent incidents recording in the 1981 survey. This figure peaked at 4,300,000 in 1995, to return to 1981 levels by 2005. It should be noted that the majority of the violent crimes recorded by the BCS are not acts of serious violence: indeed, around half of the violent crime involves acts such as pushing and shoving without any injury to the victim. The more serious violent crimes, such as attempted murder or robbery, occur very infrequently by comparison.

Moving to burglary, there were 749,000 burglaries recorded by the 1981 BCS. As with violent crime, the number of burglaries peaked at 1,770,000 burglaries in 1995, falling to 733,000 in the 2005/6 BCS. The same pattern is evident for vehicle-related theft, with approximately 1,750,000 vehicle-related thefts recorded by the 1981 BCS. Again with a peak in 1995 at just below 2,500,000, the frequency of vehicle-related theft (which includes both the theft of property from vehicles and theft of the vehicle) then fell back to 1981 levels. These fluctuations are set against a background of a year-on-year increase in the number of cars on the road.

Methodological issues in victim surveys

There are clearly many positive aspects to victim surveys, such as *The British Crime Survey*, in that they provide a reasonable picture of the type and amount of crime that is taking place. However, victim surveys are not without shortcomings. It is inevitable that the estimates they produce will underestimate the amount of crime. As they focus on offences against the person and against property they say nothing about 'white-collar crimes' such as fraud, tax evasion, and embezzlement. They are also limited with regard to the most serious crimes: at the most obvious, victims of murder cannot describe their victimisation but there are other crimes, such as domestic violence or child abuse, which victims may not wish to talk about. A lower age limit, typically 16-years-old, in many surveys means that the crimes experienced by the younger members of society are not recorded. While a sampling strategy that relies on households omits the homeless, travellers, and those who live in residential accommodation (such as children's homes or a medical facilities).

As was the case with offender surveys, the issue of respondent accuracy similarly applies to victim surveys. The respondents may have forgotten what happened, or become confused about when specific events took place, or they may wish to withhold some details. The style and conduct of the interview, the use of multiple interviews, and interviewer characteristics can all influence the information gleaned by the survey. Nonetheless, the figures produced by victim surveys remain an important source of information about the extent of crime. These surveys contribute to our understanding of crime thereby influencing academic theories and research into the crime and, perhaps more importantly, influencing political and social polices concerned with the prevention, management, and control of crime.

Another set of findings from victim surveys relates to the effects of crime on victims and public views of the criminal justice system and its various agencies. These are topics which will be returned to when considering the social issues associated with crime. The next topic, however, is the way in which psychological theories have been applied to try to give an account of crime.

Chapter summary

- Crime has costs. There are the financial costs to the public purse in paying for the elements of the criminal justice system – the police, courts, and prison and probation – as well as costs to the NHS, employers, and so on.
- Alongside financial costs, crime produces human costs in the physical and psychological suffering experienced by victims, and social costs as in the shared distress of the victim's friends and family.
- It is difficult to measure the true extent of crime. There are three methods that are used to try to estimate the numbers of crimes: (1) official statistics; (2) offender surveys; and (3) victim surveys.
- *The British Crime Survey* (BCS) is a large-scale victim survey that takes place at frequent intervals.
- The BCS reveals that, for most people in Britain victimisation is a rare occurrence, although some people are repeatedly victimised, and most crimes are relatively minor with serious violent crime particularly unusual.

Points for discussion

- Some crimes are much more readily reported by victims than others. What could be done to encourage *all* victims to report their victimisation?
- Is it really the case that the amount of crime rises year after year or are we just becoming better at reporting and recording to produce more accurate criminal statistics?
- Given what we know about the accuracy of the crime statistics, should they be used to inform criminal justice policy?

Recommended reading

Coleman, C. & Moynihan, J. (1996). *Understanding Crime Data: Haunted by the Dark Figure.* Buckingham: Open University Press.

The lighter side

'Detective work in the retired work of art theft, a rare type of crime.'
Griffiths, N. (2006). *Saving Caravaggio.* New York, NY: Viking.

Useful websites

FBI for Crime Stats www.fbi.gov/ucr/ucr.htm
Home Office/Ministry of Justice www.homeoffice.gov.uk/police/about/
EU crime figures http://epp.eurostat.ec.europa.eu/portal/page/portal/crime/data/database

References

Anderson, S. & Leitch, S. (1993). *The Scottish Crime Survey 1993: First Results.* Edinburgh: Scottish Government Publications.

Aromaa, K. (1974). *The Replication of a Survey of Victimization to Violence.* Helsinki: Institute of Criminology.

Belson, W. (1975). *Juvenile Theft: The Causal Factors.* New York, NY: Harper & Row.

Biederman, A. D., Johnson, L., McIntyre, J., & Weir, A. (1967). *Report on a Pilot Study in the District of Columbia on Victimization and Attitudes to Law Enforcement.* Washington, DC: US Government Printing Office.

Blackmore, J. (1974). The relationship between self-reported delinquency and official convictions amongst adolescent boys. *British Journal of Criminology, 14,* 172–176.

Bolling, K., Grant, C., & Donovan, J. (no date). 2007–08 British Crime Survey (England and Wales). Technical Report, Vol. I. London: Home Office.

Bottomley, K. & Pease, K. (1986). *Crime and Punishment: Interpreting the Data.* Milton Keynes: Open University Press.

Budd, T., Sharp, C., & Mayhew, P. (2005). *Offending in England and Wales: First Results from the 2003 Crime and Justice Survey.* Home Office Research Study 275. London: Home Office.

Cohen, M. A. (2005). *The Costs of Crime and Justice.* New York, NY: Routledge.

Coleman, C. & Moynihan, J. (1996). *Understanding Crime Data: Haunted by the Dark Figure.* Buckingham: Open University Press.

Congalton, A. A. & Najman, J. M. (1974). *Unreported Crime.* Sydney: New South Wales Bureau of Crime Statistics and Research.

Elliot, D. S. & Ageton, S. S. (1980). Reconciling race and class differences in self-reported and official estimates of delinquency. *American Sociological Review, 45,* 95–110.

Ennis, P. H. (1967). *Criminal Victimization in the United States: A Report of a National Survey.* Washington, DC: US Government Printing Office.

Farrall, S. (2005). Officially recorded convictions for probationers: The relationship with self-report and supervisory observations. *Legal and Criminological Psychology, 10,* 121–131.

Farrington, D. P. (1989). Self-reported and official offending from adolescence to adulthood. In M. W. Klien (Ed.), *Cross-national Research in Self-reported Crime and Delinquency* (pp. 399–423). Dordrecht: Kluwer Academic Publishers.

Farrington, D. P. & Bennett, T. (1981). Police cautioning of juveniles in London. *British Journal of Criminology, 21,* 123–35.

Farrington, D. P. & Dowds, E. A. (1985). Disentangling criminal behaviour and police reaction. In D. P. Farrington & J. Gunn (Eds.), *Reaction to Crime: The Public, the Police, Courts and Prisons* (pp. 41–72). Chichester, Sussex: John Wiley & Sons.

Freel, R. & French, B. (2008). *Experience of Crime: Findings from the 2006/2007 Northern Ireland Crime Survey.* Belfast: Northern Ireland Office.

Furnham, A. (1991). Personality and self-reported delinquency. *Personality and Individual Differences, 12,* 585–593.

Groth, A. A., Longo, R. E., & McFadin, J. B. (1982). Undetected recidivism among rapists and child molesters. *Crime and Delinquency, 28,* 450–458.

Hindelang, M. J., Hirschi, T., & Weis, J. G. (1981). *Measuring Delinquency.* Thousand Oaks, CA: Sage.

Hollin, C. R., Marsh, C., & Bloxsom, C. A. J. (2011). Anger and self-reported delinquency in university students. *European Journal of Psychology Applied to Legal Context, 3,* 1–10.

Home Office (2009). *Crime in England and Wales: Quarterly Update to December 2008.* Home Office Statistical Bulletin 06/09. London: Home Office.

Hood, R. & Sparks, R. (1970). *Key Issues in Criminology.* London: Weidenfeld & Nicholson.

Hough, M. & Mayhew, P. (1983). *The British Crime Survey: First Report.* London: HMSO.

Jansson, K. (no date). *British Crime Survey-Measuring Crime for 25 Years.* London: Home Office. Retrieved from www.homeoffice.gov.uk/rds/pdfs07/bcs25.pdf.

Jones, T., MacLean, B., & Young, J. (1986). *The Islington Crime Survey: Crime, Victimization and Policing in Inner-City London.* Aldershot, Hants: Gower.

Kershaw, C., Nicholas, S., & Walker A. (2008). *Crime in England and Wales 2007/08.* London: Home Office.

Kinsey, R. (1984). *Merseyside Crime Survey: First Report, November 1974.* Liverpool: Merseyside County Council.

Kroner, D. G., Mills, J. F., & Morgan, R. D. (2007). Underreporting of crime-related content and the prediction of criminal recidivism among violent offenders. *Psychological Services, 4,* 85–95.

Lee, M. (2007). *Inventing Fear of Crime: Criminology and the Politics of Anxiety.* Cullompton, Devon: Willan Publishing.

Lucia, S., Herrmann, L., & Killias, M. (2007). How important are interview methods and questionnaire designs in research on self-reported juvenile delinquency? An experimental comparison of Internet vs paper-and-pencil questionnaires and different definitions of the reference period. *Journal of Experimental Criminology, 3,* 39–64.

Maguire, M. (2007). Crime data and statistics. In M. Maguire, R. Morgan & R. Reiner (Eds.), *The Oxford Handbook of Criminology* (4th ed.) (pp. 241–301). Oxford: Oxford University Press.

Ministry of Justice (2008). *Criminal Statistics: England and Wales 2008.* Statistical Bulletin. London: Ministry of Justice.

Mulchandani, R. & Sigurdsson, J. (2009). *Police Service Strength: England and Wales, 31 March 2009.* Home Office Statistical Bulletin, 13/09. London: Home Office.

Palmer, E. J. & Hollin, C. R. (1998). A comparison of patterns of moral development in young offenders and non-offenders. *Legal and Criminological Psychology, 3,* 225–235.

Palmer, E. J. & Hollin, C. R. (2001a). Self-reported delinquency in persistent young offenders. *Pakistan Journal of Psychological Research, 16,* 67–83.

Palmer, E. J. & Hollin, C. R. (2001b). Sociomoral reasoning, perceptions of parenting and self-reported delinquency in adolescents. *Applied Cognitive Psychology, 15,* 85–100.

Roe, J. & Ashe, J. (2008). *Young People and Crime: Findings from the 2006 Offending, Crime and Justice Survey.* Home Office Statistical Bulletin, 09/08. London: Home Office.

Simmons, J., Legg, C., & Hoskin, R. (2003). *National Crime Recording Standards (NCRS): An Analysis of the Impact on Recorded Crime.* RDS Online Report 31/03. London: Home Office.

Smith, A. (2006). *Crime Statistics: An Independent Review.* Review chaired by Professor Adrian Smith for the Secretary of State for the Home Department. London: Home Office.

Sparks, R. F. (1981). Surveys of victimization - An optimistic assessment. In M. Tonry & N. Morris (Eds.), *Crime and Justice: An Annual Review of Research,* Vol. 3 (pp. 1–60). Chicago, IL: University of Chicago Press.

Sparks, R. F., Genn, H. G., & Dodd, D. J. (1977). *Surveying Victims: A Study of the Measurement of Criminal Victimization, Perceptions of Crime, and Attitudes to Criminal Justice.* Chichester, Sussex: John Wiley & Sons.

Swedish National Council for Crime Prevention (2007). *Youth and Crime in the Swedish Counties 1995–2005.* English Summary of Brå Report No. 2007:30. Available from Fritzes Kundservice, 106 47, Stockholm, Sweden.

Taveres, C. & Thomas, G. (2009). *Crime and Criminal Justice.* Eurostat: Statistics in Focus, 36. Luxemburg: Office for Official Publications of the European Communities.

Walker, A., Kershaw, C., & Nicholas, S. (2006). *Crime in England and Wales 2005/06.* London: Home Office.

Walker, A., Flatley, J., Kershaw, C., & Moon, D. (Eds.) (2009). *Crime in England and Wales 2008/09, Vol. 1.* Findings from the British Crime Survey and Police Recorded Crime. Home Office Statistical Bulletin, 11/09, Vol. 1. London: Home Office.

3 Psychological theories applied to crime

In this chapter, the focus is on the way in which psychological theories have been applied to formulate an understanding of criminal behaviour. In order to help appreciate the way in psychological theories have unfolded over time, the various theories are shown in chronological order in Box 3.1. It should be said that this way of presenting the flow of theory gives a rather neat appearance to what is, in truth, a far from precise process. Theories do not start and stop at exact dates and their development may be traced to an interaction between historical period and the personal characteristics of the theoretician (Simonton, 2002). There is often a period of time, during which the empirical evidence accumulates and the associated academic debate take place, before the full exposition of a given theory. Further, there is not an exact point at which a favoured theory is universally abandoned for another theory. Indeed, most of the theories discussed below, from the earliest to the most recent, are still alive and well, although sometimes in a different form to which they first appeared.

It is also the case, within and across disciplines, that not every researcher and practitioner holds the same theoretical views. In different disciplines there may be diverse means by which a theory changes and develops. Thus, contemporary psychology relies heavily on scientific method and empirical evidence as the means by which to advance theory. In philosophy, on the other hand, the picture is different, as described by Russell:

> Philosophy, as I shall try to understand the word, is something intermediate between theology and science. Like theology it consists of speculations on matters as to which definite knowledge has, so far, been unascertainable; but like science, it appeals to human reason rather than authority ... between theology and science there is a No Man's Land, exposed to attack from both sides; this No Man's Land is philosophy.
>
> (Russell, 1961: 13)

Box 3.1 A chronology of psychological theories of criminal behaviour

1800s–1930s: Free will, early biological theory, psychoanalytic theory.
1930s–60s: Operant learning theory.
1960s–70s: Personality theories.
1970s–80s: Social learning theory; cognition and crime.
1980s–2000s: Rational choice theory; social information processing; the role of gender; developmental criminology, including family factors; integrated, multi-component theories, risk-needs; evolutionary theory.

The issues surrounding theory and theoretical development are all writ large when it comes to theories of crime. The topic of crime has generated a myriad of theories across a range of disciplines. Sometimes the different disciplines share some common territory, at other times they are foreign lands. The development of theory *across* disciplines can lead, at best, to a multidisciplinary cooperation that produces theories with improved explanatory power. However, at worst, disagreements between disciplines are played out in an atmosphere of misunderstandings, name-calling, and squabbling. Kendall (2004) presents an example of a particularly vituperative polemic with high levels of disciplinary animosity, flaunting academic conventions in a highly selective use of the literature to make its arguments.

There may also be also theoretical variations *within* a discipline: for example, there are sociological theories of crime that emphasise social structure and subculture, some that are concerned with social processes such as control and labelling, and others that are more overtly political, incorporating social conflict and class struggle. These sociological theories can in some instances share some common ground while in other cases they stand diametrically opposed.

This chapter is concerned, in the main, with the psychological theories that have been used in order to attempt to understand crime or, more accurately, *criminal behaviour*. As will be seen, most psychological theories focus on the individual and their immediate social environment, it is unusual for psychological theories explicitly to incorporate the effects of social structure and political influences. The wider aspects of social influence on our behaviour are the province of criminology and sociology.

As with any discipline, psychological theories do not develop in a vacuum: psychological theory has been, at various times, aligned to theoretical developments in other mainstream disciplines such as philosophy and biology. Further, the speciality of *criminological* psychology has, of course, its own particular relationship with criminology.

Where to begin? As Hermann Ebbinghaus (1850–1909) said in 1908, 'Psychology has a short history but a long past' (Ebbinghaus, 1908: 13). The problem is when, exactly, did psychology become a discipline in its own right? The nature of philosophical enquiry by necessity involves matters psychological, however it would be stretching a point to claim figures such as René Descartes (1596–1650) and John Stuart Mill (1806–73) as early psychologists.

As Richards (1996) notes, 1879 is the traditional starting point for psychology when Wilhelm Wundt (1832–1920) founded the first psychological laboratory in Leipzig. Wundt's work was contemporary with the work of Sigmund Freud (1856–1939) and, in America, with the publication in 1890, as two volumes, of *The Principles of Psychology* by William James (1842–1910). It is safe to say that it was during the early 1900s that psychology became firmly established and began to grow into the large international enterprise which it is today.

It is not the aim here to review all the various theories that might be gathered under the umbrella of psychology. However, by taking a historical perspective we can see how the different theoretical traditions applied to explain criminal behaviour followed the lineage of mainstream psychology. As shown in Box 3.1, five broad theoretical positions can be distinguished.

These five traditions, appearing in various guises at different times, are: (1) psychobiological; (2) psychodynamic; (3) behavioural; (4) personality; and (5) cognitive. The contribution of these five traditions to explaining *criminal behaviour*, the essence of criminological psychology, will be discussed in turn. It is important to note the emphasis on the term 'criminal behaviour': a cogent theoretical account of 'crime' would necessarily involve more than any of the above five have to offer.

The psychobiological tradition

In Chapter 1, the work of the Italian criminal anthropologist Cesare Lombroso (1835–1909) was discussed. As Lilley, Cullen, and Ball (2007: 19) note, Lombroso classified criminals into four major categories, one of which was 'born criminals'. In its most elementary form, a theory of crime based solely upon genetic transmission would hold that crime is a direct product of heredity: in other words, a criminal is born not made. There are certain circumstances in which an individual's condition may be traced directly to their genetic constitution. Plomin (1990) gives the example of phenylketonuria (PKU), which is a 'recessive single-gene disease' that causes profound learning difficulties if untreated. The single-gene basis of PKU is not one that is found with other individual physical and psychological characteristics. As Plomin (1990: 19) states: 'Genetic influence on intelligence, as with height, is not due to a single gene or even a few genes … instead, hundreds of genes are known that have a small effect on individual IQ scores. However, these small effects contribute to large genetic effects on IQ scores in the population as a whole'.

If we dismiss the notion that criminal behaviour is attributable to a single gene then we have a situation, as with many other behaviours, where it is *possible* that many genes may give an overall effect which forms a part of an explanation of criminal behaviour. As Raine (1993: 48) states, it may be that 'Multiple genes, acting in combination, result in varying degrees of genetic predisposition to criminal behavior in the total population'. The key point to note is Raine's use of the term 'predisposition': a genetic predisposition requires something to activate it, a trigger to turn the predisposition into behaviour.

An important point when discussing genetic influences on behaviour lies in the distinction between the *genotype* and the *phenotype*. For any organism, the genotype is the organism's genetic constitution, the inherited instructions within its genetic code. The phenotype is any characteristic that is observable: such characteristics include the organism's development, appearance, physiological functioning, and behaviour. Phenotypes are a product of an organism's genes, the effects of the environment, and the interaction between the two. Given the role of the environment in shaping the phenotype, it follows that organisms with the same genotype will not necessarily have the same appearance or behaviour. Similarly, organisms may look alike but that does not have to mean that they have the same genotype.

An explanation of behaviour based on an interaction between genetic potential (*nature*) and the environment (*nurture*) is sometimes called the *biosocial* approach. There is a tendency in social science to be suspicious of explanations of behaviour, such as the biosocial approach, that involve a genetic influence. There may be a preference for theories and explanations of behaviour that emphasise social and environmental factors. The reason for this preference for social explanations may be historical: Rowe and Osgood (1984) make the point that at one time genetic arguments for crime were concerned with the 'defective' nature of the 'criminal gene', so that criminals were seen in terms of pathology and abnormality. This pathological approach is not compatible with contemporary thinking in social science which seeks to understand how *normal* genetic variability may account for variations in behaviour. With a complex behaviour such as criminal behaviour, any genetic influence cannot be accounted for in terms of a single gene. There is not a 'criminal gene', so any biosocial explanation for criminal behaviour that incorporates a genetic element must refer to a polygenetic influence.

The starting point with a biosocial approach to understanding criminal behaviour is to look to the evidence: there is any empirical support for a genetic or heritable predisposition to criminal behaviour? The question of the influence of heredity on human behaviour is a longstanding issue, applicable to many areas of research. Sir Francis Galton (1822–1911), a half-cousin of Charles Darwin, suggested three basic research methods by which to study the interaction between nature and nurture. Galton's three methods, still in use by present-day researchers, are: (1) family studies; (2) twin studies; and (3) adoption studies.

Family studies

There are two main reasons to study the family with regard to understanding criminal behaviour: first to consider the processes within a family in which one or more of the family members behave in a criminal manner; second, to estimate the degree of similarity between the behaviour of a specific individual and their biological relatives. The study of family processes, particularly the longitudinal studies, has provided a great deal of information about the family backgrounds of delinquents. This specific area of knowledge is discussed further in Chapter 4. However, with regard to questions of heredity, it is evidence from the second approach, the *consanguinity studies*, that is important.

The reasoning that underpins family studies is that, as biological relatives share a genetic constitution, it follows that if there is a hereditable predisposition to criminal behaviour then criminal families will tend to produce criminal children. Further, the closer the biological relationship, the greater the genetic similarity: thus, pairs of individuals that are more similar genetically, say parents and their children, should be more similar behaviourally than pairs where there is less genetic similarity, such as grandparents and grandchildren.

It is not difficult to find evidence that criminal behaviour runs in families, particularly for genetically close relationships. There are accounts from the early 1900s describing how convicted offenders came from families with a criminal history (Dugdale, 1910; Estabrook, 1916) and similar conclusions are evident in contemporary studies from several countries (Fergusson, Horwood, & Nagin, 2000; Hurwitz & Christiansen, 1983; Nijhof, de Kemp, & Engels, 2009; West & Farrington, 1977).

Farrington, Jolliffe, Loeber, Stouthamer-Loeber, and Kalb (2001) investigated offending across three generations – fathers, mothers, sons, daughters, uncles, aunts, grandfathers, and grandmothers – in a study of the concentration of offending in 1,395 families (from Pittsburgh, USA). In keeping with data from the UK (Farrington, Barnes, & Lambert, 1996), Farrington et al. reported a high concentration of offending in families: less than 10 per cent of the families accounted for more than 40 per cent of all arrested people. All relatives had some predictive power with regard to the young male's offending, although the father's offending was the strongest predictor. Bijleveld and Wijkman (2009) report the findings of a five-generation study, conducted in the Netherlands, that gathered data from 1882 to 2007 on family patterns of criminal convictions. Bijleveld and Wijkman found that, in keeping with the literature, when parents are offenders, the risk is increased that their children will also commit offences. When Bijleveld and Wijkman changed the definition of offending from any delinquency to serious delinquency, the intergenerational risk increased markedly. The association between the criminal behaviour of parents and children is not inevitable: some children from delinquent families were not convicted, while some children with non-offending parents were convicted. Bijleveld and Wijkman also found that the increased risk for the child was related to the mothers' offending and, indeed, a seriously delinquent mother increased the risk of the child's delinquency at a rate comparable with a seriously delinquent father.

Another American study, this time using data gathered in Rochester, New York, looked at intergenerational association in anti-social behaviour between parents and child (Thornberry, Freeman-Gallant, & Lovegrove, 2009). As expected, parents with (self-reported) histories of anti-social behaviour increased the risk of their children's adolescent drug-use and delinquent behaviour. However, this effect was dependent upon the level of contact between the parent and child. The effect was 'Observed for mothers, virtually all of whom live with their child, and for high-contact fathers who live with or see the child at least weekly. Interestingly, this association is not observed for absent fathers who only see the child sporadically' (Thornberry et al., 2009: 90).

The relationship between the criminal behaviour of parent and child is exacerbated when one of the parents, typically the father, is sent to prison (Murray & Farrington, 2005). Murray, Janson, and Farrington (2007) tested the accepted research finding that crime runs in families by comparing English and Swedish data. They found that parental imprisonment was a stronger risk factor for children's offending in England than in Sweden. Murray et al. suggest that an explanation for this finding may lie in social differences between the two countries, including Sweden's welfare-orientated criminal justice system.

If criminal behaviour runs in families, in that close biological relatives tend to exhibit similar behaviours, is this evidence for a heritable component? The answer to this question is simply no: a correlation between two variables, say father and son's criminal behaviour, is not evidence that a causal relationship (genetic or otherwise) exists between the two. It is possible that other variables, perhaps environmental rather than genetic, influence the behaviour of both parent and child. It could be the case that the high correlations in the criminality of family members is not a product of heredity but that the family members had in common poor schooling, or poor diets, or unemployment, or similar anti-social attitudes, lived in the same city area, and so on. In truth, there are a range of potential explanations for intergenerational continuity in crime. As shown in Box 3.2, Farrington (2002) has suggested six explanations, not necessarily mutually exclusive, for intergenerational continuity in offending.

The problem, from a research perspective, lies in disentangling the relative effects of heredity and environment on behaviour. In the laboratory, this type of problem is solved by controlling one of the factors and measuring what happens when the other one is manipulated. In real-life, this approach cannot work: researchers cannot legally, morally, or ethically exert control over an individual's heredity or environment. What researchers require is a 'natural experiment', where control occurs in the normal, everyday course of life. As Galton realised, nature has provided the basis for just such an experiment in the shape of twins.

Box 3.2 Explanations for intergenerational continuity in offending (after Farrington, 2002)

1. Exposure to multiple risk factors, in that parents may expose their children to risk factors such as low education and living in a poor neighbourhood, perpetuating the cycle of deprivation and crime.
2. Assortative mating, in that people tend to marry similar people, so that delinquents seek delinquent partners, thereby exposing their children to higher risk.
3. Family members influence each other, which may take the form of co-offending, although more generally this explanation falls under the remit of social learning.
4. Parental delinquency is transmitted through parenting styles that do not develop a strong conscience in children.
5. It is heredity that is responsible for the association between and parent and child offending.
6. The labelling of delinquent families by the police and legal authorities is responsible for the association between parent and child offending.

The twin study method has now been widely used, as can be seen, for example, in research into intelligence, personality, creativity, and school achievement; as well as in research concerning alcoholism, depression, and schizophrenia. But why are twins so special when it comes to research?

Twin studies

The foundation for twin studies lies in the genetic difference between the two types of twin. Monozygotic (MZ) twins occur when a single egg is fertilised to form one zygote (the initial cell formed when a new organism is produced through sexual reproduction), which then divides into two separate embryos. The splitting of the zygote therefore produces two genetically identical people, hence MZ twins are *identical twins*.

Unlike monozygotic twins, dizygotic (DZ) twins occur when two different eggs are independently fertilized by two different sperm cells to form two zygotes. Thus, dizygotic twins, sometimes called *fraternal twins*, are no more alike than any other pair of siblings, sharing about 50 per cent of their genetic constitution. Unlike MZ twins, DZ twins are not always of the same sex and, indeed, male-female twin pairs are the most common DZ twin combination.

The basis of twin research lies in a comparison of the functioning of MZ and DZ twins in a given psychological or behavioural domain. As Plomin (1990: 47–8) explains: 'If a trait is not influenced by heredity, identical twins should be no more similar for the trait than fraternal twins, despite the twofold greater genetic similarity of identical twins. If heredity is important, however, identical twins will still resemble each other to a greater extent than will fraternal twins'.

The match for a given characteristic between members of a twin pair may be expressed in terms of *pairwise concordance*. Concordance is usually given as a percentage: a 50 per cent concordance rate would indicate that across a total sample of, say, 20 twin pairs, 10 exhibited the target behaviour; if 15 of the 20 pairs showed the behaviour the concordance rate would be 75 per cent (15/20), and so on. As MZ twins are genetically identical, it would be predicted that for a hereditable characteristic, they will show higher rates of concordance than DZ twins.

So, do genes play a role in criminal behaviour? The German physician Johannes Lange reported the first twin study of criminal behaviour in 1929, which was followed by a string of similar studies up to the 1940s. As can be seen from Table 3.1, the seven studies before and including 1941, show a mean concordance rate of 75 per cent for MZ twins and 24 per cent for DZ twins. The five studies from 1961 and after show a mean concordance of 48 per cent for MZ twins and 20 per cent for DZ twins.

The higher rates of concordance in the earlier studies may be due to small sample sizes, with only four twin pairs in two of the studies: it is generally taken that behavioural genetic research requires large samples (Plomin, 1990). There may also be a procedural issue regarding the means by which the type of twin-pair is determined. Twin studies compare MZ twins with DZ twins of the same sex, however it can be difficult to distinguish DZ from MZ same-sex twins simply on the basis of appearance. It is possible that typing a twin-pair on the basis of appearance, as in the early studies, may lead to some confusion of MZ and DZ pairs. In contemporary studies, the use of technological advances such as single-gene markers from blood analysis can be used to make an exact match between the two members of the twin pair. However, as Plomin notes, there is a high match between judgements of twin type based on physical similarity and blood analysis.

Table 3.1 Twin studies and criminal behaviour

	MZ Twins		DZ Twins	
	No. of Pairs	*% Concordant*	*No. of Pairs*	*% Concordant*
Lange (1929)	13	77	17	12
Legras (1932)	4	100	5	0
Rosanoff et al. (1934)	37	68	60	10
Kranz (1936)	31	65	43	53
Stumpfl (1936)	18	61	19	37
Borgstrom (1939)	4	75	5	40
Rosanoff et al. (1941)	45	78	27	18
Yoshimasu (1961)	28	61	18	11
Yoshimasu (1965)	28	50	26	0
Hayashi (1967)	15	73	5	60
Dalgaard and Kringlen (1976)	31	26	54	15
Christiansen (1977)	85	32	147	12

Another procedural point when contrasting the earlier and later twin studies lies in the measure of crime. As discussed in Chapter 2, definitions of crime can change over time and across countries, which is likely to have happened between 1929 and 1977. In addition, the use of official measures of crime, such as arrest and conviction, may not tell the full story regarding the true rates of criminal behaviour. However, while the concordance is lower in the later studies, the consistent finding of a difference between MZ and DZ twins does support the hypothesis of a genetic predisposition towards criminal behaviour.

Evidence in support of a hypothesis is, of course, not absolute proof. The point can be made that it is an *assumption* of twin study methodology that high rates of concordance are a function of heredity because twins share the same environment. If this assumption is not true and MZ twins actually share more similar environments than is the case for DZ twins, then this would not support an explanation of concordance based on heredity. It is possible that precisely because they are physically identical, MZ twins are treated in a more similar fashion by those around them than is the case for DZ twins. In other words, it is plausible that MZ share an equal environment, which is not the case for DZ twins. Further, it may be that MZ twins share a closer relationship with each other than do DZ twins. Overall, it could be argued that the twins' similar behaviour can be explained as being a function of their equal environments and reciprocal social influence.

There is a methodological solution to the potential confound between equal environments and equal heredity in the study of separated twins. If the members of an MZ twin pair are separated at birth and grow up in different environments – which is a rare occurrence, Plomin (1990: 45) states that 'All the world's literature adds up to fewer than 100 pairs' – then high rates of concordance are much more likely to be due to genetic influences. There is some psychological research based on separated twin pairs but this does not include studies concerned with criminal behaviour.

Overall, the evidence from twin studies tends to favour the position that there is a genetic influence in criminal behaviour. The next question is whether the twin studies tell us just how large an influence genetic factors play in criminal behaviour. The answer to this question requires behavioural genetic studies to give estimates of the proportion of behavioural variation that is due to genetic variance. Rowe and Osgood (1984), with a sample of MZ and DZ twins, considered the relative influence on self-reported delinquent behaviour of three variables: genetic variation, as with type of twin pair; shared environmental influences, such as whether their home is broken or intact, that affect all family members equally; and specific environmental influences, such as peer group, which are particular to the individual concerned. Rowe and Osgood's behavioural genetic analysis estimated that the genetic component accounted for over 60 per cent of the relationship between the three factors, the shared environment component accounted for about 20 per cent of the relationship, specific environmental factors for just less than 20 per cent of the total relationship. Baker et al. (2007) reported a twin study investigating genetic and environmental influences on childhood (male and female) anti-social behaviour. They found that, for both genders, there were strong heritable effects on anti-social behaviour as reported by a range of sources (parents, children, and teachers).

The evidence from family and twin studies, while not without methodological shortcomings, favours the biosocial position. A third way to approach the issue of the role of genetic inheritance in criminal behaviour is to look at what happens to children who are separated from their biological parents then adopted and raised in another family.

Adoption studies

In both family and twin studies there is a confound between shared heredity and shared environment. In an adoption study (of which twins reared apart is a particular and unusual type), this confound is removed as biologically related individuals are separated, generally soon after the birth of the child, and live their lives in different environments. If the behaviour of the adopted children is a closer match to their biological rather than their adoptive parents (who are fundamental to the child's environment), then this provides evidence in favour of a genetic influence. On the other hand, if the children most closely resemble their adoptive parents, then an environmental influence is favoured.

As Blackburn (1993) notes, there are two basic types of adoption study: (1) identify convicted criminals who have given up children for adoption and compare the children's criminal behaviour with that of adopted children whose biological parents are not criminals; and (2) identify a cohort of adoptees and look at their criminal behaviour with regard to the criminality of their biological and adoptive parents.

One of the first adoption studies was reported by Crowe (1972) who compared 52 adopted children whose biological mothers had a criminal record with a matched control group of adopted children whose biological mothers did not have a criminal record. Crowe reported that almost 50 per cent of the adoptees had an arrest record (including traffic offences) by 18 years of age as compared with about 5 per cent of the control group.

Mednick, Gabrielli, and Hutchings (1984) gathered a large sample (14,427) of non-familial adoptions that had taken place between 1927 and 1947. Mednick et al. gathered court convictions for the biological families, adoptive families, and the adoptees and looked at the relationship between the criminal records of the parents and the adopted children. As shown in Table 3.2, having a biological parent who is a criminal is associated with a higher number of adoptees with a criminal conviction. Further, there is an interaction such that when *both* fathers are criminal the percentage of criminal adoptees is at its highest.

In another adoption study, Cadoret, Cain, and Crowe (1983) also investigated the interaction between the criminality of the biological parent and environmental variables on the development of anti-social behaviour. The anti-social behaviour included a range of

Table 3.2 Criminal records of adoptees and parents (after Mednick et al., 1984)

Adoptive Parents	Biological Parents	
	Criminal	*Non-criminal*
Criminal	24.5% (n = 143)	14.7% (n = 204)
Non-criminal	20.0% (n = 1,226)	13.5% (n = 2,492)

behaviours that might not be considered criminal, such as the child being rebellious, difficult to discipline, destructive, playing truant, fighting, and bullying. Cadoret et al. found that, when considered individually, genetic and environmental factors had a relatively small effect on anti-social behaviour. However, there was a 'Dramatic increase in antisocial behaviours when individuals are exposed to both genetic and environmental factors' (Cadoret et al., 1983: 309).

The findings reported by Mednick et al. and by Cadoret et al. exemplify the critical importance of the interaction between genetic and environmental factors in understanding behaviour. However, establishing that there is a genetic influence that *contributes* to criminal behaviour is not the same as *explaining* the pathway through which the genetic predisposition exerts its influence. The evidence supports the hypothesis of a genetic predisposition to anti-social and criminal behaviour but might such a predisposition work?

A genetic predisposition to what?

It is often the case that an individual displays a range of problematic behaviours so that anti-social and criminal behaviour may occur alongside, for example, illegal drug-use, alcoholism, and mental health problems. When these clusters of behaviour occur, is there any sequence, so that one behaviour precedes the others, or are there other related factors that trigger several predispositions?

There have been suggestions that the primary genetic predisposition is to alcoholism that, in turn, increases the likelihood of criminal behaviour (Bohman, 1978). Another adoption study by Cadoret and Cain (1980) showed that strongest genetic influence on anti-social behaviour was a biological relative who is either anti-social or alcoholic. However, the genetic predisposition for criminal behaviour can be evident when alcoholism is *not* present in the adoptee's biological relatives (Bohman, Cloninger, Sigvardsson, & von Knorring, 1983). In addition, the environmental factor of *adoptive* parents with problems such as psychiatric disorder, marital problems, debt, and substance misuse is strongly associated with the adopted child's anti-social behaviour (Cadoret & Cain, 1980; Cadoret et al. 1983; Cadoret, Yates, Troughton, Woodworth, & Stewart, 1995).

The more variables that are considered, the more complex the nature-nurture interaction becomes. Van Dusen, Mednick, Gabrielli and Hutchings (1983) found that the adopted child's social class has a significant effect with regard to later criminal behaviour when the genetic influence of a criminal biological parent was present. This effect was particularly evident for males from lower social classes who committed property offences.

McCartan (2007) employed behavioural genetic analysis to investigate the role of genetic influences on delinquent behaviour during late adolescence. Adolescents were drawn from the (American) National Longitudinal Survey of Youth (NLSY-Child), which collects prospective data on children from before they are born through to early adulthood. The NLSY-Child categorises related children as twins, siblings, or half-siblings. This study gathered self-reported data on delinquency, from the more serious acts such as physical aggression and serious theft, to less serious behaviours such as minor theft and truancy. The survey also gathered information on parent-child interactions and supervision, attachment between mother and child, the parents' expectations of the child within the family home (such as contributing to household chores), the influence of delinquent peers, and the economic standing of the family. The effect of intergenerational (i.e., not environmental) influences on the child's delinquency was assessed using a measure of maternal involvement in crime.

The initial level of analysis looked at the influence of the non-genetic factors on delinquency. At the second stage, the analysis was then recomputed to include factors associated with genetic influence. The first analysis showed that the strongest associates of self-reported delinquency, with males reporting a greater involvement in delinquency than females, were fewer positive interactions with parents, higher expectations at home (i.e., higher expectations are associated with higher levels of delinquency) and peer group pressure. In the subsequent analysis, the addition of the genetic factors added significantly to the explanatory power of the environmental factors in accounting for levels of delinquent behaviour. As McCartan (2007) states, the results point to the interaction of environmental and genetic factors in accounting for delinquency.

Evolutionary psychology

Duntley and Shackelford (2008) offer a broad overview of the application of Darwinian theory to behaviours that we now call criminal behaviours, such as murder, assault, and theft. They suggest that such behaviours may be a consequence of natural selection as they gave individuals an advantage in competing with others for status and resources. As will be seen in Chapter 5, evolutionary psychology has mainly been applied to violent crimes and sexual crimes.

Summary of psychobiological factors

McCartan (2007: 219) makes the point that despite studies reported in the 1980s, '[t]he body of empirical research and theorizing on genetic influence on delinquent and/or criminal behavior is relatively small'. Given this caveat, the conclusion from the evidence from family, twin and adoption studies suggests that genetic factors do have a role to play in understanding crime. There is general agreement that genetic factors are an important predisposing factor to criminal behaviour but that environmental factors are equally important in understanding how that predisposition may be realised. Thus, it is the interaction between genetic and environmental factors that is crucial in understanding criminal behaviour. The relative contribution of genes and environment remains uncertain and, indeed, may potentially vary from individual to individual.

It should be stressed that even given genetic and environmental influences that are favourable to criminal behaviour, the outcome is not inevitable. There are children born to criminal parents who experience adverse environments but do not commit crimes: conversely, there are children with non-criminal parents who experience supportive environments and who do commit crimes.

The pathway through which a predisposition to criminal behaviour may manifest itself is uncertain, although a number of possibilities have been advanced at various times. The potential pathways that have been suggested include low intelligence, personality type, learning capability, alcoholism, and other biological factors including neurological and psychophysiological functioning. As we progress through the various theories of criminal behaviour, these various factors will emerge. Further, research looking at the neurophysiological correlates of criminal behaviour has a long association with unusual acts of extreme violence, such as murder by the clinically insane (e.g., Hill & Pond, 1952). Crimes of violence are considered in Chapter 5.

The next theoretical step is an early attempt to bring together biological and psychological factors to explain criminal behaviour.

Constitutional theory

The roots of constitutional theory can be traced to Lombroso's criminal anthropology and its influence on the work of a French policeman called Alphonse Bertillon (1853–1914). Bertillon's claim to fame lies in his pioneering of the practice of *anthropometry*, later known as *Bertillonage* after its inventor. In Bertillon's system, capitalising on the possibilities afforded by photography, each criminal was identified by measurement of their head and body and by individual markings such as tattoos and scars. The recordings of these measurements could then be made available to police officers investigating a crime to help identify wanted criminals. One of the advantages of Bertillon's system was that, given precise measurement, it was possible to sort quickly through a large number of records and identify the suspect. If the system did not produce an exact match, it generated a pool of suspects, narrowing the police search and saving time and money. Bertillon's system was eventually used by police forces in both America and Britain.

The line of thought embodied in Bertillon's work incorporates the notion of a *constitution*: that is, a scheme that guides the construction of the parts to define the whole. The search for a constitutional theory would therefore involve investigation of the associations between body, mind and behaviour. The idea in itself is not remarkable and can be traced back to Aristotle and Plato: it was the application of contemporary technology, as with the use of photography, and the adaptation of scientific methods taken from anthropology that made Bertillon's approach so noteworthy and attractive to other researchers such as the German psychiatrist Ernst Kretschmer (1888–1964).

Ernst Kretschmer

While Bertillon saw the practical possibilities for police work of accurate recording of physique, Kretschmer saw similar possibilities for an association of face, skull, and body structure with character and psychiatric disorder (Gil, Weber, & Burgmair, 2002). As did Bertillon, Kretschmer used a combination of photography and anthropological techniques to measure and to describe his patients. Kretschmer eventually developed a classification of physique, described in his 1921 book *Körperbau und Charakter* (*Physique and Character*), that was based on three body types: the thin and weak *asthenic* build; the tall and muscular *athletic* build; and the stocky, even fat, *pyknic* build. (A fourth physique, *asthenic-schizothymic-leptosomic*, which was a mix of the other types was added later.)

The three physiques were, Kretschmer suggested, each associated with personality traits and, when evident in an extreme form, with particular forms of psychopathology. The thin asthenic type was introverted; the muscular athletic type was assertive; while the stocky pyknic types were highly sociable. In their extreme forms, the timid asthenic was vulnerable to becoming a withdrawn schizophrenic; the athletic type was also prone to schizophrenia; and the obese pyknic was likely to develop a manic-depressive disorder.

Kretschmer also turned his attention to criminal behaviour, classifying more than 4,000 criminal cases according to his three physiques. He concluded that the asthenic type was likely to be involved in petty theft and fraud, the athletic were violent criminals, and pyknics committed a range of crimes, mainly involving deception and fraud but sometimes also violence.

Kretschmer's findings were widely read and influenced the thinking of the American psychologist William Herbert Sheldon (1898–1977), whose name has become synonymous with constitutional theory.

William Sheldon

The essence of Sheldon's research lay in the classification of body build and determining the association between type of body build and personality (Sheldon & Stevens, 1942; Sheldon, Stevens, & Tucker, 1940).

The starting point in Sheldon's research was the classification of photographs, frontal and profile, of about 4,000 near-naked young men. From his observations, Sheldon proposed that the human physique could be classified according to the relative contribution of three fundamental elements which he called *somatotypes*. Sheldon names for the somatotypes were based on the three layers of cells found during embryogenesis (the formation and development of the embryo): the three somatotypes are therefore *endoderm* (which develops into the digestive tract), *mesoderm* (muscle, heart, and blood vessels), and *ectoderm* (skin and nervous system).

It follows that *endomorphs* are round, large, and heavy, *mesomorphs* are broad and stocky with a muscular build, and *ectomorphs* are thin and bony. Some individuals have 'pure' somatotypes, while others have a physique is an amalgam of elements from two or even three of the basic types. Sheldon used a numerical scale, from 1 to 7, to grade the varying degrees of these characteristics in a given individual: for example, a 'pure' mesomorph is rated as 7-1-1 type, a 'pure' ectomorph is 1-7-1, and an individual with characteristics of both the mesomorph and the ectomorph could be 2-6-1.

In the next step, based on interviews with hundreds of men, Sheldon classified personality characteristics into three types: (1) *viscerotonia* was manifest in a fondness for relaxation, physical comfort, food, and social contact; (2) *somatonia* was associated with physical assertiveness, competiveness, and physical activity; and (3) *cerebrotonia* relates to a pronounced need for privacy, high levels of self-awareness, and exercise of personal restraint.

As Sheldon moved to the heart of his theory, he put forward the view that each somatotype is associated with a particular type of personality. Thus, endomorphs tend towards viscerotonia to give a sociable, outgoing character; mesomorphs match with somatonia to produce an adventurous, aggressive personality; and the ectomorph fits with cerebrotonia to give a restrained, introverted individual. Any given individual will, according to their own particular *somatotype* (using the 1-7 scale), display the associated mixture of these personality traits.

The physiques that Sheldon described are familiar to us all as, indeed, are the stereotypes assigned to them as, for example, with the lazy endomorph and the socially popular mesomorph (Ryckman, Robbins, Kaczor, & Gold, 1989). However, was there any relationship between constitutional type and behaviour? Sheldon suggested the ectomorph somatotype may be associated with a predisposition towards suicide while endomorphs were at risk of severe mental disorder. The mesomorph, quick to become angry and aggressive in nature, had predisposition towards crime.

Sheldon, Hartl, and McDermott (1949) studied the somatotypes of a sample of almost 400 males in a rehabilitation establishment. The delinquents in the sample were characterised by a high prevalence of mesomorphs, some endomorphs, and an absence of ectomorphs. As this is a different pattern to that found in non-criminal samples, the conclusion was made that, indeed, there were differences in the physiques of delinquent and non-delinquent males. A 30-year follow-up study to the Sheldon et al. (1949) study reported that a mesomorphic physique was a predictor of adult crime (Hartl, Monnelli, & Eldeken, 1982). As is the case in much of the study of criminal behaviour, the research on physique was with male offenders. However, one study has compared female offenders and non-offenders and found that the offenders had a more muscular and heavier build (Epps & Parnell, 1952).

Overall, there is broad agreement with Sheldon's proposition that mesomorphs are overrepresented in delinquent populations (Cortes & Gatti, 1972; Glueck & Glueck, 1956; Hooten, 1969) and disagreement (McCandless, Persons, & Roberts, 1972; Rees, 1973; Wadsworth, 1979). However, as Madden, Walker, and Miller (2008) note, after the early 1970s interest in constitutional theory waned as attention turned away from biological theories. Madden et al. report a study in which they used body mass index (BMI), a measure of total body fat based on height and weight, as a method of somatotyping a sample of 5,000 male prisoners serving prison sentences in Arkansas. Using Sheldon's original data, Madden et al. were able to establish that BMI is a reliable measure of somatotyping. Although small in effect, Madden et al. (2008: 342) reported that there was a 'minor effect of physique on criminal offending'. The effect of somatotype was in line with the theory, so that mesomorphic prisoners were more likely to have committed a violent offence than endomorphs and ectomorphs.

Constitutional theory: summary

The theory linking physique and personality is not one that is now widely accepted. Nonetheless, the association between body-build and criminal behaviour is one that refuses to go away and the occasional new study, such as that by Madden et al. (2008), appears in the literature. *If* there is a link between physique and offending, is there another way, rather than constitutional theory, to explain it?

One alternative, as Feldman (1977) suggests, lies in criminal stereotypes. If there are stereotypes of the appearance of criminals, a suggestion with some support (Bull, 1984), then individuals whose physical features correspond with the stereotype may be attracting police attention or being disproportionately sentenced. The net result of this 'selection effect' is that certain physiques appear more frequently in offender populations.

Another explanation, suggested by Feldman and also by Raine (1993), also involves social factors. It is plausible that the muscular individual is more likely to be invited by delinquent peers to take part in criminal acts. Further, the muscular delinquent may have an increased chance of being successful at some types of criminal act, with the consequence that their anti-social behaviour results in both tangible and social reinforcement. As will be seen in Chapter 4, once anti-social behaviours become established during childhood the possibility of delinquent behaviour during adolescence is increased, in turn enhancing the likelihood of criminal behaviour in adulthood.

Psychological theories

Attention now turns to the use of mainstream psychological theory to explain criminal behaviour. The interaction between biological and psychological explanations is to be found in some of these theories.

Psychoanalytic theory

As noted in Chapter 1, Sigmund Freud is a major figure in psychology's short existence. The central tenet of Freud's psychoanalytic theory is that inner, dynamic forces drive human actions. August Aichhorn (1878–1949), a teacher who worked in Vienna with disturbed and delinquent children, was one of the first to apply the principles of psychoanalytic theory to help explain and treat children and their families. Aichhorn (1925) argued that environmental factors alone could not adequately account for a young person's delinquent acts. Aichhorn made the distinction between what he called *manifest delinquency* and *latent delinquency*. While we can see manifest acts of delinquency, their cause is to be found in an underlying predisposition, *latent delinquency*, which psychologically prepares the child for a life of crime.

Latent delinquency is held to be partially innate, partly determined by the child's early emotional relationships. Aichhorn starts with Freud's concept of the *pleasure principle*: that is, the infant's only concern is with their own comfort and well-being so that initially the child is asocial in their first dealings with the world. In the course of normal development, the child becomes increasingly socialised with the emergence of the ego and the *reality principle*: the child's behaviour falls into line with the rules of its environment. In some children, socialisation goes awry, typically explained by disturbances in early child-parent relationships, which causes an arrest in the child's development allowing the latent delinquency to become dominant. Once dominant, the child is in a state that Aichhorn calls *dissocial*, in which the failure in psychological development has allowed the latent delinquency to govern behaviour.

Franz Alexander (1891–1964), born in Hungary and professor of psychology at the University of Chicago, also drew on the reality principle to explain criminal behaviour (Alexander & Staub, 1931; Alexander & Healy, 1935). The criminal's failure to develop from the pleasure principle to the reality principle means that they are unable to postpone immediate gratification for greater gain in the long-term. Criminal behaviour in adulthood is therefore a product of the characteristics that developed during childhood.

Healy and Bronner (1936) used another concept from psychoanalytic theory, *sublimation*, to explain criminal behaviour. Sublimation is the process by which our instinctual impulses are channelled into other thoughts, emotions and behaviours. The criminal act, it is argued, results from unsatisfied desires that relate to a failure to experience strong emotional attachment with another person, usually a parent. The delinquency is an 'acting out', or sublimation, of these inner tensions and dynamic forces. Healy and Bronner reported that, compared with a non-delinquent group, children who had committed offences had less stable families and showed greater signs of emotional disturbance.

The formation of explanations for crime based on psychoanalytic principles was the dominant psychological approach up to the 1940s (e.g., Abrahamson, 1944; Friedlander, 1947). As time progressed, a broader psychodynamic framework came into use to explain the development of criminal behaviour, employing new theoretical constructs such as *self-concept* (Reckless & Dintz, 1967) and *self-esteem* (Bennett, Sorensen, & Forshay, 1971), and even new theories such as transactional analysis (Jesness, DeRisi, McCormick, & Wedge, 1972).

It is notable that many psychoanalytic accounts have an emphasis on childhood and, in particular, the child's relationship with their parents. The theme of parent-child relationship is to the fore in Bowlby's attachment theory, perhaps the most influential of contemporary psychoanalytically orientated theories of crime.

Attachment theory

The English psychiatrist and psychoanalyst John Bowlby (1907–1990) and the American developmental psychologist Mary Salter Ainsworth (1913–99) are the founders of attachment theory. Bowlby set out attachment theory in three books (Bowlby, 1969, 1973, 1980) with later additional publications by Ainsworth (1979, 1985, 1989). The essence of attachment theory lies in the emotional ties, the *attachments*, which children form with their caregivers, usually their mothers. In social interaction during the early years of life from 6 months to 2 years, infants become attached to those adults who care for them. The caregiver becomes a familiar attachment figure to the child, someone whose presence offers the child feelings of safety and security, particularly in stressful situations. A warm, trusted parent will help the child to develop their own patterns of attachment. These patterns, in turn, will guide the growing child's feelings, thoughts and expectations in their later adolescent and adult relationships. Bowlby suggested that attachment behaviours may have evolved because they have survival value for the child.

Bowlby's views on the development of criminal behaviour came from his study of 44 juvenile thieves seen at a child guidance clinic (Bowlby, 1944, 1946). These delinquent children were compared to a similar group of non-delinquent children who had also been referred to the clinic. Bowlby found that more of the children in the delinquent group (39 per cent) had experienced early maternal separation for 6 months or more in the first 5 years of their lives than was the case in the non-delinquent group (5 per cent). Thus, in keeping with the theory, the child's rejection by their mother and the loss of a warm, close and unbroken relationship with their mother (or permanent mother substitute) was to the detriment of the child's mental health and led to their delinquency.

As with any theory, there are criticisms of attachment theory. The research methodology in the two major empirical studies has been criticised on the basis of inadequate sampling, poor matching, and methods of assessment (Feldman, 1977). The theory itself has been criticised for its claim that the damage to the child caused by maternal separation is irreversible (Wootton, 1959). Attachment theory also attracted criticism from feminist critics who made the point that Bowlby had seen cases in which there was a complete absence of maternal care. It follows that any generalisation from these cases to others, as for example with day-care, where children experience a period of absence from their mothers, was a step beyond the data. The view of the mother as the preferred attachment figure also places too much emphasis on the mother, neglecting the role of other adults in the child's life and idealising a particular image of the family. Several publications have considered the theory, research, and attendant controversy concerning attachment theory (Rutter, 1981; Sluckin, Herbert, & Sluckin, 1983). The legacy of Bowlby's work can still found in some childcare policy and practice, particularly in family matters such as the impact of a broken home and the nature and quality of the child's upbringing.

Summary of psychoanalytic and psychodynamic theories

There are obvious criticisms of psychoanalytic theories including the absence of scientific method in the research base, the complexity and difficulty with measurement of many of the central concepts, and the reliance on the interpretations of the individual analyst. There are, of course, valid responses to these criticisms: there are, for example, means other than the strictly scientific by which to develop an understanding what it means to be human. The central issue from a theoretical perspective, remembering that theory influences practice, is where psychoanalytic theory locates the origin of the individual's behaviour. It is clear that within psychoanalytic theory, behaviour is the observable manifestation of a morass of inner processes, conflicts, needs, and defences. Further, these internal processes may or may not be working at an unconscious level. Thus, the basic tenet of psychoanalytic theory is that the cause of behaviour lies *inside the person*. It is currently the case, certainly within psychology although perhaps less so in psychiatry, that the use of psychoanalytic and psychodynamic theory in understanding criminal behaviour is moribund.

The next theoretical step takes us away from thinking about inner causation of criminal behaviour to considering the role played by the environment.

Learning theory: learning through association

Ivan Pavlov (1849–1936) was a Russian physiologist who, in 1904, was awarded a Nobel Prize for his research on the functioning of the digestive system. Pavlov conducted his experimental work with dogs in a laboratory and, as recounted in every introductory psychology text, he noticed that the dogs in his laboratory salivated at sounds, such as the clanking of the metal food pails, rather than at the presentation of the food. As dogs are not naturally inclined to salivate at the sound of clanking pails, Pavlov realised that something unusual was taking place. In a series of famous experiments, Pavlov demonstrated that the dogs had learned to associate the clanking of the pails with the arrival of their food. Thus, the dog's unnatural salivation cued by the clanking pails was the product of a learned association between the sound and the food, a process we now call *classical conditioning*.

As Skinner (1987) notes, the early American behaviourists, such as John B. Watson (see Chapter 1), were aware of Pavlov's work through German publications where Pavlov was often spelt *Pawlow* and cited as such (Yerkes & Morgulis, 1909). Skinner cites Watson as saying that Pavlov's ideas were not of great theoretical influence, although they did have more of an impact on the development of therapeutic techniques to change behaviour. Nonetheless, the advent of behaviourism precipitated a shift away from theories that looked for internal causes of behaviour, as with Freud's psychoanalytic theory, towards the role of the environment in shaping our actions.

If, in the early 1900s, American psychologists were aware of Pavlov's work and the notion of learning by association, then it is likely that learning by association would also have been familiar to American criminologists. It may be a coincidence but the ideas inherent in learning by association are evident in differential association theory, as formulated by the criminologist Edwin Sutherland (1883–1950). Sutherland (1939, 1947) developed his theory as new research emerged, with Donald R. Cressey (1919–87) joining him in making further revisions (Sutherland & Cressey, 1970, 1974).

Differential association theory

Sutherland spent some of his early career at the University of Chicago and the influence of the Chicago School (see Chapter 1) and its emphasis on the link between social conditions and crime is seen in some of his work. This influence is evident in the inclusion of a political dimension to understanding what is meant by the term 'crime'. Thus, crime is understood as a construct that is politically defined by those in positions of power. Some people behave in accordance with the given definitions of acceptable behaviour and so do not commit crimes: other people, criminals, have their own definition of acceptable behaviour and so act outside what the majority define as acceptable. How do some individuals acquire definitions which lead them to a life of crime? Sutherland (1947) stated nine propositions, as shown in Box 3.3, to explain criminal behaviour. Lilley et al. (2007: 42) made the comment that '[t]hese propositions compose one of the most influential statements in criminological history on the causes of crime'.

Differential association theory seeks to explain criminal behaviour as learned behaviour, with the learning taking place in a social context. The theory proposes that it is through social contact with people whose definitions favour crime, although they are not necessarily criminals themselves, the individual learns similar definitions. For example, parents may tell their children it is wrong to steal but then model dishonest behaviour by, say, not informing a shop assistant if they receive too much change. An individual may hold varying definitions of acceptable behaviour: the same person may say that it is acceptable to falsify a tax return (Sutherland invented the term 'white-collar crime') but that burglary is not to be tolerated.

Criticisms of differential association theory

Glueck (1956: 92) stated: 'The theory of differential association ... fails to organize and integrate the findings of respectable research and is, at best, so general and puerile as to add little or nothing to the explanation, treatment, and prevention of delinquency'. There were changes to the theory after 1956, leading to Lilley et al.'s (2007) highly positive appraisal, but the two principle critical points are: (1) why, even given similar conditions, does not everyone adopt the same criminal definitions? and (2) how are definitions acquired? Since the formulation of differential association theory, significant advances have been made in the study of learning and it is now possible to say with some certainty just how behaviour, criminal or otherwise, is acquired and maintained.

Box 3.3 Sutherland's nine propositions

1. Criminal behaviour is learned.
2. The learning is through association with other people.
3. The main part of the learning occurs within close personal groups.
4. The learning includes techniques to execute particular crimes and also specific attitudes, drives, and motives conducive toward crime.
5. The direction of the drives and motives is learned from perception of the law as either favourable or unfavourable.
6. A person becomes criminal when their definitions favourable to breaking the law outweigh their definitions favourable to non-violation.
7. The learning experiences – differential associations – will vary in frequency, intensity, and importance for each individual.
8. The process of learning criminal behaviour is no different from the learning of any other behaviour.
9. Although criminal behaviour is an expression of needs and values, crime cannot be explained in terms of those needs and values. (For example, it is not the need for money that causes crime, rather the method used to acquire the money; the method is learned.)

Learning through consequences

There is line of thinking in psychology that stretches back to Edward Thorndike (1874–1949) and his notion of the Law of Effect. The Law of Effect stated that the probability that a behaviour will recur is generally governed by the consequence (or effect) it produces. The consequences of a behaviour are typically something the person likes or dislikes (Thorndike, 1911).

It was the great American psychologist B. F. Skinner, whose experimental work concentrated on learning through consequences, who formulated the principles of *operant learning* (Skinner, 1938, 1953). Skinner's approach is now sometimes referred to as *radical behaviourism*. The basic principle in operant learning is that the acquisition and maintenance of a behaviour is determined by its environmental consequences. A behaviour *operates* on the environment to produce changes that, for the individual concerned, may be either reinforcing or punishing. The basic premise is deceptively simple: a behaviour that is maintained at a steady rate over time or increases in frequency over time is, by definition, being *reinforced* by its consequences. Alternatively, a behaviour that decreases in frequency over time is, by definition, being *punished* by its consequences. Skinner calls the relationship between a behaviour and its consequences a *contingency*.

Skinner defined two types of reinforcement contingency: a *positive reinforcement* contingency, in which the behaviour gains a reward; and *negative reinforcement* in which the behaviour *avoids* an aversive consequence. In both cases, the consequences act to maintain or to increase the frequency of the behaviour. There are also two punishment contingencies: with *positive punishment*, the consequences of the behaviour are aversive to the individual; with *negative punishment*, the consequence of the behaviour is the removal of something the individual finds desirable. In both cases, the consequences reduce the frequency of the behaviour. In a behavioural sense, unlike in its everyday usage, the term 'punishment' does not equate to the administration of physical pain or harsh prison regimes. The use of behaviour change techniques based reinforcement and punishment is covered in Chapter 11.

Skinner also made the point that behaviour does not occur indiscriminately: environmental cues, antecedent to the behaviour, signal when a given behaviour is liable to be reinforced or punished. The combination of three elements gives a *three-term contingency*: the *A*ntecedent conditions indicate to the individual that a particular *B*ehaviour will produce certain *C*onsequences – the *ABC* of behavioural theory. The act of answering the telephone provides a simple example: the telephone's ring is the antecedent, which signals that the operant behaviour of lifting the receiver will result in the consequence of speaking to another person. The next time the telephone rings, we lift the receiver, so the consequences are reinforcing the behaviour.

In keeping with Pavlov's learning by association, in learning by consequences, the determinants of an individual's behaviour are located the environment in which the behaviour occurs. This emphasis on the role of the environment is a marked departure from psychoanalytic and psychodynamic thinking, where the emphasis is on internal, rather the external, causes of behaviour. An individual's potential for learning, Skinner suggests, is influenced by their genetic constitution, but the *acquisition* of behaviour can be explained entirely in terms of the individual's learning history via environmental reinforcement and punishment. Does this mean that Skinner's radical behaviourism ignores or denies the existence of thoughts, emotions, and other 'private events'? As Blackman (1981) explains, a radical behavioural view is not one that sees people as puppets, their behaviour at the mercy of environmental forces and unable to enjoy or suffer private experiences. The issue is rather more theoretical: it is clear that a given act of behaviour has a function for the individual and the nature of that function is dependent upon the environment and the individual's learning history. How private events fit into that system is a theoretical challenge, although cognitions are not seen as autonomous causes of behaviour. It is the ringing that leads up to answer telephone, not the thought 'there's the telephone'.

While the philosophical connotations of behaviourism were debated (e.g., Modgil & Modgil, 1987; Skinner, 1974), the theory was applied in many areas including criminal behaviour. The principles of operant learning provided a means by which to answer some of the questions raised by differential association theory. In particular, an attempt could be made to answer the question of how criminal behaviour was acquired. Jeffery (1965) took this next step, formulating a new approach, which he called differential reinforcement theory.

Differential reinforcement theory

If criminal behaviour is seen as an operant behaviour, then it must be maintained by the consequences it produces for the individual criminal. A large percentage of crimes take some form of stealing so that, for these crimes, the obvious rewarding consequences are material and financial gain. However, the consequences of crime can also be social gain: for example, within delinquent groups, an individual's repeated criminal acts may gain social approval from peers and enhance status within the group (Short, 1968). In these examples, the material, financial, and social gains are *positively* reinforcing the criminal behaviour.

Negative reinforcement contingencies may also maintain criminal behaviour. The gains from stealing may have the consequence of avoiding the effects of poverty such as the loss of a home or the break-up of a family. Nagin, Farrington, and Moffitt (1995) note that stealing is most likely to occur when an individual is unemployed. Acts of violence may also be negatively reinforced: hitting someone is an excellent way to stop an argument, brandishing a weapon is an effective way to remove the victim's resistance to handing over their wallet.

As well as reinforcing outcomes, criminal behaviour can also produce aversive consequences such as being arrested, being sent to prison, having to report to a probation officer and family breakdown. These aversive consequences may, in a behavioural sense, have a punishing effect on the criminal behaviour in that they suppress the criminal behaviour so that it stops or becomes less frequent. However, given the high rates of reoffending after a period of imprisonment, it is doubtful that the punishments administrated by the criminal justice system are truly punishing in the sense that they change behaviour. The effectiveness of punishment within the criminal justice system will be considered in Chapter 11.

Jeffery (1965: 295) comments: 'The theory of differential reinforcement states that a criminal act occurs in an environment in which in the past the actor has been reinforced for behaving in this manner, and the aversive consequences attached to the behaviour have been of such a nature that they do not control or prevent the response'. Thus, differential reinforcement theory maintains that it is the balance of reinforcement and punishment in an *individual's* learning history that explains their criminal behaviour.

The emphasis on the individual is critically important: some individuals will have consistently gained rewards for criminal acts, others will have experienced aversive consequences. For different individuals, the pattern of reinforcement and punishment is unlikely to have been constant over time. Even within broadly similar social groups or subcultures there will be individual differences in peer group interactions, family processes, experiences at school, and so on. The focus on the individual can help to explain why even within similar environments, there are some people who behave in a criminal manner while others do not.

The force of behaviourism was to stress the importance of the environment in maintaining the individual's behaviour. The next development within learning theory, *social learning theory*, introduced an emphasis on cognitive processes in learning. Social learning theory has also been applied to study of criminal behaviour.

Social learning theory

Although many of the ideas intrinsic to social learning theory had been around for some time (Rotter, 1945; Miller & Dollard, 1941), it was the American psychologist Albert Bandura who articulated the contemporary form of social learning theory (Bandura, 1977). Social learning theory incorporates operant principles but places an emphasis on the role of cognition. While operant theory maintains that behaviour is acquired through reinforcement and punishment from the environment, social learning theory extends the ways that new behaviours may be acquired by including learning through observing the actions of other people (who are referred to as *models*). The process of learning through observation is enhanced if the model is someone the observer regards as competent at what they are doing or of high status.

Social learning theory extends the notion of reinforcement by introducing the concept of *motivation*: Bandura (1977) describes three aspects of motivation: these are *external reinforcement* (i.e., rewards from the environment, as in operant theory), *vicarious reinforcement* and *self-reinforcement*. Vicarious reinforcement occurs when an individual is motivated by seeing another person's behaviour being reinforced or punished. Self-reinforcement takes places when an individual's behaviour is motivated by a sense of pride or achievement in their own behaviour. In addition, social learning theory introduces *expectancy*: when a behaviour has previously been reinforced, there is an expectation that it will continue to be reinforced in the future.

The potential for the application of social learning theory to criminal behaviour was seen by both psychologists (Nietzel, 1979) and sociologists (Akers, 1973). A social learning approach to crime suggests that observational learning takes place primarily in three contexts: these are the family, the prevalent subculture, and through cultural symbols such as television and books that form part of the social environment. It follows that explanations for the acquisition of criminal behaviour may be found in the types of behaviour modelled within families, or through the influence of the peer group, and/or by images shown in the visual media. Of course, criminal behaviour is always reinforced by the tangible rewards it may bring for the criminal.

Summary of learning theories

Sutherland's inclusion of learning as a way to understand criminal behaviour has been refined by advances in learning theory. The foundations laid by differential association theory were followed by operant learning and then by social learning theory to providing increasingly fine-grained explanations for the acquisition and maintenance of criminal behaviour. The key point to take from a learning theory approach is that it primarily works at an individual level, emphasising each individual's uniqueness. The individual's behaviour is understood in terms of their learning history, their patterns of reinforcement and punishment, and by the consequences of the specific criminal act. This approach does not seek to offer broad explanations of the effects of culture or social structure as may be found elsewhere in mainstream criminology.

There are various criticisms of accounts of criminal behaviour based on learning theory, mostly with a focus on what is *not* explained by this approach. A comment from Nietzel (1979: 110–11) provides a good example of this type of criticism: 'We are all quite aware of the potentially rewarding consequences of property offences; however, few of us steal'. Similarly, Rutter and Giller (1983: 253) suggest that learning theories avoid sex differences, developmental change, and do not account for '[t]he observation that punishment is less effective with antisocial children and may actually *increase* their antisocial behaviours'.

These criticisms raise three basic points. First, the focus of learning theory is the behaviour of the individual, it does not set out to formulate general rules to account for specific types of behaviour such as stealing or tax evasion, nor to explain *en masse* the behaviour of anti-social children. Second, an understanding of an individual's behaviour relies on an assessment of how developmental factors *for that individual*, including gender and relevant biological factors, help explain the behaviour. Third, in operant theory the technical use of the word 'punishment' – a contingency in which behaviour is *decreasing* in frequency – is not the same as in general use where punishment means experiencing something most people would see as unpleasant. The high recidivism rates among young people subjected to punishment though the legal system suggests that these punishments are not punishing. This point will be taken up again in Chapter 11.

The essential issue with learning theory, particularly radical behaviourism, lies at a philosophical level with the question it raises of what it means to be human (Ions, 1977; Modgil & Modgil, 1987) and whether our actions are determined by environmental contingencies or do we act of our own free will? The theoretical shift that sees cognition playing a fundamental role in determining behaviour reflects the dilemma 'external' or 'internal' causation. As mainstream theory and research returned to cognition as the driver of behaviour, so too did the field of criminological psychology.

Cognition and crime

The relationship of cognition with offending is implicit in suggestions that thinking styles, such as 'impulsive' or 'concrete', are characteristic of criminal populations (e.g., Glueck & Glueck, 1950). Several researchers were at the forefront of the move towards explicitly including cognition in explanations of criminal behaviour (e.g., Sarason, 1968; Yochelson & Samenow, 1976). A central issue, apparent in the early work, lies in the varied use of the term 'cognition': in general terms, cognition refers to concepts such as memory, imagery, intelligence, and reasoning, although perhaps it is most widely used as a synonym for thinking. Indeed, Yochelson and Samenow describe various styles and errors of thinking that they see as characteristic of criminals, such as concrete thinking, a failure to emphasise with other people, irresponsible decision-making, and perceiving themselves as victims.

Ross and Fabiano (1985) made the distinction between *im*personal cognition and *inter*personal cognition: the former is that aspect of cognition that 'deals with the physical world'; the latter is concerned with 'understanding people and their actions' (now perhaps more familiar as *social cognition*). Impersonal cognition may play a part in the development of criminal behaviour: for example, when delinquents are compared with non-delinquents they may give lower scores on IQ tests (e.g., West & Farrington, 1973, 1977). However, Ross and Fabiano argue that interpersonal cognition may be the more important in understanding crime. They review the social cognition literature with criminal populations and describe several types or styles of cognition that characterise offenders.

Interpersonal cognition

There are several aspects of interpersonal cognition that have been linked with criminal behaviour. A failure of *self-control* may produce impulsive behaviour: Ross and Fabiano (1985: 37) suggest that impulsivity is a 'failure to insert between impulse and action a stage of reflection, a cognitive analysis of the situation'. An absence of self-control may be due to not learning when or how to stop and think, or not learning 'effective thinking'.

The term *locus of control* refers to whether an individual perceives their behaviour to be under their own *internal* control, or under the *external control* of fate or people in authority. The balance of findings in the literature is that offenders tend to external control in that they see their behaviour as determined by influences beyond their personal control.

Social perspective-taking refers to our ability to see events from another person's point of view, in turn linked to the ability to feel *empathy* for others. Some offenders show limited perspective-taking and empathy (Jolliffe & Farrington, 2004), as seen with a lack of appreciation of the effects of their actions upon other people. Social perspective-taking is an element of *social perception*, the ability to discriminate social cues, make sense of their meaning and use this information to decide upon a suitable course of action.

Finally, *social problem-solving* refers to the ability to deal effectively with interpersonal difficulties. There is a longstanding literature on social problem-solving (e.g., Spivack, Platt, & Shure, 1976), which extends into many areas of mental health and criminal justice research and practice (McGuire, 2005). There is some evidence that offenders show poorer social problem-solving skills than non-offenders (Antonowicz & Ross, 2005; Hollin & Palmer, 2006).

Social information-processing

The sequence of perceiving social cues, understanding the social situation, solving social problems, and deciding upon an appropriate response demands a set of complex cognitive skills. The notion of *social information-processing* brings together these various elements of cognition and it has been applied to anti-social and criminal behaviour. The explanatory power of a social information-processing approach is best illustrated specifically with reference to aggressive behaviour in children and adolescents (Dodge, 1986) and is described in Chapter 6.

The rational decision-maker

It is an obvious truism that for an offender to commit a crime, he or she must be presented with the opportunity to break the law. However, given the same opportunity, not everyone would commit a crime: a criminal is someone who decides to take advantage of the opportunity (and in some cases has the skills to do so). The view of 'crime as opportunity' was the basis for routine activity theory (Cohen & Felson, 1979; Felson, 1994), which looked at how the environment offered opportunities for criminal behaviour. The opportunity to offend may be due to our personal carelessness as, for example, in leaving one's car unlocked with shopping in view on the rear seat. Alternatively, broad social changes may create opportunities for crime: for example, the opportunities for burglary are increased if more members of a household go out to work leaving houses empty for longer periods of the day.

When an opportunity for crime presents itself, the individual has to make the decision to seize that opportunity. Cornish and Clarke (1986) took the individual's perception of the opportunity for crime as a starting point for a number of assumptions: (1) offenders seek to benefit themselves by their criminal behaviour; (2) taking the opportunity involves choices and making decisions; and (3) given the limits of time and available information, these choices and decisions are rational. The approach advocated by Cornish and Clarke therefore depicts the offender as a rational decision-maker, a *reasoning criminal*, not an empty organism acting on whim or impelled by genetic or environmental forces.

The notion of human behaviour as an exercise of rational choice has been applied to behaviours as diverse as economic decision-making and racial discrimination (Banton, 1995). Rational choice theory has been applied to a range of crimes, from car theft (Mayhew, Clarke, Sturman, & Hough, 1976) to robbery (Feeney, 1986). However, the main legacy of this approach, discussed in Chapter 12, lies in its translation into strategies for preventing crime, generally grouped under the rubric of *situational crime prevention*.

Control theories

The approach taken by the theories discussed thus far is to try to explain the acquisition of criminal behaviour. Another approach is to ask why offending does *not* take place, even when all the conditions for committing a successful crime are present. The notion of not offending is central to a group of theories within mainstream criminology that see crime as a failure of *control*.

The idea at the heart of control theories is, given that we all have the opportunity to commit crimes, why do some people, perhaps the majority of people, not offend? In other words, what *controls* our propensity to seize the opportunity to offend?

The early control theories, sociological in emphasis and heavily influenced by the writings of Émile Durkheim (1858–1917) on the n*ormality of crime*, saw social disorganisation and economic disadvantage as acting to weaken social and personal controls (Reiss, 1951). The term *social control* refers to the effect of structures within society, such as the family, religious organisations, and school, which act to contain the individual's tendency to offend. Hirschi (1969) saw social bonds, the association between the individual and the conventional structures and groups within society, as binding the person to social norms. The term *personal control* refers to the internalised values and beliefs that allow us to delay gratification and control any impulse to commit a crime.

Gottfredson and Hirschi (1990) set out a general theory of crime that, while sociological in orientation, pivots on the psychological notion of self-control. Although whether a crime follows an individual's lack of self-control or is an active choice according to their moral standards is debatable (Wikström & Trieber, 2007). From psychology, there are two particular theories involving self-control that have been applied to criminal behaviour: the first is based on moral development, the second on personality.

Moral development and criminal behaviour

Moral development forms a part of several theories of child development (e.g., Piaget, 1932, 1977), however, it is the views of moral development proposed by the American psychologist Lawrence Kohlberg (1927–87) that have been most frequently applied to criminal behaviour.

Kohlberg (1964, 1984), like Piaget, proposed that moral reasoning develops in a sequential manner as the child matures. Kohlberg described three levels of moral development, with two stages at each level. As shown in Box 3.4, at the lowest level, moral reasoning is

---

Box 3.4   Kohlberg's theory of moral development

Level 1: Pre-morality

Stage 1   *Punishment and obedience:* Moral behaviour is concerned with deferring to authority and avoiding punishment.

Stage 2   *Hedonism*: Concern with one's own needs irrespective of other people.

Level 2: Conventional conformity

Stage 3   *Interpersonal concordance: Concern with general conformity and gaining social approval.*

Stage 4   *Law and order:* Commitment to social order for its own sake and deference to authority.

Level 3: Autonomous principles

Stage 5   *Social contract:* Acknowledgement of individual rights and the democratic process in setting laws.

Stage 6   *Universal ethical principles:* A moral judgement based on justice, respect, and trust may transcend the law.

---

basic and concerned with oneself, moving to conventional social conformity at the intermediate level, and progressing to more abstract concepts, such as 'justice' and 'rights', at the highest level.

Kohlberg proposed that delinquent behaviour is related to a delay in the development of moral reasoning. This developmental delay means that the individual is functioning at a low level of moral reasoning, so that when there is the opportunity for criminal behaviour they do not have the internal mechanisms to regulate their behaviour.

Alongside criticisms of the theory itself – see Palmer (2003) for an overview – Kohlberg's theories have generated a body of empirical work mainly comparing the moral judgements of delinquent and non-delinquents. The evidence in support of the theory is variable (Campagna & Harter, 1975; Jurkovic, 1980; Thornton & Reid, 1982), which is not surprising given the complexity of the interactions between moral functioning, other psychological and environmental influences, and offending. As Jurkovic (1980: 724) comments: 'Not only do they (delinquents) vary from one another in stage of moral judgement, but they also fluctuate in their own reasoning level on different moral problems'. Further, as Ross and Fabiano (1985: 169) suggest: 'One can argue eloquently and convincingly about social/moral issues yet have a personal set of values which are entirely self-serving, hedonistic or anti-social'. The psychology literature contains some famous studies showing how people will act in ways that they believe are wrong (Asch, 1956; Milgram, 1963).

As Gibbs (1993) points out, moral reasoning does not function in a vacuum: an individual's level of moral reasoning functions alongside other aspects of cognition. Gibbs suggests that the way in which the individual processes social information is an important consideration in understanding moral reasoning. Gibbs put forward the notion of *cognitive distortions*, which are '[a]ttitudes or beliefs pertaining to the self or one's social behaviour' (Gibbs, 1993: 165), as the means by which an individual can support their amoral attitudes and temper any cognitive dissonance.

An example of self-centred moral reasoning is 'if I want it, I take it': Gibbs calls this a *primary distortion*, from which may come secondary cognitive distortions that function to rationalise and to mislabel the behaviour. Thus, the primary cognitive distortion 'I want it,

I take it', might be rationalised (secondary cognitive distortion) by blaming others: if people leave their cars unlocked then they deserve to have them stolen and, in any case, car theft can be explained away (mislabelled) as 'just a laugh' or 'nothing serious'. Similarly, victims of violence 'could have had it worse' and 'no real damage was done'. Such distortions may be shared and supported by the offender's peer group.

Gibbs' notion of cognitive distortions sits comfortably alongside another theory from mainstream criminology, *neutralisation theory* (Sykes & Matza, 1957).

Neutralisation theory

Many offenders hold conventional values and they are not impervious to guilt and to social demands to conform to the norm. However, these conventional values exist alongside the values and attitudes that support criminal behaviour. In the same way that most criminals are not continually involved in crime, they may drift between deviant and conventional thinking. It follows that, as Sykes and Matza suggest, the offender has find excuses to rationalise and justify their criminal behaviour: as shown in Box 3.5, there are various techniques of neutralisation that may be used to this effect. It is likely that these techniques are learned and supported by the offender's peers and, over time, become an effective way for the individual to resolve their feelings of guilt and remorse.

There have been attempts to relate theories of personality, such as the 'Big Five' (Heaven, 1995), to delinquency. However, Eysenck's personality theory, remains the most fully articulated with respect to criminal behaviour and is based on the notion of control.

Eysenck's personality theory

Eysenck's theory of personality incorporates biological, social, and individual factors. The basis of the theory is that through heredity there is variation between individuals in the functioning of the cortical and autonomic nervous systems. This variability, in turn, is related to each individual's ability to learn from, or more properly to *condition* to (in a Pavlovian sense), environmental stimuli. Thus, an individual's behaviour is influenced by both biological and social factors, the combination of which characterises that person's *personality*. Eysenck (1959) defined two dimensions of personality, *extraversion* (E) and *neuroticism* (N) – terms used by the Swiss psychiatrist Carl Gustav Jung (1875–1961) – and these two dimensions are at the heart of his theory. The two dimensions are seen as a continuum – E has a range from high (extravert) to low (introvert), N ranges from high (neurotic) to low (stable) – with most people falling in the middle of the range and comparatively fewer people at the extremes.

Box 3.5 Techniques of neutralisation

1. *Denial of responsibility*: 'It was not my fault'; 'I didn't have a choice'.
2. *Denial of injury*: 'It's not so bad'; 'They are insured'.
3. *Denial of victim*: 'They had it coming'; 'They had a bad attitude'.
4. *Condemn the condemners*: 'Everybody does it'; 'Why pick on me?'
5. *Appeal to higher loyalties*: 'Only cowards lose face'; 'I protect my own'.

The theory links extraversion with the functioning of the part of the brain stem called the reticular activating system. The reticular activating system regulates the arousal of the cerebral cortex, the area of the brain where higher level functioning such as thinking and memory are located. The extravert is congenitally cortically under-aroused as the reticular activating system fails to maintain optimum levels of arousal. The extravert therefore persistently seeks stimulation in order to maintain their cortical arousal at an optimal level: thus, the extravert's behaviour is impulsive and characterised by risk-taking. The introvert functions in just the opposite way to the extravert in that their reticular activating system produces cortical *over*-arousal. The introvert tries to avoid stimulation so that their cortical arousal is maintained at a comfortable level, hence the introvert's behaviour is quiet and reserved.

Neuroticism, sometimes called emotionality, is related to the functioning of the autonomic nervous system (ANS). Those individuals high in N have a highly labile ANS, which causes them to experience strong emotional reactions to any stressful or painful stimuli: high N individuals are characterised by anxious and moody behaviour. The Low N individual has a highly stable ANS and, even when under stress, their behaviour is calm and even-tempered.

Eysenck (1959) developed a psychometric test, The Maudsley Personality Inventory, which produces a score for both E and N, allowing an individual's position on the personality scales to be plotted into one of four quadrants – High E-High N, Low E-High N, High E-Low N, Low E-Low N – as shown in Figure 3.1.

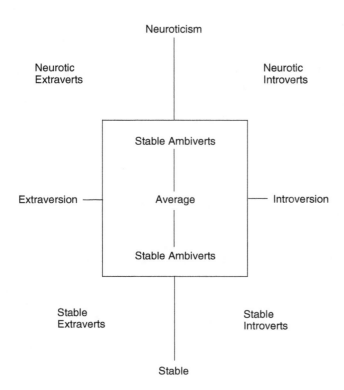

Figure 3.1 Eysenck's dimensions of personality.

The theory sees personality as playing a critical part in the process of socialisation. Eysenck took the position that we learn primarily through Pavlovian conditioning, through the associations between our actions and the accompanying environmental events. It is taken that children learn to control their anti-social behaviour as they develop a 'conscience': this conscience, Eysenck maintains, is a set of conditioned emotional responses to adverse environmental events that the individual associates with their anti-social behaviour. For example, if a child misbehaves and is scolded by a parent, the fear and pain from the reprimand is associated with the anti-social act. Thus, through learning the association between the behaviour and the adverse event, the child's behaviour becomes socialised.

The speed and efficiency of the child's socialisation is dependent upon their conditionability: introverts condition more efficiently than extraverts; less anxious, stable individuals condition more efficiently than those high in neuroticism. As the individual personality dimensions are component parts of the full personality, it follows that stable introverts (Low N-Low E) will condition best, stable extraverts (Low N-High E) and neurotic introverts (High N-Low E) will be at a mid-point; while neurotic extraverts (High N-High E) will condition least well.

In terms of criminal behaviour, Eysenck's theory concerns the development of *anti-social behaviour*: as discussed in Chapter 1, the processes by which anti-social behaviour becomes *criminal* behaviour involve a variety of legal and social factors. Further, as Eysenck (1977) points out, not all crimes are anti-social in the general sense of the term: there are politically motivated crimes, crimes committed by mentally disordered offenders and so on.

Eysenck described and refined the relationship between personality and crime over several years (Eysenck, 1964, 1970, 1977), later adding a reflective summary (Eysenck, 1996). The theory holds that as High E-High N is related to poor conditionability, so individuals with this type of personality will develop poor social control and become more likely to behave in an anti-social manner. Through the process of law, anti-social behaviour leads to criminal prosecution so that the High E-High N grouping will be overrepresented in offender populations. Conversely, as Low E-Low N leads to effective socialisation, so this personality configuration will be underrepresented in offender groups. The remaining two combinations, High E-Low N and Low E-High N, fall at some intermediate level and so may be expected in both offender and non-offender groups.

Eysenck later added a third personality dimension, psychoticism (P), to accompany E and N (Eysenck & Eysenck, 1968). P was originally conceived as indicating a vulnerability to psychoses, although it was later suggested that P might better denote psychopathy than psychoticism (Eysenck & Eysenck, 1972). The biological basis for P is not formulated as clearly as for E and N (Eysenck & Eysenck, 1968, 1976), although this aspect has been developed (Corr, 2010). The P scale assesses individual characteristics such as a preference for solitude, a lack of feeling for others, sensation-seeking, toughmindedness, and aggression (Eysenck, Eysenck, & Barrett, 1985). P is related to offending, particularly with crimes which involve hostility towards other people.

In summary, Eysenck (1977: 58) states:'In general terms, we would expect persons with strong antisocial inclinations to have high P, high E, and high N scores'. A study by Heaven, Newbury, and Wilson (2004) supported and refined Eysenck's position. Heaven et al. found that for young males and females, aged 15–16 years, P correlated with a range of anti-social acts including drinking alcohol and not paying fares on public transport. For older, 17- to 23-year-old males and females, P was most closely related to serious acts of anti-social behaviour such as drug-use and damage to property.

One the strengths of Eysenck's theory of crime is that it offers testable hypotheses and from the time it was first published it has generated a great deal of empirical research. There are several reviews of the research up to the early 1980s that showed that compared with non-offenders, offenders score highly on P and on N (Bartol & Bartol, 2005; Eysenck, 1977; Feldman, 1977; Eysenck & Gudjonnson, 1989; Powell, 1977). However, the evidence was less clear for E with some studies finding, as predicted, higher E scores in offender samples, but other studies finding no difference between offender and non-offender samples and a small number reporting *lower* E scores in offender groups. The general pattern for P, E, and N was similar for young and adult offender groups.

Eysenck and Eysenck (1971) suggested that the mixed findings for E may be explicable by considering the subcomponents of E: E comprises two subscales, *sociability* and *impulsiveness*, and it is the latter that is related to offending. In accordance with the theory, Eysenck and McGurk (1980) found that offenders scored higher than the non-offender sample on impulsiveness but there was no difference in sociability.

The first studies of Eysenck's early investigations had several shortcomings: the personality traits were considered individually rather than in combination, and few studies controlled for type of crime. (It will be recalled that Eysenck's theory concerns E and N in combination and should be applied to 'anti-social crimes'.) The next set of studies took these aspects of the theory into consideration.

Hindeland and Weis (1972) found that High E-High N was significantly associated with general deviancy such as petty theft and vandalism but not with major theft and aggression. Eysenck, Rust, and Rust (1977) compared the P, E, and N scores of offenders grouped by type of crime, finding that 'conmen' scored lowest on P, property and violent offenders lowest on N, but there were no differences on E.

Allsopp and Feldman (1974, 1976) reported positive relationships between a self-report measure of anti-social behaviour and E, N, and P for young males and females. McGurk and McDougall (1981) used a more complex statistical approach with a cluster analysis of the P, E, and N scores of 100 delinquents and 100 non-delinquent college pupils. The analysis showed four personality clusters in each group: both groups contained Low E-High N and High E-Low N clusters, but the clusters predicted to be related to criminal behaviour – High E-High N and High P-High E-High N – were very much evident in the delinquent sample. The Low E-Low N group, which the theory predicts to be highly socialised, was prevalent in the non-delinquent group. Another two studies using a similar methodology reported broadly similar clusters (McEwan, 1983; McEwan and Knowles, 1984). McEwan (1983) reported that offenders with a high P score had the greatest number of previous convictions but McEwan and Knowles (1984) failed to find any significant variation offence types according to personality cluster.

The balance of empirical evidence tends to support Eysenck's position on the relationship between personality and crime. As Eysenck has acknowledged that there are, as with any theory, limitations: the theory is not applicable to all crime and all criminals and the emphasis on classical conditioning and socialisation does not include other types of learning. There may also be other personality traits and dimensions associated with criminal behaviour (see Chapter 4). Nonetheless, Eysenck's theory of criminal behaviour is important given its emphasis on the interaction between hereditary, biological functioning, the environmental, and child development. As Bartol and Bartol (2005: 115) comment: 'Eysenck's theory is unique because it represents one of the few attempts by a psychologist to formulate a general, universal theory of criminal behaviour'.

Conclusion

A criticism of psychological theories and the research they generate is that they attempt to specify specific *causes* – biological, or psychological, or social, or a mixture of all three – of criminal behaviour. Research with a focus on causal relationships is often allied to scientific philosophies and methodologies that aim to control, measure, and determine relationships between sets of variables. The aim of such scientific research is to produce empirical findings that are reliable, verifiable, and replicable. This approach to research is characteristic of a positivism, a style of social research with a long history (Halfpenny, 1982/1992). It has become fashionable in some quarters to disparage positivism (Smith, 2004) although, as Halfpenny (1982/1992: 11) states: 'There are differences among anti-positivists, who use the term loosely and indiscriminately to describe all sorts of disfavoured forms of inquiry'.

Another criticism of psychological research applied to criminal behaviour, stretching back to Lombroso and Freud, is that there is an undue stress on defects, deficits, and developmental delays. Thus, rather than Durkheim's normality of crime, psychological theories stress the ways in which the offender is different to the normal, non-criminal population. This emphasis had an effect on the way a psychological perspective was appraised by some criminologists: 'Psychological theories are useful as explanations of the behavior of deeply disturbed, impulsive, or destructive people. However, they are limited as general explanations of criminality. For one thing, the phenomenon of crime and delinquency is so widespread that to claim that all criminals are psychologically disturbed is to make that claim against the vast majority of people' (Siegal, 1986: 175–6). Siegal's point regarding psychological disturbance and criminal behaviour is further discussed in Chapter 8.

The approach to explaining criminal behaviour as seen so far is one of applying a theory to criminal behaviour then setting about the task of research. However, a different approach is to use empirical research to formulate an understanding of criminal behaviour. The longitudinal research investigating the development of anti-social and criminal behaviour, has added significantly to our appreciation of the aetiological complexity of these forms of behaviour. The longitudinal research, including the work of David Farrington and Terrie Moffitt, is discussed in the following chapter.

Chapter summary

- There are five theoretical traditions within psychology that have been applied to criminal behaviour: these are: (1) psychobiological; (2) psychodynamic; (3) behavioural; (4) personality; and (5) cognitive.
- Psychobiological theories of criminal behaviour, once deeply unpopular, are now more widely accepted under the rubric of behavioural genetics.
- There is strong evidence that crime runs in families. The explanation for this is likely to be a mixture of hereditary, parenting, and social and economic factors.
- Learning theory and personality theory, in particular Eysenck's theory of personality, have both been applied to produce cogent theories of criminal behaviour.
- Social learning theory, incorporating cognition and emotion, is the predominant contemporary psychological theory applied to understand criminal behaviour.

Points for discussion

- Given that crime runs in families, is it only of interest to academics whether the causal balance is principally genetic or environmental?

- Do psychological theories of criminal behaviour based on cognition support the notion of free will?
- Despite the supporting evidence, explanations for criminal behaviour based on personality theory have fallen out of fashion. Why is this the case?

Essential reading

Plomin, R. (1990). *Nature and Nurture: An Introduction to Human Behavioral Genetics.* Pacific Grove, CA: Brooks/Cole.
There are several books available on behavioural genetics for the non-specialist: this slim text is an excellent introduction.

The lighter side

Eysenck, H. J. (1997). *Rebel with a Cause.* Piscataway, NJ: Transaction Publishers.
We often read books and papers without any sense of the writer. Hans Eysenck was a leading British psychologist, some might say *the* leading British psychologist, and one of the foremost proponents of trait theory. In his autobiography there is much to discover that's not in the academic papers and books.

Skinner, B. F. (1987). *Upon Further Reflection.* Englewood Cliffs, NJ: Prentice-Hall.
Skinner's contribution to psychology was immense. In this book, he presents a range of articles and essays written on a variety of themes but all – as, for example, in the essay 'Why we are not acting to save the world' – with the central message of using behavioural theory to help understand large-scale issues.

Useful websites

John Bowlby developed attachment theory, which has had an immense influence on practice, perhaps particularly among those who work with children. The Bowlby Centre website gives a great a deal of information relevant to attachment theory and to practice, http://thebowlbycentre.org.uk.
http://www.somatype.org gives a wealth of detail concerning constitutional theory.

References

Abrahamson, D. (1944). *Crime and the Human Mind.* New York, NY: Columbia University Press.
Aichhorn, A. (1925). *Verwahrloste Jungend.* Wien: Internationaler Psychoanalytischer Verlag. (Translated as Wayward Youth (1955), New York, NY: Meridian Books.)
Ainsworth, M. D. S. (1979). Attachment as related to mother-infant interaction. *Advances in the Study of Behaviour, 9,* 2–52.
—— (1985). Attachments across the life span. *Bulletin of the New York Academy of Medicine, 61,* 792–812.
—— (1989). Attachment beyond infancy. *American Psychologist, 44,* 709–716.
Akers, R. L. (1973). *Deviant Behavior: A Social Learning Approach.* Belmont, CA: Wadsworth.
Alexander, F. & Healy, W. (1935). *Roots of Crime.* New York, NY: Knopf.
Alexander, F. & Staub, H. (1931). *The Criminal, the Judge and the Public.* New York, NY: Macmillan.
Allsopp, J. F. & Feldman, M. P. (1974). Extraversion, neuroticism and psychoticism and anti-social behavior in school girls. *Social Behavior and Personality, 2,* 184–190.

—— (1976). Personality and anti-social behaviour in school-boys. *British Journal of Criminology, 16*, 337–351.

Antonowicz, D. H. & Ross, R. R. (2005). Social problem-solving deficits in offenders. In M. McMurran & J. McGuire (Eds.), *Social Problem Solving and Offending: Evidence, Evaluation and Evolution* (pp. 91–102). Chichester, Sussex: John Wiley & Sons.

Asch, S. E. (1956). Studies of independence and conformity: A minority of one against a unanimous majority. *Psychological Monographs, 70*, (whole no. 416).

Baker, L. A., Jacobson, K. C., Raine, A., Lozano, I., & Bezdjian, S. (2007). Genetic and environmental bases of childhood antisocial behavior: A multi-informant twin study. *Journal of Abnormal Psychology, 116*, 219–235.

Bandura, A. (1977). *Social Learning Theory.* New York, NY: Prentice-Hall.

Banton, M. (1995). Rational choice theories. *American Behavioral Scientist, 38*, 476–497.

Bartol, C. R. & Bartol, A. M. (2005). *Criminal Behavior: A Psychosocial Approach* (7 th ed.). Upper Saddle River, NJ: Pearson Prentice-Hall.

Bennett, L., Sorensen, D., & Forshay, H. (1971). The application of self-esteem measures in a correctional setting. *Journal of Research in Crime and Delinquency, 8*, 1–10.

Bijleveld, C. C. J. H. & Wijkman, M. (2009). Intergenerational continuity in convictions: A five generation study. *Criminal Behaviour and Mental Health, 19*, 142–155.

Blackburn, R. (1993). *The Psychology of Criminal Conduct: Theory, Research and Practice.* Chichester, Sussex: John Wiley & Sons.

Blackman, D. E. (1981). The experimental analysis of behaviour and its relevance to applied psychology. In G. Davey (Ed.), *Applications of Conditioning Theory* (pp. 1–28). London: Methuen.

Bohman, M. (1978). Some genetic aspects of alcoholism and criminality. *Archives of General Psychiatry, 35*, 269–276.

Bohman, M., Cloninger, C. R., Sigvardsson, S., & von Knorring, A. -L. (1983). Gene-environment interaction in the psychopathology of adoptees: Some recent studies of the origin of alcoholism and criminality. In D. Magnusson & V. Allen (Eds.), *Human Development: An International Perspective* (pp. 265–278). London: Academic Press.

Borgstrom, C. A. (1939). Eine serie von kriminellen zwillingen. *Archiv für Rassenbiologie, 12*, 18–44.

Bouchard, T. J., Jr., Lykken, D. T., McGue, M., Segal, N. L., & Tellegen, A. (1990). Sources of human psychological differences: The Minnesota study of twins reared apart. *Science, 250* (4978): 223–228.

Bowlby, J. (1944). Forty-four juvenile thieves. *International Journal of Psychoanalysis, 25*, 1–57.

—— (1946). *Forty-four Juvenile Thieves: Their Characters and Home-Life.* London: Bailliere, Tindall & Cox.

—— (1969). *Attachment and Loss, Vol. 1: Attachment.* New York, NY: Basic Books.

—— (1973). *Attachment and Loss, Vol. 2: Separation.* New York, NY: Basic Books.

—— (1980). *Attachment and Loss, Vol. 3: Loss, Sadness and Depression.* New York, NY: Basic Books.

Bull, R. H. C. (1984). Physical appearance and criminality. In D. J. Müller, D. E. Blackman, & A. J. Chapman (Eds.), *Psychology and Law.* Chichester, Sussex: John Wiley & Sons.

Cadoret, R. J. & Cain, C. A. (1980). Sex differences in predictors of antisocial behavior in adoptees. *Archives of General Psychiatry, 37*, 171–175.

Cadoret, R. J., Cain, C. A., & Crowe, R. R. (1983). Evidence for a gene-environment interaction in the development of adolescent antisocial behavior. *Behavior Genetics, 13*, 301–310.

Cadoret, R. J., Yates, W. R., Troughton, E., Woodworth, G., & Stewart, M. A. (1995). Genetic environmental interaction in the genesis of aggressivity and conduct disorders. *Archives of General Psychiatry, 52*, 916–924.

Campagna, A. F. & Harter, S. (1975). Moral judgement in sociopathic and normal children. *Journal of Personality and Social Psychology, 31*, 199–205.

Christiansen, K. O. (1977). A preliminary study of criminality amond twins. In S. Medrick & K. O. Christiansen (Eds.), *Biosocial Bases of Criminal Behavior* (pp. 89–108). New York, NY: Gardner Press.

Cohen, L. E. & Felson, M. (1979). Social change and crime rate trends: A routine activities approach. *American Sociological Review, 44,* 651–669.

Cornish, D. B. & Clarke, R. V. G. (Eds.) (1986). *The Reasoning Criminal: Rational Choice Perspectives on Crime.* New York, NY: Springer-Verlag.

Corr, P. J. (2010). The psychoticism-psychopathy continuum: A neuropsychological model of core deficits. *Personality and Individual Differences, 48,* 695–703.

Cortes, J. B. & Gatti, F. M. (1972). *Delinquency and Crime: A Biopsychosocial Approach.* New York, NY: Seminar Press.

Crowe, R. R. (1972). The adopted offspring of women criminal offenders. *Archives of General Psychiatry, 27,* 600–603.

Dalgaard, O. S. & Kringlen, E. (1976). A Norwegian twin study of criminality. *British Journal of Criminology, 16,* 213–33.

Dodge, K. A. (1986). A social-information processing model of social competence in children. In M. Perlmutter (Ed.), *Minnesota Symposium on Child Psychology* (pp. 77–125). Hillsdale, NJ: Erlbaum.

Dugdale, R. (1910). *The Jukes.* New York, NY: Plenum Press.

Duntley, J. D. & Shackelford, T. K. (2008). Darwinian foundations of crime and law. *Aggression and Violent Behavior, 13,* 373–382.

Ebbinghaus, H. (1908). *Psychology: An Elementary Text-Book* (M. Meyer, Ed. and trans.). Boston, MA: D.C. Heath.

Epps, P. & Parnell, R. W. (1952). Physique and temperament of women delinquents compared with women undergraduates. *British Journal of Medical Psychology, 25,* 249–255.

Estabrook, A. (1916). *The Jukes in 1915.* Washington, DC: Carnegie Institute of Washington.

Eysenck, H. J. (1959). *Manual of the Maudsley Personality Inventory.* London: University of London Press.

—— (1964). *Crime and Personality.* London: Routledge & Kegan Paul.

—— (1970). *Crime and Personality* (2 nd ed.). London: Granada.

—— (1977). *Crime and Personality* (3 rd ed.). London: Routledge & Kegan Paul.

—— (1996). Personality and crime: Where do we stand?. *Psychology, Crime and Law, 2,* 143–152.

Eysenck, H. J. & Eysenck, S. B. G. (1968). A factorial study of psychoticism as a dimension of personality. *Multivariate Behavioural Research* (Special Issue), 15–31.

—— (1976). *Psychoticism as a Dimension of Personality.* London: Hodder & Stoughton.

Eysenck, H. J. & Gudjonnsson, G. H. (1989). *The Causes and Cures of Criminality.* London: Plenum Press.

Eysenck, S. B. G. & Eysenck, H. J. (1971). Crime and personality: Item analysis of questionnaire responses. *British Journal of Criminology, 11,* 49–62.

—— (1972). The questionnaire measurement of psychoticism. *Psychological Medicine, 2,* 50–55.

Eysenck, S. B. G., Eysenck, H. J., & Barrett, P. (1985). A revised version of the psychoticism scale. *Personality and Individual Differences, 6,* 21–29.

Eysenck, S. B. G. & McGurk, B. J. (1980). Impulsiveness and venturesomeness in a detention centre population. *Psychological Reports, 47,* 1299–1306.

Eysenck, S. B. G., Rust, J., & Eysenck, H. J. (1977). Personality and the classification of adult offenders. *British Journal of Criminology, 17,* 169–79.

Farrington, D. P. (2002). Families and crime. In J. Q. Wilson and J. Petersilia (Eds.), *Crime: Public Policies for Crime Control* (pp. 129–148). Oakland, CA: Institute for Contemporary Studies Press.

Farrington, D. P., Barnes, G. C., & Lambert, S. (1996). The concentration of offending in families. *Legal and Criminological Psychology, 1,* 47–63.

Farrington, D. P., Jolliffe, D., Loeber, R., Stouthamer-Loeber, M., & Kalb, L. M. (2001). The concentration of offenders in families, and family criminality in the prediction of boys' delinquency. *Journal of Adolescence, 24,* 579–680.

Feeney, F. (1986). Robbers as decision-makers. In D. B. Cornish & R. V. G. Clarke (Eds.), *The Reasoning Criminal: Rational Choice Perspectives on Crime* (pp. 53–71). New York, NY: Springer-Verlag.

Feldman, M. P. (1977). *Criminal Behaviour: A Psychological Analysis*. Chichester, Sussex: John Wiley & Sons.

Felson, M. (1994). *Crime and Everyday Life: Implications for Society*. Thousand Oaks, CA: Pine Forge Press.

Fergusson, D. M., Horwood, L. J., & Nagin, D. S. (2000). Offending trajectories in a New Zealand birth cohort. *Criminology, 38*, 525–552.

Friedlander, K. (1947). *The Psychoanalytic Approach to Juvenile Delinquency*. London: Routledge & Kegan Paul.

Gibbs, J. C. (1993). Moral-cognitive interventions. In A. P. Goldstein & C. R. Huff (Eds.), *The Gang Intervention Handbook* (pp. 159–185). Champaign, IL: Research Press.

Gil, F. P., Weber, M. M., & Burgmair, W. (2002). Images in psychiatry: Ernst Kretschmer (1888–1964). *American Journal of Psychiatry, 159*, 1111.

Glueck, S. (1956). Theory and fact in criminology. *British Journal of Delinquency, 7*, 92–109.

Glueck, S. & Glueck, E. (1950). *Unraveling Juvenile Delinquency*. New York, NY: Harper & Row.

—— (1956). *Physique and Delinquency*. New York, NY: Harper & Row.

Gottfredson, M. R. & Hirschi, T. (1990). *A General Theory of Crime*. Stanford, CA: Stanford University Press.

Halfpenny, P. (1982/1992). *Positivism and Sociology: Explaining Social Life*. London: George Allen & Unwin/Aldershot, Hants: Gregg Revivals.

Hartl, E., Monnelli, E., & Eldeken, R. (1982). *Physique and Delinquent Behavior*. New York, NY: Academic Press.

Hayashi, S. (1967). A study of juvenile delinquency in twins. *Bulletin of the Osaka Medical School, 12*, 373–78.

Healy, W. & Bronner, A. F. (1936). *New Light on Delinquency and its Treatment*. New Haven, CN: Yale University Press.

Heaven, P. C. L. (1995). Personality and self-reported delinquency: Analysis of the "big five" personality dimensions. *Personality and Individual Differences, 20*, 47–54.

Heaven, P. C. L., Newbury, K., & Wilson, V. (2004). The Eysenck psychoticism dimension and delinquent behaviours among non-criminals: Changes across the lifespan?. *Personality and Individual Differences, 36*, 1817–1825.

Hill, D. & Pond, D. A. (1952). Reflections on a hundred capital cases submitted to electroencephalography. *Journal of Mental Science, 98*, 23–43.

Hindelang, M. J. & Weis, J. G. (1972). Personality and self-reported delinquency: an application of cluster analysis. *Criminology, 10*, 268–294.

Hirschi, T. (1969). *Causes of Delinquency*. Berkeley, CA: University of California Press.

Hollin, C. R. & Palmer, E. J. (2006). The adolescent problems inventory: A profile of incarcerated English male young offenders. *Personality and Individual Differences, 40*, 1485–1495.

Hooten, E. A. (1969). *The American Criminal: An Anthropological Study*. New York, NY: Greenwood Press.

Hurwitz, S. & Christiansen, K. O. (1983). *Criminology*. London: Allen & Unwin.

Ions, E. (1977). *Against Behaviouralism: A Critique of Behavioural Science*. Oxford: Blackwell.

James, W. (1890). *The Principles of Psychology* (2 vols.). New York, NY: Henry Holt.

Jeffery, C. R. (1965). Criminal behavior and learning theory. *Journal of Criminal Law, Criminology and Police Science, 56*, 294–300.

Jesness, C. F., DeRisi, W., McCormick, P., & Wedge, R. (1972). *The Youth Center Research Project*. Sacramento, CA: California Youth Authority.

Jolliffe, D. & Farrington, D. P. (2004). Empathy and offending: A systematic review and meta-analysis. *Aggression and Violent Behavior, 9*, 441–476.

Jurkovic, G. J. (1980). The juvenile delinquent as moral philosopher. *Psychological Bulletin, 88*, 709–727.

Kendall, K. (2004). Dangerous thinking: A critical history of correctional cognitive behaviouralism. In G. Mair (Ed.), *What Matters in Probation* (pp. 53–89). Cullompton, Devon: Willan Publishing.

Kohlberg, L. (1964). Development of moral character and moral ideology. In M. Hoffman & L. Hoffman (Eds.), *Review of Child Development Research, Vol. 1* (pp. 381–343). New York, NY: Russell Sage Foundation.

—— (1984). *Essays on Moral Development: The Psychology of Moral Development.* San Francisco, CA: Harper & Row.

Kranz, H. (1936). *Lebensschicksale Kriminellen Zwillinge.* Berlin: Julius Springer.

Kretschmer, E. (1921). *Körperbau und Charakter.* Berlin: J. Springer. (Translated as *Physique and Character,* 1925.)

Lange, J. (1929). *Verbrechen als Sochicksal.* Leipzig: Verlag.

Legras, A. M. (1932). *Psychese en Criminaliteit bij Twellingen.* Utrecht: Keminken Zoon N. V.

Lilley, J. R., Cullen, F. T., & Ball, R. A. (2007). *Criminological Theory: Context and Consequences* (4 th ed.). Thousand Oaks, CA: Sage.

McCandless, B. R., Persons, W. S. III, & Roberts, A. (1972). Perceived opportunity, delinquency, race, and body build among delinquent youth. *Journal of Consulting and Clinical Psychology, 38,* 281–287.

McCartan, L. M. (2007). Inevitable, influential, or unnecessary? Exploring the utility of genetic explanations for delinquent behavior. *Journal of Criminal Justice, 35,* 219–233.

McEwan, A. W. (1983). Eysenck's theory of criminality and the personality types of young delinquents. *Personality and Individual Differences, 4,* 201–204.

McEwan, A. W. & Knowles, C. (1984). Delinquent personality types and the situational contexts of their crimes. *Personality and Individual Differences, 5,* 339–344.

McGuire, J. (2005). Social problem solving: Basic concepts, research, and applications. In M. McMurran & J. McGuire (Eds.), *Social Problem Solving and Offending: Evidence, Evaluation and Evolution* (pp. 3–29). Chichester, Sussex: John Wiley & Sons.

McGurk, B. J. & McDougall, C. (1981). A new approach to Eysenck's theory of criminality. *Personality and Individual Differences, 2,* 338–40.

Madden, S., Walker, J. T., & Miller, J. M. (2008). Does size really matter? A re-examination of Sheldon's somatotypes and criminal behavior. *The Social Science Journal, 45,* 330–344.

Mayhew, P., Clarke, R. V. G., Sturman, A., & Hough, J. M. (1976). *Crime as Opportunity.* Home Office Research Study 34. London: HMSO.

Mednick, S. A., Gabrielli, W. F., & Hutchings, B. (1984). Genetic influences in criminal convictions: Evidence from an adoption study. *Science, 224,* 891–894.

Milgram, S. (1963). Behavioral study of obedience. *Journal of Abnormal and Social Psychology, 67,* 371–378.

Miller, N. & Dollard, J. (1941). *Social Learning and Imitation.* New Haven, CT: Yale University Press.

Modgil, S. & Modgil, C. (Eds.) (1987). *B. F. Skinner: Consensus and Controversy.* New York, NY: Falmer Press.

Murray, J. & Farrington, D. P. (2005). Parental imprisonment: Effects on boys' antisocial behaviour and delinquency through the life-course. *Journal of Child Psychology and Psychiatry, 46,* 1269–1278.

Murray, J., Janson, G. -J., & Farrington, D. P. (2007). Crime in adult offspring of prisoners: A crossnational comparison of two longitudinal samples. *Criminal Justice and Behavior, 34,* 133–149.

Nagin, D. S., Farrington, D. P., & Moffitt, T. E. (1995). Life-course trajectories of different types of offenders. *Criminology, 33,* 111–139.

Nietzel, M. T. (1979). *Crime and its Modification: A Social Learning Perspective.* Oxford: Pergamon Press.

Nijhof, K. S., de Kemp, R. A. T., & Engels, R. C. M. E. (2009). Frequency and seriousness of parental offending and their impact on juvenile offending. *Journal of Adolescence, 32,* 893–908.

Palmer, E. J. (2003). *Offending Behaviour: Moral Reasoning, Criminal Conduct and the Rehabilitation of Offenders.* Cullompton, Devon: Willan.

Piaget, J. (1932). *The Moral Judgement of the Child.* London: Routledge & Kegan Paul.

—— (1977). *The Development of Thought: Equilibration of Cognitive Structures.* New York, NY: Viking Press.

Plomin, R. (1990). *Nature and Nurture: An Introduction to Human Behavioral Genetics*. Pacific Grove, CA: Brooks/Cole.

Powell, G. E. (1977). Psychoticism and social deviancy in children. *Advances in Behaviour Research and Therapy, 1*, 27–56.

Raine, A. (1993). *The Psychopathology of Crime: Criminal Behavior as a Clinical Disorder*. New York, NY: Academic Press.

Reckless, W. C. & Dintz, S. (1967). Pioneering with self-concept as a vulnerability factor in delinquency. *Journal of Criminal Law, Criminology and Police Science, 58*, 515–523.

Rees, L. (1973). Constitutional factors and abnormal behaviour. In H. J. Eysenck (Ed.), *Handbook of Abnormal Psychology* (pp. 344–392). London: Pitman Medical.

Reiss, A. J. (1951). Delinquency as a failure of personal and social controls. *American Sociological Review, 16*, 196–207.

Rotter, J. B. (1945). *Social Learning and Clinical Psychology*. Englewood Cliffs, NJ: Prentice-Hall.

Rosanoff, A. J., Handy, L. M., & Rosanoff, F. A. (1934). Crime and delinquency in twins. *Journal of Criminal Law and Criminology, 24*, 923–934.

Rosanoff, A. J., Handy, L. M., & Plesset, I. (1941). The etiology of child behavioral difficulties, juvenile delinquency and adult criminality with special reference to their occurrence in twins. *Psychiatric Monographs* (California) No. 1, Sacramento Department of Institutions, Sacramento, California.

Ross, R. R. & Fabiano, E. A. (1985). *Time to Think: A Cognitive Model of Delinquency Prevention and Offender Rehabilitation*. Johnson City, TN: Institute of Social Sciences and Arts.

Rowe, D. C. & Osgood, D. W. (1984). Heredity and sociological theories of delinquency: A reconsideration. *American Sociological Review, 49*, 526–540.

Russell, B. (1961). *A History of Western Philosophy* (2nd ed.). London: Allen & Unwin.

Rutter, M. (1981). *Maternal Deprivation Reassessed* (2nd ed.). Harmondsworth: Penguin Books.

Rutter, M. D & Giller H. (1983). *Juvenile Delinquency: Trends and Perspectives*. Harmondsworth: Penguin Books.

Ryckman, R. M., Robbins, M. A., Kaczor, L. M., & Gold, J. A. (1989). Male and female raters' stereotyping of male and female physiques. *Personality and Social Psychology Bulletin, 15*, 244–251.

Sarason, I. G. (1968). Verbal learning, modelling and juvenile delinquency. *American Psychologist, 23*, 254–266.

Sheldon, W. H. & Stevens, S. S. (1942). *The Varieties of Temperament: A Psychology of Constitutional Differences*. New York, NY: Harper & Row.

Sheldon, W. H., Hartl, W. M., & McDermott, E. (1949). *Varieties of Delinquent Youth*. New York, NY: Harper & Row.

Sheldon, W. H., Stevens, S. S., & Tucker, W. B. (1940). *The Varieties of Human Physique: An Introduction to Constitutional Psychology*. New York, NY: Harper & Row.

Short, J. F. (Ed.) (1968). *Gang Delinquency and Delinquent Subcultures*. New York, NY: Harper & Row.

Siegal, L. J. (1986). *Criminology* (2nd ed.). St. Paul, MN: West Publishing.

Simonton, D. K. (2002). *Great Psychologists and Their Times*. Washington, DC: American Psychological Association.

Skinner, B. F. (1938). *The Behavior of Organisms*. New York, NY: Appleton-Century-Crofts.

—— (1953). *Science and Human Behavior*. New York, NY: Macmillan.

—— (1974). *About Behaviourism*. London: Cape.

—— (1987). Pavlov's influence on psychology in America. In B. F. Skinner (Ed.), *Upon Further Reflection* (pp. 185–191). Englewood Cliffs, NJ: Prentice-Hall.

Sluckin, W., Herbert, M., & Sluckin, A. (1983). *Maternal Bonding*. Oxford: Blackwell.

Smith, D. (2004). The uses and abuses of positivism. In G. Mair (Ed.), *What Matters in Probation* (pp. 34–52). Cullompton, Devon: Willan.

Spivack, G., Platt, J. J., & Shure, M. B. (1976). *The Problem-Solving Approach to Adjustment*. San Francisco, CA: Jossey-Bass.

Stumpfl, F. (1936). *Die Usprunge des Verbrechens om Lebenshauf von Zwillingen*. Leipzig: Georg Thieme Verlag.

Sutherland, E. H. (1939). *Principles of Criminology*. Philadelphia, PA: Lippincott.

—— (1947). *Principles of Criminology* (4th ed.). Philadelphia, PA: Lippincott.

Sutherland, E. H. & Cressey, D. R. (1970). *Principles of Criminology* (8th ed.). Philadelphia, PA: Lippincott.

—— (1974). *Principles of Criminology* (9th ed.). Philadelphia, PA: Lippincott.

Sykes, G. & Matza, D. (1957). Techniques of neutralization. *American Sociological Review, 22*, 664–670.

Thornberry, T. P., Freeman-Gallant, A., & Lovegrove, P. J. (2009). Intergenerational linkages in anti-social behaviour. *Criminal Behaviour and Mental Health, 19*, 80–93.

Thorndike, E. L. (1911). *Animal Intelligence: Experimental Studies*. New York, NY: Macmillan.

Thornton, D. M. & Reid, R. L. (1982). Moral reasoning and type of criminal offence. *British Journal of Social Psychology, 21*, 231–238.

Van Dusen, K. T., Mednick, S. A., Gabrielli, W. F., & Hutchings, B. (1983). Social class and crime in an adoption cohort. *Journal of Criminal Law and Criminology, 74*, 249–269.

Wadsworth, M. E. J. (1979). *Roots of Delinquency*. New York, NY: Barnes and Nobel.

West, D. J. & Farrington, D. P. (1973). *Who Becomes Delinquent?* London: Heinemann Educational.

—— (1977). *The Delinquent Way of Life*. London: Heinemann Educational.

Wikström, P. -O. & Trieber, K. (2007). The role of self-control in crime causation: Beyond Gottfredson and Hirschi's *General Theory of Crime*. *European Journal of Criminology, 4*, 237–264.

Wootton, B. (1959). *Social Science and Social Pathology*. London: Allen & Unwin.

Yerkes, R. M. & Morgulis, S. (1909). The method of Pawlow in animal psychology. *Psychological Bulletin, 6*, 257–273.

Yochelson, S. & Samenow, S. E. (1976). *The Criminal Personality, Vol. 1: A Profile for Change*. New York, NY: Jason Aronsen.

Yoshimasu, S. (1961). The criminological significance of the family in light of the studies of criminal twins. *Acta Criminologiae et Medicinae Legalis Japanica, 27*, 117–141.

—— (1965). Criminal life curves of monozygotic twin-pairs. *Acta Criminologiae et Medicinae Legalis Japanica, 31*, 9–20.

4 The development of criminal behaviour

The previous chapter looked at the way psychological theories have been applied to criminal behaviour. In this chapter, the focus shifts from theory to research as the primary means by which to progress towards an understanding of criminal behaviour. Since the early 1990s, studies that have utilised longitudinal research designs have contributed significantly to our understanding of the complex processes involved in the development of anti-social and criminal behaviour. This research has not only increased our knowledge of the way in which criminal behaviour develops but has also influenced the theory.

Longitudinal research

There is a strong argument that in order to understand criminal behaviour it is necessary to study the complete life history of offenders. The body of research that takes just such a life-span approach is often referred to as *criminal career* research (Piquero, Farrington, & Blumstein, 2003). The investigation of criminal behaviour across the life-span relies on a suitable research methodology. One possible approach is to use a cross-sectional methodology in which groups of people of different ages are compared on a range of variables. However, a cross-sectional approach, comparing groups of different ages, introduces the problem of confounding between-group differences: once formed, do the groups allow comparison of like with like? An answer to the potentially confounding effect of group differences is to use an experimental design in which individual are randomly allocated to different groups. The problem in longitudinal research, of course, is an individual cannot be randomly allocated an age! Another approach to controlling for confounding between-group differences is to use groups matched on key variables: however, as shown by the example in Box 4.1, the process of matching when using quasi-experimental group comparison designs is far from straightforward.

Another solution to the problem of finding a satisfactory control, as often used in some areas of applied psychology, is to use a research design in which the individual is their own control. This design is frequently found in clinical research where there is interest in determining, say, whether an individual's behaviour has changed before and after treatment (Barlow & Hersen, 1984; Long & Hollin, 1995). In *longitudinal research* the same idea, the individual as their own control, is used but the focus is on changes over time for a group, or *cohort*, rather than the individual as in single-case designs. Thus, in longitudinal research, the measure is of change in a cohort's behaviour over a period of time, typically years, so that rather than a cross-sectional snapshot there is a home movie, a natural history, of an individual's life.

As Loeber and Farrington (1994) note, longitudinal research has several advantages when looking at the development of anti-social behaviour: (1) It may be possible to identify typical

Box 4.1 Issues in cross-sectional design

Research question: Is there any relationship between educational background and stealing cars?
Methodology: Find a sample of car thieves and look at measures of educational background:
let's say it's found that the car thieves' educational backgrounds are characterised by high levels
of truancy and low educational attainment.

Problem: Knowledge of the car thieves' educational background but with nothing to compare it
with does not really say a great deal: it is possible that there are lots of truants with low educational attainment who don't steal cars.
Solution: Find a *control group* of people who do not steal cars and compare them, using the
same measures, with the car thieves.

Problem: A valid comparison relies on the two groups being as similar as possible. To take an
extreme example, if one group of car thieves was all male and the other all female, the group
differences could be due to the confounding effect of gender rather than educational differences.
Solution: Match two groups.

Problem: How to match the groups? There are a range of potentially important variables to
match such as age, personality, family background, peer group, and so on *ad infinitum*.
Solution: Select key variables to control (say age and IQ) and match pairs from each group.

Problem: Critically important variables may not be controlled and one-to-one matching may
cause practical difficulties in finding exact matches between pairs unless there are samples large
enough to allow the matched groups to be formed.
Solution: An alternative to one-to-one matching is to use population-based matching with multivariate analyses used to control statistically sample differences on selected variables (Rossi,
Freeman, & Lipsey, 1999).

developmental sequences associated with anti-social behaviour; (2) the association between
critical developmental periods and pathways, life events, and anti-social behaviour may
become evident; and (3) it may be possible to predict criminal behaviour in later life from
earlier information.

An inherent problem with longitudinal research is that it takes a long time to carry out and
can be financially expensive. The necessarily long time scale may have the consequence of
'dating' a study in its later years: the state-of-the-art variables at the onset of the study may
not grow old and fail to include those that later research will show to be important. A good
example of 'growing old' is to be found with research into the effects of childhood abuse on
delinquent behaviour in early life. As discussed in Chapter 6, research primarily from the
1980s onwards has shown that childhood abuse may play an important role in the aetiology
of delinquency. As the evidence on child abuse collected during the 1980s was obviously not
available to researchers in the 1960s, the effects of childhood abuse are not included as part
of the longitudinal studies started in the 1960s and 1970s.

There are two principal designs in longitudinal research: these are *retrospective studies*
and *prospective studies*, although the two can be combined within a single piece of research.

Retrospective longitudinal studies

A retrospective study is, by definition, conducted after the event. The researchers first identify a cohort relevant to the research, say people who have committed a certain type of crime.

Once a cohort is assembled, the research progresses either through interviews in which people are asked to recall the past, or by collecting archival information, such as criminal records, details of parents, and school history, which stretch back over the group's lifetime. There are several disadvantages with this design: interviews rely on the vagaries of memory, while archival data may be lost, incomplete or inaccessible. Nonetheless, there are occasions when a retrospective design is appropriate, typically when the research is concerned with an unusual or rare event.

McNally (1995) inspected official government records (England and Wales) compiled during the decade 1982–92 to gather information on cases where juveniles, aged 10–16 years, had been convicted of murder or manslaughter. McNally identified 236 such cases of which 95 per cent were males: of these cases, almost 40 per cent had been sentenced for murder, the remainder for manslaughter. From analysis of the archival data, McNally was able to describe a range of details about the cases: for example, the most common method of killing was with a sharp instrument while the use of firearms was rare, many of the juveniles had a previous diagnosis of conduct disorder, and a very high number came from homes that were not intact at the time of the offence. McNally (1995: 341) concluded that many of the young people who had killed had experienced poor parenting, including abandonment, leading to his recommendation that: 'Key targets for ministerial action should be a convergence of initiatives promoting family stability, improving parenting skills, and violence reduction schemes'.

Prospective longitudinal studies

A prospective design overcomes many of the limitations inherent in a retrospective design. The cohort, with their consent and if necessary consent from their parents or legal guardian, is regularly followed up over a period of time beginning in childhood (sometimes starting before childbirth), through adolescence and into adulthood. A range of ways of gathering data are typically used, including psychometric testing, interviews with the member of the cohort and their parents or teachers, and monitoring official records. The great advantage of a prospective approach is that it allows forward-planning, so that the researchers may define exactly what data are to be gathered, thereby allowing the characteristics and experiences of the cohort to be precisely and reliably documented over time. Although not without its own problems (Loeber & Farrington, 1994), when conducted to a high standard this methodology can produce extremely informative data. As well as delinquency (Farrington, 2006), prospective longitudinal studies have been used in a variety of areas of research including temperament and personality, schizophrenia, and drug-use (Rutter & Smith, 1995).

One way of considering the wealth of findings from longitudinal studies is to look at what they say about juvenile offending, then to consider how that knowledge informs understanding of criminal behaviour in later, adult life. This methodology therefore allows risk factors for adult offending to be identified during childhood and adolescence. A substantial number of longitudinal studies have been conducted in several countries: in the UK, the Cambridge Study in Delinquent Development is the most influential longitudinal study and provides an excellent exemplar of this type of research.

The Cambridge Study in Delinquent Development

The Cambridge Study in Delinquent Development started in 1961 with a cohort of 411 young males, aged 8–9 years, and in 2010 is in progress with a large proportion of the cohort still alive. As the Cambridge cohort are all males, its findings are restricted to male patterns of behaviour. The Cambridge Study involved testing and interviewing the cohort, along with interviews with their parents, peers, and school teachers. Access to official records provided data on convictions. In 2002, Farrington noted that testing had so far taken place when the cohort were aged 8, 10, 14, 16, 18, 21, 25, 32, and 48 years. In the time spanned by the study there have been some deaths: at age 48, 394 of the original 411 were alive. A vast amount of data has been collected in the Cambridge Study which is available in around 200 academic publications.

Juvenile crime

In juvenile crime there is a distinction to be made between *status* offences and *index* (or *notifiable*) offences. Status offences are offences that by definition apply only to young people: this includes offences such as truancy, purchasing alcohol, and driving a motor vehicle underage. Index offences are the more serious offences, such as assault, burglary, arson, and theft, which are criminal acts for anyone over the age of criminal responsibility.

If status and index offences are combined, there are estimates as high as 80 per cent of the adolescent population are committing offences. Farrington (1987: 34) suggests that if unrecorded offences were added then this would '[u]ndoubtedly push these figures close to 100 per cent'. However, the balance of types of offence committed by adolescents is weighted towards status offences rather than serious index offences. The uncertainty associated with by unrecorded crimes leaves open the possibility that adolescents are committing more serious offences than the figures suggest but it is highly unlikely that the number of serious offences is even close to the high levels of status offences.

In Chapter 1, the distinction was made between *prevalence* and *incidence*: specifically for juvenile crime, prevalence refers to the number of young people committing offences; incidence refers to the number of offences committed by each young person. This distinction is important in understanding the relationship between age and offending as shown by the longitudinal studies.

The relationship between age and crime, as illustrated in Figure 4.1, is one that has been found consistently across the literature. Among children and adolescents the rate of offending increases from around 8 years of age, reaches a peak at about 16–17 years, then rapidly declines into the late teens and early 20s. This age-crime relationship, which is similar for both males and females, is explained by increasing prevalence (more young people committing offences) rather than a rise in incidence (young offenders committing increasing numbers of offences as they grow older). Kyvsgaard (2003: 66) comments: 'It is an indisputable fact that prevalence varies with age. All studies agree that the prevalence is highest among the young and lowest among the elder citizens of any society.' Similarly, Wolfgang, Thornberry, and Figlio (1987: 44), commenting on the findings from their longitudinal study carried out in the USA, said that the peak in rates of offending at 16–17 years was due '[a]lmost entirely to an increase in the number of active offenders and not to an increase in their annual "productivity"'.

An important contribution of the longitudinal studies is that they have identified a number of risk factors that are predictive of long-term offending.

Predictors of long-term offending

When the longitudinal data have been collected, the investigators can try to identify any individual factors or significant life events that may be associated with offending. In the

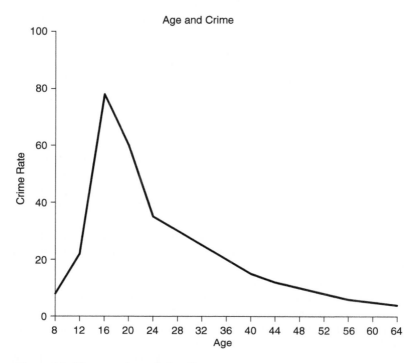

Figure 4.1 The age-crime relationship.

Cambridge Study, approximately 20 per cent of the cohort were convicted as juveniles, a figure increasing to around 33 per cent by 25 years of age. As discussed in Chapter 2, self-reported delinquency corresponded reasonably well with official convictions: the young men who were convicted of an offence also self-reported a higher number of delinquent acts. So, what were the features that distinguished the juvenile-delinquents-to-be from their peers?

Juvenile offenders

If childhood is taken to be up to the age of 10 years (the age of criminal responsibility in England and Wales), there were marked effects of particular childhood experiences. Farrington and West (1990) noted that the future juvenile delinquents were more likely to have criminal parents and delinquent older siblings. The delinquents tended to be from broken homes and from poorer, larger-sized families; they were more likely to have been neglected physically by their parents; and were more likely to be living in low-quality housing. They were also more likely to have been rated as troublesome and dishonest at primary school.

For the delinquents, a picture emerged of a childhood characterized by broken homes and harsh parenting, together with an experience of school where their behaviour – impulsive acts, hyperactivity, poor attention and concentration, and daring risk-taking – was seen as troublesome by teachers. The delinquents, scoring lower than their non-delinquent peers on tests of intelligence, do not do well academically at school and are generally unpopular with their fellow pupils.

Box 4.2 Childhood predictors of offending in later life (after Farrington, 1995)

1. Anti-social childhood behaviour, including troublesomeness in school, dishonesty, and aggressiveness.
2. Hyperactivity, impulsivity, and attention deficit, including poor concentration, restlessness, daring, and psychomotor impulsivity.
3. Low intelligence and poor school attainment.
4. Family criminality, including convicted parents, delinquent older siblings, and siblings with behaviour problems.
5. Family poverty, including low family income, large family size, and poor housing.
6. Poor parental child-rearing behaviour, including harsh and authoritarian discipline, poor supervision, parental conflict, and separation from parents.

The young person's delinquent behaviour is unlikely to stand in isolation: Stattin and Magnusson (1995) found relationships between delinquency and other educational, behavioural, social, and interpersonal problems. They make the comment that, 'The age at onset of offending is intimately connected in time with the emergence of problem behaviour generally' (Stattin & Magnusson, 1995: 440). It is also evident that when problem behaviours reach a critical stage, as seen with a formal diagnosis of *conduct disorder*, then the child's difficulties are highly likely to persist over a number of years (Lahey et al., 1995).

Farrington (1995) noted that the most important predictors of offending in later life as evident at age 8–10 years (whether measured by convictions or self-report) fell into the six categories shown in Box 4.2. Those young males who committed their first serious offence at an early age and those who accumulated more than six criminal convictions were at the greatest risk of progressing to an adult criminal career (Farrington, 1983).

The Cambridge Study suggested that various adversities in early life (the particular role of harsh parenting is considered in Chapter 6) are associated with social difficulties generally and anti-social behaviour specifically. The intensity and severity of such disadvantage is predictive of chronic offending – including aggressive and violent offending (Kingston & Prior, 1995) – in later life.

Adult criminals

When data are collected over a long period, it is possible to focus on those young people who become adult criminals. A comparison of the characteristics and circumstances of the adult offenders with non-offenders reveals details of the pathway from juvenile delinquency to adult crime.

When the young men in the Cambridge Study of Delinquent Development had reached 18 years of age, the persistent adult offenders – who had mainly committed less serious crimes involving motor vehicles, theft, group violence, and vandalism – had a lifestyle that was characterised by heavy drinking, sexual promiscuity, and drug-use. These offenders were not likely to hold educational or other formal qualifications, and they were employed in unskilled manual jobs punctuated by frequent periods of unemployment. They committed more crimes during periods of unemployment, typically theft, burglary, and fraud for financial gain. At 32 years of age, the persistent offenders had an extensive history of fines,

---

Box 4.3.   Persistent offenders at age 32

'*Convicted* men differed significantly from unconvicted ones at age 32 in most respects of their lives: in having less home ownership, more residential mobility, more divorce or separation from their wives, more conflict with their wives or cohabitees, more separation from their children, more unemployment, lower take-home pay, more evenings out, more fights, more heavy smoking, more drunk driving, more heavy drinking, more drug-taking, more theft from work, and more other types of offences ... While convicted and unconvicted men were significantly different in many respects, it should not be concluded that all convicted men were more deviant than all unconvicted men. The two groups overlapped significantly' (Farrington & West, 1990: 126).

---

probation and prison sentences; they were not likely to be home-owners, they had low paid jobs, they used a wide range of drugs, and some of the men had physically assaulted their partner.

In all, their life histories and current circumstances suggest that the persistent offenders were not leading fulfilling lives. As shown in Box 4.3, Farrington and West (1990) paint a bleak picture of life at age 32 for those adolescents who grew up to become convicted as adults.

Farrington, Ttofi, and Coid (2009) reported the fate of the adolescents in the Cambridge Study as they reached 48 years of age. At 48, the lives of the persistent offenders were not dissimilar to how they had been 16 years previously (see Box 4.3). In terms of the antecedents to persistent offending, Farrington et al. (2009: 159) note: 'In predicting persistent offenders compared with adolescence-limited offenders, the most important risk factors were heavy drinking at age 18, hyperactivity at ages 12–14, low popularity at ages 8–10, and harsh parental discipline at ages 8–10'. There were 237 men (57.7 per cent of the cohort) who had not received a criminal conviction by age 48.

Evidently two groups emerge from the longitudinal research: the first group commits offences as a juvenile and then grows out of crime; the second is composed of those who progress from offending juvenile to adult offending. However, there are two interesting subgroups nested within these two groups: one subgroup is *childhood-limited* offenders, the other is a *late onset* subgroup.

Childhood-limited offenders

When considering persistent offenders, the observation has been made that not all of those children who display high levels of anti-social behaviour continue with this behaviour into adolescence (Moffitt, Caspi, Harrington, & Milne, 2002). This pattern may be explicable by the force of protective factors during adolescence (see Box 4.4), or by the development of more profound conditions, such as mental disorder, that mask low levels of anti-social behaviour.

Late onset offenders

Not all those people who commit crimes as adults started offending in adolescence, some begin their criminal career in later life. Several studies have looked at these 'late onset

Box 4.4 Issues in the relationship between neurocognition and anti-social behaviour (after Raine et al., 2005)

1. Do offenders show impairments in both spatial and verbal functioning?
2. Do offenders show impairments in memory functioning?
3. Do life-course persistent offenders show neuropsychological impairment but not adolescent-limited offenders?
4. Do neurocognitive impairments characterise childhood-limited anti-social behaviour?
5. Are the neurocognitive impairments actually due to other disorders or injuries?

offenders'. Elander, Rutter, Simonoff and Pickles (2000) note that across a number of studies, around 10 per cent of males who are followed from an early age began offending in later life. Elander et al. suggest three potential explanations for late onset offending: (1) the earlier crimes were not detected, meaning that 'late onset' is not actually the case; (2) criminality in later life could be explained by mental disorders, particularly those associated with drug and alcohol abuse; (3) there is an absence of childhood and psychiatric problems so that it is other circumstances that lead to offending.

Elander et al. looked at the criminal records of a group of 13 males and females who were part of a larger cohort and were late onset offenders. They concluded, favouring the first explanation above, that there was a strong association between undetected early anti-social behaviour and late onset criminal behaviour. However, this study used a sample drawn from referrals to child psychiatric services: it is debatable how far these findings would generalise to mainstream offender populations.

Farrington et al. (2009) found that late onset offenders had some of the individual and social risk factors characteristic of persistent offenders, including those present during adolescence. A longitudinal study conducted in Finland also found that late onset offenders were similar to non-offenders in terms of home background and social functioning (Pulkkinen, Lyyra, & Kokko, 2009). The late onset offenders differed from the non-offenders in that they gave higher scores on measures of neuroticism, extraversion, and aggressiveness. Farrington et al. (2009: 162) have also commented on neuroticism in late onset offenders: 'Their high nervousness and neuroticism may have protected them against offending in adolescence and the teenage years ... As they were more likely than the other categories of males to still be living at home at age 18, their family may have cocooned them'.

Physical health

Childhood experiences and lifestyle relate not only to anti-social behaviour but also to other areas of life such as physical health. Shepherd, Shepherd, Newcombe, and Farrington (2009) noted that the Cambridge Study highlighted a potential association between an anti-social life style and poor physical health. There were 17 members of the Cambridge Study cohort who had died before the age of 48 years, 13 of whom had criminal convictions: of these 13, 3 had died in accidents, 6 from illnesses such cancer, 1 from a drug overdose, 1 from suicide, and 2 from unknown causes. A further 17 men were registered disabled, 2 from injuries sustained in accidents, the others as a result of illness. The best discriminators between those men who were healthy at age 48 years and those who were dead or disabled were anti-social behaviour at age 8–10 years and a conviction at age 10–18 years.

A full explanation for the association between early anti-social and criminal behaviour and adverse health and early death remains to be established. The factors associated with early offending are precursors to a later lifestyle that is characterised by alcohol and drug use, periods of imprisonment, low income and poor quality housing, broken relationships, and experience of violence. It is not unreasonable to suggest that this highly adverse mixture of factors, rather than a single factor such as alcohol use, played a role in the adverse health outcomes. The trend for an inverse relationship between health problems and anti-social behaviour may exacerbated, as Shepherd et al. (2009) suggest, by the more delinquent individuals being less likely to seek medical advice and enter hospital for treatment.

Protective factors

The longitudinal studies have described many of the factors associated with the development of criminal behaviour. However, they have also shown that there are some young people who experience adverse experiences in childhood and adolescence but do not become criminals as adults. Farrington and West (1990) commented on the phenomenon of 'good boys from bad backgrounds', referring to young men for whom all the risk factors pointed to a criminal career but who were never convicted as adults. Farrington (2002) notes that by age of 32, about one-quarter of the vulnerable, high-risk males in the Cambridge Study had not been convicted. What is it that protects these individuals from their 'criminogenic backgrounds'?

In the Cambridge Study, the best predictors of *not* offending were none or only a few friends at age 8 years, parents who were not convicted offenders and siblings who did not display problem behaviours. The non-offenders were also characterised by their shyness during adolescence, allied to a tendency towards social withdrawal, so that the young men spent most of their leisure time at home.

The formation of close romantic relationships in early adulthood may also be a protective factor. King, MacMillan, and Massoglia (2007) also looked at the effects of marriage, for both males and females, on offending. They reported that marriage had the effect of reducing offending for males but that this effect was less marked for females. Theobald and Farrington (2009) used data from the Cambridge Study to look at the effects of getting married on offending up to the age of 48 years. This study focussed on the 162 convicted males in the cohort: of these men, 133 been married, 11 had cohabited but not married, 3 had had casual relationships but had not married or cohabited, and 15 had not had a relationship. Of the men who had married, 22 were excluded as their marriage had not lasted for at least 5 years, leaving a sample of 140 men (111 married and 29 not married). The overall effect of marriage was a significant reduction in the number of convictions after marriage compared with before marriage. This effect was evident when the men were married between the ages of 18 and 24 but it was not found for those men who married after 25 years of age. The effect of marriage on the men's offending may be the result of maturation and bonding with societal conventions, or the result of a change of peer group and use of leisure time, or their wives actively curbing their offending. However, if the man's spouse is also an offender this may prolong the man's offending or at least discourage their desistance from offending (Farrington & West, 1995).

When researching criminal behaviour, there is a natural tendency to focus on the predictors of offending. On the positive side, the longitudinal studies also reveal details about those individuals who lead successful lives.

Life success

Farrington et al. (2009) used a composite measure of life success, incorporating social, financial, health, and desistence from offending, to consider the fate of those taking part in the Cambridge Study at age 48. The majority of the non-offenders, the adolescent-limited offenders, and the late onset offenders were leading successful lives. However, the persistent offenders did not fare so well compared with the other groups: fewer were leading successful lives, with particularly marked disadvantages in their standard of accommodation, employment, drug use, and being involved in fights.

Summary

From the above overview, it is clear that the longitudinal studies have contributed a wealth of findings to advance our understanding of the development of anti-social and criminal behaviour. A significant contribution of the longitudinal research lies in the identification of predictors, or risk factors, present during childhood and adolescence that are associated with an increased likelihood of adult offending.

The identification of risk factors is only part of the task: we can ask how, once identified, do the various risk factors act to *cause* criminal behaviour? Of course, there are different ways of understanding the developmental interplay between age and crime: for example, Blonigen (2010) considers the age-crime relationship from the perspective of personality theory. However, the major shift towards an understanding of the interplay between biological, psychological, and social factors in the aetiology of criminal behaviour began with Moffitt's (1993) seminal paper.

Informing theory: Moffitt's position

In the opening paragraph Moffitt makes her position absolutely clear:

> Many people behave antisocially, but their antisocial behavior is temporary and situational. In contrast, the antisocial behavior of some people is very stable and persistent. Temporary, situational antisocial behavior is quite common in the population, especially among adolescents. Persistent, stable antisocial behavior is found among a relatively small number of males whose behavior problems are also quite extreme. The central tenet of this article is that temporary versus persistent antisocial persons constitute two qualitatively distinct types of persons. In particular, I suggest that juvenile delinquency conceals two qualitatively distinct categories of individuals, each in need of its own distinct theoretical explanation.
>
> (Moffitt, 1993: 674)

Moffitt uses the term *adolescence-limited* to describe those young people who act in a delinquent manner during childhood and adolescence then grow out of offending as they reach adulthood. The term *life-course persistent* is used to describe those juvenile offenders whose criminal careers continue into adulthood. It is Moffitt's thesis that these two groups, adolescence-limited offenders and life-course persistent offenders, are fundamentally different in terms of aetiology and development as evinced by their social and psychological functioning.

Adolescent-limited offenders

Moffitt applies the notion of 'social mimicry' to account for adolescent-limited offending. The concept of social mimicry originates in ethology, where it is used to describe the process whereby one species adopts the behaviour of another species in order to gain a desired resource. Moffitt suggests that adolescent delinquency can be seen as a social mimicry, with persistent delinquents as behavioural models for behaviour that gains the adolescent valuable resources. These resources, Moffitt suggests, include the perception by peers of the adolescent's mature status and the adolescent establishing their independence from parents and other adults in positions of authority. The adolescent-limited offender may well acquire the social and educational skills to engage successfully with the wider world. Thus, when the contingencies change with age, when it is time to conform to society's rules and the rewards of delinquency pale, the young person is in the position of having the skills and qualifications to form relationships, find employment, and join society.

Life-course persistent offenders

The evidence from the longitudinal studies suggests that for some individuals anti-social, delinquent behaviour is a stable behaviour that is evident in childhood and continues through adolescence to become criminal behaviour during adulthood. Given this evidence for the continuity of behaviour, Moffitt (1993: 680) suggests: 'Investigators are compelled to look for its roots early in life, in factors that are present before or soon after birth. It is possible that the etiological chain begins with some factor capable of producing individual differences in the neuropsychological functions of the infant nervous system'.

There are many consequences of neurological dysfunction on human functioning, some relatively minor, others of significant magnitude. The effects of neurological dysfunction in early life may be evident in the child's unstable temperament, low intelligence and verbal ability, poor attentional performance, lack of temper control, and impulsive and aggressive behaviour (a constellation of features often associated with conduct disorder). An infant or young child who displays behaviours of the type associated with neuropsychological dysfunction will not be an easy child for parents and guardians to nurture. As Moffitt suggests, even those parents with financial resources and social support can find it difficult to look after a child with neuropsychological difficulties. When the parents do not have the personal, social, or financial resources to cope effectively with a 'difficult' child then they may resort to harsh measures to control the child, or let the child run uncontrolled, or reject the child from the family. It is evident that a child with such levels of personal difficulties will struggle when they reach school age and are required to function within a school environment.

As the adolescent delinquent approaches adulthood they may have experienced a childhood and adolescence characterised by parental rejection, school failure, experience of aggression, and association with delinquent peers. The child's impoverished social-cognitive development may be evident in adult psychological traits such as a lack of empathy for other people (including victims of crime), poor social problem-solving skills, delayed moral development, and difficulties with impulse and anger control. This self-centred, perhaps hostile, style of psychological functioning may bring more difficulties such as maintaining close relationships, being a successful parent, and keeping a job; it may also be associated with a tendency to aggression (see Chapter 5), and with problematic drinking and drug-use.

The force of Moffitt's thesis was that it gave a theoretical shape to the extant evidence at the time of its publication. It has been supported by the evidence supporting the distinction between adolescent-limited and life-course persistent offenders (e.g., Nagin, Farrington, & Moffitt, 1995). Moffitt brought attention to the role of neuropsychological functioning in the aetiology of criminal behaviour, perhaps as the starting point from which later events unfold.

Neuropsychological functioning

What do we mean by the term *neuropsychological*? Meier (1974) suggested that neuropsychology is the study of brain-behaviour relationships. This suitably broad view allows the term to include the physical structures and physiological functioning of the nervous system and their relationship with some aspects of psychological development and functioning. There are naturally occurring variations and similarities in neuropsychological functioning that are due to heredity: parents and their children may share neurological similarities in terms of both physical structure and functioning.

Neuropsychological functioning may be adversely affected by events at any stage of life. Some aspects of foetal neural development may be affected by maternal drug-taking, alcohol use or poor diet, while complications during birth can result in brain injury. The infant's development may be disrupted by poor nutrition, impoverished stimulation, and a lack of affection. Physical abuse can take many forms, such as shaking a baby and severe and extreme physical punishment, some of which can cause brain injury and impact severely on of the child's development.

Moffitt (1993) suggests that the evidence favours the view that the children and adolescent persistent offenders have impaired neuropsychological functioning. Specifically, Moffitt suggests that evidence favours the position that there are two types of neuropsychological deficit associated with anti-social behaviour. The first type of deficit can be seen in the evidence on deficient verbal functioning, such as reading, writing, problem-solving, and self-expression, in anti-social children and adolescents. Indeed, Trzesniewski, Moffitt, Caspi, Taylor, and Maughan (2006) suggest that the frequently found relationship between reading and anti-social behaviour, more evident in males and females, is due to common environmental factors. The second type of deficit is in executive functioning, as seen from the evidence showing poor concentration, attention, and control of impulsivity in anti-social children and adolescents.

Eme (2009) has reviewed the neurodevelopmental factors associated with life-course persistent anti-social behaviour, ranging from conditions such as attention deficit hyperactivity disorder (ADHD) to low IQ and verbal deficits. Eme (2009: 354) makes the point that '[m]ales exceed females in acquired neuropsychological deficits', which can be seen in the greater vulnerability of males to deficits in psychological functioning. The reasons for this greater vulnerability of males, Eme suggests, lie in the biological consequences of the way in which the genetic composition of males and females has evolved. Whether the neurodevelopmental differences between males and females can fully explain gender differences in anti-social and criminal behaviour is discussed in Chapter 12.

In 1993, when Moffitt's paper appeared, there was a somewhat diverse body of research on the relationship between biochemical and neurological factors and anti-social and criminal behaviour. The longitudinal research that produced the notion of life-course persistent offenders prompted a fresh look at the role of neuropsychological functioning in the context of anti-social and criminal behaviour. This research includes studies with a focus on violent behaviour, which will be discussed in Chapter 6, and on psychopathy which will be considered in Chapter 8.

The reason for this renewed interest in the neuropsychological aspects of anti-social behaviour lay in the view that lay neurocognitive functioning, and neurocognitive deficits in particular, could be the pathway through which genetic and environmental influences act in the development of anti-social and ultimately criminal behaviour. Raine et al. (2005) provide a good example of this line of theorising with the suggestion that deficits in visuospatial functioning at a very early age may compromise the infant's ability to orientate to and to recognise its mother's facial expressions. The failure to acquire a sensitive understanding of facial expression in infancy may, in turn, lead in later life to a lack of empathy and sensitivity to other people's feelings. This developmental failure could, Raine et al. suggest, then lead to affectionless anti-social behaviour.

As shown in Box 4.4, Raine et al. suggest that there are five questions to be answered to make progress in understanding the link between neurocognitive functioning and persistent anti-social behaviour.

Raine et al. (2005) addressed these questions in a study of 325 males aged 16–17 years. A range of neurocognitive measures – assessing verbal and spatial IQ, verbal memory, and visual-spatial memory – were administered to the males. Anti-social behaviour, rated for seriousness, was measured using parent, teacher and self-ratings taken every 6 months from ages 7–11 years then every 12 months until age 17. In addition, for each individual, note was made of any formal psychiatric diagnosis, along with any records of child abuse and neglect, head injury, poverty, and parental psychopathology.

The analysis of the measures of anti-social behaviour indicated two large groupings within the sample: these groupings were defined on the basis of the presence or absence of anti-social behaviour. These two groups could be further subdivided so that as well as the group with no (or very low) anti-social behaviour, a second group showed high levels of anti-social behaviour by late adolescence (adolescent-limited), a third group had high levels of anti-social behaviour up to age 11, which then declined (childhood-limited), and a fourth group started with high levels of anti-social behaviour, which became higher during adolescence (life-course persistent).

In terms of the questions set out in Box 4.4, Raine et al. (2005) reported that offenders showed impairments in both their spatial and verbal functioning, an impairment that extended to memory functioning. When compared with the group that did not display anti-social behaviour, the life-course persistent offenders were notably impaired in neurocognitive functioning and were disadvantaged on the social factors. Neurocognitive impairment was a characteristic of those who displayed anti-social behaviour, a finding which remained stable when other disorders or injuries were taken into account.

Biopsychosocial theories

The longitudinal studies, along with a diverse range of other empirical work, have led to many advances in the understanding of the individual and social factors that may culminate in anti-social and criminal behaviour. However, a complete understanding of criminal behaviour that takes into account the causal relationships between biological factors, psychological factors, and social factors is out of reach. It is possible, however, to construct a blueprint of what such a fully articulated theory may have to include. A complete biopsychosocial theory would have to give an account of how biological factors interact with social and cultural factors to produce individual differences in psychological functioning and anti-social behaviour. As is clear from the work of Dodge and Pettit (2003) and Moffitt (2005), clarifying and understanding the myriad of interrelations between the *bio* the *psycho* and the *social* is a daunting task. Indeed, just the *bio* and the *psycho* can create ample empirical difficulties as seen in Raine and Yang's (2006) 'neural moral model' of anti-social behaviour.

The complexity inherent within a biopsychosocial theory is plain to see from research that attempts to disentangle the elements of the model. It is the case that the evidence broadly supports the view that neuropsychological deficits, in interaction with adverse and disadvantaged home and family settings, predict life-course persistent offending. However, Turner, Hartman, and Bishop (2007) make the point that this biosocial interaction may not be the same in different neighbourhoods. To test this hypothesis, Turner et al. drew on data from the American National Longitudinal Survey of Youth (NLSY) to look more closely at the potential varying effects of neighbourhood. They found that, as anticipated, the biosocial interaction predicted life-course persistent offending *but* only among young people (males and females) living in the most disadvantaged neighbourhoods. Further, the effect was not uniform across all young people living within a disadvantaged neighbourhood: 'The biosocial interaction was only significant in predicting life-course-persistent offending for non-Whites living is disadvantaged neighbourhoods' (Turner et al., 2007: 1256). Turner et al. suggest that their findings may indicate that the overarching, structural effects of the neighbourhood may attenuate the family and individual risks for serious offending.

Studies such as those reported by Turner et al. (2007) illustrate the complexity in seeking to moving from risk factors to causal explanations: is neuropsychological deficit a risk factor that signals the likelihood of offending or does the deficit actually play some causative role in bring about offending? A study by McGloin, Pratt, and Piquero (2006) of maternal cigarette smoking during pregnancy further highlights these issues.

As McGloin et al. note, it is easy to assume that it is biological damage to the unborn child that is the start of the individual's progression towards criminal behaviour. It is established that maternal cigarette smoking during pregnancy is linked with a substantial number of problems for the child, including early onset and chronic anti-social and criminal behaviour. It is tempting to assume that the causal mechanism that explains the association between the risk factor of maternal smoking during pregnancy and the child's later behaviour is biological in nature. It could be hypothesised that the mother's smoking increases the likelihood of neurological deficit in the child, these acquired neurological deficits then impact on the child's development, the unfavourable impact development leads to poor social adjustment, and so on to anti-social behaviour. This line of thought is supported by the evidence for neuropsychological deficits within persistent offender populations. It is not difficult to make a hypothetical connection between smoking, deficit, and anti-social and criminal behaviour. In such a hypothesised causal chain, the neuropsychological deficit would be seen as playing a mediating role between the antecedent risk factor (smoking) and the outcome (criminal behaviour). McGloin et al. suggest that, while this causal chain is plausible, it cannot be assumed to be true and requires empirical verification. There are other potential explanations for the above chain of events: for example, perhaps mothers who smoke during pregnancy will have a certain style of parenting that influences their child's socialisation.

McGloin et al. conducted a study, involving both male and female offenders, looking at the nature of the association between maternal cigarette smoking (MCS) and offending in light of other factors such as low birth weight, birth complications and socioeconomic variables such as the income and occupation of the head of the household. The findings suggested a strong interrelationship between MCS and neuropsychological deficit, and a similarly strong association between neuropsychological deficit and life-course persistent offending. However, it was *not* the case that the neuropsychological deficit functioned as a mediating factor between the maternal smoking and the child's criminal behaviour. As McGloin et al. (2006: 422) explain: 'It should be recognized that the purported link between MCS and LCP offending has been embedded within the larger assumption that damage to the developing fetus is what starts the developmental pathway. The findings presented here, however, question this assumption and instead indicate that our attention should shift elsewhere, perhaps to parenting and/or self-control'.

In keeping with McGloin et al., Ratchford and Beaver (2009) also looked at neuropsychological deficit and self-control. As noted in Chapter 3, Gottfredson and Hirschi (1990) have presented a general theory of crime that pivots on the notion of self-control. Thus, Ratchford and Beaver follow the line that self-control is related to neurological functioning: this relationship may be related specifically the functioning of the brain's prefrontal cortex, or to birth complications, or to low birth weight.

Drawing on longitudinal data from the American National Survey of Children, Ratchford and Beaver examined the interrelationships between a range of biological risk factors, such as neuropsychological deficit and low birth weight, alongside social factors such as level of family rules and punishment, and living in a disadvantaged neighbourhood. The findings revealed, as expected, that biological markers such as low birth weight and birth complications were related to neuropsychological deficit. In turn, neuropsychological deficits were related to self-control, although the specific biological markers were *not* related. As also expected, low-self-control was related to delinquent behaviour but none of the biological variables had a direct significant influence on delinquent behaviour. The social factors of parental punishment, family rules, and neighbourhood were independently related to self-control. Ratchford and Beaver conclude that self-control has its roots in both biological and social factors and that self-control is the expression of this biosocial interaction. Thus, Ratchford and Beaver's findings are in keeping with the view that a direct line from biology to behaviour is not supported by the evidence, save perhaps for some forms of serious violent behaviour. Beaver, DeLisi, Vaughn, and Wright (2010: 38) provided further evidence in support of a view of anti-social behaviour resulting from '[g]enetic factors, neural substrates, and environmental factors working independently and synergistically'.

Conclusion

The longitudinal studies have had perhaps two, related, effects on our understanding of criminal behaviour. The first effect lies in the systematic gathering of empirical data to identify those factors that increase the likelihood of a progression from anti-social behaviour in adolescence to criminal behaviour in adulthood. The second effect is seen in the beginnings of the formulation of a comprehensive theory that integrates the biological, psychological, and social to produce an explanation of the causal links between these various elements. The shift from the identifying risk factors to the articulation of causal links has brought about a generation of studies attempting to search out the fine details of the causal relationships within a biopsychosocial approach to anti-social and criminal human behaviour. The implications of such a theory for law, the criminal justice system, and crime prevention may be profound (Raine, 2008). This is a point that will be picked up again later in the text.

As shown consistently by the crime surveys, the majority of criminal acts are relatively trivial in that they involve minor damage to property or thefts that are worth only small sums of money. This is not to trivialise such acts – some victims of minor crimes are deeply affected by their experience, although in most such cases the victim regains their equilibrium when their initial anger and feelings of loss have subsided. However, there are crimes against property and crimes against the person that are highly likely to threaten the well-being of the victim with their subsequent adverse long-term effects. Such crimes encompass serious criminal behaviours that threaten life and have potentially highly damaging long-term consequences. Three types of serious crime, which have some degree of overlap, are discussed in the next three chapters. These are arson, violent crime, and sexual crime.

Chapter summary

- Research that uses a *longitudinal* design has the advantages of the individual acting as their own control and in monitoring behaviour over a long period of time. However, this type of research is often financially expensive to conduct.
- The Cambridge Study in Delinquent Development started in England in 1961 with a cohort of 411 young males, aged 8–9 years. The study is still in progress, with a large proportion of the cohort still alive and it has produced several hundred research papers.
- Two significant findings from the longitudinal research have been the discovery of the age-crime curve and the associated account of two main types of criminal career.
- The age-crime curve shows that, for both males and females, the prevalence of delinquency peaks around the age of 17 years then rapidly declines so that fewer people are committing crimes.
- The search for the distinguishing features of those who individuals who stop offending in adolescence (adolescent-limited) and those who become life-course persistent offenders has led to a new line of theory based on neurodevelopmental functioning.

Points for discussion

- In the UK, the Cambridge Study in Delinquent Development is the major longitudinal study concerned exclusively with criminal behaviour, from which a great deal has been gained. Given the financial costs involved in this type of research, should plans be laid for a new longitudinal study?
- The various theories of criminal behaviour encompass an enormous range of variables, including biological, individual, and social factors. Will a unified theory of criminal behaviour ever be achieved?
- If some delinquency is 'adolescent-limited', should we simply be more tolerant of some juvenile crime or should all adolescents be subject to the same legal sanctions?

Essential reading

Eme, R. (2009). 'Male life-course persistent antisocial behaviour: A review of neurodevelopmental factors'. *Aggression and Violent Behavior*, *14*: 348–358.
An admirably brief overview of the various neurodevelopmental factors associated with enduring anti-social behaviour.

Moffitt, T. E. (1993). Adolescence-limited and life-course-persistent antisocial behavior: A developmental taxonomy. *Psychological Review*, *100*, 674–701.
The seminal paper on the development of offending from childhood to adolescence to adulthood.

Lighter Side

There are many novels about the pains of adolescence and wayward behaviour: J. D. Salinger's 'The Catcher in the Rye' and Mark Twain's 'Huckleberry Finn' spring to mind.

In more recent times, Ken Loach's film 'The Angels' Share' tells of a young man's escapades while serving a Community Service Order.

References

Barlow, D. H. & Hersen, M. (Eds.) (1984). *Single Case Experimental Designs: Strategies for Studying Behavior Change*. Elmsford, NY: Pergamon Press.

Beaver, K. M., DeLisi, M., Vaughn, M. G., & Wright, J. P. (2010). The intersection of genes and neuropsychological deficits in the prediction of adolescent delinquency and low self-control. *International Journal of Offender Therapy and Comparative Criminology, 54*, 22–42.

Blonigen, D. M. (2010). Explaining the relationship between age and crime: Contributions from the developmental literature on personality. *Clinical Psychology Review, 30*, 89–100.

Dodge, K. A. & Pettit, G. S. (2003). A biopsychosocial model of the development of chronic conduct problems in adolescence. *Developmental Psychology, 39*, 349–371.

Elander, J., Rutter, M., Simonoff, E., & Pickles, A. (2000). Explanations for apparent late onset criminality in a high-risk sample of children followed up in adult life. *British Journal of Criminology, 40*, 497–509.

Eme, R. (2009). Male life-course persistent antisocial behaviour: A review of neurodevelopmental factors. *Aggression and Violent Behavior, 14*, 348–358.

Farrington, D. P. (1983). Offending from 10 to 25 years of age. In K. Teilman Van Dusen & S. A. Mednick (Eds.), *Prospective Studies of Crime and Delinquency* (pp. 17–38). The Hague: Kluwer-Nijhoff.

—— (1986). Age and crime. In M. Tonry & N. Morris (Eds.), *Crime and Justice: An Annual Review of Research, Vol. 7* (pp. 189–250). Chicago, IL: University of Chicago Press.

—— (1987). Epidemiology. In H. C. Quay (Ed.), *Handbook of Juvenile Delinquency* (pp. 325–82). New York, NY: Wiley.

—— (1995). The development of offending and antisocial behaviour from childhood: Key findings from the Cambridge Study in Delinquent Development. *Journal of Child Psychology and Psychiatry, 36*, 929–964.

—— (2002). Key results from the first forty years of the Cambridge Study in Delinquent Development. In M. D. Krohn & T. P. Thornberry (Eds.), *Taking Stock of Delinquency: An Overview of Findings from Contemporary Longitudinal Studies* (pp. 137–74). New York, NY: Kluwer Academic Publishers/ Plenum Press.

—— (Ed.) (2005). *Integrated Developmental and Life-Course Theories of Offending*. New Brunswick, NJ: Transaction.

—— (2006). Key longitudinal-experimental studies in criminology. *Journal of Experimental Criminology, 2*, 121–141.

Farrington, D. P., Loeber, R., & van Kammen, W. B. (1990). Long-term criminal outcomes of hyper-activity-impulsivity-attention deficit and conduct problems in childhood. In L. Robins & M. Rutter (Eds.), *Straight and Devious Pathways from Childhood to Adulthood*. New York, NY: Cambridge University Press.

Farrington, D. P., Ohlin, L. E., & Wilson, J. Q. (1986). *Understanding and Controlling Crime*. New York, NY: Springer-Verlag.

Farrington, D. P., Ttofi, M. M., & Coid, J. W. (2009). Development of adolescent-limited, late-onset, and persistent offenders from age 8 to age 48. *Aggressive Behavior, 35*, 150–163.

Farrington, D. P. & West, D. J. (1990). The Cambridge Study in Delinquent Development: A long-term follow-up of 411 London males. In H. J. Kerner & G. Kaiser (Eds.), *Criminality: Personality, Behaviour, and Life History* (pp. 115–138). Berlin: Springer-Verlag.

—— (1995). Effects of marriage, separation and children on offending by adult males. In J. Hagan (Ed.), *Current Perspectives on Aging and the Life Cycle. Vol. 4: Delinquency and Disrepute in the Life Course* (pp. 249–281). Greenwich, CT: JAI Press.

Gottfredson, M. R. & Hirschi, T. (1990). *A General Theory of Crime.* Stanford, CA: Stanford University Press.

Hollin, C. R. (1990). *Cognitive-Behavioral Interventions with Young Offenders.* Elmsford, NY: Pergamon Press.

King, R. D., MacMillan, R., & Massoglia, M. (2007). The context of marriage and crime: Gender, the propensity to marry, and offending in early adulthood. *Criminology, 45*, 33–65.

Kingston, L. & Prior, M. (1995). The development of patterns of stable, transient, and school-age onset aggressive behaviour in young children. *Journal of the American Academy of Child and Adolescent Psychiatry, 34*, 348–358.

Kyvsgaard, B. (2003). *The Criminal Career: The Danish Longitudinal Study.* Cambridge: Cambridge University Press.

Lahey, B., Loeber, R., Frick, P. J., Hart, E. L., Applegate, B., Zhang, Q., Green, S. M., & Russo, M. F. (1995). Four-year longitudinal study of conduct disorder in boys: Patterns and predictors of persistence. *Journal of Abnormal Psychology, 104*, 83–93.

Loeber, R. & Farrington, D. P. (1994). Problems and solutions in longitudinal and experimental treatment studies of child psychopathology and delinquency. *Journal of Consulting and Clinical Psychology, 62*, 887–900.

Loeber, R., Green, S. M., Keenan, K., & Lahey, B. B. (1995). Which boys will fare worse? Early predictors on the onset of conduct disorder in a six-year longitudinal study. *Journal of the American Academy of Child and Adolescent Psychiatry, 34*, 499–509.

Long, C. G. & Hollin, C. R. (1995). Single case methodology: A review and analysis of current trends. *Clinical Psychology and Psychotherapy, 2*, 177–191.

Nagin, D. S., Farrington, D. P., & Moffitt, T. E. (1995). Life-course trajectories of different types of offenders. *Criminology, 33*, 111–139.

McGloin, J. M., Pratt, T. C., & Piquero, A. R. (2006). A life-course analysis of the criminogenic effects of maternal cigarette smoking during pregnancy: A research note on the mediating impact of neuropsychological deficit. *Journal of research in Crime and Delinquency, 43*, 412–426.

McNally, R. (1995). Homicidal youth in England and Wales 1982–1992: Profile and policy. *Psychology, Crime, and Law, 1*, 333–342.

Meier, M. J. (1974). Some challenges for clinical neuropsychology. In R. M. Reitan & L. A. Davidson (Eds.), *Clinical Neuropsychology: Current Status and Applications* (pp. 289–324). New York, NY: Wiley.

Moffitt, T. E. (1993). Adolescence-limited and life-course-persistent antisocial behavior: A developmental taxonomy. *Psychological Review, 100*, 674–701.

—— (2005). The new look of behavioral genetics in developmental psychopathology: Gene-environment interplay in antisocial behaviors. *Psychological Bulletin, 131*, 533–554.

Moffitt, T. E., Caspi, A., Harrington, H., & Milne, B. J. (2002). Males on the life-course persistent and adolescent-limited pathways: Follow-up at age 26 years. *Development and Psychopathology, 14*, 179–207.

Piquero, A. R., Farrington, D. P., & Blumstein, A. (2003). The criminal career paradigm. In M. Tonry (Ed.), *Crime and Justice: A Review of Research, Vol. 30* (pp. 359–506). Chicago, IL: University of Chicago Press.

Pulkkinen, L., Lyyra, A. -L., & Kokko, K. (2009). Life success of males on nonoffender, adolescence-limited, persistent, and adult-onset antisocial pathways: Follow-up from age 8 to 42. *Aggressive Behavior, 35*, 117–135.

Raine, A. (2008). The biological crime: Implications for society and the criminal justice system. *Revista de Psiquiatria do Rio Grande do Sul, 30*, 1–5.

Raine, A. & Yang, Y. (2006). Neural foundations to moral reasoning and antisocial behavior. *SCAN, 1*, 203–213.

Raine, A., Moffi tt, T. E., Caspi, A., Loeber, R., Stouthamer-Loeber, M., & Lynam, D. (2005). Neurocognitive impairment in boys on the life-course persistent antisocial path. *Journal of Abnormal Psychology, 114*, 38–49.

Ratchford, M. & Beaver, K. M. (2009). Neuropsychological deficits, self-control, and delinquent involvement: Towards a biosocial explanation of delinquency. *Criminal Justice and Behavior, 36*, 147–162.

Rossi, P. H., Freeman, H. E., & Lipsey, M. W. (1999). *Evaluation: A Systematic Approach* (6th ed.). Thousand Oaks, CA: Sage.

Rutter, M. & Smith D. J. (Eds.) (1995). *Psychosocial Disorders in Young People: Time Trends and Their Causes.* Chichester, Sussex: John Wiley & Sons.

Shepherd, J. P., Shepherd, I., Newcombe, R. G., & Farrington, D. (2009). Impact of antisocial lifestyle on health: Chronic disability and death by middle age. *Journal of Public Health, 31*, 506–511.

Stattin, H. & Magnusson, D. (1995). Onset of official delinquency: Its co-occurrence in time with educational, behavioural, and interpersonal problems. *British Journal of Criminology, 35*, 417–449.

Theobald, D. & Farrington, D. P. (2009). Effects of getting married on offending: Results from a prospective longitudinal survey of males. *European Journal of Criminology, 6*, 496–516.

Trzesniewski, K. H., Moffitt, T. E., Caspi, A., Taylor, A., & Maughan, B. (2006). Revisiting the association between reading achievement and antisocial behavior: New evidence of an environmental explanation from a twin study. *Child Development, 77*, 72–88.

Turner, M. G., Hartman, J. L., & Bishop, D. M. (2007). The effects of prenatal problems, family functioning, and neighbourhood disadvantage in predicting life-course-persistent offending. *Criminal Justice and Behavior, 34*, 1241–161.

West, D. J. (1969). *Present Conduct and Future Delinquency.* London: Heinemann Educational.

—— (1982). *Delinquency: Its Roots, Careers and Prospects.* London: Heinemann Educational.

West, D. J. & Farrington, D. P. (1973). *Who Becomes Delinquent?* London: Heinemann Educational.

—— (1977). *The Delinquent Way of Life.* London: Heinemann Educational.

Wolfgang, M. E., Thornberry, T. P., & Figlio, R. M. (1987). *From Boy to Man, from Delinquency to Crime.* Chicago, IL: University of Chicago Press.

5 Psychological approaches to understanding serious crime I

Arson

As stated in the previous chapter, the majority of criminal acts are relatively trivial in that they involve minor damage to property or thefts that are worth only small sums of money. In most such cases, the victim regains their equilibrium when their initial anger and feelings of loss have subsided. However, there are crimes against property and crimes against the person that are highly likely to produce immediate threats to the well-being of the victim and are likely to have subsequent adverse long-term effects. This chapter and the two that follow are concerned with serious criminal acts which threaten life and which have potentially highly damaging long-term consequences.

Arson

Is it right to view arson as a serious crime? There are two ways to answer this question: first, does arson cause injury and death on a significant scale; second, what are the financial costs of arson?

The statistics from the Office of the Deputy Prime Minister (ODPM, 2003) and from the Arson Control Forum (ACF) – a government-led national body that aims to reduce the harm caused by arson – suggest that since the early 1990s, more than 3,500 incidents of arson have caused 32,000 injuries and 1,200 deaths. In stark terms, in an average week in England and Wales there are 55 injuries and two deaths associated with arson. The highest proportion of deaths and injuries due to arson are when the fire takes place in a dwelling: in 2006, 68 people died in an arson attack on their place of residence (Department for Communities and Local Government, 2008).

The financial cost of arson is a direct result of the damage and loss of property it causes. If a deliberately set fire destroys a public building, such as a school or a hospital, it will cost millions of pounds to replace lost buildings and equipment. An arson attack on a factory may destroy machinery and stock, costing millions of pounds to replace. If a factory closes, then employees will lose their jobs – it has been estimated by the Department for Communities and Local Government (2006) that 75–80 per cent of businesses never recover from the losses caused by arson – with all the resultant costs to society.

As is often the case with other types of offence, instances of arson are generally clustered in distinct geographical locations, typically the more socially deprived, poorer areas of the country (Home Office, 2006). However, as described in Box 5.1, woodland and open spaces are another type of location open to arson. Wildland or bushfires can sweep across huge amounts of land with grave consequences. The scale of bushfires in Australia is seen in figures published by the Australian Institute of Criminology (AIC, 2009) that show an annual average of almost 54,000 fires of which 40 per cent are estimated to be deliberately set or are of suspicious origin.

Box 5.1 Wildfires (aka bushfires)

As well as buildings being set on fire, a fire may be deliberately set in order to destroy woodland and crops. In some parts of the world, setting fire to woodland is a major issue. The California Department of Forestry reported that in 2003–4 there were more than 700 wildfires caused by arson, which caused great damage to the forests and the wildlife. In Australia there is a similar issue with deliberately set bushfires (Christensen, 2007/8). These wildfires fires can cause great damage to the land and animals as well as threatening property and human life.

When arson is directed at a domestic property, the fire will damage or destroy a home and its contents, again costing large sums of money to repair or replace. The commercial and domestic costs of property insurance reflect the financial costs associated with arson. In addition, there are the costs to the fire services in dealing with the fires, costs to the NHS in treating those injured by fire, the police costs in investigating the offence, the legal costs as the case moves through court, and so on. The range and variation of the costs involved make it difficult to estimate exactly the financial impact of arson. The official estimates for the cost to society that are due to arson in an average week vary from £25 million to more than £40 million.

The seriousness of the crime of arson, in terms of the threat it poses to property and to life, is reflected in the maximum punishment of imprisonment for life if it is proven that the perpetrator intended to endanger lives or was reckless enough to cause lives to be endangered.

Arson: what is it?

The term *arson* is difficult to define. In English law, as applied in England, Wales, and Northern Ireland, the crime of arson is established within the Criminal Damage Act 1971 (in Northern Ireland by the 1997 Criminal Damage (Northern Ireland) Order) as destruction or damage to property caused by fire. Arson is generally taken to be a crime in which a fire is deliberately set in order to cause damage to property and that may also endanger life. In Scotland, the legal understanding of the act of arson is the same as for the rest of the UK but the offence is known as *fire-raising*. As arson is a crime against property, incidents such as fires in abandoned cars and other vehicles with no registered owners, and fires in derelict buildings are not covered by the Criminal Damage Act 1971.

Firesetting is another term frequently found in the literature: it is often used to refer to the acts of juveniles below the age of criminal responsibility who deliberately set fires (e.g., Fineman, 1980). The term *firesetting* will be used here to refer to the acts of juveniles below the age of criminal responsibility, while *arson* is used denote acts of firesetting within the scope of criminal law.

Prevalence

In England, the official statistics for arson are recorded by both the Fire Rescue Services (FRS) and the police. In the statistics, the distinction is made between *primary* and *secondary* fires. A primary fire is defined as one that involves buildings or non-derelict vehicles, storage facilities or plant machinery; there may be casualties and the extent of the fire

Table 5.1 Fires recorded by FRS and police (after ODPM, 2005)

	FRS deliberate	Police recorded	FRS deliberate
	Primary fires	*Arsons*	*Secondary fires*
2002/3	108,000	53,200	209,100
2003/4	99,500	57,200	256,000

requires at least five fire appliances to bring it under control. A secondary fire is typically a small fire, generally occurring outdoors as with a fire in an abandoned vehicle, which does not involving casualties and is attended by four appliances at most.

The definitional issue can lead to procedural problems within the criminal justice system. As shown in Table 5.1, a report published in 2005 by the ODPM noted that the police consistently recorded up to half fewer offences of arson than the FRS. This discrepancy is in large part due to different recording procedures: the FRS categorise a fire as being deliberately started if they suspect deliberate ignition; the police require a higher burden of proof if a charge of arson is to be brought against a suspect.

As was discussed in Chapter 2, reliable crime statistics are important at a national level as they can be used to inform decisions about resource allocation: it follows that different counts of the same crime from different arms of government is not helpful. The 2005 report from the ODPM seeks to unify the way in which the two services measure arson.

The FRS operational statistics for England during 2008–9 (see Table 5.2), as collated by the Department for Communities and Local Government (which replaced the ODPM in 2006), show the numbers of primary and secondary fires over a 3-year period (Department for Communities and Local Government, 2009). It is notable from Table 5.2 that, although the figures cover only a short period, the number of primary fires is decreasing year-on-year, and that the number of secondary fires is extremely large.

An individual arsonist's pattern of setting fires may vary: some arsonists will only set a single fire while others will set multiple fires. Further, the way in which multiple fires are set may vary. Some arsonists may be thought of as *mass arsonists*, in that they set several fires (three at a minimum) over a very short period of time, generally measured in hours, with the fires typically at the same location. A second type, the *spree arsonist*, is when the same person sets several fires in a relatively short period of time, say within a day. Finally, a *serial arsonist* sets fires over a much longer period of time, weeks, months, or even years, at a variety of different locations.

Firesetting and arson is of interest to many groups including the police, fire fighters, and insurance companies. The central concern is just who commits arson and why do they do it? What is known about what motivates arsonists and what are the characteristics of arsonists?

Motivation for arson

The literature is liberally sprinkled with lists of the motivations associated with arson: Prins (1994, 1995) has presented a comprehensive summary of the motives for arson, which are shown (with several additions) in Box 5.2.

Inspection of Box 5.2 suggests an interesting dichotomy in the motives of arsonists. As will also be seen in Chapter 6 with regard to violent crime, the motivations of some arsonists

Table 5.2 Fires (thousands) responded to by the FRS

	2005/06	*2006/07*	*2007/08*
Primary fires	137.7	129.1	115.2
Secondary fires	191.4	201.5	172.3

are rational in the sense that the fire in instrumental is bringing about some desired outcome such as revenge or financial gain. In other cases it is the fire itself, along with its psychological and social consequences, that drives the arsonist. It is probably not the case that the various motivations are always independent of each other: it is not difficult to see that, for example, setting fire to a school can be an exciting act of revenge.

Box 5.2 Motivations for arson

Concealing a crime
A fire is an excellent way to remove any incriminating evidence left at the scene of a crime. A fire can be used to try to disguise the fact that a burglary has taken place, or to remove fingerprints and other evidence from a stolen car, or to destroy incriminating computer and paper records.

Economic
Arson is a crime against property and property invariably has a value. A fire may trigger a fraudulent insurance claim for the building and its contents, which is either straight monetary profit or a means by which to eliminate debt and close down a failing business. A fire is also an effective way to close down a business rival.

Excitement
As is evident each year on 5 November, many people find the sight and sound of fire exciting. The arsonist may find that setting fires brings thrills along with a sense of power as the person who started the fire resulting in the actions of the fire fighters. Those who set fires for excitement may even volunteer to help at the scene of the fire, or find it satisfying that their actions are the cause of the confusion. It is possible that the scale of the arson attacks may escalate as the arsonist becomes tired of setting nuisance fires in dustbins and abandoned cars, and seeks bigger thrills with larger fires in homes and industrial buildings.

'Political'
A fire may be set in the name of a political, social, or even religious cause. Such fires, often called the work of extremists or terrorists, may be set in government buildings or places of worship, as well as establishments such as abortion clinics and laboratories where animal experimentation takes place.

Revenge
The damage and fear caused by fire makes it an excellent means by which to gain revenge for a personal injustice. The revenge for some slight, real, or imagined, may be against a particular person or group of people, an institution such as a school, or against society in general.

Vandalism
Vandalism fires, most often associated with juvenile firesetters, are set for fun. These fires are often set by a group of young people, with peer group pressure an obvious factor, typically targeted at schools, empty buildings, or woodland.

Self-harm and suicide

The use of fire to inflict self-harm or as a means of suicide seems so extreme as to be highly unlikely. Nonetheless, there are documented cases where individuals have inflicted self-injury and committed suicide by using fire (Jacobson, Jackson, & Berelowitz, 1986; Shkrum & Johnston, 1992; Stoddard, Pahlavan, & Cahners, 1985).

Lari and Alaghehbandan (2003) reviewed 1,236 cases of patients aged 14 and over admitted to a burn centre in Tehran, Iran. Of these cases, 110 (8.9 per cent) had attempted suicide by self-immolation, most often with the use of a flammable liquid such as kerosene. These patients had median age of 25 years, ranging from 14 to 68 years, and suffered severe burns: almost half had a previous psychiatric diagnosis, most frequently depression.

A similar American study reported by Reiland, Hovater, McGwin, Rue, and Cross (2006) reviewed retrospectively intentional burns (self-inflicted burn and assault) in 96 patient records in a hospital burn centre. Information pertaining to demographic and injury characteristics were obtained. It was found that, compared with other burn admissions, those individuals with intentional burn injuries had a greater amount of their body area burnt. This was, in turn, congruent with a longer stay in hospital, more inhalational injury, and twice the mortality rate (at 20 per cent of admissions). The self-inflicted and assault burn patients were more likely to be men (86 per cent compared with 56 per cent), more likely to have an elevated blood alcohol content and more likely to screen positive for drugs. Reiland et al. concluded that those who suffer intentional burns tend to have more severe burns and to experience a worse outcome than those with accidental burns.

I have recorded a case in which a young man, probably under the influence of alcohol, attempted suicide by setting fire to the house he was in (Hollin, 1990). He survived and was charged with arson and received a custodial sentence.

There are cases of self-immolation by fire, typically associated with religious or political causes. For example, in 2001, five people in Tiananmen Square, Beijing, poured petrol over themselves and set themselves alight in an act of group self-immolation. This act, which received international media attention, was a protest against government actions. Two of the five protestors died, the remaining three survived but with serious injuries and disfigurements.

Another way to consider those individuals who set fires is to look at their individual characteristics. The literature on individuals who set basically falls into three groupings: (1) juvenile firesetters; (2) adult arsonists; and (3) mentally disordered firesetters.

Juvenile firesetters

One of the features of fire is that, as we see every year on 5 November, flames can be exciting to watch and even to play with. The materials needed to light a fire are readily available and it does not demand any specials skills to set a fire. It is not difficult for a child to find matches to play with and to set small, exciting fires well away from adult supervision. However, the trouble with small exciting fires is that they have a habit of becoming big, exciting fires: given the right conditions a small fire can very quickly become a highly dangerous large fire. A large fire can cause extensive damage and endanger life with the consequence that that very quickly the police become involved and the child and their parents may be facing a very difficult situation.

There are a range of studies, conducted in several countries, which have looked at the demographic, psychological, and social characteristics of juvenile firesetters (Dadds &

Fraser, 2006; Hollin, Epps, & Swaffer, 2002; Kennedy, Vale, Khan, & McAnaney, 2006; Kolko, 1985; Klein, Mondozzi, & Andrews, 2008; McCarty & McMahon 2005; Pollinger, Samuels, & Stadolnik, 2005; Martin Bergen, Richardson, Roeger, & Allison, 2004; Räsänen, Hirvenoja, Hakko, & Vaeisaenen, 1995). These studies present a reasonably coherent picture, as outlined below, of the juvenile firesetter.

All the research points to the fact that juvenile firesetters are most likely to be male, particularly so when the same juvenile has set more than one fire. This point regarding gender is reinforced by figures from the Home Office that suggest that in England and Wales the majority of juveniles aged between 10 and 13 years who are cautioned for or found guilty of arson are males (Home Office, 2002).

Juvenile firesetting is frequently associated with a range of problem behaviours including other types of anti-social behaviour, particularly acts of violence, cruelty to animals, and drug and alcohol abuse. It is also the case, not surprisingly, that children who set fires display an interest and curiosity in fire from a very early age, This fascination with fire, which may manifest itself in playing with matches and setting off fire alarms, is associated with later firesetting (Kolko & Kazdin, 1992).

A range of psychological factors have been associated with juvenile firesetting including poor interpersonal skills, impulsivity, high levels of anger, and poor assertion and problem-solving skills. Chen, Arria, and Anthony (2003) found that the three-way combination of aggressiveness, feelings of being rejected by peers, and shyness was strongly associated with firesetting and arson in a sample of American adolescents. Firesetting is also associated with a range of childhood psychiatric problems. A study in Australia of children aged 4–9 years found that firesetting was associated with a range of problems including conduct disorder and hyperactivity. The girls who set fires also showed signs of anxiety and depression (Dadds & Fraser, 2006).

Juvenile firesetters are likely to have a disrupted education, with marked levels of academic underachievement, truancy, and suspensions from school. Hollin et al. (2002) found that adolescent male and female firesetters had often moved from school to school, so that by age 15 years they had typically attended three or four schools. The school careers of these young people were marked by truancy, school suspensions, assaults on teachers, and a range of other difficulties including bullying.

The family lives of juvenile firesetters may be disrupted: Hollin et al. (2002) reported that the 15-year-old male firesetters had experienced about four placements, such as foster and residential homes, away from the family home, while by the same age the females had experienced nine such placements. The family life of young firesetters is likely to be characterised by high frequencies of dysfunctional parental relationships that are characteristic of high levels of parental conflict and family stress. The child's firesetting may be associated with a lack of parental supervision and lax or highly punitive, even abusive, discipline. Root MacKay, Henderson, Del Bove, and Warling (2008) found that children with a history of maltreatment – including physical abuse, physical neglect, and sexual abuse – were more likely than non-maltreated children to be involved in firesetting. Hickle and Roe-Sepowitz (2010) confirmed this pattern of findings with a sample of female juvenile arsonists. Noblett and Nelson (2001) and Dickens et al. (2007) similarly noted a high level of abuse among female arsonists referred for psychiatric assessment. The maltreated children showed versatility in their firesetting both in terms of the way fires were set and the targets for their fires. Root et al. (2008) suggest that the maltreatment has heightens the child's negative affect, typically through anxiety and anger, and the firesetting is an expression of poor affect regulation alongside other behavioural difficulties.

It is highly likely that young people who set fires will be involved in more than one incident of firesetting. Kolko, Herschell, and Scharf (2006) looked at the predictors of recidivism for a group of young male firesetters, aged 5–13 years, in Pittsburgh, USA. They found that the strongest predictors of recidivistic firesetting were the child's level of curiosity and interest in fire and previous incidents of playing with matches and firesetting, so supporting the maxim that 'nothing predicts behaviour like behaviour'.

Knowledge of juvenile firesetting is reasonably comprehensive, although two issues remain uncertain. First, there is a marked similarity between the social and psychological characteristics of juvenile firesetters and juvenile delinquents. This prompts the question, what are the critical factors that are antecedent *specifically* to setting fires? It is evident an early interest in fire is one very early antecedent but there is more to learn about how and why some children develop such an interest. The second issue concerns the degree of continuity between childhood firesetting and arson in adulthood. Do children who set fires go on to become adult arsonists? In practice, this latter question is difficult to answer given the complex interrelationships between childhood problems, mental disorder in adulthood, and a range of anti-social behaviours, including setting fires, across the life-span. A longitudinal study would be one way to disentangle the intertwined antecedent factors that culminate in arson.

Adult arsonists

As discussed below, there is a substantial literature on the overlap between mental disorder and firesetting. As noted in Chapter 1, individuals with a mental disorder may fall under the jurisdiction of mental health law rather than criminal law: mentally disordered firesetters are covered in the following section.

In their report, published in 2002 by the ODPM, Canter and Almond make the point that most instances of arson can be accounted for in one of two ways: first, the arson is a means by which to cover up evidence of another crime; second, the arson is for financial gain. In the first case, when the aim of the arson is to cover up another crime, the purpose of the fire is to destroy evidence and it is doubtful whether the individual has any real interest in the fire itself. The target for such fires may be a home, a vehicle, or business premises. In cases of burglary, the fire may be used to add confusion to attempts to determine what was stolen, while in murder, the purpose of the fire may be to destroy evidence and obscure the identity of the victim (Davies & Mouzos, 2007).

Canter and Almond suggest that there are three broad types of person who are prepared to commit arson for financial profit: (1) 'professional' arsonists, with varying degrees of experience, who are paid to commit the crime; (2) business or property owners who intend to make money from an insurance claim; and (3) business owners covering their losses. As the aim of this type of arson is the destruction of property, rather than an interest in the fire itself, the arson may well be efficiently planned and executed with the use of accelerants and the fire ignited at several points to achieve maximum destruction before the arrival of the fire services. Flanagan and Fisher (2008) note that glue, butane, and petrol are the volatile substances frequently associated with arson. The use of a 'professional arsonist' makes it difficult to prove that the property owner was involved as, for example, he or she can ensure that they have a sound alibi for the time when the fire started. Where the arson is planned, particularly if the property is a domestic residence, the owner may remove items of personal significance and financial value before the fire is started.

As discussed above, the most widespread approach in research into arson is to offer classification systems for the motivations of those who set fires. An alternative approach is to move away from classifications of inferred motives and instead to focus on the arsonist's behaviour. The style of research in this tradition – typically using the techniques of multidimensional scaling and smallest space analysis, as exemplified by the work of David Canter – is referred to as the *arson action system* approach. The understanding of arson that comes from this approach is, not surprisingly, called the *action system model of arson* (Fritzon, Canter, & Wilton, 2001).

Canter and Fritzon (1998) suggested that arsonists are likely to show behavioural consistencies in setting fires and that these behavioural patterns are important in understanding arson. Canter and Fritzon conducted an analysis of the crime reports and witness statements, using the techniques noted above, from 175 solved cases of arson. They reported two broad themes, each with two variations. The first theme is where the arson is person-orientated: one variation of this theme, termed 'expressive', is when the purpose of the fire is to inflict self-harm (see Box 5.2); the second, termed 'instrumental', is when the aim is to hurt someone else. The second theme is where the fire was directed against an object, such as a building: one variation of this theme, again with an 'expressive' flavour, is when the fire is aimed at a building that has some personal or symbolic significance, such as a school or church; the second, 'instrumental', type is when the building is set on fire for personal gain, either to avoid detection for another crime or for financial benefit.

Canter and Fritzon also reported several associations between offender characteristics and type of theme. Arson attacks against people tended to be carried out by offenders with a psychiatric history. However, attacks on buildings with some symbolic value were perpetrated by serial arsonists.

A Finnish study reported by Häkkänen, Puolakka, and Santilla (2004) looked at 189 cases of arson using the same methodology as Canter and Fritzon. Häkkänen et al. reported similar findings to Canter and Fritzon with respect to the person-object and expressive-instrumental themes that emerged from their analysis. Interestingly, Häkkänen et al. (2004: 204) found that of those arsonists who gave a motive for their firesetting the most frequent 'motive was reported to be revenge, hatred or jealously'. As will become evident in due course, revenge, hatred, and jealousy are often as the heart of other violent crimes.

Almond, Duggan, Shine, and Canter (2005) offered a further test of the action system model in a study with 65 male offenders serving prison sentences, all of whom had either previous or a current conviction for arson. Almond et al. replicated the findings of Canter and Fritzon with the same themes emerging as in the original study.

Serial arsonists

Some arsonists will set more than one fire and, if they are not apprehended, they may be involved in multiple instances of arson stretching out over a long period of time. Kocsis and Cooksey (2002) analysed case material, from police jurisdictions in Australia, for arsonists who had set three or more fires. They reported that the serial arsonists demonstrated a high degree of planning for the crime and sophistication in its execution. The arsonists' forethought was seen in their bringing accelerants and other combustible material to the scene of the crime and then by targeting specific items within the building. The arsonist often entered the building in order to set the fire, sometimes stealing available items, and then set small fires in selected areas of the building, allowing them to evade anyone in the building, and attempting to bypass security systems and fire retardation devices such as sprinkler devices.

Canter and Larkin (1993) developed the notion of 'criminal range' and 'home range' to describe the activities of serial offenders. Criminal range refers to the environmental area encompassed by the individual's offending; the home range is the area in which the offender lives, works, shops, and so on. Some serial offenders, called 'commuters', have a large criminal range, while for others, 'marauders', there is a substantial overlap between where they commit their offences and where they live.

An Australian study of serial offenders, including serial arsonists, found that most offenders lived in cities and fell into the marauder pattern in that they committed their offences close to home (Kocsis & Irwin, 1997). Fitzon (2001) reported not dissimilar findings for serial arsonists in England. Edwards and Grace (2006) reported a study of 44 male and female serial arsonists, responsible for 214 (known) offences, in New Zealand. Unlike previous studies, Edwards and Grace did not find that the serial arsonists were primarily marauders in that they appeared to travel further from home to commit their offences. Fritzon (2001) found that the English marauder-arsonists set fires within a mean of 2 km from their home, while for the New Zealand arsonists the mean distance travelled was more than 6 km. Edwards and Grace make the important point that distance is relative and what we mean by 'close to home' is not the same everywhere in the world: 'One difference between the current study and prior research is that our sample was obtained across a wider geographical range (from Whangarei in the far north of New Zealand to Invercargill in the deep south) and there was greater variability in terms of offenders residing in urban versus rural areas. Thus, one possible reason for our failure to find a consistent geographical pattern in offence site locations was the heterogeneity of the New Zealand environment' (Edwards & Grace, 2006: 224–5).

Wachi et al. (2007) reported a study of female serial arsonists in Japan. Wachi et al. note that in Japan, the frequency of arson is rising so that in 2004 there were more than 2,000 cases of arson. The information held by the police on solved cases suggested that there were 708 serial arsonists (defined in this study as having committed at least five instances of arson). These 708 serial arsonists accounted for 6 per cent of the total number of convicted arsonists: of the 708 serial arsonists, 83 (6 per cent) were women. Wachi et al. looked in detail at these 83 female serial arsonists, using the expressive-instrumental dichotomy noted above.

They reported that most of the women (66 per cent) fell into the category of an expressive type of arsonist: these arsonists, often in a state of emotional distress, typically set fires in residential properties close to their own home and said that they becoming excited at seeing the fire. The expressive arsonists set multiple fires over a short period of time, staying close to the fires to watch the situation unfold. The smaller number of women in the instrumental category typically targeted buildings some distance from where they lived and planned the fire either as revenge, say for being fired from work, or to conceal another crime, typically theft. As Gannon (2010) points out, a great deal more understanding of female arsonists is much needed from a treatment perspective.

Criminal careers

When an individual is convicted of arson what happens after they have served their sentence? Do they continue to set fires, or commit other types of crime, or do they become law-abiding citizens?

Soothill and Pope (1973) reported a 20-year follow-up of all those, a total of 74 people, convicted for arson in 1951 in England and Wales. Of these 74 convicted arsonists there was only one woman, and there was a very low rate of reconviction, less than 5 per cent, for further crimes of arson. However, almost half of the arsonists did receive a later conviction for another offence not related to arson. The low reconviction rate for convicted arsonists was also found in a study conducted in Germany (Barnett, Richter, & Renneberg, 1999).

Soothill, Ackerley, and Francis (2004) presented a replication of the Soothill and Pope study by looking at the criminal careers of three cohorts – 1,352 in 1963–5, 5,584 in 1980–1, and 3,335 in 2000–1 – convicted for arson in England and Wales. As Soothill et al. note, the remarkable rise in the number of convictions for arson may reflect increases in the number of successful investigations and prosecutions rather than an actual rise in offending.

The characteristics of the convicted arsonists had changed over time: compared with the 1950s, the arsonists of the 1980s were younger and were more likely to be female. In terms of sentencing, Soothill et al. note that, while the raw numbers had increased since the early 1950s, the proportion of offenders receiving custodial sentences had declined. They comment that this finding 'illustrates the paradox that the courts have become less punitive since the 1950s but the prison population continues to rise' (Soothill et al., 2004: 39). After conviction, the 1980s arsonists were more likely to be reconvicted for a criminal offence: a small number for another arson (about 11 per cent), although this is twice the rate found for the 1950s cohort, the remainder for a range of other offences. The increase in further offences may be a function of the younger age of the 1980s cohort but, as Soothill et al. (2004: 40) state: 'From three arson recidivists emerging in the 1951 series to an average of 300 arson recidivists emerging in each year from the 1980–1 series, it is difficult to mask or explain away the scale of the problem'.

Jayaraman and Frazer (2006) also looked at variations in the characteristics of arsonists, contrasting their sample of 34 individuals with a sample from an earlier study carried out in the same part of England (Rix, 1994). The data in both these studies were drawn from pre-trial psychiatric reports, conducted to inform the court about the mental health status of the accused. The individuals referred for psychiatric reports were predominately male with a mean age of about 30 years, which is younger than in Rix's earlier study. There were reasonably high numbers of previous convictions for a range of offences, which included arson. There were high levels of alcohol and drug abuse in the sample along with a range of psychiatric disorders, predominately personality disorder. The presence of personality disorder was consistent with Rix's earlier study.

The work of Soothill and colleagues informs us about mainstream offenders who commit arson, the studies based on psychiatric reports speak to a different population. There is a longstanding overlap between firesetting and mental disorder.

Mentally disordered firesetters

As various commentators have noted, a great deal of the literature on arson is concerned with mentally disordered firesetters. Prins (1995) makes the comment that psychiatric reports are often requested in cases of arson and it may be that this practice simply detects mental disorder before sentencing, with the result that the arsonist is placed in a secure hospital. It should be stated at the outset that when a person with some form of mental disorder sets fires, it cannot be assumed that the disorder is necessarily a causal factor to their actions. Further, there is no rule that says mental disorders must occur singly: it is often the case that while an individual is given a primary diagnosis, this primary disorder is comorbid with one or more other disorders.

Nevertheless, it is the case that firesetting is evident among mentally disordered populations, particularly those held in secure hospital facilities. The figures from several European countries, including Finland (Repo, Virkkunen, Rawlings, & Linnoila, 1997), Sweden (Fazel

& Grann, 2002), and the UK (Coid Kahtan, Gault, Cook, & Jarman, 2001), suggest that about 1 in 10 of those admitted to forensic psychiatric services have committed arson. A survey of the views of psychiatrists about the dangers posed by firesetters suggested that the greatest professional concern was when intention to endanger life was apparent and when the fires were set in occupied buildings (Sugarman & Dickens, 2009).

There are, as discussed below, a range of mental disorders associated with arson. However, there is a diagnosable mental disorder, *pyromania*, which is specifically concerned with pathological firesetting.

Pyromania

The DSM-IV-TR (APA, 2000) diagnostic criteria for pyromania are shown in Box 5.3. Falling into the general category of Impulse-control Disorder, the rare disorder of pyromania is characterised by the individual's curiosity and fascination with fire which leads them impulsively to start fires. The arson is not for gain, revenge, criminal purposes, or to make a political point: rather its purpose is either to relieve psychological tension or to experience excitement.

A Finnish study reported by Lindberg, Holi, Tani, and Virkkunen (2005) looked at the medical and forensic examination of 401 arsonists referred to Helsinki University Hospital for psychiatric assessment prior to their appearance in court. Of these 401 arsonists there were 90, all male, who were repeat arsonists having set at least two fires. Lindberg et al. used DSM-IV-TR criteria to look for the presence of pyromania among these 90 repeat arsonists. (The DSM criteria for pyromania specify 'Deliberate and purposeful firesetting on more than one occasion'.) Following DSM criteria, they excluded 56 individuals who presented any symptoms of psychosis, mental retardation, organic brain syndrome, and anti-social personality disorder. (In the UK, the term *learning disability* is used rather than mental retardation.) Of the remaining 34 arsonists, 12 appeared to fulfil the DSM-IV-TR diagnostic criteria for pyromania. However, Lindberg et al. found that 9 of these 12 individuals were under acute alcohol intoxication when they committed their index arson – the DSM criteria state that a pyromania should be excluded when the fire is set 'as a result of impaired

---

Box 5.3 DSM-IV-TR diagnostic criteria for pyromania

a   Deliberate and purposeful firesetting on more than one occasion.
b   Tension or affective arousal before the act.
c   Fascination with, interest in, curiosity about, or attraction to fire and its situational contexts (e.g., paraphernalia, uses, consequences).
d   Pleasure, gratification, or relief when setting fires, or when witnessing or participating in their aftermath.
e   The firesetting is not done for monetary gain, as an expression of sociopolitical ideology, to conceal criminal activity, to express anger or vengeance, to improve one's living circumstances, in response to a delusion or hallucination, or as a result of impaired judgment (e.g., in dementia, mental retardation, substance intoxication).
f   The fire setting is not better accounted for by conduct disorder, a manic episode, or anti-social personality disorder.

judgment (e.g., in dementia, mental retardation, substance intoxication)' – leaving three genuine pyromaniacs. Thus, these three individuals, referred to by Lindberg et al. as 'pure arsonists', account for less than 1 per cent of the original sample of 401 arsonists. It is evident from these findings that pyromania is a rare phenomenon.

A sample of three is too small from which to draw any generalisations, however Lindberg et al. make the observation that all three men worked as volunteer fire fighters and had a special interest in fire aside from arson.

Rice and Harris (1991) reviewed the clinical files of 243 male firesetters – of which only one individual fulfilled the diagnostic criteria for pyromania – admitted to conditions of maximum security in a Canadian psychiatric facility. A total of 27 people had died as a result of the fires set by the detained firesetters, alongside many other injuries and damage to mainly residential property. There were 98 individuals who had set one fire (that was known about), leaving 145 repeat firesetters. A comparison of these two groups showed that at a mean of 26 years, the repeat firesetters were younger by 4 years than the first-time firesetters. The repeat firesetters also had a more disturbed personal history, including instances of other types of criminal behaviour such as violence.

The characteristics of the firesetters were compared with a control group admitted to the same facility but without a history of firesetting. The firesetters were younger than the comparison group and had a history, stretching back to childhood, of an unusual interest in fire, were more likely to have been involved in acts of violence, and were more likely to have spent time in an institution. The most common diagnoses among the firesetters were personality disorder, at over half of the sample, followed by schizophrenia, which was the diagnosis for about one-third of the sample.

Harris and Rice (1996) used the same data set as in their 1991 study to look for a typology of mentally disordered firesetters. As shown in Table 5.3, Harris and Rice identified four groups or types of firesetter: *psychotics* formed the largest group with high rates of schizophrenia and alcohol problems; the next most common group were called *unassertives* and were men with unremarkable backgrounds, having progressed through edcuation and held employment, and who had set fire as an act of revenge or in anger; *multi-firesetters* were the youngest group with the most disturbed backgrounds and set fires in a range of locations; the *criminals*, as the name implies, had the most extensive criminal history including acts of violence. Those individuals who formed the *criminals* group were the most likely to set fires and commit other offences after release from security.

Rice and Harris (1996) returned to the issue of recidivism, looking at the outcomes for the 243 male firesetters in the original 1991 study. The overall rate of recidivism for firesetting was low: at almost 8 years follow-up after discharge from security, there was a 16 per cent

Table 5.3 Types of mentally disordered firesetter (after Harris & Rice, 1996)

Psychotics	Unassertives	Multi-firesetters	Criminals
33% of sample	28%	23%	16%
Schizophrenic	PD	PD	PD
Low crime	Low crime	Low crime	High crime
Delusional	Anger/revenge	Anger/excitement	-------
Low alcohol	High alcohol	Low alcohol	High alcohol

chance of another instance of arson. The strongest predictors of recidivistic firesetting were associated with the intensity of the individual's firesetting history. The younger firesetters, particularly those of lower intelligence and without a background of violent behaviour, who had a high incidence of firesetting formed the group with the highest risk of further firesetting. The factors contributing to the risk of further firsetting were different to the predictors of violent and non-violent recidivism, leading Rice and Harris (1996: 372) to make the comment that their findings 'support the idea that firesetting is an act different from both violent and nonviolent crime, but especially from violent crime'.

Dickens et al. (2009) looked at predictors of recidivism in a sample of 167 male and female adult arsonists who were referred to psychiatric services in England. They found that those arsonists known to have set more than one fire were younger and had childhood and adolescent histories characterised by disrupted education and family life, and by higer levels of criminal activity and contact with the criminal justice system. The psychiatric diagnoses of personality disorder and learning disability were more frequent among multiple firesetters than for those who had set only a single fire.

As is evident from the above, there are a range of mental disorders, sometimes comorbid, frequently associated with arson, including personality disorders, psychosis, learning disability, and substance misuse. Enayati, Grann, Lubbe, and Fazel (2008) reviewed the diagnostic information on 214 arsonists, 59 women and 155 men, referred for in-patient psychiatric assessment in Sweden over a 5-year period. Enayati et al. reported that the most frequently observed diagnoses, which were similar for males and females, were for substance-use disorders, personality disorders, and psychosis (typically schizophrenia). However, the type of substance-use disorder was different for females and males, with alcohol use disorder more prevalent in the female arsonists. With the exception that learning difficulties were more frequently found among arsonists, Enayati et al. did not find marked diagnostic differences between the arsonists and a sample of violent offenders. This latter finding appears to be different to that reported by Rice and Harris (1996) who stressed the differences between firesetters and violent offenders. However, there are procedural, as well as legal and cultural, differences between the two studies in terms of their sampling and methodology.

Schizophrenia is another mental disorder that is often associated with serious crime (see Chapter 8), including arson (Ritchie & Huff, 1999), and perhaps particularly so with women (Jamieson Butwell, Taylor, & Leese, 2000). A Swedish study reported by Anwar, Långström, Grann, and Fazel (2009) looked at the incidence of schizophrenia among a large sample of 1,340 men and 349 women convicted for arson over a 13-year period. They found that, compared with a control group drawn from the general population, those individuals with schizophrenia and other psychoses showed a significantly increased risk of being convicted for arson. Indeed, Anwar et al. noted that the likelihood of being diagnosed with schizophrenia was 20 times greater for the arsonists than for the controls. In keeping with the trend in the literature, Anwar et al. reported a higher rate of schizophrenia among the female arsonists.

Finally, Dickens et al. (2008) looked at the relationship between low IQ and arson in a sample of 202 men and women referred for psychiatric assessment. They reported that 88 of the sample had an IQ of 85 or below: these low-IQ arsonists set more fires than individual of a higher IQ, although often to items such as rubbish rather than buildings, and they did not differ in the range or extent of their previous criminal convictions compared with those of a higher IQ.

It is clear that the act of firesetting is one that is carried out for a diverse range of motives and by a broad cross-section of the population. However, a great deal of research activity, psychological and psychiatric alike, has been directed at specific groups such as children and those with a mental disorder. These particular features of the research are perhaps reflected in the theoretical literature.

Theories of arson

Psychodynamic

Fire has an elemental quality and, like water, it is central to human existence. Freud (1932) suggested an association between fire, enuresis, and sexual desire, while other psychodynamic accounts of arson made use of instinctual drives such as aggression and anxiety to explain firesetting (Kaufman, Heims, & Reiser, 1961; Macht & Mack, 1968).

The empirical evidence does not offer unqualified support to psychodynamic theories, accepting that this theory is one that is difficult to verify through traditional experimental methods. There is little support for the proposition that those who set fires find the act sexually arousing (Rice & Harris, 1991; Quinsey, Chaplin, & Upfold, 1989), or that there is a high rate of enuresis amongst arsonists (Bradford, 1982).

Learning theory

Jackson, Glass, and Hope (1987) provide a functional analytic view of arson that considers the reinforcing consequences of firesetting. The consequences of firesetting can be positively reinforcing, as with the social rewards when the act is committed with a peer group, or in seeing the reactions of other people to the fire and the arrival of the fire service. The consequences of firesetting may be negatively reinforcing in that they allow the individual to avoid a difficult situation such as debt or bankruptcy. A negative reinforcement contingency may also explain why schools are frequently the target for arson: reducing one's school to ashes is an effective way of making educational demands go away.

From the perspective of social learning theory, we may look for models that make fire attractive. An American study by Curri et al. (2003) made the point that while children are taught that fire is dangerous and must be treated with caution, there are images directed at children on toy packaging that depict fire as fun and exciting. Curri et al. carried out a study in a national toy store in which they inspected the packaging on toys for images of flames, noting whether the toys were intended for boys or girls. The survey revealed 404 toys with packaging showing images of fire, of which 97 per cent were targeted at boys: video games most frequently used pictures of fire, followed by toy cars and trucks. Curri et al. make the point that boys are receiving a consistent message from the toy's packaging that fire is fun. Curri et al.'s comment that these advertisements are contributing to the higher incidence of fire-related injuries in boys is entirely consistent with social learning theory.

Another American study by Greenhalgh and Palmieri (2003) also looked at popular accounts in the media of fire and its effects. Again following a line consistent with social learning theory, Greenhalgh and Palmieri suggested that the media can have an influence on the behaviour of children and adults by portraying fire as cool, fun, and of little real consequence. Greenhalgh and Palmieri reviewed both printed material and television programmes with respect to coverage of fire, the injuries caused by burns and burn prevention. The material was categorised as one of comics, advertisements, articles that made light of burns and television shows that portrayed behaviour that would risk burn injury. Comics and advertisements were the most common source of burn-related material. In keeping with Curri et al., Greenhalgh and Palmieri make the point that flames are mostly used in advertising directed at boys and young men – frequent sufferers from burn injuries – for items such as clothes, skateboards, and hot rods. Greenhalgh and Palmieri accuse the media of being callous in ignoring or making fun of fire and its injurious effects and also for producing advertisements that show people on fire or taking risks with fire that could lead to injury.

Evolutionary theory

It is the case that fire has been an aspect of existence since the beginnings of life: many animals have evolved to fear and avoid fire given its inherent dangers to life and survival. However, humans have learned to control fire and to use it as part of their everyday existence. The evolutionary anthropologist Daniel Fessler (2006) makes the point that humans may have evolved psychological mechanisms dedicated to learning about and controlling fire. Fessler suggests that, because relationships with fire will differ across ecosystems, then these psychological mechanisms may not be the same for everyone. Thus, differences might be predicted between societies where fire is an everyday tool and children encounter fire on a daily basis, and typical Western societies where fire is encountered less frequently.

Fessler (2006: 438) recounts his fieldwork in a 'semi-traditional Bengkulu Malay fishing village on the west coast of Sumatra': he notes that children's interactions with fire, which is used for cooking, begin early childhood, particularly playing with fire in order to practice managing and using it. The child achieves the skills of mastery and control over fire by middle childhood. Thus, in this society fire has a utilitarian purpose, it is a tool, and it holds no intrinsic value as a means of achieving entertainment or excitement. This utilitarian approach to fire contrasts sharply with children's use and understanding of fire in Western societies. The dangers, as noted above, of children playing and experimenting with fire – a fascination that may extend into adulthood – can be related to their inexperience with fire and the effects of media images of fire.

Conclusion

There can be little doubt, firesetting is an activity that can profoundly affect the lives of those it touches. The psychological research has primarily focused on two populations, children and those with a mental disorder, and so we know rather a lot about both of these groups. Similarly, psychological theories have tended to emphasise the more esoteric aspects, such as children's experimentation with firesetting and our general fascination with fire. While cultural values and popular images of fire are undoubtedly important, there is also the stark reality that for mundane reasons, such as revenge and profit, the crime of arson regularly destroys property and takes lives.

Chapter summary

- Arson is a highly dangerous and costly offence in terms of both human suffering and financial cost. Arson can lead to loss of life, horrific injuries to survivors, high levels of damage to residential and commercial property, and environmental damage.
- Some arsonists set only a single fire, however *spree arsonists* set several fires with a short period of time, typically hours, while *serial arsonists* set many fires over a much longer period.
- Pyromania is a morbid fascination with firesetting and is included in some classification systems of mental disorder. It is a condition that is rarely found in practice.

- There are several motivations for arson including *concealing a crime, economic reasons (including financial gain), excitement, political, revenge,* and *vandalism.*
- There is some concern that media portrayals of fire may influence some young people have a view of fire which minimises the harm it harm it can do and maximises the 'fun' element.

Points for discussion

- Why are some children fascinated by fire?
- Is understanding the motivation of arsonists helpful in terms of preventing fires?
- Should there be regulations about the use of fire in advertising children's toys?

Essential reading

Fessler, D. M. T. (2006). A burning desire: Steps toward an evolutionary psychology of fire learning. *Journal of Cognition and Culture, 6*: 429–451.
This is an interesting paper to read for two reasons: first, it offers a very different perspective to mainstream psychology; second, it may be seen as over-elaborating or bypassing some basic psychology. Do different cultures behave differently because of an evolutionary imperative or because of the more immediate effects of social learning?

Kennedy, P. J., Vale, E. L. E., Khan, S. J., & McAnaney, A. (2006). Factors predicting recidivism in child and adolescent fire-setters: A systematic review of the literature. *Journal of Forensic Psychiatry and Psychology, 17*: 151–164.
A comprehensive review of the features of juvenile firesetting.

Kolko, D. (Ed.) (2002). *Handbook on Firesetting in Children and Youth.* New York, NY: Academic Press. Covers all the major issues concerning juvenile firesetting.

Useful websites

The Arson Control Forum (ACF) – www.arsoncontrolforum.gov.uk
The ACF began in April 2001 and is a UK government-led national body seeking to reduce arson-related deaths, injuries, and damage. It brings together agencies such as the fire service, local authorities, the police service, insurance companies, and government departments.
The ACF aims to:

- raise public awareness of arson prevention and investigation;
- reduce the number of deliberate fires and related deaths, injuries, and damage;
- maintain a strategic overview of arson prevention and investigation;
- develop, monitor, and support initiatives which improve the prevention and detection of arson;
- promote partnership and co-ordinate efforts among the various agencies to develop policy on arson prevention and investigation;
- monitor and contribute to improvements in the recording and detection of arson;
- monitor and contribute to the prevention and investigation of arson as conducted by other European and international bodies.

The Australian Institute of Criminology – www.aic.gov.au
This website carries a range of facts and figures about crime down under, including a link to the Bushfire Arson Bulletin. This bulletin provides a range of factsheets giving information on several aspects of this particular form of arson.

Centre for Violence Prevention, Karolinska – www.cvp.se

References

Almond, L., Duggan, L., Shine, J., & Canter, D. (2005). Test of the arson action system model in an incarcerated population. *Psychology, Crime, & Law, 11*, 1–15.

American Psychiatric Association (APA) (2000). *Diagnostic and Statistical Manual of Mental Disorders* (4th ed., text revised). Washington, DC: American Psychiatric Association.

Anwar, S., Långström, N., Grann, M., & Fazel, S. (2009). Is arson the crime most strongly associated with psychosis? A national case-control study of arson risk in schizophrenia and other psychoses. *Schizophrenia Bulletin, 37*, 580–586.

Australian Institute of Criminology (AIC) (2009). The number of fires and who lights them. *BushFIRE Arson Bulletin*, No. 59. Canberra: Australian Institute of Criminology.

Barnett, W., Richter, P., & Renneberg, B. (1999). Repeated arson: Data from criminal records. *Forensic Science International, 101*, 49–54.

Bradford, J. M. (1982). Arson: A clinical study. *Canadian Journal of Psychiatry, 27*, 188–193.

Canter, D. & Fritzon, K. (1998). Differentiating arsonists: A model of firesetting actions and characteristics. *Legal and Criminological Psychology, 3*, 73–96.

Canter, D. & Larkin, P. (1993). The environmental range of serial rapists. *Journal of Environmental Psychology, 13*, 63–69.

Chen, Y., Arria, A. M., & Anthony, J. C. (2003). Firesetting in adolescence and being aggressive, shy, and rejected by peers: New epidemiologic evidence from a national sample survey. *Journal of the American Academy of Psychiatry and Law, 31*, 44–52.

Christensen, W. (2007/8). The prevention of bushfire arson through target hardening. *Flinders Journal of Law Reform, 10*, 693–713.

Coid J., Kahtan, N., Gault, S., Cook, A., & Jarman, B. (2001). Medium secure forensic psychiatry services: Comparison of seven English health regions. *British Journal of Psychiatry, 178*, 55–61.

Curri, T. B., Palmieri, T. L., Aoki, T. H., Kaulkin, C. K., Lunn, M. E., Gregory, C. M., & Greenhalgh, D. G. (2003). Playing with fire: Images of fire on toy packaging. *Journal of Burn Care and Rehabilitation, 24*, 163–165.

Dadds, M. R. & Fraser, J. A. (2006). Fire interest, fire setting and psychopathology in Australian children: A normative study. *Australian and New Zealand Journal of Psychiatry, 40*, 581–586.

Davies, M. & Mouzos, J. (2007). *Fatal Fires: Fire-Associated Homicide in Australia, 1990–2005. Trends and Issues in Crime and Criminal Justice, No. 340*. Canberra, ACT: Australian Institute of Criminology.

Department for Communities and Local Government (2006). *A Special Report from the Arson Control Forum: Good Practice Conference*. London: Corrine Fleming Associates.

—— (2008). *Fire Statistics, United Kingdom 2006*. London: Department for Communities and Local Government.

—— (2009). *Fire and Rescue Service: Operational Statistics Bulletin for England 2008/09*. London: Department for Communities and Local Government.

Dickens, G., Sugarman, P., Ahmad, F., Edgar, S., Hofberg, K., & Tewari, S. (2007). Gender differences amongst adult arsonists at psychiatric assessment. *Medicine, Science, and Law, 47*, 233–238.

—— (2008). Characteristics of low IQ arsonists at psychiatric assessment. *Medicine, Science, and Law, 48*, 217–220.

Dickens, G., Sugarman, P., Edgar, S, Hofberg, K., Tewari, S., & Ahmed, F. (2009). Recidivism and dangerousness in arsonists. *Journal of Forensic Psychiatry and Psychology, 20*, 621–639.

Edwards, M. J. & Grace, R. C. (2006). Analysing the offence locations and residential base of serial arsonists in New Zealand. *Australian Psychologist, 41*, 219–226.

Enayati, J., Grann, M., Lubbe, S., & Fazel, S. (2008). Psychiatric morbidity in arsonists referred for forensic psychiatric assessment in Sweden. *Journal of Forensic Psychiatry and Psychology, 19*, 139–147.

Fazel, S. & Grann M. (2002). Older criminals: A descriptive study of psychiatrically examined offenders in Sweden. *International Journal of Geriatric Psychiatry, 17*, 907–913.

Fessler, D. M. T. (2006). A burning desire: Steps toward an evolutionary psychology of fire learning. *Journal of Cognition and Culture, 6*, 429–451.

Fineman, K. R. (1980). Firesetting in childhood and adolescence. *Psychiatric Clinics of North America, 3*, 483–499.

Fitzon, K. (2001). Examination of the relationship between distance travelled and motivational aspects of firesetting behavior. *Journal of Environmental Psychology, 21*, 45–60.

Flanagan R. J. & Fisher D. S. (2008). Volatile substance abuse and crime: Data from UK press cuttings 1996–2007. *Medicine, Science, and Law, 48*, 295–306.

Freud, S. (1932). The acquisition of power over fi re. *International Journal of Psychoanalysis, 13*, 405–410.

Fritzon, K., Canter, D., & Wilton, Z. (2001). The application of an action system model to destructive behaviour: The examples of arson and terrorism. *Behavioral Sciences and the Law, 19*, 657–690.

Gannon, T. G. (2010). Female arsonists: Key features, psychopathologies, and treatment needs. *Psychiatry, 73*, 173–189.

Gannon, T. A. & Pina, A. (2010). Firesetting: Pathology, theory and treatment. *Aggression and Violent Behavior, 15*, 224–238.

Greenhalgh, D. G., & Palmieri, T. L. (2003). The media glorifying burns: A hindrance to burn prevention. *Journal of Burn Care & Research, 24*, 159–162.

Häkkänen, H., Puolakka, P., & Santilla, P. (2004). Crime scene actions and offender characteristics in arsons. *Legal and Criminological Psychology, 9*, 197–214.

Harris, G. T. & Rice, M. E. (1996). A typology of mentally disordered firesetters. *Journal of Interpersonal Violence, 11*, 351–363.

Hickle, K. E. & Roe-Sepowitz, D. E. (2010). Female juvenile arsonists: An exploratory look at characteristics and solo and group arson offences. *Legal and Criminological Psychology, 15*, 385–399.

Hollin, C. R. (1990). *Cognitive-Behavioral Interventions with Young Offenders*. New York, NY: Pergamon Press.

Hollin, C. R., Epps, K., & Swaffer, T. (2002). Adolescent firesetters: Findings from an analysis of 47 cases. *Pakistan Journal of Psychological Research, 17*, 1–16.

Home Office (2002). Some facts and figures about arson. Home Office Crime Reduction website, www.crimereduction.homeoffice.gov.uk/arson/arson2.htm. Last accessed 15 June 2012.

—— (2006). *The Arson Control Forum Update*. London: Home Office.

Jackson, H., Glass, C., & Hope, S. (1987). A functional analysis of recidivistic arson. *British Journal of Clinical Psychology, 26*, 175–185.

Jacobson, R., Jackson, M., & Berelowitz, M. (1986). Self-incineration: A controlled comparison of in-patient suicide attempts: Clinical features and history of self-harm. *Psychological Medicine, 16*, 107–116.

Jamieson, E., Butwell, M., Taylor, P., & Leese, M. (2000). Trends in special (high-security) hospitals: 1: Referrals and admissions. *British Journal of Psychiatry, 176*, 253–259.

Jayaraman, A. & Frazer, J. (2006). Arson: A growing inferno. *Medicine, Science, and Law, 46*, 295–300.

Kaufman, I., Heims, L., & Reiser, D. E. (1961). A re-evaluation of the psychodynamics of firesetting. *American Journal of Orthopsychiatry, 31*, 123–136.

Kennedy, P. J., Vale, E. L. E., Khan, S. J., & McAnaney, A. (2006). Factors predicting recidivism in child and adolescent fire-setters: A systematic review of the literature. *Journal of Forensic Psychiatry and Psychology, 17*, 151–164.

Klein, J. J., Mondozzi, M. A., & Andrews, D. A. (2008). The need for a juvenile fire setting database. *Journal of Burn Care & Research, 29*, 955–958.

Kolko, D. J. (1985). Juvenile firesetting: A review and methodological critique. *Clinical Psychology Review, 5*, 345–376.

Kolko, D. J., Herschell, A. D., & Scharf, D. M. (2006). Education and treatment for boys who set fires: Specificity, moderators, and predictors of recidivism. *Journal of Emotional and Behavioral Disorders, 14*, 227–239.

Kolko, D. J. & Kazdin, A. E. (1992). The emergence and recurrence of child fire setting: A one-year prospective study. *Journal of Abnormal Child Psychology, 20,* 17–37.

Kocsis, R. N. & Irwin, H. J. (1997). An analysis of spatial patterns in serial rape, arson and burglary: The utility of the circle theory of environment range of psychological profiling. *Psychiatry, Psychology and Law, 4,* 195–206.

Kocsis, R. N. & Cooksey, R. W. (2002). Criminal psychological profiling of serial arson crimes. *International Journal of Offender Therapy and Comparative Criminology, 46,* 631–656.

Lari, A. R. & Alaghehbandan, R. (2003). Epidemiological study of self-inflicted burns in Tehran, Iran. *Journal of Burn Care & Research, 24,* 15–20.

Lindberg, N., Holi, M. M., Tani, P., & Virkkunen, M. (2005). Looking for pyromania: Characteristics of a consecutive sample of Finnish male criminals with histories of recidivist fire-setting between 1973 and 1993. *BMC Psychiatry, 5/47,* available at: www.biomedcentral.com/1471-244X/5/47. Last accessed 12 June 2012.

McCarty, C. A. & McMahon, R. (2005). Domains of risk in the developmental continuity of fire setting. *Behavior Therapy, 36,* 185–195.

Macht, L. B. & Mack, J. E. (1968). The firesetter syndrome. *Psychiatry, 31,* 277–288.

Martin, G., Bergen, H. A., Richardson, A. S., Roeger, L., & Allison, S. (2004). Correlates of firesetting in a community sample of young adolescents. *Australian and New Zealand Journal of Psychiatry, 38,* 148–154.

Noblett, S. & Nelson, B. (2001). A psychosocial approach to arson: A case controlled study of female offenders. *Medicine, Sciences and the Law, 41,* 325–330.

Office of the Deputy Prime Minister (ODPM) (2002). *The Burning Issue: Research and Strategies for Reducing Arson.* London: Office of the Deputy Prime Minster.

—— (2003). *Arson Control Forum Annual Report.* London: Office of the Deputy Prime Minster.

—— (2005). *Arson Terminology.* London: Office of the Deputy Prime Minster.

Pollinger, J., Samuels, L., & Stadolnik, R. (2005). A comparative study of the behavioral, personality, and fire history characteristics of residential and outpatient adolescents (ages 12–17) with firesetting behaviors. *Adolescence, 40,* 345–353.

Prins, H. (1994). *Fire-raising: Its Motivation and Management.* London: Routledge.

—— (1995). Adult fire-raising: Law and psychology. *Psychology, Crime, & Law, 1,* 271–281.

Quinsey, V. L., Chaplin, T. C., & Upfold, D. (1989). Arsonists and sexual arousal to firesetting: Correlation unsupported. *Journal of Behavior Therapy and Experimental Psychology, 20,* 203–209.

Räsänen, P., Hirvenoja, R., Hakko, H., & Vaeisaenen, E. (1995). A portrait of the juvenile arsonist. *Forensic Science International, 73,* 41–47.

Reiland, A., Hovater, M., McGwin, G. Jr., Rue, L. W. III, & Cross, J. M. (2006). The epidemiology of intentional burns. *Journal of Burn Care & Research, 27,* 276–280.

Repo, E., Virkkunen, M., Rawlings, M., & Linnoila, M. (1997). Criminal and psychiatric histories of Finnish arsonists. *Acta Psychiatrica Scandinavcia, 95,* 318–323.

Rice, M. E. & Harris, G. T. (1991). Firesetters admitted to a maximum security psychiatric institution: Offenders and offenses. *Journal of Interpersonal Violence, 6,* 641–675.

—— (1996). Predicting the recidivism of mentally disordered offenders. *Journal of Interpersonal Violence, 11,* 364–375.

Ritchie, E. L. & Huff, T. G. (1999). Psychiatric aspects of arsonists. *Journal of Forensic Science, 44,* 733–740.

Rix, K. J. (1994). A psychiatric study of adult arsonists. *Medicine, Science, and Law, 34,* 21–34.

Root, C., MacKay, S., Henderson, J., Del Bove, G. & Warling, D. (2008). The link between maltreatment and juvenile firesetting: Correlates and underlying mechanisms. *Child Abuse & Neglect, 32,* 161–176.

Shkrum, M. & Johnston, K. (1992). Fire and suicide: A three-year study of self-immolation deaths. *Journal of Forensic Sciences, 37,* 208–221.

Soothill, K. L., Ackerley, E., & Francis, B. (2004). The criminal careers of arsonists. *Medicine, Science, and Law, 44*, 27–40.

Soothill, K. L. & Pope, P. J. (1973). Arson: A twenty-year cohort study. *Medicine, Science, and Law, 18*, 247–254.

Stoddard, F., Pahlavan, K., & Cahners, S. (1985). Suicide attempted by self-immolation during adolescence. *Journal of Adolescent Psychiatry, 12*, 251–280.

Sugarman, P. & Dickens, G. (2009). Dangerousness in firesetters: A survey of psychiatrists' views. *Psychiatric Bulletin, 33*, 99–101.

Wachi, T., Watanabe, K., Yokota, K., Suzuki, M., Hoshino, M., Sato, A., & Fujita, G. (2007). Offender and crime characteristics of female serial arsonists in Japan. *Journal of Investigative Psychology and Offender Profiling, 4*, 29–52.

6 Psychological approaches to understanding serious crime II

Violent crime

We are never very far away from violence: every day there is violence, both real and fictional, on television; there are violent video games to provide entertainment; there is violence both within sport, as seen in football, and for sport as with boxing; there is human violence against other species as with hunting; there is violence inside the family home and there is violence in public places; there is violence against children and against adults; there is violence against men and violence against women; there is violence that overwhelms nations and communities; and there is violence against the individual. In his Foreword to the World Health Organization (WHO) *World Report on Violence and Health* (Krug, Dahlberg, Mercy, Zwi, & Lozano, 2002) – a publication that refers to violence as a 'global public health problem' – Nelson Mandela wrote: 'The twentieth century will be remembered as a century marked by violence. It burdens us with its legacy of mass destruction, of violence inflicted on a scale never seen and never before possible in human history' (Krug et al., 2002: ix).

This reference to history is appropriate when discussing violence. The archaeologist Steven LeBlanc puts forward the view that fighting, particularly in the form of warfare, has always been a part of the human condition as our ancestors continually fought over scarce resources (LeBlanc & Register, 2003). Archer (2009) discusses aggression from an ethological perspective, tracing the evolution of aggression and suggesting that it has adaptive functions in humans as it does in other animals. Archer (2009: 207) makes the point that human aggression is a natural human characteristic but, like other characteristics, can vary in ways that are 'abnormal in an adaptive sense'. Archer does not press the point, but perhaps for humans these abnormal variations include acts of violence that bring about extreme harm to other people. In keeping with this line of thought, Patterson (2008) makes the point that violence serves functional needs at the level of both the state and the individual. The state goes to war to expand its territories and wealth; the violent person aggresses to gain, socially and materially, by their actions.

The WHO report describes three types of violence – (1) *self-directed violence*, (2) *inter-personal violence*, and (3) *collective violence* – with several kinds of violent act nested within each type. The first of these types, self-directed violence, can take the form of suicidal behaviour and self-abuse or self-harm and there is a considerable literature on these topics (Williams, 1997, 2001). However, as self-harm and suicide are not criminal acts – in the UK the act of suicide was decriminalized in 1961, although it remains a crime to assist another person to commit suicide – they fall outside the scope of this book. Collective violence, which refers to violence perpetrated by large groups of people or by states, is subdivided into three subtypes: (1) social violence, such as crimes of hate or acts of terrorism; (2) political violence which includes war; and (3) economic violence as seen with acts that are intended to interfere with economic activity producing disruption to economic unity. These various forms of collective violence – with notable exceptions as seen in research into terrorism by Max Taylor and John Horgan (e.g., Horgan, 2005; Taylor & Horgan, 2000) – have not received a great deal of attention from psychologists.

The attention of most psychological research and theory concerned with violence has been directed towards the third type of violence, interpersonal violence. The WHO report divides interpersonal violence into two broad categories – violence against a family member or a partner, and violence within the broader community – also noting that the violence may be physical or sexual. The focus here is on the broad domain of interpersonal violence, including deprivation and neglect, sexual violence is considered in the following chapter.

However, before moving to these issues a more fundamental point lies in agreeing what we mean when we use the word *violence*.

Aggression or violence?

The immediate problem in trying to arrive at an understanding of violent crime lies in the variability in terminology in the literature: there are two terms in common, sometimes interchangeable, use, which are *aggression and violence* (of which *criminal violence* is a particular subset). The problems with arriving at a shared understanding of the terms aggression and violence are not academic niceties. The development of theory depends on a collective understanding of the terms involved, the design of assessments for aggressive/violent behaviour relies on a common meaning to ensure comparable measurement across studies. The design and evaluation of interventions to reduce aggression depend on a sound operational understanding of what is being changed.

The term aggression is one that is used in a wide range of contexts with a corresponding diversity of meanings. For example, we may talk about an aggressive form of an illness, we describe some predatory animals as aggressive hunters, sports teams may be said to have an aggressive style of play, the business world talks about aggressive takeovers of one company by another, and we describe some people as aggressive individuals. In the animal kingdom generally, aggression has been described as an instinct that leads members of the same species, including humans, to fight each other (Lorenz, 1966).

In humans, the intention of the act is important. Thus, aggression has been used to refer to the intention to hurt or gain advantage over another person without necessarily involving physical injury (Siann, 1985). Similarly, Anderson and Bushman (2002: 28) define human aggression as 'any behaviour directed toward another individual that is carried out with the *proximate* (immediate) intent to cause harm'.

Aggressive behaviours can take different forms and may be of differing intensity. Goldstein (2002) describes 'low-level aggression' as consisting of acts such as ostracism, gossiping, and teasing: these forms of aggression are commonplace in settings, such as schools or the workplace, where people meet and interact on a regular basis. These acts of low-level aggression may include offensive words and verbal abuse, as with using obscene and abusive language, or 'hate speech' such as racial insults and sexual harassment (Jay, 2009).

The term 'low-level' does not mean that these forms of aggression should be lightly dismissed. As Jay (2009: 83) notes: 'Harms experienced by victims of hateful speech … include psychological and physiological symptoms similar to posttraumatic stress disorder (PTSD): panic, fear, anxiety, nightmares, intrusive thoughts of intimidation and denigration'. These reactions to aggression may be made worse for the victim if their family, friends or work colleagues observe the aggressive act taking place.

Types of aggressive behaviour

As shown in Box 6.1, Parrot and Giancola (2007) have compiled from the literature a list of various subtypes of aggressive behaviour. This is not to say, of course, that all these subtypes meet with universal approval. A common distinction is made between reactive (or hostile) aggression and proactive (or instrumental) aggression: reactive aggression generally refers to acts that are impulsive and where the aggressor's state is of one of negative affect such as anger; proactive acts are premeditated and are carried out in order to achieve the aggressor's personal goal such as financial gain. The validity of the reactive-proactive dichotomy distinction has come into question (Bushman and Anderson, 2001) and the distinction has no legal force (Fontaine, 2007). Nonetheless, there is some evidence in support of the validity of the distinction (Polman, Orobio de Castro, Koops, van Boxtel, & Merk, 2007) and, as discussed below, an aggressor may act when in an angry state.

It can be seen from Box 6.1 that a part of the conceptual issue lies around the 'internal' and 'external' features of human aggression. Is aggression to be understood in terms of a process *within* the individual such as, say, an instinct or an intention, or is it an internal process accompanied by *external* element, such as a verbalisation or a physical action?

If aggression can be described in such a diversity of ways, when is the line crossed so that aggression becomes violence? Anderson and Bushman (2002: 29) see the distinction between aggression and violence in terms of the intention of the aggressor: they describe violence as 'aggression that has extreme harm as its goal (e.g., death)'.

When it comes to crime, the law is primarily concerned with specific *acts* accompanied by *mens rea*. So if violence may be taken to refer to an act that involves the use of physical force against another person, the *criminal* violence is harmful behaviour directed against another person and that is forbidden in law. As the central concern of law is criminal violence, the term violence, rather than aggression, will be used from this point.

The issue of what, exactly, counts as criminal violence is not straightforward. In the publication *Crime in England and Wales*, Smith and Hoare (2009) divide violent crime into two types: (1) *violence with injury*, which includes acts such as wounding, assault with injury and robbery that results in injury; (2) *violence without injury*, which includes assault without injury and robberies that do not result in injury. Smith and Hoare (2009: 24) state: 'Violence against the person offences contain the full spectrum of assaults, from pushing and shoving

---

Box 6.1 Subtypes of aggression (after Parrott & Giancola, 2007)

Active vs passive aggression
Annoyance-motivated vs incentive-motivated aggression
Anti-social vs pro-social aggression
Direct vs indirect aggression
Overt vs covert aggression
Overt vs relational aggression
Physical vs verbal aggression
Proactive vs reactive aggression
Rational vs manipulative aggression
Relational vs social aggression
Targeted vs targetless aggression

Table 6.1 Violent crime with and without injury (after Smith & Hoare, 2009)

Assault without injury
Assault without injury on a constable
Racially/religiously aggravated assault without injury
Assault with minor injury
Less serious wounding
Racially/religiously aggravated less serious wounding
Inflicting grievous bodily harm (GBH) without intent
Actual bodily harm (ABH) and other injury
Racially or religiously aggravated inflicting GBH without intent
Racially or religiously aggravated ABH or other injury
Poisoning or female genital mutilation
Wounding
More serious wounding or other act endangering life
Inflicting grievous bodily harm (GBH) with intent
Use of substance or object to endanger life
Possession of items to endanger life
Robbery
Robbery of personal property

that result in no physical harm, to murder. Even within the same offence classification, the degree of violence varies considerably between incidents'.

As shown in Table 6.1, a range of acts are included within this 'full spectrum' of violent crimes, to which can be added acts so extreme that they bring about the death of another person.

Aggression and gender

As with crime generally, it is also the case with violent crime that men are seen to be more involved than women. This gender divide would certainly be true if relying on the criminal statistics for violent crime, where the numbers of men convicted for violent crime far outweighs the number of women with similar convictions. Nonetheless, it is the case that women do perpetrate acts of violence, although how much this is a function of gender, as opposed to gender roles, remains to be established (Richardson & Hammock, 2007). The commission of acts of violence by young women is a particular concern, as reflected in a comprehensive report from the US Department of Justice (Zahn et al., 2008).

While a man or a woman may be convicted for the same violent crime, it does not follow that the factors associated with the violence are the same for men and women (Collins, 2010; Rossegger et al., 2009). Hollin and Palmer (2003) reported a study of male violent offenders using the Level of Service Inventory-Revised (LSI-R; Andrews & Bonta, 1995). The LSI-R assesses a range of factors, such as substance use, accommodation and financial problems, which are predictive of offending. When compared with non-violent offenders, the LSI-R profiles of the violent offenders were characterised by a more serious criminal history, a greater level of association with companions involved in crime, lower levels of education and employment, and higher levels of alcohol and drug use. Given the variation in LSI-R scores between male and female offenders (Hollin & Palmer, 2006), it is not surprising that the there are differences between male and female violent offenders. An American study using the LSI-R with male and female serious violent offenders found gender differences on pro-social atti-tudes and emotional problems (Manchak, Skeem, Douglas, & Siranosian, 2009). Several commentators have suggested that social cognition is an important element in understanding violent behaviour (e.g., Carlo Mestre, Samper, Tur, & Armenta, 2010; Gannon, 2009) and that the finer social cognitive skills generally shown by women are associated with their lower rates of violence (Bennett, Farrington, & Huesmann, 2005).

In order to consider violent crimes from a psychological perspective, three broad types of violent crime will be discussed: (1) taking the life of another person in an act of homicide; (2) acts of assault against another person; and (3) the use of violence for personal gain.

Criminal violence: homicide

The term *homicide*, as used in the Homicide Act 1957, encompasses the offences of murder, manslaughter, and infanticide. *Murder* is an act that is deemed in law to be *mala in se*: that is, an act that is evil in itself. In common law, the act of murder must be accompanied by intent. This emphasis on intent is crucial: if a life is taken without premeditated intent to kill, then the act is not one of murder but may be one of manslaughter. The offence of *manslaugh-ter* can take three forms, the first is sometimes called *voluntary manslaughter*, the other two are *involuntary manslaughter*: (1) with voluntary manslaughter, the killing is with intent, as for murder, but a partial defence can be made in terms of provocation, diminished responsi-bility or killing in the context of a suicide pact; (2) involuntary manslaughter may be an act that results in death and was grossly negligent; or (3) an unlawful act involving a risk of harm, that results in death.

There are other offences that fall under the rubric of homicide, such as causing death by dangerous driving, infanticide, and corporate manslaughter (or corporate homicide in some jurisdictions). The latter offence refers to cases in which failings in the way that an organisa-tion is managed brings about a person's death. Corporate manslaughter is equivalent to a breach of the duty of care owed by the organisation to the deceased. As the offender is an organisation, no one individual is held to be culpable and the legal penalty is a fine.

The person's competence with respect to intent to kill is important. In England and Wales, Part I of the Homicide Act 1957 states: 'Where a person kills or is a party to the killing of another, he shall not be convicted of murder if he was suffering from such abnormality of mind (whether arising from a condition of arrested or retarded development of mind or any inherent causes or induced by disease or injury) as substantially impaired his mental respon-sibility for his acts and omissions in doing or being a party to the killing'. It is sometimes a matter for the courts to decide whether an act was premeditated and therefore one of murder not manslaughter. The topic of mentally disordered offenders in covered in Chapter 8.

How common is homicide?

As with crime statistics generally, answering the question of how many homicides are committed in a given period of time, generally annually, is not a straightforward exercise. Smith et al. (2010: 10), with reference to the figures for England and Wales, note: 'In 2008/09, 670 deaths were initially recorded as homicide, a decrease of 14 per cent on the previous year. Where the police initially record an offence as homicide it remains classified unless the police or courts decide later that a lesser offence, or no offence, took place. Of the 670 offences first recorded in 2008/09, 19 were no longer recorded as homicide by 24 November 2009'.

The low figures for homicide in comparison with many other crimes can make it difficult to see trends in the figures for murder and, as Smith et al. note, exceptional cases can blur matters. The case of the GP Harold Shipman – referred to by Soothill and Wilson (2005: 685) as '[p]robably the most prolific serial killer in British history and sometimes headlined as "the world's most prolific serial killer"' – provides an example of just such an exceptional case (Gunn, 2010). There were 173 murders attributed to Shipman in 2002/03 and recorded by the police, massively inflating the figure for that year (Walker et al., 2003), although the offences themselves took place over a much longer period of time. The number of murders attributed to Shipman eventually rose to at least 215 (Gunn, 2010).

It is also the case that the homicide rate varies considerably from country to country, as does the legal understanding of homicide and the recording practices of its occurrence: the website nationmaster.com (see 'Useful websites' at the end of this chapter) provides many international comparisons, including murder rates. As shown in Table 6.2, Smith et al. (2010) give the homicide rates per 100,000 of the population, averaged over 2005–7, for the 15 countries that were members of the European Union during that period.

There are likely to be many reasons for the international variations in the homicide rate. Blatier, Gimenez, Paulicand, and Pullin (2010) compare the situation in France with other countries. As Blatier et al. note, France has a homicide rate that is in the middle range for Europe (see Table 6.2) and is much lower than countries such as Colombia and Russia. Blatier et al. (2010: 266) suggest the reason for the comparatively low French rate may lie either in a national 'reticence towards homicidal acts, judging them to be so extreme and immoral', or in the strong penalties for violence dispensed by the French courts.

In the USA, the homicide rate has been steady for about a decade at around at 5.6 per 100,000 of the population. In a country as large and complex as the USA there are, as might be expected, variations in the rate on a state-by-state basis. The figures in the FBI *Uniform Crime Report* for 2008 (FBI, 2009) allow a state-by-state comparison of the homicide

Table 6.2 EU homicide rates (after Smith et al., 2010)

Country	Rate per 100,000 of the Population
Austria	0.64
Belgium	2.04
Denmark	1.17
Finland	2.23
France	1.46
Germany	0.90
Greece	1.05
Ireland	1.45
Italy	1.13
Luxembourg	1.42
The Netherlands	1.06
Portugal	1.47
Spain	1.12
Sweden	1.05
UK	
England and Wales	1.43
Scotland	2.17
Northern Ireland	1.59

rate to be made. In 2008, Louisiana remained as the state with the highest homicide rate at 11.9 per 100,000 of the population, down from the previous year's rate of 14.2. The next highest rates were in Maryland (8.8) and Mississippi (8.1). The lowest homicide rate was in North Dakota (0.5) followed by New Hampshire (1.0) and Utah (1.4).

The reasons for such disparity in the homicide rates may be due to reasons such as population density, the number of big cities in a given state or country, the availability of firearms, an increased acceptance of violence across some sections of society, social structure and economic deprivation, and the prevalence of social groupings such as cults and gangs. The function of these social factors in accounting for homicide have been considered by criminologists and sociologists (Beeghley, 2003; D'Cruze, Walklate, & Pegg, 2006; Diem & Pizarro, 2010; Fox, Levin, & Quinet, 2007; McCall, Parker, & MacDonald, 2008).

The study reported by McCall et al. (2008) is particularly interesting in that it investigated the relationship between the homicide rate in the USA and a range of economic, political, and social factors. McCall et al. compared changes in the homicide rate at the start of four decades (1970, 1980, 1990, and 2000): they present data showing that, averaged across 83 large cities in the USA, from 1970 to the mid-1990s, the annual average homicide rate rose steadily, peaking around the mid-1990s and then falling precipitously so that by 2000 it was below the 1970 level. What caused such large fluctuations to occur?

McCall et al. suggest that changes in criminal justice policies may have had a role to play. The 1970s saw the introduction of tough measures to try control crime, including increases in the number of police officers and a massive expansion in the use of custodial sentences, including life sentences. With regard to social structure, McCall et al. (2008: 731) conclude that their analysis suggests 'that changes in homicide rates are related to intra-city changes in the relative size of the young crime-prone population and the effects of urban decay and poverty'. It is these cultural, political, and structural conditions that set the context within which the dynamic, interpersonal aspects of homicide are played out.

Agha (2009) disaggregated the homicide arrest figures from 48 countries according to the gender of the suspect. As expected, males were involved more frequently than females, although the magnitude of the difference varied markedly from country to country. The influence of social structure, as assessed through variables such as financial wealth, urbanization, and numbers of people per household, was found to be equivalent for men and women. Heide and Solomon (2009) suggest that the involvement of young women under the age of 18 years in violent crime is increasing, although the figures specifically for homicide show substantial annual fluctuation.

The recidivism rate for homicide is very low: it is highly unusual for an individual convicted of homicide, with the attendant likelihood of a long prison sentence, to commit another homicide after the first conviction. Roberts, Zgoba, and Shahidullah (2007) investigated the recidivism of 336 homicide offenders, 238 males and 98 females, who were released from prison in New Jersey, USA, between 1990 and 2000. At a minimum of 5 years after release from prison, none of the offenders had been reconvicted for homicide. However, more than half of the prisoners had committed other types of crime after their release, principally drug offences and parole violations.

The dynamics of killing

In seeking to understand the dynamics of the act of murder, there is a range of questions to ask. Where and in what context do homicides takes place? Who is most likely to be involved in a killing? What are the characteristics of those individuals who commit homicide?

Wolfgang (1958) analysed the situations in which 588 homicides took place in Philadelphia between 1948 and 1952. In more than one-third of the homicides, the killing followed an apparently trivial event such as an argument, a threat or an insult. In most of the homicides, the offender and victim knew each other, were likely to have been drinking, and were almost always of the same race. The majority of perpetrators were male, generally less than 35 years of age, and most had previous arrest records, usually for violent crime. A knife was the most frequently used weapon. The victim was also likely to be male – overall males account for more than two-thirds of homicide victims – although the most violent incidents involved a husband and wife. The killing most frequently occurred in a domestic setting during the summer months, mainly between Saturday evening and the early hours of Sunday.

Goldstein's (1986) analysis of the motives for homicide, using American crime figures, suggested that about one-fifth of homicides were in the context of another crime such as robbery (see below) but more than two-fifths of homicides occurred while people were arguing with each other. Clark's (1995) analysis of lone and multiple offending in homicide found that when there is one offender, the situation is likely to be a domestic setting but with multiple offenders, the situation is likely to be a concurrent crime.

There is a longstanding association between alcohol and violent behaviour (Collins, 1982). This association has two aspects: first, there is an increased risk of violence in situations where people are drinking; second, people who drink heavily and habitually are more likely to behave in a violent manner. The link between alcohol and violence extends to acts of homicide. A survey reported by Shaw et al. (2006) highlighted the frequency with which alcohol and murder are connected. In addition to alcohol, there are associations between high levels of gambling and perpetration of violent acts, particularly those against family members (Afifi, Brownridge, MacMillan, & Sareen, 2010).

Shaw et al. surveyed 1,594 individuals convicted of homicide in England and Wales between 1996 and 1999. They gathered information from psychiatric records and court reports about the murderers, their alcohol and drug use, and the role of alcohol and drugs in the offence. Across the sample, 42 per cent of the convicted murderers had a history of alcohol misuse or dependence, and 40 per cent had a history of drug misuse or dependence. Shaw et al. also reported that alcohol or drug use, with cannabis the most common drug, was a contributory factor in 40 per cent of the cases. In addition, 17 per cent of the homicides were carried out by an individual with comorbid severe mental illness and substance misuse.

Varno, McCluskey, Patchin, and Bynum (2004) described two ways in which drug use and homicide may be associated from their analysis of homicides between 1999 and 2002 in Detroit. In the first instance there is what Varno et al. call *drug-motivated homicides*. The central characteristic of this type of homicide is that it revolves around the sale or use of drugs. The second type of homicide Varno et al. called *peripheral drug homicides*, in which drugs were present at the scene of the crime but were not the primary cause of the killing.

Shaw et al.'s (2006) national survey also provides details about the people involved in the homicide. As might be anticipated, 90 per cent of the perpetrators were male and their ages ranged from 10 to 77 years. Stabbing was the most frequent means of killing and close to half of the victims were young men aged between 18 and 35 years. Almost one-third of the perpetrators had killed a member of their family or a current or former partner, another third of the perpetrators had killed an acquaintance, and strangers were the next most common victims.

A similar general pattern was evident in a Finnish investigation of adolescents who commit homicide (Hagelstam & Häkkänen, 2006). In most cases, the victim was an acquaintance, most frequently killed with in knife in an argument or a robbery, and in the majority of cases the offender had been drinking at the time of the offence. As in many crimes, there is some overlap in the characteristics of homicide offenders and victims and in lifetime experiences of maltreatment (Broidy, Daday, Crandall, Sklar, & Jost, 2006; Dobash, Cavanagh, Smith, & Medina-Ariza, 2007).

Soothill, Francis, and Liu (2008) considered the relationship between homicide and other forms of serious crime. They looked at those individuals, of which there were 67,052, convicted for a serious crime (arson, blackmail, kidnapping, and threats to kill) in England and Wales between 1979 and 2001. Across the whole sample, there were 353 subsequent homicides after the conviction for a serious offence. This level of homicide is far in excess of that found across the general population, with the kidnappers showing the greatest level of risk of homicide after conviction for their index offence.

There are a number of juveniles convicted for homicide each year. Rodway et al. (2010) carried out a survey of those convicted for homicide in England and Wales between 1996 and 2004. They considered more than 4,000 homicide cases, of which 363 had been committed by juveniles aged 17 years and under: the majority (331 cases) of perpetrators were white males as were the majority of victims (306 males). The victims were mainly older than the perpetrators and in most cases victim and perpetrator knew each other, in only a small number of cases (35) a family member was killed. The most common means of inflicting death was through the use of a sharp instrument, followed by hitting and/or kicking, with firearms rarely used (12 cases). There was a small number of female perpetrators (32) who, compared with males, were more likely to kill a female or a family member, mostly their own child. Half of the perpetrators, more males than females, had a previous conviction, mainly for acquisitive offences, and one-fifth had a conviction for a violent offence.

The picture of a typical homicide that emerges from the literature is of a crime that commonly takes place between people who know each well or are, at least, reasonably well-acquainted. The situation is likely to be one in which an argument, perhaps accompanied by drinking or drug use, has taken place. It is also likely that the perpetrator will be a male although, of course, women also commit acts of homicide. A Swedish study reported by Yourstone, Lindhome, and Kristiansson (2008) compared 43 male and 43 female perpetrators of homicide. They found that both males and females shared troubled backgrounds in terms of their family life, education, and mental health. Further, males tended to have backgrounds characterised by criminal activity, while the females had experienced high levels of abuse, including sexual abuse. In terms of the offence, the females were more likely to have sought help before committing their crime and were also more likely to kill someone to whom they were closely related.

Multiple murder

Some murderers kill more than one person: these multiple murderers can be divided into three categories, based primarily on the time that elapses between killings (Gresswell & Hollin, 1994).

Mass murderers kill a number of people in a very short period of time. In 1984, the American mass murderer James Huberty shot and killed 21 people in a sustained act of violence lasting 77 minutes in a McDonald's restaurant in San Diego. In 1996, Thomas Hamilton walked into the town's primary school in Dunblane, Scotland, and opened fire in several classrooms killing 16 children and 1 teacher. In 1969, the mass murderer Charles Manson and his followers, known as 'The Family', broke into a house in California and killed several people, including the actress Sharon Tate (who was married to the film director Roman Polanski), with the aim of starting a counterrevolution. The horrific nature of the killings alongside the high public profile of Tate and Polanski ensured that the crime received maximum publicity with a steady stream of books and articles in the years that followed. Atchison and Heide (2010) present an overview of this episode from a sociological perspective.

Spree murderers also kill several people but over an extended period of time, typically hours, in several locations. In 1987, in the town of Hungerford, Berkshire, a heavily armed man, Michael Ryan, shot and killed his first victim just after midday. From that time until just before 7 that evening, when he shot himself in an act of suicide, Ryan had killed another 15 people, including his own mother. A feature of this episode was that Ryan walked around the town during the course of the day, killing people on the street, in their cars, while they were walking on the nearby town common, and in their homes and gardens. Several people were also shot and injured or managed to escape, although one further victim died later from shock.

As I was writing this book, in 2010, there was a similar incident that started in the town of Whitehaven in Cumbria. A local taxi driver, Derrick Bird, embarked on a shooting spree, travelling between several locations, in which he killed 12 people, including his twin brother, and injured 11 other people. After his spree, Bird drove to a secluded location and committed suicide.

Serial murderers can kill over a substantial period of time, stretching over years, rather than in a short or a sustained outburst as with mass and spree killers. A serial killer may terrorise a city, as seen with the Peter Sutcliffe, the 'Yorkshire Ripper' in Leeds, who murdered 13 women (attacking and injuring seven other women) over a 5-year period between 1975 and 1981, although it is possible that he had been active over a much longer period.

David Berkowitz, popularly known as 'Son of Sam', was a serial killer who killed six people and wounded several others in New York City in the 1970s. Kenneth Bianchi and Angelo Buono – collectively known as 'The Hillside Strangler' as the police and media initially thought there was one killer – abducted, tortured, sexually assaulted, and killed 10 women in Los Angeles, California between 1977 and 1978. The Bianchi case is notable for the role played by psychologists as expert witnesses at the trial (see Chapter 10). There have been other serial murderers, such as Ian Brady and Myra Hindley, and Fred and Rose West who, like Kenneth Bianchi and Angelo Buono, committed their crimes in pairs. Forensic history is littered with men and the occasional woman who became serial murderers (Gurian, 2011; Jenkins, 1988).

Vaughn, DeLisi, Beaver, and Howard (2009) analysed the criminal careers of 160 convicted murderers who had killed two or more people. They suggested that there were three classes of offender: (1) a low-offending group of 64 murderers with few previous offences; (2) 51 severe offenders who were the most violent and persistent criminals; and (3) 45 'moderate' offenders who were similar to the severe offenders but without the pronounced history of criminal activity.

It seems unlikely that there are large numbers of serial murderers at large at any one time. Nonetheless, doubtless because of the extreme and horrific nature of their actions, serial murderers attract a great deal of attention from both the media and academics. Some serial killers have become household names (see Box 6.2), while others have had popular books written about them, such as *Killing for Company* (Masters, 1985) about Dennis Nilsen who murdered at least 15 times, keeping the bodies of his mutilated lovers in his apartment before disposing of them in his garden. As well as films about fictional serial murderers – Hannibal Lecter has enjoyed a great deal of celluloid fame – there are films based on real serial murderers such as *Henry: Portrait of a Serial Killer*, which owed much to the American serial murderer Henry Lee Lucas who killed an unknown number of people (he was convicted of 11 murders and confessed to hundreds more).

Box 6.2 Some infamous serial murderers

Real Name	*Known As*
Beverley Allitt	Angel of Death
David Berkowitz	Son of Sam
Andrei Chikatilo	Rostov Ripper
Albert DeSalvo	Boston Strangler
John Wayne Gacy	Killer Clown
John George Haigh	Acid Bath Murderer
William Heirens	Lipstick Killer
Alexander Pichushkin	Chessboard Killer
Richard Ramirez	Night Stalker
Gary Ridgway	Green River Killer
John Edward Robinson	Cyber Sex Killer
Harold Shipman	Dr Death
Peter Sutcliffe	Yorkshire Ripper
Steve Wright	Suffolk Strangler
Graham Young	Teacup Poisoner

There are many, many internet sites that are given to the topic of serial murderers: serial murder knows no international boundaries and there are sites that give lists of murderers by country, or by number of victims, or by whether they were caught, along with as many details about the crimes as you can tolerate reading.

Why do the people, mainly men, who commit such extreme crimes attract such a level of interest? It is true that many forms of extreme behaviour, good as well as bad, will attract public attention but it is highly unusual for other types of criminal to be given such graphic monikers as serial murderers – although this does occasionally happen, as with the two juvenile delinquents nicknamed 'Rat Boy' and 'Spiderman' – and to hold such a position in popular culture. Why this level of fame exists is open to speculation but it seems that serial murderers have a special place in our more doubtful affections.

Sexual murder

In law there is no such crime as 'sexual murder', but it is the case that sex can be attached to murder (Beech, Fisher, & Ward, 2005; Carter & Hollin, 2010; Langevin, Ben-Aron, Wright, Marchese, & Handy, 1988; Proulx, Beauregard, Cusson, & Nicole, 2005). As pointed out by Häkknäen-Nyholm, Repo-Tiihonen, Lindberg, Salenius, and Weizmann-Henelius (2009) in their study of sexual homicide in Finland, there are variations across countries in the rates of sexual homicide.

Sexual murder can take place for several reasons: it may be the means by which a man takes revenge or seeks to redress their resentment against a specific women or even women in general. It may be that an attack that started as a sexual assault ends in the women's death because the man tries to silence the woman during the offence or as a way to try to avoid detection. Finally, the sexual murder may be the result of the man enacting their violent, even sadistic, fantasies (Maniglio, 2010).

As with other types of crime, most sexual murderers are men, often white men, in their 20s or 30s with childhood histories frequently characterised by physical (including sexual) abuse, social isolation, and a range of problems at home and at school. As adults they may have a string of criminal convictions and a history of contact with psychiatric services. At the time of the offence, the man is unlikely to have a relationship and is likely to be heavily using drugs or alcohol. The most frequent method of killing is strangulation, followed by stabbing and physical beating, with the use of firearms notably absent (Chan & Heide, 2008; Langevin et al., 1988).

Homicide followed by suicide

This form of murder, which often makes the news headlines, is often a tragedy in which a parent kills their children and then kills him or herself. The pioneering book in about this phenomenon, *Murder Followed by Suicide*, was written by Donald West, an academic psychiatrist at Cambridge University (West, 1965). Since the publication of West's book there have been more studies of this form of homicide, reviewed by Liem (2010), in Australia, several European counties, Hong Kong, Japan, and the USA.

As suicide is not a crime, the time span between the homicide and the suicide is not legally defined. As Liem notes, some studies use a time of 24 hours between the homicide and the suicide while other studies use days, weeks, or no specified time. The incidence of homicide-suicide varies from country to country: the rate is lowest in England and Wales (Flynn et al., 2009) and highest in Japan (Hata et al., 2001). These international differences may reflect behaviour in different cultures, or different crime recording practices, or varying rates of social change. Hata et al. suggest that the variations in homicide-suicide in different regions of Japan may be explained by the different rates of urbanisation across the Japanese nation.

Box 6.3 Homicide followed by suicide (after Liem, 2010)

Intimate partner: The most frequent form of homicide followed by suicide and mostly committed by men, sometimes suffering from depression, who kill their partner by shooting. The act may result from pathological jealousy if the partner is suspected of infidelity, or because of life stresses such as bankruptcy that threaten the family unit, or because of the partner's ill-health or terminal illness.

Child: The next most common form and may involve both men and women who may be clinically depressed. Women use less violent means of killing, such as poison or suffocation, while men typically use weapons. The child's death may be part of destroying the family unit or an act of revenge against an estranged partner.

Family: An unusual form in which the perpetrator, usually male, kills his partner and children, often also destroying family possessions and household pets. This act is often associated with financial problems where the man sees the family's future as ruined and beyond redemption.

Extrafamilial: This form is seen in acts such as school shootings, such as at Columbine, Colorado, where there may be several heavily armed perpetrators. The stimulus for the act can be 'payback' for some slight, real or imagined, against people such as teachers or mangers against whom the perpetrator holds a grudge.

Other types: The other types include suicide after killing a parent or sibling. While Liem's review does not include suicide bombing, perhaps because the homicide and suicide occur at the same instant, it is the case that this act does kill large numbers of people and result in the death of the perpetrator (see Gambetta, 2005).

The act of homicide followed by suicide can take several forms, as shown in Box 6.3.

As Liem, Postulart, and Nieuwbeerta (2009) point out, the evidence suggests that those who commit homicide-suicide cannot be taken to be similar to other perpetrators of homicide.

Infanticide

Infanticide refers to the murder of a child and can take several forms: *filicide* is when a parent kills their own child (Bourget, Grace, & Whitehurst, 2007; Liem & Koenraadt, 2008; Palermo, 2002), sometimes followed by suicide (Liem, de Veta, & Koenraadt, 2010); *neonaticide* is when a child is killed within the first 24 hours of its life (Beyer, McAuliffe, Joy, & Shelton, 2008; Spinelli, 2001; Stanton & Simpson, 2005); and *siblicide* is killing by biologically close relatives (Gebo, 2002), specifically *sororicide* is the killing of a sister and *fratricide* the killing of a brother. It is also the case that, in an act of *parricide* (Heide & Petee, 2007; Malmquist, 2010), children can kill their parents.

Brookman and Nolan (2006) make the point that infants under the age of 1 year are the group at the highest rate of homicide victimisation in England and Wales. They reviewed all the recorded cases of infanticide in England and Wales between 1995 and 2002: there were 298 such recorded cases during that period, although not all had been confirmed as homicide. Indeed, Brookman and Nolan point to the difficulties that may occur in establishing whether a very young child's death is a homicide. In particular, they point to sudden infant death syndrome (SIDS), an enigmatic diagnosis (Byard & Jensen, 2008) colloquially known as 'cot death', as a complicating factor in determining whether a young child's death is from natural or unnatural causes. A study of child abuse fatalities in France, reported by Tursz, Crost, Gerbouin-Rérolle, and Cook (2010), made the point that medical, court and investigative processes can lead to misclassifications of the cause of death. A study conducted by Töro, Fehér, Farkas, and Dunay (2010), looked at homicides against infants in the city of Budapest between 1960 and 2005. Töro et al. noted 363 cases – 193 male infants and 170 female infants – with suffocation the most frequent cause of death. Töro et al. also noted that the frequency of infant homicides fell sharply after the mid-1970s: they suggest that this fall is due to improved policy and practice within the primary care system.

Brookman and Nolan (2006) reported that more men than women committed homicides with their own child, rather than a step-child, as the victim. In the large majority of cases, the circumstances surrounding the case involved child abuse.

Flynn, Shaw, and Abel (2007) collected information on 112 people convicted in England and Wales of infant homicide between 1996 and 2001. They found that most perpetrators were the child's parents, typically in their mid-20s, and that men were more likely than women to kill their child. There were eight cases of neonaticide of which seven were carried out by young mothers aged from 14 to 25 years. About one-third of those who killed had been diagnosed as mentally ill, mainly with affective disorder and schizophrenia, before the crime; one-quarter were diagnosed with a mental illness, mainly depression, at the time of the offence. Flynn et al. reported that almost two-thirds of the perpetrators were convicted of manslaughter and that most of the sample received a custodial sentence.

Eldercide

As the mean age of the population in many Western countries creeps steadily upwards, so the murder of those at the upper end of the age range becomes proportionately more likely. The older members of society may be murder victims for several reasons (Krienert & Walsh,

2010). They may be frail or socially isolated, so that being the victim of a violent act that they would have survived when they were younger becomes fatal (Falzon & Davis, 1998). This type of death among older people is often seen in the context of another crime such as burglary when the criminal is disturbed and hits out in order to escape. It may also be the case that caring for the aging person becomes a personal and financial burden to the immediate family and they bring their elderly relative's life to a premature end.

While homicide is perhaps the most extreme type of violence, there are other much more common forms of violent behaviour. These violent acts can be grouped under the general heading of violent assault.

Violent assault

While the form that a violent assault may take – punching, kicking, sometimes with the use of a weapon – to inflict physical harm on another person is readily apparent, it is the context within which the violent behaviour occurs and who is assaulted by whom that is of interest.

Henderson (1986) reported an analysis of violent incidents described in interviews by 44 prison inmates serving sentences for assaultive behaviour including wounding, attempted murder, grievous bodily harm, and actual bodily harm. The content of the interviews was analysed to look at variables such as the victim's age and sex and the time and location where the incident occurred. A cluster analysis of the 246 violent incidents described by the interviewees revealed eight distinct types of incident. The violent men gave details of their personal involvement in several different types of violence that had taken place in a variety of settings involving a range of victims. There were four broad situational categories within which the violence occurred: (1) violence in conjunction with another crime; (2) family violence; (3) violence in a public place; and (4) violence in an institution.

Violence with another crime

There are two broad types of situation in which violence is connected with another crime. The first is where violence, or at least the threat of violence, is an integral and premeditated part of the crime. The second is where violence is not planned but arises as a crime takes place. The first of these situations is exemplified by the crime of robbery, the second is seen when a domestic burglary is interrupted by another person such as a resident.

Robbery

Walker, Flatley, Kershaw, and Moon (2009: 53) suggest: 'Robbery is an offence in which force or the threat of force is used either during or immediately prior to a theft or attempted theft. It covers a wide variety of different incidents such as bank robbery, mobile phone robbery and street robbery, regardless of the amount of money or property stolen'. The Home Office Counting Rules for Recorded Crime (Home Office, 2010), as shown in Box 6.4, separate robbery into two types.

The frequency of robbery, as with the counting of crimes generally (see Chapter 2), varies between the official figures and those found in crime surveys with the general public. Walker et al. (2009) note that in the year prior to the publication of their report, the police recorded 80,104 offences that were classified as robbery. Almost all of these robberies were of personal property, with the remainder being robberies of business property such as goods from a shop or money being transported between two locations.

Box 6.4   Home Office legal definition and counting rules for robbery (Home Office, 2010)

Legal definition of robbery: Theft Act 1968 Sec 8(1):
A person is guilty of robbery if he steals, and immediately before or at the time of doing so, and in order to do so, he uses force on any person or puts or seeks to put any person in fear of being then and there subjected to force.

Robbery of a business property
This crime is defined as a robbery in which the stolen goods belong to a business or other type of company (not by the location of the robbery).

Robbery/theft from the person
The use or threat of force in a theft from the person is robbery: if the victim or a bystander offers any resistance, or if anyone is assaulted, then this is taken to constitute force. When property is stolen with force from the victim's physical possession but the force is directed to the property not to the victim, as with a 'bag snatch', this is theft from the person not robbery.

The act of robbery from the person may take place in a number of locations, such as parks, public houses and subways, as well as on the street (where it is colloquially known as 'mugging'). As described by Bennett and Brookman (2010), street robbery may target a range of items with money being the obvious target, alongside bags, wallets, jewellery, watches, and mobile phones. The majority of those individuals who carry out street robberies are mainly young white men, given some variation according to geographical region, and most victims are also young white men.

There have been several descriptions and classifications of those who commit robbery. Conklin (1972) described three types of robber: (1) the *professional robber*, who makes their living from perhaps three or four robberies a year, most probably as a member of an organised team with crimes carefully planned in advance and targeted at a commercial business; (2) the *opportunist robber*, who acts spontaneously, stealing small amounts of property, when a vulnerable target is available; and (3) *addict* and *alcoholic robbers*, who steal to fund the purchase of drugs or drink, they target 'easy' victims and the robberies are unlikely to be planned or organised.

Porter (2010) makes the observation that some street robberies involve groups of assailants who are organised to the extent that they have their own structures and hierarchies. Porter (2010: 537) suggests that the focus of street robbery for these offenders is to maintain 'a "party" lifestyle involving excitement and hedonism, with minimal responsibilities or forward thinking'. The maintenance of such a lifestyle demands fast access to status symbols, such as jewellery and particular styles or makes of clothes, as well as a steady supply of money. It seems that patterns of robbery remain relatively constant from country to country (Ceccato & Oberwittler, 2008).

A large-scale robbery of a commercial property is the type of crime that is liable to reach the public's attention because of the level of violence used during the crime or the amount of money stolen (or both). Some robbers and their robberies have become famous: the Great Train Robbery in 1963, in which an estimated £2.6 million was stolen, gave rise to a steady flow of books, television programmes and films that made household names of some the criminals involved (see Box 6.5).

Box 6.5 The Great Train Robbery, 1963

The 1963 Great Train Robbery was an audacious crime in which a train carrying the Royal Mail from Glasgow to London was stopped in mid-journey by a gang of 15 robbers who had rigged a signal to stay on red. The robbers boarded the stationary train and forced the driver, who was hit with an iron bar during the raid, to take the train to another location where they had a vehicle waiting. The robbers removed more than 100 sacks of mail, netting £2.6 million in used bank-notes. After a large-scale police investigation, 12 of the robbers were caught within a relatively short period of time and later stood trial receiving long prison sentences. Several of the gang, such as Buster Edwards (the eponymous hero of the film *Buster*, in which he was played by Phil Collins), Bruce Reynolds, Ronnie Biggs (who, oddly, sang with the Sex Pistols post-Johnny Rotten), and Jimmy White, subsequently became well-known through a string of media articles, books and television programmes, as well as their prison escapes and subsequent contact with the media from other countries. In the years after the robbery, various members of the gang served further prison sentences for crimes committed after their release from custody; one of the gang, Charlie Wilson, met a violent death at the hands of other criminals; Buster Edwards, who after prison sold flowers outside Waterloo Railway Station, was found hanged and may have taken his own life; Ronnie Biggs escaped from prison and lived in Australia and Brazil before returning to England in 2001 an ill man. He was imprisoned on his return and in 2009 he was granted compassionate leave from prison and moved to a care home.

The majority of robberies are rather more mundane affairs than the Great Train Robbery, although they may still have a profound effect on the victims. As Matthews (2002: 91–2) notes: 'The level of personal injury sustained in commercial robberies is surprisingly low, while the degree of trauma suffered by victims can be extremely high and long lasting'. However, since the time of the Great Train Robbery, the targets for commercial robbery have changed: Hobbs (2010: 293) states: 'Before the criminal fraternity turned their attention fully to banks, post offices and building societies, robbery with violence in the form of wage snatches was a popular and startlingly simple way of accessing considerable sums of money'.

The move from wage snatches to robbing banks was brought about by many employers switching from paying their employees with cash to payment of wages using a bank transfer. The initial high rate of success of robberies on banks, post offices and building societies has been reduced by the increased use of increasingly sophisticated security measures such as closed circuit television (CCTV), alarm systems, heavily locked safes, and so on. (See Chapter 12 for discussion of crime prevention.)

When preventative measures make a target harder to offend against then criminal activity may be displaced to other, softer, targets, or the criminals may respond with harder measures to crack the harder targets. Hobbs notes that in response to improved security the target for robbery shifted, yet again, to the 'point of transfer' of large quantities of cash or valuables. The robbery in 1983 near Heathrow Airport, in which £26 million of gold bullion was taken from the Brinks-Mat depot, is an example of the targeting of the point of transfer.

The use of firearms during a robbery is one means by which criminals can change their methods in order to overcome harder targets. Hobbs (2010) suggests that in the 1960s *armed robbery* became a subculture with armed robbers among the elite of the criminal classes with extravagant lifestyles and a 'professional' status. The subculture surrounding robbery, particularly armed robbery, took on a fashionable meaning of its own to the point where it entered popular culture as seen with television programmes and films, such as *The Sweeney* and *The Italian Job*. Armed robbers mainly used their weapons, shotguns often being the weapon of choice, to intimidate rather than to inflict injury, although the weapons were sometimes used.

The passage of time has seen changes – Matthews (2002) writes of a *demise*, Hobbs (2010) speaks of a *decline* – in the execution of armed robberies. The response made by armed police, the emergence of the 'supergrass', and the impact of security technology has changed the face of armed robbery. Again, Hobbs (2010: 301–2) offers a succinct view, describing how armed robbery 'became haphazard, essentially amateur excursions ... performed with minimal planning, base levels of competence and, most importantly, no commitment to specialised criminality'. Professional criminals have moved on to the drug trade while armed robbery, now available to all given the ready accessibility of firearms, has fallen from the criminal professionalism seen in the Great Train Robbery, to the mundane and muddled robberies of shops, restaurants, and garages.

Theft

There are many forms of theft that do not directly involve violence but where there is a risk that violence may arise. A common example of this occurrence is when a burglar, perhaps in a highly anxious state or having been drinking, is caught in the act by a resident. The resident tries to apprehend the burglar and violence ensues. The burglar may be carrying a weapon (in which case the crime is aggravated burglary) and a fight takes place during which the resident may be seriously injured or, perhaps as seen more frequently with elderly people or those with a physical illness, fatally injured. The victim who fights back is also seen in other forms of crime such as mugging, car theft, and pickpocketing.

When the victim fights back, there is a debate as to how much force they can reasonably use to defend themselves and their property. There are occasional cases of people using guns to fight off burglars or chasing after them to deliver retribution. The issue hinges on the understanding of 'reasonable' and when reasonable become gratuitous: is it reasonable to struggle physically with a burglar, or to use a weapon, or to shoot them as they run away? The high profile case of Tony Martin, who in 1999 acted against intruders attempting to burgle his home, provides an example of the issues that can arise when an individual defends their property. With a pump-action shotgun, Martin shot and killed a 16-year-old man and seriously injured his 29-year-old accomplice as they attempted to burgle his property. The Martin case polarised public opinion with supporters and detractors of both his actions and his jail sentence for manslaughter.

Family violence

Violence within a family household can broadly be divided into three types (Tolan, Gorman-Smith, & Henry, 2006): (1) violence directed at an intimate partner; (2) violence involving children; and (3) violence aimed at elderly people. As discussed in Chapter 2, there are difficulties in knowing generally just how many crimes are committed in any given period. This point is particularly true when specifically considering crimes within the family. There are several reasons why families may present themselves as untroubled to the outside world while violence occurs regularly within the home. The recipient of the violent acts may fear reprisals if they speak out, or they may wish to avoid the police becoming involved, or fear the attention and possible social stigma that may result. Smith et al. (2010), reporting findings from *The British Crime Survey* (BCS), noted the reasons most often given for not reporting partner abuse to the police: these included the abuse being 'too trivial or not worth reporting to the police', or that was a 'private matter or family matter', or it was 'not police business'; even when it was reported they 'didn't think the police could help'. It is clear that family violence is an area in which the official statistics are particularly likely to be an underestimate of the true prevalence (Alhabib, Nur, & Jones, 2010). Indeed, the issue of domestic violence is one that has attracted attention across the members of the European Commission (2010).

Violence against a partner

Despite longstanding concern about this form of violence (e.g., Dutton, 1995), the lack of clarity that surrounds this type of violence is compounded by the many terms with which it is associated. Among the various terms used in the literature, Robinson (2010: 245) lists: 'Wife abuse, battered women, domestic violence, domestic abuse, spousal abuse, spousal assault, family violence, violence against women, intimate partner violence, gender-based violence'. Some of these terms have become outdated: for example, it is now judged entirely appropriate to include within this grouping partners who are not married and partners of the same sex alongside those who are married.

There is grave concern in many countries about the extent of intimate partner violence and its consequences (e.g., Alaggia, Regehr, & Rischchynski, 2009; Bartels, 2010; Edlin, Williams, & Williams, 2010; Ishida et al., 2010). In England and Wales, the extent of intimate partner abuse may be considered with reference to the findings of the BCS (Roe, 2010). The BCS data on intimate partner abuse, including details of any experience of emotional, financial, or physical abuse, sexual assault, and stalking, is gathered from adults aged from 16 to 59 years using self-reporting rather than interviews. The survey findings give an estimate of about one in four women and around one in six men who have experienced domestic abuse – defined as any emotional, financial, or physical abuse, sexual assault, or stalking by a partner or family member – since the age of 16 years. Roe states that if these figures are used to give a population estimate, then there are 4.5 million female and 2.6 million male victims of domestic abuse. Although often thought of in terms of male violence against women, there are female perpetrators of intimate partner violence (Carney, Buttell, & Dutton, 2006). The BCS found that almost one-third of the victims of partner abuse had been abused by more than one partner and women were more likely to have endured longer periods of partner abuse, repeat victimisation, physical injury and emotional damage. Despite the gravity and scale of this violence, only 16 per cent of victims had reported the abuse to the police in the previous 12 months.

The violent behaviour typically consists of punching and kicking, resulting in injuries such as black eyes, bruising, and scratches: the injuries may be more serious, as with teeth knocked out and broken bones, and in the most serious cases there is a homicide (Dobash, Dobash, & Cavanagh, 2009; Elisha, Idisis, Timor, & Addad, 2010; Reckdenwald & Parker, 2010). The emotional and psychological consequences of repeated physical abuse are likely to be seen in increased levels of fear and depression, social withdrawal, and taking time away from work. It is likely that the severity of the violence will escalate over time.

Acts of physical violence against pregnant women are of particular concern given the dangers to both the woman and the unborn child. Taillieu and Brownridge (2010) suggest that this form of violence against women, evident in many countries, is closely associated with physical abuse of the woman before the pregnancy. It may be that this particular form

Table 6.3 Triggers for intimate partner violence (after Krug et al., 2002)

Failing to obey
Arguing
Not looking after the home
Not looking after the children
Asking questions about money
Queries about other women
Going out without asking
Turning down sexual demands
Suspicions of infidelity

of violence against women is one manifestation of the wider issue of aggressively masculine men targeting women (Anderson & Anderson, 2008).

Dobash and Dobash (1984) described the dynamics of violence between intimate partners. Drawn from interviews with more than 100 women and from official records, Dobash and Dobash constructed a pattern to describe a typical incident. The episode, most often occurring in the family home, often began with a verbal confrontation between the man, who may be under the influence of drink or drugs (Kraanen, Scholing, & Emmelkamp, 2009), and the woman, typically about some aspect of her behaviour, or her failure to carry out some task, or her perceived challenge to the man's authority (see Table 6.3).

As events unfold, the woman, aware of what is potentially to come, may try to turn away from the confrontation by attempting to withdraw from the situation or by trying to talk things through. As the slapping, punching, and butting starts, the woman may continue to attempt to negotiate her way out of the situation. In only a few cases does the woman physically strike back, being aware that such an action may provoke an increased level of violence.

Dobash and Dobash note that there may be bystanders, often children, in the majority of assaults: witnessing assault within their family can have a profound effect upon the child. The bystanders may try to help the woman by pleading with the man to stop or by leaving to try to find someone to help. When the attack is over, the men were said to act as if nothing had happened, with only a few men expressing any remorse. The injured women sought contact with friends, social and medical agencies, or voluntary bodies for comfort and medical assistance. Dobash and Dobash make the point that when such contact is made, a condemnation of the violence is more supportive than implicitly blaming the woman by discussing how she might have caused the violence.

The perpetrators of intimate violence are a heterogeneous group: some perpetrators are violent only towards their partners but others are violent in other contexts and, indeed, commit a range of crimes. Klein and Tobin (2008) carried out a study of 342 men arrested in Massachusetts between 1995 and 2004 for domestic violence. They reported that more than half of the men had criminal records for crimes against the person, which included and extended beyond their intimate partners. Some men had committed serious acts of violence, with 10 per cent having been convicted for murder, armed robbery, or rape. In the 10 years after their arrest, almost three-quarters of the men were rearrested for a range of crimes, including domestic abuse. Studies concerned with the risk factors for continued partner abuse have highlighted a range of characteristics – ranging from number of children in the family, the quality of the relationship, previous violence, substance use, and poverty – which are associated with prolonged abuse, even after a prison sentence (Hilton, Harris, Rice, Houghton, & Eke, 2008; Hilton, Harris, Popham, & Lang, 2010; Tolan et al., 2006).

Physical child abuse

There are incidents of physical abuse of children, such as the 'Baby P' case in London (see Box 6.6), where there is absolutely no doubt that the child has suffered extreme physical harm. There are other cases where the child may be subject to prolonged periods of physical abuse that do not culminate in the child's death, and there is 'everyday' corporal punishment of children. There are no problems in agreeing that the extreme levels of physical harm, as in the Baby P case, are abusive and hence should be dealt with under law. However, the issue becomes cloudier and distinctly more heated when corporal punishment is under scrutiny.

The physical abuse of children is of two types: first, the direct use of physical force to injure the child; second, neglect in providing for the child's safety. Stith et al. (2009: 14) define child physical abuse as 'non-accidental injury (including bruises, welts, cuts, burns, broken bones, or other tissue damage) to the child inflicted by the parent or a caregiver in a parenting role'. While child neglect is 'a failure of a parent or a caregiver in a parenting role to provide adequate supervision, safety, medical care, education, or other necessities to the child' (Stith et al., 2009: 14).

There is nothing new about adults abusing children, physically or otherwise: as the notion of childhood as a discrete stage in one's life is a relatively recent notion, so too is the idea of protecting children from the hardships of the adult world (Cunningham, 2006). As Krug et al. (2002) note, the physical abuse of children is not restricted by international boundaries: they state that 'harsh physical punishment of children by their parents exists in significant amounts wherever it has been examined' (Kurg et al., 2002: 63).

If we first consider physical abuse then, as Frude (1989) notes, the classic contemporary paper describing the 'battered child syndrome' was written in 1962 (Kempe, Silverman, Steele, Droegemuller, & Silver, 1962), since when a great deal has been learned about the physical abuse of children. It is difficult to know exactly how many children are abused, physically or otherwise (Fallon et al., 2010) and, as may be anticipated, self-report produces higher estimates of abuse than official records (Smith, Ireland, Thornberry, & Elwyn, 2008). It is also the case that an individual child may suffer several forms of abuse. Finkelhor, Ormrod, and Turner (2009) use the term 'poly-victim' for those children who have a high level of victimisation in terms of both frequency and type of abuse.

What is certain, however, is that physical abuse damages the child, physically and psychologically, and when the abuse is severe it can be fatal. Further, children who are physically abused are at a greater risk of committing acts of violence, including intimate partner violence, in later life (Renner & Slack, 2006). It is hard to ascertain exactly how many children die as a result of physical abuse (Palusci, Wirtzb, & Covington, 2010). An American study by Klevens and Leeb (2010) looked at deaths reported to the National Violent Death Reporting System (NVDRS). The NVDRS provides detailed information

---

Box 6.6   The 'Baby P' case

The death of the 17-month-old child Peter Connelly (Baby P) in 2007 was a shocking and extreme example of physical child abuse. The post-mortem examination revealed that the infant had swallowed a tooth following a punch to his face: the child's other injuries included broken bones in his back and ribs, and the tips of his fingers had been sliced off and his nails pulled out. The child's mother and her boyfriend were found guilty in court of causing or allowing the child's death and they both received substantial custodial sentences.

about children and adults who meet violent deaths. Klevens and Leeb reported that between 2003 and 2006 there were 600 recorded child deaths that were considered to be due to child maltreatment: half of these deaths were of children under the age of 1 year, 59 per cent of all deaths were male children, 42 per cent of the children were white, 38 per cent black, and 18 per cent Hispanic. In two-thirds of cases where the child was aged 5 years or younger the fatality was classified as being caused by abusive head trauma, with other types of physical abuse the next most frequent cause of death. One in 10 deaths was a consequence of neglect. The child's father (or step-father or the mother's partner) was more likely than the mother to be seen as responsible for physical abuse; mothers were more likely to be judged to be responsible for neglect.

Moving from direct physical abuse to emotional abuse and neglect brings yet more uncertainty into the picture. How is emotional abuse defined? What is meant by the term 'neglect'? How can the incidence of this type of abuse be reliably measured?

Iwaniec (2006) describes six forms of emotional abuse as shown in Box 6.7.

It is impossible to know exactly how many children are subject to the various forms of abuse listed in Box 6.7. It is not surprising therefore that attempts to estimate the levels of neglect and emotional abuse have arrived at widely differing estimates. It is, however, possible to look at numbers of abused children (of all types) via various official records, such as the Child Protection Register. However, as with other forms of crime, there are various social and recording filters operating so that the official record is highly likely to be but a fraction of the true extent of the issue.

Corporal punishment

As with the death penalty, the question of whether it is right or wrong to use corporal punishment with children is guaranteed to raise strong opinions (see Benjet & Kazdin, 2003). A cursory internet search simply using the terms 'smacking' and 'spanking' will identify a multitude of sites where opinions are expressed in forcible terms. The arguments in favour of smacking are along the lines of 'it never did me any harm', 'parents not governments/ social workers/the politically correct should discipline their children as they see fit', 'it teaches respect', 'it creates a safer world', 'any fit parent knows the difference between smacking and child abuse', and 'it has been an accepted practice for hundreds of years'. There are also a range of arguments against smacking: these include the view that smacking

---

Box 6.7 Types of emotional abuse (after Iwaniec, 2006)

1. Spurning: Belittling, shaming, or ridiculing the child; rejecting or abandoning the child.
2. Terrorising: Putting the child in danger and fear, threatening the child or someone they care for.
3. Isolating: Restricting the child's social contacts and separating them from the rest of their family.
4. Exploiting/corrupting: Facilitating the development of anti-social attitudes and behaviours, including anti-social and criminal acts.
5. Denying emotional responsiveness: Ignoring the child and dismissing the child's wish for closeness and affection.
6. Mental health, medical and educational neglect: Failing to monitor and provide for the child's health and personal development.

is not an effective form of discipline, smacking teaches children that physical force is an acceptable way to impose your will on another person, smacking desensitises children to hitting, smacking causes psychological harm, and smacking contravenes the child's human rights (Douglas & Straus, 2007; Straus, 1994, 2005; Straus & Paschall, 2009). There is also the view that corporal punishment and physical abuse are not disconnected so that use of the former increases the likelihood of the latter (Garbarino, 1977).

In essence, the debate centres on two issues: first, is corporal punishment an effective means by which to encourage the child's development? and second, is corporal punishment morally defensible? The first question is an empirical question that, on inspection, raises a raft of complex research issues. How could it be definitively shown that corporal punishment acts to the advantage or the detriment of a child's long-term development? As Gershoff and Bitensky (2007: 234) state: 'How corporal punishment should foster children's long-term compliance or moral internalization is unclear from psychological theory and research'.

Gershoff (2002) conducted a meta-analysis of 88 studies of the effects of corporal punishment. One aspect of Gershoff's analysis considered the potential trade-off between the positive and negative effects of corporal punishment. It was found that corporal punishment did increase the child's immediate compliance with parental commands. However, the short- and longer-term effects of corporal punishment were pronounced. Gershoff (2002: 544) gives the following list of undesirable correlates of the use of corporal punishment: 'Decreased moral internalization, increased child aggression, increased child delinquent and antisocial behavior, decreased quality of relationship between parent and child, decreased child mental health, increased risk of being a victim of physical abuse, increased adult aggression, increased adult criminal and antisocial behavior, decreased adult mental health, and increased risk of abusing own child or spouse'.

As Gershoff notes, and as is emphasised by Baumrind, Larzelere, and Cowan (2002) in their comment on Gershoff's meta-analysis, demonstration of an association between corporal punishment and undesirable consequences for the child is not proof of causality. It may be that a third variable, say parental style or family dynamics, mediates the relationship between the administration of corporal punishment and its long-term effects on the child. Nonetheless, parental use of corporal punishment as a means of disciplining children remains widespread across a range of countries and cultures (Gershoff et al., 2010).

The question of whether corporal punishment is morally defensible is one that has been addressed in a large number of countries (Gershoff & Bitensky, 2007). Is it right, for whatever purpose, that parents, caregivers, or teachers inflict physical pain upon a child? This question has been addressed in legal terms with respect to international human rights law by the United Nations and the Council of Europe. The position shifts and changes, as monitored by organisations such as The Global Initiative to End All Corporal Punishment of Children (see 'Useful websites' at the end of this chapter), with a growing number of countries implementing legal bans of corporal punishment of children.

Violence in a public place

There are a number of public arenas in which acts of violence may be played out: these settings include schools, the workplace, public transport, sporting events, streets, and clubs and public houses. The violence may be between two individuals or it may involve groups of people, while those involved may be acquainted or strangers. The form taken by violence in public places is both varied and culturally dependent. This latter point is illustrated by a report from the US Department of Justice which records crimes in schools and colleges over a 5-year period (Noonan & Vavra, 2007). In recording the types of weapon used, Noonan and Vavra's report notes the not-uncommon use of handguns, shotguns, and explosives: annually there are about 400 recorded incidents of the use of a handgun in schools. In this light it is not surprising that, although uncommon, homicides (and suicides) occur consistently in American schools (Schonfeld, 2006). The situation in America contrasts markedly with the UK, where firearms in schools are a rarity: Smith et al. (2010) noted just 13 instances where firearms had been stolen, obtained, or handled dishonestly in schools.

Violence in the workplace may take a number of forms, ranging from physical assault to bullying and intimidation (Barling, Dupré, & Kelloway, 2009; LeBlanc & Barling, 2005). There are some professions, such as police and prison officers, where the risk of violence is heightened because of the context of the occupational tasks. In other instances, the risk of violence towards staff is increased because of the stressful nature of the environment, as with in wards in psychiatric hospitals and hospital accident and emergency departments (Ferns, 2007). Those individuals working in other settings where there are interactions with the public – such as shops, public houses, banks, and public transport – may also be at a higher risk of encountering violence.

Violence in institutions

The issues surrounding interpersonal violence in institutions have been highlighted by research looking at violence in prisons. The violence may be between fellow inmates or between staff and inmates and the violence can range from bullying and assault to grievous injury and death. The act of violence may be spontaneous, arising from exchanges between individuals or groups of individuals, or planned in advance. However, homicide in prisons is unusual: Cunningham, Sorensen, Vigen, and Woods (2010) note that the annual homicide rate in American prisons is on average four per 100,000 inmates. In England and Wales, the *Safety in Custody Statistics 2008/2009* (Ministry of Justice, 2010a) noted that there were no homicides committed in prison custody in 2009.

If homicide is rare in prisons, the prevalence of bullying between prisoners is at the opposite extreme (Connell & Farrington, 1996; Leddy & O'Connell, 2002). Bullying in prisons may take various forms, sometimes perpetrated by gangs (Wood, Moir, & James, 2009), ranging from intimidation and assault to sexual violence including rape (Struckman-Johnson & Struckman-Johnson, 2000, 2002). Alongside its physical and psychological effects, the consequences of bulling for any victim may include self-harm and suicide (Blaauw, Winkel, & Kerkhof, 2001).

Bullying is also prevalent in schools and there are other forms of violence to be found in and around the classroom (Schonfeld, 2006). There have been several national and international surveys of violence in schools that give figures for the incidence of violent, including sexually violent, acts (e.g., Moore, Jones, & Broadbent, 2008; Noonan & Vavra, 2007). School violence may take place between any combination of pupils, teachers, and parents: there are also occasions where schools have been the setting for atrocities such as that in Dunblane, Scotland, discussed above.

Other types of violence

Kidnapping

There are many reasons why people go missing, as many do: an Australian study by Henderson, Henderson, and Kiernan (2000) stated that 30,000 people are reported missing annually (the majority are located within 1 week) for reasons ranging from running away from home, peer pressure, and dementia. However, a small number of those people who go missing will have been taken against their will.

As described by Soothill, Francis, and Ackerley (2007), the criminal statistics for England and Wales group three offences under the rubric of kidnapping. There is the offence of kidnapping which Soothill et al. (2007: 70) note to be 'The taking away of one person by another, by force or fraud, without the consent of the person taken, and without lawful excuse'. There are two offences allied to kidnapping: first, false *imprisonment*, which is unlawfully to detain or restrain an individual's liberty; second, the rare offence of *hijacking*, which concerns behaviour on aircraft (and in the UK, Anglo-French Channel Tunnel trains) including taking control of an aircraft (or train), causing damage to or destroying an aircraft (or train), or endangering an aircraft's safety. In the UK, the crime of *child abduction* (see below) has its own classification within the category of violence against the person rather than kidnapping.

Kidnapping is not a common offence: the *Offender Management Caseload Statistics 2008* (Ministry of Justice, 2009) recorded 57 kidnappings/abductions that resulted in a conviction in 2007–8, falling to 21 in 2008–9. The *Caseload Statistics* note that in England and Wales in 2008 the number of people in prison was 98,820, of which 217 (208 men and 9 women) had been convicted of kidnapping.

Soothill et al. (2007) analysed the criminal histories, using official records, of the 7,042 males and 545 females who had been convicted for kidnapping between 1979 and 2001. Only a small number of kidnappers (10 men and 14 women) had more than one conviction for kidnapping. The kidnappers were on average aged in their mid-20s and more than half of the men and one-third of the women had previous convictions for other offences, mainly theft and violent offences. In contrast to the popular view of kidnapping for ransom, most kidnappings were conducted for sexual and violent purposes.

Child abduction

Newiss and Fairbrother (2004) analysed 798 police recorded instances of child abduction in England and Wales during 2002–3. They coded four types of child abduction – parental (23 per cent), stranger attempted (47 per cent), stranger successful (9 per cent), and other (22 per cent) – for which the children's average age was nine years and most children were male (56 per cent).

When compared with other types of child abduction, children who were subject to parental abduction were more likely to be from ethnic minority groups. Newiss and Fairbrother (2004: 2) suggest that this latter finding 'is closely associated with partners from different nationalities, races or cultural backgrounds disputing the custody of their children [however], the issue is complex and multifaceted, incorporating problems of domestic violence and abuse as well as concerns with cultural identity and ways of living'.

Erikson and Friendship (2002) used information from police records at New Scotland Yard to review the cases of 149 offenders convicted of child abduction between 1993 and 1995. The offenders were classified according to their relationship with the child and their motivation for taking the child. Erikson and Friendship identified four types of child abduction which they called *sexual* (60 per cent of cases), *custodial* (18 per cent), *maternal desire* (12 per cent), and *other* (10 per cent). The sexually motivated perpetrators were the only abductors with a history of child abduction and they had the most previous convictions, including convictions for sexual and violent offences. These particular child victims were predominately female and, with an average age of 10 years, the oldest of the four categories. All of the offenders in maternal desire group were female and unrelated to the child: these women were the youngest perpetrators and abducted the youngest children, Erikson and Friendship (2002: 119) suggest that these women appeared 'to be motivated by a need to fulfil a maternal role'. The offences associated with disputes over child custody were all family affairs involving disputes between estranged parents: there were more abductions by fathers than by mothers or other relatives. The final group contained child abductions conducted for religious motives, as with members of a religious sect, to stealing a car with children in the back seat.

Any abduction of a child is highly alarming for all those concerned, however those rare cases where the abducted child is sexually assaulted and then murdered generate huge levels of public concern. Heide, Beauregard, and Myers (2009) reviewed the literature relevant to this type of abduction, suggesting that this crime is typically committed by strangers to the child and their family. Unlike those offenders whose sexual murder involves an adult, the child abductors who kill are less likely to be under the influence of drugs or alcohol but are more likely to groom their victim and plan their offence. An American study reported Beasley et al. (2009) looked at 750 individuals who had abducted children: 311 offenders had abducted a child who was later found alive and 439 offenders had abducted a child who had either been murdered or was still missing but presumed dead. The majority of abductions were carried out by white males, with women responsible for 31 of the abductions where the child was found alive and 10 of the cases in which the child was murdered. Overall, three-quarters of the offenders had a prior arrest for a wide range of crimes including assault, larceny, burglary, breaking and entering, sex offences, drug offences, weapon law violations, motor vehicle theft, robbery, and kidnapping. Beasley et al. suggest that in some cases there was a progression from a continued involvement in sexual crimes to the abduction.

Stalking

Stalking is a generic term for a range of behaviours in the overall context of sexual harassment. The publication *Statistics on Women in the Criminal Justice System* (Ministry of Justice, 2010b: 21) describes stalking as 'obscene and/or threatening unwanted letters or phone calls, waiting or loitering around home or workplace, following or watching, or interfering with or damaging personal property by any person including a partner or family member'. An American study, reported by Baum, Catalano, Rand, and Rose (2009) considered stalking as encompassing a range of behaviour: thus, stalking consisted of making unwanted phone calls, sending unsolicited or unwanted letters or emails, following or spying on the victim, showing up at places without a legitimate reason, waiting at places for the victim, leaving unwanted items, presents or flowers, and posting information or spreading rumours about the victim on the internet, in a public place, or by word of mouth.

Those people, mainly women, who are the targets of these types of behaviour will experience distress and fear as well as disruption to their everyday routines and social life. There are substantial numbers of people who experience stalking: the findings on stalking from *The British Crime Survey* (BCS), as presented in the report from the Ministry of Justice (2010b), provide information on prevalence of stalking over the previous 12 months for men and women aged between 16 and 59 years. The prevalence rates are given as the proportion of respondents who experience stalking out of the population of England and Wales aged between 16 and 59. Thus, the 2006–7 BCS gave a proportion of 5.9 for women, followed by

4.4 in 2008–9; for men the corresponding figures were 4.2 and 2.8. A higher rate of stalking of women was also reported by Baum et al. (2009) who calculated that, over a 12-month period, an estimated 14 people per 1,000 of the population were victims of stalking.

Given these figures, there is increasing concern about stalking – Spitzberg (2002) reported that the incidence of stalking is increasing over time (which may be a result of growing awareness and willingness to report) – as seen in the surveys from the UK and the USA, as well as from several European countries (e.g., Dressing, Kuehner, & Gass, 2005; Stieger, Burger, & Schild, 2008).

The victims of stalking include those people with high public profiles, such as pop stars, royalty, and presidential candidates (James et al., 2009; Phillips, 2007), as well as members of the helping professions (Gentile, Asamen, Harmell, & Weathers, 2002; Kamphuis et al., 2005). Further, there are locations where there are large numbers of women, such as a university campus, which may be hot spots for stalking (Jordan, Wilcox, & Prichard, 2007; Kirkland, 2002). Those victims at greatest risk of violence are those for whom the stalking stretches over a long period of time, where the previous relationship was intimate in nature, and where the stalker has previous convictions for violent crimes (McEwan, Mullen, & Purcell, 2007).

There have been several meta-analyses of the literature on stalking. Spitzberg (2002) conducted a meta-analysis of 103 studies of stalking, giving a cumulative total of more than 70,000 people who had experienced stalking. The average prevalence rate of stalking across the studies was 23.5 per cent for women and 10.5 per cent for men, and more than 75 per cent of the stalking victims were women. The average duration of the stalking was close to 2 years. In three-quarters of cases, the stalking appeared after an acquaintanceship between the stalker and the victim, and in half of cases this had been a romantic relationship. In 42 studies, the mean incidence of physical violence was 33 per cent, while in 17 studies the mean incidence of sexual violence was 10 per cent. Rosenfeld (2004) found a very similar rate of violence to that reported by Spitzberg, and also noted that a previous intimate relationship between offender and victim was often a precursor to the stalking.

The role of a previous relationship in stalking was also emphasised by McEwan, Mullen, and MacKenzie (2009) in their study of the predictors of the persistence of stalking. The strong predictors of persistant stalking were a previous intimate relationship with the victim, being over the age of 30, sending unsolicited materials, and psychosis. Similarly, Meloy, Davis, and Lovett (2001) found that the risk of violence increased significantly when the stalker had had a previous sexually intimate relationship with the victim. It has been suggested that stalkers are not secure in their romantic relationships because of childhood difficulties in forming attachments (Patton, Nobles, & Fox, 2010).

Spitzberg and Cupach (2007) reported a meta-analysis of 175 studies of stalking. The familiar pattern emerged of women as the most frequent victims (from 60 to 80 per cent of victims were women) with each stalking episode lasting about 2 years. There was the use of threat in just over half of the cases, with about one-third of cases involving physical violence and about 1 in 10 involving sexual violence. In the majority of cases, the offender and victim knew each other and in half of the cases there had been a romantic relationship. Spitzberg and Cupach make the distinction between stalkers drawn from clinical and forensic samples and those drawn from surveys of the general population. The use of threat was much more likely to be found in the clinical and forensic samples.

There have been several attempts to provide typologies of stalkers (Mullen, Pathé, Purcell, & Stuart, 1999): a large-scale typology study, based on an analysis of more than 1,000 stalkers, was reported by Mohandie, Meloy, McGowan, and Williams (2006).

Mohandie et al. suggested a twofold typology based on a previous relationship with the victim and none or limited previous contact. The first type was subdivided into those cases where the relationship had been intimate, as in married, cohabiting or dating, and those cases where the relationship was as an acquaintance or work colleague. The second type was subdivided into cases where the victim was either a public figure or private figure. Mohandie et al. labelled these four categories *intimate, acquaintance, public figure*, and *private stranger*.

A minority of stalkers exhibit some form of psychiatric disorder, typically a delusional or personality disorder: these individuals are therefore subject to mental health law rather than criminal law (Pinals, 2007). The consensus is that the majority of stalkers are adult males, although some stalkers are young people (Purcell, Moller, Flower, & Mullen, 2009; Ravensberg & Miller, 2003) and others are women (Purcell, Pathé, & Mullen, 2001). As with their adult counterparts, most young stalkers are male and their victims mostly females: the stalking took the form of physical approaches, telephone calls, or text messaging, with frequent threats and some physical and sexual assaults. The context of adolescent stalking was often bullying, retaliation, or a reaction to being rejected. Female stalkers were more likely than male stalkers to select victims of the same sex, often with the specific aim of becoming intimate with their victim.

Weapons

The use of weapons in a violent exchange increases the likelihood of injury and death: Felson and Messner (1996) suggest that, compared with assaults without weapons, the likelihood of death is increased 40 times by the presence of firearms and four times by the presence of a knife. The presence of a weapon at the scene of a violent encounter can prime aggressive thoughts among those involved, precipitating the use of the weapon (Bartholow, Anderson, Carnagey, & Benjamin, 2005).

Brennan and Moore (2009) note that in both the USA and the UK, weapons are used in about one-quarter of all violent incidents. Why are weapons present at some violent situations and not others? In some instances, such as school shootings, the violent act is defined by the presence of a type of weapon (Wike & Fraser, 2009). In other situations, the offender purposefully brings the weapon: the premeditated use of a weapon is typically for instrumental reasons. Thus, a weapon may be carried for protection in case of personal attack or bullying, or to threaten, coerce, and intimidate other people as well as in, say, a robbery or drug dealing, or with the intention of inflicting harm on another person. Weapons may also be carried as symbols of power or, perhaps particularly by younger people, to signal peer group membership, status, and attractiveness to the opposite sex (Barlas & Egan, 2006; Hallsworth & Silverstone, 2009; McClusky, McClusky, & Bynum, 2006).

Violence to animals

There is a body of research that compares aggressive acts perpetrated by humans and by animals in order to understand more about the concept of aggression (Lederhendler, 2003). However, there is another body of research that is concerned with the use of violence against both animals and people. As a species, we humans are not the kindest of creatures when it comes to relations with our fellow animals: we hunt for pleasure, we exploit animals as a resource, and we destroy the habitats of many unfortunate creatures. At a less global level, we are capable of extreme acts of cruelty to the domesticated animals with which we share our everyday lives. Given our propensity to cruelty to animals as well as to members of our own species, a number of researchers have considered whether there are any associations between an individual's mistreatment of people and animals.

In their review of the literature, Peterson and Farrington (2007) make the point that cruelty to animals is frequently noted as a feature of the childhood histories of violent offenders. Further, Peterson and Farrington note that claims have been made by bodies, such as the National Society for the Prevention of Cruelty to Children (NSPCC) and the Royal Society for the Prevention of Cruelty to Animals (RSPCA), that cruelty to animals is associated with several forms of abuse of people, including child abuse. While it is undoubtedly the case that many people abuse animals, it is less certain that such people will graduate to be violent towards other people. The nature of the psychological features and processes that may link cruelty to animals and violence towards people also remain uncertain (McPhedran, 2009; Tallichet & Hensley, 2009). As Peterson and Farrington (2007: 35) state: 'It is unclear whether a specific theory of animal cruelty is needed, or whether animal cruelty is merely one symptom of a more general underlying antisocial personality'.

Theories of violence

There are several different emphases prevalent in the literature relevant to understanding violence. These theories move from those primarily concerned with the individual, to those that stress social interaction, and finally those that advance complex multimodal models of violence.

In Chapter 3, the use of longitudinal designs to investigate a range of influences associated with the development of anti-social and criminal behaviour was discussed. The longitudinal studies identified a range of individual and social variables associated with the onset of anti-social and criminal behaviour and with typical patterns of an individual's involvement in crime over their lifetime. In particular, Moffitt's work identifying adolescent-limited and life-course persistent offenders has had a significant influence on the development of theory and the explanatory weight accorded to neuropsychological factors.

There is a history of using longitudinal studies to look specifically at the development of violent behaviour (e.g., Farrington, 1989; Loeber & Farrington, 1998). Huesmann, Dubow, and Boxer (2009: 136) make the observation: 'One of the most consistent findings in aggression and criminology research is that aggression is a relatively 'stable,' self-perpetuating behavior that begins early in life'. McAuliffe, Hubbard, Rubin, Morrow, and Dearing (2006) found evidence for the stability over time of both reactive and proactive aggressive behaviour. As described previously, reactive aggression is a response to a real or perceived threat typically involving high levels of unregulated emotional arousal and impulsivity; proactive aggression is more regulated, premeditated, and carried out for instrumental purposes in anticipation of a positive outcome. The distinction between these two types of aggression is important given that proactive aggression is associated with other problems such as drug use (Fite, Colder, & Lochman, 2007) and a high need to control other people (Winstok, 2009).

In their longitudinal study, based on data from Columbia County, USA, Huesmann et al. (2009) looked at the continuity of physical aggression for males and females, as measured through peer reports of mildly aggressive acts such as pushing and shoving and self-reports of more serious acts such as punching, kicking, and use of weapons. They found a moderate degree of continuity of aggression from childhood (8 years of age) to middle adulthood (48 years), which was more pronounced for males than for females. In keeping with the findings on anti-social behaviour generally, the life-course persistent individuals who were aggressive across the span of the study had worse outcomes, both socially and in terms of criminal conduct, than those individuals who fell into the adolescent-limited category. There was also a 'late-onset' group of a small number of people who (unlike the other groups) were mostly females and became *more* aggressive after 30 years of age. In later life, these late-onset individuals were characterized by depression, excessive drinking, and poor physical health.

A 30-year Canadian longitudinal study, reported by Temcheff et al. (2008), also looked at violence within the family across the lifespan, both male and female, from school age into early adulthood (low 30s). Males who showed childhood aggression progressed from aggression towards peers during time at school to later violence towards partners and children. For those females who became mothers, their level of childhood aggression was predictive of violence towards their own children. The predictors of violent behaviour included low levels of educational attainment and a punitive parenting style but not family income. The continuity of violence through families has been an issue that theorists and researchers have grappled with since Widom's (1989) seminal review. A study reported by Kokko, Pulkkinen, Huesmann, Dubow, and Boxer (2009), compared longitudinal data from Finland and Columbia, USA, and also found that, for males and females in both countries, childhood aggression was significantly associated with physical aggression and low self-control of anger in adulthood.

The role of biological factors in understanding criminal behaviour in general was discussed in Chapter 2, while in Chapter 3 the role of early neuropsychological dysfunction was seen in the context of in life-course persistent offending. There are parallel research literatures concerned specifically with violent behaviour, sometimes specified as extremely violent acts: as in Chapter 2, biological factors provide a starting point.

Biologically based theory

The literature, looked at from a historical perspective, is wide and extremely varied: a range of biological functions have been associated with violent behaviour including genetic syndromes such as the XYY syndrome (Sandberg, Koepf, Ishiara, & Hauschka, 1961; Witkin et al., 1976), EEG (Hill & Pond, 1952; Williams, 1969), brain tumours (Kletschka, 1966), neuropsychological functioning (Golden, Jackson, Peterson-Rhone, & Gontkovsky,1996; Séguin, Phil, Harden, Tremblay, & Boulerice, 1995), and minimal brain damage (Monroe, 1978). There are several methodological issues with the early work in this area, such as the use of highly selected samples and the methods used in the assessment and measurement of biological functioning. Nonetheless, as the sophistication of the technology has increased, alongside a perceptible shift within mainstream psychology towards biology and neuroscience, so research concerned with biological factors and anti-social and criminal behaviour has grown more sophisticated with a concomitant influence on theory.

In his review of biosocial studies of violent behaviour, Raine (2002: 311) lists studies 'from the areas of genetics, psychophysiology, obstetrics, brain imaging, neuropsychology, neurology, hormones, neurotransmitters, and environmental toxins'. Raine's use of the term *biosocial* highlights the need to consider the role of biological factors within a social context. There are interactions between biological functioning and the many facets of the social environment and it is the nature of these interactions which is critical in understanding behaviour (Mendes, Mari, Singer, Barros, & Mello, 2009).

Genetics

As with criminal behaviour generally, there is a body of evidence showing that violent behaviour crosses generations of the same family (Putkonen, Ryynänen, Eronen, &

Tiihonen, 2007). There is also the associated longstanding view that this generational effect is underpinned by genetic factors, perhaps accounting for 50 per cent of the variance, to the family transmission of violent behaviour (Miles & Carey, 1997; Rhee & Waldman, 2002). Indeed, a genetic basis to conduct disorder that then unfolds over time to become aggressive behaviour is a likely sequence of events (Burt, 2009; Dodge, 2009).

The point has also been made that the role of genetic and environmental factors may be different for according to the type of aggression (Yeh, Coccaro, & Jacobson, 2010). In this light, Craig and Halton (2009) offer a review of the evidence, which they begin by separating out two familiar types of aggression. The first type is *instrumental* or *proactive* aggression, which is often described as acts of aggression that are calculated and premeditated; the second type is *reactive* aggression, which is when the aggression arises within a given situation, typically from a perceived threat, and is associated with an uncontrolled emotional state. Craig and Halton argue that aggression, in both forms, has evolved over eons and may have gender-specific functions that are advantageous to the species: for females aggression can be used to protect offspring against threats, for males high aggression may allow access to a range of resources. Baker, Raine, Liu, and Jacobson (2008) have provided evidence in support of gender-specific differential genetic influences on proactive and reactive aggression.

A twin study reported by Tuvblad, Raine, Zheng, and Baker (2009) was concerned with variations in the development of reactive and proactive aggression. They used parental ratings of the two forms of aggression in order to estimate the genetic and environmental contributions to the stability and changes in aggression between childhood, taken as 9 to 10 years, and early adolescence, taken as 11 to 14 years. Across the sample, the parents' rating of reactive aggression ratings decreased over time while ratings for proactive aggression remained stable: the individual differences in the two forms of aggression remained stable. The analysis showed variations between the two types of aggression with respect to genetic and non-shared influences on their patterns over time, leading Tuvblad et al. to suggest that reactive and proactive aggression have different aetiologies that become more pronounced with age.

Craig and Halton (2009) describe the candidates for the specific genes involved in aggression and the pathways by which they influence behaviour. The association between being male and aggressive behaviour obviously brings biological characteristics associated with males, such as the Y chromosome and testosterone, into the equation. Craig and Halton describe several biological systems potentially associated with aggression: these systems include the hypothalamus and the pituitary and adrenal axis, which is involved in emotional regulation; the links between the neurotransmitter serotonin and glucose and alcohol in the pathway to violent behaviour; and the monoamine oxidases MAOA and MAOB, which are partially responsible for metabolising neurotransmitters. Ferguson and Beaver (2009) note that in addition to MOAO, there are several genes associated with anti-social and criminal behaviour, including violent behaviour. These genes are associated with the neurotransmitter functioning, including the neurotransmitters dopamine and serotonin, although the evidence is not unequivocal (Booij et al., 2010).

Ferguson (2010) reported a meta-analysis, drawing on the findings of 38 studies published between 1996 and 2006, examining the genetic contribution to 'anti-social behaviour and personality' (ABP). This analysis used a wide-ranging definition of ABP that included both the individual differences associated with anti-social behaviour and the anti-social behaviour that included but was not restricted to acts of aggression. Ferguson reported that more than half of the variation in ABP can be accounted for through genetic influences.

Ferguson also raises the issue of how the influence of genes on behaviour, including violent behaviour, is to be understood, contrasting behavioural genetics and evolutionary perspectives (see Buss & Shackleford, 1997; Gottschalk & Ellis, 2009). Ferguson (2010: 163) suggests: 'Arguably, behavioral geneticists prefer to focus on proximate explanations for behavior (i.e. specific genes), whereas evolutionary psychologists look at ultimate causes of behavior (i.e., natural selection)'. Although, as Ferguson continues, there is good reason to consider that the long view of evolution may enhance the immediate concerns of behavioural genetics.

The fast pace of progress in understanding the physical and functional aspect of human genetic functioning, as exemplified by the Human Genome Project, make it likely that this aspect of understanding crime generally and violent behaviour specifically is one in which knowledge and understanding will grow exponentially in years to come.

Brain anatomy

The advent of the brain imaging techniques functional magnetic resonance imaging (fMRI) and positron emission tomography (PET) gave rise to studies concerned with brain anatomy in violent offenders. Raine, Stoddard, Bihrle, and Buchsbaum (1998), for example, used PET with a sample of murderers: they reported that, compared with controls, some murderers showed reduced prefrontal functioning. A Finnish study reported by Tiihonen et al. (2010) collated data gathered using magnetic resonance techniques to look at the brain anatomy of male persistent violent offenders. They found that compared with a sample of healthy men the violent men 'present markedly abnormal white and grey matter regional brain volumes ... substantially larger regional volumes in the posterior brain areas were observed among violent offenders with a history of antisocial behavior going back to childhood' (Tiihonen et al., 2010: 210).

DeLisi, Umphress, and Vaughn (2009) suggest that the functioning of the amygdala, a part of the limbic system active in emotion, may be involved in anti-social behaviour. As the amygdala plays a role in learning associated with aversive stimuli, such as aversive conditioning, and in the regulation of fearful emotions, it may have an explanatory role in criminal behaviour. While DeLisi et al. suggest that the processing of emotionally laden stimuli may play a role in anti-social behaviour generally, their main concern is specifically with psychopathy and so will be returned to in Chapter 8.

Siegel and Victoroff (2009) consider two types of aggressive behaviour, which they call *defensive rage* and *predatory attack*, which are seen in many species of animals, including humans. Defensive rage, as the name suggests, is a response to an attack and is impulsive in nature; predatory attack is triggered by the presence of prey and may involve planning and the use of strategy. Siegel and Victoroff note that there is evidence to suggest that in humans the limbic structures and the hypothalamus are involved in aggression. The neurological functioning of the limbic system and the hypothalamus relies on a complex neurochemistry to operate as an integrated system (Siegel, 2005; Siever, 2008).

Brain injury and dysfunction

The anatomy of the brain can, of course, be affected by traumatic injury. The typical causes of traumatic brain injury (TBI) are through accidents (motorcycle injuries are a prime example) or through physical or pharmacological abuse. Twardosz and Lutzker (2010) consider the complex interplay between the development of the brain from an early age, child maltreatment, and subsequent behavioural and mental health problems. While physical mal-treatment is an obvious cause of damage to the child's brain, Twardosz and Lutzker argue that abuse and neglect may lead the brain to develop in a way that in later life brings about a heightened awareness of threat. This awareness and sensitivity to threat is then implicated in later psychological and social development.

Slaughter, Fann, and Edhe (2003) looked at the presence of TBI in a sample of 69 offend-ers held in the county jail in Tacoma, USA. Slaughter et al. used neuropsychological tests and structured psychiatric diagnostic interviews to screen for TBI. They found evidence for TBI in 60 of the offenders with a further 25 reporting TBI within the previous year. The offenders with recently acquired injury scored significantly lower on assessments of anger and aggression than the other offenders and they showed a higher prevalence of psychiatric disorders than the offenders with no TBI.

Another study of the prevalence of TBI in offender populations was reported by Perron and Howard (2008) with a sample of 720 male and female young offenders drawn from rehabilitation facilities in Missouri, USA. The findings, based mainly on archival and inter-view data, showed that close to 20 per cent of the young offenders reported a TBI. The strong predictors of TBI were being male and frequency of previous victimisation involving interpersonal violence.

As well as TBI, brain dysfunction can be brought about by conditions such as epilepsy and tumours. Siegel and Victoroff (2009) list a string of studies that have indicated that temporal lobe epilepsy and dysfunction of the hypothalamus are implicated in human aggression.

As noted above, a genetic predisposition to aggressive behaviour must act through a biological pathway, so this must also be the case for those areas of the brain, such as the temporal lobe and limbic systems, associated with aggression. The neurological correlates of aggressive behaviour include the neurotransmitters dopamine and serotonin (Booij et al., 2010; Ferguson & Beaver, 2009).

With an emphasis on homicidal violence, Fabian (2010) also noted the range of ways in which violence is classified in the literature and how these classifications can be applied to produce different accounts of homicidal violence. Fabian remarks on the evidence regarding the role of the limbic system and the temporal lobes, alongside brain dysfunction and neuropsychological impairment, and its role in understanding violent behaviour.

Physical size

The discussion of constitutional theory in Chapter 3 looked at the associated between body build, personality, and criminal behaviour. There is a body of research to indicate an asso-ciation between heavy weight at birth and later conduct problems and criminal behaviour (e.g., Moffitt, Caspi, Dickson, Silva, & Stanton, 1996). A Finnish study in this tradition with a focus on violent offending was reported by Ikäheimo et al. (2007). This study used data from a birth cohort study in which more than 5,500 males were followed up from birth to age 31 years with regular measurements of body size. Ikäheimo et al. found that the measure-ment at the very early age of 12 months of a high body mass index (BMI), calculated from height and weight, and a small head circumference were both associated with an increased risk of violent behaviour as measured by having a conviction for a violent offence. Neither BMI nor head circumference was associated with committing a non-violent crime. Ikäheimo et al. (2007: 849) conclude: 'Because measures of body mass at 12 months were stronger predictors of later violent behaviour than BMI at age 14, this association is more likely explained by genetic and early environmental factors, than by social learning'. This conclusion stands in contrast with Sheldon's constitutional theory and with social processes such as stereotyping (see Chapter 3).

Summary

Since the 1990s, there has been increasing interest from researchers in the role of biological factors in crime generally and violent crime specifically. This burgeoning interest has quickly produced a diffuse empirical literature exploring a wide range of variables across a range of populations. This rapid expansion in knowledge brings its own issues in attempting to make sense of the evidence. As is often the case with new areas of research, the emerging literature encompasses a variety of populations (e.g., offenders, people with personality disorders and those with brain injury), research design of different complexity (e.g., cross-sectional and longitudinal designs), different technologies (e.g., type of brain scan), and differing theoretical assumptions (e.g., behavioural genetics and evolution). This jumble of issues is typical of a new field of enquiry as it begins to focus on the most pertinent research questions and align its methodologies.

Psychologically based theories

The distinction between different theoretical approaches is not always clear cut, a point that is exemplified by the longstanding notion that some behaviours can be explained as instinctual.

Instincts

The idea that some patterns of behaviour are the result of an innate instinctual drive has a long history in evolutionary biology when used in reference to animal behaviours such as mothering, territoriality, courtship and mating, migration, and aggression. Within this frame of reference, instinctual behaviours are actions, probably selected over time, driven by a strong innate component. The most celebrated researchers in this field are perhaps the joint Nobel Prize winners Konrad Lorenz (1903–89), Nikolaas Tinbergen (1907–88), and Karl von Frisch (1886–1982), widely regarded as the founders of the discipline of ethology. In his book *On Aggression*, Lorenz (1966) proposed that aggression is the result of a 'fighting instinct' that has evolved as it has benefits for the survival of the species, including the species *Homo sapiens*.

The idea of an instinct as a force that drives behaviour from within was used by Freud in his proposition that human behaviour is driven by two basic instincts, the life instinct and the death instinct. Freud called the life instinct *Eros*, while the death instinct was later called *Thanatos*. Storr (1989: 67) explains that 'Freud considered that aggression was derived from the death instinct being redirected towards the external world'. Following Freud, psychologists freely used the concept of an instinct or a drive as a means by which to explain behaviour. It was not until the mid-1950s that the American scholar Frank Ambrose Beach (1911–88) argued that more sophisticated analysis would make redundant the concept of an instinct as an explanation for behaviour (Beach, 1955).

Drive theory

Dollard, Doob, Miller, Mowrer, and Sears (1939) presented an account of aggression, known as the *frustration-aggression hypothesis*, which incorporated elements from psychoanalytic theory and early behavioural psychology. In essence, the theory suggests that through learning we come to anticipate that certain behaviours will produce certain rewarding outcomes. At a given time, gaining that reward may be a goal, however, if our way to achieving that goal is blocked by some external agency and the expected reward is not forthcoming then we become frustrated. The internal state of frustration instigates a state of aggression, so leading to aggressive or violent behaviour that may be directed at either the perceived source of the frustration, or alternatively at other targets that are seen as having a relationship with the primary source of the frustration.

The idea that a drive towards a given goal could be acquired through experience takes the focus away from purely innate causes of behaviour. The research generated by the frustration-aggression hypothesis led to reformulations of the theory (Berkowitz, 1965; Miller, 1941). Thus, in contrast to the original theory, Berkowitz (1965) suggested that frustration acts to produce a state of emotional arousal, which in turn creates the potential for aggressive behaviour. As Berkowitz (1993: 20) explains, in this context the term *anger* is used to refer to a set of feelings triggered by an anger-eliciting cue or stimulus: 'These feelings stem in large part from the internal physiological reactions and involuntary emotional expressions produced by the unpleasant occurrence [and] are probably also affected by the thoughts and memories that arise at the time'. As Berkowitz makes plain, aggression can occur with or without anger, hence the longstanding dichotomy of emotional or angry aggression versus goal-directed or instrumental aggression. The environmental cues that precipitate the angry arousal may be the words and actions of other people or adverse environmental conditions. The advances in the understanding of the role of anger that followed Berkowitz's emphasis on the affective aspects of aggressive behaviour are discussed below.

The revisions of the frustration-aggression hypothesis suggest that for the individual concerned the cues present during the unpleasant incident become associated with both the event and its cognitive and emotional consequences. However, as psychological theory advanced so there was a continued movement away from instincts and drives as other theoretical perspectives came into play.

Personality

As with crime generally, personality theorists have addressed violent behaviour generally and, more specifically, through understanding the interplay between personality disorder and violence. The subject of personality disorder is addressed in Chapter 8.

Undercontrol and overcontrol

Megargee (1966) suggested that violence occurs when the level of provocation to violence exceeds the individual's level of control of their aggressive feelings. The *undercontrolled* individual has low levels of inhibition and when provoked they are quick to become angry and to act in a violent manner. The *overcontrolled* person has extremely high levels of inhibition and it takes intense or prolonged provocation to stir them to violence (Davey, Day, & Howells, 2005). Thus, the undercontrolled individual is involved in many relatively minor skirmishes while the overcontrolled individual explodes infrequently into acts of extreme violence. There is some support for Megargee's theory, although mainly from research conducted with samples drawn from secure psychiatric provision (Blackburn, 1968; Henderson, 1983a; Quinsey, Maguire, & Varney, 1983).

Another approach within personality theory looks for types or clusters of offenders according to their scores on various measures of personality. This line of research is exemplified by studies using the Minnesota Multiphasic Personality Inventory (MMPI).

MMPI

Originally devised more than half a century ago (Hathaway & McKinley, 1940), the MMPI consists of several scales, including *psychoticism*, *dominance*, and *hostility*, and has been widely used in psychological research. Blackburn (1971) conducted a cluster analysis of MMPI scores from 56 male murderers detained in a secure psychiatric hospital. There were four clusters of violent offenders, grouped under the two classifications of *undercontrolled* and *overcontrolled*. The undercontrolled group contained a *psychopathic* cluster, characterised by poor impulse control, high extraversion, outward-directed hostility, low anxiety and few psychiatric symptoms; and a p*aranoid-aggressive* cluster also with high impulsivity and aggression, but with high levels of psychiatric, particularly psychotic, symptoms. These two groupings are referred to as *primary psychopaths* and *secondary psychopaths*. The overcontrolled group contained a *controlled-repressor* cluster, marked by a high degree of impulse control and defensiveness and low levels of hostility, anxiety, and psychiatric symptoms; and a *depressed-inhibited* cluster characterised by low levels of impulsivity and extraversion, inward-directed hostility, and high levels of depression.

A number of subsequent studies have replicated Blackburn's original finding with psychiatric patients in secure conditions (Blackburn, 1975, 1986) and with violent offenders serving prison sentences (Henderson, 1982; McGurk, 1978). Studies with non-violent prisoners have found rather similar personality clusters (Henderson, 1983b; Holland & Holt, 1975; McGurk & McGurk, 1979; Widom, 1978). It may be that the four personality clusters are characteristic of offender populations generally, rather than violent offenders exclusively. The research with mainstream violent offenders based on personality theory has rather faded away, although without quite disappearing (Chambers, 2010), as social learning theory came to prominence. Nonetheless, as will be seen in Chapter 8, this approach has continued strongly in the field of personality disorder and offending.

Social learning theory

Social learning theory seeks to incorporate social and cognitive variables to understand behaviour: this approach is analogous to a social-cognitive view of aggression (Anderson & Huesmann, 2003). The starting point for social learning theory is that aggressive behaviour, for males and females, is no different to any other behaviour in terms of its aetiology and functioning (Snethen & Van Puymbroeck, 2008). Thus, there are there are three phases to consider: (1) the origins of the individual's *acquisition* of the aggressive behaviour; (2) the *instigation* of a given episode of aggressive behaviour; and (3) the conditions that *regulate* aggression (Bandura, 1968, 1973).

Acquisition

As discussed in Chapter 3, social learning theory fuses principles from operant learning with aspects of cognitive psychology. One of the consequences of this theoretical development was the view that behaviour could be acquired through observing other people as well as by the established means of reinforcement. The classic 'Bobo doll study' showed that young children will imitate the actions of models they observe behaving in an aggressive manner towards an inflatable doll (Bandura, Ross, & Ross, 1961). Thus, the acquisition of aggressive behaviour, like any other behaviour, is the outcome of a combination of observational learning and direct reinforcement. The real-life models for aggression may be people behaving aggressively who are seen personally, or models observed symbolically as on television or computer games.

Instigation

The instigation of an episode of aggressive behaviour relies on several factors. There are certain background environmental conditions, such as a high temperature (Anderson, 2001; Bushman, Wang, & Anderson, 2005), which are related to an increased likelihood of aggression. Indeed, it appears that just the mention of words related to hot temperatures can increase the likelihood of aggressive thoughts (DeWall & Bushman, 2009). Given the ubiquity of the temperature of any environment so, as Anderson (2001) points out, as the planet becomes hotter it may be expected that increased levels of violence will be one of the negative social consequences of global warming. There are other environmental conditions, such as lunar cycles, that are popularly seen as having an association with violence but for which the empirical evidence is not forthcoming (Biermann et al., 2009; Schafer, Varano, Jarvis, & Cancino, 2010).

How does environmental temperature increase the likelihood of aggression? As Anderson explains, incidents of heat-related aggression:

> Result from distortion of the social interaction process in a hostile direction. Heat-induced discomfort makes people cranky. It increases hostile affect (e.g., feelings of anger), which in turn primes aggressive thoughts, attitudes, preparatory behaviors (e.g., fist clenching), and behavioral scripts (such as 'retaliation' scripts). A minor provocation can quickly escalate, especially if both participants are affectively and cognitively primed for hostility by their heightened level of discomfort. A mild insult is more likely to provoke a severe insult in response when people are hot than when they are more comfortable.
>
> (Anderson, 2001: 36)

Anderson's comments about the effects of temperature raises two related issues: first, the importance of environmental factors in understanding acts of aggression; second, the need to consider a social dimension in acts of interpersonal violence.

There are other environmental factors, such as crowding and poor air quality, associated with violence. It is not difficult to think of real-life examples of instances where environmental conditions are implicated in violent outbursts: hot weather may precipitate riots in crowded prisons; and passengers trapped in closed conditions for a lengthy period, such as a crowded airport or a tube train in a tunnel, may well become aggressive with each other and with transport staff. Of course, not everyone reacts in the same way to provocation so there are likely to be individual differences in responses to provoking conditions (Bettencourt, Talley, Benjamin, & Valentine, 2006).

The social dimension to the instigation of violence lies in the words and actions of other people. When the actions of another person are perceived as insulting or provoking this may well lead to exchanges that culminate in violence. Toch (1969) conducted research with violent men and described different contexts for violence such as alleviating the tension within problematic social exchanges and a defence of status and personal reputation. The violence typically takes place when another person is seen as a threat and so action is taken to respond; when the other person reacts so the interaction escalates towards violence. On occasions, these exchanges may follow the 'rules of disorder', as illustrated by research on the rules of engagement followed by football (Marsh, Rosser, & Harré, 1978).

Other accounts, mainly from sociologists rather than psychologists, have concentrated more closely on the social setting. The social aspects of violence have been taken further by some criminologists who describe subcultures where violence, generally involving young men, is a legitimate norm (Wolfgang & Ferracuti, 1967).

Regulation

From a social learning theory perspective, the regulation of behaviour, including aggression, is through external reinforcement, vicarious reinforcement, and self-reinforcement. In terms of *external reinforcement*, i.e., rewards from the environment, violence is an effective way in the short-term to gain tangible and social rewards. *Vicarious reinforcement* takes place through seeing another person's violent behaviour producing rewards. *Self-reinforcement* is when an individual's actions are motivated by a sense of pride or achievement in their own behaviour. A perfect example of self-reinforcement is provided by Jimmy Boyle in the first volume of his autobiography (Boyle, 1977). Jimmy Boyle was a violent criminal, active in the 1960s, who later became a sociologist and a writer. With candid insight Boyle (1977: 107) describes his thoughts when, as a young man, he served a long prison sentence: 'The sentence that I was doing was quite big for a guy of my age with no prison sentence before but I wasn't really horrified at it. There was a sort of pride in it as I felt really good to be in beside lots of hard men as I was on the way to being one myself'. Indeed, the development of such patterns of cognition which are congruent with violent behaviour may function as a mediating link between adverse environmental conditions and involvement in violence (Pettit, 2004). As pointed out by Polaschek, Calvert, and Gannon (2009), there is much still to be understood about violent offenders' cognitions with respect to their own violent behaviour.

We are able most of the time to regulate our behaviour, the conditions that lead to the instigation of violent behaviour must, therefore, be able to override our regulatory inhibitions. The breakdown of regulation of behaviour may be a consequence of changes in physiological processes, as with too much alcohol, or changes in emotional state (or both!). Thus, adverse environmental conditions, such as extreme heat or overcrowding, can have the effect of increasing an individual's level of anger arousal. This rise in emotional arousal has an effect on cognition, intensifying angry thoughts and curtailing the regulatory processes that would ordinarily keep behaviour under control.

The role of anger

The role of anger in acts of violence has received considerable attention from researchers considering violent crimes against the person (Zamble & Quinsey, 1997), violent acts by young people (Sigfusdottir, Farkas, & Silva, 2004), and property offences such as arson (Kolko & Ammerman, 1988). The most psychologically complete model of anger has been devised and refined by the American psychologist Raymond Novaco. In a series of publications spanning several decades, Novaco has explained how social and individual factors can interact to produce anger-fuelled acts of aggression (Novaco, 1975, 1994, 2006; Novaco & Welsh, 1989). The experience of anger is not necessarily a bad thing: anger may have a positive function as, for example, with regard to individual and group survival (Novaco, 1994). Anger becomes *dysfunctional* when it has a negative effect on the individual and other people. It should be noted that, of course, dysfunctional anger and involvement in anti-social behaviour is not restricted to convicted violent offenders (Hollin, Marsh, & Bloxsom, 2011).

As shown in Figure 6.1, Novaco's model begins with the environmental cues that engage the individual's attention: these cues, typically the words and actions of other people, are set against the prevailing environmental conditions with respect to temperature, crowding, and so on. The individual's perception of these environmental cues, sometimes erroneously misperceiving signs of threat (Baumann & DeSteno, 2010), then sets into train a series of cognitive and physiological processes. If the other person's actions are appraised as insulting or provocative, then the individual may begin to become aroused both physiologically and psychologically. The appraisal of the other person's actions and intent may not be accurate: it is possible that the psychological characteristics of the individual concerned, as for example with a suspicious, hostile attitude to others, may lead to a misperception of the other person's actions and intentions. This stage in the process, which is akin to social information processing, is critical in understanding the offender's actions (Lösel, Bliesener, & Bender, 2007).

A hostile appraisal of a situation may lead to physiological changes, such as increased heart rate and muscle tension, of which the individual becomes aware and so labels their internal state as 'becoming angry'. The reciprocal relationship between cognition and affect

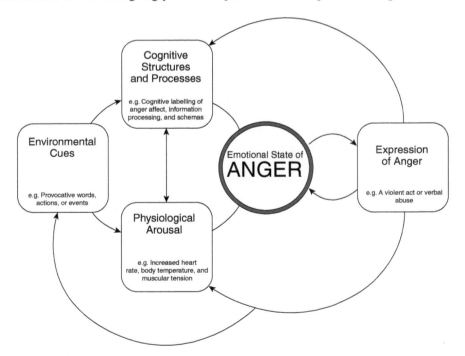

Figure 6.1 Schematic representation of Novaco's model of anger (after Novaco, 1994). Reproduced from Hollin and Bloxsom, 2007, with permission.

means that as the individual sees themselves as becoming angry, so levels of physiological arousal increase in intensity and cognitions become more hostile. The individual then begins selectively to attend to specific cues and to process information in an angry manner, seeing further evidence of threat and hostility in the other person's words and acts. As the individual's angry state intensifies so the likelihood recedes of finding rational ways to deal with the situation and the individual becomes increasingly focussed on dealing with matters in an aggressive manner.

An interaction for the perceived provocateur may open with words ('What are you looking at?'), followed by a challenge ('What are you going to do about it?'), then confirmation that matters may escalate ('You looking for a fight?'), before pushing, jostling, and throwing punches as a fight develops. The actions of onlookers may intensify the interactions – 'He's asking for it, give him a slap' – while the presence of a weapon may significantly change the outcome of a violent exchange.

There are individual differences in the way people are able to regulate their anger and in levels of rumination about the episode that made them angry. Chronic levels of rumination are not healthy as they produce prolonged physiological arousal with the consequence that anger is associated with various medical conditions including hypertension, coronary heart disease, and carotid and coronary atherosclerosis (Kubzansky, Cole, Kawachi, Vokonas, & Sparrow, 2006).

The social dimension of many violent acts is vividly described by Luckenbill (1977). With data gathered on more than 70 murders in California, Luckenbill analysed the close interactions between offender and victim in the time immediately before the killing. Luckenbill described six stages, which he called 'transactions resulting in murder', in the progression from the first exchanges to the death of one of those involved.

In stage one, the victim-to-be makes the opening move with a verbal comment, or an act such a flirting, or a refusal to comply with a request (mainly when the victim was a child). In some cases it was evident that an insult was intended, while in other cases the offender-to-be perceived the other person's behaviour as offensive. In stage two, the offender seeks confirmation of the perceived insult, either by asking the victim or talking to anyone else who was present: alternatively, the victim's continuance of the behaviour can serve as confirmation of the insult. In some instances the offender infers the 'confirmation': for example, a child's continued screaming may be seen as confirming their refusal to comply with the instruction to be quiet. At stage three, the offender decides not to retreat and stands their ground and retaliates: the retaliation may be a show of anger and verbal comment, although in a minority of cases it is physical and the murder results. At stage four, the victim replies to the retaliation with a verbal counter-challenge or a physical attack, often supported by onlookers, as if agreeing with the offender that their transaction was a contest suited to violence. In stage five, battle commences, usually with a weapon to hand: the final act is typically brief, Luckenbill (1977: 185) describes how in more than half of the murders, the offender 'dropped the victim in a single shot, stab, or rally of blows'. In the sixth and final stage, the murderer voluntarily waits for the police, or is held by others, or flees the scene. Luckenbill's analysis is of a crime that is not explained by looking at the actions of just one person, 'rather, murder is the outcome of a dynamic interchange between an offender, victim, and, in many cases, bystanders' (Luckenbill, 1977: 185).

The suggestion that the victim plays a role, perhaps even a causative role, in determining their fate does not apply to all types of violence. Savitz, Kumar, and Kahn (1991) classified 197 homicides, drawn from police records in Philadelphia, as either a 'Luckenbill' or 'non-Luckenbill' type of killing. Savitz et al. reported that 61 per cent of the 197 homicides were 'Luckenbill' types.

There are two main points to take from Luckenbill's notion of situated transactions. First, an explanation for some violent acts, including homicide, will come from understanding the social psychology of the situation and the exchanges within it. Second, not all violent acts can be understood using Luckenbill's framework and it is not always the case that the victim is an architect of their victimization. Dobash and Dobash (1984) make the point that 'blaming the victim' in the context of male violence perpetrated against women is not acceptable.

Luckenbill points to the role that a weapon can play in a violent exchange. A study conducted in Scotland by Michie and Cooke (2006) collected information, based on the MacArthur Community Violence Screening Instrument (Monahan et al., 2001), from 250 men serving custodial sentences for violent crimes (excluding sexual violence). Michie and Cooke's analysis considered the structure of the men's violent behaviour: they pointed to a superordinate factor of general violence that was underpinned by two correlated, but distinct, lower order factors. One lower order factor was associated with more severe violence, typically entailing the use of a weapon, and the other factor with less serious forms of violence.

The use of a weapon in a crime, typically a knife or a gun, increases the likelihood of a serious injury to those involved. Brennan, Moore, and Shepherd (2010) note that weapons, principally knifes, are used in about one-quarter of violent crimes in England and Wales with a corresponding number of injuries to victims. Brennan et al. looked at a small sample of offenders who had used weapons and reported that, compared with offenders who had not used weapons, they had more extensive criminal histories, greater trait aggression and were more risk-seeking. A study conducted in Colorado, USA, suggested that adolescent school bullies, both male and female, carry guns and knives, which they are prepared to use on their fellow students (Dukes, Stein, & Zane, 2010).

The importance of interpersonal behaviour alongside personal characteristics in understanding violent acts is clearly seen in explanations of family violence.

Family violence

Family violence in the form of physical abuse may be carried out by adults against other adults, by adults against children, and between siblings.

Adult family members

There are three levels of explanation for violence between adults within a family: first, the qualities of the perpetrator; second, the nature of the relationship between the adults; third, contextual and situational factors.

With regard to violence between intimate partners, which includes homosexual and heterosexual relationships, the reliable predictors of continued abuse at an individual level include characteristics such as low impulse control (Kantor & Jasinski, 1998), a history imbued with the experience of aggression (Olsen, Parra, & Bennett, 2010), and biological markers such as neuropsychological functioning (Pinto et al., 2010). Relationships that descend into violence are likely to be characterised by low levels of relationship skills such as communication, conflict resolution, and dealing with stress (Capaldi & Gorman-Smith, 2003). Finally, individuals and their relationships exist in context: there is evidence to suggest that poverty and financial constraints are the backdrop to violence against partners (Fox & Benson, 2006: 172/25).

Family violence and the child

The child may experience violence within their family in two ways: first, the child may directly experience violence by being verbally abused and physically hit; second, the child may be exposed to physical violence through witnessing their parents or caregivers being violent towards each other or towards their siblings.

As in explanations of criminal behaviour generally (see Chapters 3 and 4), the physical abuse of children can be understood from a broad social perspective or from a more narrow interpersonal standpoint. Thus, Stith et al. (2009) note that at various times explanations have been put forward for physical child abuse that emphasise the nature of parent-child interactions, parental characteristics independent of the child, child characteristics, and family factors including income and socioeconomic status. A satisfactory explanation of the physical abuse of children is likely to include all of these factors, given the potency of a person-environment in explaining behaviour, although not all factors will necessarily carry the same explanatory weight.

Why do parents hit their children? Those parents who smack their children may claim that corporal punishment is in the child's best interests. As parents, it is their task to teach their children right from wrong and as parents they must determine the best way to teach their children. In other words, some parents hit their child in order to coerce him or her to be compliant with their instructions: the child learns to avoid physical chastisement by complying with what their parents want them to do. The use of coercion by parents, using threats or physical force, is widespread throughout many societies. However, there are countries, such as Sweden and Finland, in which it is illegal for anyone, including parents, to hit a child but these are in a minority. There is not a universal consensus that hitting children is wrong. Knox is clear and to the point:

> In contrast to the growing disapproval of violence against women, social sanctions for violence against children still remain strong in the United States. In the United States, it is against the law to hit prisoners, criminals, or other adults. Ironically, the only humans it is still legal to hit are the most vulnerable members of our society — those we are charged to protect – children. Although the labels commonly used for hitting children soften their true meaning, 'spanking,' 'paddling,' and 'whuping' are, by definition, hitting, either with a hand or with an instrument. Hitting children is at least as cruel and harmful an act as hitting adult women.
>
> (Knox, 2010: 103).

Tedeschi and Felson (1994) present a theory of coercive actions through which they describe parental use of force against their children as a form of social control. The exercise of coercive tactics by parents may be successful in the short-term as they are highly likely to bring the child's behaviour under immediate control. Thus, the immediate consequences of coercing a child to behave in a certain way are highly reinforcing for the parent (Patterson, 2002). It is an axiom of behavioural theory that behaviours that are immediately reinforced are highly likely to be repeated. However, as is often the case in life generally, short-term benefits do not necessarily translate into long-term gains (Chan & Yeung, 2009).

There are two immediate problems with using physical force as a coercive tactic with children: first, the child learns that coercion is an acceptable form of behaviour; and second, there are effects other than compliance that accompany parental force. An American study reported by Simons and Wurtele (2010) looked at parental use of corporal punishment and their childrens' endorsement of spanking and hitting other children. They found that those children who experienced corporal punishment were likely to endorse aggressive means of solving social problems with their peers and siblings. As Simons and Wurtele suggest, this finding is evidence for the intergenerational transmission of aggression (see below). In addition, there is the risk that, given certain circumstances, the parental smacking spirals out of control becoming excessively forceful or abusive.

Combs-Orme and Cain (2008) conducted a study in Tennessee, USA with a sample of 224 mothers of children aged 6–13 months to determine what factors best predicted spanking. They found that spanking was used by the younger mothers, aged around 21 years, and by those mothers who endorsed fewer alternatives to corporal punishment. In addition, those mothers who saw their infant child as 'difficult' were much more likely to spank. However, in contrast to this use of physical admonishment, one-third of the mothers said that their child was 'too young to misbehave'.

Combs-Orme and Cain raise an important point with this observation with respect to the child's level of functioning. If parents believe that infants of 6 months can act deliberately and wilfully then, they may argue, smacking is entirely justified. The risk attached to this mistaken view of an infant's capabilities is that if smacking does not bring the child's behaviour under control then the obvious answer is to hit harder. As Combs-Orme and Cain state, professionals such as nurses and social workers should take particular note of parents who think that infants warrant being smacked. Further emphasis to this position is provided by studies which show that for both men and women there are adverse long-term physical and mental health consequences that follow maltreatment as a child (Fuller-Thomson, Brennenstuhl, & Frank, 2010; Hamby, Finkelhor, Turner, & Ormrod, 2010; Olaya, Ezpeleta, de la Osa, Granero, & Doménech, 2010; Springer, Sheridan, Kuo, & Carnes, 2007) as well as associations with later delinquent and criminal behaviour (Currie & Telkin, 2006).

Parental factors

The majority of parents do not abuse their children, physically or otherwise, so what are the circumstances that lead to abuse? It is the case that many parents who physically abuse their children will have been abused themselves in their own childhood. The mother's own experience of violence is associated with a range of child behaviour problems. An American study reported by Thompson (2007) found that the mother's history of violent victimization during childhood, although not during adulthood, was a powerful predictor of their own child's behaviour problems.

A study of the link between maternal experience of violence and the use of physical punishment with their children was conducted in Peru by Gage and Silvestre (2010). This study considered the use of disciplinary tactics that did not involve any physical punishment, or slapping and spanking, or both slapping and spanking together with beating the child. It was found that the mother's own childhood history of physical punishment, together with emotional and physical abuse from their current intimate partner, were significant factors in increasing the likelihood that a mother would use physical punishment with her children. Further, when the mother had also experienced physical violence by someone other than her current partner, this experience was also a significant factor in her beating her children rather than using non-physical punishment.

It is evident that parental use of force and physical aggression towards their children is associated with their own experience of violence victimisation. However, there are also likely to be situational factors that play an important role at the time the abuse takes place.

A Canadian study of child maltreatment (including emotional and sexual as well as physical abuse) by Wekerle, Wall, Leung, and Trocmé (2007) considered the role of five caregiver characteristics in reported cases of child abuse: these were (1) substance abuse, (2) criminal activities, (3) mental health issues, (4) physical health issues, and (5) lack of social support. The greater the number of these characteristics present, the greater the likelihood that the reported abuse would be substantiated. Of the five factors, Wekerle et al. report that substance misuse made the largest single contribution to the report of abuse being substantiated. This latter finding is consistent with the more general literature on substance use and violence (Kuhns & Clodfelter, 2009) and the specific literature on substance use and physical abuse (Walsh, MacMillan, & Jamieson, 2003).

When a child witnesses and experiences family violence the chances are increased that they too will act in a violent fashion (Knox, 2010; Simons & Wurtele, 2010). It is not difficult to offer an understanding of why this may be the case: children who experience violence within their family are perceiving potent models, their parents or guardians, acting in a violent manner, learning that violence is a legitimate means to solve problems and resolve interpersonal conflicts. If the child's learning to use coercive, aggressive tactics is limited to the short-term then, while clearly not in the child's best interests, at least the harm may be temporary. However, as with the effects of involvement in violence on the child's later health, it may well be the case that learning to use aggressive behaviour persists into later life, as is indicated by the longitudinal studies. Indeed, witnessing domestic violence as a child may increase the chances of later intimate partner assault (Ernst et al., 2009).

The notion of a *cycle of violence* through which young victims of violence become adults with a strong propensity to use violence has a certain intuitive appeal. In a seminal paper, Widom (1989) considered the associated arguments since when the topic has continued to generate debate (Colman, Mitchell-Herzfeld, Kim, & Shady, 2010; Widom & Brzustowicz, 2006). As explained by Ertem, Leventhal, and Dobbs (2000), there are various methodological issues, ranging from experimental design to formation of control groups length of follow-up, in untangling the data relevant to this issue. Nonetheless, concern remains about the effects on children of their observing and experiencing violence.

Margolin and Gordis (2000: 449) commented that violence 'may result in primary effects, such as anxiety, depression, or PTSD symptoms, which cause secondary reactions by disrupting children's progression through age-appropriate developmental tasks'. The idea of using post-traumatic stress disorder (PTSD) as an explanatory mechanism by which to understand the effects of violence on children is one that has several advantages. There is sufficient evidence to suggest that experiencing physical abuse and witnessing family violence can produce behaviours in the child that are indicative of PTSD. In addition, it is clear that direct involvement in the perpetration of acts of violence can also produce PTSD symptomatology. At an individual level, a combination of the experience of abuse as a child, witnessing acts of violence, and direct involvement in the perpetration of interpersonal violence may combine to give violent young offenders with PTSD (Welfare & Hollin, in press).

Conclusion

It is plain to see that violence is a complex, wide-ranging topic at many levels: violence is present in many forms, is found in many contexts, and demands multifaceted explanations. The explanations prevalent in the contemporary psychological literature (e.g., Anderson & Bushman, 2002; Nietzel, Hasemann, & Lynam, 1999) seek to draw on interactions between a wide range of explanatory factors, typically over an individual's lifespan. It is also evident

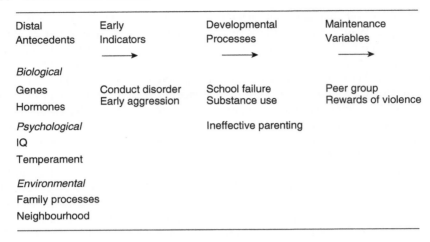

Distal Antecedents	Early Indicators ⟶	Developmental Processes ⟶	Maintenance Variables ⟶
Biological			
Genes	Conduct disorder	School failure	Peer group
Hormones	Early aggression	Substance use	Rewards of violence
Psychological		Ineffective parenting	
IQ			
Temperament			
Environmental			
Family processes			
Neighbourhood			

Figure 6.2 Developmental model of violence (after Nietzel et al., 1999)

that the importance of these factors will vary according to other variables such as the gender of the violent person. This explanatory approach is illustrated in Figure 6.2, in which each stage becomes the precursor for what follows. Of course, to take us back to where we started, this developmental process at the level of the individual can be further elaborated in terms of evolution, culture, and so on.

Chapter summary

- The World Health Organization describes three types of violence: (1) *self-directed violence*, (2) *interpersonal violence*, and (3) *collective violence*, with several subtypes within each of the three.
- Criminological psychology is principally concerned with criminal acts of interpersonal violence of which two types can be distinguished, *violence with injury*, which includes acts such as wounding, and *violence without injury*, such as robberies that do not result in physical injury.
- Homicide is the most serious form of interpersonal violence and can be committed for various reasons including revenge and sexual motivation.
- Violence can take occur in a wide range of settings including the family home, where violence may be between adult partners or directed by parents at their children. Whether hitting children as a means of discipline should be allowed raises strong opinions.
- There are several psychological models of violent behaviour: it is important to include the social context in which the violence takes place as well as the psychological characteristics of the aggressor.

Points for discussion

- Given the levels of serious violence, should we really be concerned about tackling instances of 'low-level violence'?
- Would changing the law to prohibit the sale of alcohol to young people have a significant effect on the prevalence of violence?

- In numerical terms, serial killers are a rare type of criminal: why are we so fascinated by this type of offender?

Essential reading

LeBlanc, S. A. & Register, K. E. (2003). *Constant Battles: Why we Fight*. New York, NY: St. Martin's Griffin.
This book takes a look at the long history of warfare and offers a wide view of why civilizations and societies engage in violence towards each other.

Krug, E. G., Dahlberg, L. L., Mercy, J. A., Zwi, A. B., & Lozano, R. (Eds.) (2002). *World Report on Violence and Health*. Geneva: World Health Organization.
This report contains a wealth of information about many forms of violence.

McVicar, J. (1974). *By Himself.* London: Arrow Books.
John McVicar, now a journalist and writer with a postgraduate degree from the University of Leicester, was an armed robber who in the 1960s was, according to the police, 'Public Enemy No. 1'. His auto-biography, later made into a film starring Roger Daltrey, gives an honest account of life as a violent criminal.

Craig, I. W. & Halton, K. E. (2009). Genetics of human aggressive behaviour. *Human Genetics, 126,* 101–113.
This paper offers a comprehensive and accessible review of genetic influences on human aggression.

Gottschalk, M. & Ellis, L. (2009). Evolutionary and genetic explanations of violent crime. In C. Ferguson (Ed.), *Violent Crime: Clinical and Social Implications* (pp. 57–74). Thousand Oaks, CA: Sage.
This chapter by Martin Gottschalk and Lee Ellis gives an excellent overview of the meta-issue of the context within which to understand the role of genetic influences on violent behaviour.

Berkowitz, L. (1993). *Aggression: Its Causes, Consequences and Control*. New York, NY: McGraw-Hill.
Although published some time ago, Berkowitz's excellent book provides a readable and detailed over-view of theories of aggression.

The lighter side

Any of the Hannibal Lecter novels by Thomas Harris (or the films, particularly *Red Dragon*). Michael Moore's film *Bowling for Columbine* (2002) explores a country's fascination with weapons. The *Death Wish* sequence (five films) takes on the issue of vigilante payback for a violent attack: the first in the sequence, released in 1974 and starring Charles Bronson, is probably the best. Christopher Priest's 1998 novel, *The Extremes*, is based in a seaside town where a spree murder has taken place.

Useful websites

Murderuk.com has just about everything you'll ever need to know about murder. It also has material on real-life cases of both missing persons and known murders, www.murderuk.com/index.html.

There are considerable variations in the murder rate across countries: the Nationmaster link gives details of these international variations, www.nationmaster.com/graph/cri_mur-crime-murders

The FBI has lots of stats about violent crime at www.fbi.gov/ucr/ucr.htm.

Launched in 2001, the Global Initiative to End All Corporal Punishment of Children aims to speed the end of corporal punishment of children across the world, www.endcorporalpunishment.org.

There are many websites given to the topic of stalking: www.stalkingbehavior.com has a fantastic list of references, of which more can be found at www.ncvc.org/scr/main.aspx?dbID=DB_Annotated_Stalking_Bibliography344.

References

Afifi, T. O., Brownridge, D. A., MacMillan, H., & Sareen, J. (2010). The relationship of gambling to intimate partner violence and child maltreatment in a nationally representative sample. *Journal of Psychiatric Research, 44*, 331–337.

Agha, S. (2009). Structural correlates of female homicide: A cross-national analysis. *Journal of Criminal Justice, 37*, 576–585.

Alaggia, R., Regehr, C., & Rischchynski, G. (2009). Intimate partner violence and immigration laws in Canada: How far have we come? *International Journal of Law and Psychiatry, 32*, 335–341.

Alhabib, S., Nur, U., & Jones, R. (2010). Domestic violence against women: Systematic review of prevalence studies. *Journal of Family Violence, 25*, 369–382.

Anderson, C. A. (2001). Heat and violence. *Current Directions in Psychological Science, 10*, 33–38.

Anderson, C. A. & Anderson, K. B. (2008). Men who target women: Specificity of target, generality of aggressive behavior. *Aggressive Behavior, 34*, 605–622.

Anderson, C. A. & Bushman, B. J. (2002). Human aggression. *Annual Review of Psychology, 53*, 27–51.

Anderson, C. A. & Huesmann, L. R. (2003). Human aggression: A social-cognitive view. In M. A. Hogg & J. Cooper (Eds.), *The Sage Handbook of Social Psychology* (pp. 296–323). Thousand Oaks, CA: Sage.

Andrews, D. A. & Bonta, J. (1995). *LSI-R: The Level of Service Inventory -Revised.* Toronto, Canada: Multi-Health Systems.

Archer, J. (2009). The nature of human aggression. *International Journal of Law and Psychiatry, 32*, 202–208.

Atchison A. J. & Heide, K. M. (2010). Charles Manson and the Family: The application of sociological theories. *International Journal of Offender Therapy and Comparative Criminology, 55*(5), 771–798.

Baker, L. A., Raine, A., Liu, J., & Jacobson, K. C. (2008). Differential genetic and environmental influences on reactive and proactive aggression in children. *Journal of Abnormal Child Psychology, 36*, 1265–1278.

Bandura, A. (1968). Social learning theory of aggression. *Journal of Communication, 28*, 12–29.

——. (1973). *Aggression: A Social Learning Analysis.* Englewood Cliffs, NJ, Prentice-Hall.

Bandura, A., Ross, D., & Ross, S. A. (1961). Transmission of aggression through imitation of aggressive models. *Journal of Abnormal and Social Psychology, 63*, 575–582.

Barlas, J. & Egan, V. (2006). Weapons carrying in British teenagers: The role of personality, delinquency, sensational interests, and mating effort. *Journal of Forensic Psychiatry and Psychology, 17*, 53–72.

Barling, J., Dupré, K. E., & Kelloway, E. K. (2009). Predicting workplace aggression and violence. *Annual Review of Psychology, 60*, 671–692.

Bartels, L. (2010). *Emerging Issues in Domestic/Family Violence Research.* Research in Practice, Report No. 10. Canberra, Australian Institute of Criminology.

Bartholow, B. D., Anderson, C. A., Carnagey, N. L., & Benjamin, A. J. (2005). Interactive effects of life experience and situational cues on aggression: The weapons priming effect in hunters and non-hunters. *Journal of Experimental Social Psychology, 41*, 48–60.

Baum, K., Catalano, S., Rand, M., & Rose, K. (2009). *Stalking Victimization in the United States.* Bureau of Justice Statistics Special Report. Washington, DC: US Department of Justice.

Baumann, J. & DeSteno, D. (2010). Emotion guided threat detection: Expecting guns where there are none. *Journal of Personality and Social Psychology, 99*, 595–610.

Baumrind, D., Larzelere, R. E., & Cowan, P. A. (2002). Ordinary physical punishment: Is it harmful? Comment on Gershoff (2002). *Psychological Bulletin, 128*, 580–589.

Beach, F. A. (1955). The descent of instinct. *Psychological Review, 62*, 401–410.

Beasley, J. O., Hayne A. S., Beyer, K., Cramer, G. L., Berson, S. B., Muirhead, Y., & Warren, J. I. (2009). Patterns of prior offending by child abductors: A comparison of fatal and non-fatal outcomes. *International Journal of Law and Psychiatry, 32*, 273–280.

Beech, A. R., Fisher, D., & Ward, T. (2005). Sexual murderers' implicit theories. *Journal of Interpersonal Violence, 20*, 1366–1389.

Beeghley, L. (2003). *Homicide: A Sociological Explanation.* New York, NY: Rowman and Littlefield.

Benjet, C. & Kazdin, A. E. (2003). Spanking children: The controversies, findings, and new directions. *Clinical Psychology Review, 23*, 197–224.

Bennett, S., Farrington, D. P., & Huesmann, L. R. (2005). Explaining gender differences in crime and violence: The importance of social cognitive skills. *Aggression and Violent Behavior, 10*, 263–288.

Bennett, T. & Brookman, F. (2010). Street robbery. In F. Brookman, M. Maguire, H. Pierpoint, & T. Bennett (Eds.), *Handbook on Crime* (pp. 270–289). Cullompton, Devon: Willan Publishing.

Berkowitz, L. (1965). The concept of aggressive drive: Some additional considerations. In L. Berkowitz (Ed.), *Advances in Experimental Social Psychology, Vol. 2* (pp. 301–329). New York, NY: Academic Press.

—— (1993). *Aggression: Its Causes, Consequences and Control.* New York, NY: McGraw-Hill.

Bettencourt, B. A., Talley, A., Benjamin, A. J., & Valentine, J. (2006). Personality and aggressive behavior under provoking and neutral conditions: A meta-analytic review. *Psychological Bulletin, 132*, 751–777.

Beyer, K., McAuliffe, S., Joy, M., & Shelton, L. (2008). Investigative analysis of neonaticide: An exploratory study. *Criminal Justice and Behavior, 35*, 522–535.

Biermann, T., Asemann, R., McAuliffe, C., Ströbel, A., Keller, J., Sperling, W., Bleich, S., Kornhuber, J., & Reulbach, U. (2009). Relationship between lunar phases and serious crimes of battery: A population-based study. *Comprehensive Psychiatry, 50*, 573–577.

Blaauw, E., Winkel, F. W., & Kerkhof, J. F. M. (2001). Bullying and suicidal behavior in jails. *Criminal Justice and Behavior, 28*, 279–299.

Blackburn, R. (1968). Personality in relation to extreme aggression in psychiatric offenders. *British Journal of Psychiatry, 114*, 821–828.

—— (1971). Personality types among abnormal homicides. *British Journal of Criminology, 11*, 14–31.

—— (1975). An empirical classification of psychopathic personality. *British Journal of Psychiatry, 127*, 456–460.

—— (1986). Patterns of personality deviation among violent offenders. *British Journal of Criminology, 26*, 254–269.

Blatier, C., Gimenez, C., Paulicand, M., & Pullin, W. (2010). Homicide and violent delinquency in France: An overview framed within an international context. *Aggression and Violent Behavior, 15*, 261–266.

Booij, L., Tremblay, R. E., Leyton, M., Séguin, J. R., Vitaro, F., Gravel, P., & Benkelfa, C. (2010). Brain serotonin synthesis in adult males characterized by physical aggression during childhood: A 21-year longitudinal study. *PLoS One, 5*, 1–9.

Bourget, D., Grace, J., & Whitehurst, L. (2007). A review of maternal and paternal filicide. *Journal of the American Academy of Psychiatry and the Law, 35*, 74–82.

Boyle, J. (1977). *A Sense of Freedom.* London: Pan Books.

Brennan, I. R. & Moore, S. C. (2009). Weapons and violence: A review of theory and research. *Aggression and Violent Behavior, 14*, 215–225.

Brennan, I. R., Moore, S. C., & Shepherd, J. P. (2010). Aggression and attitudes to time and risk in weapon-using violent offenders. *Psychiatry Research, 178*, 536–539.

Brookman, F. & Nolan, J. (2006). The dark figure of infanticide in England and Wales: Complexities of diagnosis. *Journal of Interpersonal Violence, 21*, 869–889.

Broidy, L. M., Daday, J. K., Crandall, C. S., Sklar, D. P., & Jost, P. F. (2006). Exploring demographic, structural, and behavioral overlap among homicide offenders and victims. *Homicide Studies, 10*, 155–180.

Burt, S. A. (2009). Are there meaningful etiological differences within antisocial behavior? Results of a meta-analysis. *Clinical Psychology Review, 29*, 163–178.

Bushman, B. J. & Anderson, C. A. (2001). Is it time to pull the plug on the hostile versus instrumental aggression dichotomy? *Psychological Review, 108*, 273–279.

Bushman, B. J., Wang, M. C. & Anderson, C. A. (2005). Is the curve relating temperature to aggression linear or curvilinear? Assaults and temperature in Minneapolis reexamined. *Journal of Personality and Social Psychology, 89*, 62–66.

Buss, D. M. & Shackleford, T. K. (1997). Human aggression in evolutionary psychological perspective. *Clinical Psychology Review, 17*, 605–619.

Byard, R. W. & Jensen, L. L. (2008). Is SIDS still a "diagnosis" in search of a disease? *Australian Journal of Forensic Sciences, 40*, 85–92.

Carlo, G., Mestre, M. V., Samper, P., Tur, A., & Armenta, B. E. (2010). Feelings or cognitions? Moral cognitions and emotions as predictors of prosocial and aggressive behaviors. *Personality and Individual Differences, 48*, 872–877.

Capaldi, D. M. & Gorman-Smith, D. (2003). The development of aggression in young male/female couples. In P. Florsheim (Ed.), *Adolescent Romantic Relations and Sexual Behavior: Theory, Research, and Practical Implications* (pp. 243–278). Mahwah, NJ: Erlbaum.

Carney, M., Buttell, F., & Dutton, D. (2007). Women who perpetrate intimate partner violence: A review of the literature with recommendations for treatment. *Aggression and Violent Behavior, 12*, 108–115.

Carter, A. J. & Hollin, C. R. (2010). Characteristics of non-serial sexual homicide offenders: A review. *Psychology, Crime and Law, 16*, 25–45.

Ceccato, V. & Oberwittler, D. (2008). Comparing spatial patterns of robbery: Evidence from a Western and an Eastern European city. *Cities, 25*, 185–196.

Chambers, J. C. (2010). An exploration of the mechanisms underlying the development of repeat and one-time violent offenders. *Aggression and Violent Behavior, 15*, 310–323.

Chan, H. C. & Heide, K. M. (2008). Weapons used by juveniles and adult offenders in sexual homicides: An empirical analysis of 29 years of US data. *Journal of Investigative Psychology and Offender Profiling, 5*, 189–208.

Chan, Y. & Yeung, J. (2009). Children living with violence within the family and its sequel: A meta-analysis from 1995–2006. *Aggression and Violent Behavior, 14*, 313–322.

Clark, R. D. (1995). Lone versus multiple offending in homicide: Differences in situational context. *Journal of Criminal Justice, 23*, 451–460.

Colman, R. A., Mitchell-Herzfeld, S., Kim, D. H., & Shady, T. A. (2010). From delinquency to the perpetration of child maltreatment: Examining the early adult criminal justice and child welfare involvement of youth released from juvenile justice facilities. *Children and Youth Services Review, 22*, 839–871.

Collins, J. J. (Ed.) (1982). *Drinking and Crime.* London: Tavistock Publications.

Collins, R. E. (2010). The effect of gender on violent and nonviolent recidivism: A meta-analysis. *Journal of Criminal Justice, 38*, 675–684.

Combs-Orme, T. & Cain, D. S. (2008). Predictors of mothers' use of spanking with their infants. *Child Abuse & Neglect, 32*, 649–657.

Conklin, J. (1972). *Robbery and the Criminal Justice System.* New York, NY: Lippincott.

Connell, A. & Farrington, D. P. (1996). Bullying among incarcerated young offenders: Developing an interview schedule and some preliminary results. *Journal of Adolescence, 19*, 75–93.

Craig, I. W. & Halton, K. E. (2009). Genetics of human aggressive behaviour. *Human Genetics, 126*, 101–113.

Cunningham, H. (2006). *The Invention of Childhood.* London: BBC Books.

Cunningham, M. D., Sorensen, J. R., Vigen, M. P., & Woods, S. O. (2010). Inmate homicides: Killers, victims, motives, and circumstances. *Journal of Criminal Justice, 38*, 348–358.

Currie, J. & Telkin, E. (2006). *Does Child Abuse Cause Crime?* Andrew Young School of Policy Studies Research Paper Series. Working Paper 06-31, available at: http://aysps.gsu.edu/publications/2006/index.htm.

D'Cruze, S., Walklate, S., & Pegg, S. (2006). *Murder.* Cullompton, Devon: Willan Publishing.

Davey, L., Day, A., & Howells, K. (2005). Anger, over-control and serious violent offending. *Aggression and Violent Behavior, 10,* 624–635.

DeLisi, M., Umphress, Z. R., & Vaughn, M. G. (2009). The criminology of the amygdala. *Criminal Justice and Behavior, 36,* 1241–1262.

DeWall, C. N. & Bushman, B. J. (2009). Hot under the collar in a lukewarm environment: Words associated with hot temperature increase aggressive thoughts and hostile perceptions. *Journal of Experimental Social Psychology, 45,* 1045–1047.

Diem, C. & Pizarro, C. (2010). Social structure and family homicides. *Journal of Family Violence, 25,* 521–532.

Dobash, R. E., & Dobash, R. P. (1984). The nature and antecedents of violent events. *British Journal of Criminology, 24,* 269–288.

Dobash, R. E., Dobash, R. P., & Cavanagh, K. (2009). "Out of the blue": Men who murder an intimate partner. *Feminist Criminology, 4,* 194–225.

Dobash, R. P., Dobash, R. E., Cavanagh, K., Smith, D., & Medina-Ariza, J. (2007). Onset of offending and life course among men convicted of murder. *Homicide Studies, 11,* 243–271.

Dodge, K. A. (2009). Mechanisms of gene-environment interaction effects in the development of conduct disorder. *Perspectives on Psychological Science, 4,* 408–414.

Dollard, J., Doob, L. W., Miller, N. E., Mowrer, O. H., & Sears, R. R. (1939). *Frustration and Aggression.* New Haven, CT: Yale University Press.

Douglas, E. M. & Straus, M. A. (2007). Discipline by parents and child psychopathology. In A. R. Felthous & H. Sass (Eds.), *International Handbook of Psychopathology and the Law* (pp. 303–317). New York, NY: John Wiley & Sons.

Dressing, H., Kuehner, C., & Gass, P. (2005). Lifetime prevalence and impact of stalking in a European population: Epidemiological data from a middle-sized German city. *British Journal of Psychiatry, 187,* 168–172.

Dukes, R. L., Stein, J. A., & Zane, J. I. (2010). Gender differences in the relative impact of physical and relational bullying on adolescent injury and weapon carrying. *Journal of School Psychology, 48*(6), 511–532.

Dutton, D. G. (1995). Male abusiveness in intimate relationships. *Clinical Psychology Review, 15,* 567–581.

Edlin, A., Williams, B., & Williams, A. (2010). Pre-hospital provider recognition of intimate partner violence. *Journal of Forensic and Legal Medicine, 17,* 359–362.

Elisha, E., Idisis, Y., Timor, U., & Addad, M. (2010). Typology of intimate partner homicide: Personal, interpersonal, and environmental characteristics of men who murdered their female intimate partner. *International Journal of Offender Therapy and Comparative Criminology, 54,* 494–516.

Erikson, M. & Friendship, C. (2002). A typology of child abduction events. *Legal and Criminological Psychology, 7,* 115–120.

Ernst, A. A., Weiss, S. J., Hall, J., Clark, R., Coffman, B., Goldstein, L., & Valdez, M. (2009). Adult intimate partner violence perpetrators are significantly more likely to have witnessed intimate partner violence as a child than nonperpetrators. *American Journal of Emergency Medicine, 27,* 641–650.

Ertem, I. O., Leventhal, J. M., & Dobbs, S. (2000). Intergenerational continuity of child physical abuse: How good is the evidence? *Lancet, 356,* 814–819.

European Commission (2010). *Domestic Violence Against Women: Report.* Eurobarometer 73.2. Brussels, TNS Opinion & Social.

Fabian, J. M. (2010). Neuropsychological and neurological correlates in violent and homicidal offenders: A legal and neuroscience perspective. *Aggression and Violent Behavior, 15,* 209–223.

Fallon, B., Trocmé, N., Fluke, J., MacLaurin, B., Tonmyr, L., & Yuan, Y. (2010). Methodological challenges in measuring child maltreatment. *Child Abuse & Neglect, 34,* 70–79.

Falzon, A. L. & Davis, G. G. (1998). A 15-year retrospective review of homicide in the elderly. *Journal of Forensic Sciences, 43*, 371–374.

Farrington, D. P. (1989). Early predictors of adolescent aggression and adult violence. *Violence and Victims, 4*, 79–100.

Federal Bureau of Investigation (FBI) (2009). *Uniform Crime Report, 2008*. Washington, DC: FBI.

Felson, R. B. & Messner, S. F. (1996). To kill or not to kill? Lethal outcomes in injurious attacks. *Criminology, 34*, 519–545.

Ferguson, C. J. (2010). Genetic contributions to antisocial personality and behavior: A meta-analytic review from an evolutionary perspective. *Journal of Social Psychology, 150*, 160–180.

Ferguson, C. J. & Beaver, K. M. (2009). Natural born killers: The genetic origins of extreme violence. *Aggression and Violent Behavior, 14*, 286–294.

Ferns, T. (2007). Considering theories of aggression in an emergency department context. *Accident and Emergency Nursing, 15*, 193–200.

Finkelhor, D., Ormrod R. K., & Turner, H. A. (2009). Lifetime assessment of poly-victimization in a national sample of children and youth. *Child Abuse & Neglect, 33*, 403–411.

Fite, P. J., Colder, C. R., & Lochman, J. E. (2007). Pathways from proactive and reactive aggression to substance use. *Psychology of Addictive Behaviors, 21*, 355–364.

Flynn, S., Shaw, J. J., & Abel, K. M. (2007). Homicide of infants: A cross-sectional study. *Journal of Clinical Psychiatry, 68*, 1501–1509.

Flynn, S., Swinson, N., While, D., Hunt, I. M., Roscoe, A., Rodway, C., Windfuhr, K., Kapur, N., Appleby, L., & Shaw J. (2009). Homicide followed by suicide: A cross-sectional study. *Journal of Forensic Psychology and Psychiatry, 20*, 306–321.

Fontaine, R. G. (2007). Disentangling the psychology and law of instrumental and reactive subtypes of aggression. *Psychology, Public Policy, and Law, 13*, 143–165.

Fox, G. L. & Benson, M. L. (2006). Household and neighborhood contexts of intimate partner violence. *Public Health Reports, 121*, 419–427.

Fox, J. A., Levin, J., & Quinet, K. (2007). *The Will to Kill: Making Sense of Senseless Murder* (3rd ed.). Upper Saddle River, NJ: Allyn & Bacon.

Frude, N. (1989). The physical abuse of children. In C. R. Hollin & K. Howells (Eds.), *Clinical Approaches to Violence* (pp. 155–181). Chichester, Sussex: John Wiley & Sons.

Fuller-Thomson, E., Brennenstuhl, S., & Frank, J. (2010). The association between childhood physical abuse and heart disease in adulthood: Findings from a representative community sample. *Child Abuse & Neglect, 34*, 689–698.

Gage, A. J. & Silvestre, E. A. (2010). Maternal violence, victimization, and child physical punishment in Peru. *Child Abuse & Neglect, 34*, 522–523.

Gambetta, D. (Ed.) (2005). *Making Sense of Suicide Missions*. Oxford: Oxford University Press.

Gannon, T. A. (2009). Social cognition in violent and sexual offending: An overview. *Psychology, Crime & Law, 15*, 97–118.

Garbarino, J. (1977). The human ecology of child maltreatment: A conceptual model for research. *Journal of Marriage and the Family, 39*, 721–735.

Gebo, E. (2002). A contextual exploration of siblicide. *Violence and Victims, 17*, 157–168.

Gentile, S. R., Asamen, J. K.., Harmell, P. H., & Weathers, R. (2002). The stalking of psychologists by their clients. *Professional Psychology: Research and Practice, 33*, 490–494.

Gershoff, E. T. (2002). Corporal punishment by parents and associated child behaviors and experiences: A meta-analytic and theoretical review. *Psychological Bulletin, 128*, 539–579.

Gershoff, E. T. & Bitensky, S. H. (2007). The case against corporal punishment of children. *Psychology, Public Policy and Law, 13*, 231–272.

Gershoff, E. T., Grogan-Kaylor, A., Lansford, J. E., Chang, L., Zelli, A., Deater-Deckard, K., & Dodge, K. A. (2010). Parent discipline practices in an international sample: Associations with child behaviors and moderation by perceived normativeness. *Child Development, 81*, 487–502.

Golden, C. J., Jackson, M. L., Peterson-Rhone, A., & Gontkovsky, S. T. (1996). Neuropsychological correlates of violence and aggression: A review of the clinical literature. *Aggression and Violent Behavior, 1*, 3–25.

Goldstein, A. P. (2002). *The Psychology of Group Aggression.* Chichester, Sussex: John Wiley & Sons.

Goldstein, G. H. (1986). *Aggression and Crimes of Violence* (2nd ed.). Oxford: Oxford University Press.

Gottschalk, M. & Ellis, L. (2009). Evolutionary and genetic explanations of violent crime. In C. Ferguson (Ed.), *Violent Crime: Clinical and Social Implications* (pp. 57–74). Thousand Oaks, CA: Sage.

Gresswell, D. M. & Hollin, C. R. (1994). Multiple murder: A review. *British Journal of Criminology, 34,* 1–14.

Gunn, J. (2010). Dr Harold Frederick Shipman: An enigma. *Criminal Behaviour and Mental Health, 20,* 190–198.

Gurian, E. A. (2011). Female serial murderers: Directions for future research on a hidden population. *International Journal of Offender Therapy and Comparative Criminology, 55,* 27–42.

Hagelstam, C. & Häkkäen, H. (2006). Adolescent homicides in Finland: Offence and offender characteristics. *Forensic Science International, 164,* 110–115.

Hallsworth, S. & Silverstone, D. (2009). "That's life innit": A British perspective on guns, crime and social order. *Criminology and Criminal Justice, 9,* 359–377.

Häkknäen-Nyholm, H., Repo-Tiihonen, E., Lindberg, N., Salenius, S., & Weizmann-Henelius, G. (2009). Finnish sexual homicides: Offence and offender characteristics. *Forensic Science International, 188,* 125–130.

Hamby, S., Finkelhor, D., Turner, H., & Ormrod, R. (2010). The overlap of witnessing partner violence with child maltreatment and other victimizations in a nationally representative survey of youth. *Child Abuse & Neglect, 34,* 734–741.

Hata, N., Kominato, Y., Shimada, I., Takizawa, H., Fujikura, T., & Sato, Y. (2001). Regional differences in homicide patterns in five areas of Japan. *Legal Medicine, 3,* 44–55.

Hathaway, S. R. & McKinley, J. C. (1940). A multiphasic personality schedule (Minnesota): I construction of the schedule. *Journal of Psychology, 10,* 249–254.

Heide, K. M., Beauregard, E., & Myers, W. C. (2009). Sexually motivated child abduction murders: Synthesis of the literature and case illustration. *Victims and Offenders, 4,* 58–75.

Heide, K. M. & Petee, T. A. (2007). Parricide: An empirical analysis of 24 years of US data. *Journal of Interpersonal Violence, 22,* 1382–1399.

Heide, K. M. & Solomon, E. P. (2009). Female juvenile murderers: Biological and psychological dynamics leading to homicide. *International Journal of Law and Psychiatry, 32,* 244–252.

Henderson, M. (1982). An empirical classification of convicted violent offenders. *British Journal of Criminology, 22,* 1–20.

—— (1983a). Self-reported assertion and aggression among violent offenders with high or low levels of overcontrolled hostility. *Personality and Individual Differences, 4,* 671–677.

—— (1983b). An empirical classification of non-violent offenders using the MMPI. *Personality and Individual Differences, 4,* 671–677.

—— (1986). An empirical typology of violent incidents reported by prison inmates with convictions for violence. *Aggressive Behavior, 12,* 21–32.

Henderson, M., Henderson, P., & Kiernan, C. (2000) Missing persons: Incidence, issues and impacts. *Trends & Issues in Crime & Criminal Justice,* No. 144. Canberra, Australian Institute of Criminology.

Hill, D. & Pond, D. A. (1952). Reflections on a hundred capital cases submitted to electroencephalography. *Journal of Mental Science, 98,* 23–43.

Hilton, N. Z., Harris, G. T., Popham, S., & Lang, C. (2010). Risk assessment among incarcerated male domestic violence offenders. *Criminal Justice and Behavior, 37,* 815–832.

Hilton, N. Z., Harris, G. T., Rice, M. E., Houghton, R. E., & Eke, A. W. (2008). An in-depth actuarial assessment for wife assault recidivism: The *Domestic Violence Risk Appraisal Guide. Law and Human Behavior, 32,* 150–163.

Hobbs, D. (2010). Stealing commercial cash. In F. Brookman, M. Maguire, H. Pierpoint, & T. Bennett (Eds.), *Handbook on Crime* (pp. 290–307). Cullompton, Devon: Willan Publishing.

Holland, T. R. & Holt, N. (1975). Personality patterns among short-term prisoners undergoing presentence evaluations. *Psychological Reports, 37,* 827–836.

Hollin, C. R. & Bloxsom, C. A. J. (2007). Treatments for angry aggression. In T. A. Gannon, T. Ward, A. R. Beech, & D. Fisher (Eds.), *Aggressive Offenders' Cognition: Theory, Research and Practice.* Chichester, Sussex: John Wiley & Sons.

Hollin, C. R., Marsh, C., & Bloxsom, C. A. J. (2011). Anger and self-reported delinquency in university students. *European Journal of Psychology Applied to Legal Context, 3*, 1–10.

Hollin, C. R. & Palmer, E. J. (2003). Level of service inventory-revised profiles of violent and non-violent prisoners. *Journal of Interpersonal Violence, 18*, 1075–1086.

—— (2006). Criminogenic need and women offenders: A critique of the literature. *Legal and Criminological Psychology, 11*, 179–195.

Home Office (2010). *Home Office Counting Rules for Recorded Crime: Robbery.* Available at: http://rds.homeoffi ce.gov.uk/rds/pdfs10/countrobbery10.pdf.

Horgan, J. (2005). *The Psychology of Terrorism.* London: Routledge.

Huesmann, L. R., Dubow, E. F., & Boxer, P. (2009). Continuity of aggression from childhood to early adulthood as a predictor of life outcomes: Implications for the adolescent-limited and life-coursepersistent models. *Aggressive Behavior, 35*, 136–149.

Ikäheimo, P., Räsänen, P., Hakko, H., Hartikainen, A., Laitinen, J., Hodgins, S., & Tiihonen, J. (2007). Body size and violent offending among males in the Northern Finland 1966 birth cohort. *Social Psychiatry and Psychiatric Epidemiology, 42*, 845–850.

Ishida, K., Stupp, P., Melian, Serbanescu, M., Goodwin, F., & Krug, M. (2010). Exploring the associations between intimate partner violence and women's mental health: Evidence from a population-based study in Paraguay. *Social Science & Medicine, 71*, 1653–1661.

Iwaniec, D. (2006). *The Emotionally Abused and Neglected Child: Identification, Assessment and Intervention. A practice handbook* (2nd ed). Chichester, Sussex: John Wiley & Sons.

James, D. V., Mullen, P. E., Pathé, M. T., Meloy, J. R., Preston, L. F., Darnley, B., & Farnham, F. R. (2009). Stalkers and harassers of royalty: The role of mental illness and motivation. *Psychological Medicine, 39*, 1479–1490.

Jay, T. (2009). Do offensive words harm people? *Psychology, Public Policy, and Law, 15*, 81–101.

Jenkins, P. (1988). Serial murder in England 1940–1985. *Journal of Criminal Justice, 16*, 1–15.

Jordan, C. E., Wilcox, P., & Pritchard, A. J. (2007). Stalking acknowledgement and reporting among college women experiencing intrusive behaviors: Implications for the emergence of a "classic stalking case". *Journal of Criminal Justice, 35*, 556–569.

Kamphuis, J. H., Galeazzi, G. M., De Fazio, L., Emmelkamp, P. M. G., Farnham, F., Groenen, A., James, D., & Vervaeke, G. (2005). Stalking–perceptions and attitudes amongst helping professions: An EU cross-national comparison. *Clinical Psychology and Psychotherapy, 12*, 215–225.

Kantor, G. K. & Jasinski, J. L. (1998). Dynamics and risk factors in partner violence. In J. L. Jasinski & L. M. Williams (Eds.), *Partner Violence: A Comprehensive Review of 20 Years of Research* (pp. 3–31). Thousand Oaks, CA: Sage.

Kempe, C. H., Silverman, F. N., Steele, B. B., Droegemuller, W., & Silver, H. K. (1962). The battered child syndrome. *Journal of the American Medical Association, 181*, 17–24.

Kirkland, C. J. (2002). *Campus Stalking.* Sacramento, CA, California Coalition Against Sexual Assault (CALSASA).

Klein, A. R. & Tobin, T. (2008). A longitudinal study of arrested batterers, 1995–2005: Career criminals. *Violence Against Women, 14*, 136–157.

Kletschka, H. D. (1966). Violent behaviour associated with brain tumours. *Minnesota Medicine, 49*, 1853–1855.

Klevens, J. & Leeb, R. T. (2010). Child maltreatment fatalities in children under 5: Findings from the National Violence Death Reporting System. *Child Abuse & Neglect, 34*, 262–266.

Kokko, K., Pulkkinen, L., Huesmann, L. R., Dubow, E. F., & Boxer, P. (2009). Intensity of aggression in childhood as a predictor of different forms of adult aggression: A two-country (Finland and United States) analysis. *Journal of Research in Adolescence, 19*, 9–34.

Kolko, D. J. & Ammerman, R. T. (1988). Firesetting. In M. Hersen & C. G. Last (Eds.), *Child Behavior Therapy Casebook* (pp. 243–262). New York, NY: Plenum Press.

Knox, M. (2010). On hitting children: A review of corporal punishment in the United States. *Journal of Paediatric Health Care, 24*, 103–107.

Kraanen, F. L., Scholing, A., & Emmelkamp, P. M. G. (2009). Substance use disorders in perpetrators of intimate partner violence in a forensic setting. *International Journal of Offender Therapy and Comparative Criminology, 54*, 430–440.

Krienert, J. L. & Walsh, J. A. (2010). Eldercide: A gendered examination of elderly homicide in the United States, 2000–2005. *Homicide Studies, 14*, 52–71.

Krug, E. G., Dahlberg, L. L., Mercy, J. A., Zwi, A. B., & Lozano, R. (Eds.) (2002). *World Report on Violence and Health*. Geneva: World Health Organization.

Kubzansky, L. D., Cole, S. R., Kawachi, I., Vokonas, P., & Sparrow, D. (2006). Shared and unique contributions of anger, anxiety, and depression to coronary heart disease: A prospective study in the normative aging study. *Annals of Behavioral Medicine, 31*, 21–29.

Kuhns, J. B. & Clodfelter, T. A. (2009). Illicit drug-related psychopharmacological violence: The current understanding within a causal context. *Aggression and Violent Behavior, 14*, 69–78.

Langevin, R., Ben-Aron, M. H., Wright, P., Marchese, V., & Handy, L. (1988). The sex killer. *Annals of Sex Research, 1*, 263–301.

LeBlanc, M. M. & Barling, J. (2005). Understanding the many faces of workplace violence. In S. Fox & P. E. Spector (Eds.), *Counterproductive Work Behavior: Investigations of Actors and Targets* (pp. 41–63). Washington, DC: American Psychological Association.

LeBlanc, S. A. & Register, K. E. (2003). *Constant Battles: Why we Fight*. New York, NY: St. Martin's Griffin.

Leddy, J. & O'Connell, M. (2002). The prevalence, nature and psychological correlates of bullying in Irish prisons. *Legal and Criminological Psychology, 7*, 131–140.

Lederhendler, I. I. (2003). Aggression and violence: Perspectives on integrating animal and human research approaches. *Hormones and Behavior, 44*, 156–160.

Liem, M. (2010). Homicide followed by suicide: A review. *Aggression and Violent Behavior, 15*, 153–161.

Liem, M., de Veta, R., & Koenraadt, F. (2010). Filicide followed by parasuicide: A comparison of suicidal and non-suicidal child homicide. *Child Abuse & Neglect, 34*, 558–562.

Liem, M. & Koenraadt, F. (2008). Filicide: A comparative study of maternal versus paternal child homicide. *Criminal Behaviour and Mental Health, 18*, 306–318.

Liem, M., Postulart, M., & Nieuwbeerta, P. (2009). Homicide-suicide in the Netherlands: An epidemiology. *Homicide Studies, 13*, 99–123.

Loeber, R. & Farrington, D. P. (Eds.) (1998). *Serious and Violent Juvenile Offenders: Risk Factors and Successful Interventions*. Thousand Oaks, CA: Sage.

Lorenz, K. (1966). *On Aggression*. New York, NY: Harcourt, Brace & World.

Lösel, F., Bliesener, T., & Bender, D. (2007). Social information processing, experiences of aggression in social contexts, and aggressive behavior in adolescents. *Criminal Justice and Behavior, 34*, 330–347.

Luckenbill, D. F. (1977). Criminal homicide as a situated transaction. *Social Problems, 25*, 176–186.

Manchak, S. M., Skeem, J. L., Douglas, K. S., & Siranosian, M. (2009). Does gender moderate the predictive utility of the Level of Service Inventory-Revised (LSI-R) for serious violent offenders? *Criminal Justice and Behavior, 36*, 425–442.

Maniglio, R. (2010). The role of deviant sexual fantasy in the etiopathogenesis of sexual homicide: A systematic review. *Aggression and Violent Behavior, 15*, 294–302.

Malmquist, C. P. (2010). Adolescent parricide as a clinical and legal problem. *Journal of the American Academy of Psychiatry and the Law, 38*, 73–79.

Margolin, G. & Gordis, E. B. (2000). The effects of family and community violence on children. *Annual Review of Psychology, 51*, 445–479.

Marsh, P., Rosser, E., & Harré, R. (1978). *The Rules of Disorder*. London: Routledge & Kegan Paul.

Masters, B. (1985). *Killing for Company: The Story of a Man Addicted to Murder*. London: Random House.

Matthews, R. (2002). *Armed Robbery*. Cullompton, Devon: Willan Publishing.

McAuliffe, M. D., Hubbard, J. A., Rubin, R. M., Morrow, M. T., & Dearing, K. F. (2006). Reactive and proactive aggression: Stability of constructs and relations to correlates. *Journal of Genetic Psychology, 167*, 365–382.

McCall, P. L., Parker, K. F., & MacDonald, J. M. (2008). The dynamic relationship between homicide rates and social, economic, and political factors from 1970 to 2000. *Social Science Research, 37*, 721–735.

McClusky, C. P., McClusky, J. D., & Bynum, T. S. (2006). Early onset offending and later violent and gun outcomes in a contemporary youth cohort. *Journal of Criminal Justice, 34*, 531–541.

McEwan, T., Mullen, P. E., & MacKenzie, R. (2009). A study of the predictors of persistence in stalking situations. *Law and Human Behavior, 33*, 149–158.

McEwan, T., Mullen, P. E., & Purcell, R. (2007). Identifying risk factors in stalking: A review of current research. *International Journal of Law and Psychiatry, 30*, 1–9.

McGurk, B. (1978). Personality types among normal homicides. *British Journal of Criminology, 19*, 31–49.

McGurk, B. J. & McGurk, R. E. (1979). Personality types among prisoners and prison officers: An investigation of Megargee's theory of control. *British Journal of Criminology, 19*, 31–49.

McPhedran, S. (2009). A review of the evidence for associations between empathy, violence, and animal cruelty. *Aggression and Violent Behavior, 14*, 1–4.

Megargee, E. I. (1966). Undercontrolled and overcontrolled personality types in extreme antisocial aggression. *Psychological Monographs, 80* (3 whole no. 611).

Meloy, J. R., Davis, B., & Lovett, J. (2001). Risk factors for violence among stalkers. *Journal of Threat Assessment, 1*, 3–16.

Mendes, D. D., Mari, J. J., Singer, M., Barros, G. M., & Mello, A. F. (2009). Study review of the biological, social and environmental factors associated with aggressive behavior. *Brazilian Journal of Psychology, 31* (Supplement II): S77–S85.

Michie, C. & Cooke, D. (2006). The structure of violent behavior: A hierarchical model. *Criminal Justice and Behavior, 33*, 706–737.

Miles, D. R. & Carey, G. (1997). Genetic and environmental architecture of human aggression. *Journal of Personality and Social Psychology, 72*, 207–217.

Miller, N. E. (1941). The frustration-aggression hypothesis. *Psychological Review, 48*, 337–342.

Ministry of Justice (2009) *Offender Management Caseload Statistics 2008*. London: Ministry of Justice.

—— (2010a). *Safety in Custody Statistics 2008/2009*. London: Ministry of Justice.

—— (2010b). *Statistics on Women in the Criminal Justice System*. London: Ministry of Justice.

Moffitt, T. E., Caspi, A., Dickson, N., Silva, P., & Stanton, W. (1996). Childhood-onset versus adolescent-onset antisocial conduct problems in males: Natural history from ages 3 to 18 years. *Developmental Psychopathology, 8*, 399–424.

Mohandie, K., Meloy, J. R., McGowan, M. G., & Williams, J. (2006). The RECON typology of stalking: Reliability and validity based upon a large sample of North American stalkers. *Journal of Forensic Science, 51*, 147–155.

Monahan, J., Steadman, H., Silver, E., Appelbaum, P., Robbins, P. C., Mulvey, E. P., et al. (2001). *Rethinking Risk Assessment: The MacArthur Study of Mental Disorder and Violence*. New York, NY: Oxford University Press.

Monroe, R. R. (1978). *Brain Dysfunction in Aggressive Criminals*. Lexington, MA: D. C. Heath.

Moore, K., Jones, N., & Broadbent, E. (2008). *School Violence in OECD Countries*. Woking, Surrey: Plan Limited.

Mullen, P. E., Pathé, M., Purcell, R., & Stuart, G. W. (1999). Study of stalkers. *American Journal of Psychiatry, 156*, 1244–1249.

Newiss, G. & Fairbrother, L. (2004). Child abduction: Understanding police recorded crime statistics. *Findings, 225*. London, Home Office.

Nietzel, M. T., Hasemann, D. M., & Lynam, D. R. (1999). Behavioral perspective on violent behavior. In V. B. Van Hasselt & M. Hersen (Eds.), *Handbook of Psychological Approaches with Violent*

Offenders: Contemporary Strategies and Issues (pp. 39–66). New York, NY: Kluwer Academic Publishers/Plenum Press.

Noonan, J. H. & Vavra, M. C. (2007). *Crime in Schools and Colleges: A Study of Offenders and Arrestees Reported via National Incident-Based Reporting System Data.* Washington, DC: US Department of Justice, Federal Bureau of Investigation.

Novaco, R. W. (1975). *Anger Control: The Development and Evaluation of an Experimental Treatment.* Lexington, MA: D. C. Heath.

—— (1994). Anger as a risk factor for violence among the mentally disordered. In J. Monahan & H. J. Steadman (Eds.), *Violence and Mental Disorder: Developments in Risk Assessment* (pp. 21–59). Chicago, IL: University of Chicago Press.

—— (2006). Anger dysregulation: Its assessment and treatment. In T. A. Cavell & K. T. Malcolm (Eds.), *Anger, Aggression, and Interventions for Interpersonal Violence* (pp. 3–54). Mahwah, NJ: Erlbaum.

Novaco, R. W. & Welsh, W. N. (1989). Anger disturbances: Cognitive mediation and clinical prescriptions. In K. Howells & C. R. Hollin (Eds.), *Clinical Approaches to Violence* (pp. 39–60). Chichester, Sussex: John Wiley & Sons.

Olaya, B., Ezpeleta, L., de la Osa, N., Granero, R., & Doménech, J. M. (2010). Mental health needs of children exposed to intimate partner violence seeking help from mental health services. *Children and Youth Services Review, 41*, 465–478.

Olsen, J. P., Parra, G. R., & Bennett, S. A. (2010). Predicting violence in romantic relationships during adolescence and emerging adulthood: A critical review of the mechanisms by which familial and peer influences operate. *Clinical Psychology Review, 30*, 411–422.

Palermo, G. B. (2002). Murderous parents. *International Journal of Offender Therapy and Comparative Criminology, 46*, 123–143.

Palusci, V. J., Wirtzb, S. J., & Covington, T. M. (2010). Using capture-recapture methods to better ascertain the incidence of fatal child maltreatment. *Child Abuse & Neglect, 34*, 396–402.

Parrott, D. J. & Giancola, P. R. (2007). Addressing "the criterion problem" in the assessment of aggressive behavior: Development of a new taxonomic system. *Aggression and Violent Behavior, 12*, 280–299.

Patterson, G. R. (2002). The early development of coercive family process. In J. B. Reid, G. R. Patterson, & J. Snyder (Eds.), *Antisocial Behavior in Children and Adolescents: A Developmental Analysis and Model for Intervention* (pp. 25–44). Washington, DC: American Psychological Association.

—— (2008). A comparison of models for interstate wars and for individual violence. *Perspectives on Psychological Science, 3*, 203–223.

Patton, C. L., Nobles, M. R., & Fox, K. A. (2010). Look who's stalking: Obsessive pursuit and attachment theory. *Journal of Criminal Justice, 38*, 282–290.

Perron, B. E. & Howard, M. O. (2008). Prevalence and correlates of traumatic brain injury among delinquent youths. *Criminal Behaviour and Mental Health, 18*, 243–255.

Peterson, M. L. & Farrington, D. P. (2007). Cruelty to animals and violence to people. *Victims and Offenders, 2*, 21–43.

Pettit, G. S. (2004). Violent children in developmental perspective: Risk and protective factors and the mechanisms through which they (may) operate. *Current Directions in Psychological Science, 13*, 194–197.

Phillips, R. T. M. (2007). Celebrity and presidential candidates. In D. A. Pinals (Ed.), *Stalking: Psychiatric Perspectives and Practical Approaches* (pp. 227–250). New York, NY: Oxford University Press.

Pinals, D. A. (Ed.) (2007). *Stalking: Psychiatric Perspectives and Practical Approaches.* New York, NY: Oxford University Press.

Pinto, L. A., Sullivan, E. L., Rosenbaum, A., Wyngarden, N., Umhau, J. C., Miller, M. W., & Taft, C. T. (2010). Biological correlates of intimate partner violence perpetration. *Aggression and Violent Behavior, 15*, 387–398.

Polaschek, D. L. L., Calvert, S. W., & Gannon, T. A. (2009). Linking violent thinking: Implicit theory-based research with violent offenders. *Journal of Interpersonal Violence, 24*, 75–96.

Polman, H., Orobio de Castro, B., Koops, W., van Boxtel, H. W., & Merk, W. W. (2007). A meta-analysis of the distinction between reactive and proactive aggression in children and adolescents. *Journal of Abnormal Child Psychology, 35*, 552–535.

Porter, L. E. (2010). Robbery. In J. M. Brown & E. A. Campbell (Eds.), *The Cambridge Handbook of Forensic Psychology* (pp. 534–542). Cambridge: Cambridge University Press.

Proulx, J., Beauregard, É., Cusson, M., & Nicole, A. (Eds.) (2005). *Sexual Murderers: A Comparative Analysis and New Perspective. (*Translated by Steven Sacks.). Chichester, Sussex: John Wiley & Sons.

Purcell, R., Moller, B., Flower, T., & Mullen, P. E. (2009). Stalking among juveniles. *British Journal of Psychiatry, 194*, 451–455.

Purcell, R., Pathé, M., & Mullen, P. E. (2001). A study of women who stalk. *American Journal of Psychiatry, 158*, 2056–2060.

Putkonen, A., Ryynänen, O., Eronen, M., & Tiihonen, J. (2007). Transmission of violent offending and crime across three generations. *Social Psychiatry and Psychiatric Epidemiology, 42*, 94–99.

Quinsey, V. L., Maguire, A., & Varney, G. W. (1983). Assertion and overcontrolled hostility among mentally disordered murderers. *Journal of Consulting and Clinical Psychology, 51*, 550–556.

Raine, A. (2002). Biosocial studies of antisocial and violent behaviour in children and adults: A review. *Journal of Abnormal Child Psychology, 30*, 311–326.

Raine, A., Stoddard, J., Bihrle, S., & Buchsbaum, M. (1998). Prefontal glucose deficits in murderers lacking psychosocial deprivation. *Neuropsychiatry, Neuropsychology, and Behavioral Neurology, 11*, 1–7.

Ravensberg, V. & Miller, C. (2003). Stalking among young adults: A review of the preliminary research. *Aggression and Violent Behavior, 8*, 455–469.

Reckdenwald, A. & Parker, K. F. (2010). Understanding gender-specific intimate partner homicide: A theoretical and domestic service-oriented approach. *Journal of Criminal Justice, 38*, 951–958.

Renner, L. M. & Slack, K. S. (2006). Intimate partner violence and child maltreatment: Understanding intra- and intergenerational connections. *Child Abuse & Neglect, 30*, 599–617.

Rhee, S. H. & Waldman, I. D. (2002). Genetic and environmental influences on antisocial behavior: A meta-analysis of twin and adoption studies. *Psychological Bulletin, 128*, 490–529.

Richardson, D. S. & Hammock, G. S. (2007). Social context of human aggression: Are we paying too much attention to gender? *Aggression and Violent Behavior, 12*, 417–426.

Roberts, A. R., Zgoba, K. M., & Shahidullah, S. M. (2007). Recidivism among four types of homicide offenders: An exploratory analysis of 336 homicide offenders in New Jersey. *Aggression and Violent Behavior, 12*, 493–507.

Robinson, A. (2010). Domestic violence. In F. Brookman, M. Maguire, H. Pierpoint, & T. Bennett (Eds.), *Handbook on Crime* (pp. 245–269). Cullompton, Devon: Willan Publishing.

Rodway, C., Norrington-Moore V., While, D., Hunt, I. M., Flynn, S., Swinson, N., Roscoe, A., Appleby, L., & Shaw, J. (2010). A population-based study of juvenile perpetrators of homicide in England and Wales. *Journal of Adolescence, 34*, 19–28.

Roe, S. (2010). Intimate violence: 2008/09 BCS. In K. Smith, J. Flatley, K. Coleman, S. Osborne, P. Kaiza, & S. Roe (Eds.), *Homicides, Firearm Offences and Intimate Violence 2008/09: Supplementary Volume 2 to Crime in England and Wales 2008/09*. London: Home Office.

Rosenfeld, B. (2004). Violence risk factors in stalking and obsessional harassment: A review and preliminary meta-analysis. *Criminal Justice and Behavior, 31*, 9–36.

Rossegger, A., Welti, N., Urbaniok, F., Elbert, T., Cortoni, F., & Endrass, J. (2009). Women convicted for violent offences: Adverse childhood experiences, low levels of education and poor mental health. *BMC Psychiatry, 9*, 81–92.

Sandberg, A. A., Koepf, G. F., Ishiara, T., & Hauschka, T. S. (1961). An XXY human male. *Lancet, 262*, 488–489.

Savitz, L. D., Kumar, K. S., & Zahn, M. A. (1991). Quantifying Luckenbill. *Deviant Behavior: An Interdisciplinary Journal, 12*, 19–29.

Schafer, J. A., Varano, S. P., Jarvis, J. P., & Cancino, J. M. (2010). Bad moon on the rise? Lunar cycles and incidents of crime. *Journal of Criminal Justice, 38*, 359–367.

Schonfeld, I. S. (2006). School violence. In E. K. Kelloway, J. Barling, & J. J. Hurrell (Eds.), *Handbook of Workplace Violence* (pp. 169–229). Thousand Oaks, CA: Sage.

Séguin, J. R., Phil, R. O., Harden, P. W., Tremblay, R. E., & Boulerice, B. (1995). Cognitive and neuropsychological characteristics of physically aggressive boys. *Journal of Abnormal Psychology, 104*, 614–624.

Shaw, J., Hunt, I. M., Flynn, S., Amos, T., Meehan, J., Robinson, J., Bickley, H., Parsons, R., McCann, K., Burns, J., Kapur, N., & Appleby, L. (2006). The role of alcohol and drugs in homicides in England and Wales. *Addiction, 101*, 1117–1124.

Siann, G. (1985). *Accounting for Aggression: Perspectives on Aggression and Violence*. London: Allen & Unwin.

Siegel, A. (2005). *The Neurobiology of Aggression and Rage*. Boca Raton, FL: CRC Press.

Siegel, A. & Victoroff, J. (2009). Understanding human aggression: New insights from neuroscience. *International Journal of Law and Psychiatry, 32*, 209–215.

Siever, L. J. (2008). Neurobiology of aggression and violence. *American Journal of Psychiatry, 165*, 429–442.

Sigfusdottir, I. D., Farkas, G., & Silva, E. (2004). The role of depressed mood and anger in the relationship between family conflict and delinquent behaviour. *Journal of Youth and Adolescence, 33*, 509–522.

Simons, D. A. & Wurtele, S. K. (2010). Relationships between parents' use of corporal punishment and their children's endorsement of spanking and hitting other children. *Child Abuse & Neglect, 34*, 639–646.

Slaughter, B., Fann, J. R., & Edhe, D. (2003). Traumatic brain injury in a county jail population: Prevalence, neuropsychological functioning and psychiatric disorders. *Brain Injury, 17*, 731–741.

Smith, C. A., Ireland, T. O., Thornberry, T. P., & Elwyn, L. (2008). Childhood maltreatment and antisocial behavior: Comparison of self-reported and substantiated maltreatment. *American Journal of Orthopsychiatry, 78*, 173–186.

Smith, K., Flatley, J., Coleman, K., Osborne, S., Kaiza, P., & Roe, S. (2010). *Homicides, Firearm Offences and Intimate violence 2008/09. Supplementary Volume 2 to Crime in England and Wales 2008/09*. London: Home Office.

Smith, K. & Hoare, J. (Eds.) (2009). *Crime in England and Wales 2008/09: Volume 2, Explanatory Notes and Classifications*. London: Home Office.

Snethen, G. & Van Puymbroeck, M. (2008). Girls and physical aggression: Causes, trends, and intervention guided by Social Learning Theory. *Aggression and Violent Behavior, 13*, 346–354.

Soothill, K., Francis, B., & Ackerley, E. (2007). Kidnapping: A criminal profile of persons convicted 1979–2001. *Behavioral Sciences and the Law, 25*, 69–84.

Soothill, K., Francis, B., & Liu, J. (2008). Does serious offending lead to homicide? Exploring the interrelationships and sequencing of serious crime. *British Journal of Criminology, 48*, 522–537.

Soothill, K. & Wilson, D. (2005). Theorising the puzzle that is Harold Shipman. *Journal of Forensic Psychiatry & Psychology, 16*, 685–698.

Spinelli, M. G. (2001). A systematic investigation of 16 cases of neonaticide. *American Journal of Psychiatry, 158*, 811–813.

Spitzberg, B. H. (2002). The tactical topography of stalking victimization and management. *Trauma, Violence, & Abuse, 3*, 261–288.

Spitzberg, B. H. & Cupach, W. R. (2007). The state of the art of stalking: Taking stock of the emerging literature. *Aggression and Violent Behavior, 12*, 64–86.

Springer, K. W., Sheridan, J., Kuo, D., & Carnes, M. (2007). Long-term physical and mental health consequences of childhood physical abuse: Results from a large population-based sample of men and women. *Child Abuse & Neglect, 31*, 517–530.

Stanton, J. & Simpson, A. (2002). Filicide: A review. *International Journal of Law and Psychiatry, 25*, 1–14.

Stieger, S., Burger, C., & Schild, A. (2008). Lifetime prevalence and impact of stalking: Epidemiological data from Eastern Austria. *European Journal of Psychiatry, 22*, 235–241.

Stith, S. M., Liu, T. L., Davies, C., Boykin, E. L., Alder, M. C., Harris, J. M., & Des, J. E. M. E. G. (2009). Risk factors in child maltreatment: A meta-analytic review of the literature. *Aggression and Violent Behavior, 14*, 13–29.

Storr, A. (1989). *Freud: A Very Short Introduction.* Oxford: Oxford University Press.

Straus, M. A. (1994). Ten myths that perpetuate corporal punishment. In M. A. Straus (Ed.), *Beating the Devil Out of Them: Corporal Punishment in American Families* (pp. 149–167). San Francisco, CA: Jossey-Bass/Lexington.

——. (2005). Children should never, ever, be spanked no matter what the circumstances. In D. R. Loseke, R. J. Gelles, & M. M. Cavanaugh (Eds.), *Current Controversies about Family Violence* (2nd ed.) (pp. 137–157). Thousand Oaks, CA: Sage.

Straus, M. A. & Paschall, M. J. (2009). Corporal punishment by mothers and development of children's cognitive ability: A longitudinal study of two nationally representative age cohorts. *Journal of Aggression, Maltreatment & Trauma, 18*, 459–483.

Struckman-Johnson, C. & Struckman-Johnson, D. (2000). Sexual coercion rates in seven Midwestern prison facilities for men. *The Prison Journal, 80*, 379–390.

—— (2002). Sexual coercion reported by women in three midwestern prisons. *The Journal of Sex Research, 39*, 217–227.

Taillieu, T. L. & Brownridge, D. A. (2010). Violence against pregnant women: Prevalence, patterns, risk factors, theories, and directions for future research. *Aggression and Violent Behavior, 15*, 14–35.

Tallichet, S. E. & Hensley, C. (2009). The social and emotional context of childhood and adolescent animal cruelty. *International Journal of Offender Therapy and Comparative Criminology, 53*, 596–606.

Taylor, M. & Horgan, J. (Eds.) (2000). *The Future of Terrorism.* London: Frank Cass & Co.

Tedeschi, J. T. & Felson, R. B. (1994). *Violence, Aggression, & Coercive Actions.* Washington, DC: American Psychological Association.

Temcheff, C. E., Serbin, L. A., Martin-Storey, A., Stack, D. M., Hodgins, S., Ledingham, J., & Schwartzman, A. E. (2008). Continuity and pathways from aggression in childhood to family violence in adulthood: A 30-year longitudinal study. *Journal of Family Violence, 23*, 231–242.

Thompson, R. (2007). Mothers' violence victimization and child behavior problems: Examining the link. *American Journal of Orthopsychiatry, 77*, 306–315.

Tiihonen, J., Rossi, R., Laakso, M. P., Hodgins, S., Testa, C., Perez, J., & Frisoni, G. B. (2010). Brain anatomy of persistent violent offenders: More rather than less. *Psychiatry Research: Neuroimaging, 163*, 201–212.

Toch, H. (1969). *Violent Men.* Chicago, IL: Aldine.

Tolan, P., Gorman-Smith, D., & Henry, D. (2006). Family violence. *Annual Review of Psychology, 57*, 557–583.

Töro, K., Fehér, S., Farkas, K., & Dunay, G. (2010). Homicides against infants, children and adolescents in Budapest (1960–2005). *Journal of Forensic and Legal Medicine, 17*, 407–411.

Tursz, A., Crost, M., Gerbouin-Rérolle, P., & Cook, J. M. (2010). Underascertainment of child abuse fatalities in France: Retrospective analysis of judicial data to assess underreporting of infant homicides in mortality statistics. *Child Abuse and Neglect, 34*, 534–544.

Tuvblad, C., Raine, A., Zheng, M., & Baker, L. A. (2009). Genetic and environmental stability differs in reactive and proactive aggression. *Aggressive Behavior, 35*, 437–452.

Twardosz, S. & Lutzker, J. R. (2010). Child maltreatment and the developing brain: A review of neuroscience perspectives. *Aggression and Violent Behavior, 15*, 59–68.

Varno, S. P., McCluskey, J. D., Patchin, J. W., & Bynum, T. S. (2004). Exploring the drugs-homicide connection. *Journal of Contemporary Criminal Justice, 20*, 369–392.

Vaughn, M. G., DeLisi, M., Beaver, K. M., & Howard, M. O. (2009). Multiple murder and criminal careers: A latent class analysis of multiple homicide offenders. *Forensic Science International, 183*, 67–73.

Walker, A., Flatley, J., Kershaw, C., & Moon, D. (Eds.) (2009). *Crime in England and Wales 2008/09, Volume 1. Findings from the British Crime Survey and Police Recorded Crime.* London: Home Office.

Walsh, C., MacMillan, H. L., & Jamieson, E. (2003). The relationship between parental substance abuse and child maltreatment: Findings from the Ontario Health Supplement. *Child Abuse & Neglect, 27*, 1409–1425.

Wekerle, C., Wall, A., Leung, E., & Trocmé, N. (2007). Cumulative stress and substantiated maltreatment: The importance of caregiver vulnerability and adult partner violence. *Child Abuse & Neglect, 31*, 427–443.

Welfare, H. & Hollin, C. R. (in press). Involvement in extreme violence and violence-related trauma: A review with relevance to young people in custody. *Legal and Criminological Psychology*.

West, D. J. (1965). *Murder Followed by Suicide*. London: Heinemann Educational.

Widom, C. S. (1978). An empirical classification of female offenders. *Criminal Justice and Behavior, 5*, 35–52.

—— (1989). Does violence beget violence? A critical examination of the literature. *Psychological Bulletin, 106*, 3–28.

Widom, C. S. & Brzustowicz, L. M. (2006). MAOA and the "cycle of violence": Childhood abuse and neglect, MAOA genotype, and risk for violent and antisocial behavior. *Biological Psychiatry, 60*, 684–689.

Wike, T. L. & Fraser, M. W. (2009). School shootings: Making sense of the senseless. *Aggression and Violent Behavior, 14*, 162–169.

Williams, D. (1969). Neural factors relating to habitual aggression. Consideration of differences between habitual aggressives and other who have not committed crimes of violence. *Brain, 92*, 503–520.

Williams, J. M. G. (1997). *Cry of Pain: Understanding Suicide and Self-Harm*. London: Penguin Books.

—— (2001). *Suicide and Attempted Suicide*. London: Penguin Books.

Winstok, Z. (2009). From self-control capabilities and the need to control others to proactive and reactive aggression among adolescents. *Journal of Adolescence, 32*, 455–466.

Witkin, H. A., Mednick, S. A., Schulsinger, F., Bakkstrøm, E., Christiansen, K. O., Goodenough, D. R., & Stocking, M. (1976). Criminality in XYY and XXY men. *Science, 193*, 547–555.

Wolfgang, M. E. (1958). *Patterns in Criminal Homicide*. Philadelphia, PA: University of Pennsylvania Press.

Wolfgang, M. E. & Ferracuti, F. (1967). *The Subculture of Violence: Towards an Integrated Theory in Criminology*. London: Tavistock Publications.

Wood, J., Moir, A., & James, M. (2009). Prisoners' gang-related activity: The importance of bullying and moral disengagement. *Psychology, Crime & Law, 15*, 569–581.

Yeh, T., Coccaro, E. F., & Jacobson, K. C. (2010). Multivariate behavior genetic analyses of aggressive behavior subtypes. *Behavior Genetics, 40*, 603–617.

Yourstone, J., Lindhome, T., & Kristiansson, M. (2008). Women who kill: A comparison of the psychosocial background of female and male perpetrators. *International Journal of Law and Psychiatry, 31*, 374–383.

Zamble, E. & Quinsey, V. L. (1997). *The Criminal Recidivism Process*. Cambridge: Cambridge University Press.

Zahn, M. A., Brumbaugh, S., Steffensmeier, D., Feld, B. C., Morash, M., Chesney-Lind, M., & Kruttschnitt, C. (2008). *Violence by Teenage Girls: Trends and Context*. Washington, DC: US Department of Justice, Office of Justice Programs, Office of Juvenile Justice and Delinquency Prevention, available at: www.ojp.usdoj.gov/ojjdp.

7 Psychological approaches to understanding serious crime III

Sexual crime

As seen in the previous chapter, violent crime presents itself in a range of guises. The focus in this chapter is on a particular type of violent crime: those crimes where there is a sexual element attached to the violence so that, in law, there is a sexual offence. Not all sexual offences are violent in a physical sense, which is not to say that they do not bring distress to those involved. For example, exhibitionism (colloquially known as 'flashing') may involve a man exposing his genitals to an unsuspecting woman; while voyeurism ('peeping') entails spying on an unsuspecting person, often while they are undressing or having sex.

Arriving at a legal definition of sexual crime is not straightforward. In that criminal law reflects a society's moral values, so the laws concerning sexual behaviour illustrate that moral values concerning sexual behaviour can fluctuate over time. Myhill and Allen (2002) charted some of the legislative changes regarding sexual offences in England and Wales since the mid-1950s, noting the legalisation of homosexuality in 1967, the lowering of the age of consent for homosexual males from 21 to 18 years in 1994, and then in 2000 the age of consent was set at 16 years for both homosexual and heterosexual sexual behaviours.

There are two further notable examples of legal changes regarding sexual behaviour. First, in 1991, the principle of marital rape exemption, which dates back to 1736, was abolished in England and Wales, thereby making rape within marriage illegal. This exemption had been based on the view that through marriage women consent sexual intercourse within their marriage and so cannot later retract their assent. Second, the legal definition of rape was changed in 1994 to include penile penetration of the anus, so bringing rape of a male within criminal law.

The rapid pace of technological change necessitates change in many areas of law, such as copyright law and regulation of the electronic distribution of literature, music, images, and films. The impact of technology in the domain of sex offending is readily seen, for example, in way in which obscene images can be distributed electronically. The availability of the internet opens up a range of possibilities for offenders, including sex offenders.

Beech, Elliott, Birgden, and Findlater (2008) suggest that the sexual abuse of children can take place over the internet in a number of ways. The abuse may take place through the dissemination of sexualised images of children, or through virtual social networks allowing contact between those with a sexual interest in children, or by facilitating inappropriate sexual communication with children, or as a means by which to find children to abuse. The use of the internet for 'online grooming' of children has become an activity that has generated significant concern in a number of countries (Choo, 2009). Sheldon and Howitt (2007) make the point that the 'internet sex offender' is a new style of sex offender unconstrained by parochial rules of ethics or law. It is, however, unlikely that men who use child pornography are a heterogeneous group, sexually dependent only upon digital images of children (McCarthy, 2010; Seto, Reeves, & Jung, 2010).

There are women who commit sexual offences (Fazel, Sjöstedt, Grann, & Långström, 2010; Gannon, Rose, & Ward, 2008; Krahé, Scheinberger-Olwig, & Bieneck, 2003), although the rate of recidivism for female sex offenders is lower than that for men. An American study by Sandler and Freeman (2009) reported a sexual reconviction rate of 1.9 per cent with a sample of 1,466 female sex offenders followed-up for 5 years after their first conviction. This rate of reconviction is much lower than the 10–15 per cent rate typically found for male sex offenders after the same time (Hanson & Morton-Bourgon, 2004). Sexual offences can be perpetrated by men against men (Scarce, 1997): same-sex sexual offending is often associated with institutions such as prisons (Neal & Clements, 2010; Struckman-Johnson & Struckman-Johnson, 2006) but it may also be prevalent in male-dominated organisations such as the military (Turchik & Wilson, 2010). However, the majority of sexual offences are perpetrated by men against women and children.

Legal definitions of sexual offences

In England and Wales, the Sexual Offences Act 2003 states the sexual behaviours that are prohibited by law (Stevenson, Davies, & Gunn, 2003). As shown in Table 7.1, the Sentencing Council guidelines for the 2003 Sexual Offences Act (Sentencing Guidelines Secretariat, 2007) categorises sexual offences under several broad headings. These guidelines introduced an expanded range of offences relating to sexual activity with a child less than 16 years of age.

As seen from Table 7.1, sexual offending encompasses a varied range of behaviours: at one extreme there are non-contact offences, such as voyeurism, at the other extreme there

Table 7.1 Sexual offences in 2003 Act (after Sentencing Guidelines Secretariat, 2007)

Non-consensual offences
- Rape and assault by penetration
- Sexual assault
- Causing or inciting sexual activity
- Other non-consensual offences

Offences involving ostensible consent
- Offences involving children
- Offences against vulnerable adults

Preparatory offences
- Sexual grooming
- Committing another offence with intent
- Trespass with intent
- Administering a substance with intent

Other offences
- Sex with an adult relative
- Sexual activity in a public lavatory
- Exposure
- Voyeurism
- Intercourse with an animal
- Sexual penetration of a corpse

Exploitation offences
- Indecent photographs of children
- Abuse of children through prostitution and pornography
- Exploitation of prostitution
- Trafficking

are acts of physical violence, as with rape. As seen in Chapter 6, there are also sexual murders (Carter & Hollin, 2010; Knoll & Hazelwood, 2009; Meloy, 2000) although these are not defined as such in criminal law.

The legal definition of a sexual offence varies from country to country, making international comparisons of crime statistics difficult to interpret. This definitional issue is compounded by the variations in victim reporting, as discussed below, that particularly surround sexual offending.

Sex offences and crime statistics

Official figures

In Chapter 2, the point was made that, for a variety of reasons, victims do not always report to the police the crime in which they were involved. Given the obvious sensitivities surrounding sexual crime, for both adult and child victims, it is likely that sexual offences are one of the crimes least likely to be reported. Hoare and Jansson (2007) estimated that only 11 per cent of those who were victims of serious sexual assault reported the crime to the police. The reasons that victims of sexual assault give for not reporting the crime are varied: they may feel humiliated and not wish to draw any attention to the fact that they have been involved in a sex offence; they may think that the police would be unable to help; they may not want to face being questioned about the crime; they may fear reprisals if they report the crime; there may be a perception that the offence is a family matter and therefore there is no need to involve the police; and parents may seek to spare child victims from questioning. It is also possible that the victim does not perceive the forced sexual act as a crime, perhaps blaming themselves for what has happened.

It was also noted in Chapter 2 that crimes can be 'lost' in the official recording process: this process of attrition applies equally to sexual offences (Kelly, Lovett, & Regan, 2005). There are several reasons why the number of sexual crimes reported is less than the number eventually recorded in the official statistics: on investigation the police may correctly conclude that no sexual offence took place; it may be that a crime did occur but there is insufficient supportive evidence; or the complainant may decide to withdraw their complaint.

There are, of course, official figures available on the prevalence of sex offences in England and Wales: there were just over 62,000 sex offences in 2005/6 and 53,500 in 2007/8 (Hoare & Povey, 2008); in 2008/09 the police recorded 12,129 offences of rape against women (Ministry of Justice, 2010). How close are these official figures to the real prevalence of sex offending? The general population surveys, although not without limitations, allow a broader picture to emerge.

Survey figures

When general population surveys are conducted through personal interviews, the respondents may, as is the case with reporting to the police, be reluctant to disclose their personal involvement in some types of violent and sexually violent crimes. This point may be particularly true when the violent assault is by an intimate partner (Povey, Coleman, Kaiza, Hoare, & Jansson, 2008). Thus, surveys based primarily on interview data may produce unreliable findings with regard to sexual offences (Hoare & Povey, 2008). In order to overcome this methodological limitation, confidential self-completion questionnaires have been used. From 1998, this type of confidential methodology was used by the *British Crime*

Survey (BCS) to ask respondents about their experiences of intimate violence, including experiences of serious sexual assault (Myhill & Allen, 2002).

The report *Statistics on Women and the Criminal Justice System* (Ministry of Justice, 2010), draws together the figures (including BCS figures) on sexual offences. Thus, for women aged between 16 and 59 years, the figures for 2006–9 showed an annual prevalence of just fewer than 3 per cent of women experiencing one or more sexual assaults; the comparable figure for men was less than 1 per cent. Similarly focusing on lifetime experience, 19.5 per cent of women reported an experience of sexual assault since the age of 16 years; the comparable figure for men was 2.8 per cent. This Ministry of Justice report also specifically considered serious sexual assault – where 'serious sexual assault is defined to include rape or assault by penetration, including attempts' (Ministry of Justice, 2010: 24) – and concluded that 4.9 per cent of women and less than 1 per cent of men had experienced an attempted or actual serious sexual assault, and 4 per cent of women had been raped (not including attempted rape).

The advances in gathering and sharing information offered by the internet have led to international efforts to pool data, including crime statistics, allowing comparisons to be made across a vast range of variables. The United Nations Office on Drugs and Crime (UNODC) collates crime and criminal justice statistics for more than 120 countries. The UNODC website (see 'Useful websites' at the end of this chapter) makes available crime statistics collated from different parts of the globe. The figures in Box 7.1 show the aggregated data for all types of sexual violence, taken to be 'rape and sexual assault, including offences against children', for 2008. In reading these figures it should be taken into account that there will be significant variations across countries in terms of legal definition of sexual violence, levels of reporting, and police recording procedures.

The comparable figure for the UK: England and Wales (which is reported separately to the UK: Northern Ireland) was 74.8.

Offences against children

Attempts to quantify the prevalence of sex offences involving children are particularly problematic. There are the familiar reporting issues, as is the case with crime generally and sex offences specifically, however with children the picture is even less clear for several reasons. Young children may not understand the nature and gravity of sexual acts in which they are involved, they may not have the resources to report abuse, or they may fear for their family stability if they report their abuse.

Box 7.1 Total police recorded sexual violence (rape and sexual assault, including offences against children): rate per 100,000 population for 2008 (after UNDOC)

Highest rate		*Lowest rate*	
Sweden	155.8	Kyrgyzstan	0.2
Maldives	152.4	Egypt	0.3
Iceland	116.7	Mongolia	0.7
Canada	75.3	Syrian Arab Republic	0.4
Israel	63.8	Armenia	2.0

Table 7.2 Recorded crime 2007/8: sexual offences against children (adapted from Home Office, no date)

	Against Males	Against Females
Sexual assault on individual aged 13 and over	1,315	15,790
Sexual assault on a child aged under 16	1,118	3,976
Rape of a child aged under 13	427	1,472
Rape of a child aged under 16	235	2,418
Sexual activity involving a child under 13	1,836[1]	
Sexual activity involving a child under 16	3,100[1]	
Sexual grooming	272[1]	
Abuse of children through prostitution or pornography	110[1]	

[1] These offences are not gender-specific so separate figures are not available for males and females.

The assessment of the prevalence of sex offences against children in England and Wales has relied mainly on the crime statistics taken from police recording of reported crime. As noted above, the Sexual Offences Act 2003 introduced changes to the definition of some sex offences, including offences against children. These definitional changes mean that comparison of figures before and after the Act is not straightforward. However, since 2004, the figures recorded by police are available for a range of sexual offences involving children. These figures for the year 2007–8, as shown in Table 7.2, along with other statistics which can be gleaned from unpublished data provided by the Home Office (Home Office, no date).

In terms of international comparisons, the figures from Box 7.1 can be disaggregated to show sexual offences specifically against children (see Box 7.2). The comparable figure for the UK: England and Wales (reported separately from the UK: Northern Ireland) was 27.6.

The respondents taking part in the BCS are all 16 years of age and above and they are specifically asked about any offences they may have experienced *after* the age of 16. However, there are other population surveys, generally of a smaller scale than the BCS, that shed some light on sex offences against children. A study conducted on behalf of the National Society for the Prevention of Cruelty to Children (NSPCC) included information about sexual crimes involving children (Cawson, Wattam, Brooker, & Kelly, 2000). This survey found that sexual abuse is most commonly perpetrated by people who are acquainted with the victim: about one in ten of the NSPCC sample said that they had been sexually abused by an acquaintance, of which a smaller proportion (about one in 25) said they had been abused by parents, carers, or relatives; similarly, a small proportion of respondents (about

---

Box 7.2 Police recorded sexual violence against children: rate per 100,000 population for 2008 (after UNDOC)

Highest rate		Lowest rate	
Maldives	152.4	Syrian Arab Republic	0.1
UK (NI)	59.7	Egypt	0.2
Israel	40.3	Kyrgyzstan	0.2
New Zealand	33.4	Mongolia	0.5
Iceland	32.3	Belarus	2.0

one in 25) experienced a sex offence committed by a stranger. Finkelhor (1986) noted that females are at higher risk than males and that children are victimised at all ages from birth to 18 years (after which the abuse is of an adult not a child). There are peaks of vulnerability to abuse at 6–7 years and during the prepubescent ages of 10–12 years.

Finkelhor (1984, 1986) interviewed men and women who had been victims of abuse as children: they reported that the most common type of assault was genital fondling, including adult contact with the child's genitals using either hand or mouth, or the child's contact with the adult's genitals. Sexual activities such as masturbation and exhibitionism were also frequently experienced, although penetrative sex was not as frequent, perhaps because of the risk of physical injury to the child. Finkelhor (1986) noted that in many cases the sexual abuse was a single, unpleasant experience after which the child avoided the adult or told their parents who dealt with the matter. However, in some cases the sexual abuse became episodic, occurring on regular basis over weeks, months, or even years. As with other types of crime, family factors are associated with the sexual abuse of children. The risk of child sexual abuse is heightened when the family is disrupted by parental conflict or separation, or when the child has a poor relationship, as characterised by low levels of attachment, with their parents (Aspelmeier, Elliott, & Smith, 2007; Finkelhor, 1984, 1986). It should be recognised that some families in which abuse occurs are struggling with a range of problems including coping with a low income, mental health problems, and substance use. The welfare of children at risk of abuse within a family is best understood in the context of being nested within a tangle of psychological and social problems (Abracen, Looman, & Anderson, 2000; Feelgood, Cortoni, & Thompson, 2005; Leue, Borchard, & Hoyer, 2004). This latter statement, which speaks to the complexity of the issues involved, should not be taken as diminishing the gravity of the offending or denying that there are some adults who deliberately and actively target children.

Juvenile sex offenders

Not all sex offences against children are perpetrated by adults: there are sexual offences committed against children by other juveniles (Barbaree & Marshall, 2008; Hunter, Hazelwood, & Slesinger, 2000). As with crime generally and perhaps sex offences specifically, it is difficult to know exactly what percentage of sex offences are committed by juveniles. Hudson and Ward (2001: 364) suggest: 'Estimates of the incidents of sexual assaults perpetrated by adolescents range from 20% to 30% of rapes and from 30% to 60% of instances of child molestation'.

Notwithstanding the many issues associated with accurate measurement, it is not controversial to say that sexual crimes are widespread. However, one of the issues faced in reading the wider literature is that the generic term 'sex offence' is sometimes used in a broad sense to encompass offences against children *and* offences against adults. However, as there is no *prima facie* reason to suggest that sex offences against children are committed by the same individuals who commit sex offences against women, the two will be considered separately. Thus, the next section of this chapter considers sex offences against children, followed by sex offences against women.

Sex offences against children

An early concern with child sexual and physical assault is seen in the work of Auguste Ambroise Tardieu (1818–79), a leading French pathologist and forensic medical scientist.

Tardieu recognised a pattern of repeated injuries inflicted on infants and young children by their parents and guardians: these injuries including bruising specifically to the lower back and buttocks, injuries from burning, multiple fractures that had occurred at different times and abdominal injuries frequently to the spleen or the liver. Tardieu noted that these physical injuries were sometimes accompanied by signs of neglect and malnutrition. This pattern of injuries was observed with sufficient frequency for Tardieu to suggest that it could be understood as a syndrome of repeated intentional injuries. The syndrome he described now bears his name, *Tardieu's Syndrome* (Labbé, 2005).

Indeed, the features of the Baby P case discussed in Chapter 6 bear a remarkable similarity to the cases described over a century ago by Tardieu. This similarity is not surprising, it is highly likely that, as with physical abuse, adult sexual activity with children has been prevalent for centuries. In mid-19th century England children as young as 10 years of age could legally consent to (hetero)sexual acts. The changing moral values in England as the 20th century approached led to a growth in concern about the involvement of children in sexual activity. An increase in the age of consent to protect children was generally seen as desirable: however, the difficult practical issue is to determine the age at which children are no longer children and therefore may be deemed to have the capacity knowingly to consent to sex (Waites, 2005). Is the age of consent best determined by chronological age, the onset of puberty, or the age at which a society judges marriage to be appropriate? The practical issues in legally defining a 'child' may be seen in two areas: first, the changes in the age of consent over time *within* a legal framework (as discussed above for England and Wales); second, in international variations *across* jurisdictions in the age of consent.

The age of consent in most Western societies lies in the range 15 to 18 years of age: in Spain it is 13 years, in England and Wales it is 16 years, and in Turkey it is 18 years. In the USA, the age of consent varies from 16 to 18 years on a state-by-state basis, while in Africa it varies from 12 (Angola) to 20 years (Tunisia), with similar variations evident across the continents of Asia, Oceania, and South America. There may be caveats, again varying from jurisdiction to jurisdiction, appended to the legislation regarding, for example, the child's mental capacity, the type of sexual act, and whether the consent is to a heterosexual or homosexual act.

As seen with other crimes, the legal definition of a sexual offence against a child has shifted and changed over time. As outlined in Table 7.1, the Sentencing Council guidelines for the 2003 Sexual Offences Act (Sentencing Guidelines Secretariat, 2007) categorises sexual offences against children under a number of headings. These headings encompass a range of types of offence including rape committed against females and against males, physically violent assaults, offences committed within the family, and the use of images on the internet.

The 2003 Act removed an ambiguity that previously allowed those accused of child rape to argue that the child consented to the sexual act. From the implementation of the 2003 Act, sexual intercourse with a child under 13 years of age is treated as rape. The 2003 Act also introduced new offences regarding adult sexual activity, including both physical and non-physical contact, with a child under 16 years of age. The Act also takes account of children committing sexual crimes that involve other children. Thus, some of the offences apply equally to those under 18 years of age as well as to adults.

Child sexual abuse and the internet

A point to note about the 2003 Act is that while the more familiar sexual crimes, such as rape and sexual assault (familial and non-familial), are present, there are acts also included that involve the use of the internet. It is invariably the case that as technology advances, so crime will keep pace: this observation is as true for sexual crimes (Atkinson & Newton, 2010) as it is for identity theft, credit card scams, and online fraud (Baker, 1999; Chen et al., 2006).

The 2003 Act introduced a new offence to counter adult sexual grooming of a child over the internet: this offence is typically one where an adult becomes friendly with a child, say via a social networking site, and establishes an online rapport with the child eventually arranging a meeting with the intention of sexually abuse the child. As Jewkes (2010) points out, the phenomenon of online soliciting is simply a new variation on the longstanding issue of adult sexual interest in children. One of the challenges in policing virtual communities or networks of adults with a sexual interest in children is that they cross international boundaries so highlighting variations in law.

Those adults with a sexual interest in children may use the internet either to distribute sexual images of children or as a means of communication about abuse (Beech et al., 2008; Sheehan & Sullivan, 2010; Sheldon & Howitt, 2007; Taylor & Quayle, 2006). The distribution of images of children is of concern for two reasons: first, it reinforces a sexualised view of children; second, actual abuse of children may have taken place in order to make the images. There are a range of sexualised images of children in circulation on the internet: Taylor, Holland, and Quayle (2001) developed a nine-level typology of sexualised picture collections of children that ranged from pictures of children wearing normal everyday clothes, to explicit poses and finally to images of sexual assault, sadism, and bestiality. The sexualised images of children may be produced in large numbers to form a 'set' with the same child or group of children shown in a range of poses.

The availability of such sets has led to the phenomenon of 'collecting', whereby adults purchase or exchange images of children from the same set which they then store electronically (Sheldon & Howitt, 2007; Taylor & Quayle, 2006). While the majority view is that sexualised images of children are not acceptable, Winder and Gough (2010) found that internet sex offenders rejected the view that their actions were harmful to children.

Sex offences involving children raise many legal and moral concerns. The law continues to evolve, particularly with regard to the abusive use of technology, and will presumably continue to do so. While it is not possible to be precise about the extent of sex offending against children, public awareness of this form of criminal activity has grown over the past decades.

Sexual offending against women

Rape

The act of rape may be understood as one in which a man intentionally penetrates with his penis the vagina, anus, or mouth of a non-consenting person. The consequences of rape may be far-reaching for the woman, affecting her physical health, psychological state, relationships, and lifestyle (Culbertson & Dehle, 2001).

As noted above, the prevalence of rape is difficult to establish both within and across jurisdictions. Nonetheless, for some time researchers have suggested that there are cross-cultural variations in the prevalence of rape which may be associated with cultural and political factors (e.g., Russell, 1975; Sanday, 1981). The disaggregation of the figures in Box 7.1 to allow rates for rape to emerge provides support for the notion that rape is more prevalent in some countries than others (see Box 7.3). However, without disentangling the effects of

---

Box 7.3   Police recorded rape: rate per 100,000 population for 2008 (after UNDOC)

Highest rate		*Lowest rate*	
Lesotho	91.6	Egypt	0.1
Sweden	53.2	Azerbaijan	0.2
New Zealand	30.9	Armenia	0.2
USA	28.6	Syrian Arab Republic	0.5
Austria	26.3	Japan	2.0

---

international variations in legal definitions, rates of reporting, and police recording, it is impossible to be precise about the meaning of these differences.

The comparable figure for the UK: England and Wales was 24.1.

Offence analysis

What are the circumstances in which rape occurs? As with most crime, the answer to this question is dependent upon several variables ranging from the country concerned to the nature of the relationship between the rapist and the victim. Surveys conducted in America have found that in large cities the victim's home is most likely location for rape, while in small cities, a motor vehicle is most common location (Chappell, Geis, & Geis, 1977). This difference in location may be explained in part by the victimisation of hitch-hikers who are more likely to accept lifts in country areas than in large cities.

In England and Wales, Myhill and Allen (2002) reported that more than half of rapes took place in the victim's home. A similar finding has also been recorded in New York (Ploughman & Stensrud, 1986). The high frequency of the home as a location for rape is because many rapes are committed by the victim's partner or ex-partner who has access to the victim's home. In close to half of reported cases, the victim and offender are acquainted prior to the rape, which may be an underestimation, as those victims who are related to their attacker may be less willing to report the offence. When the victim knows their attacker it is most often as an acquaintance previously encountered in either the victim or offender's home or at a place of work, or an ex-husband or boyfriend.

Myhill and Allen (2002) note that when the rape was committed by a stranger, the location was most often a public place. However, when the offence was sexual assault, the position was reversed so that most assaults took place in a public place such as a pub, club, park, street, or car park.

The surveys indicate that rape most frequently takes place on Saturdays between 8 pm and 2 am – peak times for alcohol consumption and social interaction in pubs and clubs – which means that the attack often takes place in darkness. In offences where the victim does not know the attacker, an obvious advantage of darkness from the man's perspective lies in minimising the chance of identification. It is also possible that darkness helps the offender to 'deindividualise' the attack, setting aside any feelings of guilt and seeing the victim as an object not a person.

The demographic characteristics of the rape victim have been described in several reviews. With regard to England and Wales, Myhill and Allen (2002: 21) make the observation: 'Age is the biggest risk factor for being a victim of a sexual offence. Young women aged 16 to 19 are most likely to be victimised. Women aged 20 to 24 have an almost equally high risk of experiencing some form of sexual victimisation. With regard to rape, 16 to 19-year-old women were over four times as likely as women from any other age group to report being raped in the last year. The risks for these younger women are statistically significant'. The higher risk for younger women of a sexual offence may be a function of a lifestyle that involves high levels of social interaction with males under 25 years, the age group most likely to be involved in rape. Myhill and Allen also note that rape victims are likely to have a low income, live in rented accommodation, and have poor health. Women who are married or cohabiting are at the lowest risk of sexual victimisation generally but specifically for rape, the risk was greatest for women who are divorced.

There is a general consensus across the (mainly American) wider literature that rape victims are young, typically between 16 and 25 years, and rarely over the age of 65 years. Victims are likely to be single with a low income or unemployed and, in the American surveys, there is an overrepresentation of black women (Chappell et al., 1977; Ploughman & Stensrud, 1986). Ploughman and Stensrud (1986: 320) suggested that '[u]nmarried women are more likely to be victimized than married women because of their greater exposure to potential rape situations (traveling alone, living alone, living in lower income areas, etc.)'.

Understanding sex offences

One approach to understanding sex offences is to focus on variations in the nature of the offence or characteristics of the offenders. Thus, for offenders against children, various distinctions have been drawn in the literature: these distinctions include *child rape* and *child molestation*, child rape involves coercion accompanied by violence, while with molestation the child is coerced by non-violent means and the harm to the child may be psychological rather than physical; *preference molesters* whose primary sexual orientation is towards children and *situational molesters* who have heterosexual adult relationships but, perhaps impulsively, take advantage of an opportunity to commit a sexual act with a child; *homosexual* and *heterosexual* offenders; and *incestuous* and *non-incestuous* child sex offenders.

As with offences against children, there have been attempts to categorise sexual offences against women. In a study based on 500 rapists, Groth (1979) described three pathways towards the fusion of sexual and violent behaviour that culminated in rape. An *anger rape* typically follows arguments, sexual jealousies and social rejection by a woman so that before the attack the offender feels wrongly treated and angry. In this type of rape, the man uses physical force far in excess of the amount necessary to make the woman comply: the man's intention is to inflict physical injury with the perpetration of the sexual act an additional way of inflicting pain and humiliation. Groth estimated that 40 per cent of the sample could be classified as anger rapists. The *power rape* is different to *anger rape* in that sexual conquest is the objective and physical force is used to the extent necessary to force the woman's compliance. Groth suggests that the goal in this type of rape is the experience of power, rather sexual gratification, which alleviates the offender's personal insecurities and allows them to assert their manhood and heterosexuality. Groth suggested that 55 per cent of the sample were power rapists. Finally, with *sadistic rape* there is a reciprocal relationship between sexuality and aggression so that the man finds the victim's humiliation and suffering to be sexually exciting. In this type of rape the victim is made to suffer, typically by being tied, tormented, sexually abused, and tortured: at 5 per cent of the sample, this was the least common type of rape. Although it is an uncommon form of sexual offending, the issue of sexual sadism continues to exercise researchers (Marshall & Kennedy, 2003).

Box 7.4 Types of rape from Scully and Marolla (1985)

(1) The man's concern is with revenge and punishment: following a perceived indiscretion from their wife or girlfriend the man raped another woman to 'get even'. These rapists reported extreme anger when committing the offence and physically as well as sexually assaulted their victims.
(2) The rape is seen a 'bonus' to another offence, such as burglary, when a women is found to be a vulnerable to an attack.
(3) So-called 'date rape' in which the men said that they were sexually motivated and believed that the woman was sexually available: when consensual sex was not forthcoming the man took what he saw he was entitled to take.
(4) The man enjoys the experience of impersonal power and domination: the rape provides an experience of control and dominance avoiding the emotions associated with intimacy.
(5) A group of men rape as an act of recreation and adventure, and the rape is seen simply as another form of criminal activity. There are social rewards, such as praise and group status, for participating in these group acts. The victims were typically hitch-hikers, women abducted at night, or women who believed they had a date with a gang member but were taken to a predetermined location and raped by the gang.

Scully and Marolla (1985) interviewed 114 convicted rapists and based on the men's accounts of their offence described five types of rape as shown in Box 7.4. Scully and Marolla reported that the rapists said they had little or no compassion for the women they raped, most said that after the offence they 'felt good', 'relieved', or 'nothing', and very few expressed pity for the woman. The reasons the men gave for their abusive actions contain elements of revenge, power and opportunity, showing that rape occurs for a complex interplay of reasons, with different men raping for different reasons and to achieve different rewards.

Mann and Hollin (2007) analysed the accounts given by a sample of sex offenders explaining their own offence. The various explanations were refined to a list of 10 categories such as 'impulsive', 'sexual desire', and 'need for respect' and the offence accounts of a further 100 sex offenders (35 rapists and 65 child molesters) sorted according to these 10 categories. It was found that child molesters most often explained their offending as due to their need for sexual gratification, a desire to improve their negative emotional state or a wish to experience intimacy. The rapists most often explained their offending as due to a grievance, an impulsive act, or sexual need. Mann and Hollin suggested that some of the categories, such as grievance and need for respect/control, reflected the offenders' wider views about themselves, other people and their social world and, as such, could be seen as schema.

Mann and Hollin (2010) looked more closely at the potential role that schema may play in sexual offending. A schema was understood as a cognitive structure based on previous experience, centred on a coherent theme, and composed of attitudes, beliefs, rules, and assumptions. A schema may guide the interpretation of social cues and so influence cognitive functioning when encountering similar situations to those previously experienced. Mann and Hollin (2010) used factor analysis to explore the explanations for their offending given by 657 imprisoned sex offenders. The analysis allowed the construction of a 43-item questionnaire, called *My Life*, to assess schemas in sex offenders. The questionnaire contained two strong factors, which were labelled *dominance* and *disadvantaged* (see Box 7.5).

Box 7.5 Items from the *My Life* questionnaire (Mann & Hollin, 2010)

Dominance factor
When others treat me badly they deserve some sort of punishment.
When people don't respect me, I feel a need to show them they're wrong.
People who threaten me need to be shown that they can't get away with it.
Violence is sometimes the only way to sort everything out. Some people that I have hurt deserved it.
When I want sex I feel I should be able to have it.
When I get angry I want to get back at people.

Disadvantaged factor
I've had more pain and loss in my life than most people.
In my life I've often needed to be able to talk about my problems but not had the opportunity.
I haven't had what I deserve in life.
I've had no help in life.
Any bad things I've done are usually because of the things that have happened to me in my life.
Women are mainly responsible for the hurt I feel in my life.

The scores of the sex offenders on the dominance factor correlated significantly with a measure of behavioural hostility and with a measure of sexual entitlement that, in turn, is also related to sexual hostility. Thus, dominance may be seen as related to violent behaviour in that it is associated with hostility in appraising situations in terms of whether they cause the person to feel diminished and threatened. A perception of threat may be followed by anger if the person decides that another person has violated their rules: any appraisal of rule violation leads to a wish to punish the transgressor. Those individuals high on dominance are likely to use violence as a strategy for dealing with a perceived lack of respect from other people. Dominance was found to be related to age, being less prevalent among older men. The scores of the sex offenders on the dominance scale did not differ significantly from other types of male offenders or, indeed, from a non-offender sample of men. The ubiquity of dominance across these different groups reflects the commonality of aggressive thoughts and beliefs among men. However, dominance did differentiate the higher risk from the lower risk sex offenders.

The disadvantaged factor can best be understood as a perception of one's self-identity as someone who has been damaged by other people. Thus, those who score highly on this factor believe that during their life they have not received the help and support that they deserve. This perception leads to hypersensitivity in seeing oneself as being let down or cheated by other people. When they perceive that others have failed to meet their standards, they become anxious and seek a comforting experience, such as sexual activity. The scores of the sex offenders on the disadvantaged factor did not correlate significantly with age, so it is unlikely that maturity leads to a change in this particular aspect of self-perception. However, the scores of the sex offenders on the disadvantaged factor correlated significantly with measures of a distrust of women and lack of openness with other adults, and with impulsive behaviour and a sense of helplessness. The non-offender comparison group had significantly lower scores than both the sexual and non-sexual offender groups. The disadvantaged factor did not correlate with a measure of risk.

It is evident that sex offences are a complex fusion of sexual and violent behaviour directed at children and adults. The traditional distinction in the literature, as discussed above, is between sex offenders against children and sex offenders who offend against adult women. However, the problem with this distinction is that sex offenders, like most other offenders, do not always fall neatly into a single category but cross over several categories.

Crossover offenders

There are offenders whose sexual interest and offending is stable and confined to, say, images available on the internet, or to children, or to adults, or to males, or to females. However, some sex offenders will cross a range of boundaries in their sexual offending: the boundary may be age, so that offences are committed against adults or children, or gender with offences against females and males, or type of relationship as in offending against family members, acquaintances and strangers (Heil, Ahlmeyer, & Simons, 2003).

Cann, Friendship, and Gozna (2007) conducted a study in which they looked at a sample of 1,345 adult male sex offenders who had committed two or more offences involving several victims and who were discharged from custody in England and Wales between 1992 and 1996 after serving a minimum 4-year sentence. Through access to police records and other Home Office databases, victim details were gathered for each sexual conviction for each individual offender. The data revealed that 330 (24.5 per cent) of the sex offenders had a criminal history that showed evidence of crossover with respect to victim gender, victim age, and relationship (or not) with the victim. When Cann et al. looked in detail at these 330 offenders, it was found that 108 had offended against both adults and children, 121 had offended against females and males, and 189 had offended both within and outside their own family. There were 74 sex offenders who had crossed two boundaries, with age and relationship the most common, and there were seven sex offenders had crossed all three (age, gender, and relationship) boundaries. As assessed using the Static-99 (Hanson & Thornton, 1999), the crossover offenders were of significantly higher risk of reoffending than the non-crossover offenders.

An Australian study by Sim and Proeve (2010) looked at a sample of 128 adult male child sexual offenders who had all offended against multiple victims. The victims were grouped by age into the three categories of 5 years of age and below, 6–12 years, and 13 years and older, and also by gender and relationship to the offender. Sim and Proeve reported that more than half of the offenders had crossed over in at least one domain, with offending against different ages the most frequently recorded pattern.

Understanding sex offences

As is the case with crime generally, psychological theories are but one of a range of theoretical perspectives that have been applied to understand sex offending. These theories include, for example, *feminist theories* and *evolutionary theories*. In feminist theories, sexual crimes are understood as a form of patriarchal domination and associated patterns of male socialisation through which men suppress women (Brownmiller, 1975) and exert power over children (Cossins, 2000). On the other hand, *evolutionary theories* see rape as a behaviour that has value as an evolutionary strategy (Malamuth & Heilman, 1998; Thornhill & Palmer, 2000).

Set against these broad theories, psychological research and theory has perhaps been narrower in focus, with the offender at centre of concerns rather than, say, the forces of evolution. The psychological literature, following Ward, Polaschek, and Beech (2006), can be considered in terms of accounts based primarily on one specific factor, and explanations based on interactions between multiple factors.

Single factor approaches

A wide range of psychological and individual factors are associated with sex offending: these factors include cognitive processes such as cognitive distortions, sexual fantasy, and victim empathy; aspects of sexual functioning such as the cues the offender finds sexually preferable and arousing; and some features of social functioning as with relationship skills and the use of alcohol and other substances. In seeking to refine measurement of these factors, for both clinical and research purposes, some complex methods to aid have been developed.

Cognitive distortions

The study of sex offenders has always been cognisant of the need to understanding the thinking of men who commit sex offences. Burt (1980) developed the *Attitudes Towards Sex and Violence Scale* and the *Rape Myth Acceptance Scale* for this purpose. In the context of sex offending, the term *cognitive distortion* was first used by Abel, Becker, and Cunningham-Rather (1984) to refer to those aspects of thinking that are supportive of sexual offending. Abel et al. identified seven attitudes and beliefs expressed by child molesters to which they applied the term 'cognitive distortions'. As is evident from Table 7.3, these cognitions may serve to minimise and rationalise the sexual act, to cope with any feelings of guilt, and to deny any suggestion of deviancy.

In order to assess cognitive distortions, Abel et al. (1989) developed the *Abel and Becker Cognitions Scale*, which contains 29 offense-supportive beliefs. There are now several questionnaires that assess cognitive distortions: the *MOLEST* scale, incorporating some items derived from the Abel and Becker Scale, contains 38 items that are rated using a four-point Likert scale (Bumby, 1996); and the 22-item *Child Molester Scale* uses a five-point Likert scale to rate items such as 'Children usually outgrow any problems resulting from a sexual experience they had as a child', which may be used to justify sex offences against children (McGrath, Cann, & Konopasky, 1998).

The empirical evidence for cognitive distortions among sexual offenders is varied in its support for the utility of the concept (Gannon & Polaschek, 2006; Gannon, Ward, & Collie, 2007).

Table 7.3 Cognitive distortions in child molesters (after Abel, Becker, & Cunningham-Rather, 1984)

Genital fondling is not really sex so no harm is done.
Children don't tell because they enjoy the sex.
Sex enhances a relationship with a child.
Society will eventually see that sex with a child is acceptable.
A child enquiring about sex means that he or she wants to experience sex.
Physical sex is a good way of teaching children about sex.
A lack of physical resistance means that the child wants sex.

This lack of convincing evidence may in part be due to the imprecision of the term: in the context of rape, would a man's view of women as being available for sex be a cognitive distortion or a justification or excuse used after the crime?

The theoretical development, informed by schema theory, that followed the idea of cognitive distortions lies in the notion of *implicit theories*.

Implicit theories

Ward (2000) suggested that cognitive distortions are a result of the offender's schema with respect to the individual's beliefs about themselves and others. As these cognitions are held to be outside conscious awareness, Ward uses the term *implicit*. Polaschek and Ward (2002) have suggested five implicit theories for rapists (see Table 7.4): this suggestion has received some empirical support (Polaschek & Gannon, 2004).

Victim empathy

The term empathy may be taken to encompass two related processes: *cognitive* empathy is the ability to understand another person's emotions; *affective* empathy is the ability to feel or share another person's emotions (Jolliffe & Farrington, 2004). The suggestion has been made that sexual offenders lack empathy, particularly for members of their preferred victim group, and this deficiency is a contributory factor to their offending (Marshall, Hamilton, & Fernandez, 2001).

The research findings do not indicate that there are marked differences in empathy between sex offenders, non-sex offenders, and non-offenders (Polaschek, 2003). Indeed, Jolliffe and Farrington's (2004) meta-analysis of the relationship between empathy and offending found a relatively weak relationship between empathy and sexual offending specifically. However, Jolliffe and Farrington did report that compared with non-sex offenders, sex offenders show a greater discrepancy in cognitive empathy than affective empathy.

Sexual arousal

It is evident simply from the numbers of convicted offenders that there are adults who are sexually aroused by children or by sexual violence towards women. These deviant sexual

---

Table 7.4 Implicit theories of rapists (after Polaschek & Ward, 2002)

Women are unknowable: Women are different to men, so therefore men cannot understand them. This means that heterosexual relations are by definition adversarial and women will try to deceive men about their intentions.

Women are sex objects: Although they may not realise it, women are always receptive to men's sexual needs.

The male sex drive is uncontrollable: Men need sexual release, without which their sexual energy may increase to dangerous levels. Thus, once sexually aroused men must reach a sexual climax.

Entitlement: One's needs are more important than those of other people so that men are entitled to sexual access to women, if access is not forthcoming then men are entitled to take what they want by force.

Dangerous world: The world is perceived to be a hostile place so there is a need to take anticipatory action to avoid rejection and hostility.

---

preferences – given that what society judges to be 'deviant' may vary by time and place – can result from childhood exposure to deviant sexual stimuli (Laws & Marshall, 1990). Sexual fantasy may play a role in maintaining deviant sexual interest through cognitive rehearsal of the arousing stimuli. When a deviant sexual fantasy is paired with sexual arousal through the use of pornography and masturbation, then the arousal to the specific stimuli is reinforced. When the individual acts out their fantasies in real life, then an offence occurs (Marshall & Eccles, 1991), allowing that the nature of the fantasy and the type of victim may be important in this regard (Sheldon & Howitt, 2008).

The assessment of sex offenders, say for the purpose of risk assessment, would benefit from a reliable and valid means by which to determine an offender's sexual preferences. One approach to measuring sexual preference relies on assessing change on various indices of physical change associated with sexual arousal in response to exposure to different cues. The technique of *penile plethysmography* (PPG), widely used with sex offenders, entails measuring changes in penile volume (the *volumetric* method) or diameter (the *circumferenential* method) in response to stimuli that may be variously presented as still and moving visual images, sounds, prompted self-imagery, and virtual reality. PPG, developed in the 1960s and 1970s (Freund, Sedlack, & Knob, 1965; Barlow, Becker, Leitenberg, & Agras, 1970), has subsequently generated an extensive literature raising a range of technical and conceptual issues (Laws, 2009; Marshall & Fernandez, 2003).

There is a myriad of technical issues associated with PPG assessment: these issues include the precise nature of the test stimuli, validation and mode of presentation of the stimuli, and the degree to which the man can inhibit and exert voluntary control over their erectile response. There are ethical issues, such as how to manufacture images and other stimuli, particularly those depicting sexual contact with children and sexual violence, for use in PPG assessment. There are issues with the legal standing of such assessments and their admissibility in court. As discussed in Chapter 10, the admissibility is this type of assessment is also found with polygraph testing of offenders, including sex offenders (Ben-Shakar, 2008; Grubin, 2008).

There is also the matter of whether arousal to deviant stimuli is the sole province of sex offenders. Some studies have reported that rapists are more highly aroused than non-rapists by scenes of rape but given certain conditions, such as not being caught and punished, men who are not sex offenders can become aroused by images of rape (Malamuth, 1981; Quinsey, Chaplin, & Varney, 1981). It is clear that there is a complex relationship, involving both individual differences and social factors, between arousal and sexual offending.

Intimacy deficits

Marshall (1989) suggests that the reason why many sex offenders have personal difficulties in forming and maintaining intimate relationships lies in their attachment style. Thus, the sex offender's intimacy deficits arise from the development during childhood of an insecure attachment with their parents. This insecure attachment style leads, in turn, to low self-esteem, poor social skills, and a view of the world as a rejecting and hostile place. The overall effect of these developments during childhood is that it becomes difficult as an adult to establish and maintain intimate relationships, which results in emotional loneliness. Marshall suggests that the interaction between an insecure attachment style and social and cultural influences such as exaggerated masculine attitudes and pornography can intensify the consequences of an insecure attachment style. Thus, the man seeks intimate behaviours in an inappropriate way, such as with children or aggressively with adults.

In support of this view, there is evidence that sexual offenders may show insecure attachment styles (Rich, 2006; Simons, Wurtele, & Durham, 2008). It is also evident that the childhoods of some sex offenders are characterised by neglect, abuse, and family disruption, all of which are associated with the development of an insecure attachment to parents (Craissati, McClurg, & Browne, 2002). Further, high levels of emotional loneliness have been found among sexual offenders (Bumby & Hansen, 1997).

With respect to forming relationships, it is generally the case that some degree of social skill and competence is a needed to interact with other people. An individual with impaired social skills may have difficulties in meeting people socially and so has limited opportunity to find a sexual partner (Graves, Openshaw, & Adams, 1992). There is some evidence that sex offenders, particularly those who offend against children, show poor social skills when compared with non-offenders (Segal & Marshall, 1985).

The strength of the single factor approach is that it highlights the role of specific psychological and behavioural characteristics that may play a role in sexual offending. However, it is highly unlikely that a complex behaviour such as sex offending can be universally explained by a solitary individual feature. In seeking a more complete explanation of sexual offending, it is much more likely that interactions between a range of individual and social factors will need to be considered. Ward, Polaschek, and Beech (2006) examine several examples of this approach to explaining sex offending: two examples are discussed below to illustrate the range and depth of this approach.

Multifactor approaches

Finkelhor's precondition model

Finkelhor (1984) developed one of the most influential multifactor theories, specifically for sex offences against children, which includes the offender, the victim, the family, and social and cultural factors. Finkelhor's approach, called the *precondition model*, is concerned with four complementary processes – each including individual, physiological, and sociocultural variables – each of which must occur in sequence before the individual acts to abuse children.

The first precondition is the individual's *motivation to sexually abuse children*. Finkelhor suggests that there are three aspects to this motivation: first, *emotional congruence*, in that the individual finds children a source of emotional gratification perhaps because children are not threatening or because of the individual's low self-esteem and immaturity; second, *sexual arousal* to children, which may be a consequence of early learning, including sexual abuse, or the use of child pornography; third, *blockage* in seeking adult partners, perhaps because of social anxiety or poor social skills, leads to children becoming sexual outlets.

Once an individual has acquired the motivation to abuse children, the second precondition lies in their overcoming *internal inhibitors*. It is one thing to be sexually attracted by children, it is quite another thing to act on that attraction. The offender must overcome both their own moral restraints against such behaviour and the strong social disapproval of such actions. There are several routes to *disinhibition*, such as alcohol use and high level of stress, which may act in a given situation to mitigate inhibitions and allow the offence to take place. The third precondition, *overcoming external inhibitors*, lies in creating the conditions in which the offence takes place. There are several ways by which this precondition may be contrived by the offender, such as gaining a family's trust, grooming a child, or planning to gain access to a child when they are alone or unsupervised.

The fourth precondition, once the other three are satisfied, lies in *overcoming the child's resistance*. The individual may seek to overcome the child's resistance to sexual contact by gaining their trust and gradually introducing them to the idea of sex, or by creating a context where the child emotionally depends on the adult, or by misusing a position of authority.

Finkelhor's precondition model is important because it seeks to understand the process by which sexual offence takes place, drawing on social as well as individual factors. The social factors range from children left unsupervised because of the absence of social support for families, parents' work patterns due to financial pressures, and the availability of child pornography on the internet.

Marshall and Barbaree's integrated theory

The theory originally developed by Marshall and Barbaree (1990), which may be applied to all types of sexual offence, has been revised in light of further research findings (Marshall, Anderson, & Fernandez, 1999; Marshall & Marshall, 2000). This theory seeks to accommodate early learning experiences, biological and psychological variables alongside the immediate situational factors in the context of the prevalent political and economic climate.

Marshall and Barbaree propose that sex offending is a consequence of the psychological vulnerabilities developed during childhood, alongside the social and biological changes during puberty, that may interact with disinhibiting factors when there is an opportunity to offend. According to Marshall and Barbaree, psychological vulnerabilities, such as poor interpersonal skills and problems with emotional self-regulation, can develop from adverse early experiences. In turn, these vulnerabilities may precipitate difficulties in forming social, emotional, and sexual attachments to other people. Thus, the vulnerabilities may cause problems for the adolescent male in that his poor social skills lead to rejection of genuine attempts at sexual intimacy; this rejection then leads to the development of deviant sexual fantasies. If the adolescent male does not learn to distinguish his feelings of aggression and sexual interest then, given the right circumstances, there is an increased likelihood of sexually aggressive behaviour.

Marshall and Barbaree suggest that for a sex offence to occur, the male's vulnerabilities must interact with situational and emotional disinhibitors such as substance use, anger, sexual frustration or rejection and loneliness, the availability of a victim, and the opportunity to offend. Continued sex offending can be accounted for by direct reinforcement of the offence behaviour and by the cognitive distortions the offender uses to rationalise his behaviour.

Conclusion

Sexual offences are a cause of a great deal of harm and distress across many cultures and societies. The research discussed in this chapter has moved forward our understanding of the social and psychological factors associated with these types of crime. As will be seen in Chapter 11, there have been attempts to translate this knowledge into practice in the formulation of strategies to reduce sexual offending.

Chapter summary

- Legal classifications and definitions of sexual crime change over time and may include non-consensual offences such as rape; offences involving ostensible consent such as those involving children; preparatory offences such as sexual grooming; and exploitation offences such as abuse of children through prostitution and pornography.

- The occurrence of a sexual offence is often hidden from the official records because the victim, often physically harmed, is too frightened or ashamed to report the crime. Sexual offences are significantly underrepresented in the official statistics.
- The advent of the internet has produced a new means by which sex offending can take place though, for example, grooming potential victims, exchanges of information between sex offenders and traffic in illegal images.
- Some psychological theories have considered the motivation of the sex offender leading to typologies such as preference and situation child molesters and anger, power, and sadistic rapists.
- The large-scale integrated theories seek to include a range of background, social, and psychological factors to give an account of sexual offending.

Points for discussion

- Does the use of the internet by sex offenders against children mean that there should be tighter internet controls?
- Is rape primarily a violent or a sexual crime?
- Why are do some sex offenders 'cross over' in terms of their type of victim?

Essential reading

Sheldon, K. & Howitt, D. (2007). *Sex Offenders and the Internet*. Chichester, Sussex: John Wiley & Sons.
A good overview of the use of the internet in facilitating sex offending.

Myhill, A. & Allen, J. (2002). *Rape and Sexual Assault of Women: The Extent and Nature of the Problem. Findings from the British Crime Survey*. Home Office Research Study 237. London: Home Office.
An excellent review of the crime statistics is given in this Home Office Research Study.

The lighter side

The novel *Comfort of Strangers* by Ian McEwan (published in 1981 by Jonathan Cape) looks at the fusion of sexual attraction and sadism, while McEwan's short story *Butterflies* (in the collection *First Love, Last Rites*, published in 1981 by Jonathan Cape) tragically combines loneliness, sexual attraction to a child, and guilt.

Useful websites

The United Nations Office on Drugs and Crime has a considerable amount of information on a range of crimes, including sexual offences, collated from many countries, www.undoc.org.

In England and Wales, the Home Office and Ministry of Justice websites carry a range of reports and statistics concerned with serious crime, including sex offences, www.homeoffice.gov.uk and www.justice.gov.uk.

The Federal Bureau of Investigation website has many sections, including pages on forcible rape and on crimes against children, which provide a wealth of statistical information and other details, www.fbi.gov/hq/cid/cac/crimesmain.htm.

The International Criminal Police Organization (INTERPOL) website has a document providing legislation across the member countries, of which there are many, summarising the various applicable legal texts regarding child sexual abuse. The information available covers age for legal purposes, type of child sex abuse including rape, child prostitution, use of the internet, and child pornography, www. interpol.int/public/children/sexualabuse/nationallaws/default.asp.

References

Abel, G. G., Becker, J. V., & Cunningham-Rather, J. (1984). Complications, consent, and cognitions in sex between children and adults. *International Journal of Law and Psychiatry, 7*, 89–03.

Abel, G. G., Gore, D. K., Holland, C. L., Camp, N., Becker, J. V., & Rathner, J. (1989). The measurement of the cognitive distortions of child molesters. *Annals of Sex Research, 2*, 135–153.

Abracen, J., Looman, J., & Anderson, D. (2000). Alcohol and drug abuse in sexual and nonsexual violent offenders. *Sexual Abuse: Journal of Research and Treatment, 12*, 263–274.

Aspelmeier, J. E., Elliott, A. N., & Smith, C. H. (2007). Childhood sexual abuse, attachment, and trauma symptoms in college females: The moderating role of attachment. *Child Abuse & Neglect, 31*, 549–566.

Atkinson, C. & Newton, D. (2010). Online behaviours of adolescents: Victims, perpetrators and Web 2.0. *Journal of Sexual Aggression, 16*, 107–120.

Baker, C. R. (1999). An analysis of fraud on the internet. *Internet Research: Networking Applications and Policy, 9*, 348–359.

Barbaree, H. E. & Marshall, W. L. (Eds.) (2008). *The Juvenile Sex Offender*. New York, NY: Guildford Press.

Barlow, D. H., Becker, R., Leitenberg, H., & Agras, W. S. (1970). A mechanical strain gauge for recording penile circumference change. *Journal of Applied Behavior Analysis, 6*, 355–366.

Beech, A. R., Elliott, I. A., Birgden, A., & Findlater, D. (2008). The internet and child sexual offending: A criminological review. *Aggression and Violent Behavior, 13*, 216–228.

Ben-Shakar, G. (2008). The case against the use of polygraph examinations to monitor post-conviction sex offenders. *Legal and Criminological Psychology, 13*, 191–207.

Brownmiller, S. (1975). *Against Our Will: Men, Women and Rape*. New York, NY: Simon & Schuster.

Bumby, K. M. (1996). Assessing the cognitive distortions of child molesters and rapists: Developments and validation of the MOLEST and RAPE scales. *Sexual Abuse: A Journal of Research and Treatment, 8*, 37–54.

Bumby, K. M. & Hansen, D. J. (1997). Intimacy deficits, fear of intimacy and loneliness among sexual offenders. *Criminal Justice and Behavior, 24*, 315–331.

Burt, M. (1980). Cultural myths and support for rape. *Journal of Personality and Social Psychology, 39*, 217–230.

Cann, J., Friendship, C., & Gozna, L. (2007). Assessing crossover in a sample of sexual offenders with multiple victims. *Legal and Criminological Psychology, 12*, 149–163.

Carter, A. J. & Hollin, C. R. (2010). Characteristics of non-serial sexual homicide offenders: A review. *Psychology, Crime, & Law, 16*, 25–45.

Cawson, P., Wattam, C., Brooker, S., & Kelly, G. (2000). *Child Maltreatment in the United Kingdom: A Study of the Prevalence of Abuse and Neglect*. London: NSPCC.

Chappell, D., Geis, R., & Geis, G. (Eds.) (1977). *Forcible Rape: The Crime, the Victim, the Offender*. New York, NY: Columbia University Press.

Chen, Y., Chen, P. S., Hwang, J., Korba, L., Song, R., & Yee, G. (2006). An analysis of online gaming crime characteristics. *Internet Research, 16*, 246–261.

Choo, K. -K. R. (2009). *Online Child Grooming: A Literature Review on the Misuse of Social Networking Sites for Grooming Children for Sexual Offences*. AIC Reports, Research and Public Policy Series 103. Canberra: Australian Institute of Criminology.

Cossins, A. (2000). *Masculinities, Sexualities and Child Sexual Abuse*. The Hague: Kluwer Law International.

Craissati, J., McClurg, G., & Browne, K. D. (2002). Characteristics of perpetrators of child sexual abuse who have been sexually victimized as children. *Sexual Abuse: A Journal of Research and Treatment, 14*, 225–240.

Culbertson, K. A. & Dehle, C. (2001). Psychological sequela of sexual assault as a function of relationship to perpetrator. *Journal of Interpersonal Violence, 16*, 992–1007.

Fazel, S., Sjöstedt, G., Grann, M., & Långström, N. (2010). Sexual offending in women and psychiatric disorder: A national case-control study. *Archives of Sexual Behaviour, 39*, 161–167.

Feelgood, S., Cortoni, F., & Thompson, A. (2005). Sexual coping, general coping and cognitive distortions in incarcerated rapists and child molesters. *Journal of Sexual Aggression, 11*, 157–170.

Finkelhor, D. (1984). *Child Sexual Abuse: New Theory and Research*. New York, NY: Free Press.

—— (1986). *A Sourcebook on Child Sexual Abuse*. Beverly Hills, CA: Sage.

Freund, K., Sedlack, F., & Knob, K. (1965). A simple transducer for mechanical plethysmography of the male genital. *Journal of the Experimental Analysis of Behavior, 8*, 169–170.

Gannon, T. A. & Polaschek, D. L. L. (2006). Cognitive distortions in child molesters: A re-examination of key theories and research. *Clinical Psychology Review, 26*, 1000–1019.

Gannon, T. A., Rose, M. R., & Ward, T. (2008). A descriptive model of the offense process for female sexual offenders. *Sexual Abuse: A Journal of Research and Treatment, 20*, 352–374.

Gannon, T. A., Ward, T., & Collie, R. M. (2007). Cognitive distortions in child molesters: Theoretical and research developments over the past two decades. *Aggression and Violent Behavior, 12*, 402–416.

Graves, R., Openshaw, D. K., & Adams, G. R. (1992). Adolescent sex offenders and social skills training. *International Journal of Offender Therapy and Comparative Criminology, 36*, 139–153.

Groth, A. N. (1979). *Men Who Rape: The Psychology of the Offender*. New York, NY: Plenum Press.

Grubin, D. (2008). The case for polygraph testing of sex offenders. *Legal and Criminological Psychology, 13*, 177–189.

Hanson, R. K. & Morton-Bourgon, K. (2004). *Predictors of Sexual Recidivism: A Meta-Analysis of Sexual Offender Recidivism Studies*. Use Report 2004–02. Ottawa: Department of the Solicitor General of Canada.

Hanson, R. K. & Thornton, D. (1999). *Static-99: Improving Actuarial Risk Assessments for Sex Offenders*. User Report 99–02. Ottawa: Department of the Solicitor General of Canada.

Heil, P., Ahlmeyer, S., & Simons, D. (2003). Crossover sexual offenses. *Sexual Abuse: A Journal of Research and Treatment, 15*, 221–236.

Hoare, J. & Jansson, K. (2007). Extent of intimate violence, nature of partner abuse and serious sexual assault, 2004/05, 2005/06, 2006/07 BCS. In D. Povey, K. Coleman, P. Kaiza, J. Hoare, & K. Jansson (Eds.), *Homicides, Firearm Offences and Intimate Violence 2006/07* (3rd ed.), Home Office Statistical Bulletin 03/08. London: Home Office.

Hoare, J. & Povey, D. (2008). Violent and sexual crime. In C. Kershaw, S. Nicholas, & A. Walker (Eds.), *Crime in England and Wales 2007/08*. Home Office Statistical Bulletin 07/08. London: Home Office.

Home Office (no date). *A Summary of Recorded Crime Data from 2002/03 to 2007/08*. Retrieved 20 November 2008, from www.homeoffi ce.gov.uk/rds/recordedcrime1.html.

Hudson, S. M. & Ward, T. (2001). Adolescent sexual offenders: Assessment and treatment. In C. R. Hollin (Ed.), *Handbook of Offender Assessment and Treatment* (pp. 363–377). Chichester, Sussex: John Wiley & Sons.

Hunter, J. A., Hazelwood, R. R., & Slesinger, D. (2000). Juvenile-perpetrated sex crimes: Patterns of offending and predictors of violence. *Journal of Family Violence, 15*, 81–93.

Jewkes, Y. (2010). Much ado about nothing? Representations and realities of online soliciting of children. *Journal of Sexual Aggression, 16*, 5–18.

Jolliffe, D. & Farrington, D. P. (2004). Empathy and offending: A systematic review and meta-analysis. *Aggression and Violent Behavior, 9*, 441–476.

Kelly, L., Lovett, J., & Regan, L. (2005). *A Gap or a Chasm? Attrition in Reported Rape Cases*. Research Study 293. London: Home Office.

Knoll, J. L. & Hazelwood, R. R. (2009). Becoming the victim: Beyond sadism in serial sexual murderers. *Aggression and Violent Behavior, 14*, 106–114.

Krahé, B., Scheinberger-Olwig, R., & Bieneck, S. (2003). Men's reports of nonconsensual sexual interactions with women: Prevalence and impact. *Archives of Sexual Behavior, 32*, 165–175.

Labbé, J. (2005). Ambroise Tardieu: The man and his work on child maltreatment a century before Kempe. *Child Abuse & Neglect, 29*, 311–324.

Laws, D. R. (2009). Penile plethysmography: Strengths, limitations, innovations. In D. Thornton & D. R. Laws (Eds.), *Cognitive Approaches to the Assessment of Sexual Interest in Sexual Offenders* (pp. 7–29). Chichester, Sussex: John Wiley & Sons.

Laws, D. R. & Marshall, W. L. (1990). A conditioning theory of the etiology and maintenance of deviant sexual preference and behavior. In W. L. Marshall, D. R. Laws, & H. E. Barbaree (Eds.), *Handbook of Sexual Assault: Issues, Theories, and Treatment of the Offender* (pp. 209–230). New York, NY: Plenum Press.

Leue, A., Borchard, B., & Hoyer, J. (2004). Mental disorders in a forensic sample of sexual offenders. *European Psychiatry, 19*, 123–130.

Malamuth, N. M. (1981). Rape proclivity among males. *Journal of Social Issues, 37*, 138–157.

Malamuth, N. M. & Heilman, M. F. (1998). Evolutionary psychology and sexual aggression. In C. B. Crawford & D. L. Krebs (Eds.), *Handbook of Evolutionary Psychology: Ideas, Issues, and Applications* (pp. 515–542). Mahwah, NJ: Lawrence Erlbaum and Associates.

Mann, R. E. & Hollin, C. R. (2007). Sexual offenders' explanations for their offending. *Journal of Sexual Aggression, 13*, 3–9.

——. (2010). Self-reported schemas in sexual offenders. *Journal of Forensic Psychiatry & Psychology, 21*, 834–851.

McCarthy, J. A. (2010). Internet sexual activity: A comparison between contact and non-contact child pornography offenders. *Journal of Sexual Aggression, 16*, 181–195.

McGrath, M. L., Cann, S., & Konopasky, R. J. (1998). New measures of defensiveness, empathy, and cognitive distortions for sexual offenders against children. *Sexual Abuse: A Journal of Research and Treatment, 10*, 25–36.

Marshall, W. L. (1989). Intimacy, loneliness and sexual offenders. *Behaviour Research and Therapy, 27*, 491–503.

Marshall, W. L., Anderson, D., & Fernandez, Y. (1999). *Cognitive Behavioural Treatment of Sexual Offenders*. Chichester, Sussex: John Wiley & Sons.

Marshall, W. L. & Barbaree, H. E. (1990). An integrated theory of the etiology of sexual offending. In W. L. Marshall, D. R. Laws & H. E. Barbaree (Eds.), *Handbook of Sexual Assault: Issues, Theories, and Treatment of the Offender* (pp. 257–275). New York, NY: Plenum Press.

Marshall, W. L. & Eccles, A. (1991). Issues in clinical practice with sex offenders. *Journal of Interpersonal Violence, 6*, 68–93.

Marshall, W. L. & Fernandez, Y. M. (2003). Sexual preferences: Are they useful in the assessment and treatment of sexual offenders? *Aggression and Violent Behavior, 8*, 131–143.

Marshall, W. L., Hamilton, K., & Fernandez, Y. M. (2001). Empathy deficits and cognitive distortions in child molesters. *Sexual Abuse: A Journal of Research and Treatment, 13*, 123–130.

Marshall, W. L. & Kennedy, P. (2003). Sexual sadism in sexual offenders: An elusive diagnosis. *Aggression and Violent Behavior, 8*, 1–22.

Marshall, W. L. & Marshall, L. E. (2000). The origins of sexual offending. *Trauma, Violence, and Abuse, 1*, 250–263.

Meloy, J. R. (2000). The nature and dynamics of sexual homicide: An integrative review. *Aggression and Violent Behavior, 5*, 1–22.

Ministry of Justice (2010). *Statistics on Women and the Criminal Justice System*. London: Ministry of Justice.

Myhill, A. & Allen, J. (2002). *Rape and Sexual Assault of Women: The Extent and Nature of the Problem. Findings from the British Crime Survey*. Home Office Research Study 237. London: Home Office.

Neal, T. M. S. & Clements, C. B. (2010). Prison rape and psychological sequelae: A call for research. *Psychology, Public Policy, and Law, 16,* 284–299.

Ploughman, P. & Stensrud, J. (1986). The ecology of rape victimization: A case study of Buffalo, New York. *Genetic, Social, and General Psychology Monographs,* 112, 303–325.

Polaschek, D. L. L. (2003). Classification. In T. Ward, D. R. Laws, & S. M. Hudson (Eds.), Sexual Deviance: *Issues and Controversies* (pp. 154–171). Thousand Oaks, CA: Sage.

Polaschek, D. L. L. & Gannon, T. A. (2004). The implicit theories of rapists: What convicted offenders tell us. *Sexual Abuse: A Journal of Research and Treatment, 16,* 299–314.

Polaschek, D. L. L. & Ward, T. (2002). The implicit theories of potential rapists: What our questionnaires tell us. *Aggression and Violent Behavior, 7,* 385–406.

Povey, D., Coleman, K., Kaiza, P., Hoare, J., & Jansson, K. (2008). *Homicides, Firearm Offences and Intimate Violence 2006/07* (3rd ed.), (Supplementary Volume 2 to Crime in England and Wales 2006/07). Home Office Statistical Bulletin 03/08. London: Home Office.

Quinsey, V. L., Chaplin, T. C., & Varney, G. W. (1981). A comparison of rapists' and non-sex offenders' sexual preferences for mutually consenting sex, rape, and physical abuse of women. *Behavioural Assessment, 3,* 127–135.

Rich, P. (2006). *Attachment and Sexual Offending.* Chichester, Sussex: John Wiley & Sons.

Russell, D. E. H. (1975). *The Politics of Rape.* New York, NY: Stein & Day.

Sanday, P. R. (1981). The socio-cultural context of rape: A cross-cultural study. *Journal of Social Issues, 37,* 5–27.

Sandler, J. C. & Freeman, N. J. (2009). Female sex offender recidivism: A large-scale empirical analysis. *Sexual Abuse: A Journal of Research and Treatment, 21,* 455–473.

Scarce, M. (1997). *Male on Male Rape: The Hidden Toll of Stigma and Shame.* New York, NY: Perseus Books.

Scully, D. & Marolla, J. (1985). "Riding the bull at Gilley's": Convicted rapists describe the rewards of rape. *Social Problems, 32,* 251–263.

Segal, Z. V. & Marshall, W. L. (1985). Heterosexual social skills in a population of rapists and child molesters. *Journal of Consulting and Clinical Psychology, 53,* 55–63.

Sentencing Guidelines Secretariat (2007). *Sexual Offences Act 2003: Definitive Guidelines.* London: Author.

Seto, M. C., Reeves, L., & Jung, S. (2010). Explanations given by child pornography offenders for their crimes. *Journal of Sexual Aggression, 16,* 169–180.

Sheehan, V. & Sullivan, J. (2010). A qualitative analysis of child sex offenders involved in the manufacture of indecent images of children. *Journal of Sexual Aggression, 16,* 143–167.

Sheldon, K. & Howitt, D. (2007). *Sex Offenders and the Internet.* Chichester, Sussex: John Wiley & Sons.

—— (2008). Sexual fantasy in paedophile offenders: Can any model explain satisfactorily new findings from a study of internet and contact sexual offenders? *Legal and Criminological Psychology, 13,* 137–158.

Sim, D. J. & Proeve, M. (2010). Crossover and stability of victim type in child molesters. *Legal and Criminological Psychology, 15,* 401–413.

Simons, D. A., Wurtele, S. K., & Durham, R. L. (2008). Developmental experiences of child sexual abusers and rapists. *Child Abuse and Neglect, 32,* 549–560.

Stevenson, K., Davies, A., & Gunn, M. (2003). *Blackstone's Guide to the Sexual Offences Act 2003.* Oxford: Oxford University Press.

Struckman-Johnson, C. & Struckman-Johnson, D. (2006). A comparison of sexual coercion experiences reported by men and women in prison. *Journal of Interpersonal Violence, 21,* 1591–1615.

Taylor, M., Holland, G., & Quayle, M. (2001). Typology of paedophile picture collections. *The Police Journal, 74,* 97–107.

Taylor, M. & Quayle, E. (2006). *Child Pornography: An Internet Crime.* Hove, Sussex: Brunner-Routledge.

Thornhill, R. & Palmer, C. T. (2000). *A Natural History of Rape: Biological Bases of Sexual Coercion.* Boston, MA: MIT Press.

Turchik, J. A. & Wilson, S. M. (2010). Sexual assault in the US military: A review of the literature and recommendations for the future. *Aggression and Violent Behavior, 15,* 267–277.

Ward, T. (2000). Sexual offenders' cognitive distortions as implicit theories. *Aggression and Violent Behavior, 5,* 491–507.

Ward, T., Polaschek, D. L. L., & Beech, A. R. (2006). *Theories of Sexual Offending.* Chichester, Sussex: John Wiley & Sons.

Waites, M. (2005). *The Age of Consent: Young People, Sexuality and Citizenship.* London: Palgrave Macmillan.

Winder, B. & Gough, B. (2010). "I never touched anybody–that's my defence": A qualitative analysis of internet sex offender accounts. *Journal of Sexual Aggression, 16,* 125–141.

8   Mental disorder and crime

In Chapter 1, it was noted that a crime has two elements: *actus reus*, the criminal act, and *mens rea*, the intent to commit the act or 'guilty mind'. It was also noted that there are instances where some individuals, such as children below the age of criminal responsibility, are judged not to have the capacity for criminal intent and therefore do not face criminal proceedings. Another class of people who may not have the capacity for criminal intent are those people with a mental disorder.

The law and the mentally disordered offender

The notion of a mentally disordered offender has a reasonably long history in English law, with the case of Daniel M'Naghten (1813–65) generally taken to be the beginning of mental health legislation with regard to criminal acts (Quen, 1968). The name M'Naghten is spelt differently in various sources where it appears as McNaughton, M'Naghten, M'Naughton (in the original trial report), McNaughton, and McNaughten (in the records from Bethlem and Broadmoor Hospitals): the family spelling was McNaughtan and the extant example of M'Naghten's signature is spelt McNaughtun.

An overview of the M'Naghten case is given in Box 8.1.

The verdict in the M'Naghten trial of not guilty on the ground of insanity caused a public outcry and even an expression of concern from the reigning monarch, Queen Victoria. In response to these pressures, the House of Lords ordered the Lords of Justice of the Queen's Bench to produce a definition of criminal insanity. The Lords of Justice concluded that, in order to establish a defence on the ground of insanity, it must be clearly proved that at the time of committing the act the accused was labouring under such a defect of reason from disease of the mind that they did not to know the nature and quality of the act their actions; or, if they did know of their actions, then they did not know that what they were doing was wrong. This conclusion has become enshrined in law and is known as the *M'Naghten Rules*.

The M'Naghten case is significant in legal history because it gave rise to the first serious attempt to modify criminal law with respect to mentally incompetent defendants. It is now held that the M'Naghten Rules embody two tests: first, it is the responsibility of the defence to show that at the time of the offence the accused did not know the nature and quality of their actions; second, that the accused did not know that their actions were wrong. In those cases where these tests are satisfied, then the accused may be judged to be 'not guilty by reason of insanity' and the sentence of the court may be a period of treatment, sometimes indeterminate, in a secure hospital rather than a punitive disposal such as a fine or imprisonment.

The M'Naghten Rules continue to hold sway in England and Wales and there are similar legal conventions in other parts of the world. In the USA, the trial in 1881 of Charles Guiteau,

Box 8.1 Daniel M'Naghten

A great deal of the detail about Daniel M'Naghten has been gathered from records of the evidence given at his trial and the various newspaper reports of the time.

M'Naghten was born in 1813 in Scotland, probably Glasgow, the illegitimate son of a Glasgow woodturner and landlord, also called Daniel M'Naghten. When his mother, Ada, died M'Naghten went to live with his father's family and worked at his father's workshop in Glasgow: he eventually left his father's employ and, after a 3-year sojourn as an actor he set up his own woodturning workshop in Glasgow in 1835. The business ran successfully for 5 years until in 1840 he sold it and spent the following 2 years in London, Glasgow, and France.

It appears that M'Naghten was hardworking and careful with his money. He attended classes and became educated, taught himself French, and is recorded as holding somewhat radical political opinions. His sympathies lay with the Chartists, a working-class organisation advocating profound social and political reform in Great Britain and Ireland and who were involved in the General Strike of 1842.

In 1841, while resident in Glasgow, he variously complained to his father, to the Glasgow commissioner of police, and to an MP that he was being persecuted and spied upon by the Tories. His claims were not believed and was seen to be deluded.

M'Naghten's place in legal history was sealed on the afternoon of 20 January 1843. On that date the Prime Minister's private secretary, a civil servant called Edward Drummond, was walking from Charing Cross towards Downing Street. M'Naghten approached him from behind, drew a pistol and fired into Drummond's back from close range; before he could fire a second pistol he was overcome by a police constable. It is assumed that M'Naghten thought that he had shot the Prime Minister, Robert Peel. At first it appeared that Drummond's wounds were not fatal but there were complications and he died 5 days later.

M'Naghten appeared at Bow Street Magistrates' Court the morning after the shooting. In a brief statement he told the court how his persecution by the Tories had driven him to the violent act. His trial for 'wilful murder' took place in 1843 at the Old Bailey in London. When asked in court to plead, M'Naghten said 'I was driven to desperation by persecution' and 'I am guilty of firing'.

At his trial the prosecution and the defence agreed that M'Naghten suffered from delusions of persecution. They therefore both advanced their case on the basis of what constituted a legal defence of insanity. The prosecution took the position that, regardless of his delusions, M'Naghten was able to distinguish right from wrong and it therefore followed that was responsible for the crime. The defence argued, supported by the testimony of medical experts, that M'Naghten's delusions had led to a breakdown of his moral sense and his loss of self-control and so that he could not be held as reasonable and responsible for his actions.

The prosecution elected not to produce any medical witnesses to testify against the defence and the trial was stopped. The judge, Chief Justice Tindal, informed the jury that that if they returned a verdict of not guilty on the ground of insanity, then M'Naghten would receive proper care. The jury duly returned a verdict of not guilty on the ground of insanity.

M'Naghten was taken from the Old Bailey to the State Criminal Lunatic Asylum at Bethlem Hospital under the 1800 Act for the Safe Custody of Insane Persons Charged with Offences. It is recoded that his hospital admission documents stated 'Imagines the Tories are his enemies, shy and retiring in his manner'. M'Naghten spent 21 years at Bethlem and in his later years developed diabetes and a heart condition. An ill man, he was moved in 1864 to the newly opened Broadmoor Asylum where he died on 3 May 1865.

who assassinated President James A. Garfield (who actually died several months after the shooting), raised similar issues. It can be surmised from the historical records that Guiteau was mentally disordered and today would probably have been diagnosed with paranoia. Guiteau was executed by hanging, but his high-profile case raised awareness of how best in law to deal with the mentally disordered offender. In the USA, rules similar to the M'Naghten Rules were as adopted in most jurisdictions (Kelly, 2009), but legislatures and courts eventually modified the rules so that there is now some variation across the USA.

In the time since the formation of the M'Naghten Rules, the law in England and Wales with regard to individuals with a mental disorder who commit a criminal act is contained in the Mental Health Act. As with most other legislation, the Mental Health Act has moved through several revisions since it was first introduced, as seen with the 1959 and 1983 Mental Health Acts. The 1957 Homicide Act also introduced the notion of *diminished responsibility*, allowing a defence for homicide to be made on the basis of proof of substantially impaired mental responsibility.

The 1983 Mental Health Act made the distinction between four types of mental disorder, namely mental illness, mental impairment, severe mental impairment, and psychopathic disorder. The most recent Mental Health Act of 2007 has, as summarised in Table 8.1, made a number of changes to the 1983 Act.

While the legislation may change both over time and from jurisdiction to jurisdiction, the legal systems of many counties – including England and Wales (Bradley, 2009; James, 2010), Ireland (Duffy, Linehan, & Kennedy, 2006), Germany (Konrad & Lau, 2010), Sweden (Svennerlind et al., 2010), the European Community generally (Salize, Dreßing, & Kief, 2007), Australia (Richardson & McSherry, 2010), Japan (Yoshikawa et al., 2007) – continue to grapple with the issues posed by the mentally disordered offender.

The association between mental disorder and crime

There is no doubt that there is a section of population who have a diagnosable mental disorder and who also commit criminal acts (Hodgins, 1993; Markowitz, 2011). The evidence in support of this statement comes both from surveys of mental disorder in offender populations and from surveys of criminal behaviour in mentally disordered populations.

Gunn, Robertson, Dell, and Way (1978) used a combination of questionnaire and interview to assess the psychiatric morbidity of more than 600 prisoners in two English prisons. They found that between 20 and 30 per cent of the prisoners had a marked or severe psychiatric condition: depression was prevalent in almost half of the diagnosed cases; anxiety states were evident in a further one-third; drug and alcohol problems were widespread; and schizophrenia was less common. This type of survey is important in giving a snapshot of the penal population at a given time (see also Brugha et al., 2005; Singleton, Meltzer, Gatward,

Table 8.1 Some of the changes introduced by the 2007 Mental Health Act

The 2007 Act abolished the four categories of mental disorder used in the 1983 Act – mental illness, mental impairment, severe mental impairment and psychopathic disorder – and replaced them with 'any disorder or disability of the mind'.

The types of mental disorders included in the 2007 Act are specifically noted as mental illnesses such as schizophrenia, bipolar disorder, anxiety or depression, personality disorders, eating disorders, autistic spectrum disorders and learning disabilities. A brain disorder or disability is *not* taken to be a mental disorder unless it also gives rise to a disability or disorder of the mind.

Coid, & Deasy, 1998; Sirdifield, Gojkovica, Brooker, & Ferriter, 2009). The pattern of a high prevalence of mental disorder, widespread alcohol and drug addiction, and physical health problems has been recorded in several studies of prison populations, both male and female, in several European countries (Dressing, Kief, & Salize, 2009; Eytan et al., 2011; Fotiadou, Livaditis, Manou, Kaniotou, & Xenitidis, 2006).

However, as shown by Prins (1980) in his overview of studies of the prevalence of mental disorder in offender populations, there can be wide variations in findings. This variation may be a function of the year when the study took place, the population included in the study, and the country in which the study took place. These variations serve as a reminder that the generalisation of research findings over time may be problematic given changes in the law regarding the definition and disposal of mentally disordered offenders. Further, the process of diagnosis may vary across studies according to both the date of the study and the country in which it was conducted. Nonetheless, the levels of psychiatric problems among imprisoned offenders are above the levels evident in the general population.

An American study of a prison population reported by Silver, Felson, and Vaneseltine (2008) looked at the relationship between mental health problems and violence. It was found that mental illness was likely to be associated with violent offences and sexual offences (violent and non-violent). The offences of mentally ill prisoners were also likely to be more deviant in that they were perpetrated against younger victims or the offender's own child. Silver et al. (2008: 423) conclude: 'Our evidence, therefore, suggests that mental illness is a causal factor in deviant behavior, some of which involves violence, and that the more deviant the behavior, the greater the effect of mental illness'. Another American study found that those prisoners with mental health problems are also likely to return to prison sooner than those without such problems (Cloyes, Wong, Latimer, & Abarca, 2010).

Surveys have also considered the prevalence of intellectual disability and psychopathy in prison populations. Fazel, Xenitidis, and Powell (2008) conducted a systematic review of the literature on the prevalence of intellectual disabilities among prisoners. This review included the findings from 10 surveys – variously conducted between 1988 and 1997 in Australia, Dubai, England and Wales, New Zealand, and the USA – with an overall sample size of 11,969 male and female prisoners. Fazel et al. reported that their findings indicated that between 0.5 per cent and 1.5 per cent of prisoners had a clinical diagnosis of an intellectual disability. This level of intellectual disability is comparable with levels found among the general population.

Finally, a number of surveys have been concerned with the prevalence of personality disorder and psychopathy (see below for a discussion of psychopathy) in prison populations. The estimates of psychopathy vary considerably from country to county: Coid et al. (2009a: 134) commented that '[t]here are remarkable differences in reported prevalence rates of psychopathy among samples of prisoners in different countries within a range of 3% to 73%'. Coid et al. (2009a) conducted a survey of the prevalence of psychopathy in a sample of 496 male and female prisoners in England and Wales. They found that the prevalence of psychopathy was 7.7 per cent in the male prisoners and 1.9 per cent in the female prisoners. This rate is much higher than would be expected in the general population, which is approximately 0.6 per cent (Coid et al., 2009b). However, given that the standard measure of psychopathy, the Psychopathy Checklist-Revised (PCL-R; Hare, 2003), includes items relating to anti-social behaviour and traits such as lying and impulsivity, it is not surprising that elevated prevalence rates are found in prison populations.

As several commentators have noted, a high prevalence of mental disorder in offender populations may be a function of disproportionate rates of arrest (Constantine et al., 2010), or the mentally disordered person being more likely to be charged or to plead guilty in court, if only for their own protection (Feldman, 1977). Further, the presence of a mental disorder when an offender is in prison does not necessarily mean that the disorder was present at the time of the crime. It is possible that the highly aversive conditions in many prisons may lead to the onset of or exacerbate a mental disorder (Yang, Kadouri, Révah-Lévy, Mulvey, & Falissard, 2009; Wormith, 1984).

As well as offenders within the criminal justice system, there are also patients resident within the psychiatric health care system who have committed criminal acts: these patients, including female patients (Long, Hall, Craig, Mochty, & Hollin, 2011), are evident within low security and community psychiatric services as well as high security services (Logan & Blackburn, 2009). In the same way as national statistics are gathered about offenders within the criminal justice system, so the same is true of mentally disordered offender. The Ministry of Justice publishes an annual bulletin that gives details of offenders subject to restriction orders or detained in secure psychiatric hospitals. The Ministry of Justice Bulletin for 2008 states that the total number of mentally disordered offenders detained in hospital at the end of 2008 in England and Wakes was 3,937: this population was composed of 3,460 males and 477 females (Ministry of Justice, 2010).

In England and Wales there are three high security hospitals: Ashworth Hospital in Liverpool, which has beds for about 500 patients; Broadmoor Hospital in Surry, which has about 250 patients; and Rampton Hospital in Nottinghamshire with about 400 patients. Scotland has a high security hospital for about 140 patients at Carstairs, South Lanarkshire, which also receives patients from Northern Ireland. These high security hospitals, previously known as *special hospitals*, are for those people with a mental disorder who are judged to be too great a risk to the community to be at liberty. There are several infamous people, including Beverley Allitt, Ian Brady, and Peter Sutcliffe, who are currently residing in the secure hospital system.

The high security hospitals are the tip of a large iceberg when considering the numbers of people detained in conditions of varying levels of security. A Ministry of Justice Report (2010: 3) notes that at the end of 2008 there were 3,937 people detained in hospital: the report comments that this figure 'represents a one per cent increase on the 2007 figure and the highest figure for the last decade. There has been a general increase in the number of restricted patients detained over the last ten years'. The relative percentage of male and female patients has, however, remained reasonably consistent at 11–13 per cent for females and 87–89 per cent for males.

There are people with a mental disorder who commit acts that, through due process of law, lead to their detention in secure hospital conditions for the safety of the wider community. However, the association between mental disorder and criminal behaviour requires an explanation: is it simply the case that mental disorder and criminal behaviour may occasionally coincide, in which case their relationship is correlational; or can mental disorder be the cause of the criminal behaviour?

The relationship between mental disorder and crime

The relationship between mental disorder and criminal behaviour is one that is likely to unfold over the individual's lifespan. The aetiology of the relationship may be complex involving an interplay between disorders of childhood and adolescence such as attention-deficit/hyperactivity disorder (ADHD), anti-social behaviour, educational difficulties, social dysfunction and emerging major psychiatric disorders (Hofvander et al., 2011; Schilling, Walsh, & Yun, 2010). In addition, traumatic events such as childhood abuse may be associated with the development of both mental disorder and anti-social and criminal behaviour (Silberman,

2010). As well as adults, there are juveniles, both male and female, who commit crimes and who also have a psychiatric disorder (McReynolds, Schwalbe, & Wasserman, 2010). It is also the case that conduct disorders in childhood and adolescence may be antecedent to the development of schizophrenia (see Hodgins, 2008).

The causality game is a difficult one to play in the social sciences generally and, given the complexity of the issues, especially so in relation to mental disorder and crime. Thus, there are discussions to be had about the separation of mind (with the familiar debate about the concept of mind) and body in accounting for human behaviour; about the role of environmental, social, cultural, and biological variables; and about satisfying the conditions of research designs that may help to infer causality between two factors (Anckarsäter, Radovic, Svennerlind, Höglund, & Radovic, 2009; Buchanan & Zonana, 2009; Dahlin, Gumpert, Torstensson-Levander, Svensson, & Rodovic, 2009). The philosophical and other concerns regarding the origin, nature, and limits of human knowledge are not without practical implications. Buchanan and Zonana (2009) make the point that legal support for mental disorder as a cause of crime and as a criterion for culpability have been erratic. They provide the example of the inconsistencies by which different jurisdictions within the USA vary in the way they treat the nature of the relationship between mental disorder and criminal behaviour in formulation of a defence on the grounds of insanity.

The evidence that informs our understanding of criminal behaviour by individuals with a mental disorder should be seen against the backdrop of the shifting debate regarding the nature of the relationship between mental disorder and criminal behaviour. This shift, as shown in Table 8.1, is exemplified by the abolition in the Mental Health Act 2007 of the various categories of mental disorder contained in the 1983 Act and their replacement by the generic 'any disorder or disability of the mind'. Nonetheless, with this legal change in mind, the old categories of *mental illness*, *mental impairment*, and *psychopathic disorder* provide a useful way of ordering the literature. In practice, an individual may be diagnosed with two concurrent or *comorbid* mental disorders: for example, it is not uncommon for psychosis to be comorbid with alcohol or drug addiction.

Mental illness and crime

The term *mental illness* encompasses a wide range of conditions including psychosis, depression, and anxiety states. The criminological literature, however, is dominated by research concerned with the relationship between psychosis and criminal behaviour, particularly violent behaviour.

Psychosis

The term 'psychosis' does not refer to a specific mental disorder, rather to a cluster of disturbances of psychological functioning. Douglas, Guy, and Hart (2009: 681) offer a succinct explanation: 'Psychosis is a syndrome found in mental disorders such as schizophrenia, delusional disorders, bipolar mood disorder, and some forms of severe depression. The syndrome comprises symptoms reflecting profound disturbances in thought, perception, and behaviour'.

Disturbances in thought include delusions and disruption in the process of making associations between thoughts. The nature of the perceptual disturbances can be seen in hallucinations, which may be visual or tactile but are most commonly auditory and typically experienced as hearing voices. The behavioural disturbances may be bizarre facial grimaces, repeated gesturing, excited physical agitation, or holding an unusual posture for a long period. In addition, affect can be flat and expressionless or inappropriate to the situation.

These disturbances cluster to form three domains: (1) a *positive* domain characterised by the presence of disturbances such as delusions; (2) a *negative* domain as seen in the absence of affect; (3) a disorganised domain as with disordered communication and displays of inappropriate affect.

The criminological research in this area is not uniform, with some studies concentrating on a specific disorder, as for example with the substantial literature given to schizophrenia, while some studies prefer the broader term psychosis and others use the generic mental illness. In the following section, the exact nature of the condition is specified where possible.

Hodgins (2008: 2505) opens her overview of violent behaviour among people with schizophrenia with the following statement: 'There is now robust evidence demonstrating that both men and women with schizophrenia are at elevated risk when compared to the general population to be convicted of non-violent criminal offences, at higher risk to be convicted of violent criminal offences, and at even higher risk to be convicted of homicide'. There is a substantial body of research evidence that Hodgins draws upon in support of this position, including large-scale cohort studies focussed on a specific type of crime, systematic reviews, and meta-analyses. Exemplars of these types of study are discussed below. While most studies are concerned with violence in the community, it is also the case that violence, sometimes serious violence, occurs within in-patient settings (Hodgins, Alderton, Cree, Aboud, & Mak, 2007; Hodgins, Cree, Alderton, & Mak, 2008).

Cohort studies

An Australian study by Wallace, Mullen, and Burgess (2004) compared the criminal records, over a 25-year period, of a cohort of 2,861 male and female patients who had contact with psychiatric services for schizophrenia with a matched sample drawn from the same community. It was found that the patients with schizophrenia were more likely to have received a criminal conviction than the comparison group (21.6 per cent and 7.8 per cent): this pattern was evident for both the male and female patients. With regard to type of crime, the frequency of violent offending was higher in the schizophrenic patients than the comparison group (8.2 per cent and 1.8 per cent), with the majority of the violent offences in both groups committed by men. There were four schizophrenic patients convicted of murder and none in the comparison group. The same basic pattern as with violent offences was found with property-related offences and substance-related offences. The male schizophrenia patients were more likely to be convicted of a sexual offence than the comparison group (1.8 per cent and 0.7 per cent), with only nine women convicted of this type of offence.

Wallace et al. also noted that 327 patients with schizophrenia had a comorbid diagnosis of substance use disorder. The rates of offending were higher among patients with a known substance abuse problem. Wallace et al. made the observation that while the patients' rates of crime rose over the 25 years spanned by the study, the same was also true of the comparison group.

A German study reported by Soyka, Graz, Bottlender, Dirschedl, and Schoech (2007) reviewed the criminal records of a cohort of 1,662 patients with schizophrenia up to 12 years after their discharge from psychiatric hospital. It was found that just over 1 in 10 patients committed one or more crimes after discharge. The majority of the crimes were non-violent, such as theft and fraud, with a smaller number of violent crimes, mainly physical assault, and one case of murder. There were a substantial number of drug offences which, as Soyka et al. suggest, most probably reflects the frequent comorbidity of schizophrenia and substance misuse. There were only two cases involving sex offences, one sexual assault and one rape. However, a study of psychotic disorders and sex offending in a Danish cohort of 358,180 people born between 1944 and 1947 reported higher levels of sex offending among those with a psychotic disorder (Alden, Brennan, Hodgins, & Mednick, 2007). Specifically, Alden et al. found that, across the cohort, 2.2 per cent of the men were admitted to psychiatric hospital with a psychotic disorder. When compared with the other, non-psychotic, men in the cohort, an interesting pattern emerged: the psychotic men were three times more likely than the non-psychotic men to have been arrested for non-physically aggressive sexual offences such as exhibitionism and voyeurism. When the psychosis was comorbid with personality disorder or substance use disorder, the risk of non-physically aggressive sexual offending, again compared with the non-psychotic men, was three to five times greater, while the risk of physically aggressive offences, such as rape, was six times greater. Alden et al. also reported that 2.6 per cent of the women in the cohort were admitted to hospital with a psychotic disorder: there were 3 women (0.07 per cent) with a psychotic disorder arrested for a sexual offences compared with 19 non-psychotic women (0.01 per cent). Thus, as found in mainstream offender populations, sexual offending among those with a psychotic disorder is primarily committed by men.

A Swedish cohort study reported by Fazel, Grann, Carlström, Lichtenstein, and Långström (2009a) looked at patients with two or more periods of hospitalisation for schizophrenia: the cohort consisted of 8,891 men and 4,951 women who were followed up over an average period of 12 years. It was found that just over 17 per cent of the men and 5.6 per cent of the women were convicted of a violent offence after their discharge from hospital. Physical assault was the most common type of crime followed by threats and harassment, with very few sexual offences: there were 109 homicides committed by men and 16 by women. The strongest risk factors for violent convictions were previous violent crime, comorbid drug, and alcohol abuse – which increased the risk by a factor of two for women and by a factor of four in men – and parental violent crime.

Systematic reviews and meta-analyses

Bonta, Law, and Hanson (1998) conducted a meta-analytic review to investigate whether the predictors of recidivism are different in mainstream and mentally disordered offender populations. The meta-analysis was conducted on 58 studies, incorporating 64 unique samples. The findings indicated that the strongest predictors of recidivism, for both general offending and violent offending, were the same for mentally disordered offenders as for mainstream offenders. The strong predictors were *criminal history* variables such as a juvenile delinquency, previous violent and non-violent offences, and the seriousness of previous offences; and *deviant lifestyle* variables such as family problems, low levels of employment, and substandard accommodation. In the personal domain, the strong predictors were age, male, antisocial personality, and a history of substance misuse. Bonta et al. (1998: 139) conclude: 'The results support the theoretical perspective that the major correlates of crime are the same, regardless of race, gender, class, and the presence or absence of a mental illness'. It follows that understanding the criminal behaviour of mentally disordered offenders requires engagement with criminology and social psychology as much, if not more, than psychopathology.

A British study reported by Phillips et al. (2005) used the findings of the Bonta et al. (1998) meta-analysis to investigate the prediction of reoffending among mentally disordered offenders. They found that it was predominately the criminogenic variables, such as age at first offence and number of previous offences, which were the most powerful predictors of all types of further offending. Clinical diagnosis alone lacked any predictive power.

Douglas et al. (2009) carried out a meta-analysis involving 204 studies concerned with psychosis as a risk factor for interpersonal violence. They found that 'psychosis was reliably associated with a 49%–68% increased likelihood of violence' (Douglas et al., 2009: 692). However, there were several moderators to take into account when looking at the overall finding: in particular, the association was significant when the psychosis was schizophrenia but it was not significant for affective psychoses. Douglas et al. make the point that it may well not be good research practice to aggregate different disorders under the generic heading of psychosis.

Large, Smith, and Nielssen (2009) conducted a meta-analysis of 25 studies concerned with the relationship between schizophrenia and homicide. They reported that approximately one in 20 homicide offenders had a diagnosis of schizophrenia, which is higher than would be anticipated from the overall prevalence of schizophrenia in the community. Large et al. suggest that this pattern of findings provides confirmatory evidence for the association between schizophrenia and homicide. However, an association does not demonstrate causality: there may be factors common to both the rate of homicide and to variations in the incidence of schizophrenia. Large et al. suggest that these factors may include the availability of weapons, social deprivation, and substance use.

Fazel, Gulati et al. (2009) conducted a systematic review and meta-analysis, incorporating 20 individual studies and involving a total of 18,423 cases, of research investigating the association between violence and schizophrenia (and other psychoses). Fazel et al. recorded four principal findings: (1) there is an increased risk of violence in those people with schizophrenia compared with the general population; (2) comorbid substance use substantially increases the risk of violence; (3) there were a cluster of variables, including whether the diagnosis was schizophrenia or other psychosis and the country in which the study took place, which did *not* influence the outcome; (4) the increased risk of violence with comorbid substance use was no different to the risk of violence for people with a primary diagnosis of substance use disorder.

The evidence concerning psychosis and criminal behaviour highlights two related areas: first, the association between schizophrenia and acts of violence; second, the high levels of co-morbidity with schizophrenia and alcohol abuse in relation to violence.

As discussed above, there are several clusters of clinical symptoms that define schizophrenia. Is there any evidence that there are any particular symptoms of schizophrenia that are related to criminal behaviour? There is some indication that certain symptoms, collectively known as 'control/threat override' – delusions such as someone is trying inflict personal harm, or control your mind, or command you to act in certain ways – are related to violence (Link, Stueve, & Phelen, 1998). However, it is debatable whether there is a direct link between these symptoms and acts of violence and the association is probably mediated by other psychological factors such as personality, the acuity of the symptoms, and previous experience of violence (Appelbaum, Robbins, & Monahan, 2000; Braham, Trower, & Birchwood, 2004; Spidel, Lecomte, Greaves, Sahlstrom, & Yuille, 2010). Skeem et al. (2006) found that it was elevated levels of anger, rather than clusters of symptoms, in the week before the violent episode that best predicted serious violence. In this respect, the acts of violence by high-risk patients are not substantially different to those found in mainstream violent populations (see Chapter 6).

Large and Nielssen (2010) reported a review and meta-analysis of nine studies concerned with violence in first episode psychosis. They found that on average one-third of those people presenting for treatment of first episode psychosis had committed an act of violence. The majority of the acts of violence were relatively minor but there were some serious incidents. The specific association between schizophrenia and homicide has been examined in several studies.

A Swedish study by Fazel, Buxrud, Ruchkin, and Grann (2010) compared 47 individuals who committed homicide within 6 months of discharge from a psychiatric hospital with 105 people who did not commit any violent offence after discharge. The diagnoses on admission were schizophrenia, bipolar disorder, and other psychoses. In comparing the two groups, the factors on admission associated with homicide included poor self-care (including not taking prescribed medication), substance misuse, previous hospitalisation for a violent episode, and having a severe mental illness for 1 year prior to admission. There was no relationship between homicide and depression or the presence of delusions or hallucinations.

In a survey of perpetrators of homicide in England and Wales, Meehan et al. (2006) reviewed the cases, including psychiatric reports, of 1,594 people who had been convicted of homicide in England and Wales between 1996 and 1999. They reported that of these 1,594 individuals there were 85 (5 per cent) with schizophrenia. Where data were available for these 85 people, just over half had been ill for less than a year, and just over one-quarter had had no previous contact with psychiatric services. In terms of the pertinent clinical features, Meehan et al. pointed the role of delusions and particularly the intensity of the individual's emotional response to their delusions in the days leading up to the offence.

There may also be gender differences in the quality of the violent acts committed by people with psychosis (Taylor & Bragado-Jimenez, 2009). Flynn, Abel, Menta, and Shaw (2011) gathered data on 4,126 men and 446 women who had been convicted of homicide in England and Wales between 1997 and 2004. They reported that significantly more of the women had a lifetime history of mental illness (which included schizophrenia, depression, and personality disorder) than the men, and that at the time the offence took place the women were more likely than the men to be to be mentally ill. There were also gender differences with regard to the victim: women were more likely to kill family members, including their own children; men were more likely to kill acquaintances or strangers.

A study of filicide by mentally ill mothers in New Zealand, reported by Stanton, Simpson, and Wouldes (2000), found that the women were experiencing their mental state as extremely distressing at the time they killed their child. The women said that they committed the offence for altruistic reasons, such as saving the child from a stressful life, or as part of their own attempted suicide.

Walsh et al. (2010) looked another form of violence, intimate partner violence, among 225 male and 111 female psychiatric patients (psychotic disorders and depression were among a range of diagnoses). They found higher rates of intimate partner violence for women but more violence towards people other than their partner among men. The men were characterised by higher levels of psychopathic traits and anti-social personality disorder as well as substance use disorders, while the women showed higher rates of borderline personality disorder and anxiety.

Alcohol abuse

Substance use, particularly alcohol and cannabis, is known to be prevalent among people with schizophrenia (Eriksson, Tengström, & Hodgins, 2006). Indeed, Volkow (2009) estimates that almost half of those with schizophrenia will have a lifetime substance use disorder.

Fazel et al. (2009a), continuing the series of studies from Sweden, considered the relationship between schizophrenia, substance abuse, and violent crime using longitudinal data gathered between 1973 and 2006. They compared the rates of conviction for a violent crime – including homicide, assault, robbery, arson, and sexual offences – of a group of 8,003 individuals after their diagnosis of schizophrenia with a non-schizophrenic control group drawn from the general population. For those people with schizophrenia, 13.2 per cent had one or more violent offences compared with 5.3 per cent of the control group. However, when the schizophrenia was comorbid with substance abuse, the rate of violent offending was three times greater than when the schizophrenia was not comorbid with substance abuse. Fazel, Gulati1, Linsell, Geddes, and Grann (2009b: 12) suggest: 'Individuals with substance use disorders may be more dangerous than individuals with schizophrenia and other psychoses, and that the psychoses comorbid with substance abuse may confer no additional risk over and above the risk associated with the substance abuse'.

As Hodgins and Janson (2002) note, there are three broad types of explanation for criminality within mentally disordered populations. The first is increased likelihood of arrest and conviction, the second is a dearth of effective treatment, and the third concerns the role of psychotic symptoms. The third of these explanations, particularly within schizophrenia research, has expanded to include neurobiological and neuropsychological correlates of mental disorder and criminal behaviour.

Neurological factors

In their overview of the literature, Naudts and Hodgins (2006a,b) point to two groups of people with schizophrenia who commit crimes. The first are adults with schizophrenia who have a stable lifetime pattern of anti-social and aggressive behaviour; the second are adults with schizophrenia but with no history of anti-social or aggressive behaviour. Naudts and Hodgins (2006b) concluded their overview by pointing to variations in functioning between these two groups: those people with schizophrenia and a lifetime history of anti-social and aggressive behaviour when compared with those with schizophrenia but no such history, perform less well on assessments of orbitofrontal functions, have fewer neurological soft signs, more abnormalities of the orbitofrontal system and of white matter in the amygdala-orbitofrontal system, and smaller reductions in hippocampal volume. Yang et al. (2010) also pointed to reduced hippocampal volumes as a characteristic of murderers with schizophrenia.

Schug and Raine (2009) conducted meta-analyses of neuropsychological functioning in anti-social schizophrenic people. They found that anti-social schizophrenic people were characterised by lower levels of intellectual functioning when compared both with people with schizophrenia who were not anti-social and with people who were not schizophrenic. The anti-social schizophrenic group were also characterised by deficits across a range of areas of functioning, including full-scale IQ, verbal and performance IQ, attention, executive function and memory. However, it was memory dysfunction that was the principal distinction between the anti-social schizophrenic and the non-anti-social schizophrenic groups. Schug and Raine (2009: 239) suggest that their analyses support the view that there may be 'an antisocial subtype of schizophrenia with a neurobiological basis'.

It is evident that a great deal remains to be understood at a biological level about the interactions between psychosis, including schizophrenia, and antisocial and violent behaviour. As Schug and Raine suggest, the enrichment of this level of understanding will play an important part in the development of effective treatment regimes.

Intellectual disability

As seen in Table 8.1, the 2007 Mental Health Act uses the broad terminology of 'any disorder or disability of the mind'. The phrase used in the Act includes a group of people who have traditionally been characterised by low levels of intellectual functioning. The name given to this group has varied over time and between countries: the following are to be found in the various diagnostic systems and in the research literature, *mentally defective, mental handicap, mental retardation,* and *learning disability.* The current terminology speaks to *developmental intellectual impairment* (learning or developmental disabilities). Holland (2004: 26) notes that the term 'developmental disability' refers to 'a highly heterogeneous group of people who have in common evidence of some delay in reaching, or a failure to reach developmental milestones, a delay in or failure to acquire living, educational and social skills as expected for their age, and evidence, on standard psychological assessment, of a significant intellectual impairment'.

As Holland explains, the emergence of the notion of development disability brings together two groups previously considered in the literature to be distinct. For one group there is a genetic or environmental explanation for their impaired functioning, such as people with diagnosable chromosomal abnormalities, head injury, or identifiable pregnancy and birth complications such as infection *in utero* as, for example, with rubella, birth complications such as anoxia, or a childhood disease such as meningitis. For the second group, a combination of adverse biological and environmental factors is involved in the learning disability.

Given the a range of terms in use across the literature, to maintain a thread within the research which focuses on intelligence, the term intellectual disability (ID) is used here, acknowledging the arguments in favour of the term developmental disability.

ID is not the same as mental illness, although the two can be co-morbid, and involves both intellectual and social ability. There is no legal level of IQ score by which to define intellectual disability. However, on standard IQ tests that give a mean score of 100, such as the Wechsler Adult Intelligence Scales (WAIS), an IQ in the region of 70 is taken as 'borderline'. An IQ of 70 or below together with a low level of social functioning may be indicative of learning disability (having eliminated other explanations such as memory loss or trauma).

There are two main approaches to considering the relationship between intellectual disability and criminal behaviour: first, to look at the intellectual functioning of offender populations; second, to examine the criminal behaviour of those with an intellectual disability. An innovative departure from these two approaches was reported in an American study that showed a correlation between IQ estimates at a state level and state-level crime rates (Beaver & Wright, 2011).

Intelligence in offender populations

As long ago as 1913, Charles Goring concluded from his study of 3,000 English convicts that criminals were generally of low intelligence. Goring's work has been replicated over the following decades, with various studies from different countries reporting an association between low IQ and criminal behaviour (e.g., Bartels, Ryan, Urban, & Glass, 2010; Beaver & Wright, 2011; Craft, 1984; Hirschi, 1969; Moffitt, Gabrielli, Mednick, & Schulsinger, 1981; West & Farrington, 1973; Woodward, 1955).

However, low intelligence, as indicated by IQ scores between 70 and 80, is not the same as intellectual disability: this point is illustrated by an American study reported by Denkowski and Denkowski (1985). Denkowski and Denkowski estimated that approximately 2.5 per cent of prisoners, across 20 states, have an IQ below 70. The importance of adaptive social functioning in intellectual disability is evident from the figures presented: in states that rely on IQ testing alone, 2.25 per cent of prisoners are classified as 'retarded'; in the five states where IQ and adaptive behaviour were assessed (using a standard psychometric test) the figure fell to 1.28 per cent of the prisoners.

In a study carried out in an English Young Offender Institution, Herrington (2009) investigated the prevalence of ID among 185 young male prisoners aged between 18 and 21 years. The prisoners completed an intelligence test and a measure of social adaptation (the Vineland Adaptive Behaviour Scales). The assessments indicated that about 1 in 10 of the prisoners had an IQ of 69, which indicates an impairment in functioning. When scores on a measure of adaptive behaviour were taken into consideration, Herrington notes that none of the offenders met the diagnostic criteria for ID but that 11 per cent were borderline ID. Herrington also makes the point that the prisoners with borderline ID were housed within the main part of the institution and that it was unlikely that their level of functioning had been recognised.

Offending in ID populations

Barron, Hassiotis, and Banes (2002) conducted a study, based in north-east London and west Essex, of 61 adults with an IQ below 80 who had offended within the previous 5 years. Alongside low IQ, the sample was marked by high levels of comorbid psychosis and lower levels of autistic symptomatology. Barron et al. reported that just over half of the sample had their first contact with the criminal justice system before the age of 16 years. The sample was characterised by high levels of family criminality, experience of abuse, conduct disorder, problems at school, and a long history of offending – all of which could be found in any mainstream offender group, low IQ or not. The type of offences most frequently found were violent offences, sex offences, and firesetting, for which more than one-quarter of the sample had served a custodial sentence. Indeed, reinforcing the point regarding similarities between ID and mainstream offenders, Gray, Fitzgerald, Taylor, MacCulloch, and Snowden (2007) found that risk assessments developed with general offenders groups functioned accurately with ID offenders.

A Scottish study of court reports completed by the Tayside learning disability service since 1986 was reported by Smith, White, and Walker (2008). There were 64 people with a learning disability who faced charges for a range of offences, most commonly public order offences with a relatively high level of arson and sexual offending. Schizophrenia was the most common comorbid diagnosis.

A Finnish study reported by Männynsalo, Putkonen, Lindberg, and Kotilainen (2009) reviewed the pre-trial forensic psychiatric reports of 44 people (36 male, 8 female) with ID over the period 1996–2006. They found that about half of the offenders had committed previous crimes, with arson the most frequent offence. There were very high levels of alcohol and drug abuse and dependency, and about half of those assessed were intoxicated when committing their crime. In addition to the comorbid substance use, about one-quarter of the sample also met the diagnostic criteria for anti-social personality disorder. The comorbidity of ID and personality disorder is one that is beginning to come to prominence (Morrissey & Hollin, 2011).

Hobson and Rose (2008) conducted a review of 14 studies concerned with the mental health of people with ID who commit offences. They concluded that a substantial proportion of people with ID had comorbid mental health problems, particularly schizophrenia and other psychotic disorders. Hobson and Rose noted that the offences committed by people with ID ranges across the full spectrum of types of crime, from property offences to acts of serious violence. However, as noted by Lindsay and Taylor (2005), it is aggression, firesetting, and inappropriate sexual behaviour that attracts the main body of attention.

When looking at offending in mentally disordered offenders, including offenders with ID, the source of the sample used in the research is important. Some mentally disordered offenders are deemed to be such a risk to the public that they are detained in conditions of high security, while others of much lower risk are accommodated in lower security or within the community. Lindsay et al. (2010) reviewed the case files of 477 people in England and Scotland with ID who were referred to offender services – including community and low, medium, and maximum security – over a 12-month period. They found that violence, both verbal and physical, was the most frequently seen behaviour: however, for those in maximum security, who were the younger members of the sample, sexual offenses were much more evident. A similar survey in the north of England found that among 60 people with ID, the most frequent offences were violence against the person, sexual offences, and arson (Crossland, Burns, Leach, & Quinn, 2005).

Sex offending

There is a longstanding history of research concerned with the high prevalence of improper sexual behaviour among low IQ groups (Day, 1993; Robertson, 1981; Walker & McCabe, 1973). In a review of the research concerned with sex offenders with intellectual and developmental disabilities, Lindsay (2002) pointed to methodological variations across studies, such differences in inclusion criteria, the source of the sample and in the way that IQ was measured, which could affect prevalence rates of sex offenders. Lindsay concludes that, overall, the research does indicate that sex offenders with ID are less discriminating in their victims, committing offences against children both male and female. Lindsay makes the point that assessment methods for sex offenders with ID, which could be used to inform the court with respect to decisions regarding sentencing and treatment, are not well developed.

Rice, Harris, Lang, and Chaplin (2008) addressed the issue of offenders with an ID who offend against children. The question they specifically addressed was do these offenders sexually assault children because of their own sexual immaturity and lack of social skills, or is it because they have a sexual preference for children? In order to answer this question, Rice et al. compared the personal characteristics, offence records, and phallometric assessment of 69 male sex offenders with an ID (IQ below 80) and a control group of 69 sex offenders (IQ average or above). In terms of offending history, the sex offenders with ID were more likely to have previous victims who were prepubescent or very young and male. However, they were no more likely than the comparison group to show a preference for highly coercive sex with children, nor were the offenders with ID any more likely to commit further violent sexual offences.

In conclusion, an explanation for the relationship between ID and anti-social and criminal behaviour may be due to a combination of various factors. The person with ID may not learn the difference between socially acceptable and unacceptable behaviour. In addition, poor social skills may mean that behaviour intended to be friendly is perceived as aggressive or hostile and so results in altercations. It is possible the person with ID is easily influenced by more able offenders and so becomes involved in crime. Finally, the person with ID may carry out the crime clumsily so that detection and arrest is made easier.

The point regarding a failure to learn to distinguish socially acceptable and unacceptable behaviour may be particularly applicable to sexual offending. The term 'counterfeit deviance' has been used to refer to behaviour that is clearly anti-social but is explicable by the individual's lack of sexual knowledge and by limitations in their social skills and opportunities to establish sexual relationships in a socially acceptable fashion. Thus, any sexually inappropriate behaviour is a consequence of sexual naïveté rather than sexual deviance (Luiselli, 2000). Nonetheless, social naïve behaviour may be seen by other people as assault, reported to the police and criminal proceedings may follow.

Personality disorder

The generic term 'personality disorder' masks a myriad of diagnostic categories. The two major diagnostic systems, the International Statistical Classification of Diseases and Related Health Problems (ICD) and Diagnostic and Statistical Manual of Mental Disorders (DSM), have both traditionally included substantial numbers of types of personality disorder. As shown in Box 8.2, following DSM conventions, it is now usual to think of clusters of personality disorders rather than a multitude of individually named disorders.

Personality disorders are relatively common across the both general population and among mentally disordered populations, where they are often comorbid with alcohol and drug problems. As might be predicted, anti-social personality disorder (APD) is highly prevalent among offender populations and is predictive of high rates of recidivism, particularly

---

Box 8.2 Personality disorders classified

ICD-10 Classification

Specific personality disorders
- Paranoid personality disorder
- Schizoid personality disorder
- Dissocial personality disorder
- Emotionally unstable personality disorder (impulsive type and borderline type)
- Histrionic personality disorder
- Anankastic personality disorder
- Anxious [avoidant] personality disorder
- Dependent personality disorder
- Other specific personality disorders
- Personality disorder, unspecified

Mixed and other personality disorders
- Mixed personality disorders
- Troublesome personality changes

DSM IV-TR
- Paranoid personality disorder
- Schizoid personality disorder
- Schizotypal personality disorder
- Anti-social personality disorder
- Borderline personality disorder
- Histrionic personality disorder
- Narcissistic personality disorder
- Avoidant personality disorder
- Dependent personality disorder
- Obsessive-compulsive personality disorder

DSM Clusters
Cluster A: 'odd or eccentric' types: paranoid, schizoid, and schizotypal personality disorders
Cluster B: 'dramatic, emotional, or erratic' types: histrionic, narcissistic, anti-social, and border-line personality disorders
Cluster C: 'anxious and fearful' types: obsessive-compulsive, avoidant, and dependent personality disorders

when comorbid with substance use disorders (Walter, Wiesbeck, Dittmann, & Graf, 2010). A survey of psychiatric morbidity among prisoners in England and Wales found that:

> Antisocial personality disorder had the highest prevalence of any category of personality disorder. This would be expected, since the category of antisocial personality disorder requires the presence of antisocial behaviour before the age of 15 years which persists into adulthood. Among the sub-sample who had a clinical interview, 63% of male remand prisoners, 49% of male sentenced prisoners and 31% of female prisoners were assessed as having antisocial personality disorder. These prevalence rates for antisocial personality disorder are broadly in line with the results of studies carried out within the United States penal system.
>
> (Singleton et al., 1998: 10)

Roberts and Coid (2010) reported that among a sample of male prisoners in England and Wales a range of personality disorders was evident. In terms of criminal behaviour, APD was associated with a range of crimes including robbery, blackmail, and burglary.

The DSM-IV-TR diagnostic criteria for APD are summarised in Table 8.2.

As may be predicted, those with APD cause a great deal of harm as given their involvement in a range of anti-social, including violent, behaviours. In addition, APD is likely to be comorbid with other psychiatric disorders, meaning that anti-social behaviour is often evident within psychiatric hospitals, alongside high rates of educational failure, family breakdown, unemployment, and other social problems.

It is established that the first signs of APD are to be found in childhood conduct disorder, followed by high levels of anti-social behaviour during adolescence (Robins, 1978). As is the case with many childhood disturbances, it is likely that an explanation for ASP lies in combination of impoverished environment, genetic constitution and biological functioning, and harsh parenting (De Brito & Hodgins, 2009).

The way in which offenders with personality disorders, including ASP, are managed and treated within the metal health and criminal justice systems is a longstanding issue. Those people diagnosed as personality disordered are difficult to manage within institutions and there is only a very small evidence-base to inform the design of effective treatments with

Table 8.2 DSM IV-TR criteria for APD

A) There is a longstanding pattern of a disregard for the rights of other people. This pattern may have been evident from childhood onwards and is indicated by three or more of the following criteria:
    i) a failure to conform to social norms with as seen by repeated behaviours that are grounds for arrest;
    ii deceitfulness as seen with repeated lying or cheating others for profit or pleasure;
    iii) impulsivity;
    iv) irritability and aggressiveness leading to repeated involvement in fights or assaults;
    v) a reckless disregard for the safety of self or others;
    vi) consistent irresponsibility in failing to hold employment respect financial obligations;
    vii) a lack of remorse for their victims.
B) The individual is at least 18 years of age.
C) There is evidence of conduct disorder with onset before the age of 15 years.
D) The occurrence of anti-social behaviour is not evident only during an episode of schizophrenia or mania.

such a complex group (see De Brito & Hodgins, 2009). In England in the late 1990s and early 2000s, concerns were being voiced that there was a reluctance to offer treatment to people, including offenders, with a personality disorder. This reluctance may have been based on the fact that some personality disordered offenders are dangerous to work with alongside the view that others were untreatable by mainstream psychiatric services. This concern lead the National Institute for Mental Health in England in 2003 to issue the best practice guide *Personality Disorder: No Longer a Diagnosis of Exclusion*. This guide addressed issues such as the assessment and treatment of personality disorder within psychiatric and forensic services. The overarching aim of the guidelines was to emphasise that people with personality disorder should be perceived as legitimate users of mental health services.

As this initiative to draw personality disorder into mainstream psychiatric services unfolded there was, paradoxically, a different agenda coming into force. This new focus was aimed at a group of people whose violence (including sexual violence) led to their being a significant danger to the community. Feeney (2003) traces the name given to this group to a statement in 1999 by the then Home Secretary, Jack Straw (1999): 'There is, however, a group of dangerous and severely personality disordered individuals from whom the public at present are not properly protected'. The notion of dangerous and severe personality disorder (DSPD) was at large even if, as Mullen (2007: s3) states, it was '[b]orn out of a populist law and order reaction, based on false premises', or as Maden (2007: s8) puts it: 'Politicians and civil servants invented dangerous and severe personality disorder in 1999'. One of the main reservations about the DSPD programme was expressed by Buchanan and Leese (2001: 1955): 'The proposals have provoked debate on the morality of preventatively detaining people who have not been convicted of an offence'.

Dangerous and severe personality disorder

As Feeney (2003) makes clear in his comprehensive review, the machinery of government churned into action with £126 million funding for a 3-year programme for the development of specialist services for DSPD. These specialist services were eventually established in both high security hospitals (Broadmoor and Rampton) and prisons (Frankland and Whitemoor). It was planned that there would be 312 beds for those male offenders who fulfilled the criteria for DSPD. Those individuals who fulfilled the criteria for DSPD could be detained in conditions of security at one of the specialist centres. All three diagnostic criteria for DSPD, as specified by the Home Office and the Department of Health (2001), should be satisfied in each individual case: (1) they are more likely than not to commit an offence within 5 years that might be expected to lead to serious physical or psychological harm from which the victim would find it difficult or impossible to recover; (2) they have a significant disorder of personality; (3) the risk presented appears to be functionally linked to the significant personality disorder. As Tyrer et al. (2010) point out, these criteria present a challenge to those who work in the field: the prediction of future offending is fraught with multiple difficulties, the assessment of dangerousness is less than straightforward, and how precisely to establish a functional relationship between personality disorder and risk posed remains uncertain.

In spite of this daunting range of conceptual and practical problems, the DSPD initiative was translated into action as the funding was made available: innovative assessments were developed, new treatment centres were built, and new treatment regimes appeared (Howells & Tennant, 2010), and screening of large numbers of prisoners was undertaken to identify those individuals with DSPD (Ullrich, Yang, & Coid, 2010).

The provision of these new services was an expensive task: Barrett et al. (2009) estimated that it cost the public purse £25,150 per patient over a 6-month period to house and treat those people contained within DSPD Units. This cost is £3,500 more expensive than keeping a prisoner in conditions of similar security.

The clinical profile of the first 203 male patients admitted to the new high security DSPD units was described by Kirkpatrick et al. (2010). A summary of the characteristics of this cohort is given in Box 8.3.

Of course, the figures about the cost of the new services are meaningless unless set against outcomes: if the DSPD initiative demonstrably and significantly reduced offending and facilitated community rehabilitation then the benefits may well outweigh the costs. However, the evaluation of the DSPD programme has proved to be a far from straightforward task. Tyrer et al. (2009) have pointed to the organisational issues that, despite the protestations from the government department charged with delivering the DSPD programme (Ramsay, Saradjian, Murphy, & Freestone, 2009), seriously compromised the evaluation that relied upon the use of a randomised control trial (RCT). Tyrer et al. (2009: 140) noted that their negative findings 'should be tempered by the observations that there were smaller numbers than expected, protocol violations meant that only a minority completed the study as planned, and certain outcomes such as retention in the treatment programme might have been more relevant outcomes for the assessment'. Indeed, the history of evaluations of forensic mental health services is blighted by the problems inherent in running RCTs (Hollin, 2008).

Psychopathic disorder

The 1983 Act defined psychopathic disorder as a 'persistent disorder or disability of mind (whether or not including significant impairment of intelligence) which results in abnormally aggressive or seriously irresponsible conduct' (section 1(2)). This definition is no longer prevalent as the 2007 Act uses the more general 'any disorder or disability of the mind'.

Box 8.3 Characteristics of the 203 males in the first DSPD cohort (from Kirkpatrick et al., 2010)

Mean age   35.7 years (SD = 8.6)

Common offences
Rape/attempted rape   31.0%
Indecent assault   26.5%
Murder   19.4%
Assault   16.9%

Personality disorder diagnoses
93.8% had a diagnosed personality disorder
75.3% had more than one personality disorder
The most common combination was anti-social personality disorder with borderline personality
    disorder (28.8%), followed by paranoid personality disorder with borderline (41.5%)

Most frequently assessed treatment needs
Violent lifestyle   97.9%
Criminal personality   96.5%
Criminal attitudes   95.1%
Work ethic   76.9%
Criminal peers   52.4%

What is a psychopath? The modern-day formulation of the notion of a person who can be identified as a psychopath (the notion has been around since the 19th century) are often credited to the American psychiatrist Hervey Milton Cleckley (1903–84). Cleckley's 1941 book, *The Mask of Sanity*, took its title from Cleckley's clinical observations that, unlike people with mental disorders such as schizophrenia or depression, the psychopath presents as sociable and personally engaging but this 'mask' of normality conceals a personality characterised by coldness and a ruthless disregard for the feelings of other people. Cleckley continued to refine the notion of the psychopath in later editions of *The Mask of Sanity*, finally producing a fifth and final edition in 1976.

The psychopath was not Cleckley's only well-known work: he seems to have had the ability to corner the market in usual psychological conditions and snappy book titles. Alongside *The Mask of Sanity*, in 1956 he was a co-author, with Corbett H. Thigpen, of *The Three Faces of Eve*, a case study about a woman with multiple personality disorder that was later made into a film.

As shown in Box 8.4, Cleckley described psychopaths as having a range of readily identifiable characteristics that typify their emotional and social emptiness.

Robert Hare and the PCL

Cleckley gave a clinically informed description of the psychopath but it was the Canadian psychologist Robert Hare who brought the formal assessment of psychopathy to the fore. Some of the terms used by Cleckley are vague and imprecise, causing difficulties for clinicians and researchers alike, so the development of a psychometrically sound scale by which to assess psychopathy has many obvious applications.

Hare (1980) conducted a factor analysis of data derived from the Cleckley criteria and found five factors. These factors offer a succinct description of the psychopath: (1) an inability to develop warm, empathic relationships; (2) an unstable lifestyle; (3) an inability to accept responsibility for anti-social behaviour; (4) an absence of intellectual and psychiatric

---

Box 8.4 Cleckley's description of the psychopath

1. Superficial charm and good intelligence.
2. Absence of delusions and other signs of irrational thinking.
3. Absence of nervousness or psychoneurotic manifestations.
4. Unreliability.
5. Untruthfulness and insincerity.
6. Lack of remorse and shame.
7. Inadequately motivated anti-social behaviour.
8. Poor judgement and failure to learn by experience.
9. Pathologic egocentricity and incapacity for love.
10. General poverty in major affective reactions.
11. Specific loss of insight.
12. Unresponsiveness in general interpersonal relations.
13. Fantastic and uninviting behaviour with drink and sometimes without.
14. Suicide threats rarely carried out.
15. Sex life impersonal, trivial and poorly integrated.
16. Failure to follow any life plan.

Box 8.5 Characteristics of the psychopath (Hare, 1980)

1. Glibness/superficial charm.
2. Previous diagnosis as a psychopath (or similar).
3. Egocentricity/grandiose sense of self-worth.
4. Proneness to boredom/low frustration tolerance.
5. Pathological lying and deception.
6. Conning/lack of sincerity.
7. Lack of remorse or guilt.
8. Lack of affect and emotional depth.
9. Callous/lack of empathy.
10. Parasitic lifestyle.
11. Short-tempered/poor behavioural controls.
12. Promiscuous sexual behaviour.
13. Early behaviour problems.
14. Lack of realistic long-term plans.
15. Impulsivity.
16. Irresponsible behaviour as a parent.
17. Frequent marital relationships.
18. Juvenile delinquency.
19. Poor probation or parole risk.
20. Failure to accept responsibility for own actions.
21. Many types of offence.
22. Drug or alcohol abuse not direct cause of anti-social behaviour.

---

problems; (5) weak behavioural control. From this analysis, Hare (1980) constructed a scale for the assessment of psychopathy in criminal populations. This scale, shown in Box 8.5, was subsequently amended and became the 20-item Psychopathy Checklist (PCL; Hare 1991), subsequently revised (PCL-R; Hare 2003). The items on the PCL-R are informed by file review and interview with the individual being assessed. Each of the 20 items is scored by the assessor on a three-point scale, with 0 indicating not present, 1 indicating possibly present, and 2 definitely present. Thus, the scale has a maximum score of 40, with a cut-off point of 30 taken to indicate psychopathy. This cut-off point of 30 may vary across countries and according to the gender of the person being assessed (Cooke & Michie, 1999; Cooke, Michie, Hart, & Clark, 2005a,b; Dolan & Völlm, 2009), although the need for adjustment by country has been called in question (Bolt, Hare, & Neumann, 2007).

The PCL-R has become a widely used assessment in clinical forensic practice (Archer, Buffington-Vollum, Stredny, & Handel, 2006; Flores-Mendoza, Alvarenga, Herrero, & Abad, 2008), used either alone or in conjunction with other measures, and particularly with regard to the assessment of risk of future violent conduct (Lestico, Salekin, DeCoster, & Rogers, 2008; Mokros, Osterheider, Hucker, & Nitschke, 2010). This widespread use of the PCL-R includes not just the assessment of women (Warren et al., 2003; Weizmann-Henelius et al., 2010) as well as men, but also children and adolescents (Salekin, Lee, Schrum Dillard, & Kubak, 2010; Stockdale, Olver, & Wong, 2010) – for whom a Youth Version has been developed (PCL: YV; Forth, Kosson, & Hare, 2003) – and mentally disordered and ID offenders (Morrissey et al., 2007; Vitacco, Rogers, Neumann, Harrison, & Vincent, 2005). These assessments are often undertaken in the context of violent and sexually violent crimes (e.g., Blackburn & Coid, 1998; Mokros et al., 2010; Vincent, Odgers, McCormick, & Corrado, 2008).

Given the predictive utility of the PCL-R a body of research, primarily with males, has investigated the factor structure of the scale.

The structure of the PCL-R

The longstanding position, based on factor analysis of PCL-R scores, was that the scale consisted of two correlated factors: factor 1 relates to interpersonal and affective functioning such as superficial charm, cheating, and lack of empathy; factor 2 concerns anti-social behaviour, impulsiveness, and irresponsibility (Harpur, Hakistan, & Hare, 1991). However, this two-factor model was called into question by Cooke and Michie (2001) who used confirmatory factor analysis with a combination of 10 Canadian and American data sets (n = 2067) to re-examine the factor structure of the PCL-R. Cooke and Michie reported a a three-factor structure underpinning the PCL-R: these three factors are (1) arrogant and deceitful interpersonal style, (2) deficient affective experience, and (3) impulsive and irresponsible behavioural style. This three-factor structure did not include PCL-R items that were concerned with anti-social and criminal behaviour. Cooke and Michie suggest that their model moves to the heart of the psychological construct of psychopathy, of which anti-social and criminal behaviour is a consequence not a core component. With the benefit of hindsight it is at about this point in the research that the debate started that would eventually lead to threats of legal proceedings.

In response to Cooke and Michie, Hare (2003) proposed a four-facet model: factor 1 was affective/interpersonal and consisted of two facets (affective and interpersonal), factor 2 (lifestyle/anti-social) also with two facets (lifestyle and anti-social). In later publications, Hare and Neumann (2008, 2009) have expounded upon this four-facet model and its implications for understanding the nature of psychopathy and how it is measured. While both sides questioned the statistical models used by their adversary, the debate, as Blackburn (2007a) has made clear, ran much deeper than statistics. Indeed, Blackburn notes his own position, remaining consistent with his own research (see Chapter 6), that the core of psychopathy reflects narcissistic and histrionic personality disorders rather more than antisocial personality disorder. However, the development of the four facet model failed to impress Cooke and Michie who, joined by Skeem, maintained their position that the PCL-R confounded personality and antisocial behaviour, two quite separate and distinct constructs, with potentially misleading consequences both theoretically and practically (Andrade, 2008; Cooke, Michie, & Skeem, 2007).

These types of exchange and polarisation of opinions are not uncommon in academic journals. However, the Cook et al. versus Hare debate about the role of criminal behaviour in psychopathy was about to take an unusual twist, as discussed in Box 8.6, with a paper by Skeem and Cooke (2010a).

Psychopathy and personality disorder

What is the relationship between psychopathy and personality disorder? Is psychopathy a type of personality disorder or is it something quite separate, a taxon i.e., a distinct grouping of individuals different in kind to other people?

Blackburn (1988) proved to be remarkably prescient with regard to the debate captured in Box 8.5 in his discussion of the 'myth of psychopathic personality'. Blackburn argues that

---

Box 8.6   When researchers disagree

It is an integral part of the scientific process that research findings challenge accepted theory and that theory evolves as the evidence accumulates. In the case of the PCL-R, Hare and his colleagues have rightly defended their position in the journals when they have been challenged (as documented by Poythress and Petrila, 2010). However, when Jennifer Skeem and David Cooke submitted a paper that, following peer review, was accepted for publication in the academic journal *Psychological Assessment*, a very different train of events ensued:

> Prior to publication, Professor Hare's counsel issued a letter to the authors and the editor of *Psychological Assessment* in which he stated that the paper 'was fraught with misrepresentations and other problems and a completely inaccurate summary of what amounts to his life's work.'[14] The letter charged that the authors of the paper 'deliberately fabricated or altered quotes of Dr. Hare, and substantially altered the sense of what Dr. Hare said in his previous publications.' The letter asserted that publication of the article 'will constitute defamation on the part of the authors, and also *Psychological Assessment*,' and issued a 'demand' that the paper be pulled from publication in its current state.
>
> The summary of events in this section is taken from a letter dated November 8, 2007, from Hare's attorney to Professors Cooke and Skeem, and to Dr. Milton E. Strauss, the editor of *Psychological Assessment*.
>
> (Poythress & Petrila, 2010: 4)

The threat of litigation against both the journal and the authors significantly changes the nature of academic debate and the freedom to publish scholarly work without fear of reprisal.

The errant paper was eventually published (Skeem and Cooke, 2010a) with comments (Hare and Neumann, 2010) and replies (Skeem and Cooke, 2010b). However, as Hart (2010) suggests, this situation leaves journal editors with much to ponder.

---

a cluster of personality traits, including egocentricity, hostility, and impulsivity, all associated with socially deviant behaviour, have attracted the label 'psychopathy'. This confluence of personality traits, Blackburn argues, suggests a *dimension* of personality which is not the same as a discrete *type*. Blackburn (1988: 510) takes the argument a stage further: 'Extremes on one dimension may characterise several personality types that differ significantly on other dimensions. The traits claimed by Cleckley and others to identify a 'distinct entity' may therefore represent a personality dimension that is common to more than one class of personality disorder'.

This question of classification continues to vex researchers (e.g., Blackburn, 2007b; Blackburn, Logan, Renwick, & Donnelly, 2005; Coid & Ullrich, 2010; Ogloff, 2006; Skeem, Poythress, Edens, Lilienfeldd, & Cale, 2003) with the consequence that the concept of psychopathy remains a matter of debate. Now, given that the concept is uncertain and therefore measurement is unsure, the development of a cogent explanation for psychopathy is a daunting task! In spite of these problems in terminology, definition, and measurement, a literature has nonetheless accumulated that examines a range of correlates of psychopathy. The familiar variables of biological influences, childhood behaviour, and family functioning have all been considered with respect to psychopathy and its development (Lynam & Gudonis, 2005). The biological research has progressed from studies of autonomic and central nervous system functioning (e.g., Blackburn, 1979) to consider genetic influences (Forsman, Lichtenstein, Andershed, & Larsson, 2008; Tikkanen et al., 2010), brain abnormalities (Weber, Habel, Amunts, & Schneider, 2008), neurological functioning (Dolan, 2010; Harenski, Harenski, Kiehl, & Shane, 2010; Nilsson et al., 2010). It seems likely that research, including biological research, has some way to go before solving the puzzle that is psychopathy.

Conclusion

The mentally disordered offender sets several challenges: there are the legal issues concerning *mens rea* and the definition of what exactly constitutes a mental disorder; there are empirical questions around the nature of the relationship between symptomatology and criminal behaviour; and there are practical issues regarding the treatment of the mentally disordered offender. The research concerned with all these aspects of the mentally disordered offender, as is evident from the range of professions with a direct interest in the area, continues to gather with some momentum. One of the priorities for the future is to use this knowledge to design effective treatment regimes.

Chapter summary

- Where there is an overlap between mental disorder and criminal behaviour, the principle of *mens rea* is not seen to be applicable. Thus, alongside criminal law, there is mental health law for those cases where the offender is mentally disordered.
- The legal definition of mental disorder has shifted and changed over time but can be seen as broadly including mental illnesses such as schizophrenia, personality disorders, and learning disabilities.
- The proportion of people with a mental disorder who commit crimes is very small. People with a mental disorder are, however, overrepresented in prison populations.
- Anti-social personality disorder (APD) is highly prevalent among offender populations and is predictive of high rates of recidivism, particularly when comorbid with substance use disorders.
- The introduction of the classification of dangerous and severe personality disorder (DSPD) and the development of associated services brought about a good deal of debate within the literature. The same is true of the topic of the psychopathic individual.

Points for discussion

- As we have mental health laws, why are so many people with a mental disorder prevalent in the prison population?
- Why is alcohol abuse often comorbid with the main psychiatric diagnosis in mentally disordered offenders?
- What was the thinking behind the introduction of the category of dangerous and severe personality disorder (DSPD)?

Essential reading

Anckarsäter, H., Radovic, S., Svennerlind, C., Höglund, P., & Radovic, F. (2009). Mental disorder is a cause of crime: The cornerstone of forensic psychiatry. *International Journal of Law and Psychiatry*, *32*, 342–347.

This paper below offers an excellent discussion of the issues surrounding the debate between the association between mental disorder and criminal behaviour.

Lindsay, W. R., Hastings, R. P., & Beech, A. R. (Eds.) (2011). Special issue: Forensic research in offenders with intellectual and developmental disabilities (parts 1 and 2). *Psychology, Crime, & Law, 17*(1 & 2).
These two volumes of the journal *Psychology, Crime, and Law* are given to the topic of offenders with intellectual and developmental disabilities.

De Brito, S. A. & Hodgins, S. (2009). Antisocial personality disorder. In M. McMurran & R. Howard (Eds.), *Personality, Personality Disorder and Violence* (pp. 133–153). Chichester, Sussex: John Wiley & Sons.
This chapter presents an excellent overview of anti-social personality disorder.

A. R. Felthous & H. Sa (2007). *International Handbook on Psychopathic Disorders and the Law: Two Volume Set*. Chichester, Sussex: John Wiley & Sons.
More than anyone could ever want to know about psychopathy is contained in these two volumes – perhaps rather wide-ranging in scope and American in flavour, they are nonetheless a wealth of information.

Lynam, D. R. & Gudonis, L. (2005). The development of psychopathy. *Annual Review of Clinical Psychology, 1*, 381–407.
A comprehensive overview of the factors involved in the aetiology of psychopathy.

The lighter side

The Three Faces of Eve, starring Joanne Woodward, is a film about a woman with multiple personality disorder.

Useful websites

Mental Health Act (2007). www.legislation.gov.uk/ukpga/2007/12/contents. Mentally Disordered Offenders, www.justice.gov.uk/publications/mentally-disordered-offenders.htm.

References

Alden, A., Brennan, P., Hodgins, S., & Mednick, S. (2007). Psychotic disorders and sex offending in a Danish birth cohort. *Archives of General Psychiatry, 64*, 1251–1258.

Anckarsäter, H., Radovic, S., Svennerlind, C., Höglund, P., & Radovic, F. (2009). Mental disorder is a cause of crime: The cornerstone of forensic psychiatry. *International Journal of Law and Psychiatry, 32*, 342–347.

Andrade, J. T. (2008). The inclusion of antisocial behaviour in the construct of psychopathy: A review of the research. *Aggression and Violent Behavior, 13*, 328–335.

Appelbaum, P., Robbins, P. C., & Monahan, J. (2000). Violence and delusions: Data from the MacArthur Risk Assessment Study. *American Journal of Psychiatry, 157*, 566–572.

Archer, R. P., Buffington-Vollum, J. K., Stredny, R. V., Handel, R. W. (2006). A survey of psychological test use patterns among forensic psychologists. *Journal of Personality Assessment, 87*, 84–94.

Barrett, B., Byford, S., Seivewright, H., Cooper, S., Duggan, C., & Tyrer, P. (2009). The assessment of dangerous and severe personality disorder: Service use, cost, and consequences. *Journal of Forensic Psychiatry & Psychology, 20*, 120–131.

Barron P., Hassiotis A., & Banes, J. (2002). Offenders with intellectual disability: The size of the problem and therapeutic outcomes. *Journal of Intellectual Disability Research, 46*, 454–463.

Bartels, J. M., Ryan, J. J., Urban, L. S., & Glass, L. A. (2010). Correlations between estimates of state IQ and FBI crime statistics. *Personality and Individual Differences, 48*, 579–583.

Beaver, K. M. & Wright, J. P. (2011). The association between county-level IQ and county-level crime rates. *Intelligence, 39*, 22–26.

Blackburn, R. (1979). Cortical and autonomic arousal in primary and secondary psychopaths. *Psychophysiology, 16*, 143–150.

—— (1988). On moral judgements and personality disorders: The myth of psychopathic personality revisited. *British Journal of Psychiatry, 153*, 505–512.

—— (2007a). Personality disorder and antisocial deviance: Comments on the debate on the structure of the Psychopathy Checklist-Revised. *Journal of Personality Disorders, 21*, 142–159.

—— (2007b). Personality disorder and psychopathy: Conceptual and empirical integration. *Psychology, Crime & Law, 13*, 7–18.

Blackburn, R. & Coid, J. W. (1998). Psychopathy and the dimensions of personality disorder in violent offenders. *Personality and Individual Differences, 25*, 129–145.

Blackburn, R., Logan, C., Renwick, S. J. D., & Donnelly, J. P. (2005). Higher-order dimensions of personality disorder: Hierarchical structure and relationships with the five-factor model, the interpersonal circle, and psychopathy. *Journal of Personality Disorders, 19*, 597–623.

Bolt, D. M., Hare, R. D., & Neumann, C. S. (2007). Score metric equivalence of the Psychopathy Checklist-Revised (PCL-R) across criminal offenders in North America and the United Kingdom: A critique of Cook, Michie, Hart, and Clarke (2005) and new analyses. *Assessment, 14*, 44–56.

Bonta, J., Law, M., & Hanson, K. (1998). The prediction of criminal and violent recidivism among mentally disordered offenders: A meta-analysis. *Psychological Bulletin, 123*, 123–142.

Bradley, K. (2009). *The Bradley Report: Lord Bradley's Review of People with Mental Health Problems or Learning Disabilities in the Criminal Justice System*. London: DH Publications.

Braham, L. G., Trower, P., & Birchwood, M. (2004). Acting on command hallucinations and dangerous behavior: A critique of the major findings in the last decade. *Clinical Psychology Review, 24*, 513–528.

Brugha, T., Singleton, N., Meltzer, H., Bebbington, P., Farrell, M., Jenkins, R., & Lewis, G. (2005). Psychosis in the community and in prisons: A report from the British National Survey of Psychiatric Morbidity. *American Journal of Psychiatry, 162*, 774–780.

Buchanan, A. & Leese, M. (2001). Detention of people with dangerous severe personality disorders: A systematic review. *The Lancet, 358*, 1955–1959.

Buchanan, A. & Zonana, H. (2009). Mental disorder as the cause of crime. *International Journal of Law and Psychiatry, 32*, 142–146.

Cleckley, H. (1941). *The Mask of Sanity*. St. Louis, MO: Mosby.

—— (1976). *The Mask of Sanity* (5th ed.). St. Louis, MO: Mosby.

Cloyes, K. G., Wong, B., Latimer, S., & Abarca, J. (2010). Time to prison return for offenders with serious mental illness released from prison: A survival analysis. *Criminal Justice and Behavior, 37*, 175–187.

Coid, J. & Ullrich, S. (2010). Antisocial personality disorder is on a continuum with psychopathy. *Comprehensive Psychiatry, 51*, 426–433.

Coid, J., Yang, M., Ullrich, S., Roberts, A., Moran, P., Bebbington, P., & Hare, R. (2009a). Psychopathy among prisoners in England and Wales. *International Journal of Law and Psychiatry, 32*, 134–141.

—— (2009b). Prevalence and correlates of psychopathic traits in the household population of Great Britain. *International Journal of Law and Psychiatry, 32*, 65–73.

Constantine, R. J., Petrila, J., Andel, R., Givens, E. M., Becker, M., Robst, J., & Howe, A. (2010). Arrest trajectories of adult offenders with a serious mental illness. *Psychology, Public Policy, and Law, 16*, 319–339.

Cooke, D. J. & Michie, C. (1999). Psychopathy across cultures: North America and Scotland compared. *Journal of Abnormal Psychology, 108*, 55–68.

—— (2001). Refining the construct of psychopathy: Towards a hierarchical model. *Psychological Assessment, 13*, 171–188.

Cooke, D. J., Michie, C., Hart, S. D., & Clark, D. (2005a). Searching for the pan-cultural core of psychopathic personality disorder. *Personality and Individual Differences, 39*, 283–295.

—— (2005b). Assessing psychopathy in the UK: Concerns about cross-cultural generalisability. *British Journal of Psychiatry, 186*, 335–341.

Cooke, D. J., Michie, C., & Skeem, J. L. (2007). Understanding the structure of the Psychopathy Checklist-Revised: An exploration of methodological confusion. *British Journal of Psychiatry, 190*(Suppl. 49), s39–s50.

Craft, M. (1984). Low intelligence, mental handicap and criminality. In M. Craft & A. Craft (Eds.), *Mentally Abnormal Offenders* (pp. 177–185). London: Baillière Tindall.

Crossland, S., Burns, M., Leach, C., & Quinn, P. (2005). Needs assessment in forensic learning disability. *Medicine, Science, and Law, 45*, 147–153.

Dahlin, M. K., Gumpert, C. H., Torstensson-Levander, M., Svensson, L., & Rodovic, S. (2009). Mentally disordered criminal offenders: Legal and criminological perspectives. *International Journal of Law and Psychiatry, 32*, 398–405.

Day, K. (1993). Crime and mental retardation: A review. In K. Howells & C. R. Hollin (Eds.), *Clinical Approaches to the Mentally Disordered Offender* (pp. 111–144). Chichester, Sussex: John Wiley & Sons.

De Brito, S. A. & Hodgins, S. (2009). Antisocial personality disorder. In M. McMurran & R. Howard (Eds.), *Personality, Personality Disorder and Violence* (pp. 133–153). Chichester, Sussex: John Wiley & Sons.

Denkowski, G. C. & Denkowski, K. M. (1985). The mentally retarded offender in the state prison system: Identification, prevalence, adjustment, and rehabilitation. *Criminal Justice and Behavior, 12*, 55–70.

Dolan, M. C. (2010). What imaging tells us about violence in anti-social men. *Criminal Behaviour and Mental Health, 20*, 199–214.

Dolan, M. & Völlm, B. (2009). Antisocial personality disorder and psychopathy in women: A literature review on the reliability and validity of assessment instruments. *International Journal of Law and Psychiatry, 32*, 2–9.

Douglas, K. S., Guy, L. S., & Hart, S. D. (2009). Psychosis as a risk factor for violence to others: A meta-analysis. *Psychological Bulletin, 135*, 679–706.

Dressing, H., Kief, C., & Salize, H. J. (2009). Prisoners with mental disorders in Europe. *British Journal of Psychiatry, 194*, 88.

Duffy, D., Linehan, S., & Kennedy, H. G. (2006). Psychiatric morbidity in the male sentenced Irish prisons population. *Irish Journal of Psychological Medicine, 23*, 54–62.

Eriksson, Å., Tengström, A., & Hodgins, S. (2006). Typologies of alcohol use disorders among men with schizophrenic disorders. *Addictive Behaviors, 32*, 1146–1163.

Eytan, A., Haller, D. M., Wolff, H., Cerutti B., Sebo, P., Bertrand, D., & Niveau, G. (2011). Psychiatric symptoms, psychological distress and somatic comorbidity among remand prisoners in Switzerland. *International Journal of Law and Psychiatry, 34*, 13–19.

Fazel, S., Buxrud, P., Ruchkin, V., & Grann, M. (2010). Homicide in discharged patients with schizophrenia and other psychoses: A national case-control study. *Schizophrenia Research, 123*, 263–269.

Fazel, S., Grann, M., Carlström, E., Lichtenstein, P., & Långström, N. (2009a). Risk factors for violent crime in schizophrenia: A national cohort study of 13,806 patients. *Journal of Clinical Psychiatry, 70*, 362–369.

Fazel, S., Gulati, G., Linsell, L., Geddes, J. R., & Grann, M. (2009b). Schizophrenia and violence: Systematic review and meta-analysis. *PLOS Medicine, 6*, 1–15.

Fazel, S., Långström, N., Hjern, A., Grann, M., & Lichtenstein, P. (2009c). Schizophrenia, substance abuse, and violent crime. *Journal of the American Medical Association, 301*, 2016–2023.

Fazel, S., Xenitidis, K., & Powell, J. (2008). The prevalence of intellectual disabilities among 12000 prisoners: A systemic review. *International Journal of Law and Psychiatry, 31*, 369–373.

Feeney, A. (2003). Dangerous severe personality disorder. *Advances in Psychiatric Treatment, 9*, 349–358.

Feldman, M. P. (1977). *Criminal Behaviour: A Psychological Analysis.* Chichester, Sussex: John Wiley & Sons.

Flores-Mendoza, C. E., Alvarenga, M. A. S., Herrero, Ó., & Abad, F. J. (2008). Factor structure and behavioural correlates of the Psychopathy Checklist-Revised [PCL-R] in a Brazilian prisoner sample. *Personality and Individual Differences, 45*, 584–590.

Forsman, M., Lichtenstein, P., Andershed, H., & Larsson, H. (2008). Genetic effects explain the stability of psychopathic personality from mid- to late adolescence. *Journal of Abnormal Psychology, 117*, 606–617.

Forth, A. E., Kosson, D. S., & Hare, R. D. (2003). *Psychopathy Checklist: Youth Version (PCL: YV).* Toronto, Ontario: Multi-Health Systems.

Fotiadou, M., Livaditis, M., Manou, I., Kaniotou, E., & Xenitidis, K. (2006). Prevalence of mental disorders and deliberate self-harm in Greek male prisoners. *International Journal of Law and Psychiatry, 29*, 68–73.

Flynn, S., Abel, K. M., Menta, H., & Shaw, J. (2011). Mental illness, gender and homicide: A population-based descriptive study. *Psychiatry Research, 185*, 368–375.

Goring, C. (1913/1972). *The English Convict: A Statistical Study.* Montclair, NJ: Patterson Smith.

Gray, N. S., Fitzgerald, S., Taylor, J., MacCulloch, M. J., & Snowden, R. J. (2007). Predicting future reconviction in offenders with intellectual disabilities: The predictive efficacy of VRAG, PCL-SV, and the HCR-20. *Psychological Assessment, 19*, 474–479.

Gunn, J., Robertson, G., Dell, S., & Way, C. (1978). *Psychiatric Aspects of Imprisonment.* London: Academic Press.

Hare, R. D. (1980). A research scale for the assessment of psychopathy in criminal populations. *Personality and Individual Differences, 1*, 111–119.

—— (1991). *The Hare Psychopathy Checklist-Revised.* Toronto, Ontario: Multi-Health Systems.

—— (2003). *The Hare Psychopathy Checklist-Revised* (2nd ed.). Toronto, Ontario: Multi-Health Systems.

Hare, R. D. & Neumann, C. S. (2008). Psychopathy as a clinical and empirical construct. *Annual Review of Clinical Psychology, 4*, 217–246.

—— (2009). Psychopathy and its measurement. In P. J. Corr & G. Matthews (Eds.), *The Cambridge Handbook of Personality Psychology* (pp. 660–686). Cambridge: Cambridge University Press.

—— (2010). The role of antisociality in the psychopathy construct: Comment on Skeem and Cooke (2010). *Psychological Assessment, 22*, 446–454.

Harenski, C. L., Harenski, K. A., Kiehl, K. A., & Shane, M. W. (2010). Aberrant neural processing of moral violations in criminal psychopaths. *Journal of Abnormal Psychology, 119*, 863–874.

Harpur, T. J., Hakistan, A. R., & Hare, R. D. (1991). Factor structure of the Psychopathy Checklist. *Journal of Consulting and Clinical Psychology, 56*, 227–232.

Hart, S. D. (2010). The dark side of peer review. *International Journal of Forensic Mental Health, 9*, 1–2.

Herrington, V. (2009). Assessing the prevalence of intellectual disability among young male prisoners. *Journal of Intellectual Disability Research, 53*, 397–410.

Hirschi, T. (1969). *Causes of Delinquency.* Berkeley and Los Angeles, CA: University of California Press.

Hobson, B. & Rose, J. L. (2008). The mental health of people with intellectual disabilities who offend. *The Open Criminology Journal, 1*, 12–18.

Hodgins, S. (Ed.) (1993). *Mental Disorder and Crime.* Newbury Park, CA: Sage.

—— (2008). Violent behaviour among people with schizophrenia: A framework for investigations of causes, and effective treatment, and prevention. *Philosophical Transactions of the Royal Society B, 363*, 2505–2518.

Hodgins, S., Alderton, J., Cree, A., Aboud, A., & Mak, T. (2007). Aggressive behaviour, victimization and crime among severely mentally ill patients requiring hospitalisation. *British Journal of Psychiatry, 191*, 343–350.

Hodgins, S., Cree, A., Alderton, J., & Mak, T. (2008). From conduct disorder to severe mental illness: Associations with aggressive behaviour, crime and victimization. *Psychological Medicine, 38*, 975–987.

Hodgins, S. & Janson, C. -G. (2002). *Criminality and Violence Among the Mentally Disordered: The Stockholm Metropolitan Project.* Cambridge: Cambridge University Press.

Hofvander, B., Ståhlberg, O., Nydén, A., Wentz, E., degl'Innocenti, A., Billstedt, E., & Anckarsäter, H. (2011). Life history of aggression scores are predicted by childhood hyperactivity, conduct disorder, adult substance abuse, and low cooperativeness in adult psychiatric patients. *Psychiatry Research, 185*, 280–285.

Holland, A. J. (2004). Criminal behaviour and developmental disability: An epidemiological perspective. In W. R. Lindsay, J. L. Taylor, & P. Sturmey (Eds.), *Offenders with Developmental Disabilities* (pp. 23–34). Chichester, Sussex: John Wiley & Sons.

Hollin, C. R. (2008). Evaluating offending behaviour programmes: Does only randomisation glister? *Criminology and Criminal Justice, 8*, 89–106.

Home Office & Department of Health (2001). *DSPD Programme: Dangerous People with Severe Personality Disorder Initiative. Progress report.* London: Home Office.

Howells, K. & Tennant, A. (2010). Ready or not, they are coming: Dangerous and severe personality disorder and treatment engagement. In A. Tennant & K. Howells (Eds.), *Using Time Not Doing Time: Practitioner Perspectives on Personality Disorder and Risk* (pp. 33–44). Chichester, Sussex: John Wiley & Sons.

James, D. V. (2010). Diversion of mentally disordered people from the criminal justice system in England and Wales: An overview. *International Journal of Law and Psychiatry, 33*, 241–248.

Kelly, B. D. (2009). Criminal insanity in 19th-century Ireland, Europe and the United States: Cases, contexts and controversies. *International Journal of Law and Psychiatry, 32*, 362–368.

Kirkpatrick, T., Draycott, S., Freestone, M., Cooper, S., Twiselton, K., & Maden, T. (2010). A descriptive evaluation of patients and prisoners assessed for dangerous and severe personality disorder. *Journal of Forensic Psychiatry and Psychology, 21*, 264–282.

Konrad, N. & Lau, S. (2010). Dealing with the mentally ill in the criminal justice system in Germany. *International Journal of Law and Psychiatry, 33*, 236–240.

Large, M. M. & Nielssen, O. (2011). Violence in first-episode psychosis: A systematic review and meta-analysis. *Schizophrenia Research, 125*, 209–220.

Large, M. M., Smith, G., & Nielssen, O. (2009). The relationship between the rate of homicide by those with schizophrenia and the overall homicide rate: A systematic review and meta-analysis. *Schizophrenia Research, 112*, 123–129.

Lestico, A. R., Salekin, R. S., DeCoster, J., & Rogers, R. (2008). A large scale meta-analysis relating Hare measures of psychopathy to antisocial conduct. *Law and Human Behavior, 32*, 28–45.

Lindsay, W. R. (2002). Research and literature on sex offenders with intellectual and developmental disabilities. *Journal of Intellectual Disability Research, 46*, 74–85.

Lindsay, W. R., O'Brien, G., Carson, D., Holland, A. J., Taylor, J. L., & Johnston, S. (2010). Pathways into services for offenders with intellectual disabilities: Childhood experiences, diagnostic information, and offense variables. *Criminal Justice and Behavior, 37*, 678–694.

Lindsay, W. R. & Taylor, J. L. (2005). A selective review of research on offenders with developmental disabilities: Assessment and treatment. *Clinical Psychology and Psychotherapy, 12*, 201–214.

Link, B., Stueve, A., & Phelan, J. (1998). Psychotic symptoms and violent behaviors: Probing the components of "threat/control override" symptoms. *Social Psychiatry and Psychiatric Epidemiology, 33*, S55–S60.

Logan, C. & Blackburn, R. (2009). Mental disorder in violent women in secure settings: Potential relevance to risk for future violence. *International Journal of Law and Psychiatry, 32*, 31–38.

Long, C. G., Hall, L., Craig, L., Mochty, U., & Hollin, C. R. (2011). Women referred for medium-secure inpatient care: A population study over a six-year period. *Journal of Psychiatric Intensive Care, 7*, 17–26.

Luiselli, J. K. (2000). Presentation of paraphilias and paraphilia related disorders in young adults with mental retardation: Two case profiles. *Mental Health Aspects of Developmental Disabilities, 3*: 42–46.

Lynam, D. R. & Gudonis, L. (2005). The development of psychopathy. *Annual Review of Clinical Psychology, 1*, 381–407.

Maden, A. (2007). Dangerous and severe personality disorder: Antecedents and origins. *British Journal of Psychiatry, 190*(Suppl. 49), s8–s11.

Markowitz, F. E. (2011). Mental illness, crime, and violence: Risk, context, and social control. *Aggression and Violent Behavior, 16*, 36–44.

Männynsalo, L., Putkonen, H., Lindberg, N., & Kotilainen, I. (2009). Forensic psychiatric perspective on criminality associated with intellectual disability: A nationwide register-based study. *Journal of Intellectual Disability Research, 5*, 279–288.

McReynolds, L. S., Schwalbe, C. S., & Wasserman, G. A. (2010). The contribution of psychiatric disorder to juvenile recidivism. *Criminal Justice and Behavior, 37*, 204–216.

Meehan, J., Flynn, S., Hunt, I. M., Robinson, J., Bickley, H., Parsons, R., & Shaw, J. (2006). Perpetrators of homicide with schizophrenia: A national clinical survey in England and Wales. *Psychiatric Services, 57*, 1648–1651.

Ministry of Justice (2010). *Statistics of Mentally Disordered Offenders 2008 England and Wales.* Ministry of Justice Statistics Bulletin. London: Ministry of Justice.

Moffitt, T., Gabrielli, W., Mednick, S., & Schulsinger, F. (1981). Socioeconomic status, IQ, and delinquency. *Journal of Abnormal Psychology, 90*, 152–156.

Mokros, A., Osterheider, M., Hucker, S. J., & Nitschke, J. (2010). Psychopathy and sexual sadism. *Law and Human Behavior, 35*, 188–199.

Morrissey, C., Hogue, T., Mooney, P., Allen, C., Johnston, S., & Taylor, J. L. (2007). Predictive validity of the PCL-R in offenders with intellectual disability in a high secure hospital setting: Institutional aggression. *Journal of Forensic Psychiatry and Psychology, 18*, 1–15.

Morrissey, C. & Hollin, C. (2011). Antisocial and psychopathic personality disorders in forensic intellectual disability: What do we know so far? *Psychology, Crime, & Law, 17*, 133–149.

Mullen, P. E. (2007). Dangerous and severe personality disorder and in need of treatment. *British Journal of Psychiatry, 190*(Suppl. 49), s3–s7.

National Institute for Mental Health in England (2003). *Personality Disorder: No Longer a Diagnosis of Exclusion. Policy Implementation Guidance for the Development of Services for People with Personality Disorder.* London: Department of Health.

Naudts, K. & Hodgins, S. (2006a). Schizophrenia and violence: A search for neurobiological correlates. *Current Opinion in Psychiatry, 19*, 533–538.

——— (2006b). Neurobiological correlates of violent behavior among persons with schizophrenia. *Schizophrenia Bulletin, 32*, 562–572.

Nilsson, T., Bromander, S., Anckarsäter, R., Kristiansson M., Forsman, A., Blennow, K., & Wass, C. (2010). Neurochemical measures co-vary with personality traits: Forensic psychiatric findings replicated in a general population sample. *Psychiatry Research, 178*, 525–530.

Ogloff, J. P. (2006). Psychopathy/antisocial personality disorder conundrum. *Australian and New Zealand Journal of Psychiatry, 40*, 519–528.

Quen, J. M. (1968). An historical view of the M'Naghten trial. *Bulletin of the History of Medicine, 42*, 43–51.

Phillips, H. K., Gray, N. S., MacCulloch, S. I., Taylor, J., Moore, S. C., Huckle, P., & MacCulloch, M. J. (2005). Risk assessment in offenders with mental disorders: Relative efficacy of personal demographic, criminal history, and clinical variables. *Journal of Interpersonal Violence, 20*, 833–847.

Poythress, N. & Petrila, J. P. (2010). PCL-R Psychopathy: Threats to sue, peer review, and potential implications for science and law. A commentary. *International Journal of Forensic Mental Health, 9*, 3–10.

Prins, H. (1980). *Offenders, Deviants, or Patients? An Introduction to the Study of Socio-Forensic Problems.* London: Tavistock Publications.

Ramsay, M., Saradjian, J., Murphy, N., & Freestone, M. (2009). Commentary on the article by Peter Tyrer and others about the assessment phase of the Dangerous and Severe Personality Disorder Programme. *Journal of Forensic Psychiatry & Psychology, 20*, 147–150.

Rice, M. E., Harris, G. T., Lang, C., & Chaplin, T. C. (2008). Sexual preferences and recidivism of sex offenders with mental retardation. *Sexual Abuse: A Journal of Research and Treatment, 20*, 409–425.

Richardson, E. & McSherry, B. (2010). Diversion down under -programs for offenders with mental illnesses in Australia. *International Journal of Law and Psychiatry, 34*, 249–257.

Roberts, A. D. L. & Coid, J. W. (2010). Personality disorder and offending behaviour: Findings from the national survey of male prisoners in England and Wales. *Journal of Forensic Psychiatry and Psychology, 21*, 221–237.

Robertson, G. (1981). The extent and pattern of crime amongst mentally handicapped offenders. *Apex: Journal of The British Institute of Mental Handicap, 9*, 100–103.

Robins, L. N. (1978). Sturdy childhood predictors of adult antisocial behavior: Replication from longitudinal studies. *Psychological Medicine, 8*, 611–622.

Salekin, R. T., Lee, Z., Schrum Dillard, C. L., & Kubak, F. A. (2010). Child psychopathy and protective factors: IQ and motivation to change. *Psychology, Public Policy, and Law, 16*, 158–176.

Salize, H. J., Dreßing, H. & Kief, C. (2007). *Mentally Disordered Persons in European Prison Systems - Needs, Programmes and Outcome (EUPRIS)*. Health & Consumer Protection Directorate General, European Commission.

Schilling, C. M., Walsh, A., & Yun, I. (2010). ADHD and criminality: A primer on the genetic, neurobiological, evolutionary, and treatment literature for criminologists. *Journal of Criminal Justice, 39*, 3–11.

Schug, R. & Raine, A. (2009). Comparative meta-analyses of neuropsychological functioning in antisocial schizophrenic persons. *Clinical Psychology Review, 29*, 230–242.

Silberman, M. (2010). Sexual abuse in childhood and the mentally disordered female offender. *International Journal of Offender Therapy and Comparative Criminology, 54*, 783–802.

Silver, E., Felson, R. B., & Vaneseltine, M. (2008). The relationship between mental health problems and violence among criminal offenders. *Criminal Justice and Behavior, 35*, 405–426.

Singleton, N., Meltzer, H., Gatward, R., Coid, J., & Deasy, D. (1998). *Psychiatric Morbidity Among Prisoners in England and Wales*. London: The Stationary Office.

Sirdifield, C., Gojkovica, D., Brooker, C., & Ferriter, M. (2009). A systematic review of research on the epidemiology of mental health disorders in prison populations: A summary of findings. *Journal of Forensic Psychiatry & Psychology, 20*(S1), S78–S101.

Skeem, J. L., Schubert, C., Odgers, C., Mulvey, E. P., Gardner, W., & Lidz, C. (2006). Symptoms and community violence among high-risk patients: A test of the relationship at the weekly level. *Journal of Consulting and Clinical Psychology, 74*, 967–979.

Skeem, J. L. & Cooke, D. J. (2010a). Is criminal behavior a central component of psychopathy? Conceptual directions for resolving the debate. *Psychological Assessment, 22*, 433–445.

—— (2010b). One measure does not a construct make: Directions toward reinvigorating psychopathy research - reply to Hare and Neumann (2010). *Psychological Assessment, 22*, 455–459.

Skeem, J. L., Poythress, N., Edens, J. F., Lilienfeldd, S. O., & Cale, E. M. (2003). Psychopathic personality or personalities? Exploring potential variants of psychopathy and their implications for risk assessment. *Aggression and Violent Behavior, 8*, 513–546.

Smith, H., White, T., & Walker, P. (2008). Offending in the learning disabled population: A retrospective audit of Tayside learning disability service court reports. *Medicine, Science, and the Law, 48*, 31–36.

Soyka, M., Graz, C., Bottlender, R., Dirschedl, P., & Schoech, H. (2007). Clinical correlates of later violence and criminal offences in schizophrenia. *Schizophrenia Research, 94*, 89–98.

Spidel, A., Lecomte, T., Greaves, C., Sahlstrom, K., & Yuille, J. C. (2010). Early psychosis and aggression: Predictors and prevalence of violent behaviour amongst individuals with early onset psychosis. *International Journal of Law and Psychiatry, 33*, 171–176.

Stanton, J., Simpson, A., & Wouldes, T. (2000). A qualitative study of filicide by mentally ill mothers. *Child Abuse & Neglect, 24*, 1451–1460.

Stockdale, K. C., Olver, M. E., & Wong, S. C. P. (2010). The Psychopathy Checklist: Youth Version and adolescent and adult recidivism: Considerations with respect to gender, ethnicity, and age. *Psychological Assessment, 22*, 768–781.

Straw, J. (1999). Severe personality disorders. *Hansard (UK Parliamentary Reports, House of Commons)*, 15 February, pp. 601–613.

Svennerlind, C., Nilsson, T., Kerekes, N., Andiné, P., Lagerkvist, M., Forsman, A., & Malmgre, H. (2010). Mentally disordered criminal offenders in the Swedish criminal system. *International Journal of Law and Psychiatry, 33*, 220–226.

Taylor, P. J. & Bragado-Jimenez, M. D. (2009). Women, psychosis and violence. *International Journal of Law and Psychiatry, 32*, 56–64.

Tikkanen, R., Auvinen-Lintunen, L., Ducci, F., Sjöberg, R. L., Goldman, D., Tiihonen, J., Ojansuu, I., & Virkkunen, M. (2010). Psychopathy, PCL-R, and MAOA genotype as predictors of violent reconvictions. *Psychiatry Research, 185*, 382–386.

Thigpen, C. H. & Cleckley, H. M. (1957). *The Three Faces of Eve*. New York, NY: McGraw-Hill.

Tyrer, P., Cooper, S., Rutter, D., Seivewright, D., Duggan, C., & Byford, S. (2009). The assessment of dangerous and severe personality disorder: Lessons from a randomised controlled trial linked to qualitative analysis. *Journal of Forensic Psychiatry & Psychology, 20*, 120–131.

Tyrer, P., Duggan, C., Cooper, S., Crawford, M., Seivewright, H., Rutter, D., & Barrett, B. (2010). The successes and failures of the DSPD experiment: The assessment and management of severe personality disorder. *Medicine, Science and Law, 50*, 95–99.

Ullrich, S., Yang, M., & Coid, J. (2010). Dangerous and severe personality disorder: An investigation of the construct. *International Journal of Law and Psychiatry, 33*, 84–88.

Vincent, G. M., Odgers, C. L., McCormick, A. V., & Corrado, R. R. (2008). The PCL: YV and recidivism in male and female juveniles: A follow-up into young adulthood. *International Journal of Law and Psychiatry, 31*, 287–296.

Vitacco, M. J., Rogers, R., Neumann, C. S., Harrison, K. S., & Vincent, G. (2005). A comparison of factor models on the PCL-R with mentally disordered offenders: The development of a four-factor model. *Criminal Justice and Behavior, 32*, 526–545.

Volkow, N. D. (2009). Substance use disorders in schizophrenia - clinical implications of comorbidity. *Schizophrenia Bulletin, 35*, 469–472.

Walker, N. & McCabe, S. (1973). *Crime and Insanity in England*. Edinburgh: Edinburgh University Press.

Wallace, C., Mullen, P. E., & Burgess, P. (2004). Criminal offending in schizophrenia over a 25-year period marked by deinstitutionalization and increasing prevalence of comorbid substance use disorders. *American Journal of Psychiatry, 161*, 716–727.

Walsh, Z., Swogger, M. T., O'Connor, B. P., Schonbrun, Y. C., Shea, M. T., & Stuart, G. L. (2010). Subtypes of partner violence perpetrators among male and female psychiatric patients. *Journal of Abnormal Psychology, 119*, 563–574.

Walter, M., Wiesbeck, G. A., Dittmann, V., & Graf, M. (2010). Criminal recidivism in offenders with personality disorders and substance use disorders over 8 years of time at risk. *Psychiatry Research, 186*, 443–445.

Warren, J. I., Burnettea, M. L., Southa, S. C., Chauhana, P., Balec, R. Friend, R., & Van Patten, I. (2003). Psychopathy in women: Structural modeling and comorbidity. *International Journal of Law and Psychiatry, 26*, 223–242.

Weber, S., Habel, U., Amunts, K., & Schneider, F. (2008). Structural brain abnormalities in psychopaths: A review. *Behavioral Sciences and the Law, 26*, 7–28.

Weizmann-Henelius, G., Putkonen, H., Grönroos, M., Lindberg, N., Eronen, M., & Häkkänen-Nyholm, H. (2010). Examination of psychopathy in female homicide offenders - confirmatory factor analysis of the PCL-R. *International Journal of Law and Psychiatry, 33*, 177–183.

West, D. J. & Farrington, D. P. (1973). *Who Becomes Delinquent?* London: Heinemann Educational.

Woodward, M. (1955). The role of low intelligence in delinquency. *British Journal of Delinquency, 6*, 281–303.

Wormith, J. S. (1984). The controversy over the effects of long-term incarceration. *Canadian Journal of Criminology, 26*, 423–437.

Yang, S., Kadouri, A., Révah-Lévy, A., Mulvey, E. P., & Falissard, B. (2009). Doing time: A qualitative study of long-term incarceration and the impact of mental illness. *International Journal of Law and Psychiatry, 32*, 294–303.

Yang, Y., Raine, A., Han, C. -B., Schug, R. A., Toga, A. W., & Narr, K. L. (2010). Reduced hippocampal and parahippocampal volumes in murderers with schizophrenia. *Psychiatry Research: Neuroimaging, 182*, 9–13.

Yoshikawa, K., Taylor, P. J., Yamagami, A., Okada, T., Ando, K., Taruya, T., Matsumoto, T., & Kikuchi, A. (2007). Violent recidivism among mentally disordered offenders in Japan. *Criminal Behaviour and Mental Health, 17*, 137–151.

9   Crime investigation and evidence

In the preceding chapters, the focus has been on the contribution psychology can make to help understand why an individual commits a crime. However, the study of crime is wider than just the criminal: the individual's actions are at the beginning of a chain of events that starts with an investigation by the police, moves through the courts, and may culminate with a sentence and disposal. The police are central to crime investigation and there is a vast literature on the police, including several academic journals given to investigations of the police and policing. The main body of research into police and policing comes principally from criminology, law, politics, and sociology (Newburn & Reiner, 2007): this work broadens out to the substantive topic of law and order (Reiner, 2007) and public confidence in the police (Jang, Joo, & Zhao, 2010; Skogan, 2009), and extends to other disciplines such as anthropology (Kania, 1983). With regard to psychology, there is a more substantial tradition of police psychology in the USA (Reiser, 1982) than in Britain, although there are contributions by British psychologists (e.g., Ainsworth, 2002; Ainsworth & Pease, 1987), and British journals publish some police psychology research (Snook, Doan, Cullen, Kavanagh, & Eastwood, 2009).

In terms of the police themselves, there are obvious international differences in the social role and accountability of the police, their organisation and powers, and such basic points as whether they routinely carry guns. Thus, as elsewhere in this book, the country of origin of the research is made clear where it is important to do so. In Britain, the investigation of crime is mainly the province of the British police force along with specialist types of police, such as the military police in the armed forces and the British transport police for railways. The modern British police force has a long history with its origins in the notion of *policing*.

The origins of modern policing

The community taking responsibility for maintaining its own peace was inherent in the culture of the Danes and Anglo-Saxons who invaded the British Isles around 900 AD. It was from this historical lineage that the tradition of community policing emerged, so that responsibility for keeping the local peace was taken by every citizen in the community (Rawlings, 2003). Thus, responsibility for keeping the peace – located within the smallest unit of local government, called the *tun* or *vill* (roughly equivalent to the modern parish) – was held by all the males resident within a given location. The men were organised for police duties in groups of about 10 families, which were called *tythings* with a *tythingman* at their head. If a member of a tything committed a crime, the rest of the group were required to produce him for trial. In turn, a tything was part of a larger group called a *hundred*, which was headed by a *hundred man* or *royal reeve* who exercised administrative and judicial powers though a *hundred court*. The control of all the hundreds in a shire belonged to the *shire reeve* or *sheriff*. The sheriff had the general responsibility under the king for keeping and maintaining the peace in the shire.

After the Norman conquest of England in 1066, these arrangements were modified under the system called *frankpledge*. Frankpledge, previously called frith-borh (meaning peace-pledge), was also a system of joint sharing of responsibility among persons associated through kinship or an oath of allegiance to a lord. The Normans acted to increase the powers of the sheriffs who were obliged twice yearly to hold a hundred court and to ensure observance of the frankpledge system. The Norman regime also required the tythingman to report any suspicions of criminal intent and suspicious character to the sheriff via a jury of 12 free men. As time passed so the central control was relaxed and local law enforcement came to the fore: the Normans encouraged communities to appoint individuals to take a prominent role in maintaining the peace. In France, the official position of *Connétable de France* was highly prized as the First Officer of the Crown of France. Thus, towards the end of the 12th century, the title of *connétable* was imported and so the *local constable* emerged. Initially responsible for keeping the peace in the tything, the local constable became the most important elected officer with powers to assist the lord of a feudal manor in controlling the affairs of the local community.

In 1285, the Statute of Winchester was passed: this statute laid out the principles of policing that were to be influential for the next six centuries. The principles contained in the Statute of Winchester are shown in Box 9.1.

The Statute of Winchester connected Saxon and Norman principles to produce the role of a constable whose duty it was to provide a service to their community and, as required, exercise their powers of arrest granted under common law. The task of constable was not a full-time occupation, each male member of the community took their turn at the office of constable. The first change to the office of constable came about with the Justices of the Peace Act of 1361, which gave Justices a mixture of police, judicial, and administrative authority. The Justices were selected by the sovereign, from whom they derived their authority, with their primary duty being to maintain the king's peace. The Peace Act marks the move from local policing to a more centralised system and in so doing lessened the power of the office of constable.

As the 15th and 16th centuries unfolded, so the wealthier members of the community, the merchants, tradesmen, and farmers, grew increasingly reluctant to take their turn at

---

Box 9.1   The principles of the Statute of Winchester

1. It was everyone's duty to keep the king's peace: any citizen could be called upon to arrest an offender. (This duty is echoed in today's notion of a citizen's arrest. In England and Wales under Section 24a of the Police and Criminal Evidence Act 1984, this is called an *any person arrest*.)
2. The unpaid, part-time constable had a special duty to arrest offenders, assisted in towns by the watchman who patrolled at night.
3. If an offender was not caught red-handed, then a hue and cry was raised whereby all of community were gathered to apprehend the lawbreaker.
4. All citizens had to keep arms with which to follow the cry when required.
5. It was the constable's duty to present the offender at the court for punishment.

performing the demanding and unpaid duties of the office of constable. The solution, which comes naturally to the wealthy, was to pay deputies to act in their place: the practice emerged of these deputies themselves paying other deputies to take their place. Thus, the once-respected position of constable now belonged to the poorest and least able members of the community. As the status of constable sank further and further, the whole system of policing fell into disrepute. Further, the Justices of the Peace were paid on the basis of the number of convictions they secured. This arrangement was exploited by many Justices who profited by extorting fees from both citizens and criminals to prevent their conviction.

Thus, the system gradually fell into disrepute, particularly in urban areas, during the 17th and 18th centuries. The social and economic upheaval precipitated by the Industrial Revolution during the 18th century, together with a doubling of England's population from 6 to 12 million, created several national crises. The City of London grew rapidly to become a massive conurbation, while vast rural areas were turned to slums, mines and factories. For the first time in British history, large populations were concentrated in small geographical areas giving rise to new levels of lawlessness. In 18th-century London, whole districts of the city were left unpoliced and became sanctuaries in which thieves and robbers enjoyed complete immunity. This untenable state of affairs led to a review the system of policing, culminating in the passing of the Metropolitan Police Act in 1829.

The origins of the modern British police force

The changes brought about by the 1829 Act built in part upon a preceding reforms that had met with some success. The establishment of the Thames River Police, first in 1798 as a private venture then in 1800 as a public service with the passing of the Thames River Police Act, was once such venture. The Thames River Police consisted of 60 salaried officers whose duty it was to keep London's port free from crime.

Another successful innovation dated back to the early part of the 19th century when the Chief Magistrate, Sir Richard Ford, had revived the idea of a previous Chief Magistrate, John Fielding, to organise a group of carefully selected officers to act as an elite force to patrol the streets of London. This patrol became known as 'The Bow Street Runners' and were joined in 1821 by a second group known as the 'Unmounted Horse Patrol'.

In 1822, the Home Secretary Sir Robert Peel set in train a reform of criminal law. In 1826, he drew up a plan for a single police system to operate within a radius of 10 miles of St. Paul's Cathedral in London. Following this and other plans, in 1829 Peel eventually presented to Parliament his 'Bill for Improving the Police in and near the Metropolis'. The principles laid down at the time to govern the new force, which still remain in force to this day, are shown in Box 9.2.

Robert Peel's Act was passed without opposition and the Metropolitan Police Act became law in July 1829. In September of that year the first 'new police' – the 1,000 new constables fondly nicknamed *Bobbies* or, less fondly, *Peelers* – began patrolling the City from their headquarters in Scotland Yard. It was a short step to the idea of a central police force, although Parliament regarded this idea with disfavour: between 1816 and 1822 several Parliamentary committees had rejected the establishment of a police force, holding that this was not compatible with the principles of British liberty.

The general public in London generally looked upon the new police with suspicion at best and outrage and as an insult to the people at worst. It was felt that the police were part of a conspiracy to put the Duke of Wellington on the throne, as he had helped with the passing of the Bill in the House of Lords. There was public hostility to the extent that policemen

Box 9.2   The principles of Peel's 1829 Bill

'It should be understood at the outset, that the object to be attained is the prevention of crime.

'To this great end every effort of the police is to be directed. The security of person and property and the preservation of a police establishment will thus be better effected than by the detection and punishment of the offender after he has succeeded in committing crime.

'He [the constable] will be civil and obliging to all people of every rank and class.

'He must be particularly cautious not to interfere idly or unnecessarily in order to make a display of his authority; when required to act, he will do so with decision and boldness; on all occasions he may expect to receive the fullest support in the proper exercise of his authority. He must remember that there is no qualification so indispensable to a police-officer as a perfect command of temper, never suffering himself to be moved in the slightest degree by any language or threats that may be user; if he do his duty in a quiet and determined manner, such conduct will probably excite the well-disposed of the bystanders to assist him, if he requires them'.

controlling the traffic were ridden down and lashed with whips. In August 1830, the first London Metropolitan policeman to be killed on duty, John Long, was stabbed to death in Gray's Inn Road.

The twin duties of the police were to maintain public order and to fight crime. The maintenance of public order included controlling the new working class and the police were used to break up political meetings and to spy on working-class movements. The London Metropolitan Police placed much emphasis on patrolling the beat: a strategy that afforded some protection from vagabonds, footpads, and gangs to the middle-class areas of London but did little for working-class areas of the city.

Peel was succeeded in 1830 by Lord Melbourne, who steered the new force through a period in 1833 when a clash between officers and a London mob resulted in the death of another constable. The jury at the inquest returned a verdict of 'justifiable homicide' but this verdict was later overturned and public opinion began to side with the police.

Expansion of the police force

In 1839, the County Police Act was passed, which permitted the counties to form police forces, although it was not mandatory. Thus, by the early 1850s half of the counties had 'new' police forces, although most major towns did not have a dedicated force. In 1856, the County and Borough Police Act made it obligatory to recruit a police force: by 1860 there were 259 separate polices forces of varying size. These forces were each under local control, with the Justices of the Peace playing a large part in their running, and there was little or no cooperation between forces. The record-keeping with respect to crime was limited simply to noting prosecutions and convictions: the offences reported to the police were not systematically recorded and hence the amount of 'official crime' remained unknown.

A major reason for the implementation of the 1856 Act was the ending of transportation overseas as a form of punishment for crime. Thus, more criminals were imprisoned in England who were eventually to be released into the community after serving their sentence. The increasing numbers of hardened criminals at large gave weight to the argument that a countrywide police force was necessary to maintain law and order given.

The period between 1870 and 1920 saw three major changes in the development of the police: first, the extension of police activity into working-class areas of cities; second, internal police reforms including improved record-keeping and improvements in working conditions of work and pay; third, the beginnings of detection *after* the crime and the formation of the Criminal Investigation Department (CID) at Scotland Yard.

Extension of activity into working-class areas

Both before and after the new police force was formed, the rich and powerful within society demanded protection from the more militant sections of the growing working class. In fact, the militia raised and led by landowners exacerbated rather than diminished class violence, so that maintenance of the peace was not possible given the level of confrontation between different sections of society. As the 'criminal element' were primarily from the working classes, so crime control was only possible if the communities were patrolled by the police. This situation led to considerable resentment and police patrols were often attacked by groups attempting to frustrate an arrest. This, not surprisingly, led to the resignation of many constables. However, by patrolling working-class communities, the police were also acting on behalf of individual working people as for the first time working people gained some protection from attack, robbery, and burglary. In time, this improvement led to increased public support for the police.

Internal reforms

Prior to the 1870s, the only criminal records kept by the police, which were often incomplete, were details of prosecutions and convictions. These records were not centralised, so that each station in London acted independently in keeping its own records and it was not until the 1870s that an official record was kept of all reported crimes. This development was associated with the establishment in 1878 of a new department of the Metropolitan Police at Scotland Yard, the Criminal Investigation Department (CID).

This period also saw efforts by police officers to improve their pay and working conditions and the police were the first body in the public sector to organise a union. The first nationwide strike by the police came just before the end of the First World War. The strike was met by fierce opposition from the Police Commissioner, who refused to talk to the men and sacked the leader of the union. A temporary wage settlement was implemented pending a review, which lowered tension, although a further strike took place in 1919. This latter strike was badly supported and eventually broken and resulted in the government banning the organising of a trade union in the police.

Formation of the Criminal Investigation Department

The police began to use plain-clothes officers almost immediately after its formation. It was obvious that patrolling uniformed men simply acted to warn pickpockets and burglars of the increased likelihood of capture. Thus, on the instructions of the Home Secretary and two Commissioners, two or three police constables from each station were temporarily assigned to plain-clothes duties. These plain-clothes policemen were also used to infiltrate organisations and to spy on political meetings. This strategy eventually became an accepted practice and by 1867, Scotland Yard had 15 men assigned to these covert duties. However, following an incident in 1877, where three plain-clothes officers were convicted of charges of corruption, a Home Office enquiry recommended the official formation of the CID. After its establishment, the CID quickly expanded and by 1886 it had a staff of 800 officers.

The police now had two arms: those officers in uniform and detectives who wore plain clothes. The primary duty of the uniformed police was to patrol the streets, to apprehend offenders on the spot, and in so doing to act as a general deterrent. On the other hand, the task of the new detectives was to take over once a crime had been reported and devote time to tracking down the offender.

The role of crime detection led to the increased use of scientific methods to police work. The use of fingerprinting as a means of identification was one of the first such scientific innovations. Sir Francis Galton presented the idea of using fingerprints to identify and apprehend criminals to a Home Office committee in 1893, and by 1894 fingerprinting was in use by the police. Galton had proved the uniqueness of each fingerprint and a system of fingerprint classification was provided in 1899 by Sir Edward Henry. The first conviction gained through the use of fingerprints was in 1902: while fingerprinting had been used internally by the CID for several years, it was inadmissible as evidence in court.

The years leading up to the present day have seen many changes, none more significant than the amalgamation of all police forces throughout the country to produce the force we have today.

The nature and role of the modern police force

There is a general notion that a police force is necessary for the maintenance of social order involving both *police* as a social institution and *policing* as a process with specific social functions.

Policing

The concept of policing generally includes both the control of crime and the maintenance of public order. In this respect, the nature of the modern police force has undergone a major change since the late 1960s and early 1970s, before which the police employed a generally 'proactive' role in detecting and preventing criminal behaviour. The police officer was out on foot patrol in the community, actively looking for evidence of criminal acts. However, as modern technology increasingly became a part of police work so there was an increasing reliance on cars, radios, telephones and so on and the police became more 'reactive'. The efficiency of the police was increasingly judged in terms of their being able to react quickly to reports of crime. This change has led to a position in which, arguably, the act of policing is carried out by the public. Members of the public 'patrol' the streets and react to crime, which they then report to the police for action. However, while some police officers do have a reactive role, other groups of officers, such as the drug, vice, and serious crimes squads, are established precisely to act 'proactively' to prevent crime.

As is the case with any large organisation, the police force will continue to change and evolve as society changes and evolves. In the next section, we move to a more psychological area, considering the ways in which psychological theory and research has been applied to police work.

With respect to the specialised field of psychology and the police there are two main elements to consider: (1) psychological studies of the police and policing; (2) psychologically informed investigative techniques applied to police work. We begin the first broad area, psychological studies of the police and policing, with the question of who would want to become a police officer. The popular stereotype is perhaps that members of the police force have a distinct type of personality and attitude which sets them apart from the rest of the population. Is this true?

Investigating the investigators: a 'police personality'?

Siegal (1986: 500) presents an American perspective in stating that the 'typical police personality is thought to include authoritarianism, suspicion, racism, hostility, insecurity, conservatism, and cynicism'. An English study by Colman and Gorman (1982) with new recruits and probationer constables with under 2 years' service employed psychometric tests alongside an open response format to questions on the contentious topics of the 'death penalty', 'coloured immigration', and 'mixed marriage'. The control group were young people who were not members of the police force. The psychometric tests showed that police were significantly more conservative and authoritarian (a belief in the rightness of those with authority at the expense of individual freedom) than the controls. The responses to the open-format questions were rated by independent judges on the scale liberal/tolerant–illiberal/intolerant: the police personnel gave the more illiberal responses to the questions on the death penalty and immigration. Colman and Gorman argued that the differences in age and education between police and controls did not account for their findings, concluding: 'The police force tends to attract to it people who are more conservative and authoritarian than those of comparable socioeconomic status' (1982: 8).

Brown and Willis (1985) also compared authoritarianism in British police recruits (one group in the north of England, another in the south) with a group of recruits to the fire service as the non-police control. The police and fire service personnel completed a psychometric measure of authoritarianism during the first week of their training, again at the end of the 12- to 13-week training period, and at a follow-up after 3 months of work experience. At first there was no significant difference between the police and fire service recruits, however, by the end of the training period, the police showed significantly *less* authoritarianism than the fire service recruits. At follow-up there was no significant difference in authoritarianism between the fire service personnel and the police officers from the northern force, while the police officers from the southern force were less authoritarian than both the other groups. Thus, both police groups began training with similar authoritarian values, which then declined after the training period. After 3 months 'on the beat', the officers from the northern force had returned to pre-training levels but the police officers from the southern force showed a significant overall decline in authoritarianism over the duration of the study. Brown and Willis suggest that their findings show that the police are no more or less authoritarian than their counterparts who join the fire service. An American study reported by Laguna, Linn, Ward, and Rupslaukyte (2010) agreed with Brown and Willis in finding that that level of authoritarianism shown by police officers were comparable with the general population and that length of service.

Gudjonsson and Adlam (1983) looked at a different set of personality variables: these were psychoticism (P), neuroticism (N), and extraversion (E) – as explained in Chapter 3, P equates to *toughmindedness*, N to *emotionality*, and E to *sociability* – and impulsiveness (I), venturesomeness (V), and empathy (Em): I is the tendency to act quickly, V is a liking for adventure, and Em is the ability to sympathise with the feelings of other people. Measures of these personality variables were administered to four groups of police officers: (1) recruits, (2) probationary constables with an average of 18 months' service, (3) constables with an average of almost 20 years' service, and (4) a group of senior police officers also with 20 years' service. When compared with normative data from the general population, the recruits were high on E, I, and V, but low on P; the probationary constables, on the other hand, were introverted and had low Em. As compared with general population norms both the experienced and the senior police officers scored very low on I, V, Em, and P. Gudjonsson and Adlam suggested that the personality profiles of the recruits showed an attraction to the image of the police as an exciting occupation. The differences between the recruits and the experienced officers may be due to which of the recruits actually pass their training and become police officers, or it may reflect the effects of real-life policing. The low scores for empathy may be a positive factor in an occupation where becoming emotionally involved with difficult situations and distressed people would otherwise be a cause of anguish. Nonetheless, the diversity of personality profiles argues against strict stereotyping of the police officer.

Salters-Pedneault, Ruef, and Orr (2010) also compared the personality profiles of recruits with the police and fire services in America. They used the Revised NEO Personality Inventory (NEO-PI-R; Costa & McCrae, 1992), which is a self-report measure of the 'Big 5' personality domains of neuroticism, extraversion, openness to experiences, agreeableness, and conscientiousness. Salters-Pedneault et al. found that the recruits to the police were higher than the fire fighters on *gregariousness*, which is an aspect of extraversion, and also on *dutifulness* and *deliberation*, which are features within conscientiousness. When compared with general population norms, both the police and the fire fighters both scored higher on *excitement-seeking*, a facet of extraversion.

'Nature or nurture?'

A central point in the discussion about a 'police personality' can be seen in the contrasting views of Colman and Gorman (1982) and Brown and Willis (1985). Colman and Gorman argue for nature as with the *predispositional model*, whereby the recruit's personality and attitudes are formed before they apply to join the police: indeed, these personal qualities may be what makes police work appear particularly attractive.

However, in the Willis and Brown study, why did the difference in authoritarianism emerge between the recruits from the north and those from the south? They both entered the police with similar levels of authoritarianism, yet 6 months later they were significantly different. Brown and Willis, on the side of nurture, favour a *socialisation model*, where the individual's personality and values are shaped by the police culture in which they spend their working life. Thus, they suggest two possible explanatory factors for the north-south divide in their study: (1) the higher base-rate of crime in the north may have hardened the new officers' attitudes; (2) differences in police style and culture with, at the time, a Chief Constable in the north who preferred a law and order approach to policing, as opposed to the south, where the ethos favoured community policing.

An American study by Austin, Hale, and Ramsey (1987) tested these two models by looking at police officers who had been made redundant. They argued that if the predispositional model is correct, then the officer's values are stable and not dependent upon being part of the police culture: it follows that leaving the police should not cause any change in values. However, if the socialisation model is correct, then leaving the police force should precipitate a change in values. Austin et al. found that there was no change in authoritarianism when officers left the police force.

It is evident from these studies that there are certain people who are attracted to police work, which is stating the obvious, because if there were not such people then there would not be a police force! If we follow a predispositional model – although it is possible of course for both models to have some validity – the next questions is why does police work appeal to authoritarian, excitement-seeking individuals? What are the perceived payoffs for joining the police?

What's the motivation?

White, Cooper, Saunders, and Raganella (2010) considered the American literature on motivations for applying to join the police. White et al. summarise the early research, mostly dating from the 1960s, as showing that, as would be true for most jobs, people joined the police for a variety of different reasons. They note a consistent theme regarding the attraction of the role of police officer to those with authoritarian personalities who see the opportunity for power and control. Job security was another frequently found motivation for joining the police, as was helping people and enforcing the law. Some people said they became police officers because they wished to work in a job that is perceived as important and exciting. In other cases, people said the joined the force because they needed a job and the police was a convenient option, or they 'drifted' into the police after a lack of success in other occupations. Another American study, reported by Schlosser, Safran, and Sbaratta (2010), found that police recruits stressed the service rather than the financial aspects of the occupation.

As White et al. note, some studies have considered the reasons given by both men and women (most research is with men) for joining the police. They state that in the main the reasons for joining given by men and women are the same, job security, helping others, and the salary. The men were more likely than women to report the influence of friends or relatives who were police officers; while women were more likely to say that they were motivated by feelings of pride, and the challenge of the work. However, as Poteyeva and Sun (2009) point out from their overview of the (mainly American) research, once they have become serving police officers, there is little difference in the attitudes of males and females.

White et al. (2010) also reported their own data, which was follow-up of their original study (Raganella & White, 2004), looking at the stability of motivations for joining the police. In a 6-year follow-up of a group of almost 200 police officers, White et al. reported that there was little change in motivation. The reasons why people joined the police were the same reasons that kept them going 6 years down the line. Nonetheless, it must be the case, as it is with any human behaviour in any walk of life, that the people employed as police officers change as a result of both their personal maturation, the organisational environment in which they work and their experiences in their day-to-day work.

Environmental influences

The socialisation model is evident in various accounts of police work that describe the personal effects of becoming a police officer. Butler and Cochrane (1977), for example, found that British police officers became more self-assertive, more independent, and more dominant with increasing socialisation into the police culture. Adlam (1981) suggested that in the first few years of being a police officer, the recruit gains experience becoming more independent and emotionally robust, gaining the professional confidence and understanding of the people they encounter that comes with experience.

Chicken or egg?

The nature (personality)-nurture (environment) debate is a mixture of the obvious and the complex when applied to the question of a police personality (Twersky-Glasner, 2005). It is evident that certain individuals are attracted to police work and the nature of this attraction is reasonably clear. It is not surprising that the police culture, as other work cultures, reinforces certain attitudes, beliefs, and behaviours: the exact definitions of these cultural values remains to be fully researched, as does the question of their relationship with personal values

---

Box 9.3   From personality to police officer

The sequence of events that takes an individual to a career as a police officer may work in a number of stages.

1. There are individuals with a range of personalities who are attracted to the idea of working as a police officer.
2. The recruitment and selection process then 'selects in' some of those people with the 'right personality', and 'selects out' those with the 'wrong personality'.
3. The period of training then builds on the selection procedure: unsuitable applicants will not progress and those with suitable personal qualities will begin their career.
4. The powerful effects of the police culture and the experiences of police work will as time passes act to shape up particular attitudes and behaviour.

---

prior to entering the police and with work-related behaviour. As Brown and Willis' research suggests, it is unlikely that the police culture is the same in all forces in Britain: this same point extends to police forces in other countries.

As shown in Box 9.3, it may be that there is a sequence of events that leads from person-ality to police officer, which incorporates both the individual and the culture within which they work.

The issue of whether or not there is a 'police personality' is not an abstract debate. There are two important practical issues associated with understanding the psychological aspects of the person in the role of police officer. The first is the selection and training of new police officers, the second is supporting officers in the more psychologically demanding aspects of police work. A range of different personality tests have been used for police selection, some appear to be more successful than others (Varela, Boccaccini, Scogin, Stump, & Caputo, 2004), sometimes in conjunction with other personal attributes such as problem-solving and decision-making (Lord & Schoeps, 2000) or even polygraph testing (Handler, Honts, Krapohl, Nelson, & Griffin, 2009).

Police selection

In occupational testing, there are two sides to selection: 'screening out' undesirable candidates and 'screening in' the right candidates. The process of selection may involve psychometric testing of personality and attitudes, an interview, and skills tests. The selection of police officers may also be concerned with the assessment of specific strengths and weaknesses (Ho, 2001). Thus, given that police work can be particularly stressful (see below) it may be advantageous to select those candidates most able to cope with stress. This selection strategy may be benefi-cial in choosing officers for high risk duties such as bomb squads and hostage negotiation.

Burbeck and Furnham (1984) compared the Eysenck Personality Questionnaire (EPQ) profiles of more than 250 successful and unsuccessful applicants with the London Metropolitan Police. It was stressed to applicants that the EPQ was being used for research purposes and not as part of the selection process. When compared with population norms, the candidates' EPQ scores showed higher extraversion and lower neuroticism and psychoticism. This pattern of scores suggests that either the applicants are a self-selected group of highly extroverted and stable people, or they are 'faking good' by giving the EPQ responses that they consider to be desirable. Burbeck and Furnham favour the faking good explanation as the very high scores on the lie scale (part of the EPQ) are indicative of faking, while applicants' scores are similar to those found when people are asked to 'fake good' on this test (Furnham & Henderson, 1982). The successful candidates were more extroverted and less neurotic than the unsuccessful candidates.

Ghazinour, Lauritz, Du Preez, Cassimjee, & Richter (2010) tested both personality and the mental health status of 103 male and female Swedish police trainees. They reported that the police trainees, particularly the females, had higher level of mental health than was the norm in the general population and, in terms of personality, showed mature levels of strength, responsibility, and reliability. These personal attributes, Ghazinour et al. suggest, indicate that the trainees have the necessary personal resources to cope with the stressful situations inherent in police work.

Personality testing can be used for purposes other than selecting new recruits as shown in a study conducted in Poland. Próchniak (2009: 104) looked at the issue of selecting Polish police officers for a peace mission in Kosovo: 'The task of the Polish forces squad is to reinforce public order in the area inhibited by Serbs, Bosnians, Gypsies and Albanian populations. Participation in the mission is very risky. Policemen's tasks are to separate aggressively disposed people within different ethnic groups, escort dangerous criminals, disarm bombs after wars in the Balkans and to eliminate drug routes from Asia to Europe'. Próchniak considered the personality and risk-taking of the officers, all of whom volunteered for the mission, using the Zuckerman-Kuhlman Personality Questionnaire, which measures the five personality traits of *impulsive sensation seeking*, *neuroticism*, *activity*, *sociability*, and *aggression/hostility* (Zuckerman, Kuhlman, Joireman, Teta, & Kraft, 1993). The volunteers' scores were compared with those of a low risk-taking group of social workers and educators. The only significant between-group difference was for impulsive sensation-seeking, with the volunteers the higher risk-takers. As Próchniak points out, a high level of impulsive risk-taking is a double-edged sword: in dangerous environments, there are occasions where it is necessary to act impulsively, however, sensation-seeking can also place oneself and others in peril. The decision to select volunteers for such a task will, of course, demand more than just psychometric scores, nonetheless the personality assessment can assist those making the selection.

One of the indices of the success of any selection procedure lies in the careers of those selected. Do the selected candidates engage with and learn from training (Detrick, Chibnall, & Luebbert, 2004)? Do those officers who graduate from training then go on to enjoy job satisfaction and progress in their careers? Do they do the job well? A number of studies have looked at the careers of police recruits over the short- and the long-term. What does the research say about which police officers enjoy success and those who experience problems?

Satisfaction and problems

Miller, Mire, and Kim (2009) looked at the relationship between personality and job satisfaction in a sample of 87 police officers from the southern USA. They found that the longer the police officers had served so their level of job satisfaction decreased accordingly. The personality measures had minimal predictive power regarding officers' level of job dissatisfaction.

Forero, Gallardo-Pujol, Maydeu-Olivares, and Andrés-Pueyoet (2009) reported a large-scale longitudinal study of 2,010 police candidates enrolled at the Catalan Institute for Public Safety for assessment and training between 1999 and 2001 and who successfully completed the training. They found that personality, in this study measured used the Sixteen Personality Factor Questionnaire (16PF-5; Cattell et al., 1993) and the Clinical Analysis Questionnaire (CAQ; Krug, 1980), best predicted performance when seen as a mediator of response to training. This is an interesting although perhaps not unexpected finding as it suggests that the individual's personality, along with other personal attributes such as intelligence, may stand them in good stead during training. However, it is what is learnt during training that best predicts performance in the line of duty.

As in any large organisation, the police will face any number of personnel problems ranging from officers who overstep their authority to corruption and illegal behaviour. It is often also the case that the majority of problems are caused by the minority of staff. Terrill and McCluskey (2002) looked at the pattern of citizen complaints against the police in St. Petersburg, Florida. The considered a range of types of complaint, which included discourtesy, the excessive use of force, and provocative stopping and interrogation. It is easy to label the officers who attracted the most complaints as problem officers but Terrill and McCluskey took a further step in looking at other aspects of the officers' performance. They found that the officers most complained about were in fact the most productive: the 'problem officers' are more active in engaging and interacting with members of the public and are more likely to stop and question people breaking the law.

Harris (2009, 2010) reported findings from a longitudinal study involving more than 1,000 police officers in the northeast of the USA who were tracked over a 14-year period. The plot of number of complaints from the public against the officers' years of experience showed a distinctive shape. The prevalence of complaints was low in the first year of service then increased steadily for the next 5 years, at which point the number of complaints gently declined year after year. As might be expected, the complaints were not evenly distributed across the cohort: Harris reports that there were no complaints against almost 20 per cent of the officers, just one or two complaints against just over 40 per cent of officers, while just less than 3 per cent of the cohort had more than ten complaints made about their behaviour. The relationship between complaints and experience described by Harris can be taken to indicate that as officers gain more experience, so their conduct becomes less problematic in terms of attracting public protest. However, as Harris points out, it could be that experienced officers become more discriminatory, learning who will and will not complain about abusive behaviour, excessive force, and so on.

The level of citizen complaints does not, of course, capture the full range of potential problem behaviours that may emerge over an officer's career. It is possible, as Harris continues, that officers will reduce their interactions with the public and avoid everyday police work, or take protracted periods of sick leave, or even engage in illegal acts such taking bribes and falsifying evidence.

As Sobol (2010) reports, the real world interactions between the attitudes of individual police officers, levels of crime, and type of neighbourhood preclude easy answers to explaining the behaviour of individual officers. This same point is also true when considering public confidence in the police. As Skogan (2009) explains, people may view the police as accountable for the level of crime in their neighbourhood: if there is a lot of crime the ready explanation is that the police are not doing a good job. A study by Jang, Joo, and Zhao (2010) of public confidence in the police in 15 countries from across the globe found that '[p]eople living in countries with higher homicide rates had lower levels of confidence in the police' (2010: 65).

Once recruited and trained, the fledgling police officer will find him or herself on the streets interacting with the public, law-abiding and criminal alike, and confronting the more unpleasant aspects of the job, such as meeting with distressed and injured victims of crime and attending the scenes of serious car accidents. The police may be called upon to use force and even deploy weapons that cause varying degrees of harm in certain situations (Sousa, Ready, & Ault, 2010). It is possible that these aspects of the job, together with the risk of personal injury, the demands of paperwork, and so on, may weigh heavily on the individual police officer. *Stress* is the ubiquitous term applied to those struggling with the demands of work (or life generally).

The effects of stress are typically poor mental and physical health as seen with feelings of anxiety and depression together with raised blood pressure and headaches. The consequences of stress may be impaired functioning, both socially and at work, and the use of dysfunctional 'coping' strategies such as heavy drinking, relationship difficulties including partner abuse, separation and divorce, and even suicide. There is a substantial literature given to stress within the police force.

Stress

In a review of police stress, Terry (1981) described four types of stressor prevalent in police work, which he termed *external, internal, task-related,* and *individual*. External stressors include frustrations such as perceived light sentences for offenders, poor public opinions, and media coverage of the police, and administrative tasks and political decisions that interfere with the job. Internal stressors are to do with the nature of the organisation such as dissatisfaction with training, equipment, promotion prospects, career structure, the amount of paperwork, and pay. Task-related stressors include fear, danger, exposure to distressing events such as accidents and child abuse, and work overload. Finally, individual stressors include concern about one's own personal competence, success, and safety.

Sources of stress

In broad agreement with the American studies, several British studies have shown that within the police force, work overload is seen as the greatest occupational stressor, followed by the burden of paperwork and having to work shifts (Collins & Gibbs, 2003; Cooper, Davidson, & Robinson, 1982; Gudjonsson, 1984; Gudjonsson & Adlam, 1985). The experience of stress may vary as a function of rank: less senior officers are primarily concerned with situations that threaten bodily harm, more senior officers with job overload and decision-making.

It is true that overwork and making difficult decisions are part of the working lives of many people and that in this respect the stressors faced by police officers are not very different from those faced in many others occupations. Like other workers, some police officers find shift work stressful (Gerber, Hartmann, Brand, Holsboer-Trachsler, & Pühse, 2010) and police work may involve stressful, even aggressive, social interactions with the public (Adams & Buck, 2010), including people with mental illness (Coleman & Cotton, 2010): in the extreme, there is the phenomenon of 'suicide by cop' (Lord & Sloop, 2010). It is evident, as with other occupations, that organisational ethos is related to police officer stress. In an American study, for example, Shane (2010) comments on the deleterious effects of a traditional and rigid military model on the lowest ranking members of the organisation. However, there are other sources of stress – such as investigating sexual crimes and exposure to images of child pornography (Krause, 2009; Perez, Jones, Englert, & Sachau, 2010), being physically attacked (Wilson & Zhao, 2008), using deadly force (Lee & Vaughn, 2010) and being first at the scene of a suicide (Koch, 2010) – that are particularly associated with police work.

Consequences of stress

An American study by Gershon, Barocas, Canton, Li, and Vlahov (2009) also found that it was organisational stressors rather than specific incidents that were most strongly associated with police stress. The police officers who reported high levels of stress were at an increased risk for adverse health issues, including anxiety and depression. Gershon et al. also reported a substantial relationship between stress and negative outcomes such as spousal abuse, aggression, and an increased intake of alcohol. A highly stressed, armed, aggressive police officer with a drink problem is a disturbing prospect.

The consequences of a prolonged period of stress or an exceptionally distressing event can be manifest in two ways: a slow period of burnout during which the officer becomes increasingly disaffected with their job and accordingly less effective (Kohan & Mazmanian, 2003); alternatively the officer becomes overwhelmed by their stressful experiences so that they become traumatised.

Prolonged exposure to stressful events, exposure to a single major event, or a combination of the two can produce a set of symptoms collectively known as post-traumatic stress disorder (PTSD). Pearlman and Saakvitne (1995: 60) describe trauma as an 'event or condition where the individual's ability to understand, process and cope with an emotional experience is overwhelmed as the individual experiences a threat to life, bodily integrity, or sanity'. PTSD is recognised by the two major diagnostic systems, International Classification of Diseases (ICD-10; World Health Organization, 1992) and the Diagnostic and Statistical Manual of Mental Disorders (DSM-IV-TR; APA, 2000). The diagnostic criteria for PTSD are shown in Box 9.4.

When exposed to extreme levels of stress, typically involving threats to life, police officers may experience the symptoms of PTSD, which, in turn, may be linked with depression

---

Box 9.4 Summary of PTSD symptoms (ICD-10 and DSM-IV-TR)

- Persistent re-experiencing of the traumatic event in the form of flashback memories or recurrent nightmares.
- An intense negative response (psychological or physiological) to any reminder of the traumatic event(s).
- Persistent avoidance of anything associated with the trauma, including thoughts, feelings, or discussion about the event(s); and avoidance of places or people that might lead to distressing memories.
- An inability to remember some or all of the traumatic events.
- A reduced involvement in everyday activities.
- A lowered capacity to experience some emotions.
- Increased physiological arousal as seen with insomnia, inability to concentrate, angry outbursts, and hypervigilance. (Hypervigilance is a heightened state of sensory sensitivity and increased anxiety as the individual is primed to detect threats to their well-being. It typically leads to mental and physical exhaustion.)
- In PTSD, these symptoms are present for more than a month and lead to clinically significant distress or impairment of everyday activities including social relationships and occupational activity.

(Wang et al., 2010) and dissociation (Aaron, 2000). The phenomenon of dissociation is a defence against trauma that takes the form of amnesia and other disruptions of normal psychological functioning (van der Kolk & Fisler, 1995). Of course, the majority of police officers who experience stress will not be affected by PTSD, and it may be that female police officers are more resilient than female civilians (Lilly, Pole, Best, Metzler, & Marmar, 2009).

However, in extreme circumstances, it is possible for PTSD to occur among members of the police force. A Brazilian study reported by Peres et al. (2010: 27) considered such extreme circumstances in which 'Sao Paulo's state police force was the target of gunfire attack on an unprecedented scale. Several officers were killed or wounded' – not surprisingly, some police officers were affected by psychological trauma. Similarly, Chapin, Brannen, Singer, and Walker (2008: 339) noted that in American policing the 'top five stressors are reported to be (a) killing someone in the line of duty, (b) a fellow officer getting killed, (c) being physically attacked, (d) working with a battered child, and (e) high-speed chases'.

Concern about stress in the police force is entirely justified, particularly so if it precipitates PTSD symptomatology, for several reasons: these causes include the well-being of the individual officer, the risk to the public that may result from an officer's decisions made under stress, and the reduced operational efficiency of a stressed police officer. In light of these undesirable consequences of stress there have been attempts to develop stress management programmes for the police.

Stress management

Stress management programmes can work at a number of levels ranging from large-scale organisational change to work with the individual officer. The notion of change at an organisational level to reduce stress is addressed by Ainsworth and Pease (1987), who identify several areas, such as equipment design, interdepartmental communication, and clarity in the definition of tasks and responsibilities, where change may reduce stress. However, programmes aimed at the person experiencing stress are perhaps most commonly used.

Any initiative aimed at reducing an individual's stress needs a reliable means by which to identify those who are in a stressed condition. Ainsworth and Pease (1987: 159) offer advice on 'how to recognise stress', presenting guidelines for police officers to assess their own stress-related behaviours, ranging from the macro of 'decreased work performance' to the micro of 'sleeplessness'. Chapin et al. (2008) designed and developed laminated pocket-sized cards for officers that gave a summary of the various warning signs that indicated stress and what could be done to ease matters. An example of the items from one such card is shown in Table 9.1.

Once the signs of stress have been reliably assessed, the next step is to have stress management strategies in place. At an individual level, a coping strategy, such as self-monitoring or

Table 9.1 Prompts for stress recognition and management (Chapin et al., 2008)

What to do about operational fatigue for yourself and your partner
- Focus on the immediate operation.
- Expect to continue duties; focus on a well-learned task or drill, follow standard operating procedures.
- Remember that operational fatigue is normal and others have it too – helps to joke about it.
- Get the facts: do not jump to conclusions or believe rumours.
- If operational stress fatigue signs do not begin to get better with good rest, tell someone you trust.

Table 9.2 Police officer-nominated factors to reduce stress

1. Better training in coping with demanding situations.
2. Greater support from senior colleagues.
3. Better familiarity with police procedures.
4. Improved police-community relations.
5. Fewer bureaucratic obstacles.

relaxation, is typically used (Sarason, Johnson, Berberich, & Siegal, 1979). In two British studies, police officers, of both senior and junior rank, were asked what they thought would reduce their experience of stress (Gudjonsson, 1983; Gudjonsson & Adlam, 1982). The most frequent responses are shown in Table 9.2: similar strategies were nominated by senior and junior officers, mostly at an organisational rather than individual level, with very few officers saying that it would be helpful to be armed.

Training

Can psychology contribute to the training and performance of police officers? There are many aspects of the work of the police that are similar to other organisations, including management skills such as leadership and motivating colleagues, performance management, interacting with 'customers' (the public at large), training and team-building, and giving assistance to distressed colleagues. It is likely that the training undertaken by the police in these areas would be recognised in other organisations.

Horncastle (1985) suggests that the involvement of psychologists in training of police officers may be actually to carry out the training, or to be involved in the design of the training without actually delivering the training. The psychologist may also advise trainers on training methods and principles (Birzer & Tannehill, 2001), or be responsible for the way in which psychology itself is incorporated into training programmes and its evaluation (Traut, Feimer, Emmert, & Thom, 2000). Thus, Taylor (1983) suggests various roles for psychology in police training: it can offer a context within which to locate professional activity, content to inform and improve practice, the means by which to integrate professional practice and theory, and the methods by which to analyse and evaluate practice.

As well as training in stress recognition, there are training programmes for the police in coping with stress. Berking, Meier, and Wupperman (2010) devised an emotion-regulation course for Swiss police officers. There are times when we all use emotion-regulation skills, with greater or lesser success, to accept and deal with negative feelings brought about by our own mistakes or by interactions with other people. Berking et al. (2010: 336) reported exploratory analyses that revealed '[p]olice officers reported having particular difficulties with (a) accepting negative emotions, (b) tolerating negative emotions, (c) supporting themselves in emotionally challenging situations, and (d) confronting situations that cue negative emotions in order to attain important goals'. Berking et al. utilised a programme called iTEC (Integrative Training of Emotion-Regulation Competencies), to help officers improve their skills in the area of emotional regulation. Arnetz, Nevedal, Lumley, Backman, and Lublin (2009) describe a similar training programme aimed at assisting police offers to become more resilient to the effects of involvement in traumatic incidents.

In addition, there are other areas of police work, such as policing large-scale public events, hostage-taking, and dealing with armed criminals, where training in specialist skills is required. The interviewing of suspects is another area in which the police engage in training to develop specialist skills, of which more below, as attention turns to the application of psychological theory and research to the tasks undertaken by the police.

Psychology for the police

Alongside their duties concerned with maintaining public order, the police also have the task of investigating criminal acts. The focus of a police investigation is to produce the evidence that will allow a decision to be made with respect to the prosecution of the suspect(s). In England and Wales, the decision about whether or not to prosecute is made by the Crown Prosecution Service (see Box 9.5), in Scotland a similar function is undertaken by the Crown Office, and in Northern Ireland by the Public Prosecution Service. In the USA, the Attorney's Office takes on a similar role.

If criminals are to be prosecuted, which is a far from straightforward decision (Gilchrist, 2006), it is vital that the police are able to gather high-quality evidence from their investigations. There are several areas in which psychological research has informed the work of the police with regard to crime investigation and the gathering of different types of evidence.

One of the first forays by psychologists into the world of investigation and evidence-gathering sought to apply what was known of the psychology of memory to real-life cases in which eyewitness evidence was a critical factor (Sporer, 2008). Starting in 1909 and ending in 1918, the psychologist Guy Montrose Whipple (1876–1941) annually published a paper on the 'psychology of testimony' (Whipple, 1909, 1918), since when the study of eyewitness memory has become a staple research topic in applied psychology.

Box 9.5　The Crown Prosecution Service

The decisions made by the Crown Prosecution Service (CPS) are guided by *The Code for Crown Prosecutors* (available via the internet). In addition, the CPS publishes its policies in the prosecution of specific crimes.[1] *The Code for Crown Prosecutors* presents the basis upon which decisions are made, of whether to refuse, discontinue or proceed with a prosecution. The two main principles that guide the decision to prosecute are: (1) the evidence allows a realistic chance of conviction; (2) it is in the public interest for the prosecution to proceed.

The police provide the staff at the CPS – who are mainly legally qualified to a high level – with the evidence they have gathered during their investigations. This evidence may be sufficient to allow a decision to be made or alternatively the prosecutor may advise the police what further evidence may help in taking the case to the standard required by the *Charging Standards* as agreed between the police and the CPS.

When the decision is made to prosecute, the next step is to decide if a prosecution would be in the public interest as determined by *The Code for Crown Prosecutors*. The default position is that prosecution will proceed unless the prosecutor is convinced that it is not in the public interest. As a general rule, the more serious the offence the more likely it becomes that a prosecution will be seen to be in the public interest. However, if the prosecutor's view is that the court is highly likely to impose just a nominal penalty or that the offence was the result of a mistake or misunderstanding they may decide to offer the offender the opportunity to have the matter dealt with out of court.

[1] There are a range of publications setting out CPS policy for prosecuting crimes such as domestic violence, disability hate crime, homophobic and transphobic hate crime, and racist and religious crime.

Eyewitness evidence

A substantial body of research evidence has established that a wide range of factors can influence the accuracy of eyewitness evidence both in terms of recall of what was seen and facial identification of those involved (e.g., Heaton-Armstrong, Shepherd, Gudjonsson, & Wolchover, 2006; Lindsay, Ross, Read, & Toglia, 2007; Loftus, 1979; Shepherd, Ellis, & Davies, 1982; Toglia, Read, Ross, & Lindsay, 2007; Wilcock, Bull, & Milne, 2008). As shown in Table 9.3, these factors can be classified as social, situational, individual, and interrogational; they may variously be influential when the person sees the incident, in the interval between perception and retrieval, and at the point of making retrieval from memory.

Some examples are drawn from the literature to illustrate the multiplicity of factors that may affect the reliability of eyewitness memory.

Witnessing the event

There are several physical factors that will affect the accuracy of eyewitness memory: these factors include the length of time the witness has to observe the event (Clifford & Richards, 1977), the level of illumination at the scene of the crime (Kuehn, 1974), which may depend on time of day (Yarmey, 1986), and how far away the witness is from the event (Lindsay, Semmler, Weber, Brewer, & Lindsay, 2008).

What happens during the witnessed event is also of relevance. Clifford and Hollin (1981) looked at both the nature and complexity of the witnessed incident. Witnesses saw one of six different scenes: three of a violent crime where a woman was attacked and her bag stolen, three of a comparable but non-violent incident: for each scene the male target was seen either alone, with two companions, or with four companions. The accuracy of recall of the appearance of the target was significantly lower in the violent scenes. In the non-violent scenes, recall was not affected by the number of people, however, in the violent scenes recall became progressively less accurate as the number of people increased.

The deleterious effect of violence on memory has been replicated (Hollin, 1981; Loftus & Burns, 1982). Another effect of violence, typically extreme violence as with murder, can be to induce complete or partial amnesia for the event (Woodworth et al., 2009).

It is not certain quite why violence sometimes affects memory. It may be that violence acts to increase emotional arousal to the detriment of memory or that high arousal narrows the range of factors to which the witness attends (Deffenbacher, Bornstein, Penrod, & McGorty, 2004). For example, the idea of *weapon focus* concerns a witness's extreme

Table 9.3 Psychological correlates of suggestibility

Psychological Factor	Relationship with Suggestibility
Acquiescence	Positive
Anxiety	Positive
Assertiveness	Negative
Facilitative coping style	Negative
Fear of negative evaluation	Positive
High expectation of accuracy	Positive
Intelligence	Negative
Memory ability	Negative
Self-esteem	Negative
Social desirability	Positive

concentration on a weapon present during the event so that they neglect other details (Mitchell, Livosky, & Mather, 1998; Steblay, 1992).

Retention interval

The common-sense view is that memory for an event becomes less accurate over time as, indeed, is found with our everyday memory for words, conversations, places we've visited, and so on. Read and Connolly (2007) suggest that when it comes to recall of a witnessed incident, the common-sense view also applies. They state that increasing the length between event and recall brings about memory change: 'These changes reflect a loss of access to information, and that loss is often accompanied by distortions in the reports provided, in the form of reduced amounts of information recalled, inconsistencies in the level of detail, or qualitative changes in the meaning and interpretation of aspects of the event or the event itself' (Read and Connolly, 2007: 143). The same point is true of recognition rather than recall, although memory for faces is more resistant to decay over accuracy with time (Shepherd, 1983).

While the length of delay is important, the events that occur in the retention interval may also be important. For example, if there is more than one witness to an incident, what happens when they discuss what they have seen, as many will do (Paterson & Kemp, 2006), before making individual statements to the police? On one hand, it may be that discussion facilitates memory performance (Warnick & Saunders, 1980); on the other hand, it is possible that discussion may introduce errors into a witness's testimony (Hollin & Clifford, 1983). The adverse effect on memory of events between witnessing the event and recollection has been called the 'misinformation effect' (Tousignant, Hall, & Loftus, 1986). Gerrie, Garry, and Loftus (2005) suggest that one of the consequences of the misinformation effect is that it brings about a false memory for what was actually seen. Baym and Gonsalves (2010) suggest that variations in encoding of true and false information may help explain the creation of false memories.

Gerrie et al. suggest that false memories may involve bringing new details into a remembered scene or changing correctly remembered details: the misinformation effect, they state, has led to witnesses in experimental studies claiming that 'they saw buildings in an empty landscape, a thief fiddling with a hammer instead of a screwdriver, or a lost child holding a green instead of a white teddy bear' (Gerrie et al., 2005: 223). The origins of false memories may lie in a number of sources including discussion with other witnesses, seeing mugshots prior to making a formal identification, leading questions, hypnosis, or from traumatic experiences and their aftermath (Loftus, 2004). The problem from an evidential perspective is that the individual believes their false memory to be true, which sets the scene for a range of errors that may waste police time and eventually lead to a miscarriage of justice. It is a difficult task in practice to distinguish true and false memories (Bernstein & Loftus, 2009).

Retrieval from memory

At some stage the eyewitness will be required to retrieve their memory for the events and for those involved. They may have to recall what happened and the characteristics of those involved, or attempt to recognise the person involved from photographs (*mugshots*) or in real-life (an *identity parade* or *line-up*). The process of retrieval will involve questioning and a great many studies have investigated the effects of questioning on eyewitness memory. It has been found that even the most subtle nuances and changes in question wording can influence testimony. For example, Loftus and Palmer (1974) asked witnesses to watch a filmed automobile accident to estimate the speed of the cars when 'they —— into each other': each group of witnesses was asked the same question but with a different verb: thus the question asked what happened when one car *contacted, hit, bumped*, or *smashed* the other car. The witnesses' estimates of the cars' speeds increased with the severity of the verbs (in the order above) from 31.8 to 40.8 mph. Those witness asked about the *smash* were later more likely to say mistakenly that they had seen broken glass at the scene of the accident.

The form in which testimony is given is important. In *narrative recall* the witness gives an account in their own words; with *interrogative recall* the witnesses give answers to specific questions. A narrative report is likely to be more accurate than an interrogative report but is liable to lack completeness. Items that are 'easy' to recall, such as hair colour or clothing, are freely given in narrative report and correctly answered in questioning; however 'difficult' items, such as actions or words spoken, are typically omitted from narrative report and are more likely to be answered incorrectly in direct questioning (Lipton, 1977).

Is it possible to assist the witness in making an accurate identification? There are two ways to answer this question: first, see if current procedures can be improved; second, look to innovative methods of enhancing accuracy.

The problems associated with identification parades provide a good illustration of the first point. When a witness sees a line-up, there are several potential sources of bias that may influence their choice of identification. As can be seen from Box 9.6, these biases may originate in several different sources (see Brewer, Weber, & Semmler, 2005; Lindsay, 1994; Memon, Vrij, & Bull, 2003).

Box 9.6 Potential sources of bias in identification parades

'The suspect must be present!' It is not unreasonable for the witness to assume that if the police have organised a line-up, then one of those in the line-up must be the person they saw. Thus, the witness feels that they must make an identification even if, in reality, the real person is not there and the police have warned them of this possibility.

'I've seen that face before.' If a witness has looked through photographs (mugshots) of potential suspects before the ID parade there is the potential for confusion a person in the line-up has been seen previously.

Who to use as foils in the ID parade? If a line-up is being constructed, should the foils look like the suspect? If the foils are too similar, the task of selecting the right person becomes very difficult, if the foils are all markedly dissimilar then the suspect stands out.

What should the members of the ID parade wear? Should all those in the ID parade wear the same clothes? Should they all wear clothes similar to those the suspect wore when the crime was committed?

How many people should be in the ID parade? The more people there are so the likelihood of the suspect being selected by chance declines. On the other hand, it is more difficult and costly to find 10 people of similar height, build, and so on than it is to find 5 or 6.

How should the witness view the ID parade? Is it preferable for the witness to see the members of the parade one at a time, making a yes/no decision; or to see all members of the parade simultaneously? Making an identification can be anxiety provoking, so is it better that the witness sees the parade via a video link?

'That's the one!' Should the person conducting the parade know which person is the suspect? This may not matter, but it is possible that the person gives non-verbal cues that influence the witnesses' selection. If the witness is given positive feedback immediately after making an identification, this may strengthen their confidence in their choice of suspect but not their accuracy (see Wright and Skagerberg, 2007).

Given these potential sources of bias, many jurisdictions have developed guidelines for best practice in gathering identification evidence (Beaudry, Lindsay, & Dupuis, 2006; Brewer & Palmer, 2010).

A live identity parade is only one means by which witnesses can try to identify a suspect. The line-up can be conducted using a videolink so that the witness does not have physically to be in the same room as the suspect. As well as identity parades, there are other means by which an identification of a suspect can be made. In a 'street identification', the police take the witness on a tour of the locality immediately after a crime seeking to identify the perpetrator (Wolchover & Heaton-Armstrong, 2006).

Alternatively, use may be made of closed circuit television (CCTV), so that the witness may be asked to look at a recording to identify a suspect. The use of CCTV in this respect can be problematic both procedurally and in terms of gathering reliable evidence (Valentine, 2006). Nonetheless, the use of CCTV is a logical progression in a line of innovations intended to facilitate identification: photofit and identikit systems were developed to assist witnesses construct a likenesses of faces (Davies, 1981), artist sketches were similarly used (Laughery & Fowler, 1980), and there are now computer-based face recognition systems with forensic applications (Zhao, Chellappa, Phillips, & Rosenfeld, 2003). However, as Wilcock et al. (2008: 178) point out: 'Innovative tools designed to help the witness do not seem to help and even when the offender is caught on camera, this does not mean that they will be easily identified'.

Witness factors

A wide range of individual differences have been associated to memory for faces, including intelligence, cognitive style, imagery ability, various aspects of personality, anxiety, sex, and race (Shepherd, 1981). It therefore follows, as Darling, Martin, Hellman, and Memon (2009) suggest, that some witnesses are better than others at remembering what happened. On occasions some witnesses will be better than others because of the circumstances of the crime, on other occasions it will be the qualities of the witness him or herself that are important.

In this context, the effect of the circumstances of the crime is seen in the same-race effect. There is evidence to support the position that the large majority of people are far better at recognising faces of their own race (Meissner & Brigham, 2001). Thus, if a witness is making an identification of a person of the same race, it may be taken that they are more likely to be correct, all else considered, than if they were identifying a person of another race.

Age

In terms of the qualities of the witness, age is an obvious consideration. In particular, a great deal of research has been focused on how children perform as witnesses. At one time the prevailing view was that young children are unreliable witnesses because they have poorer memory ability than adults and are more open to the effects of suggestion. However, a wealth of research dating from the 1990s has consistently shown that even very young children can remember events accurately (Goodman & Schaaf, 1997; Gordon, Baker-Ward, & Ornstein, 2001). A conclusion to be drawn from the research base is the importance of 'the interviewers' ability to *elicit* information and the child's willingness and ability to *express* it, rather than the child's ability to *remember* it' (Lamb, Orbach, Warren, Esplin, & Hershkowitz, 2007: 430). Thus, the emphasis has become one of finding sympathetic ways to allow children to give testimony (Goodman & Melinder, 2007; La Rooy, Lamb, & Memon, 2011).

At the other end of the continuum there are witnesses who are no longer in the first (or even second) flush of youth. For the elderly eyewitness, memory functioning may not be at its optimum with potential difficulties at the stages of encoding, storage, and retrieval (Memon, Bartlett, Rose, & Gray, 2003). As with children, the testimony of the older adult as well as other vulnerable groups may benefit from sensitive interviewing (Bull, 2010; Gudjonsson, 2010; Mueller-Johnson & Ceci, 2007). A point that also holds true in police interactions with victims of crime (e.g., Maddox, Lee, & Barker, 2011).

Children and the elderly may be thought of as vulnerable witnesses because of the weaknesses they present when taking the role of a witness. Similar vulnerabilities may apply to other witnesses such as adults with a learning disability (Murphy & Clare, 2006).

Drugs and alcohol

A crime can occur at any time in any place but it is known that the likelihood of an offence is higher in some circumstances than others. Thus, late at night in clubs and pubs is a prime time for interpersonal violence and where there's crime, there may be witnesses. What happens if the witness (who may also be the victim) has been drinking or is under the influence of drugs? An American survey of law enforcement officers reported by Evans, Schreiber Compo, and Russano (2009) reported that more than half of the officers said that they frequently had to deal with intoxicated witnesses and victims.

There is a wealth of research to show that excessive alcohol intakes acts to the detriment of memory ability in both the short and long term. As Curran (2006) points out, psychoactive drugs (including alcohol) may have an adverse effect on memory functioning. The types of drug classified as psychoactive range from prescribed drugs such as tranquillisers and antidepressants, to self-administered drugs such as alcohol and sleeping pills, to illegal drugs such as opiates, cannabis, and ecstasy. While each drug has its own effects that will interact with the user's physiology according to dosage and method of ingestion, Curran (2006: 81) points out that '[m]ost drugs that impair memory exert their major effects upon episodic memory', interfering with the development of new episodic memories. Of course, a strong episodic memory is precisely what is needed for accurate recall of an incident.

Confidence

The journalist and writer Ambrose Bierce made the comment that 'To be positive is to be wrong at the top of one's voice'! Is this true of eyewitness confidence in the accuracy of their recall? Wells and Murray (1984: 165) reviewed 31 studies and concluded: 'The eyewitness accuracy-confidence relationship is weak under good laboratory conditions and functionally useless in forensically representative settings'. Areh (2011: 562) pointed to a variation by gender in the accuracy confidence relationship, noting: 'Males tend to express unjustifiably greater confidence, making them seem more reliable and thus leading criminal investigators and judges to wrong conclusions. Females, on the other hand, tend to be less confident than males, but with equally misleading results – the information they supply is often more accurate than the information provided by males'.

However, the view has also been expressed that confidence as assessed in laboratory studies typically conducted with students may not give an accurate picture of the real-life witness (Read, Lindsay, & Nicholls, 1998). Odinot, Wolters, and van Koppen (2009) reported a study of 14 witnesses to an armed robbery in which the witnesses' accuracy could be cross-checked against recording of the event by security cameras. The witnesses were interviewed

3 months after the event and gave highly accurate recall, although accurate recall had a higher confidence level than inaccurately recalled information, the overall correlation between accuracy and confidence was rather low (0.38). However, there was a moderating factor in the accuracy-confidence relationship: the witnesses who said they had spent more time thinking about the incident had higher levels of confidence in their accuracy.

As Allwood (2010) points out, eyewitness confidence is important for several reasons. An uncertain witness may be reluctant to report what they saw to the police or to testify in court; further, a positive witness may influence decisions regarding whether or not to prosecute a case (Flowe, Mehta, & Ebbesen, 2011). If a confident witness is more likely to be perceived as correct this may increase the chances of an error and the attendant risk to the innocent (Clark & Godfrey, 2009). It should be remembered, of course, that eyewitness errors can have serious repercussions. As the American researchers Wells and Olson (2008: 277) note: 'More than 100 people who were convicted prior to the advent of forensic DNA have now been exonerated by DNA tests, and more than 75% of these people were victims of mistaken eyewitness identification'.

The force of a great deal of the research concerned with eyewitness testimony has been to point to the limitations and shortcomings of memory. This knowledge informs and alerts the legal system, including the police, to the potential frailties inherent to type of evidence. The use of innovations ranging from artist's impressions to computer-generated images has been developed in an effort to aid the eyewitness. There have been various attempts (without much success) to use more radical methods such as hypnosis to probe witness memory (Haward & Ashworth, 1980; Mazzoni & Lynn, 2007).

The thinking behind the use of techniques such as hypnosis is that if the individual cannot access their memory for a particular event, such as a personally traumatic event, so some assistance is required. The function of an aid to recall is therefore to help the person recover their lost, or *repressed*, memories. In theory, this approach appears to be advantageous with respect to gaining evidence about the traumatic event, however there is a fundamental problem with recovered memories. As Loftus, Garry, and Hayne (2008: 184) explain, one way of 'understanding claims of repressed and recovered memory is to investigate whether there are certain techniques that help people "recover" memories for experiences that never really happened'. For example, when in a hypnotic state, people may become increasingly susceptible, unknowingly incorporating suggestions into their memory and believing them to be true. Indeed, this principle underpins the humour when hypnosis is used in a stage show: the person's bewilderment as they respond to suggestions planted under hypnosis – 'when I tap my nose your chair will become red hot' – leads to much merriment when the hypnotist touches their nose and the unsuspecting person leaps to their feet clutching their rear. The danger of hypnosis from an evidential standpoint lies in the possibility that the individual's memory could be changed through suggestion while they are in a hypnotised state.

Another way in which repressed memories can be recovered is through therapy. In some cases, this can be personally beneficial for the individual concerned but there are two caveats. First, if memory for an event has been repressed then it is usually because of its traumatic effect on the individual: it is possible that recovered memories for traumatic experiences are prone to inaccuracies (Jacobs & Nadel, 1998). Second, as with hypnosis, there are concerns that the process of therapy may implant or distort memory for traumatic events. This latter point is highlighted by the debate, at times acrimonious (see Loftus & Ketcham, 1994), about the reliability of recovered memories of sexual abuse (Geraerts, Raymaekers, & Mercklebach, 2008).

Confession evidence

If a person freely admits to the police that they committed a crime what further evidence of guilt could possibly be needed? In a *genuine confession*, the suspect confesses truthfully that he or she committed the crime of which they are accused. A genuine confession is not problematical in itself, although the means by which the confession has been obtained is a separate issue. A *retracted confession* occurs when the suspect, having confessed, later claims that their original confession is untrue. Retracted confessions are not uncommon in criminal proceedings and suspects may retract their confession for a number of reasons, some honest others not.

One reason for retraction is the suspect's claim that they made a *false confession*. Which raises the question, why would someone say they had committed a crime if they had done nothing of the sort? There is now a body of psychological research that attempts to give an answer to this question and several extensive reviews are available (Gudjonsson, 2003; Kassin, 1997; Kassin & Gudjonsson, 2004; Kassin, Drizin, et al., 2010; Lassiter, 2004).

Kassin and Wrightsman (1985) described two types of false confession: these are *voluntary confessions* and the *coerced confessions* of which there are two subtypes, *coerced-compliant* and *coerced-internalized*.

Voluntary false confession

A voluntary false confession occurs when, in the absence of any obvious external pressure, a person freely goes to the police and confesses to a crime which they did not commit (see Box 9.7). This type of confession is not uncommon in major criminal investigations (Gudjonsson, 2003).

Alongside financial gain, Gudjonsson and MacKeith (1988) suggested several reasons for voluntary false confessions: (1) the individual is seeking publicity and fame; (2) a guilt-ridden person, for reasons real or imagined, seeks absolution by confessing; (3) the confession is intended to protect the real criminal; (4) the person is mentally distressed and confuses reality and fantasy.

Box 9.7 Voluntary false confessions

In 1932, a sensational crime took place in New Jersey with the kidnapping of Charles Augustus Lindbergh Jr. the 18-month-old son of the aviator Charles Lindbergh. Lindbergh was internationally famous for his solo non-stop flight from New York to Paris in the monoplane *Spirit of St. Louis*. While the child was missing, several people came forward claiming falsely that they were involved in the kidnapping. In this case, the motives for making a voluntary confession was hope of financial gain. (The kidnapping ended in tragedy with the child's body later found a short distance from his home.)

Another, more recent, example of a voluntary false confession involved the murder of the child beauty pageant contestant JonBenét Patricia Ramsey in 1996. The child was found dead in her family home in Boulder, Colorado, shortly after she was reported missing by her parents. In 2006, John Mark Karr, a 41-year-old former schoolteacher, confessed to the murder while being detained by the police on child pornography charges. Karr was obsessed with the Ramsey murder and he confessed to the police that he had been with JonBenét when she died. However, Karr's DNA did not match that found on JonBenét Ramsey's body and testimony from his relatives indicated that he was elsewhere when the murder took place. Karr was not charged with the murder.

Coerced false confession

A coerced false confession is one that is made under pressure, even intimidation, during police interrogation. In a *coerced-compliant false confession*, the suspect is fully aware that they are admitting to a crime they did not commit; a *coerced-internalized false confession* is made when the suspect, either temporarily or permanently, comes wrongly to believe during police interrogation that they really did commit the crime of which they are accused.

In order to explain coerced false confessions there are three elements to consider: (1) the conditions in which the interrogation takes place; (2) the process of interrogation, and (3) the characteristics of the suspect.

The conditions of interrogation

It may be the case the suspect is held in police custody for questioning. The isolation and confinement that may accompany the period of detention in police cells prior to and during interrogation can have a profound effect on the suspect. For some people, being apprehended and detained by the police is an unnerving experience, Irving (1986: 142) is to the point: 'Those people who haven't tried it should test the experience of being locked in a small bare room, not knowing what's going to happen, or when they are going to get out. It has rather startling effects on some people'. Thus, the suspect unfamiliar with police procedures may be unsure about their legal rights, be frightened about the way the police might behave, have doubts about how long they must spend in custody, and be unsure about their ability to cope with the situation.

The suspect's trust in the police may play a role: it is possible for a suspect to believe that the police do not arrest the wrong person, that the justice system does not make mistakes and that one must always obey those in positions of authority. In short, the conditions may be such as to place the suspect in a position of considerable stress resulting in psychological distress and exacerbating any problems caused by psychological and emotional difficulties or by alcohol or drug abuse.

The stressed suspect will have to try to find a way to cope with the situation in which they find themselves. However, when a stressful experience is prolonged the likelihood of abnormal responses is increased.

The process of interrogation

At its most elementary, interrogation can be seen as an exchange of questions and answers by which an interrogator seeks to learn a set of facts from a suspect. At its most complex interrogation is a rich, dynamic interaction between the interrogator and the suspect: an interaction during which the interrogator's actions and the suspect's response to the pressures of interrogation can, either wittingly or unwittingly, mould and influence the suspect's account of the 'truth'.

The aim of the questioning will in large part determine the tactics used by the interrogator. The interrogator, whose aim is to obtain an accurate account of an incident, as when questioning an eyewitness, may adopt an approach that encourages the witness to remember as much information as they can. However, the aim when interrogating someone suspected of committing a criminal offence can be quite different.

In his 1987 book *Police Interrogation: A Handbook for Investigators*, Police Superintendent John Walkley is very clear about the aim of the interrogation:

In a high proportion of interviews with suspects the interviewing officer has a very clear idea of the extent of a suspect's implication in the offence about which he is being questioned ... Frequently they [police officers] are forced to the conclusion that a particular individual has committed a crime and that the only additional evidence likely to become available which will satisfy a court is the suspect's own confession.

(Walkley, 1987: 8)

Thus, unlike the questioning of witnesses, which seeks to obtain accurate information, the interrogation of a suspect begins with the premise that the interrogator must overcome the suspect's natural resistance to tell the truth. In order to overcome this resistance, the interrogator must use a range of tactics to persuade the suspect to agree to confess. There are several accounts of the interrogational tactics, many founded in the social psychology of conformity, obedience, and persuasion, which the police may use to secure a confession from a resistant suspect (Aubry & Caputo, 1980; Inbau, Reid, & Buckley, 1986; Walkley, 1987). The intention behind these interrogational tactics is to put as much social pressure as possible on the suspect in order to make him or her conform to the interrogator's view of events. In order to make the interrogation as effective as possible, Inbau et al. provide details on setting up the interrogation room, guidelines on interrogator conduct, variations for questioning suspects whose guilt or innocence is considered doubtful as opposed to suspects whose guilt seems certain, and a note on the psychological principles of criminal interrogation.

An inspection of the psychological forces at play in this style of interrogation shows the pressure the suspect is placed under.

The use of power

There is a significant difference in power between the police interrogator and the suspect held in custody: this imbalance can be used by the interrogator to exert social pressure on the suspect. For example, Walkley (1987) recommends a number of strategies, based on the social psychology of verbal and non-verbal communication, that can be used to emphasise the authority, status, and credibility of the police interrogator. These strategies include the personal attributes of being well-dressed, articulate, thoroughly briefed, and well-mannered; the skills of reading the suspect's non-verbal cues; the preparation of the interview room, including such details as seating positions; and the essentials of interrogation by teams, such as being at pains not to contradict or undermine each other.

The social pressure on the suspect can be increased still further if the interrogator suggests that they have the power to determine what charge is appropriate, whether bail or a remand in custody will be forthcoming, whether to involve other people known to the suspect, what the charges might be against those other people and what information might be passed to other suspects involved in the crime. Such a declaration of power, on a suspect perhaps already in a state of some anxiety, may well act to increase further the stressful nature of the experience.

From the interrogator's viewpoint, the increase in stress is desirable, as Walkley (1987: 21) notes: 'The effectiveness of social pressures to conform is enhanced by mild stress, including mild fear, uncertainty due to lack of information, information overload, or mild conflict'. Although it may be said that it remains uncertain quite what constitutes 'mild stress'.

Against this background of uncertainty and isolation, in the context of a clear imbalance in social power, the interrogator will seek an account from the suspect. Walkley expresses the view that '[t]he whole technique of skilled interrogation is to build up an atmosphere in which the desire to remain silent is replaced by an urge to confide in the questioner' (1987: 50). Thus, the suspect must be encouraged not to remain silent and there are various strategies the interrogator can use to encourage talking such as not asking questions likely to frighten the suspect too much, and making neutral statements with which the suspect is likely to agree. This strategy aims to establish a rapport between interrogator and suspect, so allowing the interrogator to move on to questioning the suspect about the crime.

Types of questions

When it comes to questions about the offence, there are several types of question, such as closed questions, open questions, and echo questions, at the interrogator's disposal. While the judicious use of different types of question is good practice in interrogation, there is always the possibility that the content of the question might in some way mislead the suspect. As discussed previously, misleading questions have been extensively researched in the context of eyewitness memory. It is established that misleading questions can produce changes in memory, a point that is particularly pertinent in an interrogation.

Encouraging confessions

If the interrogator's aim is to eliminate denial and encourage confession, one way to achieve this goal is to influence the suspect's decision-making by persuading him or her that certain outcomes are contingent upon continued denial or making a confession. While some persuasive tactics such as lying, trickery, threats, and inducements are disreputable, there are other ways in which more subtle social pressures can be applied by the interrogator to encourage a confession. These pressures fall into three broad strategies regarding communication with the suspect: (1) the suspect really has no decision to make; (2) there are disadvantages to continued denial; (3) that there are advantages in making a confession.

In the first of these strategies – that the suspect has no decision to make – the interrogator implies that they have evidence that proves the case against the suspect. The suggestion can be made that accomplices have made incriminating statements, or by hinting at the existence of forensic evidence, or even, as Gudjonsson and MacKeith (1982: 261) suggest, by 'producing dummy files of "evidence"'. Walkley describes just such a scenario:

> Files of 'evidence' are examined extensively to check to see if the suspect is lying, knowing glances are exchanged between interviewers, indicating that they have access to information not communicated to the suspect, or to indicate disbelief in what he says. It is put to the suspect that he is of pretty distinctive appearance (they always seem to agree that they are) and the significance of this (ie that they have probably been seen and identified) is left hanging in the air.
>
> (Walkley, 1987: 55–6)

Inbau et al. (1986: 83) suggested that 'The interrogator should prepare and have on hand an evidence case folder, or else a simulation of one'. There are two principles guiding this tactic: first, to emphasise that the interrogator is highly prepared and competent; second, that the weight of evidence is such that the suspect has no reasonable alternative other than to confess.

Disadvantages of denial

The interrogator may stress the disadvantages of continued denial, using a *utilitarian* argument, or *social disapproval*, or by seeking to influence the suspect's *self-appraisal*. When taking a utilitarian approach, the interrogator stresses that if the suspect continues to deny the crime then this will count against them in the long run, perhaps by turning a small case into a big one. Social disapproval can be used to lead the suspect to believe that their continued silence and lying is exactly in keeping with what would be expected of a criminal and is not in their favour; or that their family and friends would disapprove of their denial because of the strain it places on them and that they may need to be interviewed; or the that vulnerable victims such as small children will be forced into the witness box if they continue to refuse to confess. These arguments all serve to make it plain to the suspect that everyone in their social network disapproves of their decision not to confess. Thus, the suspect's self-appraisal may shift so that they see themselves as selfish and become guilty about their refusal to cooperate.

Finally, the interrogator may make it clear that there are advantages to confessing: in utilitarian terms, it might be pointed out that once a confession is made then matters will be over with very quickly; or that the courts look more favourably on those who cooperate and help save time and money; or that mitigating circumstances will mean that the outcome will be much less serious than feared; or even that once a confession has been made things might stop there and then.

The interrogator may seek to influence the suspect's view of both the crime and the social reactions to their confession. The interrogator may 'normalise' the offence by suggesting that given circumstances such as peer group pressure or provocation then anyone would have reacted the way they did, or stating that there are many people who commit this type of crime. The suspect's self-appraisal and self-esteem may be influenced by suggestions that it takes great courage to confess and is an honourable thing to do, displaying admirable personal qualities such as fairness and strength of character. Irving and Hilgendorf (1980: 20) suggest that this ploy is 'especially effective with upper class or religious suspects'. The interrogator may suggest that the crime was exciting or well planned and, indeed, there is credit to be had by confessing to the act. In addition, it may be implied that making a confession will raise the suspect's status compared with their accomplices and that a confession will have a cathartic effect, relieving anxiety and guilt.

The suspect, perhaps disorientated by time spent in custody, is faced with a sophisticated interrogator, using a range of subtle persuasive tactics to elicit a confession. These tactics include playing on the suspect's uncertainty, building interpersonal trust and a wish to confide, providing information to prompt the suspect's memory, and expressing social approval and disapproval through positive and negative feedback to the suspect's answers. It is true that not all suspects are stressed, and that not all stressed suspects make false confessions; however, it is also likely that some stressed suspects do make false confessions. Do suspects who make false confessions have distinctive psychological characteristics?

The suspect

The suspect under interrogation is taking part in a highly unusual form of social interaction in that, unlike most everyday social interactions, it is a 'closed' interaction. The interrogation takes place in a closed room, the suspect is closed off from their normal surroundings, and their attention is closed in on the interrogator. Unlike most social interactions, one person (the interrogator) holds the balance of power and controls the length, content, and form of the interaction, and may well be working to persuade the suspect to confess with some highly effective persuasive strategies at their disposal.

However, the suspect is not completely helpless. Gudjonsson and Clark (1986) suggest that the suspect enters interrogation with a general cognitive set. This set may be to take a hostile approach to the interrogation, or be helpful, or to be suspicious. Depending on their cognitive set, the suspect will appraise the situation and formulate a strategy for coping with the interrogation as they see it. Gudjonsson and Clark outline two styles of initial coping response typically adopted by suspects. The first response is based on logical, considered, and realistic attempts to appraise and actively deal with the situation: this strategy, Gudjonsson and Clark suggest, may lead to resistance to the interrogator's persuasion to confess. The second coping response involves the suspect taking a passive, helpless stance, aiming to avoid confrontation with the interrogator and reduce the emotional impact of the situation: this strategy may lead the suspect to be susceptible to the interrogator's persuasive tactics.

When asked a question, the suspect is not faced simply with making a right or wrong answer; there are other factors to be considered and decisions to be made. The suspect must decide on how certain their memory is for specific details, they must decide on what answer to give the interrogator (which may not be the same as their private knowledge of events), they must decide whether they trust the interrogator to be fair in their questioning and they must decide how they expect the interrogator to react when they give their answer.

A suspect who adopts a resistant coping strategy will make different decisions to a suspect who takes a passive coping strategy. The resistant suspect will maintain their own version of the truth, rejecting the interrogator's attempts to persuade him or her to confess. However, the passive suspect may change their version of the truth so as to agree with the interrogator's version. This process of change may take two forms: (1) the suspect is aware that their public statements and private knowledge disagree, which is termed a *coerced-compliant* false confession; or (2) the suspect's private knowledge changes so that both publicly and privately they come to agree with the interrogator, which is a *coerced-internalized* false confession.

Coerced-compliant

The concept of compliance has a long history in psychological research, as seen in the social psychology of conformity and obedience (Asch, 1956; Milgram, 1974). We respond to social influences according to both our perception of the type of situation and our appraisal of the likely personal, and social consequences of compliance or non-compliance. Thus, the suspect who adopts a compliant strategy may decide to agree with the interrogator's version of events while privately knowing this to be wrong. There are three reasons for this decision: (1) an eagerness to please the interrogator and, via the interrogator's positive feedback for complying, preserve their self-esteem; (2) to avoid further confinement and contact with feared authority figures and so avoid the realisation of threats, real or imagined, of physical harm; (3) to fulfil a bargain with the interrogator that offers a reward for compliance (Vennard, 1984).

Gudjonsson (1989) developed a 20-item questionnaire to assess how compliant an individual is liable to be during interrogation. The scores on the compliance questionnaire showed a high correlation with social desirability, social conformity, emotionality and acquiescence (the tendency to answer a question in the affirmative, regardless of its content). There was no correlation between level of compliance and age and IQ: however, compliance did correlate positively with suggestibility (see below). Gudjonsson (1990) found that a group of 55 people who had made retracted confessions gave the high score on the compliance questionnaire.

Coerced-internalized

As with compliance, the concept of *suggestibility* has a long history in psychology (Gudjonsson, 1987a). In 1900, Alfred Binet (1857–1911) wrote *La Suggestibilité*, since when publications on the topic have regularly appeared (e.g., Coffin, 1941; Evans, 1967; Eysenck & Furneaux, 1945; Gheorghiu, Netter, Eysenck, & Rosenthal, 1989). The suggestible person is one who is in a state, such as hypnosis, where they are abnormally suggestible to messages and instructions from another person. Gudjonsson and Clark (1986) described *interrogative suggestibility* as the process by which during formal questioning within a closed social interaction the individual comes to accept as true the messages they are given during interrogation so leading them to change their response to questioning. Thus, publicly and privately they come to agree with the version of events offered by the interrogator.

Gudjonsson developing a test of interrogative suggestibility – the Gudjonsson Suggestibility Scale (GSS; Gudjonsson, 1983) – for use by both clinicians and researchers (see Box 9.8). In essence, the GSS is concerned with readiness to absorb into memory the suggestive information embedded in questions and sensitivity to critical comments about one's performance.

As shown in Table 9.3, there are relationships between suggestibility and several other aspects of psychological functioning such as acquiescence, poor memory recall, locus of control, low intelligence, high emotionality and anxiety, self-esteem, mental disorder and high social desirability (Forrest, Wadkins, & Larson, 2006; Gudjonsson, 1983, 1986, 1987b, 1988a,b, 1990; Gudjonsson & Lister, 1984), as well as with several types of psychological disturbance (Gudjonsson, Sigurdsson, Einarsson, Bragason, & Newton, 2010).

Case studies

There have been several infamous cases in which it seems likely that false confessions played a part in a miscarriage of justice. In England and Wales, the case of the Birmingham Six (Mullin, 1989) and the linked cases of the Guildford Four and the Maguire Seven (Gudjonsson & MacKeith, 2003) came to national attention as it became apparent the people involved had been convicted and imprisoned for long periods on the basis of flawed forensic

---

Box 9.8 Gudjonsson Suggestibility Scale (GSS)

The GSS consists of a passage that is read out to the testee, who then freely recalls as much detail as possible. This is followed by a series of 20 questions about the story in the passage: 15 of these questions are 'loaded' in that they contain different types of suggestive messages about the passage: the three types of suggestive message are *leading questions* that offer misleading information; *affirmative questions* that suggest that the correct response is affirmative; and *false alternative questions* that suggest the presence of objects, persons and events that were not contained in the passage.

The test protocol is designed to give information about two dimensions of suggestibility. The responses to the first set of questions assesses the degree to which a person *yields* to the suggestive questions. After answering the 20 questions, the testee is 'firmly told' that they have made several errors (even if there are no errors) and that it is necessary to go through the questions once more to obtain more accurate answers. The same 20 questions are repeated and the second set of answers recorded to assesses the degree to which the person *shifts* their answers as a result of the negative feedback to their performance on the first trial. The sum of the yield and shift scores gives the individual's overall suggestibility score.

practice and flimsy, inaccurate evidence, which included false confessions. However, not all miscarriages of justice reach the national press and precipitate national inquiries headed by senior members of the judiciary. The following two case studies illustrate how the psychological progress involved in false confessions may be evident in less publicised cases.

The case of FC

Gudjonsson and MacKeith (1990) present a case study of a 17-year old (FC) who falsely confessed to two murders during police interrogation. Gudjonsson and MacKeith analysed the recordings of the police interviews, which lasted for nearly 14 hours, and describe the pressure exerted by the interrogating officers, which included claims to have witnesses, accusations of lying, belittling his alleged failures with girlfriends to lower his self-esteem, and claims that they knew exactly what he had done when he committed the murders.

FC became distressed and angry prior to his self-incriminating admissions. In a second interview, FC retracted his confession, saying he had previously confessed because of persistent pressure from the police officers. The retraction brought renewed pressure over a series of interrogation sessions, clearly illustrated by Gudjonsson and MacKeith in their quotations from the record of the interviews, which culminated in a second confession.

Medical and psychiatric examination while FC was on remand failed to reveal any sign of psychiatric disorder, although he was judged immature for his age and socially awkward. FC was of average intelligence but showed a high degree of suggestibility on the GSS, indicating that he was the type of person who would not cope well with interrogative pressure.

After almost a year in custody, FC was released following withdrawal of the charges by the prosecution when another person pleaded guilty to the murders. Gudjonsson and MacKeith were therefore able to hold extensive interviews with FC shortly after his release. They report that FC gave the following reasons for his false confession at the police station: (1) the police kept on and on, with no end in sight to the questioning; (2) he wanted the questioning to stop and felt very tired; (3) he claimed to have been hit by a police officer and remained frightened throughout the interview; (4) he lost control over the situation and gave in, telling the police what he thought they wanted to hear; (5) at the time of confessing he did not realize the full implications of making a confession to such a serious crime.

Gudjonsson and MacKeith note that this case bears the hallmarks of a coerced-compliant false confession: FC is clear that he was not persuaded by the questioning that he had committed the murders, but that his confession was made in order to escape from the pressures of interrogation.

The Case of E

Gudjonsson and Lebegue (1989) present the case of an American serviceman, Sergeant E, who was charged with murdering his closest friend. Although the British police were satisfied that the death was accidental, the American Office of Special Investigation required E to take a polygraph test, which he 'failed'. After extensive interviews over a 24-hour period, E made several self-incriminating admissions: 'He said the saw two "pictures" in his mind. The first was consistent with his previous account to the British police of an accidental death. In the second, he became angry with S [the deceased] while standing on the cliff edge, began to shake him from side to side and intentionally let him fall over the cliff' (Gudjonsson & Lebegue, 1989: 263). On the basis of the failed polygraph and the self-incriminating statements, E was charged with murder.

During the pre-trial it became clear that E had been placed under considerable pressure during interrogation: he was told that the polygraph never lies; he was wrongly told that a psychiatrist had been consulted who said that E must have committed the murder; he was placed under emotional pressure when repeatedly told that he owed it to S and his family to admit guilt; and it was suggested to him that a confession would come as a great relief. E was reported to have been emotional and confused throughout the interviews, gradually came to accept that the interrogators' version of events could be right. In addition, it was highly likely that E had consumed considerable amounts of alcohol at the time of the incident.

Medical and psychological assessment revealed that E had a rather low IQ and a history of problem drinking, although his memory functioning and concentration were intact. With respect to the fatal incident, E described typical symptoms of post-traumatic stress disorder, such as recurrent images of the fall and uncontrollable crying. Having lost a close friend and feeling some degree of blame, it seems reasonable to conclude that E was in a psychologically vulnerable state. E also claimed amnesia for the interrogation, simply stating that 'I was trying hard to come up for the answers for them'. Psychometric evaluation, including tests of suggestibility and compliance, led Gudjonsson and Lebegue (1989: 266) to the view that: 'He was a suggestible individual who had major difficulties in detecting discrepancies between what he had observed and misleading information that had been suggested to him'.

Gudjonsson and Lebegue conclude that the effects of his friend's death, the failed polygraph test and the interrogational manipulations had made E susceptible to the scenario presented by his interrogators. They argue that, during questioning, E began to doubt his own memory and so accepted as true the interrogators' alternative version of events, including his murder of his friend. At the evidentiary stage, the judge concluded that E's confession was involuntary and so dismissed the case.

Police interrogational tactics

It is evident that the tactics sometimes used by the police when interviewing suspects, particularly during the 1980s, played a part in false confessions and the serious consequences that followed (Hasel & Kassin, 2009; Kassin, 2008). There have been a number of subsequent legislative changes to regulate the collection of evidence, including evidence gathered through interviewing. In England and Wales, the 1984 Police and Criminal Evidence Act (PACE; Home Office, 1985) required that all interviews are conducted to set standards and a recorded. As Kassin (2005) notes, the practice of taping interviews is also becoming increasingly prevalent in the USA – although this may sometimes have untoward effects (Ratcliff et al., 2010) – while procedures continue to evolve in Australia (Dixon, 2010), Canada (Smith, Stinson, & Patry, 2009), and the Nordic countries (Gudjonsson & Sigurdsson, 2010). There is also evidence to suggest that the police now favour less aggressive approaches to questioning (Culhane, Hosch, & Heck, 2008). It is doubtful whether changes in interviewing practice will eliminate false confessions but it is likely that they will reduce their likelihood.

Given the centrality of interviewing to gathering evidence from both witness and suspects, including children (La Rooy, Katz, Malloy, & Lambet, 2010; Leander, 2010), a body of research has looked at the processes and techniques which are involved in effective interviewing.

Interviewing

The police are, of course, not alone in having an interest in efficient and effective interviewing. Memon and Bull (1999) discuss how interviews, of varying types, can be used by many different groups for a range of purposes. The focus of many of the interviews carried out by the police is quite specific: to obtain an account of something that has already happened by asking people to access their memory and give a reliable account of what they have experienced. At first glance this seems like a relatively straightforward task: ask the witness what happened and go from there. If the interview starts with an open question, 'What did you see?', it is likely to elicit a narrative response from the interviewee. A narrative response is likely to be crime-focused and accurate but will be limited in range and in attention to detail.

The obvious alternative to asking for a narrative response is for the interviewer to use to closed questions in order to elicit information: 'Who said what to whom?', 'Who threw the first punch?', and 'What colour coat was the child wearing?' The problem with such highly specific questions is that it is often very difficult for the witness to recall exact details, particularly so in the context of a stressful formal interview. It is not our natural inclination to give highly detailed responses: we prefer to give information that we are confident is accurate, holding back on finer details where the likelihood of being incorrect increases. Further, if the interviewer has their own set of closed questions then they are unlikely to capture any information from the witness that is not addressed by the interviewer's list.

A potential solution to the problem of encouraging full and accurate recall from witnesses and victims began to emerge in the 1980s in the form of what has now become known as the Cognitive Interview.

The Cognitive Interview

The idea that witness or victim recall may be assisted rather than left to individual variation was investigated by Malpass and Devine (1981). Witnesses to an act of (staged) vandalism saw an identity parade (or *suspect line-up* as is preferred in some parts of the world) and were asked to identify the vandal. After a 5-month delay, the same witnesses were asked to view five line-up photographs: half of the witnesses were simply asked whether the vandal's photograph was present and, if so, to identify it; the other half were asked to make an identification after taking part in an interview guiding their recollection of the incident, the vandal, and their initial reactions to the incident. Malpass and Devine found that recognition accuracy was greater for those who took part in the guided memory interviews, indicating that after the delay, the guided memory procedure enhanced the identification accuracy.

The notion of guiding memory was used by two American psychologists, R. Edward Geiselman and Ronald Fisher, to inform the design of an interview protocol which became known as the *Cognitive Interview*. In a series of studies, the structure and working of the Cognitive Interview were devised during the 1980s (e.g., Geiselman et al., 1984; Geiselman, Fisher, MacKinnon, & Holland, 1985) culminating in a text published in 1992 (Fisher & Geiselman, 1992) and setting in train a line of applied research that continues to develop and influence practice (Fisher, McCauley, & Geiselman, 1994; Fisher & Schreiber, 2007; Holliday, Brainerd, Reyna, & Humphries, 2009; Memon, Meissner, & Fraser, 2010).

As described by Fisher and Schreiber (2007), the Cognitive Interview incorporates various strategies to facilitate eyewitness testimony. As shown in Box 9.9, these strategies are grouped into three main components, while the interview itself follows the set sequence of *introduction, open-ended narration, probing, review,* and *close.*

The development of more efficient and effective practice in interviewing suspects is likely to remain a stable part of the application of psychology to the work of the police (Kassin, Appleby, & Perillo, 2010). The following topic, detecting deception, is interesting at a number of levels, not least because it is one of those instances where psychological research questions widespread beliefs about everyday life.

Box 9.9   The Cognitive Interview: general principles and examples of strategies

Memory/General Cognition
   Context reinstatement: At the start of the interview, the witness is told to mentally recreate their emotional and psychological state at the time they witnessed the event.
   Varied retrieval: The witness is encouraged to remember details in different ways, such as out of temporal sequence or from different spatial positions, or in terms of their sensory properties.

Social Dynamics
   Develop rapport: Efforts are made to put the witness at ease and to reduce any intimidation the witness may feel by being interviewed by a police officer.
   Active participation: The witness should play a full part in the interview rather than being the passive recipient of questions. The witness should be listened to without interruptions and should play a full part in the proceedings. This may be particularly important with vulnerable witnesses such as child witnesses.

Detecting deception

It is axiomatic that those who commit crimes and are apprehended by the police will, at some stage, lie in order to attempt to deceive the police about their personal details (Roach, 2010) or their involvement in the offence (Vrij & Mann, 2001). It follows that the officers concerned will be at an advantage if they can detect when someone is trying to deceive them during questioning. Now, as Vrij (2008) explains, most of us believe we are good at spotting when someone is lying to us: for example, we all know that the liar's nervous behaviour and avoidance of eye contact is a dead giveaway. It follows, therefore, that professional lie detectors will be skilled at catching professional liars. Well, it is a nice idea that liars can be so easily detected but unfortunately the evidence fails to support the hypothesis. Vrij cites studies that show that police investigators who rely on non-verbal cues such as eye contact, posture, or self-adaptors such as touching one's nose or stroking one's hair, actually perform worse at detecting lies than those who do not use these types of clues to deception.

As the evidence has accumulated so it has become evident that there are advantages to having reliable methods by which to detect attempts at deception. It is possible to refine interviewers' understanding of behavioural cues to lying so that they become more discriminating during questioning (DePaulo & Morris, 2004). Thus, more rigorous approaches, such as *Statement Validity Assessment* and *Scientific Content Analysis* (see Vrij, 2008), to detecting deception and have been developed. These procedures typically involve several investigators systematically cross-checking information gleaned from both case material and interviews in order to highlight discrepancies and inconsistencies in the evidence.

In the same way as technology can be put to use by criminals, so it can be used to detect crime. The trend in science generally is towards incremental leaps in biotechnology (Kurtzweil, 2005) and Duncan (2008) has speculated on how these advances may impact on policing. The most obvious example of the application of biological advances in a forensic context is seen in the use of DNA sampling (Wilson, McClure, & Weisburd, 2010). There are several examples of how technology has been applied to policing specifically to detect deception.

Physiological detection of deception

The polygraph was invented in 1921 by John Augustus Larson (1892–1965) who was a medical student at the University of California and also a police officer in the Berkeley Police Department in California. Larson saw the possibilities of simultaneously recording several measures of physiological functioning in order to detect deception. The assumption underpinning this approach to lie detection is that when we tell lies there are associated physiological changes such as increased sweating, raised blood pressure, and respiratory fluctuations. Further, for the purposes of lie detection, it is also assumed that this pattern of changes is reasonably consistent across different people. If both these assumptions are correct then the measurement of physiological functioning during questioning may indicate when a person is lying. The machine developed for this purpose is the *polygraph*, often simply called a lie detector. Iacono (2008) makes the comment that in America 'Tens of thousands of polygraph tests are administered in this country every year, mostly by government agencies, and many of these tests are administered to resolve crimes' (p. 219). Use of the polygraph is not restricted to America: the procedure is used in criminal investigations in many countries although the test results are generally not admissible as evidence in court.

Whether the polygraph can reliably detect lies is an issue that has generated several exchanges in the literature (e.g., Iacono & Lykken, 2005; Kircher & Raskin, 2002). The doubts about the polygraph as an accurate and reliable lie detector are varied: is it the polygraph or the skilled questioning of the person administering the polygraph (there are also variations in test format such as the *Comparison Question Technique* and the *Guilty Knowledge Test*) that identifies a lie?; if the person believes the polygraph performs accurately, does this influence their responding?; there are some people who can lie without detection, there are others who become so nervous that they are identified as telling lies when they are not. Indeed, it seems that if an individual is determined and sufficiently skilled they can evade most forms of detection (e.g., Verschuere, Prati, & De Houwer, 2009). The British Psychology Society (BPS) has published a review of the evidence, concluding that 'The results of better quality research studies demonstrate that while the correct classification of deceivers can sometimes be fairly high, incorrect decisions about who is or is not being deceptive occur at rates that are far from negligible' (BPS, 2004: 7).

Nonetheless, science marches onwards and the shift from testing the autonomic nervous system, as with the polygraph, to testing the central nervous system is underway. There is an emerging debate regarding the use of functional magnetic resonance imaging (fMRI) as a tool in detecting deception in criminal cases (Langleben, 2008; Spence, 2008). It may be anticipated that, as with the polygraph, the arguments are set to run for some time.

While applying psychology to the issues of witness memory, false confessions, and so on is all well and good, can psychology be applied to the business of catching criminals? There are two associated topics to discuss in this respect: the efforts of psychologists to construct offender profiles and the development of techniques to try to link crimes that are potentially a series committed by the same person or group of people.

Offender profiling

Canter and Youngs (2009) make the point that throughout history lists of the characteristics of types of people have been made for various reasons. They give the example of the characteristics used to guide witch hunts – elderly woman, knowledge of herbs, mark of the devil, and so on – so that when these characteristic are evident in an individual it proves that she is indeed a witch. Canter and Youngs suggest that lists of this types hint at the beginnings of profiling. As history unfolds so the trend continues as seen in the writings of Lombroso, Kretschmer, and Sheldon where there is an emphasis on the classification of people as criminal or non-criminal types. The modern-day use of the term *profiling* can be traced to its usage by law enforcement agencies in America during the 1970s. In particular, the FBI Behavioral Science Unit at Quantico, Virginia was prominent in both developing profiling techniques and in training detectives to apply them to real cases.

Since the 1970s, interest in offender profiling has grown exponentially and there is now a large literature on the topic (Ainsworth, 2001; Hicks & Sales, 2006; Kocsis, 2006, 2007) with expertise in profiling specific types of crime such as rape (Canter & Gregory, 1994) and homicide (Crabbé, Decoene, & Vertommen, 2008). However, there is a lack of precision in the term 'offender profiling' and, indeed, it is often used interchangeably with other terms such as 'personality profiling' or 'psychiatric profiling'.

Canter and Gregory (1994) give a workable description of offender profiling in suggesting that, as with tangible material traces, criminals may leave psychological traces at the scene of the crime. These psychological traces give clues as to the characteristics of the person who committed the crime: these characteristics, it is claimed, can be compiled to sketch a profile of the noticeable features of the criminal.

As Ainsworth (2001) notes, there are various approaches to profiling including among others the FBI approach (Douglas & Olshaker, 1995), the style developed by David Canter (1994), and the Dutch approach (Jackson & Bekerian, 1997). The common thread that runs through these approaches is that they gather data from the crime scene with the intention of providing information to assist the police investigation. The differences between the approaches are twofold: first, the nature of the data gathered; second, the way in which sense is made of the data.

The data that are gathered to aid the construction of a profile typically include details of the victim, details of the geographical location of the crime, and information from any witness statements or CCTV footage. There are manuals to guide the process of information gathering (e.g., Douglas, Burgess, Burgess, & Ressler, 1992) and various ways of breaking down crime types and linking them to offender type (e.g., Youngs, 2004).

The method of data analysis used by profilers can be thought of as either *clinical* or *structured* in orientation. As Ainsworth (2001: 141) states with regard to those who espouse a clinical approach: 'Such practitioners will tend to view each case as distinctive and offer a "one-off" profile based upon clinical judgement'. This judgement may be informed by a perspective from mainstream psychology: for example, Alison, Bennell, Mokros, and Ormerod (2002) discuss the strengths and weaknesses of the application of personality theory to the task of offender profiling.

In contrast, a structured approach will draw upon an established theory or analytical method to make sense of the information. For example, Canter (1994) draws upon narrative theory (McAdams, 1988) as the basis for understanding a criminal's actions. Canter and Youngs (2009) provide several examples of how analysis of offenders' accounts of their crimes reveals information about their motives and psychological state when committing the crime. Canter and Young explain how such narratives express the offender's confusion as to the right thing to do when the crime was taking place, or their feelings of excitement and adventure, or their sense of helplessness in committing the crime, or their sense of extracting revenge for a wrong.

Canter also favours the application of Smallest Space Analysis (SSA; Lingoes, 1973), a multidimensional scaling procedure. The benefit of SSA is that is looks for relationships between all the pieces of available information, such as where the crimes took place, what the criminal said to the victim, what evidence was left at the crime scenes, and so on. The analysis produces a plot of the relationships between the various pieces of information that may show clusters of related variables. These clusters can be understood as *facets* of behaviour such as *who* the crimes are directed against (which may be a person or property), *how* the criminal behaves, such as furtively or with excessive force, and *where* the crimes occur, which may be within a narrow geographical location or spread over an expanding distance. Alison (2005) provides a wealth of case studies to illustrate profiling in action.

Does profiling work?

There are some strong opinions to be found on the veracity and usefulness of offender profiling and, as discussed in Box 9.10, there have been cases where profiling is called into disrepute. Torres, Boccaccini, and Miller (2006) conducted a survey of 161 forensic psychologists and psychiatrists asking for their view on offender profiling. They reported than about only one-quarter of the respondents believed that profiling was scientifically respectable. Similarly, Snook, Cullen, Bennell, Taylor, and Gendreau (2008: 1258) take

---

Box 9.10   The Colin Stagg case

On 15 July 1992, a terrible murder took place on Wimbledon Common in London. A woman, Rachel Nickell was walking on the Common with her 2-year-old son when she was attacked, sexually assaulted, and stabbed 49 times. The murder investigation focused on several men including Colin Stagg who was known to walk his dog on the Common. The police used the services of a forensic clinical psychologist, Paul Britton, to construct a profile of Nickell's murderer. It was decided that there was a match between Colin Stagg and the profile but in the absence of forensic evidence it seems a plan was devised to snare Stagg and bring him to implicate himself in the murder. The details of who devised this plan and how it was enacted are open to debate and there is more than one version of what happened. Nevertheless, Stagg was arrested but when the case went to court it was thrown out and the police operation, which included the profiler, described by the judge as a 'honeytrap' involving police entrapment. In the acrimonious public and professional debate that followed Stagg's trial, much was made of the psychologist's role in the affair and, inevitably, questions were asked about the efficacy of profiling and psychological expertise.

In 2008, another man, Robert Napper, pleaded guilty to the murder of Rachel Nickel and was duly sentenced: Stagg received substantial financial compensation for his wrongful arrest. A later report stated that Napper had been eliminated as a suspect in the Nickel case.

The Stagg case gave rise to several publications from those involved in the case (Inspector Pedder was a senior officer on the investigation), as well as a considered overview by Alison and Canter:

Alison, L. and Canter, D. (2005) 'Rhetorical shaping in an undercover operation: the investigation of Colin Stagg in the Rachel Nickell murder enquiry', in L. Alison (ed.) *The Forensic Psychologist's Casebook: Psychological Profiling and Criminal Investigation*. Cullompton, Devon: Willan Publishing, 197–234.

Britton, P. (1997) *The Jigsaw Man*. London: Bantam Press.

Pedder, K. (2002) *The Rachel Files*. London: Blake Publishing.

Stagg, C. and Kessler, D. (1999) *Who Really Killed Rachel?* London: Greenzone Publishing.

the position that profiling relies on common sense assumptions and has 'no basis in scientific theory and has meager empirical support as an investigative tool'. They suggest that support for profiling has arisen from exaggerated claims for its efficacy its proponents (see also Snook, Eastwood, Gendreau, Goggin, & Cullen, 2007). It is also the case, of course, that for purposes of entertainment the popular media have built up profiling to be rather more than it is in real life. Devery (2010: 394) suggests that profiling has 'never been an overtly scientific process' and lists a range of objections against profiling based on its lack of scientific credibility. Devery's trenchant criticisms, directed at practice in America and not the UK, include biased sampling in the cases used to demonstrate the effectiveness of profiling, weak or non-existent research designs in gathering evidence of its effectiveness, large claims for effectiveness on limited evidence, a lack of validity in offence classifications, an absence of procedural transparency, and portraying an image of the profiler as almost psychic in their ability to 'get inside the mind' of the criminal.

As Devery notes, in the UK the development of profiling has moved on from the earlier clinical and statistical approaches to what has become known as behavioural investigative advice (BIA; Alison, McLean, & Almond, 2007). Alison, Goodwill, Almond, van den Heuvel, and Winter (2010: 116) suggest that BIA 'recognizes the range of fruitful, reliable, tested, and transparent evidence-based methods by which psychologists might provide advice to the police during investigations'. As Alison et al. suggest, it seems likely that an empirical approach to assisting police investigations, driven by theory and an expanding evidence base, will be where advances are likely to be made.

Crime linkage

In the process of investigating a crime such as a rape, the police will have on file hundreds of reports from witness and victims who have either seen a rape or who have been assaulted. As many rapists will rape more than once, is it possible to determine which of the rapes in the police records have been committed by the same person (or people)? In other words, is it possible to *link* the crimes committed by the same offenders? As Woodhams and Toye (2007) suggest, searching for an answer to this question is not unlike constructing a profile for an individual criminal. In the absence of physical forensic evidence such as DNA, it is necessary to gather data from the crime scene and from witness and victim accounts and then search for behavioural patterns and other commonalities in order to attempt to link crimes.

There are several benefits to successful crime linkage: the accurate collation of information from different crime scenes adds to the weight of evidence against an offender and increases the likelihood of a conviction, while successful linkage allows a set of crimes to be investigated as a group rather than individually so allowing police resources to be used more efficiently.

Hazelwood and Warren (2003) suggest that linkage is a search for three processes: first the offender's *modus operandi*, in essence how they go about committing the crime; second the presence of any *ritual* or fantasy-behaviours; and finally the offender's *signature*, the combination of behaviours unique to the offender. Hazelwood and Warren explain that the process of crime linkage relies on five discrete assessment procedures: (1) gathering a wide range of relevant information; (2) reviewing the information and noting significant features; (3) classifying the information as either modus operandi or ritual; (4) where possible, combining the modus operandi and ritual behaviours to describe the offender's signature; (5) finally producing the written analysis and conclusions.

The evidence suggests that, while far from perfect, crime linkage can have some success in identifying behavioural consistency across crimes (Woodhams, Hollin, & Bull, 2007). However, the crime analyst can only be as good as the information to hand, which brings us back to where we started with effective interviewing, maximising witness memory, and eliminating deception and efficient recording procedures.

Conclusion

In comparison with other areas where psychological knowledge has been applied to crime and criminal behaviour, it is difficult to resist the conclusion that, in the UK at least, psychology and the police do not have many points of contact. There are notable examples, such as the work on profiling and on investigative interviewing, but these tend to be the exception rather than the rule and down to the efforts of innovative academics in partnership with police contacts.

There are other parts of the criminal justice, such as the Prison Service and the Probation Service, where psychologists make a contribution as employees of those organisations. If there were to be candidate for an area of growth in criminological psychology in the UK then, as is the case in the USA, the police force would be an excellent choice.

Chapter summary

- The police have gone through a lengthy evolution to arrive at their current role and responsibilities within society. It is only very recently that psychology has played any role in policing.
- One aspect of psychology applied to policing is concerned with the police themselves and looks at, for example, who is attracted to police work, the impact of the police culture on new recruits and types of problems faced by the police.
- Another aspect of psychology applied to policing is the use of psychological research to augment police work as, for example, with contributions to the recruitment and training of new police officers, and in stress management for serving officers.
- Psychological research into memory has been instrumental in assisting in the development of procedures for maximising the accuracy of eyewitness testimony and for interviewing witnesses and suspects.
- Some psychological techniques, such as hypnosis and offender profiling, have been a cause of some debate both professionally and operationally.

Points for discussion

- As the police force continues to evolve, what form might it take in 20 years' time?
- Is there an ideal 'police personality'?
- What is the most significant contribution that psychology has made to policing?

Essential reading

Police

Newburn, T. (Ed.) (2003). *Handbook of Policing*. Cullompton, Devon: Willan Publishing.
The collection of chapters in the *Handbook of Policing* provides a wealth of information about the organisation, tasks, and debates in the contemporary police force.

False confessions

Gudjonsson, G. H. (2003). *The Psychology of Interrogations and Confessions: A Handbook.* Chichester, Sussex: John Wiley & Sons.
Conlon, G. (1990). *Proved Innocent: The story of Gerry Conlon of the Guildford Four.* London: Hamish Hamilton.
Kee, R. (1989). *Trial and Error: The True Events Surrounding the Convictions and Trials of the Guildford Four and the Maguire Seven.* London: Penguin Books.
Gisli Gudjonsson's remarkable book, *The Psychology of Interrogations and Confessions: A Handbook*, is one of the most complete accounts of a psychological topic imaginable. There are many published accounts of miscarriages of justice, the book by Robert Kee gives a full account of two cases in which false confessions played a significant role, while Gerry Conlon's book gives the inside story of being a victim of a wrongful conviction.

Investigation

Bull, R., Valentine, T., & Williamson, T. (Eds.) (2009). *Handbook of Psychology of Investigative Interviewing.* Chichester: Wiley-Blackwell.
Canter, D. & Youngs, D. (2009). *Investigative Psychology: Offender Profiling and the Analysis of Criminal Action.* Chichester, Sussex: John Wiley & Sons.
Vrij, A. (2008). *Detecting Lies and Deceit: Pitfalls and Opportunities* (2nd ed.). Chichester, Sussex: John Wiley & Sons.
Hain, P. (1976). *Mistaken Identity: The Wrong Face of the Law.* London: Quartlet Books.

The lighter side

There are any number of police officers and detectives who we know from the printed page, some of whom make it to the small screen. Off the top of my head and in loose historical order from British TV I can think of Dixon of Dock Green ('evening all'!), Jules Maigret, Simon Templar (aka *The Saint*), Z *Cars*, *Taggart*, Chief Inspector Reginald Wexford, *Inspector Morse* then *Lewis*, *The Bill*, Detective Inspector Rebus, *Prime Suspect*, and from Sweden Inspector Kurt Wallander (Krister Henriksson is my favourite Wallander, Rolf Lassgård and Kenneth Branagh are the other two).

Clarice Starling and Dr. Eddie 'Fitz' Fitzgerald are eminent figures in the world of fictional offender profiling.

The police can also play it for laughs as in *The Pink Panther* movies and *The Thin Blue Line*.

Finally, Sherlock Holmes who, despite solving many crimes, does not qualify as, to the best of my knowledge, he was not a member of Her Majesty's Constabulary. The same point applies to other fictional luminaries such as Hercule Poirot, Lord Peter Wimsey, Miss Marple, and Dirk Gently.

Useful websites

Information about the work and responsibilities of the Crown Prosecution Service can be found at www.cps.gov.uk.

Details of the Police and Criminal Evidence Act (PACE) and the regulation of investigative interviews can be found at www.homeoffice.gov.uk/police/powers/pace-codes.

The official website of the International League of Polygraph Examiners has a great deal of information about detecting lies and deceit, www.theilpe.com.

While the case against polygraph testing can be read at www.antipolygraph.org.

The use of the internet to organise campaigns is seen in two sites, one British the other American, which campaign for those wrongfully convicted. INNOCENT is an independent English organisation, composed of families, friends, and supporters of wrongly convicted prisoners, which campaigns for innocent people in prison in the UK, www.innocent.org.uk. This American project aims to exonerate those people wrongfully convicted through DNA testing, www.innocenceproject.org.

The professional problems faced by Elizabeth Loftus in relation to her views on false memories and therapy can be found at www.psychologicalscience.org/observer/getArticle.cfm?id=2339.

References

Aaron, J. D. K. (2000). Stress and coping in police officers. *Police Quarterly, 3*, 438–450.

Adams, G. A. & Buck, J. (2010). Social stressors and strain among police officers: It's not just the bad guys. *Criminal Justice and Behavior, 37*, 1030–1040.

Adlam, R. C. A. (1981). The police personality. In D. W. Pope & N. L. Weiner (Eds.), *Modern Policing* (pp. 152–162). London: Croom Helm.

Ainsworth, P. B. (2001). *Offender Profiling and Crime Analysis.* Cullompton, Devon: Willan Publishing.

—— (2002). *Psychology and Policing.* Cullompton, Devon, Willan Publishing.

Ainsworth, P. B. & Pease, K. (1987). *Police Work.* Leicester/London: British Psychological Society/ Methuen.

Alison, L. (Ed.) (2005). *The Forensic Psychologist's Casebook: Psychological Profiling and Criminal Investigation.* Cullompton, Devon: Willan Publishing.

Alison, L., Bennell, C., Mokros, D., & Ormerod, D. (2002). The personality paradox in offender profiling: A theoretical review of the processes involved in deriving background characteristics from crime scene actions. *Psychology, Public Policy, and Law, 8*, 115–135.

Alison, L., Goodwill, A., Almond, L., van den Heuvel, C., & Winter, J. (2010). Pragmatic solutions to offender profiling and behavioural investigative advice. *Legal and Criminological Psychology, 15*, 115–132.

Alison, L., McLean, C., & Almond, L. (2007). Profiling suspects. In T. Newburn, T. Williamson, & A. Wright (Eds.), *Handbook of Criminal Investigation* (pp. 493–516). Cullompton, Devon: Willan Publishing.

Allwood, C. M. (2010). Eyewitness confidence. In P. A. Granhag (Ed.), *Forensic Psychology in Context: Nordic and International Approaches* (pp. 281–303). Cullompton, Devon: Willan Publishing.

American Psychiatric Association (APA) (2000). *Diagnostic and Statistical Manual of Mental Health Disorders-Revised* (4th ed., revised text). Washington, DC: American Psychiatric Association.

Areh, I. (2011). Gender-related differences in eyewitness testimony. *Personality and Individual Differences, 50*, 559–563.

Arnetz, B. B., Nevedal, D. C., Lumley, M. A., Backman, L., & Lublin, A. (2009). Trauma resilience training for police: Psychophysiological and performance effects. *Journal of Police and Criminal Psychology, 24*, 1–9.

Asch, S. (1956). Studies of independence and submission to group pressure: A minority of one against a unanimous majority. *Psychological Monographs, 70*, 416–688.

Aubry, A. S. & Caputo, R. R. (1980). *Criminal Interrogation.* Springfield, IL: C. C. Thomas.

Austin, T. L., Hale, D. C., & Ramsey, L. J. (1987). The effect of layoff on police authoritarianism. *Criminal Justice and Behavior, 14*, 194–210.

Baym, C. L. & Gonsalves, B. D. (2010). Comparison of neural activities that leads to true memories, false memories, and forgetting: An fMRI study of the misinformation effect. *Cognitive, Affective, and Behavioral Neuroscience, 10*, 339–348.

Beaudry, J., Lindsay, R., & Dupuis, P. (2006). Procedural recommendations to increase the reliability of eyewitness recommendations. In M. R. Kebbell & G. M. Davies (Eds.), *Practical Psychology for Forensic Investigations and Prosecutions* (pp. 25–45). Chichester, Sussex: John Wiley & Sons.

Berking, M., Meier, C., & Wupperman, P. (2010). Enhancing emotion-regulation skills in police officers: Results of a pilot controlled study. *Behavior Therapy, 41*, 329–339.

Bernstein, D. M. & Loftus, E. F. (2009). How to tell if a particular memory is true or false. *Perspectives on Psychological Science, 4*, 370–374.

Binet, A. (1900). *La Suggestibilité.* Paris: Schleicher.

Birzer, M. L. & Tannehill, R. (2001). A more effective training approach for contemporary policing. *Police Quarterly, 4,* 233–252.

Brewer, N. & Palmer, M. A. (2010). Eyewitness identification tests. *Legal and Criminological Psychology, 15,* 77–96.

Brewer, N., Weber, N., & Semmler, B. (2005). Eyewitness identification. In N. Brewer & K. D. Williams (Eds.), *Psychology and Law: An Empirical Perspective* (pp. 177–221). New York, NY: Guilford Press.

British Psychological Society (BPS) (2004). *A Review of the Current Scientific Status and Fields of Application of Polygraphic Deception Detection.* Leicester: Author.

Brown, L. & Willis, A. (1985). Authoritarianism in British police recruits: Importation, socialization or myth? *Journal of Occupational Psychology, 58,* 97–108.

Bull, R. (2010). The investigative interviewing of children and other vulnerable witnesses: Psychological research and working/professional practice. *Legal and Criminological Psychology, 15,* 5–23.

Burbeck, E. & Furnham, A. (1984). Personality and police selection: Trait differences in successful and unsuccessful applicants to the Metropolitan Police. *Personality and Individual Differences, 5,* 257–263.

Butler, A. J. P. & Cochrane, R. (1977). An examination of some elements of the personality of police officers and their implications. *Journal of Police Science and Administration, 5,* 441–450.

Canter, D. V. (1994). *Criminal Shadows: Inside the Mind of the Serial Killer.* London: HarperCollins.

Canter, D. & Gregory, A. (1994). Identifying the geographical location of serial rapists. *Journal of the Forensic Science Society, 34,* 169–175.

Canter, D. & Youngs, D. (2009). *Investigative Psychology: Offender Profiling and the Analysis of Criminal Action.* Chichester, Sussex: John Wiley & Sons.

Cattell, R. B., Cattell, A. K. & Cattell, H. E. P. (1993). *Sixteen Personality Factor Questionnaire* (5th ed.). Champaign, IL: Institute for Personality and Ability Testing Inc.

Chapin, M., Brannen, S. J., Singer, M. I., & Walker, M. (2008). Training police leadership to recognize and address operational stress. *Police Quarterly, 11,* 338–352.

Clark, S. E. & Godfrey, E. D. (2009). Eyewitness identification evidence and innocence risk. *Psychonomic Bulletin and Review, 16,* 22–42.

Clifford, B. R. & Hollin, C. R. (1981). Effects of the type of incident and number of perpetrators on eyewitness memory. *Journal of Applied Psychology, 66,* 364–370.

Clifford, B. R. & Richards, V. J. (1977). Comparison of recall of policemen and civilians under conditions of long and short durations of exposure. *Perception and Motor Skills, 45,* 503–512.

Coffin, T. E. (1941). Some conditions of suggestion and suggestibility: A study of certain attitudinal and situational factors influencing the process of suggestion. *Psychological Monographs, 53,* 1–121.

Coleman, T. G. & Cotton, D. H. (2010). Reducing risk and improving outcomes of police interactions with people with mental illness. *Journal of Police Crisis Negotiations, 10,* 39–57.

Collins, P. A. & Gibbs, A. C. C. (2003). Stress in police officers: A study of the origins, prevalence and severity of stress-related symptoms within a county police force. *Occupational Medicine, 53,* 256–264.

Colman, A. M. & Gorman, L. P. (1982). Conservatism, dogmatism, and authoritarianism in British police officers. *Sociology, 17,* 388–391.

Cooper, C. L., Davidson, M. J., & Robinson, P. (1982). Stress in the police service. *Journal of Occupational Medicine, 24,* 30–36.

Costa, P. T. & McCrae, R. R. (1992). *NEO PI-R: Professional Manual.* Odessa, FL: Psychological Assessment Resources, Inc.

Crabbé, A., Decoene, S., & Vertommen, H. (2008). Profiling homicide offenders: a review of assumptions and theories. *Aggression and Violent Behavior, 13,* 88–106.

Culhane, S. E., Hosch, H. M., & Heck, C. (2008). Interrogation technique endorsement by current law enforcement, future law enforcement, and laypersons. *Police Quarterly, 11,* 366–386.

Curran, H. V. (2006). Effects of drugs on witness memory. In A. Heaton-Armstrong, E. Shepherd, G. Gudjonsson, & D. Wolchover (Eds.), *Witness Testimony: Psychological, Investigative and Evidential Perspectives* (pp. 77–87). Oxford: Oxford University Press.

Darling, S., Martin, D., Hellman, J. H., & Memon, A. (2009). Some witnesses are better than others. *Personality and Individual Differences, 47*, 369–373.

Devery, C. (2010). Criminal profiling and criminal investigation. *Journal of Contemporary Criminal Justice, 26*, 393–409.

Davies, G. M. (1981). Face recall systems. In G. M. Davies, H. D. Ellis, & G. W. Shepherd (Eds.), *Perceiving and Remembering Faces* (pp. 227–250). London: Academic Press.

Deffenbacher, K. A., Bornstein, B. H., Penrod, S. D., & McGorty, E. K. (2004). A meta-analytic review of the effects of high stress on eyewitness memory. *Law and Human Behavior, 28*, 687–706.

DePaulo, B. M. & Morris, W. L. (2004). Discerning lies from truths: Behavioural cues to deception and the indirect pathway of intuition. In P. A. Granhag & L. A. Strömwall (Eds.), *Deception Detection in Forensic Contexts* (pp. 15–40). Cambridge: Cambridge University Press.

Detrick, P., Chibnall, J. T., & Luebbert, M. C. (2004). The Revised NEO Personality Inventory as predictor of Police Academy performance. *Criminal Justice and Behavior, 31*, 676–694.

Devery, C. (2010). Criminal profiling and criminal investigation. *Journal of Contemporary Criminal Justice, 26*, 393–409.

Dixon, D. (2010). Questioning suspects: A comparative perspective. *Journal of Contemporary Criminal Justice, 26*, 426–440.

Douglas, J. E., Burgess, A. W., Burgess, A. G., & Ressler, R. K. (1992). *Crime Classification Manual: A Standard System for Investigating and Classifying Violent Crime*. New York, NY: Simon & Schuster.

Douglas, J. E. & Olshaker, M. (1995). *Mind Hunter: Inside the FBI's Elite Serial Crime Unit*. New York, NY: Simon & Schuster.

Duncan, A. (2008). Precognition-predicting the future: Biotechnology and policing in 2020. *Australian Journal of Forensic Sciences, 40*, 25–29.

Evans, F. J. (1967). Suggestibility in the normal waking state. *Psychological Bulletin, 67*, 114–129.

Evans, J. R., Schreiber Compo, N., & Russano, M. B. (2009). Intoxicated witnesses and suspects: Procedures and prevalence according to law enforcement. *Psychology, Public Policy, and Law, 15*, 194–221.

Eysenck, H. J. & Furneaux, W. D. (1945). Primary and secondary suggestibility: An experimental and statistical study. *Journal of Experimental Psychology, 35*, 485–503.

Fisher, R. P. & Geiselman, R. E. (1992). *Memory-Enhancing Techniques in Investigate Interviewing: The Cognitive Interview*. Springfield, IL: C. C. Thomas.

Fisher, R. P., McCauley, M. R., & Geiselman, R. E. (1994). Improving eyewitness testimony with the Cognitive Interview. In D. F. Ross, J. D. Read, & M. P. Toglia (Eds.), *Adult Eyewitness Memory: Current Trends and Developments* (pp. 245–269). Cambridge: Cambridge University Press.

Fisher, R. P. & Schreiber, N. (2007). Interview protocols to improve eyewitness memory. In M. P. Toglia, J. D. Read, D. F. Ross, & R. C. L. Lindsay (Eds.), *The Handbook of Eyewitness Memory: Volume I: Memory for Events* (pp. 53–80). Mahwah, NJ: Lawrence Erlbaum and Associates.

Flowe, H. D., Mehta, A., & Ebbesen, A. B. (2011). The role of eyewitness identification evidence in felony case dispositions. *Psychology, Public Policy, and Law, 17*, 140–159.

Forero, C. G., Gallardo-Pujol, D., Maydeu-Olivares, A., & Andrés-Pueyoet, A. (2009). A longitudinal model for predicting performance of police officers using personality and behavioral data. *Criminal Justice and Behavior, 36*, 591–606.

Forrest, K. D., Wadkins, T. A., & Larson, B. A. (2006). Suspect personality, police interrogations, and false confessions: Maybe it is not just the situation. *Personality and Individual Differences, 40*, 621–628.

Furnham, A. & Henderson, M. (1982). The good, the bad, and the mad: Response bias in self-report measures. *Personality and Individual Differences, 3*, 311–320.

Geiselman, R. E., Fisher, R. P., Firstenberg, I., Hutton, L. A., Sullivan, S., Avetissian, I., & Prosk, A. (1984). Enhancement of eyewitness memory: An empirical evaluation of the cognitive interview. *Journal of Police Science and Administration, 12,* 74–80.

Geiselman, R. E., Fisher, R. P., MacKinnon, D. P., & Holland, H. L. (1985). Eyewitness memory enhancement in the police interview: Cognitive retrieval mnemonics versus hypnosis. *Journal of Applied Psychology, 70,* 401–412.

Geraerts, E., Raymaekers, L., & Mercklebach, H. (2008). Recovered memories of childhood sexual abuse: Current findings and their legal implications. *Legal and Criminological Psychology, 13,* 165–176.

Gerber, M., Hartmann, T., Brand, S., Holsboer-Trachsler, E., & Pühse, E. (2010). The relationship between shift work, perceived stress, sleep and health in Swiss police officers. *Journal of Criminal Justice, 38,* 1167–1175.

Gerrie, M. P., Garry, M., & Loftus, E. F. (2005). False memories. In N. Brewer & K. D. Williams (Eds.), *Psychology and Law: An Empirical Perspective* (pp. 222–253). New York, NY: Guilford Press.

Gershon, R. R. M., Barocas, B., Canton, A. N., Li, X., & Vlahov, D. (2009). *Mental, physical, and behavioral outcomes associated with perceived work stress in police officers. Criminal Justice and Behavior, 36,* 275–289.

Ghazinour, M., Lauritz, L. E., Du Preez, E., Cassimjee, N., & Richter, J. (2010). An investigation of mental health and personality in Swedish police trainees upon entry to the Police Academy. *Journal of Police and Criminal Psychology, 25,* 34–42.

Gheorghiu, V. A., Netter, P., Eysenck, H. J., & Rosenthal, R. (Eds.) (1989). *Suggestion and Suggestibility: Theory and Research.* Berlin: Springer-Verlag.

Gilchrist, E. (2006). Deciding to prosecute. In M. R. Kebbell & G. M. Davies (Eds.), *Practical Psychology for Forensic Investigations and Prosecutions* (pp. 166–182). Chichester, Sussex: John Wiley & Sons.

Goodman, G. S. & Melinder, A. (2007). Child witness research and forensic interviews of young children: A review. *Legal and Criminological Psychology, 12,* 1–19.

Goodman, G. S. & Schaaf, J. M. (1997). Over a decade of research on children's eyewitness testimony: What have we learned? Where do we go from here? *Applied Cognitive Psychology, 11,* S6–S20.

Gordon, B. N., Baker-Ward, L., & Ornstein, P. A. (2001). Children's testimony: A review on research of memory for past experiences. *Clinical Child and Family Psychology Review, 4,* 157–181.

Gudjonsson, G. H. (1983). Suggestibility, intelligence, memory recall and personality: An experimental study. *British Journal of Psychiatry, 142,* 35–37.

—— (1984). Fear of "failure" and "tissue damage" in police recruits, constables, sergeants and senior officers. *Personality and Individual Differences, 5,* 233–236.

—— (1986). The relationship between interrogative suggestibility and acquiescence: empirical findings and theoretical implications. *Personality and Individual Differences, 7,* 195–199.

—— (1987a). Historical background to suggestibility: How interrogative suggestibility differs from others types of suggestibility. *Personality and Individual Differences, 8,* 347–355.

—— (1987b). The relationship between memory and suggestibility. *Social Behaviour, 2,* 29–33.

—— (1988a). The relationship of intelligence and memory to interrogative suggestibility: The importance of range effects. *British Journal of Clinical Psychology, 27,* 185–187.

—— (1988b). Interrogative suggestibility: Its relationship with assertiveness, social-evaluative anxiety, state anxiety and method of coping. *British Journal of Clinical Psychology, 27,* 159–166.

—— (1989). Compliance in an interrogative situation: A new scale. *Personality and Individual Differences, 10,* 535–540.

—— (1990). The relationship of intellectual skills to suggestibility, compliance and acquiescence. *Personality and Individual Differences, 11,* 227–231.

—— (2003). *The Psychology of Interrogations and Confessions: A Handbook.* Chichester, Sussex: John Wiley & Sons.

—— (2010). Psychological vulnerabilities during police interviews: Why are they important? *Legal and Criminological Psychology, 15,* 161–175.

Gudjonsson, G. H. & Adlam, K. R. C. (1982). Factors reducing occupational stress in police officers: Senior officers' view. *Police Journal, 58*, 73–80.

—— (1983). Personality patterns of British police officers. *Personality and Individual Differences, 4*, 507–512.

—— (1985). Occupational stressors among British police officers. *Police Journal, 58*, 73–80.

Gudjonsson, G. H. & Clark, N. K. (1986). Suggestibility in police interrogation: A social psychological model. *Social Behaviour, 1*, 83–104.

Gudjonsson, G. H. & Lebegue, B. (1989). Psychological and psychiatric aspects of a coerced-internalized false confession. *Journal of the Forensic Science Society, 29*, 261–269.

Gudjonsson, G. H. & Lister, S. (1984). Interrogative suggestibility and its relationship with selfesteem and control. *Journal of the Forensic Science Society, 24*, 99–110.

Gudjonsson, G. H. & MacKeith, J. A. C. (1982). False confessions: Psychological effects of interrogation: A discussion paper. In A. Trankell (Ed.), *Reconstructing the Past: The Role of Psychologists in Criminal Trials* (pp. 253–269). Deventer, the Netherlands: Kluwer Academic Publishers.

—— (1988). Retracted confessions: Legal, psychological and psychiatric aspects. *Medicine, Science and the Law, 28*, 187–194.

—— (1990). A proven case of false confession: Psychological aspects of the coerced-compliant type. *Medicine, Science and the Law, 30*, 329–335.

—— (2003). The "Guilford Four" and the "Birmingham Six". In G. H. Gudjonsson (Ed.), *The Psychology of Interrogations and Confessions* (pp. 445–457). Chichester, Sussex: John Wiley & Sons.

Gudjonsson, G. H. & Sigurdsson, J. F. (2010). False confessions in the Nordic countries: Background and current landscape. In P. A. Granhag (Ed.), *Forensic Psychology in Context: Nordic and International Approaches* (pp. 94–116). Cullompton, Devon: Willan Publishing.

Gudjonsson, G. H., Sigurdsson, J. F., Einarsson, E., Bragason, O. O., & Newton, A. K. (2010). Inattention, hyperactivity/impulsivity and antisocial personality disorder: Which is the best predictor of false confessions? *Personality and Individual Differences, 48*, 720–724.

Handler, M., Honts, C. R., Krapohl, D. J., Nelson, R., & Griffin, S. (2009). Integration of preemployment polygraph screening into the police selection process. *Journal of Police and Criminal Psychology, 24*, 69–86.

Harris, C. J. (2009). Exploring the relationship between experience and problem behaviors: A longitudinal analysis of offi cers from a large cohort. *Police Quarterly, 12*, 192–213.

—— (2010). Problem offi cers? Analyzing problem behavior patterns from a large cohort. *Journal of Criminal Justice, 38*, 216–225.

Hasel, L. E. & Kassin, S. M. (2009). On the presumption of evidentiary independence: Can confessions corrupt eyewitness identifications? *Psychological Science, 20*, 122–126.

Haward, L. & Ashworth, A. (1980). Some problems of evidence obtained by hypnosis. *Criminal Law Review*, 469–485.

Hazelwood, R. R. & Warren, J. I. (2003). Linkage analysis: Modus operandi, ritual, and signature in serial sexual crime. *Aggression and Violent Behavior, 8*, 587–598.

Heaton-Armstrong, A., Shepherd, E., Gudjonsson, G., & Wolchover, D. (Eds.) (2006). *Witness Testimony: Psychological, Investigative and Evidential Perspectives*. Oxford: Oxford University Press.

Hicks, S. J. & Sales, B. D. (2006). *Criminal Profiling: Developing an Effective Science and Practice*. Washington, DC: American Psychological Association.

Ho, T. (2001). The interrelationships of psychological testing, psychologists' recommendations, and Police Departments' recruitment decisions. *Police Quarterly, 4*, 318–342.

Holliday, R. E., Brainerd, C. J., Reyna, V. F., & Humphries, J. E. (2009). The Cognitive Interview: Research and practice across the life-span. In R. Bull, T. Valentine, & T. Williamson (Eds.), *Handbook of Psychology of Investigative Interviewing* (pp. 137–160). Chichester, Sussex: Wiley-Blackwell.

Hollin, C. R. (1981). Nature of the witnessed incident and status of interviewer as variables influencing eyewitness recall. *British Journal of Social Psychology, 20*, 295–296.

Hollin, C. R. & Clifford, B. R. (1983). Eyewitness testimony: The effects of discussion on recall accuracy and agreement. *Journal of Applied Social Psychology, 13*, 234–244.

Home Office (1985). *Police and Criminal Evidence Act of 1984.* London: HMSO.

Horncastle, P. (1985). Psychology and police training. *Policing, 1*, 254–266.

Iacono, W. G. (2008). Polygraph testing. In E. Borgida & S. T. Fiske (Eds.), *Beyond Common Sense: Psychological Science in the Courtroom* (pp. 219–235). Oxford: Blackwell.

Iacono, W. G. & Lykken, D. T. (2005). The case against polygraph tests. In D. L. Faigman, D. H. Kaye, M. J. Saks, & J. Sanders (Eds.), *Modern Scientific Evidence: The Law and Science of Expert Testimony* (Vol. 4) (pp. 605–655). Eagan, MN: West Publishing.

Inbau, F. E., Reid, J. E., & Buckley, J. P. (1986). *Criminal Interrogation and Confessions* (3 rd ed.). Baltimore, MD: Williams & Wilkins.

Irving, B. (1986). The interrogation process. In J. Benyon & C. Bourn (Eds.), The Police: Powers, Procedures and Proprieties (pp. 136–149). Oxford: Pergamon Press.

Irving, B. & Hilgendorf, L. (1980). *Police Interrogation: The Psychological Approach.* Royal Commission on Criminal Procedure Research Study No. 1. London: HMSO.

Jackson, J. L. & Bekerian, D. A. (Eds.) (1997). *Offender Profiling: Theory, Research and Practice.* Chichester, Sussex: John Wiley & Sons.

Jang, H., Joo, H. -J., & Zhao, J. (2010). Determinant of public confidence in the police: An international perspective. *Journal of Criminal Justice, 38*, 57–68.

Jacobs, W. L. & Nadel, L. (1998). Neurobiology of reconstructed memory. *Psychology: Public Policy and Law, 4*, 1110–1134.

Kania, R. R. E. (1983). Joining anthropology and law enforcement. *Journal of Criminal Justice, 11*, 495–504.

Kassin, S. M. (1997). The psychology of confession evidence. *American Psychologist, 52*, 221–233.

—— (2005). On the psychology of confessions: Does innocence put innocents at risk? *American Psychologist, 60*, 215–228.

—— (2008). False confessions: Causes, consequences, and implications for reform. *Current Directions in Psychological Science, 17*, 249–253.

Kassin, S. M., Appleby, S. C., & Perillo, J. T. (2010). Interviewing suspects: Practice, science, and future directions. *Legal and Criminological Psychology, 15*, 39–55.

Kassin, S. M., Drizin, S., Grisso, T., Gudjonsson, G. H., Leo, R. A., & Redlich, A. D. (2010). Policeinduced confessions: Risk factors and recommendations. *Law and Human Behavior, 34*, 3–38.

Kassin, S. M. & Gudjonsson, G. H. (2004). The psychology of confessions: A review of the literature and issues. *Psychological Science in the Public Interest, 5*, 33–67.

Kassin, S. M. & Wrightsman, L. S. (1985). Confession evidence. In S. M. Kassin & L. S. Wrightsman (Eds.), The Psychology of Evidence and Trial Procedure (pp. 67–94). Beverly Hills, CA: Sage.

Kircher, J. C. & Raskin, D. C. (2002). Computer methods for the psychophysiological detection of deception. In M. Kleiner (Ed.), *Handbook of Polygraph Testing* (pp. 287–326). San Diego, CA: Academic Press.

Koch, B. J. (2010). The psychological impact on police officers of being first responders to completed suicides. *Journal of Police and Criminal Psychology, 25*, 90–98.

Kohan, A. & Mazmanian, D. (2003). Police work, burnout, and pro-organizational behavior: A consideration of daily work experiences. *Criminal Justice and Behavior, 30*, 559–583.

Kocsis, R. N. (2006). *Criminal Profiling: International Theory, Practice, and Research.* Totowa, NJ: Humana Press.

—— (Ed.) (2007). *Criminal Profiling: Principles and Practice.* Totowa, NJ: Humana Press.

Krause, M. (2009). Identifying and managing stress in child pornography and child exploitation investigators. *Journal of Police and Criminal Psychology, 22*, 24–29.

Krug, S. E. (1980). *Clinical Analysis Questionnaire Manual.* Champaign, IL: Institute for Personality and Ability Testing.

Kuehn, L. (1974). Looking down a gun barrel: Person perception and violent crime. *Perceptual and Motor Skills, 39*, 1159–1164.

Kurtzweil, R. (2005). *The Singularity is Near.* New York, NY: Viking Penguin.

La Rooy, D., Katz, C., Malloy, L. C., & Lambet, M. E. (2010). Do we need to rethink guidance on repeated interviews? *Psychology, Public Policy, and Law, 16,* 373–392.

La Rooy, D., Lamb, M. E., & Memon, A. (2010). Forensic interviews with children in Scotland: A survey of interview practices among police. *Journal of Police and Criminal Psychology, 26,* 26–34.

Lamb, M. E., Orbach, Y., Warren, A. R., Esplin, P. W., & Hershkowitz, I. (2007). Enhancing performance: Factors affecting the informativeness of young witnesses. In M. P. Toglia, J. D. Read, D. F. Ross, & R. C. L. Lindsay (Eds.), *The Handbook of Eyewitness Testimony: Vol. 1, Memory for Events* (pp. 429–451). Mahwah, NJ: Lawrence Erlbaum and Associates.

Laguna, L., Linn, A., Ward, K., & Rupslaukyte, R. (2010). An examination of authoritarian personality traits among police offi cers: The role of experience. *Journal of Police and Criminal Psychology, 25,* 99–104.

Langleben, D. D. (2008). Detection of deception with fMRI: Are we there yet? *Legal and Criminological Psychology, 13,* 1–9.

Lassiter, G. D. (Ed.) (2004). *Interrogations, Confessions, and Entrapment.* New York, NY: Kluwer Academic Publishers.

Laughery, K. R. & Fowler, R. H. (1980). Sketch artist and Identi-kit procedures for recalling faces. *Journal of Applied Psychology, 65,* 307–316.

Leander, L. (2010). Police interviews with child sexual abuse victims: Patterns of reporting, avoidance and denial. *Child Abuse & Neglect, 34,* 192–205.

Lee, H. & Vaughn, M. S. (2010). Organizational factors that contribute to police deadly force liability. *Journal of Criminal Justice, 38,* 193–206.

Lilly, M. M., Pole, N., Best, S, R., Metzler, T., & Marmar, C. R. (2009). Gender and PTSD: What can we learn from female police officers? *Anxiety Disorders, 23,* 767–774.

Lindsay, R. C. L. (1994). Biased lineups: Where do they come from? In D. R. Ross, J. D. Read, & M. P. Toglia (Eds.), *Adult Eyewitness Testimony: Current Trends and Developments* (pp. 182–200). Cambridge: Cambridge University Press.

Lindsay, R. C. L., Ross, D. F., Read, J. D., & Toglia, M. P. (2007). *The Handbook of Eyewitness Testimony: Vol. 1, Memory for People.* Mahwah, NJ: Lawrence Erlbaum and Associates.

Lindsay, R. C. L., Semmler, C., Weber, N., Brewer, N., & Lindsay, M. R. (2008). How variations in distance affect eyewitness reports and identification accuracy. *Law and Human Behavior, 32,* 526–535.

Lingoes, J. (1973). *The Guttman-Lingoes Non-Metric Program Series.* Ann Arbor, MI: Mathesis Press.

Lipton, J. P. (1977). On the psychology of eyewitness testimony. *Journal of Applied Psychology, 62,* 90–95.

Loftus, E. F. (1979). *Eyewitness Testimony.* Cambridge, MA: Harvard University Press.

—— (2004). Memories of things unseen. *Current Directions in Psychological Science, 13,* 145–147.

Loftus, E. F. & Burns, T. E. (1982). Mental shock can produce retrograde amnesia. *Memory and Cognition, 10,* 318–323.

Loftus, E. F., Garry, M., & Hayne, H. (2008). Repressed and recovered memory. In E. Borgida & S. T. Fiske (Eds.), *Beyond Common Sense: Psychological Science in the Courtroom* (pp. 177–194). Oxford: Blackwell.

Loftus, E. F. & Ketcham, K. (1994). *The Myth of Repressed Memory: False Memories and Allegations of Sexual Abuse.* New York, NY: St. Martin's Press.

Loftus, E. F. & Palmer, J. C. (1974). Reconstruction of an automobile destruction: An example of the interaction between language and memory. *Journal of Verbal Learning and Verbal Behavior, 4,* 323–334.

Lord, V. B. & Schoeps, N. (2000). Identifying psychological attributes of community-oriented, problem-solving police officers. *Police Quarterly, 3,* 172–190.

Lord, V. B. & Sloop, M. W. (2010). Suicide by cop: Police shooting as a method of self-harming. *Journal of Criminal Justice, 38,* 889–895.

Laughery, K. R. & Fowler, R. H. (1980). Sketch artist and identi-kit procedures for recalling faces. *Journal of Applied Psychology, 65*, 307–316.

Malpass, R. S. & Devine, P. G. (1981). Guided memory in eyewitness identification. *Journal of Applied Psychology, 66*, 343–350.

Maddox, L., Lee, D., & Barker, C. (2011). Police empathy and victim PTSD as potential factors in rape case attrition. *Journal of Police and Criminal Psychology, 26*, 112–117.

Mazzoni, G. & Lynn, S. J. (2007). Using hypnosis in eyewitness memory: Past and current issues. In M. P. Toglia, J. D. Read, D. F. Ross, & R. C. L. Lindsay (Eds.), *The Handbook of Eyewitness Memory: Vol. I, Memory for Events* (pp. 321–338). Mahwah, NJ: Lawrence Erlbaum and Associates.

McAdams, D. (1988). Biography, narratives and lives: An introduction. *Journal of Personality, 56*, 1–18.

Meissner, C. A. & Brigham, J. C. (2001). Thirty years of investigating the own-race bias in memory for faces: A meta-analytic review. *Psychology, Public Policy, and Law, 7*, 3–35.

Memon, A., Bartlett, J. C., Rose, R., & Gray, C. (2003). The aging eyewitness: The effects of face-age and delay upon younger and older observers. *British Journal of Gerontology, 58*, 338–345.

Memon, A. & Bull, R. (Eds.) (1999). *Handbook of the Psychology of Interviewing.* Chichester, Sussex: John Wiley & Sons.

Memon, A., Meissner, C. A., & Fraser, J. (2010). The cognitive interview: A meta-analytic review and study space analysis of the past 25 years. *Psychology, Public Policy, and Law, 16*, 340–372.

Memon, A., Vrij, A., & Bull, R. (2003). *Psychology and Law* (2nd ed.). Chichester, Sussex: John Wiley & Sons.

Milgram, S. (1974). *Obedience to Authority.* New York, NY: Harper & Row.

Miller, H. A., Mire, S., & Kim, B. (2009). Predictors of job satisfaction among police officers: Does personality matter? *Journal of Criminal Justice, 37*, 419–426.

Mitchell, K. J., Livosky, M. L., & Mather, M. (1998). The weapon focus effect revisited: The role of novelty. *Legal and Criminological Psychology, 3*, 307–323.

Mueller-Johnson, K. & Ceci, S. J. (2007). The elderly eyewitness: A review and prospectus. In M. P. Toglia, J. D. Read, D. F. Ross, & R. C. L. Lindsay (Eds.), *The Handbook of Eyewitness Memory: Vol. I, Memory for Events* (pp. 577–603). Mahwah, NJ: Lawrence Erlbaum and Associates.

Mullin, P. (1989). *Error of Judgement: The Truth About the Birmingham Bombings.* Dublin: Poolberg.

Murphy, G. H. & Clare, I. C. H. (2006). The effect of learning disabilities on witness testimony. In A. Heaton-Armstrong, E. Shepherd, G. Gudjonsson, & D. Wolchover (Eds.), *Witness Testimony: Psychological, Investigative and Evidential Perspectives* (pp. 43–60). Oxford: Oxford University Press.

Newburn, T. & Reiner, R. (2007). Policing and the police. In M. Maguire, R. Morgan, & R. Reiner (Eds.), *The Oxford Handbook of Criminology* (pp. 910–932). Oxford: Oxford University Press.

Odinot, G., Wolters, G., & van Koppen, P. J. (2009). Eyewitness memory of a supermarket robbery: A case study of accuracy and confidence after 3 months. *Law and Human Behavior, 33*, 506–514.

Peres, J. F.P., Foerster, B., Santana, L. G., Fereira, M. D., Nasello A. G., Savoia M., Moreira-Almeida, A., & Lederman, H. (2011). Police officers under attack: Resilience implications of an fMRI study. *Journal of Psychiatric Research, 45*, 727–734.

Paterson, H. M. & Kemp, R. I. (2006). Eyewitnesses talk: A survey of eyewitness discussion. *Psychology, Crime, & Law, 12*, 181–191.

Pearlman, L. A. & Saakvitne, K. W. (1995). *Trauma and the Therapist.* New York, NY: Norton.

Perez, L. M., Jones, J., Englert, D. R., & Sachau, D. (2010). Secondary traumatic stress and burnout among law enforcement investigators exposed to disturbing media images. *Journal of Police and Criminal Psychology, 25*, 113–124.

Poteyeva, M. & Sun, M. I. Y. (2009). Gender differences in police officers' attitudes: Assessing current empirical evidence. *Journal of Criminal Justice, 37*, 512–522.

Próchniak, P. (2009). Polish police officers: Personality and risk taking. *Journal of Police and Criminal Psychology, 24*, 104–107.

Raganella, A. J. & White, M. D. (2004). Race, gender, and motivation for becoming a police officer: Implications for building a representative police department. *Journal of Criminal Justice, 32*, 501–513.

Rawlings, P. (2003). Policing before the police. In T. Newburn (Ed.), *Handbook of Policing* (pp. 41–65). Cullompton, Devon: Willan Publishing.

Ratcliff, J. J., Lassiter, G. D., Jager, V. M., Lindberg, M. J., Elek, J. K., & Hasinski, A. E. (2010). The hidden consequences of racial salience in videotaped interrogations and confessions. *Psychology, Public Policy, and Law, 16*, 200–218.

Read, J. D. & Connolly, D. A. (2007). The effects of delay on long-term memory for witnessed events. In M. P. Toglia, J. D. Read, D. F. Ross, & R. C. L. Lindsay (Eds.), *The Handbook of Eyewitness Memory: Vol. I, Memory for Events* (pp. 117–155). Mahwah, NJ: Lawrence Erlbaum and Associates.

Read, J. D., Lindsay, D. S., & Nicholls, T. (1998). The relation between confidence and accuracy in eyewitness identification studies: Is the conclusion changing? In C. P. Thompson, D. J. Herman, J. D. Read, D. Bruce, D. G. Payne, & M. P. Toglia (Eds.), *Eyewitness Memory: Theoretical and Applied Aspects* (pp. 107–130). Hillsdale, NJ: Lawrence Erlbaum and Associates.

Reiner, R. (2007). *Law and Order: An Honest Citizen's Guide to Crime and Crime Control.* Cambridge: Polity Press.

Reiser, M. (1982). *Police Psychology: Collected Papers.* Los Angeles, CA: LEHI Publishing.

Roach, J. (2010). Home is where the heart lies? A study of false address giving to police. *Legal and Criminological Psychology, 15*, 209–220.

Salters-Pedneault, K., Ruef, A. M., & Orr, S. P. (2010). Personality and psychophysiological profiles of police officer and firefighter recruits. *Personality and Individual Differences, 49*, 210–215.

Sarason, I. G., Johnson, J. H., Berberich, J. P., & Siegal, J. M. (1979). Helping police officers to cope with stress: A cognitive-behavioral approach. *American Journal of Community Psychology, 7*, 593–603.

Schlosser, L. Z., Safran, D. A., & Sbaratta C. A. (2010). Reasons for choosing a correction officer career. *Psychological Services, 7*, 34–43.

Shane, J. M. (2010). Organizational stressors and police performance. *Journal of Criminal Justice, 8*, 807–818.

Shepherd, J. W. (1981). Social factors in face recognition. In G. M. Davies, H. D. Ellis, & J. W. Shepherd (Eds.), *Perceiving and Remembering Faces* (pp. 55–79). London: Academic Press.

—— (1983). Identification after long delays. In S. M. A. Lloyd-Bostock & B. R. Clifford (Eds.), *Evaluating Witness Evidence: Recent Psychological Research and New Perspectives* (pp. 173–187). Chichester, Sussex: John Wiley & Sons.

Shepherd, J. W., Ellis, H. D., & Davies, G. M. (1982). *Identification Evidence: A Psychological Evaluation.* Aberdeen: University of Aberdeen Press.

Siegal, L. J. (1986). *Criminology* (2nd ed.). St. Paul, MN: West Publishing.

Skogan, W. G. (2009). Concern about crime and confidence in the police: Reassurance or accountability? *Police Quarterly, 12*, 301–318.

Smith, S. M., Stinson, V., & Patry, M. W. (2009). Using the "Mr. Big" technique to elicit confessions: Successful innovation or dangerous development in the Canadian legal system? *Psychology, Public Policy, and Law, 15*, 168–193.

Snook, B., Eastwood, J., Gendreau, P., Goggin, C., & Cullen, R. M. (2007). Taking stock of criminal profiling: A narrative review and meta-analysis. *Criminal Justice and Behavior, 34*, 437–453.

Snook, B., Cullen, R. M., Bennell, C., Taylor, P. J., & Gendreau, P. (2008). The criminal profiling illusion: What's behind the smoke and mirrors? *Criminal Justice and Behavior, 35*, 1257–1276.

Snook, B., Doan, B., Cullen, R. M., Kavanagh, J. M., & Eastwood, J. (2009). Publication and research trends in police psychology: A review of five forensic psychology journals. *Journal of Police and Criminal Psychology, 24*, 45–50.

Sobol, J. J. (2010). Social ecology and police discretion: The influence of district crime, cynicism, and workload on the vigor of police response. *Journal of Criminal Justice, 38*, 481–488.

Sousa, M., Ready, J., & Ault, M. (2010). The impact of TASERs on police use-of-force decisions: Findings from a randomized field-training experiment. *Journal of Experimental Criminology, 6,* 35–55.

Spence, S. A. (2008). Playing Devil's advocate: The case *against* fMRI lie detection. *Legal and Criminological Psychology, 13,* 11–25.

Sporer, S. L. (2008). Lessons from the origins of eyewitness testimony research in Europe. *Applied Cognitive Psychology, 22,* 737–757.

Steblay, N. M. (1992). A meta-analytic review of the weapon focus effect. *Law and Human Behavior, 16,* 413–424.

Taylor, M. (1983). Psychology and police education. *Bulletin of The British Psychological Society, 36,* 406–408.

Terrill, W. & McCluskey, J. (2002). Citizen complaints and problem officers: Examining officer behavior. *Journal of Criminal Justice, 30,* 143–155.

Terry, W. C. (1981). Police stress: The empirical evidence. *Journal of Police Science and Administration, 9,* 61–75.

Toglia, M. P., Read, J. D., Ross, D. F., & Lindsay, R. C. L. (Eds.) (2007). *The Handbook of Eyewitness Testimony: Vol. 1, Memory for Events.* Mahwah, NJ: Lawrence Erlbaum and Associates.

Torres, A. N., Boccaccini, M. T., & Miller, H. A. (2006). Perceptions of the validity and utility of criminal profi ling among forensic psychologists and psychiatrists. *Professional Psychology: Research and Practice, 37,* 51–58.

Tousignant, J. P., Hall, D., & Loftus, E. F. (1986). Discrepancy detection and vulnerability to misleading postevent information. *Memory and Cognition, 14,* 329–338.

Traut, C. A., Feimer, S., Emmert, C. F., & Thom, K. (2000). Law enforcement recruit training at the State level: An evaluation. *Police Quarterly, 3,* 294–314.

Twersky-Glasner, A. (2005). Police personality: What is it and why are they like that? *Journal of Police and Criminal Psychology, 20,* 56–67.

Valentine, T. (2006). Forensic facial identification. In A. Heaton-Armstrong, E. Shepherd, G. Gudjonsson, & D. Wolchover (Eds.), *Witness Testimony: Psychological, Investigative and Evidential Procedures* (pp. 281–307). Oxford: Oxford University Press.

van der Kolk, B. A. & Fisler, R. (1995). Dissociation and the fragmentary nature of traumatic memories: Overview and exploratory study. *Journal of Traumatic Stress, 8,* 505–525.

Varela, J. G., Boccaccini, M. T., Scogin, F., Stump, J., & Caputo, A. (2004). Personality testing in law enforcement employment settings: A metaanalytic review. *Criminal Justice and Behavior, 31,* 649–675.

Vennard, J. (1984). Disputes within trials over the admissibility and accuracy of incriminating statements: Some research evidence. *Criminal Law Review,* 15–24.

Verschuere, B., Prati, V., & De Houwer, J. (2009). Cheating the lie detector: Faking in the autobiographical Implicit Association Test. *Psychological Science, 20,* 410–413.

Vrij, A. (2008). *Detecting Lies and Deceit: Pitfalls and Opportunities* (2 nd ed.). Chichester, Sussex: John Wiley & Sons.

Vrij, A. & Mann, S. (2001). Lying when the stakes are high: Deceptive behaviour of a murderer during his police interview. *Applied Cognitive Psychology, 15,* 187–203.

Walkley, J. (1987). *Police Interrogation: A Handbook for Investigators.* London: Police Review Publishing.

Wang, Z., Inslicht, S. S., Metzler, T. J., Henn-Haase, C. McCaslin S. E., Tong, H., Neylan, T. C., & Marmar, C. R. (2010). A prospective study of predictors of depression symptoms in police. *Psychiatry Research, 175,* 211–216.

Warnick, D. H. & Saunders, G. S. (1980). The effects of group discussion on eyewitness accuracy. *Journal of Applied Social Psychology, 10,* 249–59.

Wells, G. L. & Murray, D. M. (1984). Eyewitness confi dence. In G. L. Wells & E. F. Loftus (Eds.), *Eyewitness Testimony: Psychological Perspectives* (pp. 155–1170). Cambridge: Cambridge University Press.

Wells, G. L. & Olson, E. A. (2003). Eyewitness testimony. *Annual Review of Psychology, 54*, 277–295.

Whipple, G. M. (1909). The observer as reporter: A survey of the "psychology of testimony". *Psychological Bulletin, 6*, 153–170.

—— (1918). The obtaining of information: Psychology of observation and report. *Psychological Bulletin, 15*, 217–248.

White, M. D., Cooper, J. A., Saunders, J., & Raganella, A. J. (2010). Motivations for becoming a police officer: Re-assessing officer attitudes and job satisfaction after six years on the street. *Journal of Criminal Justice, 38*, 520–530.

Wilcock, R., Bull, R., & Milne, R. (2008). *Witness Identification in Criminal Cases: Psychology and Practice.* Oxford: Oxford University Press.

Wilson, D. B., McClure, D., & Weisburd, D. (2010). Does forensic DNA help to solve crime? The benefit of sophisticated answers to naive questions. *Journal of Contemporary Criminal Justice, 26*, 458–469.

Wilson, S. & Zhao, J. (2008). Determining the correlates of police victimization: An analysis of organizational level factors on injurious assaults. *Journal of Criminal Justice, 36*, 461–468.

Wolchover, D. & Heaton-Armstrong, A. (2006). Improving visual identification procedures under Pace Code D. In A. Heaton-Armstrong, E. Shepherd, G. Gudjonsson, & D. Wolchover (Eds.), *Witness Testimony: Psychological, Investigative and Evidential Procedures* (pp. 309–326). Oxford: Oxford University Press.

Woodhams, J., Hollin, C. R., & Bull, R. (2007). The psychology of linking crimes: A review of the evidence. *Legal and Criminological Psychology, 12*, 233–249.

Woodhams, J. & Toye, K. (2007). An empirical test of the assumptions of case linkage and offender profiling with serial commercial robberies. *Psychology, Public Policy, and Law, 13*, 59–85.

Woodworth, M., Porter, S., ten Brinke, L., Doucette, N. L., Peace, K., & Campbell, M. A. (2009). A comparison of memory for homicide, non-homicidal violence, and positive life experiences. *International Journal of Law and Psychiatry, 32*, 329–334.

World Health Organization (1992). *ICD-10: The ICD-10 Classification of Mental and Behavioural Disorders: Clinical Descriptions and Diagnostic Guidelines.* Geneva: WHO.

Wright, D. B. & Skagerberg E. M. (2007). Postidentification feedback affects real eyewitnesses. *Psychological Science, 18*, 172–178.

Yarmey, A. D. (1986). Verbal, visual and voice identification of a rape suspect under different levels of illumination. *Journal of Applied Psychology, 71*, 363–370.

Youngs, D. (2004). Personality correlates of offence style. *Journal of Investigative Psychology and Offender Profiling, 1*, 99–119.

Zhao, W., Chellappa, R., Phillips, P. J., & Rosenfeld, A. (2003). Face recognition: A literature survey. *ACM Computing Surveys, 35*, 399–458.

Zuckerman, M., Kuhlman, D. M., Joireman, J., Teta, P., & Kraft, M. (1993). A comparison of three structural models for personality: the big three, the big five, and the alternative five. *Journal of Personality and Social Psychology, 65*, 757–768.

10 Psychology in the courtroom

When the police have gathered evidence and the decision is made to prosecute the suspect – see the section on the Crown Prosecution Service in the previous chapter – then a new set of actors enter the drama. The courtroom is the stage on which they perform, playing out decisions of guilt and innocence, liberty and custody, and in some instances even life and death.

In England and Wales there are a range of courts, with varying levels of responsibility, within the justice system. These courts range from the County Court, which deals with civil cases, to the Magistrates' Court, the Crown Court, and the High Court, and ultimately to the Court of Appeal, the House of Lords, and finally the European Court of Justice and the European Court of Human Rights. There are different court systems in place all round the world (including Scotland and Northern Ireland).

The involvement of psychologists in courtroom proceedings has a long history, which Bartol and Bartol (1999) have traced to Cattell's (1895) study of the psychology of testimony. Cattell's work was the starting point for a number of studies (e.g., Binet, 1900; Bolton, 1896), which in the early 20th century grew to become a substantial body of empirical evidence on witness memory which was reviewed annually by Whipple (1909–15, 1917, 1918). Indeed, even the great Sigmund Freud showed interest in this new application of psychology, with a paper titled *Psychoanalysis and the Ascertaining of Truth in Courts of Law* (Freud, 1906). Notwithstanding the earlier work of G. F. Arnold (1906; Bornstein & Penrod, 2008), the dominant figure of the period was the American-based German psychologist Hugo Münsterberg who, in 1908, published the book *On The Witness Stand* in which he proposed that psychology could be beneficially applied to the work of the courts. Münsterberg particularly drew attention to the psychologist's understanding of perception and memory, arguing that this gave the psychologist a special insight into the vagaries of witness testimony. As is inevitably the case with any radical idea, Münsterberg's suggestions drew criticism, this time from some of the legal profession (Moore, 1907).

As chronicled by historians of the study of witness memory (Greer, 1971; Sporer, 1982), in the late 1920s the interests of psychologists – although not lawyers (Brown, 1926) – turned away from applied memory research. In the 1950s and 1960s, only occasional relevant works appeared, with very little in the way of fresh empirical data (Haward, 1963; Kubie, 1959; Marshall, 1966; Rouke, 1957; Wall, 1965). However, the late 1960s and early 1970s saw a full turn of the cycle with a return to the study of eyewitness memory, which flourished in the following decades (see Chapter 9).

Alongside witness testimony, Münsterberg (1914) also saw the jury as a suitable topic for psychological investigation. Not content with defining these two major research areas, Münsterberg, a prolific and controversial writer (Hale, 1980), was influential in making the

---

Box 10.1 Conducting courtroom research

The courtroom is not a natural home for researchers, given the safeguards that are rightly in place to protect the probity and confidentiality of proceedings. For example, in some jurisdictions direct observation or recording of jury deliberations is not allowed, nor is interviewing jurors and witnesses. As Hope (2010: 677) points out with reference to the Contempt of Court Act 1981, 'Under English law it is illegal to "obtain, disclose or solicit and particular statements made, opinions expressed, arguments advanced or votes cast by members of a jury in the course of their deliberations"'.

This situation has led researchers to adopt various procedures, such as mock trials and jury simulations, by which to study the social dynamics of the courtroom and introduce experimental manipulation of variables such as type of information, gender of the accused, and so forth. However, as is evident from the critique presented by Kerr and Bray (2005), there are a range of difficulties with these approaches. These problems include the artificiality of the simulations and the lack of ecological validity, in turn meaning that the generalisability of the research, i.e., the extent to which it tells us about real-life, is seriously compromised.

---

case for the psychologist in the courtroom as an expert witness. While not actually testifying himself, as the expert witness was not then accepted in American courts, Münsterberg did act as a consultant in two murder cases. Of course, the presence of a psychologist as an expert witness in court is now accepted in many countries, although conducting courtroom research is more difficult (Box 10.1).

The focus of this chapter will be on the three areas highlighted by Munsterberg – eyewitness testimony, the jury, and the psychologist as expert witness – which have dominated psychology in the courtroom.

Witness testimony in court

The force of much of the research over the past decades has been to illuminate the factors that might influence the accuracy of witness testimony. A number of surveys have indicated that the general public has a partial understanding of these factors and, as such, may believe that witness memory is more reliable than is actually the case (Deffenbacher & Loftus, 1982; Noon & Hollin, 1987). It is also known that mistaken eyewitness identification has been at the heart of several miscarriages of justice (Hain, 1976; Scheck, Neufeld, & Dwyer, 2001). In this light, given that some members of the public are potential jurors, a related line of research has looked at the impact of eyewitness testimony on the jury.

Loftus (1980) carried out a study in which mock jurors read one of three case summaries, containing circumstantial evidence of the defendant's guilt, of an armed robbery and a murder. In one account there was no eyewitness, in the second the eyewitness evidence was not called into question, and in the third the eyewitness was revealed to have poor vision. In the no eyewitness condition, 18 per cent of mock jurors said the defendant was guilty; in the unchallenged eyewitness condition, 72 per cent said guilty; in the discredited eyewitness condition, 68 per cent said guilty. Loftus drew two conclusions from these results: (1) eyewitness evidence can be a powerful determinant of jury decisions; (2) this power is virtually undiminished even when the witness is less than perfect.

Penrod and Cutler (1995) reviewed the evidence on witness testimony, including the witness's level of confidence, and came to the following view:

> Taken together, the survey studies, the prediction studies, and the mock juror experiments converge on a worrisome set of conclusions about jurors' abilities. Jurors appear to overestimate the accuracy of identifications ... do not distinguish accurate from inaccurate eyewitnesses, and are generally insensitive to factors that influence eyewitness identification accuracy.
>
> (Penrod & Cutler, 1995: 822)

Penrod and Cutler also make the point that, despite the equivocal nature of the relationship in practice, jurors perceive the confident witness as an accurate witness.

If eyewitness testimony can have an undue effect on the jury what can be done to readjust the balance? One solution is to bring an expert into the court in order to present an expert account of the extant evidence. This point does not, of course, just apply to psychologists. There are many instances in which what would appear to be straightforward evidence is not all that it seems. For example, it might be thought that images collected via closed circuit television (CCTV) are solid, incontrovertible evidence. However, as Porter (2009: 14) shows from his analysis of CCTV images: 'How we interpret CCTV images as evidence is also more complex than what it may appear. Establishing an understanding of what is "real or distorted", "true or untrue" requires an understanding of visual culture aspects that relate directly to forensic science'. Indeed, dealing in evidence from visual images can be a decidedly tricky business (Lassiter, 2002). The complexities of genetics in understanding behaviour may also be an issue with which the courts may have to struggle. Denno (2006) discusses a case in which an appeal against the death penalty was arguably compromised by the absence of evidence from testing for genetic deficiencies. So, if there is a role for the psychologist in court as an expert witness what would this role entail?

The psychologist as expert witness

Haward (1987) suggests that the psychologist may be called to give an expert opinion into two broad areas. First, *medical* advice to the court, which may fall into one of three categories: (1) *neurological*, as seen in the assessment of the effects of brain injury; (2) *psychiatric* in relation to mental disorder and psychological distress; (3) *psychological medicine*, as in the psychological aspects of recovery. The psychological evidence, as Haward suggests, draws on the psychologist's scientific knowledge of human functioning, including cognition, affect, sensation, and perception, alongside an understanding of individual differences and the distribution of human abilities.

In his later work, Haward refined the role of the psychologist as expert witness into four types, which he called the experimental role, the clinical (assessment) role, the actuarial role, and the advisory role (Gudjonsson & Haward, 1998). These four roles are not mutually exclusive: for example, clinical-experimental evidence may be given or actuarial evidence may be informed by experimental findings.

The experimental role

There are two sides to the experimental role. In the first, the psychologist may inform the court of the extant findings of experimental research that are relevant to a given case.

The previous discussion regarding the accuracy and reliability of eyewitness testimony provides a perfect example of this aspect of the experimental role.

The second part of the experimental role, which follows the tradition started by Münsterberg, is for the psychologist to conduct laboratory or field studies in order to resolve an issue central to the outcome of a trial. Gudjonsson and Haward (1998) present several examples of the experimental role, which may involve re-creating a given situation, then observing and recording performance in that setting to determine the degree of similarity between the evidence presented to the court and the findings from the experimental investigation. Thus, studies have been conducted to aid the court in questions of identification, the effects of drugs and alcohol, industrial hazards, faking of psychiatric symptoms, and accuracy of maritime vision. In an example of this role, Haward (1979) describes assessing whether a policeman could, as he claimed, have taken the registration numbers of four motorcycles as they travelled at high speed through a village. Using 100 people with perfect eyesight as observers, with identical lighting conditions to those at the time of the incident, Haward found that the policeman's claims were not substantiated by the experimental results.

However, as Haward notes, there is a difference between the probabilistic statements based on population sampling that result from experimental studies, and statements of 'fact' and 'truth' in a particular case which is what the court demands. Thus, Haward states:

> The fact that a hundred people found it impossible to see X in conditions Y does not prove that it was impossible for police constable Z. It may be highly improbable, but the impossibility of an event is beyond scientific proof … When the forensic scientist is asked 'Could this policeman have possibly done it?', he, as a scientist, has to reply 'Yes, it is possible', however unlikely the event.
>
> (Haward, 1979: 48)

There is a great deal of experimental evidence on eyewitness memory and there are two rationales for expert testimony on eyewitness evidence: (1) jurors are too ready to believe eyewitness evidence; (2) jurors are not always able to discriminate between reliable and unreliable witnesses and the circumstances that effect the reliability of memory. An expert witness with knowledge of the eyewitness research may be able to inform the jury about the reliability of eyewitness testimony. Martire and Kemp (2009, 2011) conducted a review of the literature on the effects on jurors of expert testimony on eyewitness testimony, including 24 studies in their review, which covers the empirical literature from 1980. They remarked on the wide range of research designs for such a small body of work and also how the strength of the research findings varied according to the design employed by individual studies. Martire and Kemp concluded that the case remains to be proven that expert testimony regarding eyewitness testimony significantly influences jury decision-making.

The clinical role

In the clinical role, the psychologist's testimony may be given individually or in conjunction with other experts. For example, in cases of brain injury, which may be related to compensation claims, medical experts may testify on the nature and extent of the physical damage, while the psychologist may inform the court of associated levels of cognitive impairment or behaviour change. The clinical psychologist may be concerned with an offender's level of psychological disturbance and state of mind or their intellectual functioning. The clinical evidence may be based on interview, case records, psychometric tests, and experimental evidence.

Clinical opinions may be relevant in a variety of types of case in both the civil and criminal courts (Campbell, 2010; Carlin, 2010).

The psychologist may also be called upon to give an opinion with respect to an individual's ability to understand the legal proceedings in which they are engaged: in the UK this is referred to as *fitness to plead*, in the USA as *competency to stand trial* (Pirelli, Gottdiener, & Zapf, 2011; Polythress & Zapf, 2009; Rogers, Blackwood, Farnham, Pickup, & Watts, 2008). The principle here is that the accused should be able to comprehend the trial proceedings in order to be able to make a proper defence, understand the evidence, and give proper instructions to his or her legal representatives. A wide range of formal tests of competence have been devised (Grisso, 2003), although they are mainly used in the USA rather than the UK.

The actuarial role

In this capacity, the psychologist may provide an estimate of the probability or of the range or average of some event. This type of evidence may be seen in the civil courts as, for example, in road traffic accident cases where loss of earnings are to be calculated. The psychologist may give evidence on the range of earnings of people of different levels of intelligence, or comment on the frequency of certain types of social behaviour.

The advisory role

In this role, the psychologist is not engaged as an expert witness by either the defence or the prosecution, rather they are outside the adversarial process in order to inform the court on technical matters. In America, it is not unusual for the psychologist to be a 'Friend of the Court', however this is much rarer in England, where it is more usual for the psychologist to sit with counsel commenting on testimony and noting points to follow up in the cross-examination of another expert witness.

Psychologists in court

The process of giving evidence, either in writing (Weiner, 1999) or verbally (Hess, 1999), demands an understanding of the functioning of the courtroom and its use of evidence alongside the skill of presenting evidence in court. Gudjonsson and Hayward (1998) discuss several surveys of psychologists' involvement in presenting evidence in court.

As shown in Table 10.1, the 1995 survey of members of the British Psychological Society showed that psychologists were involved in a wide range of issues in preparing expert witness reports for court (Gudjonsson, 1985).

One of the professional dilemmas that psychologists may face in court lies in requests to disclosure psychometric test material. Gudjonsson (1985) reported that more than one-quarter

Table 10.1 The five issues most often addressed in court reports by psychologists (after Gudjonsson & Haward, 1998)

1. Post-traumatic stress disorder (PTSD)
2. Compensation (other than PTSD)
3. Childcare
4. Sentencing/disposal (treatment)
5. Mitigation (no treatment)

of psychologists in his survey had been asked to give details of test content in open court. This topic raises a number of problems: (1) disclosure may breech client confidentiality; (2) disclosure may influence the validity and reliability of any further testing with a given individual; (3) most psychometric tests are designed to be administered and scored as a whole so that questioning the relevance of individual test items may be misleading; (4) public disclosure may create a situation in which the general public has access to test material that is not available to psychologists without the appropriate postgraduate qualifications. However, if disclosure is requested by the court then it cannot be refused, which has proved a matter of some concern (Heim, 1982; Tunstall, Gudjonsson, Eysenck, & Haward, 1982a,b).

The distribution of psychological test material in open court raises another fundamental issue: circulation of test material implicitly states that the lay public acting as jurors are qualified to comment on the validity of any given psychometric test. The inference is that psychological evidence is simply 'common sense' and therefore the psychologist as expert can be dismissed as having nothing to offer beyond what is generally understood regardless of their training in psychology.

The view which the court might hold that psychology is nothing more than common sense is of some concern. It follows from this proposition that: (a) either psychologists are fooling themselves about their specialist knowledge, or (b) the court has an incomplete understanding of psychology. It is not difficult, however, to point to areas in which the psychologist has discrete skills and knowledge, beyond what may be expected of the 'ordinary person'. Indeed, the book *Beyond Common Sense: Psychological Science in the Courtroom* (Borida & Fiske, 2008) discusses a range of topics – including prejudice, gender stereotyping, eyewitness testimony, and false confessions – where psychological knowledge outstrips common sense. It is not difficult to think of other such topics, such as neuropsychological assessment and psychological development in children, where specialist psychological knowledge is likely to be more refined and advanced than that of the layperson.

The view in the courtroom of psychological expertise as common sense may in fact be a specific instance of a more general belief in the banality of matters psychological. Colman (1981) lists more than 20 examples of findings from psychological research that show that 'common sense' is not always correct in predicting human behaviour.

To generalise or not to generalise?

Now, having made the point that there is a discrete body of knowledge labelled *psychological*, does it follow that this knowledge must necessarily be presented in court? The sticking point here is the notion of *generalisabilty*, the degree to which psychological research can be taken and applied to the 'real world'. In other words, is the realism of psychological research of such a level that its findings can be directly extrapolated to real life?

The issue of the generalisabilty of psychological research has been debated extensively for both jury studies (Kerr & Bray, 2005) and eyewitness memory (Wells & Hasel, 2008). There are a range of threats to generalisability that flow from experimental research such as the use of staged crimes, filmed sequences, mock juries, the participant's awareness of the aims of the research, and the absence of realism. Aronson and Carlsmith (1968) suggested that the realism of an experiment can be viewed in two ways: first, *experimental realism* refers to the degree of authenticity the experiment holds for the subjects; second, *mundane realism* is the extent to which laboratory conditions are likely to occur in real life. In applied research, it is highly advantageous to have high levels of both experimental and mundane realism so that each piece of evidence, each experiment, should be judged on its own merits.

Critics of experimental studies rightly point to the issue of generalization (Konečni & Ebbesen, 1986). However, there are several reasons why a good degree of generalisation from the laboratory to the real world might be expected. Take, for example, the common practice of using university students as participants in psychological experiments: generally speaking, students are above average intelligence, are familiar with laboratory and test conditions, and are used to having their performance assessed. To obtain, for example, poor memory performance with students, it might be argued, suggests equally poor, if not worse, performance in the remainder of the population.

The issue of generalisabilty can be approached empirically: do people perform significantly differently in the laboratory as in real life? Yuille and Cutshall (1986) presented a case study of eyewitness memory in which 13 of 21 real-life eyewitnesses to a shooting incident were re-interviewed 4–5 months after the incident. Yuille and Cutshall's results were contrary to what might have been predicted on the basis of laboratory findings. Does this finding mean we should dismiss the findings from laboratory research?

The problem is that field studies, interesting as they are, fall prey to criticisms that are the very strength of laboratory research, that is the degree of *control* the investigator has over the study. Thus, in the Yuille and Cutshall study, it is not known how much witnesses have talked with each other, how accurate the missing 38 per cent of witnesses would be, how much influence newspaper and television coverage has had, and so on. As with laboratory studies, considerable caution is required with the findings from real-life studies. While field studies are high in realism, there are advantages to tightly controlled experimental studies. As is generally the case in applied psychology, the strongest evidence comes from a confluence of the findings from a range of methodologies, including laboratory studies, case studies, field studies, and archival studies.

It is a fact that many psychologists now act as expert witness in a wide range of types of case in many jurisdictions. The general acceptance of the psychologist in court in the role of expert witness has led some countries to formulate rules to govern the flow of expert evidence (see Box 10.2).

The jury: a brief history

A great deal has been written about the history of the jury in England from its beginnings in the 11th century, when the notion was probably brought into England following the Norman

---

Box 10.2 Rules regarding admitting expert evidence in court (after Freckleton & Selby, 2002)

1. *Expertise:* Does the witness have the level of knowledge and experience to act as an expert witness and inform the court on a particular area?
2. *Common knowledge:* Is the expert's knowledge necessary or is it in fact generally understood and common sense?
3. *Area of expertise:* Is the expert's knowledge and expertise recognised as such by other experts?
4. *Ultimate issue:* Will the expert's evidence decide the issue? (If so, it may well be rejected by the court.)
5. *Basis rule:* Can an expert's opinion be drawn from matters outside their own observations (meaning that it cannot be evaluated by the court)?

Conquest in 1066 (Cockburn & Green, 1988). The Norman system was that a group of local individuals were placed under oath (*jurare*, to swear) to be truthful on a range of local matters. After 1066, the role of the jury in England evolved to become that of adjudicator in civil and criminal disputes. Henry II (1133–89), who ruled as King of England from 1154 to 1189, promoted the role of juries in his reforms of the English criminal justice system. At a time of much crime, the legal system then depended on the sworn accusations of individuals to bring a criminal before the court. However, this procedure held a risk for the accuser, who would be punished if the accused was found innocent. In addition, the traditional methods of determining the guilt of the accused, through trial by oath-helping and ordeal, were becoming unpopular. The procedure of oath-helping allowed the person accused to find a group of respectable people who would swear an oath avowing their trustworthiness. Trial by ordeal was based on the principle of *judicium Dei*, a judgement by God in favour of the innocent. Thus, the accused was thrown into cold water to see if he or she floated, or they were made to walk on hot irons as the innocent would emerge unscathed while the guilty suffered.

The thinking of those in power during the 12th century began to doubt both methods. The ease with which oath-helping can be manipulated is palpably obvious, but some religious men were apprehensive about trial by ordeal. It was felt that an appeal to God was unworthy because justice as judged by the people was sufficient to deal fairly with for the peoples' problems. The system evolved of selecting 12 free and lawful men from the local neighbourhood who were required to answer questions of common knowledge put to them under oath by the king's judges. These 12 men, called jurymen, were experienced in resolving various local issues with their particular knowledge of the circumstances of claims and disputes.

This system worked well and was extended to determine claims to legal ownership. Thus, a freeholder whose title to own his land was challenged could have his claim tried in the king's court. In the presence of the king's judges, 12 knights of the shire would declare under oath which of the two parties had the better case for ownership: once it was made and declared their decision was final. The use of jurymen was extended to the criminal justice system so that 12 ordinary men – men without knowledge of the law who based their decisions on ordinary common sense and therefore without doubt the most impartial judges of all – listened to the facts of a case and were required to decide whether these facts were true. It was said that, given the safeguards of the law, there could be no fairer way by which a man may be judged.

In much more recent times, the jury has been the subject of a great deal of research, including psychological research, ranging from the expansive, such as regional variations in the use of juries (Duff, 1999) and whether juries are needed at all (Lloyd-Bostock & Thomas, 1999); to the fine-grained, as seen in studies of how juries make decisions (Devine, Clayton, Dunford, Seying, & Pryce, 2000; Spellman & Kincannon, 2001). This research into juries has spanned decades, from the early investigations of Münsterberg to more contemporary landmark studies in both Britain (Baldwin & McConville, 1979) and America (Hans & Vidmar, 1986). The interests of psychologists in juries have been principally in four areas: (1) the impact of expert evidence on jury decisions; (2) the effects of extra-evidential influences on jury decisions; (3) the composition of the jury; and (4) jury decision-making. The optimum statistical methods for jury research have also been of concern: Wright, Strubler, and Vallano (2011) suggest that methods to handle multivariate data are much more appropriate for jury research than the comparative statistics often used in psychological research.

However, before considering these psychological concerns there are several general points to note about the jury itself.

Juror selection

Who can sit on a jury? In most jurisdictions there are formal criteria, such as age, eligibility to vote, residency, and not having a diagnosable mental disorder, which are used to determine whether an individual qualifies for jury service. However, an individual may satisfy these formal criteria yet, arguably, still not be ideally suited for the demands of jury service. Thus, someone may be thought unsuitable because of their extreme political or social views, or because of their exposure to pre-trial publicity, or because they are likely to react favourably or unfavourably to some characteristic of the defendant, or because it is doubtful if they would be competent to understand highly complex evidence. In the light of these possibilities, it makes sense to have a procedure to screen out those individuals unsuitable for jury service in a given trial.

The formal process of screening is called *Voir Dire* and its purpose is to allow counsel to select jurors to hear a case. The conduct of the *Voir Dire* test varies from jurisdiction to jurisdiction. In England, any objections must be well-founded, such as when a potential juror personally knows the defendant, in order to be admissible. However, in other jurisdictions, including Australia, Canada, France, the Republic of Ireland, and the USA, the defence and the prosecution are allowed a certain number of unconditional challenges without having to justify a request to reject a specific juror. These challenges may be made by the defence on the belief that jurors of professions or backgrounds that are similar to the victim's may identify and be unduly sympathetic towards them, while the prosecution may seek to exclude jurors who may display undue empathy towards the defendant. However, it is questionable whether in fact jury selection actually functions to introduce a fresh source of bias (Comiskey, 2011; Norton, Sommers, & Brauner, 2007).

In some American courts there may be the need to assemble a *death-qualified jury* for those cases where the prosecution intends to pursue the death penalty. This is a unique type of jury in that they take responsibility for determining the defendant's guilt *and* the sentence. In order to have a death-qualified jury, all members who disagree with capital punishment are removed so that the jury, should they so wish, would be willing to give a sentence of death. However, there is a potential confound inherent in this approach as death-qualified jurors may be generally more likely to be punishment-orientated (see below) and more likely to return a guilty verdict (Butler & Moran, 2007).

Scientific jury selection

If jurors are to be selected, is there a better way of doing it than relying on such broad factors as background and occupation or should more sophisticated psychological testing be used? Should the process of selection be conducted by a judge? How far should the process go in terms of questioning to 'trap' unsuitable jurors? These questions have crystallised into a debate on the merits and otherwise of *scientific jury selection* (Lieberman & Sales, 2007). Those in favour of scientific jury selection argue for a systematic, empirically-based selection method to produce the fairest outcome in court; those against hold that selection is unfair, unsafe, unethical, and improper and will produce a jury that at best is not representative of the community and at worst is potentially biased.

In an early attempt at scientific jury selection, Kassin and Wrightsman (1983) constructed a Juror Bias Scale to measure individual differences in pre-trail bias among jurors. The scale assesses each juror's pre-trial expectancies that the defendant is guilty, and their values regarding conviction and punishment. In mock juror evaluation studies, the scale reliably detected individuals who were 'prosecution biased' in that they were more ready to return a guilty verdict and held less stringent standards on reasonable doubt.

The situation in America has moved on from scales to assess bias with the advent of 'jury consultants' and 'trial consultants'. This type of consultancy has become widespread in America with substantial numbers of companies offering 'scientific jury selection services', at a considerable cost. The methods they use include a mixture of demographic analysis and social psychology to sift potential jurors so as to produce the 'perfect' panel.

Twelve good men and true?

Why other than historical precedent should a jury consist of 12 people? There are various explanations on offer without any widely accepted conclusion. Miller (1998: 632) makes the comment that: 'Although the issue has been studied and debated for more than a century, there is still no agreement about it. Scholars have traced the origins to sources as diverse as ancient Greece, the Roman Conquest, the Biblical importance of the number twelve, ancient reliance on court astrologers, the Anglo-Saxon era in England, the Norman Conquest, the Assize of Clarendon, and the Magna Carta'.

However, not all jurisdictions require 12 jurors: Scotland uses 15 jurors, Norway has 10, and in Hong Kong 7 or 9 may be used. Some American courts have experimented with five- and six-person juries, which has generated a debate about whether the reduced number is unconstitutional (Miller, 1998; Smith & Saks, 2008). In England and Wales, once a trial has started in either the Crown Court or High Court, if a juror or jurors become indisposed or is discharged then the trial may continue with up to a minimum of nine jurors.

Is there any merit in smaller juries? It could be argued, for example, that a reduction in size would not impair jury functioning, would increase their efficiency, and would certainly reduce financial costs. The counter argument is that smaller juries are less likely to be representative of the community, may not engage in group discussion, and may not consider the evidence in sufficient detail. Of the six-person jury, Winick (1979: 85) states: 'They are more likely to enter the jury room with their minds made up so that they are, in effect, polling their members rather than deliberating the case'. Saks and Marti (1997) conducted a meta-analysis of the decision-making of 6- and 12-person juries. They found that juries with 12 people spent more time deliberating the evidence, which is not surprising given that there are more people, but that their verdicts were not significantly different. Waller, Hope Burrows, and Morrison (2011) found that if the larger unit of 12 jurors was broken down in three subgroups of four, then the subgroups were more functional in terms of each individual juror making a contribution to the larger task.

As yet there is no right answer on the issue of jury size and, as seen in America, the issue may become enmeshed in issues of national jurisprudence and legal tradition regardless of what any evidence may indicate.

Extra-evidential influences

The basis of the adversarial system is that the evidence presented in the courtroom, along with judicial instructions regarding the evidence, is what provides the jurors with the information upon which to base their decision making. However, there are several extra-evidential factors that can influence juries: these include (1) pre-trial publicity; (2) the personal characteristics of the witness; (3) juror prejudices towards others in the courtroom.

Pre-trial publicity

There are some criminal cases that attract a great deal of publicity either locally, nationally, or internationally. It is not difficult to think of examples of infamous court cases: as I wrote this chapter, the Amanda Knox case, in which she and a co-defendant appealed against their sentences for murder, dominated the media with informed (and uniformed) comments on every aspect of the proceedings. Now, in the Knox case the appeal was heard by a panel of judges who would have the fair application of the process of law rather than trial by media at forefront of their thoughts. However, what of those cases where a jury is aware of and subject to the media storm surrounding a given case? There are various steps that the judge can take to try to restrict pre-trial publicity including a gag order (sometimes referred to as a gagging order or a suppression order), or restricting any of those involved – witnesses, police, courtroom personnel – from disclosing information to the press. Nonetheless, there are trials during which the charge has been made that adverse pre-trial publicity has influenced court proceedings. The concern here is that the pre-trial publicity sways the verdict of the jury and influences the length of sentence in cases of a guilty verdict (Ruva, McEvoy, & Becker-Bryant, 2007).

In a typical experimental study of pre-trial publicity, Padawer-Singer and Barton (1974) gave a group of mock jurors newspaper cuttings about a defendant's criminal record and their retracted confession. A second group of mock jurors read newspaper stories that omitted the biasing details. The two groups then listened to audio-tapes of the trial: of the jurors exposed to the pre-trial publicity, 78 per cent returned a guilty verdict; of the unexposed group, 55 per cent said guilty.

Kovera and Greathouse (2008: 263) review the psychological studies of the effects of pre-trial publicity and suggest that it 'has a negative influence on both pretrial and posttrial judgements of defendant guilt'.

There has also been concern about what has become known as the '*CSI* effect'. Kim, Barak, and Shelton (2009: 452) explain that the *CSI* effect refers to an 'alleged or supposed influence that watching television shows like *CSI: Crime Scene Investigation* has on juror decision-making during the workings of a criminal trial'. A 2008 paper by the Honourable Donald E. Shelton in the US Department of Justice, *National Institute of Justice Journal*, suggested that audiences for forensic dramas in the USA are around 100 million viewers per week. The chances are that next day some of those viewers will be reporting for jury service and some, if not all, will have been influenced by what they saw. However, as Shelton notes, the evidence suggests that while *CSI*-watching jurors had higher expectations of forensic evidence being made available, such expectations were not associated with an increased propensity to convict.

How can pre-trial influences be countered? There may be judicial instructions to jurors to ignore or forget biasing material but they do not appear to reduce the effects of the adverse material (Fein, McCloskey, & Tomlinson, 1997). Other solutions may be to try to select unbiased jurors, which would rely upon a reliable means of assessing the pre-trial knowledge and prejudice of each juror, or even changing the venue of the trial if local feelings and attendant publicity are inflamed.

Interpersonal perception

When members of a jury hear the evidence and see the defendant, the witnesses, and the families of those involved who sit in the gallery there is a strong chance that there will be various extra-evidential influences that may sway their judgements. As people, jurors may experience a range of emotions, from disgust through to sympathy, that may influence how they evaluate the evidence. Jurors will have their own individual irrational prejudices that may influence their views of the personal qualities of those involved. There are several dimensions of person perception that may influence jurors including the more obvious examples of age, gender, physical attractiveness, race, and socioeconomic status (Hans & Vidmar, 1986; Mazzella & Feingold, 1994; Sommers, 2006, 2007; Stevenson & Bottoms, 2009; Thomas, 2010).

There may be subtle interactions between the personal qualities of the jurors and the defendant. For example, in a mock jury study reported by Pozzulo, Dempsey, Maeder, and Allen (2010) the jurors were asked to give credibility ratings for a 12-year-old victim when the gender of the victim was presented as either male or female while the defendant was presented as a young (15 years) male or young female or an older (40 years) male or female. The females rated the victim higher on accuracy, truthfulness, and believability than the male jurors; while the males rated the defendant higher on reliability, credibility, truthfulness, and believability than the females. The males were more likely than female jurors to believe that the victim was complicit in and took some responsibility for the crime. The victim was seen as having more responsibility for the crime when the defendant was older rather than younger; female jurors gave higher responsibility for the offence to the defendant than did the males. Pozzulo et al. found higher ratings of guilt when the defendant was a male.

There may be other subtle influences at play. Conley, O'Barr, and Lind (1978) reported that 'powerful speech', speaking clearly and without prevarication, led to witnesses being seen as more convincing, competent, trustworthy, intelligent and truthful.

The disclosure of personal details about those involved in the trial may also influence the views of jurors. An usual study reported by Stevenson, Bottoms, and Diamond (2010) was carried out with people over the age of 18 years who had been called for jury service at courthouses in Cook County Illinois but had not been selected for trials on the day the study was conducted. The real/mock jurors were shown a tape of a sentencing hearing to determine if the defendant should be sentenced to death having been found guilty of murder and armed robbery.

The tape showed a mock trial with professional actors playing the roles of judge, attorneys, and witnesses. The judge introduced the case, informing those present that the defendant, guilty of the charges laid, had previous convictions for attempted robbery and murder. The case involved attempted robbery by the defendant and an accomplice in which the victim was shot and killed trying to resist the attack. The task of the jury was to consider whether the defendant should receive the death penalty for his conviction for murder (the law in Illinois requires that jurors should consider not just the crimes committed by the defendant but any aggravating and mitigating factors to determine whether the defendant should be executed). The mock jurors were given a full description of the crime and they heard the testimony of witnesses and the opening and closing statements from the lawyers. The defence stated that the defendant had been drinking at the time of the crime, that he had been an alcoholic from 12 years of age, and that he was physically abused by his father when he was a child. The defendant's sister testified that the defendant's violence was primarily due to alcohol and that he was good with her children. The sister also testified that she and her brother (the defendant) had as children been sexually and physically abused by their father. She also said that her brother was not a violent man except sometimes when he was very drunk, and she testified that in her view he was willing to change and accept treatment for his alcoholism. The prosecution's testimony let it be known that that the defendant had six prior convictions including two for armed robbery, while a psychiatrist testified that the defendant had a high risk of committing more offences.

Stevenson et al. were concerned to find out how the disclosure of details about the defendant's past would influence jury decision-making. Would knowledge of his childhood abuse and later alcoholism be seen as offering a degree of mitigation for the current offence? The analysis of the jurors' statements showed a belief that the defendant could have controlled any adverse effects of the childhood abuse and so his abusive experiences were not an explanation for the crime. Thus, the jurors took the position that the child abuse was *not* a mitigating factor and the defendant should be held fully responsible for his behaviour. A similar position was evident for the alcohol use: the jurors agreed that the defendant was not responsible for his actions when drunk, however he was responsible for the decision to drink excessively, which ultimately made him responsible for the crime. The jurors were also highly sceptical about the prospect of the success of any attempt at treatment of the defendant's drink problem.

The jurors who supported the use of the death penalty were more likely to discount the role of child abuse and alcoholism than those jurors without such views. Stevenson et al. (2010: 30–1) conclude that their findings 'adds a further empirical example of just how powerful attitudes toward the death penalty are; it seems they nearly function as a proxy for a general punitive worldview. In addition to relations between pro-death penalty attitudes and pro-prosecution attitudes and judgments we noted in the introduction, research finds that those who support the death penalty also tend to be higher in authoritarianism, dogmatism, a belief in a just world, and need for vengeance and retribution'.

In the real world of the courtroom it is, of course, impossible to know just how much jurors' decision-making is swayed by their perceptions of defendants, witnesses, and so on. However, estimates from both jurors and mock juror studies suggest that the actual evidence presented during the trial has by far the greatest effect on jurors (Kalven & Zeisel, 1966; Tanford & Penrod, 1982; Visher, 1987).

Jury competence: judicial instructions

The task of the jurors is to listen to the evidence, including any expert witnesses, then to assimilate what has been presented before retiring to reach a verdict. It is part of due process that the jurors must always consider the evidence within the context and boundaries of the law. Thus, there may be times during the trial when the jury is directed by the judge to ignore extra-legal influences, such as newspaper reports, and any inadmissible evidence that may have been heard. At the end of the trial, the jury is presented by the judge with a summing up of the case and associated points of law. The judge's instructions (or *jury charge* as it is sometimes called) are given to ensure that the jury is certain of the facts in the case, has knowledge of the law and knows how to apply the law to the facts. The immediate question raised by judicial instructions is whether jurors can both comprehend the judge's remarks and then apply them to their decision-making.

A substantial number of studies, using a range of methodologies – including questioning jurors directly (after the trail), field studies, and mock jury – have examined juror comprehension of judicial instructions. In their review, Ogloff and Rose (2005: 413) make the trenchant comment that '[t]he general picture that emerges from real jurors is that they genuinely seem to believe that they understand and follow judicial instructions, but also, that it is unlikely that they really do so'. Why should this be the case?

The style and the complexity of language used in court is critically important. Highly complex evidence may be very difficult to follow, while the use of legal and archaic terminology may limit how comprehensible the instructions are to jurors. Elwork, Sales, and Alfini (1982) found that 39 per cent of mock jurors who viewed a videotaped trial (in which the verdict was known) and received standard instructions made incorrect verdicts. However, if jurors were presented with instructions that were revised to increase their clarity, then only 13 per cent of mock jurors made the incorrect verdicts.

If the jurors fail to understand the judicial instructions then this is not in the interests of justice. Is it possible to take steps to assist juror comprehension of instructions and, thinking more broadly, also to eliminate the effects of other sources of bias?

Daftary-Kapur, Dumas, and Penrod (2010) suggest that there is empirical evidence to guide the presentation of judicial instructions in order to reduce confusion. Thus, it has been suggested that jurors could be provided with a written copy of the instructions, the language used in the instructions can be made clearer, jurors should be allowed to make notes to aid their memory, and decision-making trees can be provided to illustrate choices and associated consequences. Daftary-Kapur et al. acknowledge that it is much more difficult for jurors to disregard inadmissible evidence or evidence that is stricken from the record. It is impossible for jurors to wipe from their memory what they have heard, human memory does not function in that way. In extreme cases, the judge may order a mistrial and a new jury is convened: needless to say, this is a very costly option and rarely takes place.

Reaching a verdict: the process of deliberation

When the evidence is presented and judicial instructions issued the jury retires to reach their verdict. The verdict will be the product of each individual juror's initial views as they are affected by the process of discussion with the other jurors. The individual juror may change their view of guilt or innocence through discussion or their original opinion may remain unchanged throughout.

The jury deliberations typically move through three stages beginning with *orientation*, followed by *conflict* and finally *reconciliation*. At the orientation stage, the jury elect a foreperson, discuss how to proceed and air any general issues. At the conflict stage, the jurors may be either *evidence*-focused or *verdict*-focused (Hastie, Penrod & Pennington, 1983). About two-thirds of juries are evidence-focused and organise their discussions around what they have heard during the trial and may relate the evidence to a range of verdicts. This type of jury may take a straw poll of opinions on the verdict but only at a later stage in their deliberations. The verdict-focused juries are likely to begin with a poll so that opinions are declared very quickly and the discussion moves on from that point. The polls may be carried out secretly, or by verbal announcement, or by a show of hands.

Although the two types of jury set about their task quite differently – the evidence-focused jury will spend more time deliberating the evidence, while the verdict-focused jury will move more quickly to a decision – there are group processes that are common to both during the conflict stage.

The process of presenting and discussing conflicting individual views can make some jurors anxious, angry, or uncomfortable: these emotions can be exacerbated in cases where the jury has to discuss evidence of sexual offences and crimes against children. It may be that views may become personalised leading to insults, people may stubbornly refuse to change their opinion, and a minority of jurors may feel persecuted and dissociate themselves from the discussion by sitting apart from the group. As the discussion unfolds, so two social processes, normative and informational influences, become evident. Those jurors whose view is affected by normative influences will fall into line with the majority view while privately maintaining their own beliefs about the case (psychologically not unlike a coerced-compliant false confession). On the other hand, those jurors who shift their views because of informational influences will privately accept the change on the basis of the force of the arguments or increased understanding of the facts of the case. As Salerno and Diamond (2010) point out, a great deal remains to be understood about the cognitive dimension to jury deliberation.

There are other issues that may arise with jury discussions. The defendant may be talked about in ways that are outside the jury's terms of reference, such as being blamed for the disruption caused to everyone's life by having to do jury service. The jurors may also consider the consequences of returning a guilty verdict and, while sentencing is not their concern, this consideration may influence their eventual verdict (Goldman, Maitland, & Norton, 1975).

While about one-third of jurors do change their minds during the course of discussion, the best predictor of the eventual verdict is the balance of opinion at the very start of the deliberations (Hastie et al., 1983). A jury starting with 11 guilty votes, notwithstanding Henry Fonda (see 'The lighter side' at the end of this chapter), is highly unlikely to return a verdict of innocent. When a jury begins its discussions with a clear majority view, the discussion will serve to strengthen this majority view, which is a clear example of the phenomenon of *group polarization* (Lamm & Myers, 1978). This is not to say that minorities never change opinions, but when they do it is a highly unusual event.

With a verdict reached, the jury enters its final, reconciliatory phase. The foreperson will try to ensure that each member of the jury is satisfied with the verdict. Thus, support for the group decision is asserted, rifts are healed, tension is released (often through humour), and arrangements made to meet after the trial.

Reaching a verdict: do juries get it right?

It is impossible to know exactly the frequency with which juries make wrong decisions: certainly innocent men and women have been imprisoned, even executed, because of a wrong jury decision; undoubtedly guilty people have been set free. While the exact numbers can never be known, attempts have been made to estimate jury accuracy. Kalven and Zeisel (1966) compared the difference in convictions and acquittals between judges and juries in American courts. They found that in more than 3,500 trials, the judge and jury agreed on the verdict in 78 per cent of cases. In the instances of disagreement, the jury acquitted in 19 per cent of cases when the judge would have convicted; therefore in only 3 per cent of cases would the judge have acquitted when the jury returned a guilty verdict.

An English study by Baldwin and McConville (1979) arrived at similar findings to Kalven and Zeisel. Judges and juries agreed in the majority of cases and, where there was disagreement, the jury was more lenient.

Kalven and Zeisel offered a several explanations for jury leniency: (1) if the defendant did not have any previous offences then this increased the likelihood of their being given the benefit of the doubt; (2) if the jury felt sympathetic towards the defendant; (3) if the jury disagreed with the law. Baldwin and McConville noted that doubtful decisions came about when juries seemed not to appreciate the high standard of proof needed to reach a decision, or if the jury did not understand the evidence or failed to comprehend the judge's instructions.

In all, the jury appears reasonably reliable, although the difficulty with understanding evidence is noted by several authorities. The answer to this difficulty may be for the court to draw on the ability of an expert to assist in the proceedings. Recent years have seen a marked increase in the role of the psychologist as an expert witness and this is aspect of psychology in the courtroom which is now addressed.

Given the need for jurors to understand some complex concepts and assimilate a weight of argument, it is perhaps not unexpected that those juries which contain jurors of a higher cognitive ability are more likely to reach more accurate verdicts (Park, 2010).

Sentencing

If the defendant is found guilty then he or she will be sentenced by the judge to serve a penalty. In some countries, including England and Wales, the judge's sentence will follow a set of Sentencing Guidelines: these guidelines are formulated by the Sentencing Council for England and Wales (see Box 10.3).

At the time of writing the Sentencing Council website (see 'Useful websites' at the end of this chapter) provided links to 19 sets of guidelines, including guidelines for Magistrates' Court and for a range of crimes from fraud and breach of a protective order to robbery and causing death by driving. The Sentencing Council also makes available guidelines on the principles – such as determining seriousness and those for offences against children – that underpin the sentencing guidelines. These guidelines all give a great deal of detail clarifying, for example, how in determining the seriousness of an offence account should be taken of the offender's culpability and the harm which has resulted from the crime. Further, there may be a need for the judge to consider aggravating factors, such as the use of a weapon; or mitigating factors, such as high levels of provocation prior to the offence; or to allow a degree of personal mitigation when the offender shows remorse or a high degree of cooperation with the police during interviewing. These principles are evident in the sentencing guidelines as illustrated by the guidelines for causing death by driving (Box 10.4).

Judges

The judge has a complex series of tasks to perform during a trial including monitoring the questioning of all those giving evidence, giving detailed instructions to the jury before they retire to make their decision, and applying sentencing guidelines. The study of judges and

---

Box 10.3 The Sentencing Council for England and Wales

The Sentencing Council for England and Wales, an independent public body of the Ministry of Justice, formulates sentencing guidelines on a wide range of crimes to assist judges in making sentencing decisions. The availability of these guidelines does not mean that judges simply follow written rules when sentencing – the judiciary is independent and makes sentencing decisions according to the circumstances relevant to each individual case – rather that there is synchronicity between the Crown Prosecution Service's advice to prosecutors and eventual sentencing. The guidelines also aim to increase both transparency and consistency in sentencing, so promoting public confidence, while also considering the resource implications of its proposals.

The Sentencing Council for England and Wales also carries out research on the operation and effect of the sentencing guidelines.

Box 10.4 Sentencing guidelines for causing death by driving

Assessing and determining seriousness
- Awareness of risk
- Effect of alcohol or drugs
- Inappropriate speed of vehicle
- Seriously culpable behaviour of offender
- Victim
- Alcohol and drugs
- Avoidable distractions
- Vulnerable road users

Aggravating and mitigating factors
- More than one person killed
- Effect on offender
- Actions of others
- Offender's age and lack of driving experience

Personal mitigation
- Good driving record
- Conduct after the offence
- Giving assistance at the scene
- Remorse

Source: Sentencing Guidelines Council (2008). *Causing Death by Driving: Definitive Guideline*. London: Sentencing Guidelines Secretariat.

---

judging relies primarily on two methodologies, setting up scenarios for mock judges and interviewing real judges. An example of the former approach is provided by Mueller-Johnson and Dhami (2010), who carried out studies using university students as mock judges. The students were presented with scenarios featuring varying details – such as the offender's age, heath and previous convictions – and asked to make sentencing decisions concerning the guilty person. Qurashi and Shaw (2008) provide an example of the latter methodology in a study where 12 judges were interviewed with respect to their experiences and thinking regarding aspects of mental health law. A third approach does not rely on data but attempts to build models of judicial behaviour using extant research findings and theories: for example, Porter and ten Brinke (2009) applied a theory of decision-making to construct an understanding of how judges assess the credibility of witnesses. These methodologies have varying strengths and weaknesses but together help our understanding of judges and judging.

Schauer (2010: 103) makes the point that judges share three common characteristics: first, they are obviously judges; second, they are in the main lawyers; and third, 'the opinions of some attorneys and litigants notwithstanding, they are human beings'. As human beings so judges hold attitudes, even biases, of their own (Bennett & Broe, 2010; Goodman-Delahunty & Sporer, 2010) and Schauer makes the point that it is these human qualities of judges, particularly as they interact with their professional qualities, which raise questions that are of interest to psychologists.

Thus, one of the tasks that judges perform is to make decisions in the legal domain: these decisions may concern both the application of law in a given trial and, in some cases, the making of laws. How do judges make complex decisions? How do the processes underpinning their legal reasoning compare with other professional groups and, indeed, people in general? Can mainstream psychological models of decision-making be applied to the legal reasoning of the judiciary? Another interesting question is how do judges change over the course of their career? Do they mellow with experience? It must be presumed that, like any other professional, a judge's knowledge and expertise increases as their career progresses. How does this professional maturity effect the quality of their performance in the courtroom?

Is professional expertise sufficient to become a judge or are certain dispositional traits desirable in members of the judiciary? It is not unusual for people to be emotionally affected by events in the workplace and this may be true of some judges. Bennett and Broe (2010) suggest that, despite the stereotype of the impartial and dispassionate judge, in real life judges are not immune from strong emotions. In court, judges are exposed to a range of emotions including distress and anger; in making sentencing decisions judges may wish to exercise compassion, or deliver a punishment that takes away liberty or even life. It is difficult to believe that all judges can remain emotionally detached at all times: indeed, it may be thought that there is a great deal of merit in judges having refined emotional intelligence alongside their legal knowledge. King (2006) takes the argument a stage further in advancing the case that interpersonal and problem-solving skills should part of the repertoire of all judges. Yet further, the judge's influence as expressed through their communication skills may be advantageous in mental health courts in assisting offenders to understand the court procedures and eventually reduce recidivism (Wales, Hiday, & Ray, 2010).

When the evidence has been presented, the legal arguments heard and the jury has made their decision, it then falls to the judge to pass sentence on the guilty party. We accept that the court will impose a sentence but the wider question is what purpose is served by sentencing?

The purpose of sentencing

McGuire (2008) asks the question 'What's the point of sentencing?' and suggests that, as shown in Box 10.5, that there are five principal functions, not necessarily mutually exclusive, which are intended to be served by this phase of the courtroom procedures.

Box 10.5   The aims of sentencing

Retribution: The retributive aim of sentencing is plain and straightforward: to punish the individual for breaking the law.

Incapacitation: If it seems likely that an offender will commit more crimes, particularly crimes of a serious nature, then the public can be protected by taking the offender out of circulation either permanently or for a specified period of time.

Deterrence: As with retribution, the idea underpinning deterrence is plain and direct: the administration of punishment will in itself act to deter those who would commit crimes.

Correction: The imposition of the sentence may act to correct the offender's wrongdoing; alternatively, steps can be taken during the sentence to try to change the offender's propensity to commit crime.

Restoration and reparation: The sentence acts to make the offender aware of the impact of their crime on the victims and gives him or her the opportunity to apologise to the victim and offer restitution.

It is evident from even a cursory glance at Box 10.5 that a daunting range of issues, mainly of a specialist legal nature but also involving philosophy, sociology, and some psychology, is involved in sentencing (Ashworth, 2010).

Retribution

The delivery of retribution by inflicting punishment on those who break the law has a long history (Hollin, 2012). While we now accept the notion of proportionality, i.e., that the punishment should fit the crime (von Hirsch & Ashworth, 2005), this was not always the case with severe forms of punishment were administered for minor crimes. As Pettifer (1992) records, in mid-18th century England there were more than 100 offences that were punishable by death by hanging. As well as hanging, many other forms of punishment have historically been used: thus, legally sanctioned punishments included mutilation by variously cutting off limbs, ears, lips, or noses; burning to death; crushing to death; public humiliation as with the pillory; and deportation to the colonies. It was not until the 18th century, which saw the influence of classical theory as framed by Cesare Beccaria (1738–94), an Italian mathematician and economist, and the English philosopher Jeremy Bentham (1748–1832), that the notion of proportionality was applied to punishment. The basis of the argument is straightforward: if minor crimes attract the same harsh penalties as serious crimes then the administration of punishment will not deter further acts of crime. For example, if hanging is the penalty for stealing a lamb then, as the saying goes, it's as well to be hung for a sheep as for a lamb.

A consequence of proportionality is that by varying the degree of punishment according to the crime it is possible to use sentencing to prevent and reduce the harm caused by crime. This utilitarian approach to sentencing can be clearly seen in the notion of deterrence.

Deterrence

As with retribution, the idea underpinning deterrence is plain and direct: the administration of punishment should make the costs of crime outweigh the benefits that accrue from committing crime. Thus, a crime that produces a minimal gain, say shoplifting a coat, does not attract the same penalty as a crime such as robbery in which the theft is accompanied by violence. There are two sides to deterrence: (1) *general deterrence*, which holds that when offenders are punished this acts as a deterrent to the population at large so that they refrain from offending; and (2) *specific deterrence*, which maintains that the act of punishment will deter the individual offender from committing more crimes in the future.

Incapacitation

If there is a high risk that an offender will commit more crimes, particularly if his or her crimes are of a serious nature, then the public can be protected by removing the offender from the community. This removal may be either on a permanent basis or for a specified period of time. As deportation is no longer an option, incapacitation is achieved through the use of imprisonment. In those countries where it applies, the death sentence is the ultimate form of incapacitation.

Correction

The imposition of the punishment may in itself act to correct the offender's wrongdoing. Alternatively, steps can be taken during the time the offender is serving their sentence to try to change the offender's propensities to commit crime and so bring about their rehabilitation into the community.

Restoration and reparation

The punishment may include steps to make the offender aware of the physical, psychological, and financial effect that their crimes have on their victims. This awareness may be achieved by giving the offender the opportunity to apologise to the victim and to offer restitution.

A great deal of public money is spent trying to achieve these five aims of sentencing and there are several agencies charged with the task of turning these aims into reality. Who are these agencies and what happens when they get to work?

The agents of punishment

What happens to offenders after sentencing? The sentence imposed by the court will entail some degree of loss for the offender. This loss may take several forms: it may be financial, as with a fine; or social, as with loss of contact with certain people, typically children, as seen with a restriction order; it may entail a period of monitoring or supervision in the community, as with a probation order; or it may mean a loss of liberty with time spent in custody. These penalties within the criminal justice system find parallels with the mental health system with hospital orders that impose varying degrees of curtailment of liberty from the community through to institutions of conditions of low, medium and high security.

It is a fact of life that the agencies that make up the criminal justice and forensic mental health systems are, in the main, funded from the public purse and are therefore prey to the ebb and flow of political currents. The quality of the service provided, in terms of both the physical environment and the calibre of staff, within these systems is therefore dependent upon levels of government funding.

The probation service

The probation service had its beginnings in latter part of the 18th century, when increasing numbers of criminals were being released from custody into the community. Several voluntary organisations, including the Church of England Temperance Society, provided missionaries to the London Police Courts. Offenders were released on the understanding that they remained in contact with and accepted advice from their assigned missionary. In 1907, the role of the missionaries was legally sanctioned and the courts employed 'probation officers' to befriend and advise offenders.

The National Probation Service (NPS) for England and Wales is now a statutory Criminal Justice Service, funded by central government, traditionally the Home Office but since 2007 the Orwellian-sounding Ministry of Justice. The current configuration of the NPS is 42 probation areas, identical to police force areas, served by 35 Probation Trusts. Northern Ireland has its own probation service, Probation Board for Northern Ireland (PBNI), and in Scotland the criminal justice social work services are part of the social work services delivered by local authorities.

The tasks of the probation services include providing pre-sentence reports to court to advise on the background of individual offenders and to assist in deciding upon the appropriate sentence for those who are convicted. The probation service also supervises offenders in the community, either directly from court or on release from prison. In a typical year, the

NPS will supervise close to 200,000 offenders and provide one-quarter of a million pre-sentence reports. The NPS also has the task of ensuring that the victims of violent and sexual crime for which the offender received a prison sentence of more than 12 months are consulted prior to the offender's release.

Given their location in the community, probation services will often work closely with other community agencies, including voluntary agencies. Thus, probation services may work with other offender-orientated agencies, such as the National Association for the Care and Resettlement of Offenders (NACRO); or alternatively with agencies that specialise in the problems, such as alcohol and drug addiction, which are often but not exclusively found among offenders.

Prison service

For centuries people have been locked away, sometimes in the most terrible conditions, for a variety of reasons. Monarchs would cast their opponents into the deepest, darkest dungeons pending their execution, those captured during battle would be incarcerated and sometimes held hostage for a ransom, people who fell into debt were cast into debtors' prison until they or their family paid what was owed (Morris & Rothman, 1995). In more recent times, people have been deprived of their liberty as prisoners of war, as political prisoners and for protective custody.

In England, the notion of imprisoning a person as a form of punishment for a crime can be traced to the Penitentiary Act 1779 (see Soothill, 2007). This Act led to the building of two prisons in London, one for males and one for females, and eventually to the network of prisons, as described in Box 10.6, which is currently in operation. In some countries, including England and Wales, the running of some prisons has been contracted out by the state to private concerns. The privatisation of prisons, which enables the private sector to lock up citizens for financial gain, has generated a great deal of debate on the moral, social, and human rights issues involved in punishment for profit (Mehigan & Rowe, 2007).

How many people are there in prison?

As with crime statistics generally, it is difficult to be highly precise about the number of people in prison at any one time. It is the case that each individual prison establishment will each day have new prisoners entering to serve their sentence and prisoners leaving having served their time in custody. This movement of people in and out of prison, sometimes referred to as the 'churn', when multiplied over many establishments makes it difficult to be exact about numbers. Nonetheless, there are figures available: the numbers for the UK, taken from the relevant websites, are given in Box 10.7. The figures are accompanied by the date at which they were accessed because they may well change, sometimes significantly, over time.

When the figures for the number of people in prison are collated for different countries so the range of issues in collecting accurate information are multiplied exponentially. It is highly likely that different countries will have different systems, which are more or less accurate, for recording their prison population, the figures may be reported in different ways (as totals or averages), while some countries may not wish to release accurate figures.

The International Centre for Prison Studies (see 'Useful websites' at the end of this chapter) provides figures on prison populations around the world. As shown in Box 10.8, the list of the five countries with the largest recorded prison populations is topped by the USA with

Box 10.6   Prisoners and prisons in England and Wales

Adult prisoners
Male adults, aged 21 or over, are assigned a security category upon their reception into prison. These categories are based on consideration of type of crime, length of sentence, probability of escape, and danger to the public should they escape. These four categories are:

> **Category A:** prisoners requiring maximum security as their escape would be highly dangerous to the public or to national security: based on their likelihood of escaping 'Cat A' prisoners are divided into Standard Risk, High Risk and Exceptional Risk.
> **Category B:** prisoners not requiring maximum security but escape should be very difficult to achieve.
> **Category C:** prisoners who cannot be trusted in open conditions but who are unlikely to attempt to escape
> **Category D:** prisoners are those who can be reasonably trusted not to escape, these prisoners may be granted 'release on temporary licence' to allow them to work in the community or go on home leave.

Women adult prisoners are classified into four categories that are broadly similar to those for men.

Prisons are correspondingly categorised according to security levels as Category A, B, C (closed prisons), and D (open prisons). Prisoners held on remand awaiting trial are usually held in closed prisons. It is, however, more accurate to say that prison conditions, rather than prisons, are categorised as A, B, C, or D: for example, some prisons will have wings that are Cat A security level and others that are Cat B.

Young offenders and juveniles
There are four types of custodial establishment for offenders under the age of 21 years:

> **Secure training centres:** These are privately-run establishments for offenders up to age 17 years.
> **Local authority secure children's homes:** These are run by Local Authorities and provide care and accommodation for young people who have been placed under secure accommodation welfare orders.
> **Juvenile prisons:** These are run by the Prison Service for young offenders aged 15–18 years.
> **Young offender institutions:** Run by the Prison Service for 18- to 21-year-old offenders.

Box 10.7   Prisons and prisoners in the UK

The NI Prison Service currently has three operational establishments housing a population of 1,769 prisoners (1,709 men and 60 women; figures as available on 16 December 2011).

The Scottish Prison Service has 16 prisons, holding 7,891 prisoners (7,749 men and 442 women; 23 December 2011)

The Prison Service for England & Wales has 139 prisons holding 86,638 prisoners (82,553 men and 4,085 women; 6 January 2012).

Box 10.8 Worldwide prison populations

Numbers of prisoners
- USA 2,266,832
- China 1,650,000
- Russian Federation 763,700
- Brazil 513,802
- India 376,969

Prison population rates per 100,000 of the national population
- USA 730
- St. Kitts and Nevis 649
- Rwanda c.595
- Georgia 539
- Virgin Islands (USA) 539
- Russian Federation 534
- Brazil 261
- China 122
- India 31

- England and Wales 154
- Scotland 150
- Northern Ireland 101

---

more than 2.5 million people held in custody. It is unlikely that any nation has ever imprisoned its own citizens on such a scale.

However, raw numbers do not tell the full tale: given the different populations of these top five countries what happens when population statistics are taken into consideration? It can also be seen from Box 10.7 that when the prison population is considered as a rate per 100,000 of the national population then the USA remains at the head of the list but other countries come to attention.

The American prison population provides an excellent example of the complexities that lie beneath the prison population figures. As described by Blumstein (2012: 15), the rise in the prison population in the dates from the mid-1970s when the 'United States began an incarceration escalation that raised incarceration rates at an exponential rate of 6% to 8% per year'. Blumstein suggests that this rise was fuelled by a perceived failure of efforts to rehabilitate offenders and a political will to commit resources to lock more people up for longer periods: this shift in thinking about prison was seen, for example, in changes in sentencing patterns and the 'three strikes and you're out' laws that dramatically increased the number of prisoners serving life sentences.

Conclusion

A great deal of time and public money is spent on the process of determining guilt or innocence, then on those agencies charged with managing the lives of those who the courts find guilty. A fundamental question across the whole system is one of effectiveness – does the vast public expenditure provide value for money in the sense that it achieves the aims of sentencing? This issue will be addressed in considering what works in terms of attempts to reduce crime.

Chapter summary

- Although the arguments for psychology in the courtroom were first made in the early 1900s, it is only more recently that the testimony of psychologists has become more widespread in the court system.
- When called as an expert witness, psychologists typically act in one of four roles: (1) an experimental role; (2) a clinical (assessment) role; (3) an actuarial role; and (4) an advisory role.
- The psychological research into the functioning of juries has been concerned with how expert evidence may influence jury decisions, extra-evidential influences on jury decisions, the composition of the jury, and jury decision-making.
- The court will pass sentence on the guilty. Along with other disciplines, psychology has considered the purposes of sentencing in terms of retribution, incapacitation of the offender, deterrence to others, correction of the offender's wrongdoing, and restoration and reparation to victims.
- A great deal of time and public money is spent on the process of determining guilt or innocence, then on those agencies charged with managing those who the courts find guilty. The issue of the effectiveness of this process is an important issue.

Points for discussion

- Should evidence gained from a witness under hypnosis be admissible in court?
- Should punishment of the offender be the main aim of sentencing?
- Can psychologists really contribute anything important to court proceedings?

Essential reading

Kapardis, A. (1997). *Psychology and Law: A Critical Introduction*. Cambridge: Cambridge University Press.
An excellent overview of the topic.

Borgida, E. & Fiske, S. T. (Eds.) (2008). *Beyond Common Sense: Psychological Science in the Courtroom*. Oxford: Blackwell Publishing.
A wide-ranging set of chapters of the contribution psychology can make to legal matters.

Kline, D. & Mitchell, G. (Eds.) (2010). *The Psychology of Judicial Decision Making*. Oxford: Oxford University Press.
Lieberman, J. D. & Krauss, D. A. (Eds.) (2009). *Jury Psychology: Social Aspects of the Trial Process. Psychology in the Courtroom, Vol. I*. Farnham, Surrey: Ashgate Publishing.
Krauss, D. A. & Lieberman, J. D. (Eds.) (2009). *Psychological Expertise in Court*. Psychology in the Courtroom, *Vol. II*. Farnham, Surry: Ashgate Publishing.
These three books will tell you a great deal what you need to know about psychology, juries, and the courtroom.

Saks, M. (1997). What do jury experiments tell us about how juries (should) make decisions?', *Southern California Interdisciplinary Law Review, 6*, 1–53.
This paper by Saks complements the above with its fine-grained analysis of different research methodologies.

Gudjonsson, G. H. & Haward, L. R. C. (1998). *Forensic Psychology: A Guide to Practice*. London: Routledge.
In terms of the specific role of psychologists in the courtroom, the two most experienced forensic psychologists in England have pooled their experience.

The lighter side

The jury has proved a never-ending source of fascination, inspiring a steady stream of first-person accounts, films, and novels, with Henry Fonda starring in the film *Twelve Angry Men* perhaps the most famous of all. There have been several dramas based in or around the courtroom including Raymond Burr in *Perry Mason* and *Ironside*, There are many prison movies to take your pick from: my choice would be (you can also read the books) *The Green Mile* (book by Stephen King), *Papillon* (Henri Charrière), and *The Shawshank Redemption* (based on a novella by Stephen King with the stunning title *Rita Hayworth and Shawshank Redemption)*.

Useful websites

Sentencing Council (provides sentencing guidelines), http://sentencingcouncil.judiciary.gov.uk/sentencing-guidelines.htm.

The Probation Service for England and Wales, www.nationalprobationservice.co.uk.

International Centre for Prison Studies is a source of a fantastic amount of information, www.prison-studies.org.

The National Association for the Care and Resettlement of Offenders is a charity that aims to work with offenders to reduce their offending, www.nacro.org.uk.

References

Arnold, G. F. (1906). *Psychology Applied to Legal Evidence and Other Constructions of Law*. Calcutta: Thacker, Spink & Co.
Aronson, E. & Carlsmith, J. M. (1968). Experimentation in social psychology. In G. Lindzey & E. Aronson (Eds.), *The Handbook of Social Psychology* (Vol. 2) (pp. 1–79). Reading, MA: Addison-Wesley.
Ashworth, A. (2010). *Sentencing and Criminal Justice* (5th ed.). Cambridge: Cambridge University Press.
Baldwin, J. & McConville, M. (1979). *Jury Trials*. Oxford: Oxford University Press.
Bartol, C. R. & Bartol, A. M. (1999). History of forensic psychology. In I. B. Weiner & A. K. Hess (Eds.), *Handbook of Forensic Psychology* (2nd ed.) (pp. 3–23). New York, NY: John Wiley & Sons.
Bennett, H. & Broe, G. A. (2010). Judicial decision-making and neurobiology: The role of emotion and the ventromedial cortex in deliberation and reasoning. *Australian Journal of Forensic Sciences, 42*, 11–18.
Binet, A. (1900). *La Suggesestibilité*. Paris: Schleicher.
Blumstein, A. (2012). Crime and incarceration in the United States. In J. A. Dvoskin, J. L. Skeem, R. W. Novaco, & K. S. Douglas (Eds.), *Using Social Science to Reduce Violent Offending* (pp. 31–49). Oxford: Oxford University Press.
Bolton, F. E. (1896). The accuracy of recollection and observation. *Psychological Review, 3*, 286–295.
Borida, E. & Fiske, S. T. (Eds.) (2008). *Beyond Common Sense: Psychological Science in the Courtroom*. Oxford: Blackwell Publishing.
Bornstein, B. H. & Penrod, S. D. (2008). Hugo who? G. F. Arnold's alternative early approach to psychology and law. *Applied Cognitive Psychology, 22*, 759–768.
Brown, M. (1926). *Legal Psychology*. Indianapolis, IN: Bobbs-Merrill.

Butler, B. & Moran, G. (2007). The role of death qualification and need for cognition in venirepersons' evaluations of expert scientific testimony in capital trials. *Behavioral Sciences and the Law, 25,* 561–571.

Campbell, E. A. (2010). Expert witness in civil cases. In J. M. Brown & E. A. Campbell (Eds.), *The Cambridge Handbook of Forensic Psychology* (pp. 766–772). Cambridge: Cambridge University Press.

Carlin, M. (2010). The psychologist as expert witness in criminal cases. In J. M. Brown & E. A. Campbell (Eds.), *The Cambridge Handbook of Forensic Psychology* (pp. 773–782). Cambridge: Cambridge University Press.

Cattell, J. M. (1895). Measurements of the accuracy of recollection. *Science, 2,* 761–766.

Cockburn, J. S. & Green, T. A. (Eds.) (1988). *Twelve Good Men and True: The English Criminal Jury Trial, 1200–1800.* Princeton, NJ: Princeton University Press.

Colman, A. M. (1981). *What is Psychology?* London: Kogan Page.

Comiskey, M. (2011). Does Voir Dire serve as a powerful disinfectant or pollutant? A look at the disparate approaches to jury selection in the United States and Canada. *Drake Law Review, 59,* 733–759.

Conley, J., O'Barr, W., & Lind, A. (1978). The power of language: Presentation style in the courtroom. *Duke Law Journal, 27,* 1375–1399.

Daftary-Kapur, T., Dumas, R., & Penrod, S. D. (2010). Jury decision-making biases and methods to counter them. *Legal and Criminological Psychology, 15,* 133–154.

Deffenbacher, K. A. & Loftus, E. F. (1982). Do jurors share a common understanding concerning eyewitness behavior? *Law and Human Behavior, 6,* 15–30.

Denno, D. (2006). Revisiting the legal link between genetics and crime. *Law and Contemporary Problems, 69,* 209–257.

Devine, D. J., Clayton, L. D., Dunford, B. B., Seying, R., & Pryce, J. (2000). Jury decision making: 45 years of empirical research on deliberating groups. *Psychology, Public Policy, and Law, 7,* 622–727.

Duff, P. (1999). The Scottish criminal jury: A very peculiar institution. *Law and Contemporary Problems, 62,* 173–201.

Elwork, A., Sales, B. D., & Alfini, J. J. (1982). *Making Jury Instructions Understandable.* Charlottesville, VA: Michie.

Fein, S., McCloskey, A. L., & Tomlinson, T. M. (1997). Can the jury disregard that information? The use of suspicion to reduce the prejudicial effects of pretrial publicity and inadmissible testimony. *Personality and Social Psychology Bulletin, 23,* 1215–1226.

Freckleton, I. & Selby, H. (2002) *Expert Evidence: Law, Practice, Procedure and Advocacy.* Sydney: Lawbook Co.

Freud, S. (1906). *Psychoanalysis and the Ascertaining of Truth in Courts of Law: Collected Papers, Vol. 2.* New York, NY: Basic Books.

Goodman-Delahunty, G. & Sporer, S. L. (2010). Unconscious influences in sentencing decisions: A research review of psychological sources of disparity. *Australian Journal of Forensic Sciences, 42,* 19–36.

Goldman, J., Maitland, K. A., & Norton, P. L. (1975). Psychological aspects of jury performance. *Journal of Psychiatry and Law, 3,* 367–379.

Greer, D. S. (1971). The reliability of testimony in criminal trials. *British Journal of Criminology, 11,* 131–154.

Grisso, T. (2003). *Evaluating Competencies: Forensic Assessments and Instruments* (2nd ed.). New York, NY: Kluwer Academic Publishers/Plenum Press.

Gudjonsson, G. H. (1985). Psychological evidence in court: Results from the BPS survey. *Bulletin of the British Psychological Society, 38,* 327–330.

Gudjonsson, G. H. & Haward, L. R. C. (1998). *Forensic Psychology: A Guide to Practice.* London: Routledge.

Hain, P. (1976). *Mistaken Identity: The Wrong Face of the Law.* London: Quartet Books.

Hale, M. (1980). *Human Science and Social Order: Hugo Münsterberg and the Origins of Applied Psychology.* Philadelphia, PA: Temple University Press.

Hans, V. P. & Vidmar, N. (1986). *Judging the Jury*. New York, NY: Plenum Press.

Hastie, R., Penrod, S. D., & Pennington, N. (1983). *Inside the Jury*. Cambridge, MA: Harvard University Press.

Haward, L. R. C. (1963). Some psychological aspects of oral evidence. *British Journal of Criminology, 3*, 342–358.

—— (1979). The psychologist as expert witness. In D. P. Farrington, K. Hawkins, & S. M. A. Lloyd-Bostock (Eds.), *Psychology, Law and Legal Processes* (pp. 44–53). London: Macmillan.

—— (1987). The uses and misuses of psychological evidence. In G. Gudjonsson & J. Drinkwater (Eds.), *Psychological Evidence in Court. Issues in Criminological and Legal Psychology*, No. 11. Leicester: The British Psychological Society.

Heim, A. (1982). Professional issues arising from psychological evidence in court: A reply. *Bulletin of the British Psychological Society, 35*, 332–333.

Hess, A. K. (1999). Serving as an expert witness. In A. K. Hess & I. B. Weiner (Eds.), *The Handbook of Forensic Psychology* (2nd ed.) (pp. 521–55). New York, NY: John Wiley & Sons.

Hollin, C. R. (2012). A short history of corrections: The rise, fall, and resurrection of rehabilitation through treatment. In J. A. Dvoskin, J. L. Skeem, R. W. Novaco, & K. S. Douglas (Eds.), *Using Social Science to Reduce Violent Offending* (pp. 31–49). Oxford: Oxford University Press.

Hope, L. (2010). Jury decision making. In J. M. Brown & E. A. Campbell (Eds.), *The Cambridge Handbook of Forensic Psychology* (pp. 675–82). Cambridge: Cambridge University Press.

Kalven, H. & Zeisel, H. (1966). *The American Jury*. Boston, MA: Little, Brown.

Kassin, S. M. & Wrightsman, L. S. (1983). The construction and validation of a juror bias scale. *Journal of Research in Personality, 17*, 423–442.

Kerr, N. L. & Bray, R. M. (2005). Simulation, realism and the study of the jury. In N. Brewer & K. D. Williams (Eds.), *Psychology and Law: An Empirical Perspective* (pp. 322–64). New York, NY: Guildford Press.

Kim, Y. S., Barak, G., & Shelton, D. E. (2009). Examining the "CSI-effect" in the cases of circumstantial evidence and eyewitness testimony: Multivariate and path analyses. *Journal of Criminal Justice, 37*, 452–460.

King, M. S. (2006). The therapeutic dimension of judging: The example of sentencing. *Journal of Judicial Administration, 16*, 92–105.

Koneni, V. J. & Ebbesen, E. B. (1986). Courtroom testimony by psychologists on eyewitness identification issues. *Law and Human Behavior, 10*, 117–126.

Kovera, M. B. & Greathouse, S. M. (2008). Pretrial publicity: Effects, remedies, and judicial knowledge. In E. Borida & S. T. Fiske (Eds.), *Beyond Common Sense: Psychological Science in the Courtroom* (pp. 261–79). Oxford: Blackwell Publishing.

Krafka, C. & Penrod, S. (1985). Reinstatement of context in a field experiment on eyewitness identification. *Journal of Personality and Social Psychology, 49*, 58–69.

Kubie, L. (1959). Implications for legal procedure of the fallibility of human memory. *University of Pasadena Law Review, 108*, 59–75.

Lamm, H. & Myers, D. G. (1978). Group-induced polarization of attitudes and behavior. In L. Berkowitz (Ed.), *Advances in Experimental Social Psychology* (pp. 145–195). New York, NY: Academic Press.

Lassiter, G. D. (2002). Illusory causation in the courtroom. *Current Directions in Psychological Science, 11*, 204–208.

Lieberman, J. D. & Sales, B. D. (2007). *Scientific Jury Selection*. Washington, DC: American Psychological Association.

Lloyd-Bostock, S. & Thomas, C. (1999). Decline of the "little Parliament": Juries and jury reform in England and Wales. *Law and Contemporary Problems, 62*, 7–40.

Loftus, E. F. (1980). Impact of expert psychological testimony on the unreliability of eyewitness identification. *Journal of Applied Psychology, 65*, 9–15.

McGuire, J. (2008). What's the point of sentencing? In G. Davies, C. Hollin, & R. Bull (Eds.), *Forensic Psychology* (pp. 265–291). Chichester, Sussex: John Wiley & Sons.

Martire, K. A. & Kemp, R. I. (2009). The impact of eyewitness expert evidence and judicial instruction on juror ability to evaluate eyewitness testimony. *Law and Human Behavior, 33*, 225–236.

—— (2011). Can experts help jurors to evaluate eyewitness evidence? A review of eyewitness expert effects. *Legal and Criminological Psychology, 16*, 24–36.

Marshall, J. (1966). *Law and Psychology in Conflict*. New York, NY: Anchor Books.

Mazzella, R. & Feingold, A. (1994). The effects of physical attractiveness, race, socio-economic status, and gender of defendants and victims on judgements of mock jurors: A meta-analysis. *Journal of Applied Social Psychology, 24*, 1315–1344.

Mehigan, J. & Rowe, A. (2007). Problematizing prison privatization: An overview of the debate. In Y. Jewkes (ed.), *Handbook on Prisons* (pp. 356–376). Cullompton, Devon: Willan Publishing.

Miller, R. H. (1998). Six of one is not a dozen of the other: A re-examination of Williams v. Florida and the size of state criminal juries. *University of Pennsylvania Law Review, 146*, 621–686.

Moore, C. C. (1907). Yellow psychology. *Law Notes, 11*, 125–127.

Morris, N. & Rothman, D. J. (Eds.) (1995). *The Oxford History of the Prison: The Practice of Punishment in Western Society*. Oxford: Oxford University Press.

Mueller-Johnson, K. U. & Dhami, M. K. (2010). Effects of offenders' age and health on sentencing decisions. *Journal of Social Psychology, 150*, 77–97.

Münsterberg, H. (1908). *On the Witness Stand: Essays on Psychology and Crime*. New York, NY: Clark, Boardman.

—— (1914). *Psychology: General and Applied*. New York, NY: Clark: Boardman.

Noon, E. & Hollin, C. R. (1987). Lay knowledge of eyewitness behaviour: A British survey. *Applied Cognitive Psychology, 1*, 143–153.

Norton, M. I., Sommers, S. R., & Brauner, S. (2007). Bias in jury selection: Justifying prohibited peremptory challenges. *Journal of Behavioral Decision Making, 20*, 467–479.

Ogloff, J. R. P. & Rose, V. G. (2005). The comprehension of judicial instructions. In N. Brewer & K. D. Williams (Eds.), *Psychology and Law: An Empirical Perspective* (pp. 407–444). New York, NY: Guildford Press.

Padawer-Singer, A. M. & Barton, A. (1974). The impact of pre-trial publicity on jurors' verdicts. In R. J. Simon (Ed.), *The Jury System in America: A Critical Overview* (pp. 125–139). Beverly Hills, CA: Sage.

Park, K. (2010). Estimating juror accuracy, juror ability, and the relationship between them. *Law and Human Behavior, 35*, 288–305.

Penrod, S. & Cutler, S. B. (1995). Witness confidence and witness accuracy: Assessing their forensic relation. *Psychology, Public Policy, and Law, 1*, 817–845.

Pettifer, E. W. (1992). *Punishments of Former Days*. Winchester, Hants: Waterside Press. (Original edition published by the author in 1939.)

Pirelli, G., Gottdiener, W. H., & Zapf, N. G. (2011). A meta-analytic review of competency to stand trial research. *Psychology, Public Policy, and Law, 17*, 1–53.

Polythress, N. G. & Zapf, N. G. (2009). Controversies in evaluating competence to stand trial. In J. L. Skeem, K. S. Douglas, & S. O. Lilienfeld (Eds.), *Psychological Science in the Courtroom: Consensus and Controversy* (pp. 309–329). New York, NY: Guilford Press.

Porter, G. (2009). CCTV images as evidence. *Australian Journal of Forensic Sciences, 41*, 11–25.

Porter, S. & ten Brinke, L. (2009). Dangerous decisions: A theoretical framework for understanding how judges assess credibility in the courtroom. *Legal and Criminological Psychology, 14*, 119–134.

Pozzulo, J. D., Dempsey, J., Maeder, E., & Allen, L. (2010). The effects of victim gender, defendant gender, and defendant age on juror decision making. *Criminal Justice and Behavior, 37*, 47–63.

Qurashi, I. & Shaw, J. (2008). Sections 37/41 Mental Health Act 1983: A study of judges' practice and assessment of risk to the public. *Medicine, Science, and the Law, 48*, 57–63.

Rogers, T. P., Blackwood, N. J., Farnham, F., Pickup G. J., & Watts, M. J. (2008). Fitness to plead and competence to stand trial: A systematic review of the constructs and their application. *Journal of Forensic Psychiatry and Psychology, 19*, 576–596.

Rouke, F. L. (1957). Psychological research on problems of testimony. *Social Issues, 13*, 50–59.

Ruva, C., McEvoy, C., & Becker-Bryant, J. (2007). Effects of pre-trial publicity and jury deliberation on juror bias and source memory errors. *Applied Cognitive Psychology, 21*, 45–67.

Saks, M. J. & Marti, M. W. (1997). A meta-analysis of the effects of jury size. *Law and Human Behavior, 21*, 451–467.

Salerno, J. M. & Diamond, S. S. (2010). The promise of a cognitive perspective on jury deliberation. *Psychonomic Bulletin & Review, 17*, 174–179.

Schauer, F. (2010). Is there a psychology of judging? In D. Klein & G. Mitchell (Eds.), *The Psychology of Judicial Decision Making* (pp. 103–120). Oxford: Oxford University Press.

Scheck, B., Neufeld, P., & Dwyer, J. (2001). *Actual Innocence* (2nd ed.). New York, NY: Signet Printing.

Shelton, D. E. (2008). The *"CSI* Effect": Does it really exist? *National Institute of Justice Journal, 259*, 1–7.

Smith, A. & Saks, M. J. (2008). The case for overturning Williams v. Florida and the six-person jury: History, law, and empirical evidence. *Florida Law Review, 60*, 441–470.

Sommers, S. R. (2006). On racial diversity and group decision making: Identifying multiple effects of racial composition on jury deliberations. *Journal of Personality and Social Psychology, 90*, 597–612.

—— (2007). Race and the decision making of juries. *Legal and Criminological Psychology, 12*, 171–187.

Soothill, K. (2007). Prison histories and competing audiences, 1776–1966. In Y. Jewkes (Ed.), *Handbook on Prisons* (pp. 27–48). Cullompton, Devon: Willan Publishing.

Spellman, B. A. & Kincannon, A. (2001). The relation between counterfactual ("but for") and causal reasoning: Experimental findings and implications for jurors' decisions. *Law and Contemporary Problems, 64*, 241–264.

Sporer, S. L. (1982). A brief history of the psychology of testimony. *Current Psychological Reviews, 2*, 323–340.

Stevenson, M. C. & Bottoms, B. L. (2009). Race shapes perceptions of juvenile offenders in criminal court. *Journal of Applied Social Psychology, 39*, 1660–1689.

Stevenson, M. C., Bottoms, B. L., & Diamond, S. S. S. (2010). Jurors' discussions of a defendant's history of child abuse and alcohol abuse in capital sentencing deliberations. *Psychology, Public Policy, and Law, 16*, 1–38.

Tanford, S. & Penrod, S. D. (1982). Biases in trials involving defendants charged with multiple offences. *Journal of Applied Social Psychology, 12*, 453–480.

Thomas, C. (2010). *Are Juries Fair?* Ministry of Justice Research Series 1/10. London: Ministry of Justice.

Tunstall, O., Gudjonsson, G. H., Eysenck, H. J., & Haward, L. R. C. (1982a). Professional issues arising from psychological evidence presented in court. *Bulletin of The British Psychological Society, 35*, 329–331.

—— (1982b). Response to professional issues arising from psychological evidence presented in court: A reply to Dr Heim. *Bulletin of The British Psychological Society, 35*, 333.

Visher, C. A. (1987). Juror decision-making: The importance of evidence. *Law and Human Behavior, 11*, 1–17.

von Hirsch, A. & Ashworth, A. (2005). *Proportionate Sentencing: Exploring the Principles.* Oxford: Oxford University Press.

Wales, H. W., Hiday, V. A., & Ray, B. (2010). Procedural justice and the mental health court judge's role in reducing recidivism. *International Journal of Law and Psychiatry, 33*, 265–271.

Wall, P. M. (1965). *Eyewitness Identification in Criminal Cases.* Springfield, IL: C. C. Thomas.

Waller, B. M., Hope, L., Burrows, N., & Morrison, E. R. (2011). Twelve (not so) angry men: Managing conversational group size increases perceived contribution by decision makers. *Group Processes & Intergroup Relations, 14*, 835–843.

Wells, G. L. & Hasel, L. E. (2008). Eyewitness identification: Issues in common knowledge and generalization. In E. Borida & S. T. Fiske (Eds.), *Beyond Common Sense: Psychological Science in the Courtroom* (pp. 159–176). Oxford: Blackwell Publishing.

Weiner, I. B. (1999). Writing forensic reports. In A. K. Hess & I. B. Weiner (Eds.), *The Handbook of Forensic Psychology* (2nd ed.) (pp. 501–520). New York, NY: John Wiley & Sons.

Whipple, G. M. (1909). The observer as reporter: A survey of "the psychology of testimony". *Psychological Bulletin, 6*, 153–170.

—— (1910). Recent literature on the psychology of testimony. *Psychological Bulletin, 7*, 365–368.

—— (1911). Psychology of testimony. *Psychological Bulletin, 8*, 307–309.

—— (1912). Psychology of testimony and report. *Psychological Bulletin, 9*, 264–269.

—— (1913). Psychology of testimony and report. *Psychological Bulletin, 10*, 264–268.

—— (1914). Psychology of testimony and report. *Psychological Bulletin, 11*, 245–250.

—— (1915). Psychology of testimony. *Psychological Bulletin, 12*, 221–224.

—— (1917). Psychology of testimony. *Psychological Bulletin, 14*, 234–236.

—— (1918). The obtaining of information: Psychology of observation and report. *Psychological Bulletin, 15*, 217–248.

Winick, C. (1979). The psychology of the courtroom. In H. Toch (Ed.), *Psychology of Crime and Criminal Justice* (pp. 68–105). New York, NY: Holt, Rinehart, & Winston.

Wright, D. B., Strubler, K. A., & Vallano, J. P. (2011). Statistical techniques for juror and jury research. *Legal and Criminological Psychology, 16*, 90–125.

Yuille, J. C. & Cutshall, J. L. (1986). A case study of eyewitness memory to a crime. *Journal of Applied Psychology, 71*, 291–301.

11 Reducing crime

Punish or cure?

In the previous chapter, the five aims of sentencing were noted as *retribution, deterrence, incapacitation, correction,* and *restoration and reparation*. In the first part of this chapter, these five aims will be looked at more closely in the context of reducing crime. The aspect of crime reduction of concern here lies with those crimes where the actions of an individual or group of individuals inflict harm on another person's health or property. While equally important, the focus here is not on crime reduction initiatives aimed at financial crimes such as tax evasion or the theft of valuable pieces of art.

There are several approaches to crime reduction: (1) *change the offender*, such that if certain personal attributes, such as impulsiveness, are associated with criminal behaviour then helping the offender to become less impulsive may reduce their criminal behaviour; (2) *social control* relies on broad-scale social and legal change so that if, for example, the rate of unemployment correlates with the crime rate then government policies to reduce unemployment may bring about an associated fall in crime; (3) *situational change* by managing the environments in which crime is most likely to take place, thus if certain crimes takes place in dark city streets then improved lighting may reduce those crimes.

These three approaches to crime reduction are not mutually exclusive: there is a clear link between drug use and criminal behaviour (Bennett, Holloway, & Farrington, 2008), which may be approached by legislative measures to make possession of certain drugs an offence and so deter ownership, or action by customs and the police to control the flow of drugs into the country and apprehend those who distribute drugs; it may be important to educate people as to the disadvantages associated with drug use, while working with the individual offender can help him or her control their drug use and reduce offending.

In this chapter, the focus is on crime reduction by retribution and by treatment. The next chapter moves to situational crime prevention.

Retribution/punishment

The belief that those who are wronged are entitled some form of redress to the wrongdoing is widespread. The ancient principle of *lex talionis*, 'an eye for an eye', is bedded in the history of many of the world's cultures and religions. This principle may be described in different ways, such as revenge or punishment, but the aim is clear: through its sentence the court will extract retribution for the criminal act by punishing the offender.

There are two schools of thought, which have their basis in moral philosophy, on the purpose of punishment. Immanuel Kant (1724–1804) argued that crimes should be punished because of the moral wrong committed by the criminal. There should be no expectation of any further consequences of the administration of punishment. In contrast to the retributionist approach, the utilitarian position, as argued by figures such as Jeremy Bentham (1748–1832) and John Stuart Mill (1806–73), holds that punishment in and of itself is immoral, the punishment should have an outcome that is beneficial in terms of the greater good. Thus, the purpose of punishment should be to reduce crime through its deterrent effect. Further, the more serious the crime so more severe the punishment should be in order to serve the purpose of the offender receiving their just deserts. We now accept the principle of proportionality in that the degree of retribution, the punishment, should fit the crime – which was not always the case historically, when severe punishments were handed out for relatively minor crimes (Pettifer, 1992) – and we draw limits on the acceptability of certain forms of punishment.

If a retributionist stance is taken, then discussions hinge around determining proportionality: what is the appropriate retribution for, say, theft or rape? The issue also arises of what form of punishment a society judges to be morally defensible: is it justifiable that retribution takes the form of very long prison sentences or even the death penalty? However, with retribution there is no question of outcome: the delivery of the punishment *is* the outcome.

The use to which retribution is put has the potential to raise a raft of issues. It is, for example, arguably morally indefensible either to use punishment for political purposes or to impose punishments of different severity on different citizens. An American study reported by Helms (2009) looked at sentencing patterns in over 5,000 cases heard in courts across seven states. Helms found clear variations in sentence severity according to the gender and race of the defendant: Helms (2009: 18) argues that this unequal sentencing highlights the fact that '[t]he courts, in their political role, mete punishments that reflect and respond to localized environmental pressures'.

In England there have been, as discussed in Box 11.1, similar claims of political interference in the judicial process following the trials of those accused of being involved in the riots that took place in several cities during 2011.

Political parties have much to gain by being seen as tough on crime and bringing down the rate of crime. Hedderman (2008) shows how penal policy, crime statistics, and political rhetoric can become conflated to suit a political end. The building of more prisons can be seen as taking a populist stance as being tough on crime. However, as Hedderman (2008:10) argues, this is an expensive way to create more offenders: 'Of course, any calls to limit the prison population are likely to be portrayed by the popular press negatively as being soft on

---

Box 11.1 Politics and the court

The point made by Helms (2009) regarding political influence on court proceedings was seen in England with the riots which took place in some parts of the country in 2011. It was reported in the media that courts were advised to put sentencing guidelines aside to allow unduly heavy sentences to be given for offences such as theft. There was highly favourable political commentary on the severity of the sentences, some of which were changed on appeal, which led to expressions of unease from some MPs and civil rights groups. There were also complaints from within the legal profession about the actions of the Crown Prosecutor Service in opposing bail more often than usual.

While the right and wrongs and who did what and what actually happened after the riots can be debated, the point remains that grave concerns were expressed about the actions of politicians and the process of justice.

crime but that is not a good enough reason to conceal the damaging financial and public safety consequences of our increasing use of custody. The consequence of pandering to "penal populism" in the short term by building more prison places is that the financial costs of the building programme will be much greater than the forecast because it will feed rather than meet demand'.

In modern society, punishment is based around the notion of loss: the criminal may lose assets, as with a fine; their liberty, as with supervision in the community or a custodial sentence; or even their life in those jurisdictions where the death penalty is available. In order to impose punishment, there must be mechanisms within the criminal justice system by which the punishment is delivered: how does this work in practice?

Supervision in the community

In England and Wales, if an offender is judged not to be a highly significant risk to the public then he or she may receive the sentence of a Community Order. This sentence, as the name implies, is served in the community rather in custody. The exact requirements of a Community Order, in accordance with the Criminal Justice Act 2003, may vary according to the characteristics of both the offender and their offence. Thus, a Community Order may specify a range of alternatives for different offenders: a *prohibited activity* bans the offender from taking part in events such as attending football matches or entering public houses; with a *specified activity* the offender must take part in certain activities such as employment training, education, debt counselling or victim reparation. If necessary, the offender may be required to partake in treatment for problem drinking or can be advised to participate in mental health treatment. Those offenders between the ages of 18 and 25 years of age can be required as part of their Community Order to spend between 12 and 36 hours a week at an *Attendance Centre*. While at an Attendance Centre, offenders will take part in various constructive activities intended to develop their sense of personal responsibility and help learn new skills.

Finally, the offender may be required to observe a *curfew* requiring them to be at a specific location at a specified time. A curfew requirement, which may be for at least 2 hours and up to 12 hours per day (often overnight), can last for up to 6 months and may entail electronic monitoring or *tagging* (Nellis, 2000). Monitoring a person's whereabouts can be achieved by fitting the offender with an electronic tag that they must always wear (usually around the ankle) and installing a monitoring box in their place of residence. If the offender does not return home for the prescribed curfew hours and engage the tag and monitoring box, an electronic signal is sent to the supervisor who then investigates. If the offender breaks their curfew they may be in breach of their Community Order and so returned to court.

The means of electronic monitoring has progressed from radio frequencies to global positioning systems (GPS). GPS systems provide a much more precise form of surveillance in terms of pinpointing the offender's exact location: this method has been used in North America with sex offenders (Payne & DeMichele, 2010). Finally, the offender may take part in *unpaid work* (often thought of as community work): this typically means carrying out work such as clearing rubbish or removing graffiti from a public place for the general good of the community (Palmer, Hollin, & Caulfield, 2005). There are indications from research conducted in the Netherlands that community service can be more effective than a short prison sentence in reducing recidivism (Wermink, Blokland, Nieuwbeerta, Nagin, & Tollenaar, 2010).

Intensive supervision

Gendreau, Goggin, and Fulton (2001) describe the advent of the notion of an Intensive Supervision Programme (ISP) in North America. As seen in Box 11.2, the term ISP has been used to encompass a range of activities intended, as Gendreau et al. suggest, 'to turn up the heat' on offenders. Further, as found by Lowenkamp, Flores, Holsinger, Makarios, and Latessa (2010) in a study of 58 ISPs, the philosophy underpinning the delivery of the programmes varied between rehabilitation, punishment, and deterrence.

In England and Wales, ISPs have been used with young offenders, typically aged between 10 and 17 years with, as noted by Gray et al. (2005), the main aim of reducing recidivism. As with the North American programmes, these ISPs include a range of interventions and activities.

Imprisonment

The court has a range of custodial options available for sentenced offenders ranging from short sentences of a few months duration to much longer sentences up to and including life imprisonment. If the offence is one, such as murder, that carries a mandatory life sentence then the trial judge will specify a period of imprisonment, known as the 'minimum term', to ensure that the appropriate punishment for the crime is delivered. In the most serious offences the judge may make a *whole life order*, so that the offender may never be released from prison. Those individuals serving whole life prison sentences include criminals such as the Moors Murderer Ian Brady and the serial killer Dennis Nilsen.

In many jurisdictions, imprisonment is the most severe form of punishment for those convicted of breaking the law. As described by Slobogin and Fondacaro (2000), there are various justifications for imposing a sentence of loss of liberty that hinge on mixture of punishment, prevention, and protection. There is, however, some debate about what else prisoners should lose alongside their liberty. Should prisoners retain all their civil and human rights? This is a far-reaching question, touching on human rights legislation, the use of torture and cruel and degrading forms of treatment, freedom to vote, contact with families, and the use of medical and psychological interventions. Coyle (2008) discusses these and other

---

Box 11.2 Elements and purpose of ISPs

Elements
- High frequency of reporting to supervising officer
- Electronic tagging
- Home confinement
- Curfews
- Random drug testing
- Victim restitution

Purpose
- Retribution
- Deterrence
- Correction

associated issues, particularly with regard to the application and enforcement of international standards such as the Universal Declaration of Human Rights and the UN Standard Minimum Rules for the Protection of Prisoners.

Prison plus

In addition to deprivation of liberty, schemes may be introduced to attempt to make prison sanctions even more punishing then can be achieved just by loss of liberty. In decades past, the pains of imprisonment were increased by subjecting prisoners to various forms of hard labour and long periods of solitary confinement. In more recent times, prison regimes have been designed with the intention of providing imprisoned young offenders with a highly unpleasant experience. The institutions running these regimes became known as boot camps.

Boot camps

The history of boot camps can be traced back to the USA when they were introduced in 1983 in Georgia and Oklahoma principally for young non-violent offenders who did not have an extensive criminal history. The thinking informing the development of boot camps was plain: crime would be reduced by exposing the offenders to a military ethos, in settings where the staff have military titles and both staff and prisoners wear military uniforms, with an atmosphere of strict discipline, and where days are spent practising marching drills and taking part in physical training and hard labour. As the idea caught on so the number of boot camps grew so that by 1994 they were to be found in 36 American states.

Short, sharp shocks

Although obviously influenced by the American boot camps, the *short, sharp shock* regime in England rested on an altogether more refined pedigree. The designation 'short, sharp shock' was taken from a Gilbert and Sullivan opera, where the phrase refers to the act of beheading, and used in early 1980s as the moniker for a boot camp style of prison regime for young offenders. As with boot camps, the short, sharp shock custodial regime was based on the notion that a brief highly unpleasant custodial sentence would jolt the young offender and so deter them from a life of crime.

A decade later, a similar idea to the short, sharp shock was tried with young offenders at two English custodial establishments, the Thorn Cross High Intensity Treatment (HIT) regime and the Colchester Military Corrective Training Centre (MCTC). In the HIT regime, the young offenders faced a full and exacting 16-hour day, beginning with military style drills before breakfast then on to an activity packed daily programme that ended at 10 at night. The MCTC regime, as the name suggests, was based on the conditions which prevailed for military prisoners from the Army, the Royal Navy, the Royal Marines, and the Royal Air Force. As may be anticipated, the MCTC regime has an emphasis on physical training, physical fitness and, of course, marching drills.

The point of these regimes, as explained by various Home Secretaries, was to reduce crime through the exposure of offenders to regimes built on discipline, physical activity, hard work, and strict standards of behaviour (see Farrington et al., 2002). The conditions in the institutions were austere and the rules of the regime were strictly enforced. The young offenders were allowed very few personal possessions. The claim was made by government that exposure to a combination of deterrence, discipline, and training would reduce the criminal activity of the young people who experienced the harsh regime. The cost of the building work to prepare the institutions to run the new regimes ran to several million pounds.

Deterrence

The notion of deterrence has generated a considerable theoretical and empirical literature (Kennedy, 2009). As Kennedy points out, 'Deterrence is at the heart of the criminal-justice enterprise ... [it] is particularly at the heart of the preventative aspiration of criminal justice' (2009: 1). There are many ways by which the criminal justice system can act to increase deterrence: steps can be taken to increase the chances of being caught, such as by an increased police presence or more rigorous crime investigation; and sentencing practices can become more severe to introduce, say, larger fines and lengthy prison sentences.

Special deterrence refers to the effect of punishment on the individual offender: an offender who has been punished should be deterred from committing further crimes. Thus, in the case of boot camps and short, sharp shocks, the offenders exposed to those regimes should be deterred from further offending. On the other hand, *general* deterrence refers to effect of punishment in discouraging criminal activity across the population at large. In this case, the introduction of more punitive sanctions should be reflected in a lower crime rate.

Does punishment work?

Special deterrence

Does the punished offender cease offending? If punishment has a deterrent effect then we should expect that offenders will stop offending after they have been punished. There are two ways to consider whether punishment has a special deterrent effect: (1) do offenders stop offending after they have been punished? and (2) can any particular effect be demonstrated for projects such as the short, sharp, shock regime?

Reconviction after punishment

At first glance this appears relatively straightforward: how many offenders go on to commit more offences after they have been punished? The problem comes with deciding how to measure reconviction: how is reconviction measured, by official figures or self-report?; over what period of time should we expect the effect of punishment to last?; should we take account of the age and gender of the offender?; does the seriousness of the offence matter – would an arsonist reconvicted for burglary count the same as a shoplifter reconvicted for murder? If that's not enough, there is also the problem of 'pseudo reconvictions', which are convictions after, say, release from prison but which relate to offences committed before the prison sentence.

There are no easy answers to these questions as seen in the 2011 Statistical Bulletin published by the Ministry of Justice, which gives an analysis of adult reconvictions as recorded by the Police National Computer. An appendix to the 2011 Statistical Bulletin provides the overall 2-year reconviction rates of offenders convicted, with both community and prison sentences, over the period between 2000 and 2008. The reconviction rate remained reasonably stable with a low of 51.9 per cent in 2006 and a high of 58.5 per cent in 2002. The 2-year reconviction rate in noticeably higher than the 1-year rate, which is around 40 per cent and it would almost certainly be the case that the 3-year rate would be higher than the 2-year rate and so on. If these figures are reliable then it appears that within a 2-year period about half of those punished by the courts commit more crimes. In fact, the figure is likely to be greater than this, given the vagaries in reporting and cording crime. Nonetheless, as Nagin, Cullen, and Johnson (2009: 187) observe, given the numbers of people imprisoned and the cost to the public purse: 'It is remarkable that so many democratic societies, most especially the United States, incarcerate so many people without good estimates of the effects of this very expensive sanction on macro-level and individual-level crime rates'. This conclusion drawn by Nagin et al. is in sympathy with the findings of Marsh and Fox (2008: 403) whose analysis of the UK prison data led them to the view that, compared with community provision, 'Standard prison sentences are not an economically efficient means for reducing re-offending'.

Do studies that look at the effect of specific punitive measures give a better idea of whether punishment works? Gendreau, Goggin, and Fulton reviewed the evidence on ISPs and arrived at the view that 'When it comes to the matter of reducing offender recidivism, the conclusion is inescapable. ISPs have little effect on offenders' future criminal activity' (2001: 198). However, the same may not be the case for electronic monitoring. A large-scale study of more than 7,000 offenders in Florida reported by Padgett, Bales, and Blomberg (2006) found that both electronic (radio frequency) and GPS monitoring reduced reoffending and hence lowered the risk of harm to the community when offenders are not incarcerated. A Swiss study of 240 offenders randomly assigned either to community service or to electronic monitoring was reported by Killias, Gilliéron, Kissling, and Villettaz (2010). They found that when offenders completed their sanction, those assigned to electronic monitoring reoffended marginally less frequently than those assigned to community service. It is also the case that not all offenders serving community sentences pose the same level of risk of further offending. Thus, lower-risk offenders can be managed effectively in the community with less supervision than their higher risk counterparts (Barnes et al., 2010).

Moving to prison regimes, Thornton, Curran, Grayson, and Holloway (1984) found no effect of the *short, sharp shock* regime on the reconviction rate of the young offenders who experienced it. Farrington et al. (2002) conducted a reconviction study of the HIT and MTCT regimes for young offenders (YOs). For the HIT regime they reported that the 2-year reconviction figures revealed that 'The 70 per cent reconviction probability of these YOs is similar to the 72 per cent figure for all male offenders aged 18–20 serving a sentence of over 12 months up to four years released from prison in 1997' (Farrington et al., 2002: 15). The evaluation of the MTCT was hindered by the fact that the decision was made to close the centre after 1 year, meaning that only a small number of offenders passed through the regime. With due reservations given this important limitation on the strength of their findings, Farrington et al. (2002: 60) conclude: 'There was no evidence that Colchester YOI succeeded in reducing actual reconviction rates'.

In the USA, there have been several evaluative studies of boot camps, most notably by Doris Layton MacKenzie (see Wilson, MacKenzie, & Mitchell, 2008). MacKenzie, Brame, McDowall, and Souryal (1995) carried out the first large-scale evaluation of boot camps, mostly for young non-violent offenders without a previous extensive serious criminal history, across eight American states. MacKenzie et al. reported that the staff at the boot camps were highly enthusiastic about the programmes, seeing their role as being supportive in enabling offenders to take responsibility for their actions and to change for the better. The young inmates found the rules, discipline and activities stressful, especially in the first few weeks, and they also complained about verbal abuse and harsh treatment by staff. In light of such complaints, Benda, Toombs, and Peacock (2003: 548) suggested: 'Boot camps have been severely criticized for summary punishments that include physical abuse, humiliating verbal confrontations using belittling names such as "maggot" or "scumbag", and threats of being returned to prison where sexual victimization would likely be experienced'.

However, it is also evident that while at boot camp the young people increased their levels of physical fitness and were free from drugs. Further, compared with control inmates, boot camp inmates became more hopeful about the future, particularly their chances of getting a job. Probation and parole staff were rather sceptical, pointing to the difficulties the young people would face when they returned to their dysfunctional families, drug-using friends, and poor employment opportunities.

MacKenzie et al. (1995) found that compared with controls in other institutions the recidivism rates for the eight boot camp inmates were lower in three states, higher in one state, and no different in four states. The boot camps with the lower recidivism rates were those that gave most time to rehabilitative activities and those with more intensive supervision after release.

Meade and Steiner (2010) conducted a systematic review of the effects of boot camps. They note that the initial enthusiasm in the 1980s for boot camps based on quasi-military routines – by the 1990s, 30 states were sending young people to such institutions – quickly dissipated and a 'second generation' of boot camps emerged during the 2000s. As Meade and Steiner explain, these second generation boot camps 'place more emphasis on rehabilitative programming, and a number of programs have added an aftercare component' (2010: 843). A telling conclusion from their comprehensive review was that in the short-term, the boot camp regime changes the young peoples' attitudes and behaviour in a positive manner. However, the experience of a boot camps, in and of itself, does not have a consistent or significant long-term effect on the likelihood of recidivism. In terms of financial expenditure, Bierie (2009) reported that boot camps are cheaper to run than a traditional prison. Bierie also reported that the boot camp inmates showed a lower rate of recidivism. However, the numbers involved in Bierie's study are rather small with an overall total of 102 convictions (63 from the inmates from traditional prison and 39 from the boot camp).

In conclusion, the literature does not suggest that the militaristic elements of boot camp prisons are effective in reducing recidivism. Further, it is doubtful that turning a short, sharp, shock into a long, sharp, shock would have any effect on levels of juvenile recidivism (Winokur, Smith, Bontrager, & Blakenship, 2008).

The position does not change significantly if we move from juveniles to adults. Bonta and Gendreau (1990) argued that there are noteworthy individual differences in the way prisoners adapt to and manage a period of incarceration. There is little doubt that for some prisoners, a period in custody is a deeply adverse and stressful experience as seen, for example, in levels of self-harm and suicide that are above the norm (Pratt, Piper et al., 2006). However, the pains associated with imprisonment cannot be assumed to present for all prisoners, nor can they be assumed to be related to adverse prison conditions such as overcrowding. If there is a range of reactions to imprisonment might these have any relationship with the effects of imprisonment on reoffending? Chen and Shapiro (2007) considered whether harsh prison conditions in American federal prisons had an impact on recidivism. They concluded: 'We find no evidence that harsher confinement conditions reduce recidivism. If anything, our estimates suggest that moving an inmate over a cutoff that increases his assigned security level from minimum to above minimum security tends to increase his likelihood of rearrest following release' (Chen and Shapiro, 2007: 3). Essentially the same point holds true for white-collar criminals, those people typically convicted of economic crimes such as fraud, income tax evasion, and bank embezzlement. It might be thought that such middle-class criminals would be deterred from further offending by a period of imprisonment but

Weisburd, Waring, and Chayet (1995) found that prison does not have a specific deterrent effect upon these offenders.

Nonetheless, since the early 1980s the use of so called 'supermax' prison conditions has become increasingly widespread across most American states (Mears & Bales, 2009). As described by Mears and Bales (2010: 546), the characteristics of supermax prisons include 'twenty to twenty-four hour-per-day single-cell confinement with limited to no programming, services, or visitation for an indefinite period of time, in a setting that relies on substantially more intensive security measures than used in other facilities'. It remains a moot question whether the supermax facilities have any impact on rates of reoffending.

In Canada, Cook, and Roesch (2011) have expressed concerns regarding the advent of punitive, get-tough policies including long prison sentences, which it is claimed will reduce crime. Doob and Webster (2003) considered the specific general deterrent effect of the severity of sentences imposed by the court. They pick their way through a literature plagued by a morass of problems with measurement of key variables, conflicting explanatory accounts, and data gathering finally reaching the conclusion: 'Severity of sentences does not affect crime levels' (Doob & Webster, 2003: 191).

Why should punishment reduce offending?

The evidence that punishment deters criminals from committing more crimes is far from conclusive. If we step back from the empirical evidence, we can ask on what basis should punishment deter the individual from committing more crimes? In one way this is an odd question to ask: Kennedy (2009: 9) makes the observation: 'In fact, the world is soaked in deterrence, something that easily escapes notice because of its utter ordinariness. The class of people who persistently put their hands on hot stoves, cross the street without looking, and steal cars in front of police officers is very small'. All these points are undoubtedly true, so why does punishment not consistently and reliably deter the individual offender?

An answer to the question of does punishment reduce criminal behaviour can be formulated by drawing on some basic psychological research (Axlerod & Apsche, 1983; Hollin, 2002). If we reframe the issue of reducing recidivism as one of changing behaviour in terms of decreasing its frequency then we can apply learning theory. Skinner's operant learning (Skinner, 1938, 1974) considers the characteristics of a contingency in which a given behaviour decreases in frequency. As can be seen from Box 11.3, there are five empirically verified characteristics that define effective punishment (using the term punishment in an operant sense, i.e., behaviour that is decreasing in frequency).

Box 11.3   Characteristics of effective punishment contingencies

1. The punishing consequence of the behaviour immediately follows the behaviour.
2. The punishing consequence of the behaviour is inevitable and therefore follows *every* occurrence of the behaviour.
3. The punishing consequence of the behaviour should be intense.
4. The punishment should be demonstrably effective.
5. Punishment is most effective when another form of behaviour is available that results in a different consequences.

It is not difficult to see how real-life is at variance with the ideal conditions for effective punishment. The process of detection and prosecution makes it impossible for the aversive consequences that follow sentencing to be in close temporal proximity to the crime (which is not likely to be the case when stealing a car in front of a police officer). Thus, unlike putting one's hand on a hot stove, the consequences of a crime are much delayed (if and when they occur) rather than instant. The number of crimes committed by a typical offender is many more than they are sentenced for, meaning that punishment for criminal behaviour is by no means inevitable. The consequences that follow a criminal sentence are not likely to be intense at the onset, rather the offender is likely to work their way up the tariff from more lenient to harsher sentences. It is likely that what constitutes an 'effective' punishment will vary from individual to individual. However, it is beyond the capability of the criminal justice system to design punishment on an individual basis. The final point regarding the availability of alternative behaviours is important: the criminal behaviour will produce rewarding outcomes, how is the offender going to obtain those outcomes without recourse to crime? Finally, punishment tends to suppress behaviour rather than eliminate it: this means that the person may find new ways to gain what they want, which in the case of criminal behaviour may be more devious, risky, and harmful than was originally the case. Thus, punishment is most likely to be effective in reducing crime when the offender is able to develop a new type of behaviour that produces legitimate rewarding consequences.

One way of looking at the points made above is to say that what is required for effective criminal justice sanctions is even more severe sentences. This point is a familiar one to those who read certain national newspapers, or those who attend to political rhetoric, particularly when an election is in the offing. If there were to be more severe sentences then what would they look like? As the evidence on boot camps and the like does not support their continued use (as is the case in the USA), what would a truly aversive sentence involve? The obvious response is to return to former days and have prison regimes that inflict physical pain and suffering. There are two points to make in this regard: (1) short of the death penalty, it is doubtful whether physically demanding regimes would reduce offending; (2) if physical torment is the best response to crime we can come up with in the 21st century then something, somewhere has gone very badly wrong.

General deterrence

General deterrence hinges on the thesis that the population's perceived likelihood of being punished for committing a crime will act to deter them from committing crimes. This general deterrent effect is extremely difficult to investigate because, as McGuire (2008b: 271) points out, 'societies are scarcely likely to embark on large-scale experiments in which they temporarily suspend their laws for hypothesis testing purposes'. There are, however, occasions when the powers of deterrence temporarily take a large-scale break.

In several countries, the police have taken strike action and during times of large-scale civil unrest the forces of law and order may be powerless to act. It appears that what happens on such 'police-less' occasions can vary from location to location. Pfuhl (1983) suggested that overall there were minimal changes in the crime rate when the police were on strike in 11 American cities, although in some cities there were an increased numbers of crimes. McGuire notes that a similar pattern was evident when there was a police strike in Finland in 1976 (Makinen & Takala, 1980).

Another test of general deterrence rests on changes in crime following the introduction of punitive measures, such as changes in sentencing practice, which are intended to increase deterrence. Now, it is clear that the prevalence of different types of crime, say as measured by the crime statistics, do ebb and flow over time. However, these fluctuations occur for a range of reasons, including the prevailing economic conditions, levels of employment, and so on, so that showing cause and effect between the imposition of punitive criminal justice policies and changes in offending is extremely difficult to demonstrate empirically (Farrington & Langan, 1992). If we focus on harsh punishments for specific low volume crimes, such as murder, then it becomes possible to say a little more about the general deterrent effect of harsh sentences. The best example in this instance is to be found with the use of the death penalty.

The death penalty

It is impossible to know exactly how many people are legally executed each year. In some parts of the world, very precise figures are available: for example, America provides exact figures about its executions. The quote below is taken from the US Department of Justice publication *Capital Punishment, 2010 – Statistical Tables*:

> Between January 1 and December 19, 2011, 13 states executed 43 inmates, which was 3 fewer than the number executed as of the same date in 2010. Three states accounted for more than half of the executions carried out during this period: Texas executed 13 inmates; Alabama executed 6; and Ohio executed 5. Of the 43 executions carried out during this period, all were by lethal injection. No women were executed during this period.
>
> (US Department of Justice, 2011: 2)

McCann (2008) provides evidence to suggest that the disparity across American states in the use of the death penalty (convictions and executions) is positively linked to state conservatism as assessed by political affiliation, presidential voting, and other measures. As with previous studies of the use of sentencing, it is difficult to be certain that the courts are impartial politically on certain matters.

However, not all countries wish to be so open as America about the number of executions within their borders and do not make the figures publically available. There are various estimates available, compiled by organisations such as the United Nations and Amnesty International, but these figures are necessarily drawn from a range of sources and many not be highly reliable. Indeed, in its report *Death Sentences and Executions 2010*, Amnesty International (2011) states: 'The figures presented in this report are the largest that can safely be drawn from our research, although we emphasise that the true figures are significantly higher. Some states intentionally conceal death penalty proceedings; others do not keep or make available figures on the numbers of death sentences and executions'. The Amnesty report suggests that as a minimum estimate in 2010 there were 17,833 people under sentence of death and there were 527 executions. However, this figure is certainly an underestimation: China does not make available its crime statistics but the number of executions within China is said to be in the thousands. The number of executions in Japan is similarly shrouded in secrecy (Johnson, 2006).

Lu and Zhang (2005) discuss the use of the death penalty in China. They suggest that the death penalty has a long history in China and that its use increases in times of political and economic change depending on the circumstances: 'During Mao's time, the primary target of the death penalty was political offenses – the counterrevolutionaries. The 1979 Criminal

Law included twenty-eight capital offenses. Among these capital offenses, fifteen were counterrevolutionary offenses' (Lu and Zhang, 2005: 372). In more recent times, there has been a crime wave in China associated with economic reform and the accompanying 'open door' policy. In response to the social unease brought about by these reforms, in 1997 China increased the number of capital offenses from 28 to 68. A rise in the numbers of people executed was the inevitable consequence.

The use of the death penalty is bound into cultural norms and beliefs so that there are varying levels of support in different countries for its use. As in China, there is strong support for the death penalty in Russia (Semukhina & Galliher, 2009) but there are contrasting views in China, Japan, and America (Jiang, Lambert, Wang, Saito, & Pilot, 2010). It is not difficult to find divided opinions about the death penalty among a wide range of groups as defined by, for example, gender (Cochran & Sanders, 2009), feminist beliefs (Pope, 2002), race (Cochran & Chamlin, 2006), and social status (Whitehead, Blankenship, & Wright, 1999).

In those jurisdictions which apply the death penalty it is not always clear that it is used without discrimination. A study of the use of the death penalty in Louisiana reported by Smith (1987) looked at the race of the offender and victim and at the sex of the victim. Smith reported clear signs of discrimination in the use of the death penalty according to the race of the victim: those charged with the murder of a white victim, regardless of their own race, were twice as likely to receive a death sentence as those who killed a black victim. Further, those offenders who killed a female were more likely to receive a sentence of death. As Smith (1987: 283) says: 'In simple terms, risk of the death penalty was essentially influenced by *who* was murdered'.

There are a range of arguments for and against the use of the death penalty. There are moral arguments with respect to the state taking the life of one of its citizens (Sorrell, 1987). It can be argued that it is paradoxical for the state to engage in the behaviour it is seeking to punish. Amnesty International are opposed to the death penalty as they claim it is a violation of two fundamental human rights – the right to life and the right not to endure inhuman or degrading punishment – as detailed in the Universal Declaration of Human Rights. Similarly, there are religious arguments about the use of the death penalty: as Wozniak and Lewis (2010: 1082) note: 'Some of the earliest abolitionists viewed the crusade to eliminate capital punishment as a Christian imperative, while many of their pro-death penalty opponents cited the Bible to argue that capital punishment was an acceptable exercise of state power under God's law'.

As Wiecko and Gau (2008) point out, to proclaim oneself 'pro-life' in respect to abortion would suggest an opposition to killing of any type. However, the seemingly paradoxical nature of human thinking shows that this is not so: Wiecko and Gau suggest that those who hold pro-life/pro-death penalty views constitute about 5 per cent of the American population. How can these conflicting beliefs possibly be rationalised? The answer lies not so much in religious belief but in line with what Wiecko and Gau call 'Biblical literalism', an inflexible view of God's justice: 'Thus, the answer to the question "How do pro-life/pro-death penalty advocates reconcile these conflicting beliefs?" could be that they simply do not think about it much. A literal, retributivist orientation toward the Bible and a belief that God approves of vengeance is all that is necessary for a pro-death penalty stance ... and probably also for the idea that abortion is never acceptable' (Wiecko and Gau, 2008: 557).

Why do people support the death penalty? There are two main reasons given by members of the public, retribution and deterrence, which cross international borders (Bohm, 1992; Jiang, Lambert, & Nathan, 2009). As Bohm (1992) observes, the public's understanding of

---

Box 11.4   Wrongful executions

There are many examples from all over the world of men and women who have been wrongfully executed. The two English cases below are famous not just because of the wrongful deaths but because of the long fight for justice undertaken by relatives, friends, and journalists.

Derek Bentley, who was reported to have 'a mental age of 10', was hanged in 1953 at the age of 19, for his part in a robbery. Bentley's accomplice was carrying a gun and when they were challenged by the police Bentley was alleged to have shouted 'Let him have it!' and his 16-year-old companion, Christopher Craig, then shot and killed a policeman. The defence said that Bentley wanted his accomplice to hand over the gun; while the prosecution said Bentley was giving an instruction to shoot. After a long campaign by his sister, in 1993 Bentley received a posthumous pardon and 5 years later his conviction was overturned by the Court of Appeal.

Timothy Evans was found guilty of the murder of his wife and daughter and hanged in 1950. The murders were later found to have been committed, as Evans had claimed, by his neighbour the serial killer John Christie. The police investigation had failed to discover the other human remains buried in Christie's garden and the police were said to have coerced a false confession from Evans. Evans was granted a posthumous royal pardon in 1966 but his conviction has not been quashed despite his innocence being accepted.

---

retribution is far from simple: among others, retribution may be taken to mean simple revenge for the wrong committed, i.e., *lex talionis*, or alternatively the delivery of *just deserts* in that the offender pays back for the wrong they have committed.

It is a fact of life that nothing devised by man or woman is infallible. In the case of the death penalty, this means that wrongful executions are inevitable. Given the history of wrongful executions in many countries (see Box 11.4 for two English examples), there is a pragmatic argument to say that evidence presented in court can never lead to a judgment so far beyond reasonable doubt that justifies such an extreme act as the death sentence. Further, at a more prosaic level, given the costs of a death penalty case – Roman, Chalfin, and Knight (2009: 570) estimate that '[o]n average, a death notice adds about $1,000,000 in costs over the duration of a case'– making the wrong decision is a very expensive mistake to make.

There is no doubt that the continued use of the death penalty is often justified by recourse to proclaiming its general deterrent effect. There is a great deal of research into the deterrent effect of the death penalty because its adoption and abolition provides a natural experiment into the general deterrent effects of punishment. The hypothesis in favour of the death penalty is that its use deters those crimes – primarily murder although some argue for its use with sex offenders (Mancini & Mears, 2010) – for which it applies. Thus, is possible to compare the pre-post murder rate in countries, or even cities (Hjalmarsson, 2008; Zimring, Fagan, & Johnson, 2010), which have had the death penalty and abolished it. This deceptively simple 'pre-post change' hypothesis has generated a substantial and contradictory literature using a plethora of complex statistical techniques to grapple with a wide range of variables (Donohue & Wolfers, 2009).

Dezhbakhsh, Rubin, and Shepherd (2003: 344) used a system of simultaneous equations to arrive at the precise conclusion: 'Our results suggest that capital punishment has a strong deterrent effect; each execution results, on average, in eighteen fewer murders – with a margin of error of plus or minus ten'. Frakes and Harding (2009) arrive at a similar conclusion, a deterrent effect of the death penalty, specifically for child murder. On the other hand,

Doob and Webster (2003: 145) make the comment: 'Indeed, it was only after several decades of research producing consistent results in different periods and places and using multiple measures and methods that most social scientists abandoned the notion that capital punishment deters'.

Yang and Lester (2008) conducted a meta-analysis of 95 studies of the deterrent effect of the death penalty. They concluded that the death penalty did have a deterrent effect but its presence was dependent upon the type of analysis used in the primary studies. Those studies that used a cross-sectional methodology, studies of the impact of single executions, and studies of the effect of media publicity did not show a deterrent effect. However, studies that used time-series analysis and panel studies (which rely on longitudinal data) did show a deterrent effect, although in both cases the effect size was small. Yang and Lester (2008: 459) conclude: 'Even if executions are shown to deter potential murderers, alternative strategies to reduce the murder rate may be more effective and more ethically acceptable, depending on one's theory of the etiology of murder (such as stricter gun control, elimination of poverty, legalization of drugs, etc.)'.

Radelet and Lacock surveyed a number of distinguished criminologists asking for their views on the death penalty: the view from the experts was 'In short, the consensus among criminologists is that the death penalty does not add any significant deterrent effect above that of long-term imprisonment' (2009: 504). This doubt about the deterrent effect of the death penalty, along with the other arguments against its use, has led some eminent criminologists to argue for its global abolition (Hood, 2001) and others for, at least, its abolition for juvenile offenders (Morreale & English, 2004).

So, where does this all leave the deterrent effect of sentencing? Pratt, Cullen et al. (2006) reported a meta-analysis of empirical studies of deterrence theory that showed that deterrence is, of itself, unlikely to impact hugely on levels of crime. It may be that it is difficult within the criminal justice system to produce the optimum conditions for effective deterrence or that for reasons of humanity we refrain from the harshest of punitive measures that would have a deterrent effect.

However, there is another explanation, which is that we obey the law not to avoid being caught but for other, perhaps more constructive, reasons. Tyler (2006) looked at why people obey the law and found that most people said that they conformed with the law not because of a fear of punishment but because they respected the legitimate authority that the law embodies.

Incapacitation

If an offender is given a sentence that involves a period where they are, as it were, taken out of circulation, then it must surely follow that their offending will be reduced while they are incapacitated. This statement is true as far as the general public is concerned but it is also the case prisons are not 'crime neutral', indeed they are full of potential victims. An American study by Sorensen and Davis (2011) presented evidence in support of the truism that 'nothing predicts behaviour like behaviour'. They found that prisoners who were convicted of violent crimes such as assault and robbery were more likely than inmates convicted of property crimes to commit violent acts against both fellow inmates and prison staff. These acts included assault and fighting of varying degree of severity, threatening behaviour, extortion, possession and use of weapons, sexual abuse, rioting, and homicide. Indeed, there is a strong support for the notion that prisoners will display similar to, or *parallel*, behaviours on the inside as they exhibit outside security (Daffern, Jones, & Shine, 2010).

There is little doubt that more and more offenders are being taken out of circulation in some parts of the world. For example, Weiss and MacKenzie (2010: 269) make the startling observation that 'Even though the United States makes up just 5% of the world's population, it houses 25% of the world's prison population'. In numerical terms, Weiss and MacKenzie state that in 2008 the American prison population was more than 2.3 million people. As Weiss and MacKenzie observe, a rise and fall in the prison population has been a feature of several Western democracies but the scale of issue in America is unprecedented in recent times. The moot question is whether these levels of incarceration really do reduce the crime rate? Is it possible to lock up enough criminals so as to see a demonstrable fall in the number of crimes committed? This is a very difficult question to answer for several reasons. There is the issue of an accepted method by which to measure crime but the main problem lies in ascribing cause and effect to patterns of changes in two measures, i.e., the numbers in prison and the crime rate. There are several social factors that can shift over time that are associated with levels of crime and the size of the prison population: these include the unemployment rate, population demographics, police funding and priorities, the government's criminal justice policy, and so on. Piquero and Blumstein (2007) draw attention to the lack of consensus about the long-term effectiveness of incarceration. They also draw attention to the financial costs associated with a growing prison population. There are the obvious costs in terms of professional and civilian staff, building maintenance, and so on, but there are also human issues to consider.

A growing prison population focuses attention on prisoners with special needs as they become more prevalent in the prison population. As shown in Box 11.5, The United Nations' *Handbook on Prisoners with Special Needs* (United Nations, 2009) includes eight categories of this prisoners with needs above and beyond the majority of prisoners.

Corrections

The philosophy underpinning corrections is that it is possible to change the offender in order that he or she may live a life free from crime: an approach that is of benefit to the community as well as the offender (Raynor & Robinson, 2009). The genesis of idea in its modern format can be traced in Britain to the impact of the great prison reformers, such as Jonas Hanway (1712–86), John Howard (1726–90), and Elizabeth Fry (1780–1845), who campaigned for humane conditions in prisons and argued strongly that they should serve a useful purpose in reforming the prisoner through education, developing work skills and through learning self-discipline, and to treat other people with respect. There were similar figures, such as Enoch Cobb Wines (1806–79), Theodore William Dwight (1822–92), and Samuel J. Barrows (1845–1909), making the same case for prison reform in the USA.

Psychotherapeutic methods

As the reform movement gathered pace in the early 19th century, so psychological theories and their associated methods of change were applied to criminal populations, especially young offenders. This step took the process of reform into the realms of psychological treatment so that, as may be anticipated, the first therapeutic work with delinquents was from a psychoanalytic tradition (e.g., Aichhorn, 1955, orig. 1925). These first psychological accounts understood delinquent behaviour as a consequence of a failure in psychological development. Thus, it was aim of the psychologist, in the role of therapist, to correct this

---

Box 11.5   United Nations' categories of adult prisoners with special needs

1. *Prisoners with mental health care needs.* These prisoners are particularly vulnerable with complex needs with respect to protection of their human rights and provision of appropriate mental health care.
2. *Prisoners with disabilities.* These prisoners have long-term physical, mental, intellectual, or sensory impairments that require attention at both physical and psychological levels.
3. *Ethnic and racial minorities and indigenous peoples.* Prisoners from minority groups may differ from the majority of prisoners due to their ethnicity, race, and descent, which may be reflected for example in religious and cultural practices and languages. Penal policies and practices must seek to eliminate any discriminatory element.
4. *Foreign national prisoners.* These are prisoners who do not carry the passport of the country where they are in prison. They may have lived for extended periods in the country of imprisonment (but not naturalized) or be recently arrived. The foreign national prisoner faces many difficulties from language barriers to not understanding the criminal justice system of the country in which they are held.
5. *Lesbian, gay, bisexual, and transgender prisoners.* This group of prisoners can be discriminated against in terms of both their access to justice and physical victimisation.
6. *Older prisoners.* As life expectancy increases so the number of prisoners serving full life sentences increases accordingly. An aging prison population brings its own issues with an increased demand for specialist physical and mental health services. The typical physical prison environment is not designed architecturally for older prisoners: the stairs that are a feature of many prison wings are not suited to wheelchairs or walking frames; older prisoners who are physically frail are more vulnerable; and older prisoners may require particular types of diet. The older prisoner leaving prison after decades of imprisonment, perhaps with few or no family contacts, will need high levels of support in returning to a society that will have changed dramatically since they last lived in the community.
7. *Prisoners with terminal illness.* The numbers prisoners who face an early death is rising worldwide, in part due to the global increase in tuberculosis and HIV/AIDS. These prisoners will have particular medical needs according to their illness alongside the need for psychological and spiritual support as death draws closer.
8. *Prisoners under sentence of death.* In those countries that retain the death penalty, it is possible that the prisoner sentenced to death will have a long wait, up to a decade, awaiting execution. These delays may be caused by appeals against execution and due the due process of law. A prisoner sentenced to death will need access to informed legal services, interpreters if they are in a foreign country, and assistance in coping with the physical and mental anguish in being held in alone knowing that death may be imminent. Indeed, the period of isolation and uncertainty about the time of execution has been referred to as the 'death row phenomenon', with the associated psychological effects on the prisoner. The UN Handbook notes that 'The "death row phenomenon" has also been found to amount to cruel, inhuman and degrading punishment in violation of international human rights law by the European Court of Human Rights' (United Nations, 2009: 161).

---

developmental failure and so reduce delinquency. Psychodynamic methods of treatment with offenders became increasingly widespread: group and milieu therapies – including group counselling, psychodrama, reality therapy, transactional analysis, and therapeutic communities – were widely used in Britain and America in the 1940s, 1950s, and 1960s (Lester & Van Voorhis, 2004a). However, as discussed in Box 11.6, there is the thorny question of what, exactly, we mean by the term 'treatment'.

The therapeutic community (TC) has also used been used with offenders. TCs are typically based around communalism, democratisation, permissiveness, and reality confrontation, so that those living in the community take responsibility for their own behaviour while appreciating the rights of others (Rapoport, 1960). TCs have been used, without a great deal of success in terms of a reduction in recidivism, with a range of offenders (Lipton, 2001). There have been TCs in residential establishments for young offenders (e.g., Cornish & Clarke, 1975) and in prisons, there have been experiments in which wings are turned into TCs (Smith, 1984). The most famous example in Scotland was the Special Unit at Barlinnie Prison in Glasgow (Cooke, 1989), which housed Jimmy Boyle, a notorious criminal who later became a journalist and writer (Boyle, 1977). Grendon Prison in England functions as a psychotherapeutic unit according to TC principles (Shuker & Sullivan, 2010). TCs have also been used with violent offenders (Day & Doyle, 2010), sex offenders (Ware, Frost, & Hoy, 2009), and drug-using mentally ill offenders (Sacks, Sacks, McKendrick, Banks, & Stommel, 2004).

The American Cambridge-Somerville Youth Study (Powers & Witmar, 1951) was an intervention for young males at risk of delinquency and their families. Starting in 1939, counsellors were assigned to the delinquent's family and visited on average twice a month, although families were able to call for assistance as necessary. The treatment group had access to a range of support services including academic teaching, medical and psychiatric care, counselling, and various community programmes. The treatment lasted for between 2 and 8 years. A control group simply provided information about themselves without access to services. McCord (1978) traced more than 500 men who had participated in the study: while those in the treatment group expressed fond memories of the project and their counsellors, there was no difference in the rate of offending, either as juveniles or adults, of the treatment and control groups. Yet further, McCord lists seven *adverse* effects of treatment, including more signs of mental illness, more evidence of alcoholism, and a tendency to die at a younger age. McCord suggests that the intervention may have fostered a dependency on outside assistance that caused problems when it was removed. McCord (1978: 289) concludes: 'Intervention programmes risk damaging the individuals they are designed to assist'. It remains the case that well-intentioned interventions can produce unwanted effects. Gottfredson (2010) showed how an after-school programme at an American school was actually providing 'deviancy training' rather than reinforcing pro-social attitudes and behaviours.

Box 11.6 What do we mean by *treatment*?

The term 'treatment' is frequently used in the context of working with offenders to reduce levels of offending. Its use in this way attracts criticism for its overtones of pathology: i.e., that offending is pathological and so offenders need to be cured. While some treatment programmes may begin from this perspective, it is not a view that is universally held. The word 'treatment' can legitimately be used in a broader sense as in the sense of managing an issue or seeking to bring about positive change. For example, teaching an offender to learn to read may bring a change that will reduce their offending, the same may be said for teaching problem-solving skills: neither education or acquiring cognitive skills implies a pathology. Of course, the same could be said about punishment: the imposition of penalties to attempt to reduce offending is to treat offenders in a particular way.

Behaviour modification

While the popularity of psychotherapeutic methods in the criminal justice system has waned, the practice of forensic psychotherapy remains, although perhaps as a speciality requiring high levels of professional training (Lester & Van Voorhis, 2004b). As psychotherapeutic methods faded from correctional practice, the replacements which emerged in the 1970s methods were based on behavioural theory (Milan, 2001). The use of behaviour modification techniques such as the token economy – a system in which 'good behaviour' gains points that can later be exchanged for rewards such as cigarettes or access to leisure activities, television, and so on – spread through in American prisons with the explicit 'managerial' aim of increasing conformity to institutional rules. These token economy programmes (Milan & McKee, 1976; Milan, Throckmorton, McKee, & Wood, 1979) attracted a great deal of hostile criticism on both legal and ethical grounds. After a series of lawsuits and congressional hearings, these programmes faded from use.

However, behavioural methods continued to be applied in a range of settings, from residential homes to the community, often with young offenders (Hollin, 1990). The use of behavioural methods led to a number of innovative projects for young offenders as seen with Achievement Place in Kansas (Kirigin, Braukmann, Atwater, & Wolf, 1982) and the use of social skills training (SST; Henderson & Hollin, 1986). Further, Howells (1986) noted the potential of SST with adult offenders, particularly violent and sexual offenders.

Family therapy

The use of family therapy with delinquents has proved popular: Kazdin (1987) identifies two broad types of family therapy, parent management training (PMT) and functional family therapy (FFT). In PMT, the focus is on training the parental skills required to manage the child or adolescent's problem behaviour and to reinforce desirable behaviour. In FFT, the focus shifts to changing the interactive processes within the family system: thus, rather than parent skills, the aim is to increase the family's understanding of family issues, enabling them to generate effective and agreeable solutions to family problems (Alexander & Parsons, 1982).

Cognitive-behavioural methods

The next phase saw the field shift to the use of cognitive therapies with offenders, as research suggested that certain aspects of interpersonal cognition were related to offending (Ross & Fabiano, 1985). These cognitive interventions typically relied on cognitive-behavioural methods of change such as coping skills training, stress inoculation training, and self-instructional training. The introduction of anger management training to ameliorate the harmful effects of high levels of emotional arousal was another development in this tradition (Novaco, 1975).

Nothing works

A number of reviews of the effects of treatment suggested that interventions do not lead to a reduction in crime (Bailey, 1966; Brody, 1976). However, it was a paper by Martinson (1974), based on a larger review of 231 studies by Lipton, Martinson, and Wilks (1975), which was to prove the most influential. The basis of this paper was that the case had not been proven that treatment-orientated interventions had any marked or sustainable effect.

While this view and its supporting evidence was strongly challenged (Gendreau & Ross, 1979, 1987; Thornton, 1987) and, indeed, Martinson later modified his views (Martinson, 1979), the message was widely accepted that 'nothing works' and any attempt at rehabilitation through treatment was doomed to failure. The net effect within the criminal justice system was a period during the 1980s where rehabilitation disappeared to be replaced by punitive regimes offering nothing more than 'just deserts' (Hudson, 1987).

What works?

The resurrection of treatment in the 1990s is directly attributable to the impact of the meta-analyses of the offender treatment literature. Meta-analysis is a statistical technique for reviewing the accumulated results of a large number of primary research studies. Unlike traditional qualitative reviews of research, meta-analysis can control for variations and potential biases in the primary studies, allowing a quantifiable treatment effect to emerge (Cohen, 1988; Glass, McGraw, & Smith, 1981). Thus, meta-analyses of the offender treatment literature have developed coding systems to account for variations across studies in variables such as offender group, offence type, follow-up period, criterion of outcome and treatment setting (e.g., Lipsey, 1992; Redondo, Sánchez-Meca, & Garrido, 2002). A meta-analysis produces a statistic called an effect size from which the magnitude of the difference in outcome between treated groups and controls can be calculated (Marshall & McGuire, 2003).

Garrett (1985) reported a meta-analysis of the effects of residential treatment with delinquents that was the forerunner of 70 meta-analytic studies of offender treatment (for reviews see McGuire, 2002, 2008). A meta-analysis can offer a summary of a substantial literature: for example, Lipsey's (1992) study incorporated 443 treatment studies of offenders aged from 12 to 21 years.

The meta-analyses yielded a 'net effect' of treatment of all kinds (which includes deterrence, boot camps, group therapy, and so on) as a mean effect size (ES) with respect to recidivism, which was of the order of a 10–12 per cent reduction in reoffending (Lösel, 1996). However, again with reoffending as an outcome, Lipsey (1992) reported that interventions that were multi-modal, behavioural, cognitive-behavioural, or skills-oriented in nature had a positive ES; deterrence-based interventions had a negative ES. Further, effective offender interventions take the form of structured programmes with specific aims and objectives, involve offenders with a high risk of reoffending, are delivered with high levels of treatment integrity by trained staff, and enjoy high levels of organisational support (Lowenkamp, Flores, et al., 2010).

Since the first meta-analyses with their emphasis on young offenders the same methodology has been applied to a range of offender populations. There are now meta-analyses of the effects of interventions with women offenders (Dowden & Andrews, 1999), sexual offenders (Hanson, Bourgon, Helmus, & Hodgson, 2009; Lösel & Schmucker, 2005), drink-drivers (Wells-Parker, Bangret-Downs, McMillen, & Williams, 1995), juvenile offenders (Lipsey, 2009), violent offenders (McGuire, 2008a), men who are violent to their partners (Babcock, Green, & Robie, 2004), and drug abusing offenders (Mitchell, Wilson, & MacKenzie, 2007; Prendergast, Podus, Chang, & Urada, 2002).

Principles of effective practice

In coining a phrase from the title of Martinson's (1974) paper, the collective interest in applying the lessons from the meta-analyses to inform rehabilitative practice with offenders became known as '*What Works?*' (McGuire, 1995). The principles of effective practice informing 'What Works' came from syntheses of the findings of the meta-analyses (e.g., Andrews, 1995; Gendreau, 1996; Hollin, 1999; Lösel, 1996), reconfirmed by later analysis (Smith, Gendreau, & Swartz, 2009)

The first principle is the *risk principle*: intensive (and expensive) services are necessary for offenders with a high risk of reoffending; a lighter touch is needed for offenders with a low risk of reoffending. The second principle is the *needs principle*: interventions should target offenders' criminogenic needs: if an intervention is to reduce offending then it must target those aspects of an offenders' functioning which are related to their offending. This principle does not suggest that non-criminogenic needs should be ignored, rather there must be clarity in what outcome an intervention can be expected to achieve: interventions that target non-criminogenic needs will be seen to 'fail' when they do not reduce offending.

The third principle, *the responsivity principle*, highlights the need for a close match between the delivery of the intervention and offender characteristics such as age (Bogestad, Kettler, & Hagan, 2009; Ozabaci, 2011), culture (Sharkey, Sander, & Jimerson, 2010), intellectual ability (Taylor, Thorne, Robertson, & Avery, 2002), and gender (Blanchette & Brown, 2006; see Chapter 12 for further discussion of gender sensitive crime prevention). Andrews (1995) noted the need to include *treatment integrity* – a close match between treatment design and actual service delivery (Hollin, 1995) – alongside the three principles of effective practice.

The combination of risk, need, and responsivity became known as the Risk-Need-Responsivity (RNR) model of offender assessment and rehabilitation (Andrews, Bonta, & Wormith, 2006). The RNR model is now the predominant model in the field of offender rehabilitation and can arguably inform work in other areas of applied psychology (Andrews & Bonta, 2010). There are other models of offender rehabilitation: for example, the Good Lives Model (GLM; Ward & Brown, 2004) is a 'strengths-based' approach that seeks to enable offenders to achieve legitimately the primary goals they currently gain through crime. Therefore, when set against the standards of interventions that stem from the RNR model, the GLM is lacking a solid empirical base, is theoretically weak, and adds little if anything to the RNR model (Andrews, Bonta, & Wormith, 2011). While popular with some practitioners, the GLM also faces a presentational problem: the *realpolitik* is that it is one thing for governments to use public funds for evidence-based programmes to reduce risk to the community, quite another to use the same funds with the aim of helping the offender to lead a good life when it is less than clear than the general public (i.e., voters) are supportive of offender rehabilitation (Perelman & Clements, 2009).

Research into practice: risk and need

The application of the risk principle and the need principle to practice relies, by definition, upon a means of measuring risk and need. The Level of Supervision Inventory (Andrews, 1982) was designed for this task and was developed in Canada as the Level of Service Inventory, later becoming the Level of Service Inventory–Revised (Andrews & Bonta, 1995). The use of the LSI-R is explained in Box 11.7.

The LSI-R has been used extensively (Vose, Cullen, & Smith, 2008): it is both to be valid and reliable in England (Hollin, Palmer, & Clark, 2003) and able to differentiate the criminogenic needs of violent and non-violent offenders (Hollin & Palmer, 2003). The risk principle has been shown to be critically important in the delivery of effective interventions (Andrews & Dowden, 2006; Lewis, Maguire, Raynor, Vanstone, & Vennard, 2007; Lowenkamp, Latessa, & Holsinger, 2006; Palmer et al., 2009).

Box 11.7   The LSI-R

The LSI-R consists of 54 items, completed through interview with the offender and file review, which assess 10 criminogenic needs:

Accommodation	Alcohol/Drug Problems
Attitudes/Orientation	Companions
Criminal History	Education/Employment
Emotional/Personal	Family/Marital
Finance	Leisure/Recreation

The items are scored to give a total for each area of need, so specifying where interventions should be targeted; the total score gives an estimate of risk of reoffending.

The measurement of risk in relation to offending has occupied a great deal of attention (Hanson, 2009; Jones, Brown, & Zamble, 2010; Singh & Fazel, 2010; Vrieze & Grove, 2010) with a range of risk assessment instruments available for recidivism generally and for specific offences such as violent crimes (Campbell, French, & Gendreau, 2009; Singh, Grann, & Fazel, 2011) and sexual crimes (Hanson & Thornton, 2000). In England and Wales, use is made of the Offender Assessment System (OASys; Home Office, 2006) and the Offender Group Reconviction Score (OGRS; Copas & Marshall, 1998; Howard, Francis, Soothill, & Humphreys, 2009) to inform risk management and sentence planning. Given the level of need among prisoners, particularly newly sentenced prisoners (Stewart, 2008), there is a pressing need for clear assessment. However, one of the problems with good assessment is that it can identify levels of need that stretch beyond the resources allocated for services to meet those needs.

Structured interventions

The use of treatment manuals to guide the delivery of an intervention is established in mainstream clinical psychology (Wilson, 1996). In the field of offender treatment, *Reasoning and Rehabilitation* (R&R) was the first manualised offending behaviour programme to be widely used with offenders. This structured, programmed approach to intervention, based on cognitive-behavioural principles (Lipsey, Landenberger, & Wilson, 2007; Polaschek, 2011), has become widespread throughout the criminal justice system in both prison and community services (Hollin & Palmer, 2006b).

Reasoning and Rehabilitation

R&R was developed in Canada by Robert Ross and Elizabeth Fabiano (Ross, Fabiano, & Ewles, 1988; Ross, Fabiano, & Ross, 1989) and was the first evidence-based, structured cognitive-behavioural programme intended to reduce offending. R&R is based on research which suggests an association between cognition and offending (Ross & Fabiano, 1985). R&R aims to enable the offender to learn new ways of thinking so promoting the thinking patterns and skills that are associated with pro-social behaviour. Through the use of techniques such as role-playing, rehearsal, modelling, reinforcement, and cognitive exercises R&R seeks to change offenders' self-control, social problem-solving skills, social perspective-taking, critical reasoning, and the attitudes and beliefs that support criminal behaviour. There is an emphasis on applying the newly acquired skills to everyday life.

R&R is designed to be delivered by a range of staff, including prison and probation officers, not just professional therapists. There is an intensive training process for those who are to deliver the programme and video monitoring of sessions to assist feedback to staff and to help maintain treatment integrity. R&R has been used in both institutional and community settings in Canada, England and Wales, Scotland, Spain, Germany, Scandinavia, Australia and New Zealand, and the USA. To date, there have been several evaluations that show positive results in terms of reduced offending (Antonowicz, 2005; Tong & Farrington, 2006).

Straight Thinking on Probation (STOP)

Mid-Glamorgan Probation Service in Wales took the bold step of running an adaptation of the R&R programme in 1991 (Knott, 1995). An evaluation of the programme reported that the actual and the predicted rates of reconviction were the same for those allocated to treatment and the comparison group at 12-months follow-up (Raynor & Vanstone, 1996). However, for those offenders who actually completed the programme there was a significantly lower reconviction rate than predicted, along with a significant lower rate of custodial sentences upon reconviction.

Enhanced Thinking Skills (ETS)

ETS is also a cognitive skills programme, developed within the English and Welsh Prison Service, to addresses similar targets to R&R. Initially used within the Prison Service, since 2000 it has been used in the National Probation Service in England and Wales. As with R&R, evaluations have shown ETS to be effective in institutional settings with adult male offenders who complete the programme (Friendship, Blud, Erikson, Travers, & Thornton, 2003; Sadlier, 2010).

Think First

The Think First programme is a third general cognitive skills programme developed in England and Wales (McGuire, 2005): it is similar in content to R&R and ETS but has a more explicit focus on offending behaviour. The design of Think First includes pre-group sessions to prepare the offender to take part in the programme and post-group sessions to work at preventing relapse.

An evaluation of Think First in the English and Welsh Probation Service (when it was called *Offence-Focused Problem Solving*) found significant decreases in criminal attitudes and locus of control and significant increases in self-esteem after participating in the programme (McGuire & Hatcher, 2000). Several large-scale evaluations of all three programmes, under the generic title of cognitive skills programmes, conducted in the English and Welsh Probation Service have shown significant decreases in reconviction (Hollin et al., 2008; Hollin & Palmer, 2009; Palmer et al., 2007; McGuire et al., 2008). These evaluations also prompted a methodological discussion of the utility of different research designs in programme evaluation (Hollin, 2008) and exploration of the adverse effects on outcome when the risk principle is bypassed (Palmer et al., 2009).

Alongside cognitive skills programmes, interventions building on What Works and the RNR model were designed within England and Wales for use with a range of types of offender in the criminal justice system. As well as the examples discussed below of programmes for sex offenders and violent offenders, there were programmes for domestic violence (Bowen, 2011), drink-impaired drivers (Palmer, Hatcher, McGuire, Bilby, & Hollin, 2012), life-sentenced prisoners (Ruddell, Broom, & Young, 2010), substance-using offenders (Palmer et al., 2011; McMurran, Riemsma, Manning, Misso, & Kleijnen, 2011), and offenders on probation in the community (Bruce & Hollin, 2009; Pearson, McDougall, Kanaan, Bowles, & Torgerson, 2011).

Sex Offender Treatment Programme (SOTP)

Originally a single programme, SOTP has developed into a suite of programmes within the English and Welsh prison service: these variations on a theme address the criminogenic needs of sex offenders of lower levels of intellectual functioning offenders; provide an intensive version for sexual offenders of high risk and need alongside a version for *low*-risk sexual offenders; and a booster programme for offenders who may need further intervention after completing one of the other versions (Mann & Fernandez, 2006). The outcome research has found mixed results (Beech & Mann, 2002). Where positive results in terms of sexual reconviction have been found, these have typically been among medium-low and medium-high risk men who have been responsive to treatment (Beech, Erikson, Friendship, & Ditchfield, 2001; Friendship, Mann, & Beech, 2003).

Aggression Replacement Training (ART)

The ART programme was developed by Arnold Goldstein and colleagues (Goldstein, Glick, & Gibbs, 1998, 2004; Goldstein & Glick, 2001). ART incorporates skills training, anger control, and moral reasoning training to assist the offender to learn how to control their violent behaviour. ART was used successfully by the English and Welsh Probation Service with adult male violent offenders in the community (Hatcher et al., 2008).

The research into the effectiveness of rehabilitative programmes has highlighted new questions for researchers to answer. It has become clear, for example, that when offenders drop out of programmes their recidivism rate is poor compared with those who complete treatment (McMurran & McCulloch, 2007; McMurran & Theodosi, 2007; Olver, Stockdale, & Wormith, 2011). It follows that understanding more about which offenders drop out of treatment and why will inform efforts to increase retention rates. The positive findings have also prompted theoretical questions about why, exactly, cognitive-behaviour interventions are effective (Vaske, Galyean, & Cullen, 2011).

Organisational issues

As the English and Welsh Prison Service attempted to translate the What Works? principles into practice it became evident that much was to be gained from clear criteria to determine if a given programme is fit for purpose. The need for standards led to the formulation of the process of accreditation whereby accreditation criteria (see Box 11.8) could be used to assess the suitability of a programme with regard to its anticipated effect in reducing offending (Lipton, Thornton, McGuire, Porporino, & Hollin, 2000; Maguire, Grubin, Losel, & Raynor, 2010). These standards and the processes for ensuring they are met were later adopted by other agencies, such as the Scottish Prison Service (SPS, 2003), and later introduced for criminal justice community programmes (for a full discussion see Hollin & Palmer, 2006a). As well as programmes being fit for purpose, the implementation and running of the programmes within criminal justice settings is critically important (Bourgon & Armstrong,

---

Box 11.8   Accreditation criteria

Outline of CSAP accreditation criteria for offending behaviour programmes:
1. Programmes must have a clear model of change.
2. The selection of offenders must be justified.
3. Target a range of dynamic risk factors.
4. Programmes should use effective methods of change.
5. Programmes should be skills oriented.
6. Sequencing, intensity, and duration of treatment should be justified.
7. Attention should be given to the engagement and motivation of offenders taking part in the programme.
8. Continuity of programmes and services within sentence planning.
9. Programmes should show how they will maintain integrity.
10. There should be procedures to allow the continued evaluation of a programme.

2005; Lipsey & Cullen, 2007). The best designed programme in the world will fail if it is not implemented and conducted in the correct way by highly trained and supervised staff (Dowden & Andrews, 2004). However, achieving and maintaining organisational coherence and standards of delivery for effective service delivery is neither simple or straightforward (Gendreau, Goggin, & Smith, 2001) but is critically important (Andrews, 2011).

One of many issues to be faced, as so splendidly phrased by Gendreau, Smith, and Thériault (2009), lies in 'correctional quackery and the law of fartcatchers'. Gendreau et al. discuss how a great deal of practice in corrections is based on whimsy and rhetoric, rather than evidence, promoted by those in positions of authority but without the specialist knowledge to be critical of the policies and practice they endorse (see Box 11.9).

Box 11.9   Fartcatchers and correctional quackery

What is correctional quackery? Gendreau et al. (2009: 386) describe it as those 'common sense' fix-it cures for crime that permeate the criminal justice system: 'There are a multitude of other commonsense programs that have surfaced in the media that have escaped evaluation, such as acupuncture, the angel-in-you therapy, aura focus, diets, drama therapies, ecumenical Christianity, finger painting, healing lodges, heart mapping, horticulture, a variety of humilia-tion strategies (e.g., diaper baby treatment, dunce cap, cross dressing, John TV, sandwich board justice, Uncle Miltie treatment), no frills prisons, pet therapy, plastic surgery, and yoga ... [more instances] ... such as brain injury reality, cooking/baking, dog sledding, handwriting, interior decorating in prisons (e.g., pink and teddy bear décor), classical music, and ritualized tapping'.

How could such a litany of fads be allowed to happen? Again, Gendreau et al. provide an explanation, this time with reference to research showing a null effect of boot camps, of how this quackery can occur: 'Reacting to the study (research on the lack of effectiveness of military boot camps), a spokesman for Governor Zell Miller said that "we don't care what the study thinks" – Georgia would continue to use its boot camps. Governor Miller is an ex-Marine, and says that the Marine boot camps he attended changed his life for the better: he believes that the boot camp experience can do the same for wayward Georgia youth ... "Georgia's Commissioner of Corrections" ... also joined the chorus of condemnation, saying that academics were too quick to ignore the experiential knowledge of people "working in the system" and rely on research findings' (quote cited from Vaughn, 1994: 2).

The exercise of 'common sense' allows scientific evidence to be dismissed in favour of anecdote, fashion, and personal experience so that the solution to a complex problem, such as criminal behaviour, is reduced to a single shot, evidence-free, magic bullet. The exercise of common sense places personal values and experience above knowledge and results in expensive and potentially damaging poor practice. The 'fartcatchers' are those who stand downwind and allow banal practice to spread (the word originally referred to obsequious servants who, like Uriah Heep, trail after their masters, with cloying humility, fawning, and eager to please).

The fact that practice without an evidence base can flourish in the criminal justice system raises two immediate issues. First, it calls into question the probity of those running the system: if health services allowed such unproven, unscientific practices with people with physical ailments there would, rightly, be a public outcry. Second, it is inevitable that this quackery will have no effect on offending thereby providing fuel for those who wish to return to nothing works (Cullen, Smith, Lowenkamp, & Latessa, 2009).

Mentally disordered offenders

The mentally disordered offender is detained not for punishment but for treatment in order to reduce their risk to the community. The treatment will necessarily be focused on their mental disorder but attention to the offending behaviour is also important. In some cases, the nature of the offence and the risk to the public may require close control and security. Mainstream psychiatric hospitals are not equipped to manage such offenders and, of course, prisons are not appropriate as the mentally disordered offender is not a criminal. As some mainstream offenders held in prisons are mentally disordered – Fazel and Danesh (2002: 548) reviewed 62 surveys from 12 countries and suggested that 'Typically about one in seven prisoners in western countries have psychotic illnesses or major depression ... and about one in two male prisoners and about one in five female prisoners have antisocial personality disorders'– so there are attempts to divert those with a mentally disorder from the criminal justice system (James, 2010). Nonetheless, the fact remains that some offenders with a mental disorder are sent to prison. There are substantial problems in attempting to treat mental disorder within the criminal justice system (Chandler, Peters, Field, & Juliano-Bult, 2004) so that in practice there is a steady movement of prisoners between the criminal justice system and the health service.

There is a need to keep some offenders with a mental disorder in conditions of high security. The means by which this is achieved is through the maximum security psychiatric hospital: these institutions are variously known as State Hospitals or Special Hospitals.

High security hospitals

In England and Wales, there are three Special Hospitals and one in Scotland that also serves Northern Ireland: each hospital houses more than 100 patients, mainly males but with some females. The first special hospital, Broadmoor Hospital in Berkshire, opened in 1863, followed by Rampton Hospital in Nottinghamshire in 1910. Ashworth Hospital near Liverpool is the third Special Hospital and was formed from a merger of Moss Side Hospital, which dates back to 1914 as an institution for 'shell shocked' soldiers from the Great War, and Park Lane Hospital, which opened much later in 1974 (Greenland, 1969). Carstairs is the State Hospital in Scotland. It remains a moot point as to whether high security hospitals can cater for the specific needs of women (Thomas et al., 2005).

Special Hospitals have held and continue to detain some of the most infamous cases in recent criminal history (see Box 11.10).

Box 11.10   Infamous Special Hospital patients

Beverley Allitt, Rampton Hospital: Nurse known to have killed at least four children.

Ian Brady, Ashworth Hospital: Responsible with Myra Hindley for the 'Moors Murders' of five children.

Charles Bronson, Ashworth Hospital: Armed robber known as 'the most violent person in Britain'.

Ian Huntley, Rampton Hospital: Responsible for the 'Soham Murders' of two young girls.

Ronald Kray, Broadmoor: With his twin brother, Reggie, a violent gangster involved in organized crime and murder: Ronald Kray died in 1995.

Peter Sutcliffe, Broadmoor: Serial killer known as the 'Yorkshire Ripper' known to have killed 13 women.

Graham Young, Broadmoor: Murdered at least three people, including his father and sister, by poisoning: he died in 1990.

Black (1982) reported a 5-year follow-up study of 125 male patients discharged from Broadmoor. He found that of the 125 patients, 101 had had no readmission to any psychiatric hospital, 97 had no record of imprisonment, and 70 had no further court appearances. Jamieson and Taylor (2004) conducted a follow-up study of 197 Special Hospital patients (167 men and 30 women). They found that 74 of the patients were convicted after discharge, typically within a 2-year period, most often for property and violent offences. Buchanan, Taylor, and Gunn (2004) investigated a sample of 40 patients who were discharged from an English special hospital between 1987 and 1991 and then were convicted of a serious offence by 1993. Of these 40 patients, eight had been discharged from special hospital with no arranged psychiatric follow-up, and there were only informal arrangements for a further five patients. For 27 patients discharged under supervision, 11 dropped out of that supervision in the period between leaving hospital and the offence. In comparison with a matched group of un-convicted patients, the convicted patients were significantly younger, less likely to have attended mainstream education, more likely to have a history of alcohol use, to have a diagnosis of psychopathic disorder and to have more criminal convictions. Similar findings have been recorded in a follow-up of patients from a high security hospital in Norway (Bjørkly, Sandli, Moger, & Stang, 2012).

Medium secure hospitals

The high-risk mentally disordered offender presents a two-sided problem: (1) do all mentally disordered offenders have to go to (highly expensive) high security regardless of the degree of risk they pose to the community?; (2) where do patients go when they have been treated and no longer require high levels of security? The solution lies in facilities which have a medium degree of security: these hospitals, known as Regional Secure Units (RSUs), were established across in England and Wales in the 1980s (Coid, Kahtan, Cook, Gault, & Jarman, 2001a,b). As RSUs are spread around the country, they have the advantage that the majority of patients can remain close to their own home. Similarly, close links can be made with low security and community psychiatric services to foster a high degree of continuity of patient care and risk management.

Cope and Ward (1993) looked at the outcomes for patients transferred from high to medium security over a 10-year period. They found that one-third of the patients returned directly to high security. Cope and Ward also found that just over 10 per cent of patients had serious reconvictions, with personality disordered patients responsible for most of the reconvictions. Similar findings were presented by Quinn and Ward (2000) with more than one-quarter of patients returning from medium to high security and with a similar rate of serious reconvictions. Blattner and Dolan (2009) carried out a follow-up study of 72 patients who had moved from high security and were being discharged into the community after a stay in medium security. They found a high rate of returns to high security, with 46 per cent of the patients going back to high security. The 15 per cent reconviction rate for serious offences was comparable with the other two studies.

Of course, some patients enter and leave medium security without experiencing high security. Maden et al. (1999) followed-up a group of 234 first admissions to medium security: they found that almost one-quarter of the patients had been reconvicted at a mean of 6.6 years follow-up, 9 per cent of patients had died, and 74 per cent had been readmitted to hospital. Maden et al. (2004) followed up a sample of 959 patients over a 2-year period and found a 15 per cent reconviction rate. Davies, Clarke, Hollin, and Duggan (2007) reported a follow-up of 550 patients discharged from medium security over a 20-year period. They reported that almost half of the patients were reconvicted (14 per cent for a grave offence) and almost two-fifths of the patients were readmitted to secure care. Davies et al. also looked at how well the patients fared after discharge: they found the 57 (10 per cent) patients had died and that 18 of these deaths were recorded as suicide: the risk of death was six times greater than the standard mortality rate for the general population. Clarke, Davies, Hollin, and Duggan (2011) looked in more detail at the high suicide rate and found that, as set against the standard mortality rate, the women patients and patients with a mental illness were especially at risk of suicide.

There are some mentally disordered offenders who, like any other group or type of offenders, will commit further offences after the sanction, be it under criminal or health legislation. A group of studies have looked at predictors of further offending among mentally disordered offenders.

Predicting recidivism with the mentally disordered offender

Bonta, Law, and Hanson (1998) conducted a meta-analysis of studies of recidivism in mentally disordered offenders published between 1959 and 1995. They found that the significant predictors of recidivism were of three types: (1) *individual* variables such as being male, age, being single, employment problems, family dysfunction, and substance, particularly alcohol, abuse; (2) *clinical* variables such as previous hospitalisations and number of days in hospital, and a diagnosis of antisocial personality disorder; and (3) *criminological* variables such as criminal history, including juvenile and adult convictions. An American study by Castillo and Alarid (2011) found that those individuals whose illness had required residential treatment and who had a more extensive criminal history were at a higher risk of further offending than those suitable for probation. Alcohol misuse was the variable most closely associated with violent reoffending.

A Swedish study reported by Nilsson, Wallinius, Gustavson, Anckarsater, and Kerekes (2011) looked at violent reoffending among a group of 100 mentally disordered patients committed to psychiatric care. They found that, within a maximum of 73 months follow-up, 20 patients committed further violent crimes. They reported that age at first conviction, substance use, and some structured risk assessments were moderately associated with violent recidivism. However, further analysis showed that 'Criminological risk factors tended to be the best predictors of violent relapses' (Nilsson et al., 2011: 1). However, this is not to dismiss the importance of variables associated with the mental disorder in predicting further offending. Hodgins and Riaz (2011) looked at offending in a sample of 251 patients from several countries with a diagnosis of schizophrenia or schizo-affective disorder. They reported that 'The findings confirmed again that even after taking account of the well-known predictors of aggressive behavior such as age, sex, and previous and current antisocial behavior and illicit drug use, that each additional clinically relevant positive symptom increased the risk of aggressive behavior' (Hodgins & Riaz, 2011: 522).

While most studies of violent behaviour are concerned with reoffending after discharge, it is the case that violence is a behaviour that is a consistent across settings. Thus, the violent person is likely to be violent towards other patients and staff with a secure setting (Logan & Blackburn, 2009; Nicholls, Brink, Greaves, Lussier, & Verdun-Jones, 2009).

Risk assessment

Given that there are a range of factors associated with offending, particularly violent offending, in people with a mental disorder, the development of methods of risk assessment for this population is an obvious step (Scott & Resnick, 2006). As shown in Box 11.11, there is a range of assessment tools designed specifically for this purpose, although some standard assessment instruments for mainstream offender populations function reasonably well with mentally disordered offenders (Ferguson, Ogloff, & Thomson, 2009). There are other widely used assessment methods including patient observation to determine the likely cues associated with the onset and maintenance of violent behaviour (Hornsveld, Nijman, Hollin, & Kraaimaat, 2007).

Box 11.11   Risk assessment with mentally disordered offenders

CANFOR: Camberwell Assessment of Need – Forensic Version (Thomas et al., 2003)
   CANFOR is a needs assessment for people with mental health problems in contact with forensic services. It assess need in 25 areas covering health, social, clinical, and functional domains. There is also a version for use in secure forensic settings (Long, Webster, Waine, Motala, & Hollin, 2008).

HCR-20: Historical-Clinical Risk (Webster, Douglas, Eaves, & Hart, 1997)

The HCR-20 is a 20-item checklist to assess the risk for future violent behaviour in criminal and psychiatric populations: it considers past, present, and likely future considerations in predicting violence.

Iterative Classification Tree: ICT (Monahan et al., 2000)

This approach to risk assessment uses a series of questions, each contingent on the answer to the previous question, to classify an individual's risk of violence as low or high.

Psychopathy Checklist-Revised: PCL-R (Hare, 1991)

The PCL-R uses a combination of file review and semi-structured to assess psychopathy, a feature of high (particularly violent) recidivism.

VRAG
   The VRAG was developed from patients in a Canadian maximum security hospital: it uses 12 items, including PCL-R score, to assess the risk of violent conduct (Quinsey, Harris, Rice, & Cormier, 1998).

Treatment and the mentally disordered offender

The treatment of the mentally disordered offender must deal with the psychiatric disturbance while ensuring that the risk of reoffending is also reduced. In practice, this may mean a combination of psychotropic medication and psychological therapy. As with mainstream offenders, the association between substance use, particularly alcohol, and offending is evident in the mentally disordered offender population. Indeed, several of the studies discussed above have noted that substance use is often comorbid with another disorder. Gumpert et al. (2010) looked at the reoffending of 403 male offenders with suspected mental disorder and substance abuse over a 52-month period, comparing those who had participated in substance abuse treatment with those who had not taken part in treatment. They found that those who had completed more than 6 weeks of substance abuse treatment had a significantly reduced risk of committing a new crime, including violent crime.

As is evident from the example of the role of alcohol treatment programmes for mentally disordered offenders, the treatment goals for this population are not very different to those for mainstream offenders. Thus, Ashford, Wong, and Sternbach (2008) targeted similar aspects of cognitive functioning as would be found with mainstream offenders; while Tapp, Fellowes, Wallis, Blud, and Moore (2009) adapted a standard cognitive skills programme for use with mentally disordered offenders in high security. It is important to note that while the treatment targets remain the same, the delivery of the intervention has to be tailored to the requirements of the patients, more obviously so perhaps in the case of offenders with intellectual impairment (e.g., Taylor et al., 2002), to ensure responsivity and effectiveness.

The development of treatment for the violent mentally disordered offender is seen in two studies conducted in a high security hospital reported by Jones and colleagues (Braham, Jones, & Hollin, 2008; Jones & Hollin, 2004). The targets for change in these interventions are anger control, social problem solving and skill development – as would be found in most interventions for violent offenders – with the pace of delivery and levels of personal support tailored to the patient group. In a similar intervention, Hornsveld, Nijman, Hollin, and Kraaimaat (2008) adapted aggression replacement training for use with a forensic psychiatric population.

The point made by Gumpert et al. (2010) about the importance of treatment engagement is reflected in the findings of McCarthy and Duggan (2010) in an evaluation of treatment effects with personality disordered offenders in a MSU. McCarthy and Duggan found that almost three-quarters of the patient sample failed to complete their treatment. The patients who completed treatment had a 10 per cent reduction in their rate of reoffending compared with non-completers: McCarthy and Duggan argue that this magnitude of reduction is of clinical significance.

The treatment of offenders with personality disorders, particularly anti-social personality disorder (APD), is a pressing concern (Dowsett & Craissati, 2008). There are, for example, clinical guidelines for working with APD (National Institute for Health and Clinical Excellence, 2009) and reviews of the condition (De Brito & Hodgins, 2009) as well as reviews of the comorbidity between APD and intellectual disability (Morrissey & Hollin, 2011), however there is rather less in the way of hard evidence on treatment effectiveness. The same point may be made with respect to psychopathy where there is evidence, contrary to widespread belief, that treatment can be effective (Salekin, 2002).

Concluding remarks

It is evident that the notion that 'nothing works' has now been dispelled. However, in seeking to implement 'what works' it is also evident that while the gains in terms of crime reduction are worth having they do not come easily. There is no 'magic bullet' in effective rehabilitative work with offenders, rather a great deal of disciplined application of the principles of effective practice is required. It is also the case that a field will change and develop so that advances are incorporated as they occur. There are two examples of this process of development which are set to have an impact on the configuration of rehabilitative services for offenders.

The first lies in the traditional view that motivation is an important ingredient in effective practice so that offenders must be motivated to engage in treatment and to change as a result (e.g., Tierney & McCabe, 2002). However, the amorphous concept of motivation has come under critical scrutiny generally (Drieschner, Lammers, & van der Staak, 2004) and specifically in offender rehabilitation (Casey, Day, & Howells, 2005). It may well be that the notion of 'readiness to change' offers greater conceptual clarity to both researchers and practitioners (Casey, Day, Howells, & Ward, 2005; Chambers, Eccleston, Day, Ward, & Howells, 2008; Howells & Day, 2003).

The second issue lies in how practice evolves. Of course, the meta-analyses conducted in the 1990s could only take account of the extant evidence but progress does not stop and new evidence, new ways of thinking continue to emerge. There is, for example, the growth of the 'third wave' of cognitive behaviour therapy influenced by Eastern philosophies and Buddhism (Hayes, Follette, & Linehan, 2004), which includes concepts such as mindfulness, compassion, and forgiveness (Fehr, Gelfand, & Nag, 2010; Goetz, Keltner, & Simon-Thomas, 2010; Wade, Johnson, & Meyer, 2008) and which is beginning to influence forensic practice (Day, Gerace, Wilson, & Howells, 2008; Howells, 2010). In addition to cognitive behavioural methods, there is much to build on from other areas of practice such as family therapy (Piquero, Farrington, Welsh, Tremblay, & Jennings, 2009; Sexton & Turner, 2010) and multi-systemic therapy (Schaeffer & Borduin, 2005). While it also remains the case that low frequency types of offender, such as juvenile homicide offenders (Heide & Solomon, 2003), may require highly specialised interventions.

Restoration and reparation

The twin notions of restoration and reparation have become something of a 'must have' in criminal justice systems around the world since the turn of the century. As shown in Table 11.1, Miers (2001) lists 20 jurisdictions that have implemented restorative justice programmes. There are reports by independent think tanks (Sherman & Strang, 2007), in-house evaluations of restorative justice from, among others, Canada (Latimer, Dowden, & Muise, 2001), England and Wales (Miers et al., 2001; Shapland et al., 2008), and Scotland (Kirkwood, 2009; Viewpoint, 2009), and there is an United Nations handbook on restorative justice programmes (United Nations, 2006).

Why this rapid growth in a new and unproven technique? There are a number of interwoven strands that have made restorative justice popular. The first stems from a belief that the victim has been forgotten in a criminal justice system with a focus on the application of law and the fate of the offender. Thus, an approach that acknowledges the concerns of the victim offers something new. The second point, associated with the first, is an opposition to rehabilitation, which is seen, at best, as too offender-focused and at worst as too soft on offenders.

So, what exactly is restorative justice? A Home Office description of restorative justice refers to a process whereby the parties involved in a crime together resolve how to deal with both the aftermath of the offence and its implications for the future (Marshall, 1999). Sherman and Strang (2007: 12) suggest that 'Restorative justice is a way of thinking about what is best for the many connections among crime victims, their offenders and the criminal justice process'.

Table 11.1 Jurisdictions with restorative justice programmes (after Miers, 2001)

Australia
Austria
Belgium
Canada
Czech Republic
Denmark
Finland
France
Germany
Ireland
Italy
The Netherlands
New Zealand
Norway
Poland
Russia
Slovenia
Spain (Catalonia)
Sweden
USA

Miers et al. (2001) begin their account of their restorative justice research with a chapter headed 'Restorative justice: definitions, theory and practice'. However, a definition is not to be found, rather there is a quote from Marshall: 'Restorative justice is not, therefore, a single academic theory of crime or justice, but represents, in a more or less eclectic way, the accretion of actual experience in working successfully with particular crime problems' (Marshall, 1999: 7). Daly (2002: 58) has commented on the definitional problem and suggests that while the nature of the definitions of restorative justice vary considerably, the point of uniformity lies 'In defining restorative justice by reference to what it is *not*, and this is called *retributive justice*'.

The definitional haziness extends to theory. In the first discussions of reintegration of offenders through community conferences much was made of shame as a means by which reconciliation between victim and offender could be achieved (Braithwaite, 1989). This discussion was later followed by accounts of the historical and pan-cultural antecedents to the contemporary practice of restorative justice (Braithwaite, 1999).

Miers et al. (2001) give several examples of attempts at an explanation of restorative justice that have in common an offender, a victim, and a process by which the two are connected for the common good. This may well serve as a description but it is not a theory: indeed, Miers et al. (2001: 10) conclude that restorative justice is a 'new perspective on criminal justice', which is rather a long way from a theoretical account. Sherman and Strang (2007: 12) point in the direction of a theoretical account of how restorative justice may work in suggesting that the processes act by 'fostering remorse, not fear. The emotions of anger, shame, guilt and regret form a complex cocktail of feelings associated with crime and justice. If we are to make progress in achieving the crime prevention goals of justice, it may happen from better understanding of how we can mobilise those emotions more effectively'.

The slippery nature of the whole enterprise is exacerbated when it comes to practice as seen in the quote below where Miers et al. (2001) observed many variations on a theme, adding the comment that in some cases where contact with victims was not a high priority it is doubtful whether the scheme really is delivering restorative justice.

There are terminological differences at the international level, a plethora of descriptors for the varying practices that claim to fall within its ambit. Informal mediation, victim-offender mediation, victim-offender conferencing, victim-offender groups, family group conferencing, restorative conferencing, restorative cautions and community conferencing are only the most common names used in England and Wales. Other jurisdictions feature sentencing circles, tribal or village moots, community panels or courts, healing circles and other communitarian associations ... programme organisers typically display a strong sense of ownership for their preferred methods, which may translate into a reluctance to be dictated to by a central authority.

(Miers et al., 2001: 12–3)

The advocates of restorative justice make no claims for its originality, often suggesting that it has its beginnings in the cultural and social systems of a minority group. Braithwaite and Mugford (1994), based at an Australian university, write about 'the reintegration ceremony', suggesting that the New Zealand Maoris had employed similar practices. This claim of an historical precedent is also to be found on the Centre for Restorative Justice website (see 'Useful websites' at the end of this chapter), which states that 'Restorative Justice is an old idea with a new name. Its roots can be found in Aboriginal healing traditions and the non-retaliatory responses to violence endorsed by many faith communities'.

Daly (2002) has traced the history of the notion of restorative justice and suggests that there is a great deal of contemporary wish fulfilment in romantically and selectively rewriting history to impart the message that a superior form of justice existed before the advent of justice-based retribution. Daly gives as an example of this reworking of history the practice of conferencing in New Zealand. There are claims that the beginnings of conferencing (for a discussion of conferencing, see Rodogno, 2008) are lost in the mists of Maori cultural values but Daly suggests that in reality it emerged in the 1980s in the context of Maori challenges to white New Zealand crime and welfare systems.

Latimer et al. (2001) suggest that the delivery of restorative justice encompasses the three categories of circles, conferences, and victim-offender mediations. In their review, Sherman and Strang (2007) described several variations on a theme including face-to-face meetings between victim and offender, financial restitution, a letter of apology, and conferences with five or more family members; these proceedings would variously involve the courts, the police, or other agencies.

The processes inherent to restorative justice are intended to be of benefit to the victim and the offender: the victim's recovery comes about through experiencing a sense of redress for their suffering; while the offender makes recompense through apologising and understanding the harm they have caused. In addition, it is claimed that there are wider benefits as the community is strengthened by the renewal and reintegration of the relationship between the victim and the offender.

Evaluation

What benefits may be expected if restorative justice works? Would offenders feel remorse? Would victims experience satisfaction? Would communities be healed? Would crime be reduced? Unlike rehabilitation, where there was a large body of research available for analysis, with restorative justice the evidence has had to accrue over a relatively short period of time: for example, the earliest study in Sherman and Strang's (2007) review was published in 1998. Nonetheless, an evaluative literature has emerged that allows some conclusions to be drawn about the effectiveness of interventions with a focus on restorative justice.

The first point is to define 'effective': what would constitute an effective intervention? Latimer, Dowden, and Muise (2005) suggested that there are three classes of outcome variable by which to measure the effectiveness of restorative justice: (1) victim and offender satisfaction; (2) restitution compliance; (3) recidivism. Latimer et al. conducted a meta-analysis of restorative justice programmes using as an operational definition the following: 'Restorative justice is a voluntary, community-based response to criminal behavior that attempts to bring together the victim, the offender, and the community, in an effort to address the harm caused by the criminal behavior' (2005: 131). The literature search started from 1980 and identified 22 unique studies that complied with the definition and were conducted with predominately white, male young offenders. There was strong support for victim satisfaction: almost without exception the studies that measured victim satisfaction reported that the victims gave higher satisfaction ratings when compared with other approaches. Of the 22 studies, only eight reported compliance with restitution agreements: nonetheless, offenders who participated in restorative justice procedures did tend towards higher rates of compliance than offenders subject to other arrangements. Finally, as may be anticipated, there was a wide range of outcomes with regard to recidivism: however, the overall conclusion was that 'Restorative justice programs, on average, yielded reductions in recidivism compared to nonrestorative approaches' (Latimer et al., 2005: 137).

In keeping with Latimer et al. (2005), the weight of evidence suggests that the processes involved in face-to-face meetings are engaging for both the offender and the victim (Kuo, Longmire, & Cuvelier, 2010; Sherman et al., 2005). Is helping offenders to feel remorse and victims to have a voice an end in itself or should some reduction in crime be expected? It can be argued that from a utilitarian perspective that some long-term benefits should accrue from the costs involved. However, the research looking at the long-term outcomes of restorative justice programmes faces a familiar litany of issues.

Bergseth and Bouffard (2007) list the perennial difficulties of sampling, the formation of properly matched control groups, the definition of type and seriousness of any reoffence, and allowing an adequate follow-up time in completing outcome research. In their evaluation of a restorative justice programme, Bergseth and Bouffard (2007) found that the way the research design managed completion of the programme (25 per cent of offenders assigned to the programme did not complete) was an important determinant of outcome (see Hollin, 2008). When the outcome data were analysed according to programme assignment (i.e., assigned to treatment versus control) rather than programme completion (i.e., treatment received versus control), then the strength of the positive outcome was reduced. de Beus and Rodriguez (2007) observed that rates of completion of restorative justice programmes may be related to recidivism according to offence type. Sherman and Strang (2007) also noted that type of offence may have an influence on outcome such that in terms of reducing repeat offending restorative justice programmes work better with more serious, rather than less serious, crimes. Miers et al. (2001) suggest that it is the level of risk of reoffending that is the important determinant with regard to impact on offending: which is, of course, in keeping with the risk principle of effective practice. Thus, Miers et al. observe that 'The West Yorkshire scheme produces a small, but statistically significant, reduction in reconviction rates as compared to the control group, but that the scheme is less successful with those offenders who are in the highest risk categories for reconviction as measured by OGRS 2' (2001: x). However, the same positive effect on reconviction was not found in all the schemes in the evaluation: Miers et al. comment that the successful West Yorkshire scheme involved the most serious offenders and was marked by high levels of victim involvement. Shapland et al. (2008) examined three restorative justice schemes for adult offenders in England and reported significantly fewer reconvictions than the control group at a 2-year follow-up. However, in terms of the severity of the offence leading to the reconviction, there were no significant differences between those taking part in a restorative justice project and the controls.

While the evidence is generally supportive in terms of the effect of restorative justice on further offending, the outcome research faces the same two issues as are prevalent with the outcome studies for offending behaviour programmes. As Latimer et al. (2005) suggest, there is inevitably a self-selection bias given the voluntary nature of restorative justice schemes. This bias may mean that some third variable is actually at work to produce the effect of reduced offending. In addition, there is the problem of large rates of attrition from some programmes such that a focus on completers arguably offers a biased estimate of the effect of the programme. On the other hand, to test the effects of an intervention by looking its effects on those who do not take part in it is not really a test at all!

Concluding remarks

The notion of restorative justice has attracted a great deal of attention and resources. The evidence is broadly supportive of the effects of interventions based on the principles of restorative justice. However, there are notes of caution to be expressed on two interrelated points. First, as Daly (2002) forcefully describes, there is a great deal of almost anti-scientific wishful thinking surrounding the enterprise of restorative justice (see Box 11.12).

The second point to made flows from Daly's fourth myth, an in-built belief among some of its advocates that restorative justice 'works' and an associated disregard for evidence. This type of sentiment is hinted at by Miers et al. (2001) in the quote above: 'Programme organisers typically display a strong sense of ownership for their preferred methods, which may translate into a reluctance to be dictated to by a central authority'. A free-for-all among

---

Box 11.12 Mythical beliefs and restorative justice (after Daly, 2002)

Myth 1. Restorative justice is the opposite to retributive justice. The process of restorative justice contains elements of other justice models: the offender may be censured for their behaviour (retribution) or encouraged to think differently about what they have done in the past and their future behaviour (rehabilitation).

Myth 2. Restorative justice uses indigenous justice practices and was the dominant form of pre-modern justice. Daly refers to this as *constructing origin myths* in order to herald a return to indigenous practices after the white takeover and imposition of white retributive justice. This may or may not be the case in some parts of the world (Australia and New Zealand are the much-cited examples) but is certainly not the case in Great Britain, where a return to the practice of former days would see significant numbers of criminals publically humiliated, executed, or transported to the convict colonies in Australia.

Myth 3. Restorative justice is a 'care' (or feminine) response to crime in comparison with a 'justice' (or masculine) response. Daly suggests that this statement is a part of the power inversion of restorative justice, the movement away from white- and male-dominated approaches to the superiority of indigenous and female forms of justice.

Myth 4. Restorative justice can be expected to produce major changes in people. In truth, this is a hypothesis that is open to empirical investigation but Daly suggests that observations of 'personal and social transformations' in participants are telling an inspiring story from which to claim the desired effect.

service providers and practitioners is that last thing that's needed in the criminal justice system (or anywhere else for that matter). The steady accumulation of evidence according to good research practice, accompanied by theory building, will provide the real test of the value of restorative justice.

Are the efforts worth the costs?

The consequences of criminal behaviour include both the personal suffering of victims of crime to the financial costs of maintaining the criminal justice system. If it were possible to reduce crime, given that its elimination is highly improbable, benefits would surely follow. In order to see what these benefits might be, we need to be more exact about the cost of crime.

When considering the cost of crime there are two elements to take into account: first, estimates of the financial costs associated with crime; second, the human costs paid by victims.

Financial costs

There are a myriad of financial costs associated with crime: there are the costs of the police, the courts, and prison and probation services; there are financial costs to the health system, in terms of both physical and mental health; other public services such as the fire service and public transport may bear the cost of crime; criminal behaviour has an effect on levels of insurance premiums, on rising retail prices in shops, on employer productivity costs for employee missing days due to crime, and on the costs of security measures; and the victim may well have to bear costs such as property repairs and excess payments on insurance claims.

It is clear that society pays a substantial financial cost because of criminal behaviour. The task of estimating those costs through understanding the economics of the criminal justice system is a highly complex undertaking. At the most basic level, the value of money does not remain constant over time, the values of goods and properties shift and change, and international comparisons of financial data are difficult to make. Nonetheless, it is possible to make estimates on the costs of crime and the financial benefits that may accrue from preventing crime (Cohen, 2005; Welsh, Farrington, & Sherman, 2001).

The cost of the criminal justice system is staggeringly large, as outlined in a 2011 briefing paper from the Prison Reform Trust, which contains the following information for England and Wales gathered from a variety of government reports and statements. The National Offender Management Service (NOMS) referred to below is an executive agency of the Ministry of Justice with responsibility for the correctional services in England and Wales, principally the National Probation Service and the Prison Service: (1) the total cost of the criminal justice system rose from 2 per cent of GDP to 2.5 per cent over the last decade, which is at a higher per capita level than the USA or any EU country; (2) the resource budget for the National Offender Management Service for 2011–12 is £3.679 billion, within which the budget for public prisons is £1,870 million and £311 million for private prisons; (3) the average cost of a prison place, including costs met by NOMS but excluding expenditure from other government departments such as health and education, is £45,000; (4) in 2007–8, the cost of reoffending by all recent ex-prisoners was between £9.5 billion and £13 billion.

Now, the above figures are just for the supervision and detention of sentenced offenders. If we move to law and order, the official Home Office figure, in terms of expected spending, was £4,808,807,759 for the police for 2010–11. Once a criminal is apprehended, the decision regarding whether a case proceeds to trial is made by the Crown Prosecution Service, which has an annual budget of £672.5 million for 2009–10; the costs of running the court system are detailed on the HM Courts and Tribunals Service website: 'From April 2011 the agency employs 21,000 staff operating from around 650 locations. It has a gross annual budget of around £1.7bn, approximately £585m of which is recovered in fees and income from service users. It handles over 2 million criminal cases, 1.8 million civil claims, more than 150,000 family law disputes and almost 800,000 tribunal cases annually'. Harries (1999) estimated that the cost of the crown court process of imposing a prison sentence is approximately £30,500.

Thus, the amount of money to maintain the criminal justice system (without the additional costs for mentally disordered offenders) runs to billions and billions of pounds. If some of these costs could be reduced, a range of benefits might accrue: for example, savings to the public purse could be invested in schools, hospitals, libraries, and other institutions for the benefit of the public. In order to bring about financial change, some intervention is required to reduce expenditure. There are many ways that reduced expenditure can be achieved organisationally as with budget cuts, reorganisation, and so forth. However, another way to bring about financial savings is to reduce the amount of crime either by preventing crime occurring in the first place or by reducing reoffending by known offenders.

When considering interventions to reduce crime, the key consideration from a financial perspective is whether the intervention delivers financial savings. There are two ways in which the financial question can be addressed: (1) is the intervention cost effective? A *cost effectiveness analysis* allows an estimate to be given of the output of the intervention as, say, a reduction of 10 burglaries per £1,000 spent; (2) does the intervention bring a cost benefit? A *cost benefit analysis* considers the question of whether the cost of the intervention actually realises a saving. In fact, the latter is an extension of the former: a cost benefit analysis would answer the question of how much money was *saved* by investing the £1,000 to prevent 10 burglaries. If the £1,000 produced a saving of 10 burglaries (so it is effective) and also saved £5,000 in police time, courts, and so on, then it realises a cost *benefit*. In practice, it is easier to carry out a cost-effectiveness analysis than a cost benefit analysis as the data required for the latter are much more wide-ranging (French et al., 2008). As with psychology, economics is not an exact science but it is arguable that cost-benefits should be an important part of the equation in determining what works in crime prevention (Sherman et al., 1997).

It is possible, of course, to spend a great deal of money to reduce crime but for the costs of doing so to outweigh the savings to be made. In these circumstances, a case can be made for intervention in terms of savings in human costs but not in terms of cold cash. In field of outcome research in corrections there are a substantial number of outcome studies but comparatively few of these studies have included a cost analysis. Those examples discussed below are gathered from a range of settings and types of intervention.

Prison

As noted above, a great deal of money is spent in prisons: do prisons bring any savings? Marsh and Fox (2008) looked at the costs and benefits of the UK prisons by first considering the relative impact on reoffending of both community and prison sentences. This consideration then informed an economic analysis to formulate economic estimates of the efficiency of various sentencing options. They summarised their findings as showing that 'Diverting adult offenders from standard prison sentences to alternative interventions saves the UK public sector between £19,000 and £88,000 per offender. When victim costs are considered, diverting offenders from standard prison sentences saves UK society between £17,500 and £203,000 per offender' (Marsh and Fox, 2008: 403).

An interesting study by Zhang, Roberts, and McCollister (2009) looked at the effects of a prison-based therapeutic community (TC) on the costs of running the prison. They compared the costs of running the TC with the costs of the 'non-treatment' parts of the prison. The TC generated savings because it led to lower administrative costs for disciplinary actions and fewer inmate grievances and major disruptive incidents. Thus, aside to any rehabilitative value, the TC was instrumental in helping to control prison management costs.

Electronic monitoring (EM)

An American study by Yeh (2010) estimated that the implementation of EM plus home detention could prevent 781,383 crimes annually. The estimated social value of this level crime reduction is given as $481.1 billion or a gain of $12.70 for every dollar spent on the proposed intervention. This study is interesting because it lays out the assumptions under which the estimates are given – remembering that estimates are just that, not actual costs – and because the expression of savings per monetary unit spent is much easier to grasp than billions of dollars.

Restorative justice

Miers et al. (2001) included cost effectiveness as an element of their evaluation of seven restorative justice schemes in England. Alongside varying levels of effectiveness in terms of reduced reconvictions, Miers et al. also found that the schemes varied in cost from £244 to £451 per case. With regard to reduced reconvictions, they suggest that high-risk adult offenders are the most cost-effective group to target; the programmes for juvenile offenders were not found to be cost-effective. Shapland et al. (2008) also found considerable variation, ranging from £12,636 per month to £60,511 per month, in the costs associated with running different restorative justice schemes in England. However, it was the most expensive scheme that gave the best return in terms of cost. As in life, sometimes you get what you pay for.

Juvenile offenders

Drake, Aos, and Miller (2009) conducted a research project for Washington State to facilitate a review of interventions for adult and juvenile offenders and crime prevention programmes. The aim of the research was to inform the implementation of services to reduce the future need for prisons. They first carried out a 'what works' analysis of the literature to identify effective intervention; then an economic analysis to inform decision making on costs. The first part of the research identified the familiar interventions of cognitive-behavioural programmes, family therapy, drug programmes, and so on. The economic analysis then reveals what the financial gains may be for different approaches. Thus, for example, Drake et al. estimate that the cost of running a typical cognitive-behavioural programme for adult offenders is approximately $107 per offender. As these programmes are generally run with groups of 10–15 offenders for 40–60 hours, the estimated 6.9 per cent reduction in recidivism (as generated from the review of the evidence) equates to a benefit of $15,469. The net value of the average evidence-based cognitive-behavioural programme for adult offenders is therefore $15,361 (i.e., $15,469 – $107) per offender. However, for the functional family therapy (FFT) the parameters change: Drake et al. estimate that FFT has an average cost of $2,380 per juvenile: the cost is high because FFT is a one-to-one programme involving the FFT therapist and the young person and their family. However, if FFT reduces recidivism rates by the expected 18.1 per cent, the costs generate benefits of about $52,156, giving a net value of $49,776 for each young offender.

The importance of a solid evidence base to inform decisions regarding services for crime reduction, as stressed by Drake et al., is seen in their analysis of electronic monitoring. As an aside, Mair (2005) is pointed in his summary of the decision-making and evidence-base that led to the introduction of electronic monitoring in England and Wales. Drake et al. (2009) reviewed 12 methodologically sound evaluations of electronic monitoring and concluded that this intervention does not have a statistically significant effect on recidivism. The cost of a typical electronic monitoring programme is approximately $1,301 per offender. If the expectation is that the use of electronic monitoring will reduce crime, then the $1,301 is wasted in terms of a cost benefit. However, if electronic monitoring is used as an alternative to imprisonment then it produces an estimated net saving per offender of $926. Thus, electronic monitoring can be cost effective when used to offset the costs of a more expensive resource.

The other cost of crime lies in its effects on its victims in terms of physical and psychological pain, fear of further victimisation, reduced quality of life, and effects on family.

Personal costs

It is impossible to know how many people are victims of crime. The victim surveys discussed in Chapter 2 showed that substantial numbers of people are victims of crime but, for a range of reasons, they do not report the crime and so do not appear in any official statistics. It is easy to think of a victim of crime as someone involved in violence or who has had their property stolen but victimisation comes in many guises. Hoyle and Zedner (2007) list several types of victimisation ranging from the effects of corporate crime, white-collar crime, terrorism, and state crimes. An example of the diverse experience of victimisation is to be found in workplace victimisation. Aquino and Thau (2009) reviewed the literature on aggression in the workplace and suggested that most victimisation is psychological rather than physical. This makes sense because acts of physical violence in many work settings would lead to disciplinary action against the aggressor. As shown in Box 11.13, psychological

---

Box 11.13   Forms of workplace aggression (after Aquino & Thau, 2009)

Abusive supervision. Those in positions of supervision persistently show hostile verbal and non-verbal behaviour but are not physically aggressive.

Bullying. Where one or more people persistently see themselves as the target for hurtful behaviour from one or more persons; the target has difficulty in defending themselves against the harmful actions.

Emotional abuse. Emotional abuse, which may be communicated via verbal and non-verbal expression, is repeated over time by a person in power with the intention of harming the target.

Harassment. Harassment can take the form of repeated activities aimed to hurt, mentally and sometimes physically, those who cannot defend themselves.

Identity threat. Actions intended to challenge, call into question, or reduce the target's sense of competence, dignity, or self-esteem.

Incivility. Low-intensity duplicitous behaviour intended to harm the target by violation of everyday standards of personal respect.

Social undermining. Actions intended to hamper the target's progress in establishing and maintaining positive personal relationships, success at work and a positive reputation.

victimisation can take many forms: to which can be added the phenomenon of victimisation by cybercrimes such as computer fraud, hacking, malware infection, harassment, and cyber-stalking (Jaishankar, 2011; Ngo & Paternoster, 2011). Of course, many of these types of aggressive behaviours – what Goldstein (2002) calls *low-level aggression* – can also occur outside the workplace. As Goldstein suggests, aggressive acts such as ostracism, gossip, hazing (initiation rites), teasing, baiting, and cursing can be found in any setting – schools are a particularly good example – where people gather for a common purpose.

The consequences of victimisation are characterised by a cluster of negative emotional, physiological, and psychological signs. The emotional responses to victimisation may include diminished emotional well-being generally, lower levels of satisfaction with friends, family and life generally, self-blame, shame, and fear. The physiological consequences of victimisation can include sleep disturbance, fatigue, muscular aches, and chronic headaches. Finally, the negative psychological consequences may encompass various mental health problems such as depression and anxiety, particularly fear of further victimisation. In extreme cases, the symptoms may coalesce in the form of post-traumatic stress disorder. When the crime is of more directly threatening nature, as with burglary, physical and sexual violence, the negative personal experiences described above may be magnified in intensity as shown in a study by Romito and Grassi (2007).

Romito and Grassi investigated whether there were gender differences in the effects of violent victimisation with a sample of 502 Italian male and female students. They found that some students had been the victim of more than one violent incident, sometimes of a different type, such as physical assault and sexual violence, carried out in a range of settings including the home and school. Romito and Grassi considered a range of potential adverse mental health outcomes including depression, panic attacks, and heavy alcohol use. The males and females reported similar rates of experience of violence, although the type and setting varied: men were more likely to experience violence at school, while sexual violence was more prevalent among females. There were some profound effects on mental health with high levels of panic attacks among females and alcohol problems among males. It was the case for both men and women that the more violence they experienced so their risk of developing mental health problems rose accordingly, with marked effects if the individual had experienced three or more types of violence. In these types of cases it may be that support and treatment can play a role in recovery from the abusive experience (Taylor & Harvey, 2009; Vickerman & Margolin, 2009).

Risk of victimisation

The risk of becoming a victim of crime is not randomly distributed: there are certain factors that increase the risk of victimisation and, correspondingly, factors that reduce the likelihood of victimisation (Daigle, Beaver, & Turner, 2010). However, the first point to make is that the majority of people do not experience a serious crime, most crime is fairly low level in nature (which is not to say that its effects on the person concerned are necessarily minimal).

At a broad environment level, there are certain settings associated with an increased likelihood of crime and hence victimisation. It has been understood since the work of Shaw and McKay that certain city areas characterised by social disorganisation, high levels of mobility, low-quality housing, and so on are associated with high levels of crime. The victims of crime in such adverse environments may be people who fail to take care of their movements and so place themselves at risk, as well as those people who live in crime-prone areas.

While crime has little respect for the qualities of the individual victim, there are some personal characteristics that, given the 'right environment', act to increase the likelihood of becoming a victim of crime. Some victims are vulnerable because they find themselves in the wrong place at the wrong time, others such as children are vulnerable because they do not understand the situation and when in trouble cannot defend themselves. Some people with a mental disorder are at an increased risk of victimisation, particularly for violent and sexually violent crimes (Creighton & Jones, 2012; Hodgins, Alderton, Cree, Aboud, & Mak, 2007), which is probably best accounted for in terms of an interplay between impoverished living circumstances, alcohol abuse, and symptomatology (Teasdale, 2009).

Those individuals who commit crimes will invariably spend time in environments, both in the community and in prison, where crime takes place. It follows that there is a strong chance that criminals will encounter other criminals. When these meetings between criminals take place, further crime may ensue, as is most clearly seen with bullying and intimidation of prisoners by other prisoners (McGurk, Forde, & Barnes, 2000), thereby causing the neat conceptual divide between criminal and victim to become muddied.

Smith (2004) presents evidence from the Edinburgh Study of Youth Transitions and Crime concerning young people's experience of criminal behaviour. Smith (2004: 16) states: 'The most important factors explaining the link between victimization and offending were getting involved in risky activities and situations, and having a delinquent circle of friends'. However, as Smith points out, the chain of causality can run both ways: the victim may become an offender (see below), while the offender can become a victim. Jennings, Higgins, Tewksbury, Gover, and Piquero (2010) conducted a longitudinal study directed at young people's experience of violence. They reported a substantial overlap over time between who those were victims of physical violence and those who were offenders.

A particular feature of risky situations lies in the availability of and access to weapons. It is axiomatic that the presence of a weapon greatly increases the likelihood of an altercation turning into a serious crime. At its most extreme, this point is made by the school shootings as seen, for example, at Columbine High School in Colorado. A study conducted in America by Wells and Chermak (2011) gathered self-reported information data from more than 200, mainly male, felony probationers about their involvement in the use of guns. The offenders reported that their involvement in gun crimes was related to an increased likelihood of gun victimisation.

In other countries where there is not widespread availability of firearms, other weapons, particularly knives, may be prevalent. A study of knife-carrying by young people belonging to gangs in Scotland identified several reasons why some young people, mainly males, carry knives and other weapons such as screwdrivers, bottles, and Stanley blades (Bannister et al., 2010). A substantial number of young people said they did not intend to use their knife, while those who claimed they would use it said they had identified parts of the body, such as the buttocks, where its use would not be fatal. The majority of the young people said they carried knives for protection in case they were attacked or to enhance their reputation among peers.

Nonetheless, it is a fact of life that the best intentions go astray and the knife carried simply to impress peers may become a murder weapon. The intention just to wound the victim may go wrong, while other factors such as heightened emotion, mental instability, and intoxication can bring about a loss of self-control so that the situation quickly escalates out of control. A large scale Swedish study, reported by Stenbacka, Moberg, Romelsjö, and Jokinen (2012), looked at mortality and causes of death among violent offenders, victims, or both. Stenbacka used a nationwide representative sample of 48,834 men aged from 18 to 53 years of age followed through official records over a 35-year period. The mortality rate was substantially higher for the violent offenders (12.8 per cent), the victims (15.6 per cent), and the offender-victims (22 per cent) than the non-violent controls (4.9 per cent). Of note, the cause of death being alcohol- and drug-related was high for the three violent groups, while those without a history of violence were more likely to die from natural causes or in accidents. Indeed, the use of alcohol is a prominent feature of sexual victimisation (Franklin, 2010; Testa, Hoffman, & Livingston, 2010).

It is beyond dispute that crime exacts a heavy toll in both financial terms and in its effects on victims. While there are positive payoffs to be had from working with known offenders in order to reduce the likelihood of their committing more crimes, it remains the case that this approach is after the event. An alternative approach is to try to prevent crimes from happening in the first place.

Chapter summary

- Retribution and punishment are fundamental aspects of the criminal justice system and are often given as a justification for harsh sentencing. However, the empirical evidence suggests that little is achieved by way of crime reduction by punishing offenders.
- The death penalty, while no longer used in the UK, is used sometimes extensively in other parts of the world. Its use raises a raft of issues, including moral and religious considerations, for any society to consider.
- The idea that the criminal justice system might be of a correctional benefit to offenders, so helping them to reduce their offending, came about as part of the civic reforms of the 19th century.
- A range of types of service, drawing on education, employment training, and psychotherapeutic methods, has variously been offered to offenders in an attempt to reduce reoffending.
- The damning view that 'nothing works' in offender rehabilitation was overturned in the late 1990s by a string of meta-analyses guiding the 'what works' principles of effective practice to reduce reoffending.

Points for discussion

- Is the occasional miscarriage of justice simply a price to pay for capital punishment or is it a strong argument against state execution?
- Does there ever come a point at which a society's prison population becomes too large?
- In designing methods to reduce crime, should we be led by common sense or by the evidence?

Essential reading

Walker, N. (1991). *Why Punish?* Oxford: Oxford University Press.
It is impossible not to recommend Walker's text as an essential primer on punishment.

Oswald, M. E., Bieneck, S., & Hupfeld-Heinemann, J. (Eds.) (2009). *Social Psychology of Punishment of Crime*. Chichester, Sussex: Wiley-Blackwell.
This text gives a range of chapters on punishment from a social psychological standpoint.

Hood, R. & Hoyle, C. (2008). *The Death Penalty: A Worldwide Perspective* (4th ed.) – *Revised and Expanded*. Oxford: Oxford University Press.
Roger Hood is a world authority on the death penalty, his book is mandatory reading on this topic.

Hollin, C. R. (Ed.) (2001). *Handbook of Offender Assessment and Treatment*. Chichester, Sussex: John Wiley & Sons.
There is full coverage of a range of issues concerning assessment and treatment in this handbook.

Daly, K. (2002). Restorative justice: The real story'. *Punishment and Society, 4*, 55–79.
A Wide-ranging discussion of restorative justice.

Drake, E. K., Aos, S., & Miller, M. G. (2009). Evidence-based public policy options to reduce crime and criminal justice costs: Implications in Washington State. *Victims and Offenders, 4*, 1–35.
A absolute masterclass in evaluation.

The lighter side

The TV series *Porridge*, starring Ronnie Barker and Richard Beckinsale, is a consistently funny, if somewhat sanitised, view of life in one of HM's prisons.

Useful websites

The is a great deal of information about the death penalty at www.deathpenaltyinfo.org,

www.amnesty.org.uk/content.asp?CategoryID=78,   www.criminaljusticedegreesguide.com/features/10-infamous-cases-of-wrongful-execution.html.

There are discussions about cases of wrongful conviction to be found at www.innocenceproject.org.

All you want to know about forensic psychiatry can be found at www.forensicpsychiatry.ca/risk/instruments.htm, while www.sfu.ca/cfrj/popular.html has a wealth of information about restorative justice. Finally, there is a great deal of information about the organismal side of justice at the website of HM Courts and Tribunal Service, www.justice.gov.uk/about/hmcts.

References

Aichhorn, A. (1955, orig. 1925). *Wayward Youth* (Trans.) New York, NY: Meridian Books.
Alexander, J. F. (1973). Short-term behavioral intervention with delinquent families: Impact on family processes and recidivism. *Journal of Abnormal Psychology, 81*, 219–225.
Alexander, J. F. & Parsons, B. V. (1982). *Functional Family Therapy*. Monterey, CA: Brooks/Cole.
Amnesty International (2011). *Death Sentences and Executions 2010*. London: Amnesty International.
Andrews, D. A. (1982). *The Level of Supervision Inventory (LSI): The First Follow-Up*. Toronto: Ontario Ministry of Correctional Services.
—— (1995). The psychology of criminal conduct and effective treatment. In J. McGuire (Ed.), *What Works: Reducing Reoffending – Guidelines for Research and Practice* (pp. 35–62). Chichester, Sussex: John Wiley & Sons.
—— (2011). The impact of nonprogrammatic factors on criminal-justice interventions. *Legal and Criminological Psychology, 16*, 1–23.
Andrews, D. A. & Bonta, J. (1995). *LSI-R: The Level of Service Inventory-Revised*. Toronto: Multi-Health Systems.
—— (2010). Rehabilitating criminal justice policy and practice. *Psychology, Public Policy, and Law, 16*, 39–55.

Andrews, D. A., Bonta, J., & Wormith, J. S. (2006). The recent past and near future of risk and/or need assessment. *Crime & Delinquency, 52*, 7–27.

—— (2011). The Risk-Need-Responsivity (RNR) model: Does adding the Good Lives Model contribute to effective crime prevention? *Criminal Justice and Behavior, 38*, 735–755.

Andrews, D. A. & Dowden, C. (2006). Risk principles of case classification in correctional treatment: A meta-analytic investigation. *International Journal of Offender Therapy and Comparative Criminology, 50*, 88–100.

Andrews, D. A., Zinger, I., Hoge, R. D., Bonta, J., Gendreau, P., & Cullen, F. T. (1990). Does correctional treatment work? A clinically relevant and psychologically informed meta-analysis. *Criminology, 28*, 369–404.

Antonowicz, D. H. (2005). The *Reasoning and Rehabilitation* programme. In M. McMurran & J. McGuire (Eds.), *Social Problem Solving and Offending: Evidence Evaluation and Evolution* (pp. 163–181). Chichester, Sussex: John Wiley & Sons.

Aquino, K. & Thau, S. (2009). Workplace victimization: Aggression from the target's perspective. *Annual Review of Psychology, 60*, 717–741.

Ashford, J. B., Wong, K. W., & Sternbach, K. O. (2008). Generic correctional programming for mentally ill offenders: A pilot study. *Criminal Justice and Behavior, 35*, 457–473.

Axlerod, S. & Apsche, J. (Eds.) (1983). *The Effects of Punishment on Human Behavior*. New York, NY: Academic Press.

Babcock, J. C., Green, C. E., & Robie, C. (2004). Does batters' treatment work? A meta-analytic review of domestic violence treatment. *Clinical Psychology Review, 23*, 1023–1053.

Bailey, W. (1966). Correctional outcome: An evaluation of 100 reports. *Criminal Law, Criminology and Police Science, 57*, 153–160.

Bannister, J., Pickering, J., Batchelor, S., Burman, M., Kintrea, K., & McVie, S. (2010). *Troublesome Youth Groups, Gangs, and Knife Carrying in Scotland*. Edinburgh: The Scottish Centre for Crime and Justice Research.

Barnes, G. C., Ahlman, L., Gill, C., Sherman, L. W., Kurtz, E., & Malvestuto, R. (2010). Low-intensity community supervision for low-risk offenders: A randomized, controlled trial. *Journal of Experimental Criminology, 6*, 159–189.

Beech, A. R., Erikson, M., Friendship, C., & Ditchfield, J. (2001). *'A Six-Year Follow-up of Man Going Through Probation-Based Sex Offender Treatment Programmes'*. Home Office Research Findings No. 144. London: Home Office.

Beech, A. R. & Mann, R. E. (2002). Recent developments in the assessment and treatment of sexual offenders. In J. McGuire (Ed.) *Offender Rehabilitation and Treatment: Effective Programmes and Policies to Reduced Reoffending* (pp. 259–288). Chichester, Sussex: John Wiley & Sons.

Benda, B. B., Toombs, N. J., & Peacock, M. (2003). Discriminators of types of recidivism among boot camp graduates in a five-year follow-up study. *Journal of Criminal Justice, 31*, 539–551.

Bennett, T., Holloway, K., & Farrington, D. P. (2008). The statistical association between drug misuse and crime. *Aggression and Violent Behavior, 13*, 107–118.

Bergseth, K. J. & Bouffard, J. A. (2007). The long-term impact of restorative justice programming for juvenile offenders. *Journal of Criminal Justice, 35*, 433–451.

Bjørkly, S., Sandli, C. S., Moger, T. A., & Stang, J. (2012). A follow-up interview of patients eight years after discharge from a maximum security forensic psychiatry unit in Norway. *International Journal of Forensic Mental Health, 9*, 343–353.

Bierie, D. (2009). Cost matters: A randomized experiment comparing recidivism between two styles of prisons. *Journal of Experimental Criminology, 5*, 371–397.

Black, D. A. (1982). A 5-year follow-up study of male patients discharged from Broadmoor Hospital. In J. Gunn & D. P. Farrington (Eds.), *Abnormal Offenders, Delinquency, and the Criminal Justice System* (pp. 307–338). Chichester, Sussex: John Wiley & Sons.

Blanchette, K. & Brown, S. L. (2006). *The Assessment and Treatment of Women Offenders: An Integrative Perspective*. Chichester, Sussex: John Wiley & Sons.

Blattner, R. & Dolan, M. (2009). Outcome of high security patients admitted to a medium secure unit: The Edenfield Centre study. *Medicine, Science, and the Law, 49*, 247–256.

Bogestad, A. J., Kettler, R. J., & Hagan, M. P. (2009). Evaluation of a cognitive intervention program for juvenile offenders. *International Journal of Offender Therapy and Comparative Criminology, 54*, 552–565.

Bohm, R. M. (1992). Retribution and capital punishment: Toward a better understanding of death penalty option. *Journal of Criminal Justice, 20*, 227–236.

Bonta, J. & Gendreau, P. (1990). Reexamining the cruel and unusual punishment of prison life. *Law and Human Behavior, 14*, 347–372.

Bonta, J., Law, M., & Hanson, R. K. (1998). Prediction of criminal and violent recidivism among mentally disordered offenders: A meta-analysis. *Psychological Bulletin, 123*, 123–142.

Bourgon, G. & Armstrong, B. (2005). Transferring the principles of effective treatment into a "real world" prison setting. *Criminal Justice and Behavior, 32*, 13–25.

Bowen, E. (2011). *The Rehabilitation of Partner-Violent Men*. Chichester, Sussex: Wiley-Blackwell.

Boyle, J. (1977). *A Sense of Freedom: An Autobiography*. London: Pan Books.

Braham, L., Jones, D., & Hollin, C. R. (2008). The Violent Offender Treatment Program (VOTP): Development of a treatment programme for violent patients in a high security psychiatric hospital. *International Journal of Forensic Mental Health, 7*, 157–172.

Braithwaite, J. (1989). *Crime, Shame and Reintegration*. Cambridge: Cambridge University Press.

—— (1999). Restorative justice: Assessing optimistic and pessimistic accounts. *Crime and Justice, 25*, 1–127.

Braithwaite, J. & Mugford, S. (1994). Conditions of successful reintegration ceremonies: dealing with juvenile offenders. *British Journal of Criminology, 34*, 139–171.

Brody, S. (1976). *The Effectiveness of Sentencing: A Review of the Literature*. London: HMSO.

Bruce, R. & Hollin, C. R. (2009). Developing citizenship. *EuroVista: Probation and Community Justice, 1*, 24–31.

Buchanan, A., Taylor, P., & Gunn, J. (2004). Criminal conviction after discharge from special (high security) hospital: The circumstances of early conviction on a serious charge. *Psychology, Crime and Law, 10*, 5–19.

Campbell, M. A., French, S., & Gendreau, P. (2009). The prediction of violence in adult offenders: A meta-analytic comparison of instruments and methods of assessment. *Criminal Justice and Behavior, 36*, 567–590.

Casey, S., Day, A., & Howells, K. (2005). The application of the transtheoretical model to offender populations: Some critical issues. *Legal and Criminological Psychology, 10*, 151–171.

Casey, S., Day, A., Howells, K., & Ward, T. (2005). Assessing suitability for offender rehabilitation: development and validation of the Treatment Readiness Questionnaire. *Criminal Justice and Behavior, 34*, 1427–1440.

Castillo, E. D. & Alarid, L. F. (2011). Factors associated with recidivism among offenders with mental illness. *International Journal of Offender Therapy and Comparative Criminology, 55*, 98–117.

Chambers, J. C., Eccleston, L., Day, A., Ward, T., & Howells, K. (2008). Treatment readiness in violent offenders: The influence of cognitive factors on engagement in violence programs. *Aggression and Violent Behavior, 13*, 276–284.

Chandler, R. K., Peters, R. H., Field, G., & Juliano-Bult, D. (2004). Challenges in implementing evidence-based treatment practices for co-occurring disorders in the criminal justice system. *Behavioral Sciences and the Law, 22*, 431–448.

Chen, M. K. & Shapiro, J. M. (2007). Do harsher prison conditions reduce recidivism? A discontinuity-based approach. *American Law and Economics Review, 9*, 1–29.

Clarke, M., Davies, S., Hollin, C., & Duggan, C. (2011). Long-term suicide risk in forensic psychiatric patients. *Archives of Suicide Research, 15*, 16–28.

Cochran, J. K. & Chamlin, M. B. (2006). The enduring racial divide in death penalty support. *Journal of Criminal Justice, 34*, 85–99.

Cochran, J. K. & Sanders, B. A. (2009). The gender gap in death penalty support: An exploratory study. *Journal of Criminal Justice, 37*, 525–533.

Cohen, J. (1988). *Statistical Power Analysis for the Behavioural Sciences* (2nd ed.). New York, NY: Academic Press.

Cohen, M. A. (2005). *The Costs of Crime and Justice.* London: Routledge.

Coid, J., Kahtan, N., Cook, A., Gault, S., & Jarman, B. (2001a). Predicting admission rates to secure forensic psychiatry services. *Psychological Medicine, 31*, 531–539.

—— (2001b). Medium secure forensic psychiatry services: Comparison of seven English Health Regions. *British Journal of Psychiatry, 178*, 55–61.

Cook, A. N. & Roesch, R. (2011). "Tough on Crime" reforms: What psychology has to say about the recent and proposed justice policy in Canada. *Canadian Psychology.* Advance online publication, doi: 10.1037/a0025045.

Cooke, D. (1989). Containing violent prisoners: An analysis of the Barlinnie Special Unit. *British Journal of Criminology, 29*, 129–143.

Copas, J. & Marshall, P. (1998). The Offender Group Reconviction Scale: A statistical reconviction score for use by probation officers. *Applied Statistics, 47*, 159–171.

Cope, R. & Ward, T. (1993). What happens to special hospital patients admitted to medium security? *Journal of Forensic Psychiatry and Psychology, 4*, 14–24.

Cornish, D. B. & Clarke, R. V. G. (1975). *Residential Treatment and its Effects on Delinquency.* Home Office Research Study, no. 32. London: HMSO.

Coyle, A. (2008). The treatment of prisoners: International standards and case law. *Legal and Criminological Psychology, 13*, 219–230.

Creighton, C. D. & Jones, A. C. (2012). Psychological profiles of adult sexual assault victims. *Journal of Forensic and Legal Medicine, 19*, 35–39.

Cullen, F. T., Smith, P., Lowenkamp, C. T., & Latessa, E. J. (2009). Nothing Works revisited: Deconstructing Farabee's *Rethinking Rehabilitation. Victims and Offenders, 4*, 101–123.

Daffern, M., Jones, L., & Shine, J. (Eds.) (2010). *Offence Paralleling Behaviour: A Case Formulation Approach to Offender Assessment and Intervention.* Chichester, Sussex: John Wiley & Sons.

Daigle, L. E., Beaver, K. M., & Turner, M. G. (2010). Resiliency against victimization: Results from the National Longitudinal Study of Adolescent Health. *Journal of Criminal Justice, 38*, 329–337.

Daly, K. (2002). Restorative justice: The real story. *Punishment and Society, 4*, 55–79.

Davies, S., Clarke, M., Hollin, C., & Duggan, C. (2007). Long-term outcomes after discharge from medium secure care: A cause for concern. *British Journal of Psychiatry, 191*, 70–74.

Day, A. & Doyle, P. (2010). Violent offender rehabilitation and the therapeutic community model of treatment: Towards integrated service provision? *Aggression and Violent Behavior, 15*, 380–386.

Day, A., Gerace, A., Wilson, C., & Howells, K. (2008). Promoting forgiveness in violent offenders: A more positive approach to offender rehabilitation? *Aggression and Violent Behavior, 13*, 195–200.

de Beus, K. & Rodriguez, N. (2007). Restorative justice practice: An examination of program completion and recidivism. *Journal of Criminal Justice, 36*, 337–347.

De Brito, S. A. & Hodgins, S. (2009). Antisocial personality disorder. In M. McMurran & R. Howard (Eds.), *Personality, Personality Disorder and Violence* (pp. 133–153). Chichester, Sussex: John Wiley & Sons.

Dezhbakhsh, H., Rubin, P. H., & Shepherd, J. M. (2003). Does capital punishment have a deterrent effect? New evidence from postmoratorium panel data. *American Law and Economics Review, 5*, 344–376.

Donohue, J. J. & Wolfers, J. (2009). Estimating the impact of the death penalty on murder. *American Law and Economics Review, 11*, 249–309.

Doob, A. N. & Webster, C. M. (2003). Sentence severity and crime: Accepting the null hypothesis. *Crime and Justice, 30*, 143–195.

Dowden, C. & Andrews, D. A. (1999). What works for female offenders: A meta-analytic review. *Crime and Delinquency, 45*, 438–452.

—— (2004). The importance of staff practice in delivering effective correctional treatment: A meta-analytic review of core correctional practice. *International Journal of Offender Therapy and Comparative Criminology, 48*, 203–214.

Dowsett, J. & Craissati, J. (2008). *Managing Personality Disordered Offenders in the Community: A Psychological Approach.* London: Routledge.

Drake, E. K., Aos, S., & Miller, M. G. (2009). Evidence-based public policy options to reduce crime and criminal justice costs: Implications in Washington State. *Victims and Offenders, 4*, 1–35.

Drieschner, K. H., Lammers, S. M. M., & van der Staak, C. P. F. (2004). Treatment motivation: An attempt for clarification of an ambiguous concept. *Clinical Psychology Review, 23*, 1115–1137.

Farrington, D. P., Ditchfield, J., Hancock, G., Howard, P., Jolliffe, D., Livingston, M. S., & Painter, K. A. (2002). Evaluation of two intensive regimes for young offenders. *Home Office Research Study 239*. London: Home Office.

Farrington, D. P. & Langan, P. A. (1992). Changes in crime and punishment in England and America in the 1980s. *Justice Quarterly, 9*, 5–46.

Fazel, S. & Danesh, J. (2002). Serious mental disorder in 23,000 prisoners: A systematic review of 62 surveys. *Lancet, 359*, 545–550.

Fehr, R., Gelfand, M. J., & Nag, M. (2010). The road to forgiveness: A meta-analytic synthesis of its situational and dispositional correlates. *Psychological Bulletin, 136*, 894–914.

Ferguson, A. M., Ogloff, J. R. P., & Thomson, L. (2009). Predicting recidivism by mentally disordered offenders using the LSI-R:SV. *Criminal Justice and Behavior, 36*, 5–20.

Frakes, M. & Harding, M. (2009). The deterrent effect of death penalty eligibility: Evidence from the adoption of child murder eligibility factors. *American Law and Economics Review, 11*, 451–497.

Franklin, C. A. (2010). Physically forced, alcohol-induced, and verbally coerced sexual victimization: Assessing risk factors among university women. *Journal of Criminal Justice, 38*, 149–159.

French, M. T., Zavala, S. K., McCollister, K. E., Waldron, H. B., Turner, C. W., & Ozechowski, T. J. (2008). Cost-effectiveness analysis of four interventions for adolescents with a substance use disorder. *Journal of Substance Abuse Treatment, 34*, 272–281.

Friendship, C., Blud, L., Erikson, M., Travers, L., & Thornton, D. M. (2003). Cognitive-behavioural treatment for imprisoned offenders: An evaluation of HM Prison Service's cognitive skills programmes. *Legal and Criminological Psychology, 8*, 103–114.

Friendship, C., Mann, R. E., & Beech, A. R. (2003). Evaluation of a national prison-based treatment programme for sexual offenders in England and Wales. *Journal of Interpersonal Violence, 10*, 744–59.

Garrett, C. G. (1985). Effects of residential treatment on adjudicated delinquents: A meta-analysis. *Journal of Research in Crime and Delinquency, 22*, 287–308.

Gendreau, P. (1996). Offender rehabilitation: What we know and what needs to be done. *Criminal Justice and Behavior, 23*, 144–161.

Gendreau, P., Goggin, C., & Fulton, B. (2001). Intensive supervision in probation and parole. In C. R. Hollin (Ed.), *Handbook of Offender Assessment and Treatment* (pp. 195–204). Chichester, Sussex: John Wiley & Sons.

Gendreau, P., Goggin, C., & Smith, P. (2001). Implementing correctional interventions in the "real" world. In G. A. Bernfeld, A. W. Leschied, & D. P. Farrington (Eds.), *Inside the 'Black Box' in Corrections* (pp. 247–268). Chichester, Sussex: John Wiley & Sons.

Gendreau, P. & Ross, R. R. (1979). Effective correctional treatment: bibliotherapy for cynics. *Crime and Delinquency, 25*, 463–489.

—— (1987). Revivification of rehabilitation: Evidence from the 1980s. *Justice Quarterly, 4*, 349–408.

Gendreau, P., Smith, P., & Thériault, Y. L. (2009). Chaos theory and correctional treatment: Common sense, correctional quackery, and the law of fartcatchers. *Journal of Contemporary Criminal Justice, 25*, 384–396.

Glass, G. V., McGraw, B., & Smith, M. L. (1981). *Meta-Analysis in Social Research*. Beverly Hills, CA: Sage.

Goetz, J. L., Keltner, D., & Simon-Thomas, E. (2010). Compassion: An evolutionary analysis and empirical review. Psychological *Bulletin, 136*, 351–374.

Goldstein, A. P. (2002). *The Psychology of Group Aggression*. Chichester, Sussex: John Wiley & Sons.

Goldstein, A. P. & Glick, B. (2001). Aggression replacement training: Application and evaluation management. In G. A. Bernfeld, D. P. Farrington, & A. W. Leschied (Eds.), *Offender Rehabilitation in Practice: Effective Programs and Policies to Reduce Re-offending* (pp. 122–148). Chichester, Sussex: John Wiley & Sons.

Goldstein, A. P., Glick, B., & Gibbs, J. C. (1998). *Aggression Replacement Training* (2nd ed.). Champaign, IL: Research Press.

Goldstein, A. P., Nensen, R., Deleflod, B., & Kalt, M. (Eds.) (2004). New Perspectives on Aggression Replacement Training: Practice, Research, and Application. Chichester, Sussex: John Wiley & Sons.

Gottfredson, D. C. (2010). Deviancy training: Understanding how preventive interventions harm. *Journal of Experimental Criminology, 6*, 229–243.

Gray, E., Taylor, E., Roberts, C., Merrington, S., Fernandez, R., & Moore, R. (2005). *Intensive Supervision and Surveillance Programme: The Final Report.* London: Youth Justice Board.

Greenland, C. (1969). The three Special Hospitals in England and Wales and patients with dangerous, violent or criminal propensities. *Medicine, Science and the Law, 9*, 253–264.

Gumpert, C. H., Winerdal, U., Grundtman, M., Berman, A. H., Kristiansson, M., & Palmstierna, T. (2010). The relationship between substance abuse treatment and crime relapse among individuals with suspected mental disorder, substance abuse, and antisocial behavior: Findings from the MSAC Study. *International Journal of Forensic Mental Health, 9*, 82–92.

Hanson, R. K. (2009). The psychological assessment of risk for crime and violence. *Canadian Psychology, 50*, 172–182.

Hanson, R. K., Bourgon, G., Helmus, L., & Hodgson, S. (2009). The principles of effective correctional treatment also apply to sexual offenders: A meta-analysis. *Criminal Justice and Behavior, 36*, 865–891.

Hanson, R. K. & Thornton, D. (2000). Improving risk assessments for sex offenders: A comparison of three actuarial scales. *Law and Human Behavior, 24*, 119–136.

Hare, R. D. (1991). *The Hare Psychopathy Checklist-Revised.* Toronto: Multi-Heath Systems.

Harries, R. (1999). The cost of criminal justice. *Research Findings, No. 103.* London: Home Office.

Hatcher, R. M., Palmer, E. J., McGuire, J., Hounsome, J. C., Bilby, C. A. L., & Hollin C. R. (2008). Aggression Replacement Training with adult male offenders within community settings: A reconviction analysis, *Journal of Forensic Psychiatry and Psychology, 19*, 517–32.

Hayes, S. C., Follette, V. M., & Linehan, M. M. (Eds.) (2004). *Mindfulness and Acceptance: Expanding the Cognitive-Behavioral Tradition.* New York, NY: Guilford Press.

Hedderman, C. (2008). *Building On Sand: Why Expanding the Prison Estate is Not the Way to 'Secure the Future'.* Centre for Crime and Justice Studies, Briefing 7. London: Centre for Crime and Justice Studies, King's College London.

Heide, K. M. & Solomon, E. P. (2003). Treating today's juvenile homicide offenders. *Youth Violence and Juvenile Justice, 1*, 5–31.

Helms, R. (2009). Modeling the politics of punishment: A conceptual and empirical analysis of "law in action" in criminal sentencing. *Journal of Criminal Justice, 37*, 10–20.

Henderson, M. & Hollin, C. R. (1986). Social skills training and delinquency. In C. R. Hollin & P. Trower (Eds.), *Handbook of Social Skills Training, Volume 1: Applications Across the Life Span* (pp. 79–101). Oxford: Pergamon Press.

Hjalmarsson, R. (2008). Does capital punishment have a "local" deterrent effect on homicides? *American Law and Economics Review, 11*, 310–334.

Hodgins, S., Alderton, J., Cree, A., Aboud, A., & Mak, T. (2007). Aggressive behaviour, victimization and crime among severely mentally ill patients requiring hospitalisation. *British Journal of Psychiatry, 191*, 343–350.

Hodgins, S. & Riaz, M. (2011). Violence and phases of illness: Differential risk and predictors. *European Psychiatry, 26*, 518–524.

Hollin, C. R. (1990). *Cognitive-Behavioural Interventions with Young Offenders.* Oxford: Pergamon Press.

—— (1995). The meaning and implications of "programme integrity". In J. McGuire (Ed.), What Works: Reducing Reoffending (pp. 195–208). Chichester, Sussex: John Wiley & Sons.

—— (1999). Treatment programmes for offenders: Meta-analysis, "what works", and beyond. *International Journal of Law and Psychiatry, 22*, 361–372.

—— (2002). Does punishment motivate offenders to change? In M. McMurran (Ed.), *Motivating Offenders to Change: A Guide to Enhancing Engagement in Therapy* (pp. 225–249). Chichester, Sussex: John Wiley & Sons.

—— (2008). Evaluating offending behaviour programmes: Does only randomisation glister? *Criminology & Criminal Justice, 8*, 89–106.

Hollin, C. R. & Palmer, E. J. (2003). Level of Service Inventory-Revised profiles of violent and non-violent prisoners. *Journal of Interpersonal Violence, 18*, 1075–1086.

—— (2006a). Offending behaviour programmes: History and development. In C. R. Hollin & E. J. Palmer (Eds.), *Offending Behaviour Programmes: Development, Application, and Controversies* (pp. 1–32). Chichester, Sussex: John Wiley & Sons.

—— (Eds.) (2006b). *Offending Behaviour Programmes: Development, Application, and Controversies.* Chichester, Sussex: John Wiley & Sons.

—— (2009). Cognitive skills programmes for offenders. *Psychology, Crime & Law, 15*, 147–164.

Hollin, C. R., Palmer, E. J., & Clark, D. (2003). The Level of Service Inventory-Revised profile of English prisoners: A needs analysis. *Criminal Justice and Behavior, 30*, 422–440.

Hollin, C. R., McGuire, J., Hounsome, J. C., Hatcher, R. M., Bilby, C. A. L., & Palmer, E. J. (2008). Cognitive skills offending behavior programs in the community: A reconviction analysis. *Criminal Justice and Behavior, 35*, 269–283.

Home Office (2006). *Offender Assessment System OASys User Manual.* London: Author.

Hood, R. (2001). Capital punishment: A global perspective. *Punishment & Society, 3*, 331–354.

Hornsveld, R. H. J., Nijman, H. L. I., Hollin, C. R., & Kraaimaat, F. W. (2007). Development of the Observation Scale for Aggressive Behavior (OSAB) for Dutch forensic psychiatric inpatients with an antisocial behavior disorder. *International Journal of Law and Psychiatry, 30*, 15–27.

Hornsveld, R. H. J., Nijman, H. L. I., Hollin, C. R., & Kraaimaat, F. W. (2008). Aggression control therapy for violent forensic psychiatric patients: Method and clinical practice. *International Journal of Offender Therapy and Comparative Criminology, 52*, 206–221.

Howard, P., Francis, B., Soothill, K., & Humphreys, L. (2009). OGRS 3: The Revised Offender Group Reconviction Scale. Ministry and Justice Research Summary, 7/09.

Howells, K. (1986). Social skills training and criminal and antisocial behaviour in adults. In C. R. Hollin & P. Trower (Eds.), *Handbook of Social Skills Training, Volume 1: Applications Across the Life Span* (pp. 185–210). Oxford: Pergamon Press.

—— (2010). The "third wave" of cognitive behavioural therapy and forensic practice. *Criminal Behaviour and Mental Health, 20*, 251–256.

Howells, K. & Day, A. (2003). Readiness for anger management: Clinical and theoretical issues. *Clinical Psychology Review, 23*, 319–337.

Hoyle, C. & Zedner, L. (2007). Victims, victimization, and criminal justice. In M. Maguire, R. Morgan, & R. Reiner (Eds.), *The Oxford Handbook of Criminology* (pp. 461–495). Oxford: Oxford University Press.

Hudson, B. (1987). *Justice Through Punishment: A Critique of the `Justice' Model of Corrections.* London: Macmillan.

James, D. V. (2010). Diversion of mentally disordered people from the criminal justice system in England and Wales: An overview. *International Journal of Law and Psychiatry, 33*, 241–248.

Jamieson, L. & Taylor, P. J. (2004). A re-conviction study of special (high security) hospital patients. *British Journal of Criminology, 44*, 783–802.

Jaishankar, K. (Ed.) (2011). *Cyber Criminology: Exploring Internet Crimes and Criminal Behavior.* Boca Raton, FL: Taylor & Francis.

Jennings, W. G., Higgins, G. E., Tewksbury, R., Gover, A. R., & Piquero, A. R. (2010). A longitudinal assessment of the victim-offender overlap. *Journal of Interpersonal Violence, 25*, 2147–2174.

Jiang, S., Lambert, E. G., & Nathan, V. M. (2009). Reasons for death penalty attitudes among Chinese citizens: Retributive or instrumental? *Journal of Criminal Justice, 37*, 225–233.

Jiang, S., Lambert, E. G., Wang, J., Saito, T., & Pilot, R. (2010). Death penalty views in China, Japan and the US: An empirical comparison. *Journal of Criminal Justice, 38*, 862–869.

Johnson, D. T. (2006). Where the state kills in secret: Capital punishment in Japan. *Punishment & Society, 8*, 251–285.

Jones, D. & Hollin, C. R. (2004). Managing problematic anger: The development of a treatment programme for personality disordered patients in high security. *International Journal of Forensic Mental Health, 3*, 197–210.

Jones, N. N., Brown, S. L., & Zamble, E. (2010). Predicting criminal recidivism in adult male offenders: researcher versus parole officer assessment of dynamic risk. *Criminal Justice and Behavior, 37*, 860–882.

Kazdin, A. E. (1987). Treatment of antisocial behaviour in children: Current status and future directions. *Psychological Bulletin, 102*, 187–203.

Kennedy, D. M. (2009). *Deterrence and Crime Prevention: Reconsidering the Prospect of Sanction.* London: Routledge.

Killias, M., Gilliéron, G., Kissling, I., & Villettaz, P. (2010). Community service versus electronic monitoring – what works better? Results of a randomized trial. *British Journal of Criminology, 50*, 1155–1170.

Kirigin, K. A., Braukmann, C. J., Atwater, J. D., & Wolf, M. M. (1982). An evaluation of teaching family (Achievement Place) group homes for juvenile offenders. *Journal of Applied Behavior Analysis, 15*, 1–16.

Kirkwood, S. (2009). *Restorative Justice Cases in Scotland: Factors Related to Participation, Restorative Process, Agreement Rates and Forms of Reparation.* Edinburgh: Sacro.

Knott, C. (1995). The STOP programme: Reasoning and rehabilitation in a British setting. In J. McGuire (Ed.), *What Works: Reducing Reoffending* (pp. 115–126). Chichester, Sussex: John Wiley & Sons.

Kuo, S., Longmire, D., & Cuvelier, S. J. (2010). An empirical assessment of the process of restorative justice. *Journal of Criminal Justice, 38*, 318–328.

Latimer, J., Dowden, C., & Muise, D. (2001). *The Effectiveness of Restorative Justice Practices: A Meta-Analysis.* Research and Statistics Division Methodological Series, Department of Justice, Canada.

—— (2005). The effectiveness of restorative justice practices: A meta-analysis. *The Prison Journal, 85*, 127–144.

Lewis, S., Maguire, M., Raynor, P., Vanstone, M., & Vennard, J. (2007). What works in resettlement? Findings from seven Pathfinders for short-term prisoners in England and Wales. *Criminology & Criminal Justice, 7*, 33–53.

Lester, D. & Van Voorhis, P. (2004a). Early approaches to group and milieu therapy. In P. Van Voorhis, M. Braswell, & D. Lester (Eds.), *Correctional Counseling & Rehabilitation* (5th ed.) (pp. 85–110). Cincinnati, OH: Anderson Publishing Co.

—— (2004b). Psychoanalytic therapy. In P. Van Voorhis, M. Braswell, & D. Lester (Eds.), *Correctional Counseling & Rehabilitation* (5th ed.) (pp. 41–60). Cincinnati, OH: Anderson Publishing Co.

Lipsey, M. W. (1992). Juvenile delinquency treatment: A meta-analytic inquiry into the variability of effects. In T. Cook, D. Cooper, H. Corday, H. Hartman, L. Hedges, R. Light, T. Louis, & F. Mosteller (Eds.), *Meta-Analysis for Explanation: A Casebook* (pp. 83–127). New York, NY: Russell Sage Foundation.

—— (1995). What do we learn from 400 research studies on the effectiveness of treatment with juvenile delinquents? In J. McGuire (Ed.), *What Works: Reducing Reoffending.* Chichester, Sussex: John Wiley & Sons.

—— (2009). The primary factors that characterize effective interventions with juvenile offenders: A meta-analytic overview. *Victims and Offenders, 4*, 124–147.

Lipsey, M. W. & Cullen, F. T. (2007). The effectiveness of correctional rehabilitation: A review of systematic reviews. *Annual Review of Law and Social Science, 3*, 297–320.

Lipsey, M. W., Landenberger, N. A., & Wilson, S. J. (2007). *Effects of Cognitive-Behavioral Programs for Criminal Offenders.* Campbell Systematic Reviews.

Lipton, D. S. (2001). Therapeutic community treatment programming in corrections. In C. R. Hollin (Ed.), *Handbook of Offender Assessment and Treatment* (pp. 155–177). Chichester, Sussex: John Wiley & Sons.

Lipton, D. S., Martinson, R., & Wilks, D. (1975). *The Effectiveness of Correctional Treatment.* New York, NY: Praeger.

Lipton, D. S., Thornton, D. M., McGuire, J., Porporino, F. J., & Hollin, C. R. (2000). Program accreditation and correctional treatment. *Substance Use and Misuse, 35*, 1705–1734.

Logan, C. & Blackburn, R. (2009). Mental disorder in violent women in secure settings: Potential relevance to risk for future violence. *International Journal of Law and Psychiatry, 32*, 31–38.

Long, C. G., Webster, P., Waine, J., Motala, J., & Hollin, C. R. (2008). Usefulness of the CANFORS for measuring needs among mentally disordered offenders resident in medium or low secure hospital services in the UK: A pilot evaluation. *Criminal Behaviour and Mental Health, 18*, 39–48.

Lösel, F. (1996). Working with young offenders: The impact of the meta-analyses. In C. R. Hollin & K. Howells (Eds.), *Clinical Approaches to Working with Young Offenders* (pp. 57–82). Chichester, Sussex: John Wiley and Sons.

Lösel, F. & Schmucker, M. (2005). The effectiveness of treatment for sexual offenders: A comprehensive meta-analysis. *Journal of Experimental Criminology, 1*, 117–146.

Lowenkamp, C. T., Flores, A. W., Holsinger, A. M., Makarios, M. D., & Latessa, E. J. (2010). Intensive supervision programs: Does program philosophy and the principles of effective intervention matter? *Journal of Criminal Justice, 38*, 368–375.

Lowenkamp, C. T., Latessa, E. J., & Holsinger, A. M. (2006). The risk principle in action: What have we learned from 13,676 offenders and 97 correctional programs? *Crime & Delinquency, 52*, 77–93.

Lowenkamp, C. T., Makarios, M. D., Latessa, E. J., Lemke, E., & Smith, P. (2010). Community corrections facilities for juvenile offenders in Ohio: An examination of treatment integrity and recidivism. *Criminal Justice and Behavior, 37*, 695–708.

Lu, H. & Zhang, L. (2005). Death penalty in China: The law and the practice. *Journal of Criminal Justice, 33*, 367–376.

MacKenzie, D. L., Brame, R., McDowall, D., & Souryal, C. (1995). Boot camp prisons and recidivism in eight states. *Criminology, 33*, 327–357.

Maden, A., Rutter, S., McClintock, T., Friendship, C., & Gunn, J. (1999). Outcome of admission to a medium secure psychiatric unit. I. Short and long-term outcome. *British Journal of Psychiatry, 175*, 313–16.

Maden, A., Scott, F., Burnett, R., Lewis, G, H., & Skapinakis, P. (2004). Offending in psychiatric patients after discharge from medium secure units: Prospective national cohort study. *British Medical Journal, 328*, 1534.

Maguire, M., Grubin, D., Losel, F., & Raynor, P. (2010). "What Works" and the Correctional Services Accreditation Panel: Taking stock from an inside perspective. *Criminology and Criminal Justice, 10*, 37–58.

Mair, G. (2005). Electronic monitoring in England and Wales: Evidence-based or not? *Criminal Justice, 5*, 257–277.

Makinen, T. & Takala, H. (1980). 1976 police strike in Finland. In R. Hague (Ed.), *Policing Scandinavia* (pp. 87–106). Oslo: Universitetsforlaget.

Mancini, C. & Mears, D. P. (2010). To execute or not to execute? Examining public support for capital punishment of sex offenders. *Journal of Criminal Justice, 38*, 959–968.

Mann, R. E. & Fernandez, Y. M. (2006). Sex offender programmes: Concept, theory, and practice. In C. R. Hollin & E. J. Palmer (Eds.), *Offending Behaviour Programmes: Development, Application, and Controversies* (pp. 155–177). Chichester, Sussex: John Wiley & Sons.

Marsh, K. & Fox, C. (2008). The benefit and cost of prison in the UK. The results of a model of lifetime re-offending. *Journal of Experimental Criminology, 4*, 403–423.

Marshall, T. (1999). *Restorative Justice: An Overview.* Home Office Occasional Paper. London: Home Office.

Marshall, W. L. & McGuire, J. (2003). Effect sizes in the treatment of sexual offenders. *International Journal of Offender Therapy and Comparative Criminology, 47*, 653–663.

Martinson, R. (1974). What works? Questions and answers about prison reform. *The Public Interest, 35*, 22–54.

—— (1979). New findings, new views: A note of caution regarding sentencing reform. *Hofstra Law Review, 7*, 243–258.

McCann, S. J. H. (2008). Social threat, authoritarianism, conservatism, and US state death penalty sentencing (1977–2004). *Journal of Personality and Social Psychology, 94*, 913–923.

McCarthy, L. & Duggan, C. (2010). Engagement in a medium secure personality disorder service: A comparative study of psychological functioning and offending outcomes. *Criminal Behaviour and Mental Health, 20*, 112–128.

McCord, J. (1978). A thirty-year follow-up of treatment effects. *American Psychologist, 33*, 284–289.

McGuire, J. (Ed.) (1995). *What Works: Reducing Reoffending.* Chichester, Sussex: John Wiley & Sons.

McGuire, J. (2002). Integrating findings from research reviews. In J. McGuire (Ed.), *Offender Rehabilitation and Treatment: Effective Programmes and Policies to Reduce Re-offending* (pp. 3–38). Chichester, Sussex: John Wiley & Sons.

—— (2005). *The Think First* programme. In M. McMurran & J. McGuire (Eds.), *Social Problem Solving and Offending: Evidence Evaluation and Evolution* (pp. 183–206). Chichester, Sussex: John Wiley & Sons.

—— (2008a). A review of effective interventions for reducing aggression and violence. *Philosophical Transactions of the Royal Society B, 363*, 2577–2597.

—— (2008b). The impact of sentencing. In G. Davies, C. Hollin, & R. Bull (Eds.), *Forensic Psychology* (pp. 266–291). Chichester, Sussex: John Wiley & Sons.

McGuire, J., Bilby, C. A. L., Hatcher, R. M., Hollin, C. R., Hounsome, J., & Palmer, E. J. (2008). Evaluation of structured cognitive-behavioural treatment programmes in reducing criminal recidivism. *Journal of Experimental Criminology, 4*, 21–40.

McGuire, J. & Hatcher, R. (2000). Offence-focused problem solving: Preliminary evaluation of a cognitive skills program. *Criminal Justice and Behavior, 28*, 564–587.

McGurk, B. J., Forde, R., & Barnes, A. (2000). *Sexual Victimisation Among 15-17-Year-Old Offenders in Prison.* RDS Occasional Paper No 65. London: Home Office.

McMurran, M. & McCulloch, A. (2007). Why don't offenders complete treatment? Prisoners' reasons for non-completion of a cognitive skills programme. *Psychology, Crime & Law, 13*, 345–354.

McMurran, M., Riemsma, R., Manning, N., Misso, K., & Kleijnen, J. (2011). Interventions for alcohol-related offending by women: A systematic review. *Clinical Psychology Review, 31*, 909–922.

McMurran, M. & Theodosi, E. (2007). Is treatment non-completion associated with increased reconviction over no treatment? *Psychology, Crime & Law, 13*, 333–343.

Meade, B. & Steiner, B. (2010). The total effects of boot camps that house juveniles: A systematic review of the evidence. *Journal of Criminal Justice, 38*, 841–853.

Mears, D. P. & Bales, W. D. (2009). Supermax incarceration and recidivism. *Criminology, 47*, 1131–1166.

—— (2010). Supermax housing: Placement, duration, and time to re-entry. *Journal of Criminal Justice, 38*, 545–554.

Miers, D. (2001). *An International Review of Restorative Justice.* Crime Reduction Research Series, Paper 10. London: Home Office.

Miers, D., Maguire, M., Goldie, S., Sharpe, S., Hale, C., Netten, A., & Newburn, T. (2001). *An Exploratory Evaluation of Restorative Justice Schemes.* Crime Reduction Research Series Paper 9. London: Home Office.

Milan, M. A. (2001). Behavioral approaches to correctional management and rehabilitation. In C. R. Hollin (Ed.), *Handbook of Offender Assessment and Treatment* (pp. 139–154). Chichester, Sussex: John Wiley & Sons.

Milan, M. A. & McKee, J. M. (1976). The cellblock token economy: Token reinforcement procedures in a maximum security correctional institution for adult male felons. *Journal of Applied Behavior Analysis, 9*, 254–275.

Milan, M. A., Throckmorton, W. R., McKee, J. M., & Wood, L. F. (1979). Contingency management in a cellblock token economy: Reducing rule violations and maximizing the effects of token reinforcement. *Criminal Justice and Behavior, 6*, 307–325.

Ministry of Justice (2011). *Adult Re-Convictions: Results from the 2009 Cohort. England and Wales.* Statistics Bulletin. London: Ministry of Justice.

Mitchell, O., Wilson, D. B., & MacKenzie, D. L. (2007). Does incarceration-based drug treatment reduce recidivism? A meta-analytic synthesis of research. *Journal of Experimental Criminology, 3*, 353–375.

Monahan, J. S., Henry, J., Applebaum, P. S., Robbins, P.C., Mulvey, E. P., Silver, E., et al. (2000). Developing a clinically useful actuarial tool for assessing violent risk. *British Journal of Psychiatry, 176*, 312–319.

Morreale, M. C. & English, A. (2004). Abolishing the death penalty for juvenile offenders: A background paper. *Journal of Adolescent Health, 35*, 335–339.

Morrissey, C. & Hollin, C. R. (2011). Psychopathic and antisocial personality disorders in forensic intellectual disability: What do we know so far? *Psychology, Crime, & Law, 17*, 133–149.

Mitchell, O., Wilson, D. B., & MacKenzie, D. L. (2007). Does incarceration-based drug treatment reduce recidivism? A meta-analytic synthesis of the research. *Journal of Experimental Criminology, 3*, 353–375.

Nagin, D. S., Cullen, F. T., & Jonson, C. L. (2009). Imprisonment and reoffending. In M. Tonry (Ed.), *Crime and Justice: An Annual Review of Research* (Vol. 38) (pp. 115–200). Chicago, IL: University of Chicago Press.

Nellis, M. (2000). Law and order: The electronic monitoring of offenders. In D. Dolowitz (Ed.), *Policy Transfer and British Social Policy* (pp. 98–117). Buckingham: Open University Press.

National Institute for Health and Clinical Excellence (2009). *Antisocial Personality Disorder: Treatment, Management and Prevention.* NICE Clinical Guideline 77. London: NICE.

Ngo, F. T. & Paternoster, R. (2011). Cybercrime victimization: An examination of individual and situational level factors. *International Journal of Cyber Criminology, 5*, 773–793.

Nicholls, T. L., Brink, J., Greaves, C., Lussier, P., & Verdun-Jones, S. (2009). Forensic psychiatric inpatients and aggression: An exploration of incidence, prevalence, severity, and interventions by gender. *International Journal of Law and Psychiatry, 32*, 23–30.

Nilsson, T., Wallinius, M., Gustavson, C., Anckarsater, H., & Kerekes, N. (2011). Violent recidivism: A long-time follow-up study of mentally disordered offenders. *PLoS ONE, 6*(10): e25768.

Novaco, R. W. (1975). *Anger Control: The Development an Evaluation of an Experimental Treatment.* Lexington, MA: D.C. Heath.

Olver, M. E., Stockdale, K. C., & Wormith, J. S. (2011). A meta-analysis of predictors of offender treatment attrition and its relationship to recidivism. *Journal of Consulting and Clinical Psychology, 79*, 6–21.

Ozabaci, N. (2011). Cognitive behavioural therapy for violent behaviour in children and adolescents: A meta-analysis. *Children and Youth Services Review, 33*, 1989–1993.

Padgett, K. G., Bales, W. D., & Blomberg, T. G. (2006). Under surveillance: An empirical test of the effectiveness and consequences of electronic monitoring. *Criminology & Public Policy, 5*, 61–92.

Palmer, E. J., Hatcher, R. M., McGuire, J., Bilby, C. A. L., Ayres, T. C., & Hollin, C. R. (2011). Evaluation of the Addressing Substance-Related Offending (ASRO) program for substance-using offenders in the community. *Substance Use and Misuse, 46*, 1072–1080.

Palmer, E. J., Hatcher, R. M., McGuire, J., Bilby, C. A. L., & Hollin, C. R. (2012). The effect on reconviction of an intervention for drink-driving offenders in the community. *International Journal of Offender Therapy and Comparative Criminology, 56*, 525–538.

Palmer, E. J., Hollin, C. R., & Caulfield, L. (2005). Surveying fear: Crime, buses, and new paint. *Crime Prevention and Community Safety: An International Journal, 7*, 47–58.

Palmer, E. J., McGuire, J., Hatcher, R. M., Hounsome, J. C., Bilby, C. A. L., & Hollin, C. R. (2009). Allocation to offending behaviour programmes in the English and Welsh Probation Service. *Criminal Justice and Behavior, 36*, 909–922.

Palmer, E. J., McGuire, J., Hounsome, J. C., Hatcher, R. M., Bilby, C. A., & Hollin, C. R. (2007). Offending behaviour programmes in the community: The effects on reconviction of three programmes with adult male offenders. *Legal and Criminological Psychology, 12*, 251–264.

Payne, B. K. & DeMichele, M. T. (2010). Electronic supervision for sex offenders: Implications for work load, supervision goals, versatility, and policymaking. *Journal of Criminal Justice, 38*, 276–281.

Pearson, D. A. S., McDougall, C., Kanaan, M., Bowles, R. A., & Torgerson, D. J. (2011). Reducing criminal recidivism: Evaluation of citizenship, an evidence-based probation supervision process. *Journal of Experimental Criminology, 7*, 73–102.

Perelman, A. M. & Clements, C. B. (2009). Beliefs about what works in juvenile rehabilitation: The influence of attitudes on support for "Get Tough" and evidence-based interventions. *Criminal Justice and Behavior, 36*, 184–197.

Pettifer, E. W. (1992). *Punishments of Former Days.* Winchester, Hants: Waterside Press. (Original edition published by the author in 1939.)

Pfuhl, E. H. (1983). Police strikes and conventional crime – a look at the data. *Criminology, 21*, 489–503.

Piquero, A. R. & Blumstein, A. (2007). Does incapacitation reduce crime? *Journal of Quantitative Criminology, 23*, 267–286.

Piquero, A. R., Farrington, D. P., Welsh, B. C., Tremblay, R., & Jennings, W. G. (2009). Effects of early family/parent training programs on antisocial behavior and delinquency. *Journal of Experimental Criminology, 5*, 83–120.

Polaschek, D. L. L. (2011). Many sizes fit all: A preliminary framework for conceptualizing the development and provision of cognitive-behavioral rehabilitation programs for offenders. *Aggression and Violent Behavior, 16*, 20–35.

Pope, A. E. (2002). A feminist look at the death penalty. *Law and Contemporary Problems, 65*, 257–282.

Powers, E. & Witmar, H. (1951). *An Experiment in the Prevention of Delinquency: The Cambridge-Somerville Youth Study.* New York, NY: Columbia University Press.

Pratt, D., Piper, M., Appleby, L., Roger, W., & Shaw, J. (2006). Suicide in recently released prisoners: A population-based cohort study. *Lancet, 368*(9530), 119–123.

Pratt, T. C., Cullen, F. T., Blevins, K. R., Daigle, L. E., & Madensen, T. D. (2006). The empirical status of deterrence theory: A meta-analysis. In F. T. Cullen, J. P. Wright, & K. R. Blevins (Eds.), *Taking Stock: Advances in Criminological Theory* (pp. 367–395). New Brunswick, NJ: Transaction Publishers.

Prendergast, M. L., Podus, D., Chang, E., & Urada, D. (2002). The effectiveness of drug abuse treatment: A meta-analysis of comparison group studies. *Drug and Alcohol Dependence, 67*, 53–72.

Prison Reform Trust (2011). *Bromley Briefings Prison Factfile.* London: Prison Reform Trust.

Quinn, P. & Ward, M. (2000). What happens to special hospital patients admitted to medium security? *Medicine, Science, and Law, 40*, 345–349.

Quinsey, V. L., Harris, G. T., Rice, M. E., & Cormier, C. A. (1998). *Violent Offenders: Appraising and Managing Risk.* Washington, DC: American Psychological Association.

Radelet, M. L., & Lacock, T. L. (2009). Do executions lower homicide rates?: The views of leading criminologists. *Journal of Criminal Law and Criminology, 99*, 489–508.

Rapoport, R. (1960). *The Community as Doctor.* London: Tavistock Publications.

Raynor, P. & Robinson, G. (2009). Why help offenders? Arguments for rehabilitation as a penal strategy. *European Journal of Probation, 1*, 3–20.

Raynor, P. & Vanstone, M. (1996). Reasoning and rehabilitation in Britain: The results of the Straight Thinking on Probation (STOP) program. *International Journal of Offender Therapy and Comparative Criminology, 40*, 272–284.

Redondo, S., Sanchez-Meca, J., & Garrido, V. (2002). Crime treatment in Europe: A review of outcome studies. In J. McGuire (Ed.), *Offender Rehabilitation and Treatment: Effective Programmes and Policies to Reduce Re-offending* (pp. 113–141). Chichester, Sussex: John Wiley & Sons.

Rodogno, R. (2008). Shame and guilt in restorative justice. *Psychology, Public Policy, and Law, 14*, 142–176.

Roman, J. K., Chalfin, A. J., & Knight, C. R. (2009). Reassessing the cost of the death penalty using quasi-experimental methods: Evidence from Maryland. *American Law and Economics Review, 11*, 530–574.

Romito, P. & Grassi, M. (2007). Does violence affect one gender more than the other? The mental health impact of violence among male and female university students. *Social Science & Medicine, 65*, 1222–1234.

Rosnow, R. L. & Rosenthal, R. (1988). Focused tests of significance and effect size estimation in counseling psychology. *Journal of Counseling Psychology, 35*, 203–208.

Ross, R. R. & Fabiano, E. A. (1985). *Time to Think: A Cognitive Model of Delinquency Prevention and Offender Rehabilitation.* Johnson City, TN: Institute of Social Sciences and Arts.

Ross, R. R., Fabiano, E. A., & Ewles, C. D. (1988). Reasoning and rehabilitation. *International Journal of Offender Therapy and Comparative Criminology, 32*, 29–35.

Ross, R. R., Fabiano, E. A., & Ross, B. (1989). *Reasoning and Rehabilitation: A Handbook for Teaching Cognitive Skills.* Ottawa: The Cognitive Centre.

Ruddell, R., Broom, I., & Young, M. (2010). Creating hope for life-sentenced offenders. *Journal of Offender Rehabilitation, 49*, 324–341.

Sacks, S., Sacks, J. Y., McKendrick, K., Banks, S., & Stommel, J. (2004). Modified TC for MICA offenders: Crime outcomes. *Behavioral Science and the Law, 22*, 477–501.

Sadlier, G. (2010). *Evaluation of the Impact of the HM Prison Service Enhanced Thinking Skills Programme on Reoffending Outcomes of the Surveying Prisoner Crime Reduction (SPCR) Sample.* Ministry of Justice Research Series 19/10. London: Ministry of Justice.

Salekin, R. T. (2002). Psychopathy and therapeutic pessimism: Clinical lore or clinical reality? *Clinical Psychology Review, 22*, 79–112.

Schaeffer, C. M. & Borduin, C. M. (2005). Long-term follow-up to a randomized clinical trial of multisystemic therapy with serious and violent juvenile offenders. *Journal of Consulting and Clinical Psychology, 73*, 445–453.

Scott, C. L. & Resnick, P. J. (2006). Violence risk assessment in persons with mental illness. *Aggression and Violent Behavior, 11*, 598–611.

Scottish Prison Service (2003). *Manual of Standards and Guidelines for the Design Accreditation of Prisoner Programmes and the Implementation of Programmes in Establishments.* Edinburgh: Scottish Prison Service.

Semukhina, O. B. & Galliher, J. F. (2009). Death penalty politics and symbolic law in Russia. *International Journal of Law, Crime and Justice, 37*, 131–153.

Sexton, T. & Turner, C. W. (2010). The effectiveness of functional family therapy for youth with behavioral problems in a community practice setting. *Journal of Family Psychology, 24*, 339–348.

Shapland, J., Atkinson, A., Atkinson, H., Dignan, J., Edwards, L., Hibbert, J., & Sorsby, A. (2008). Does restorative justice affect reconviction? Ministry of Justice Research Series 10/08.

Sharkey, J. D., Sander, J. B., & Jimerson, S. R. (2010). Acculturation and mental health: Response to a culturally-centered delinquency intervention. *Journal of Criminal Justice, 38*, 827–834.

Shaw, C. & McKay, H. (1942). *Juvenile Delinquency and Urban Areas.* Chicago, IL: University of Chicago Press.

Sherman, L. W., Gottfredson, D., MacKenzie, D., Eck, J., Reuter, P., & Bushway, S. (1997). Preventing Crime: What Works, What Doesn't, What's Promising. Report to the United States Congress. *National Institute of Justice*, NCJ-165366.

Sherman, L. W. & Strang, H. (2007). *Restorative Justice: The Evidence.* London: The Smith Institute.

Sherman, L. W., Strang, H., Angel, C., Woods, D., Barnes, G. C., Bennett, S., & Inkpen, N. (2005). Effects of face-to-face restorative justice on victims of crime in four randomized, controlled trials. *Journal of Experimental Criminology, 1*, 367–395.

Shuker, R. & Sullivan, E. (2010). *Grendon and the Emergence of Forensic Therapeutic Communities: Developments in Research and Practice.* Chichester, Sussex: Wiley-Blackwell.

Singh, J. P. & Fazel, S. (2010). Forensic risk assessment: A metareview. *Criminal Justice and Behavior, 37*, 965–998.

Singh, J. P., Grann, M., & Fazel, S. (2011). A comparative study of violence risk assessment tools: A systematic review and metaregression analysis of 68 studies involving 25,980 participants. *Clinical Psychology Review, 31*, 499–513.

Skinner, B. F. (1938). *The Behavior of Organisms.* New York, NY: Appleton-Century-Crofts.

—— (1974). *About Behaviorism.* New York, NY: Knopf.

Slobogin, C. & Fondacaro, M. (2000). Rethinking deprivations of liberty: possible contributions from therapeutic and ecological jurisprudence. *Behavioral Sciences and the Law, 18*, 499–516.

Smith, D. (2004). The Links Between Victimization and Offending. Number 5: The Edinburgh Study of Youth Transitions and Crime. Edinburgh: Centre for Law and Society, The University of Edinburgh.

Smith, M. D. (1987). Patterns of discrimination in assessments of the death penalty: The case of Louisiana. *Journal of Criminal Justice, 15*, 279–286.

Smith, P., Gendreau, P., & Swartz, K. (2009). Validating the principles of effective intervention: A systematic review of the contributions of meta-analysis in the field of corrections. *Victims and Offenders, 4*, 148–169.

Smith, R. (1984). Grendon, the Barlinnie Special Unit, and the Wormwood Scrubs Annexe: Experiments in penology. *British Medical Journal, 288*, 472–475.

Sorensen, J. & Davis, J. (2011). Violent criminals locked up: Examining the effect of incarceration on behavioral continuity. *Journal of Criminal Justice, 39*, 151–158.

Sorrell, T. (1987). *Moral Theory and Capital Punishment.* Oxford: Blackwell.

Stenbacka, M., Moberg, T., Romelsjö, A., & Jokinen, J. (2012). Mortality and causes of death among violent offenders and victims – a Swedish population based longitudinal study. *BMC Public Health, 12*, 38.

Stewart, D. (2008). The Problems and Needs of Newly Sentenced Prisoners: Results from a National Survey. Ministry of Justice Research Series 16/08. London: Ministry of Justice.

Tapp, J., Fellowes, E., Wallis, N., Blud, L., & Moore, E. (2009). An evaluation of the Enhanced Thinking Skills (ETS) programme with mentally disordered offenders in a high security hospital. *Legal and Criminological Psychology, 14*, 201–212.

Taylor, J. E. & Harvey, S. T. (2009). Effects of psychotherapy with people who have been sexually assaulted. *Aggression and Violent Behavior, 14*, 273–285.

Taylor J. L., Thorne, I., Robertson, A., & Avery, G. (2002). Evaluation of a group intervention for convicted arsonists with mild and borderline intellectual disabilities. *Criminal Behaviour and Mental Health, 12*, 282–293.

Teasdale, B. (2009). Mental disorder and violent victimization. *Criminal Justice and Behavior, 36*, 513–535.

Testa, M., Hoffman, J. H., & Livingston, J. A. (2010). Alcohol and sexual risk behaviors as mediators of the sexual victimization-revictimization relationship. *Journal of Consulting and Clinical Psychology, 78*, 249–259.

Thomas, S., Harty, M., Parrott, J., McCrone, P., Slade, M., & Thornicroft, G. (2003). *CANFOR: Camberwell Assessment of Need-Forensic version.* London: Royal College of Psychiatrists.

Thomas, S. D. M., Dolan, M., Shaw, J., Thomas, S., Thornicroft, G., & Leese, M. (2005). Redeveloping secure psychiatric services for women. *Medicine, Science, and the Law, 45*, 331–339.

Thornton, D. M. (1987). Treatment effects on recidivism: A reappraisal of the "nothing works" doctrine. In B. J. McGurk, D. M. Thornton, & M. Williams (Eds.), *Applying Psychology to Imprisonment: Theory and Practice* (pp. 181–189). London: HMSO.

Thornton, D. M., Curran, L., Grayson, D., & Holloway, V. (1984). *Tougher Regimes in Detention Centres: Report of an Evaluation by the Young Offender Psychology Unit.* London: HMSO.

Tierney, D. W. & McCabe, M. P. (2002). Motivation for behavior change among sex offenders: A review of the literature. *Clinical Psychology Review, 22*, 113–129.

Tong, L. S. J. & Farrington, D. P. (2006). How effective is the 'Reasoning and Rehabilitation' programme in reducing re-offending? A meta-analysis of evaluations in four countries. *Psychology, Crime and Law, 12*, 3–24.

Tyler, T. R. (2006). *Why People Obey the Law.* Princeton, NJ: Princeton University Press.

United Nations (2006). Handbook on Restorative Justice Programmes. Criminal Justice Handbook Series. Vienna: United Nations Office on Drugs and Crime.

—— (2009). Handbook on Prisoners with Special Needs. Criminal Justice Handbook Series. Vienna: United Nations Office on Drugs and Crime.

US Department of Justice (2011). *Capital Punishment, 2010-Statistical Tables.* US Department of Justice, Office of Justice Programs, Bureau of Justice Statistics, Washington, DC.

Vaske, J., Galyean, K., & Cullen, F. T. (2011). Toward a biosocial theory of offender rehabilitation: Why does cognitive-behavioral therapy work? *Journal of Criminal Justice, 39*, 90–102.

Vaughn, M. (1994). Boot camps. *The Grapevine, 2*, 2.

Vickerman, K. A. & Margolin, G. (2009). Rape treatment outcome research: Empirical findings and state of the literature. *Clinical Psychology Review, 29*, 431–448.

Viewpoint (2009). *National Evaluation of Restorative Justice Youth Services in Scotland 2008–2009.* Bridgend, Wales: The Viewpoint Organisation.

Vose, B., Cullen, F. T., & Smith, P. (2008). The empirical status of the Level of Service Inventory. *Federal Probation, 72*, 22–29.

Vrieze, S. I. & Grove, W. M. (2010). Multidimensional assessment of criminal recidivism: Problems, pitfalls, and proposed solutions. *Psychological Assessment, 22*, 382–395.

Wade, N. G., Johnson, C. V., & Meyer, J. E. (2008). Understanding concerns about interventions to promote forgiveness: A review of the literature. *Psychotherapy: Theory, Research, Practice, Training, 45*, 88–102.

Ward, T. & Brown, M. (2004). The Good Lives Model and conceptual issues in offender rehabilitation. *Psychology, Crime, and Law, 10*, 243–257.

Ware, J., Frost, A., & Hoy, A. (2009). A review of the use of therapeutic communities with sexual offenders. *International Journal of Offender Therapy and Comparative Criminology, 54*, 721–742.

Webster, C. D., Douglas, K. S., Eaves, D., & Hart, S. D. (1997). HCR-20: Assessing the Risk for Violence (Version 2). Vancouver: Mental Health, Law, and Policy Institute, Simon Fraser University.

Wells, W. & Chermak, S. (2011). Individual-level risk factors for gun victimization in a sample of probationers. *Journal of Interpersonal Violence, 26*, 2143–2164.

Weisburd, D., Waring, E., & Chayet, E. (1995). Specific deterrence in a sample of offenders convicted of white collar crimes. *Criminology, 33*, 587–607.

Weiss, D. B. & MacKenzie, D. L. (2010). A global perspective on incarceration: How an international focus can help the United States reconsider its incarceration rates. *Victims and Offenders, 5*, 268–282.

Wells-Parker, E., Bangret-Downs, R., McMillen, R., & Williams, M. (1995). Final results from a meta-analysis of remedial interventions with drink/drive offenders. *Addiction, 9*, 907–926.

Welsh, B. C., Farrington, D. P., & Sherman, L. W. (2001). *Costs and Benefits of Preventing Crime.* Boulder, CO: Westview Press.

Wermink, H., Blokland, A., Nieuwbeerta, P., Nagin, D., & Tollenaar, N. (2010). Comparing the effects of community service and short-term imprisonment on recidivism: A matched samples approach. *Journal of Experimental Criminology, 6*, 325–349.

Whitehead, J. T., Blankenship, M. B., & Wright, J. P. (1999). Elite versus citizen attitudes on capital punishment: Incongruity between the public and policymakers. *Journal of Criminal Justice, 27*, 249–258.

Wiecko, F. M. & Gau, J. M. (2008). Every life is sacred ... kind of: uncovering the sources of seemingly contradictory public attitudes toward abortion and the death penalty. *Social Science Journal, 45*, 546–564.

Wilson, D. B., MacKenzie, D. L., & Mitchell, F. N. (2008). Effects of ional boot camps on offending. *Campbell Systematic Reviews.* Oslo, Norway: The Campbell Collaboration.

Wilson, G. T. (1996). Manual-based treatments: The clinical application of research findings. *Behaviour, Research and Therapy, 34*, 295–314.

Winokur, K. P., Smith, A., Bontrager, S. R., & Blakenship, J. L. (2008). Juvenile recidivism and length of stay. *Journal of Criminal Justice, 36*, 126–137.

Wozniak, K. H. & Lewis, A. R. (2010). Reexamining the effect of Christian denominational affiliation on death penalty support. *Journal of Criminal Justice, 38*, 1082–1089.

Yang, B. & Lester, D. (2008). The deterrent effect of executions: A meta-analysis thirty years after Ehrlich. *Journal of Criminal Justice, 36*, 453–460.

Yeh, S. S. (2010). Cost-benefit analysis of reducing crime through electronic monitoring of parolees and probationers. *Journal of Criminal Justice, 38*, 1090–1096.

Zhang, S. X., Roberts, R. E. L., & McCollister, K. E. (2009). An economic analysis of the in-prison therapeutic community model on prison management costs. *Journal of Criminal Justice, 37*, 388–395.

Zimring, F. E., Fagan, J., & Johnson, D. T. (2010). Executions, deterrence and homicide: A tale of two cities. *Journal of Empirical Legal Studies, 7*, 1–29.

12 Crime prevention

The field of crime prevention can be looked at in two ways: first, the use of broad social controls (including legal sanctions) to prevent crime; second, by utilising analysis of the situation in which the crime takes place to change the situation to prevent crime.

Crime prevention: socio-legal change

There are several instances where something that is generally accepted across society also has an association with crime. When this situation arises, the approach may be either to prohibit or to regulate. For example, as noted several times in this text, the use of alcohol is strongly associated with crime. In order to manage this relationship there are regulations about the use of alcohol, in terms who can purchase it and when. In the UK, the regulations stop short of an outright ban but in other some countries this is not the case and there is a total ban on alcohol, as was once the case in America in the prohibition era. There are, as discussed below, several areas where there is an association between an accepted social activity and criminal behaviour and where steps have been taken to prevent crime by curtailing that activity.

Drugs

The term 'drugs' spans an extensive range of types of substance, from everyday nicotine, to cannabis and amphetamines, and on to LSD and heroin with many variations therein. The relationship between drugs and crime is twofold: first, there is the illegal business of the large-scale production and selling of drugs; second, there is the connection between drug misuse at the individual level and its connection to criminal behaviour.

The first point raises a raft of issues concerning international law and drug trafficking and the use to which the finance raised by the drug trade is put. A report by the United Nations Office on Drugs and Crime (2009) discusses the association between the international trade in drugs and money-laundering which, in turn, pose a threat to the stability of financial institutions worldwide, affect economic prosperity and fund international terrorism. At a national level, the issue is one of policing the supply of drugs coming into the country and their distribution at a local level.

The second point raises two particular issues at an individual, psychological level. Is there a particular relationship between drug use and certain types of crime? If so, what are the mechanisms by which this relationship functions?

Bennett, Holloway, and Farrington (2008) conducted a meta-analysis of 30 studies of the association between drug misuse and crime. The evidence for the presence of the association

Box 12.1 Details of the drugs-crime connection (Bennett et al., 2008)

Type of drug: The drugs-crime association varies by type of drug use, such that the greatest odds of offending are for crack users, followed by heroin, cocaine, amphetamine, and marijuana.

Type of crime: The most frequently recorded crimes among drug users are crimes of acquisition, presumably to finance drug buying, including property crime, shoplifting, theft and burglary; there is also a link with prostitution.

User gender: The evidence suggests that the association between drug use and crime is strongest for females, possibly in relation to shoplifting and prostitution.

User age: Many studies do not report the age of their samples. However, on the basis of the extant research, it appears that the relationship between drugs and crime is stronger for adults than juveniles.

was marked: they reported that 'The odds of offending were between 2.8 and 3.8 times greater for drug users than non-drug users' (Bennett et al., 2008: 117). However, as shown in Box 12.1, there were a number of variations within this broad finding.

The meta-analytic research is valuable because it allows important main effects to be identified across the literature. However, smaller scale individual studies are also important in providing the fine details to accompany the big picture as seen with a French study of cannabis use. Charbol, Rodgers, Sobolewski, and van Leeuwen (2010) found, with a sample of more than 600 adolescents, 382 boys and 233 girls, that cannabis use was significantly predictive of scores on a self-report measure of delinquency. Further, cannabis use was also greatest among delinquents with higher scores on measures of depressive symptomatology and psychopathic traits. Given that drug use in adolescence is predictive of a range of life and health problems, including criminal behaviour, there are strong arguments in favour of preventing young people from having access to drugs (Odgers et al., 2008). There is also a case to be made for the treatment of drug-using offenders (Bhati & Roman, 2010; Tripodi & Bender, 2011).

The processes by which the drug-crime relationship functions is a complex one to unravel. At one level, as shown by Bennett and Holloway (2009) from interviews with drug-using offenders, there are several ways in which the connection can be made including stealing to fund buying drugs, violent crime directed at drug dealers to steal drugs, and the effects of the drugs leading to aggression and violence. However, as Boles and Miotto (2003) demonstrate with respect to violent crime, it is not sufficient only to consider the interaction between the psychopharmacological properties of the psychoactive drugs and the criminal behaviour. Boles and Miotto suggest that for some drugs, including alcohol, amphetamines, and cocaine, the evidence from laboratory and empirical studies supports the likelihood that these substances play a causal role in violent behaviour. However, alongside their psychopharmacological effects, substance use should be understood in a social context with regard to its relationship with violence. As Bennett and Holloway suggested, the drugs-violence connection may be systemic as with the social processes involved in the distribution of drugs, or acquisitive as when violence is used to gain funds to purchase or steal drugs. Thus, a complete understanding of the drug-crime connection would encompass biological and psychological processes, social dynamics, and economic forces, all in the context of the environments where drugs are obtained and consumed.

Finally, another common type of crime involving the use of drugs, including alcohol, is driving while under the influence (DUI). In 2006 in England and Wales, there were more than 101,000 arrests for drink-driving, which led to 92,671 convictions (Ministry of Justice, 2008); while of the 140,361 traffic accidents in Great Britain in 2007, 9,620 were known to be alcohol-related (Department for Transport, 2008). The human cost of drink-driving is heavy: in 2007 in Great Britain alcohol-related traffic accidents led to 14,480 casualties, of which 460 were fatal and 1,760 resulted in serious injuries (Department for Transport, 2008). The financial cost of alcohol-related traffic accidents is also substantial, estimated in 2007 at £1,250 million (Department for Transport, 2008). The efforts to reduce DUI include advertising and educational campaigns, as well as formal interventions (Palmer, Hatcher, McGuire, Bilby, & Hollin, 2012; Stein et al., 2006).

Media

No matter whether it is taken from the broad perspective of common sense or the more narrow view of social learning theory, it is plain that our behaviour is influenced, to a greater or lesser extent, by a media barrage that emanates from television, radio, films, music and music videos, newspapers and magazines, Twitter, texts, YouTube, and so on. Further, there is a steady stream of 'crime as entertainment' in the form of novels and television series (Greer & Reiner, 2012) and video games, while in advertising nothing gains our attention quite like sex and violence (Ferguson, Cruz, Martinez, Rueda, & Ferguson, 2010). The media flow is not without an audience: for example, we spend an average of more than 4 hours day watching television each day and some individuals spend even more time playing violent video games. How are these various media influences are related to criminal behaviour?

It is clear that media content helps to form and maintain attitudes and opinions about the causes and consequences of crime. This point is illustrated by the effects of coverage of terrorism by the mainstream media, which can have the effect of increasing prejudice against minority groups (Das, Bushman, Bezemer, Kerkhof, & Vermeulen, 2009). However, what effect does media have on the acquisition and maintenance of criminal *behaviour*? A main concern in the empirical literature is with the influence of the media specifically on violent behaviour that has generated a substantial research literature summarised in several meta-analyses (e.g., Paik & Comstock, 1994; Savage & Yancey, 2008). The conclusion frequently drawn from this body of literature is that persistent viewing of violence in childhood and adolescence is strongly related to later acts of physical violence in adulthood, including sexual violence (Malamuth & Check, 1981). Thus, Anderson et al. (2003: 81) are definite about the force of the evidence, the opening lines of their summary state: 'Research on violent television and films, video games, and music reveals unequivocal evidence that media violence increases the likelihood of aggressive and violent behavior in both immediate and long-term contexts'. Further, Anderson et al. state: 'The evidence is clearest within the most extensively researched domain, television and film violence. The growing body of video-game research yields essentially the same conclusions' (2003: 81). A later meta-analysis of 136 primary studies reported by Anderson et al. (2010) focused on the effects of violent video games. The analysis led the researchers to the unequivocal view that 'We believe that debates can and should finally move beyond the simple question of whether violent video game play is a causal risk factor for aggressive behavior; the scientific literature has effectively and clearly shown the answer to be 'yes' (Anderson et al., 2010: 171). This analysis was welcomed by Huesmann (2010: 181) who called for an acceptance of 'the fact that playing violent video games increases the 'risk' that the player will behave more aggressively'.

However, complete certainty is a rare commodity in social science research and, again in response to the Anderson et al. analysis, Ferguson and Kilburn (2010) list several methodological concerns with the original analysis. These methodological issues may, they suggest, have acted to inflate effect sizes and so lead to misleading conclusions. In addition, Ferguson and Kilburn also call on 'real world data' to bring certainty into doubt: 'Anderson et al. (2010) neglected to report on one very basic piece of information. Namely, as VVGs [violent video games] have become more popular in the United States and elsewhere, violent crime rates among youths and adults in the United States, Canada, United Kingdom, Japan, and most other industrialized nations have plummeted to lows not seen since the 1960s' (Ferguson & Kilburn, 2010: 176). Their standpoint, based on their own meta-analysis, led Ferguson and Kilburn (2009) to question the expressed view that the effects of media violence on behaviour are equivalent to a public health risk on a similar standing to smoking cigarettes (Huesmann, 2007). Ferguson and Kilburn point to a range of technical and conceptual problems in comparing social science research with health research. For example, there is no ambiguity in outcome in health research that uses morality rates as an outcome variable, which is in stark contrast to arguing for a causal link between viewing habits and aggression based on survey data or cognitive tests. Ferguson and Kilburn express the view: 'The concern remains that media violence effects research may continue to be driven primarily by ideological or political beliefs rather than objectivity. Media violence has a long history of being driven by ideology. Why the belief of media violence effects persists despite the inherent weaknesses of the research is somewhat of an open question' (2009: 762). In this light, Trend (2007) presents the view that there is actually a need for violence to be seen in media and that the 'war of the professors' acts to fuel public hysteria on the matter.

However, from both a methodological and theoretical perspective, the media-violence association is a complex relationship to unravel. The methodological difficulties lie in finding the optimal design to show a causal relationship between viewing, in terms of time and content, and violence in its many forms. In order to be able to demonstrate such a relationship a range of variables, including viewer characteristics (e.g., Feshbach & Tangney, 2008; Markey & Markey, 2010), need to be accounted for as well as untangling related concepts such as aggression and competiveness (Adachi & Willoughby, 2011).

Finally, it is not all bad news as far as the media is concerned: there are several studies which indicate that viewing positive, non-violent material can have beneficial effects such as increasing empathy for others and developing cognitive skills (Ferguson, 2010; Greitemeyer, Osswald, & Brauer, 2010).

Pornography

Pornography is a form of media given to the presentation of material, in written, pictorial, sound or filmed format, which is overtly sexual in nature. There are laws that regulate the production and availability of pornographic material. An exact definition of pornography for legal purposes, as seen in Box 12.2, is elusive: in the much quoted words of Potter Stewart, an Associate Justice of the US Supreme Court, hard-core pornography may be hard to define but 'I know it when I see it'.

There is little doubt that pornography is big business: Diamond (2009) cites figures to show that in the USA 10,000–15,000 pornographic movies are made each year, the sales and rentals of adult videos and DVDs are worth at least an estimated $4 billion gross annually and potentially $10 billion, while the income from phone sex lines may be in excess of $1 billion a year. In Britain, the sums involved are considerably smaller, nonetheless they have

Box 12.2 The law and pornography

In the UK, Section 63 of the Criminal Justice and Immigration Act 2008 makes it a criminal offence to possess extreme pornographic images. The Act refers to pornography as an image for which it can reasonably be assumed that it was produced solely or principally for the purpose of sexual arousal and is 'grossly offensive, disgusting or otherwise of an obscene character'. In practice, such explicit and realistic images would encompass the following:

(1) an act that threatens a person's life;
(2) an act that threatens or causes in serious injury to a person's anus, breasts, or genitals;
(3) necrophilia (sexual activity with a human corpse);
(4) zoophilia (sexual activity with a live or dead animal).

Pornographic acts are taken to include staged acts and whether or not those involved consent to the acts is immaterial. The Act does not define serious injury, leaving that to the discretion of the magistrate or jury in individual cases. The guidance provides examples of acts that include portrayals of hanging, suffocation, sexual assault accompanied by threat with a weapon, and mutilation of breasts or genitals.

been estimated at millions of pounds per year. It is the task of the British Board of Film Classification (BBFC) to regulate the material that can be made available to the public.

There are several arguments against pornography: (1) it is morally objectionable; (2) it is demeaning to those people (usually women) who are portrayed in the images; (3) it leads to social attitudes that denigrate women; (4) it plays a role in the development of criminal behaviour, particularly sexual offences; and (5) it is implicated in specific crimes.

The moral objections are just that, objections based on the grounds of decency, taste, and propriety; those in favour of pornography may argue that we have a free choice and no one is forced to consume pornography, taste is relative concept and pornography is enjoyable and prudery is outdated. The second objection again has two sides: the adult who chooses to appear in pornography, and may be paid to do so, is making a free choice as their right; alternatively, their choice may be influenced by reasons other than straight financial reward, such as threats of violence or funding a drug habit. The third objection, rather like the first, is straightforward to assert but less easy to prove. The standing of fourth and fifth objections, as discussed below, are open to empirical investigation.

Does exposure to pornography play a role in the development of criminal behaviour? The underlying assumption here is that the content of the pornography has the potential to corrupt the individual so as to turn them into an offender. As may be anticipated, the main emphasis within the research has been with the relationship between sexual pornography and sexual (including sexually violent) offending. The research in this area faces a substantial problem: how to show a relationship between an individual's exposure to a certain type of media and a specific behaviour? How is exposure to be measured? What counts as pornography? What behaviours are to be assessed? How to measure offending?

Itzin, Taket, and Kelly (2007) conducted an assessment of the evidence in relation to exposure to pornography. They divided the research literature into four broad types: (1) findings from experimental studies conducted under laboratory conditions; (2) findings from non-experimental studies; (3) research carried out with male sexual offenders; and (4) studies involving victimised women. The type of study in the first category is exemplified by that of Donnerstein and Berkowitz (1981), which found that after viewing a filmed gang rape with physical violence the participants performed at a high level on a laboratory test of aggression. The second category contains studies using surveys of past behaviour as with a retrospective longitudinal study reported by Mancini, Reckdenwald, and Beauregard (2012). Mancini et al. considered the influence of pornography at different developmental stages – adolescence, adulthood, and immediately prior to the offense – on the extent of physical injury and humiliation suffered by victims of sex crimes. They found that adolescent exposure to pornography significantly predicted raised levels of violence and an increase in humiliation of the victim. There was no effect of exposure pornography as an adult, while pornography use just before the offence was correlated with reduced lower levels of physical injury.

The research with male sex offenders typically shows high levels of consumption of pornography, including violent pornography, and deviant sexual interests and patterns of arousal: this is true for both sex offenders against children (e.g., Kingston, Fedoroff, Firestone, Curry, & Bradford, 2008) and against adults (e.g., Beauregard et al., 2004). Finally, studies of victimised women show that a high proportion of women who have experienced physical and sexual intimate partner violence report that their partners are frequent users of pornography (e.g., Cramer et al., 1998).

The weight of evidence shows an association between pornography and sex offences but an associative relationship is not necessarily a causative relationship. It is firmly established that there are high levels of consumption of a range of pornographic material across society. Given that not everyone who views pornography is or becomes a sex offender, there must be some mediating factors between the viewing and the offence. A Swiss study reported by Endrass et al. (2009) was concerned with 231 men who had been detected in a special police operation against child pornography on the internet and subsequently charged with possession of illegal material. The study looked at the recidivism rates for 'hands-on' and 'hands-off' sex offenses for the convicted men over a 6-year follow-up. The numbers involved were found to be low: applying a wide definition of recidivism, including current investigations, charges and convictions, 14 of the 231 men had committed another violent or sexual offence. Of these 14 new offences, 9 were related to hands-off sex offenses (illegal possession of pornography), 2 were hands-on sex offences (child sexual abuse), while the remaining 3 were violent offences. Endrass et al. conclude that in itself the consumption of child pornography alone is not a risk factor for hands-on sex offenses. Ferguson and Hartley (2009) reach the same conclusion with respect to the relationship between pornography and rape and sexual assault. Indeed, Ferguson and Hartley present data to show that as the number of hardcore pornography titles commercially available in the USA rose between 1998 and 2005, so the rate of rape and sexual assault fell over the same period. Ferguson and Hartley make two important points: first, that *violent* pornography is rare when set against the range of pornography widely available; second, that it suits the purposes of some politicians, lobby groups, and researchers to insist that there is a causal relationship between pornography and crime. While stopping short of making the claim themselves, Ferguson and Hartley point out that the data can actually be read as suggesting that increased consumption of pornography has a cathartic effect on sexual aggression.

If a causal link between pornography and criminal behaviour is difficult to show at a population level, what happens if we move to the final scenario, the role of pornography in specific crimes? Does pornography lead to copycat crimes? There is a literature considering the effects on violence of films such as Oliver Stone's celebrated *Natural Born Killers* (Kunich, 2000), Stanley Kubrick's *Clockwork Orange*, which achieved a certain notoriety in the 1970s for its depictions of sex and violence (Krämer, 2011), and David Cronenberg's 1996 film of J. G. Ballard's multi-layered novel *Crash*, an everyday tale of a group of people who find sexual pleasure in car accidents. Computer and video games such as *Grand Theft Auto* (Frasca, 2003) have also been associated with individual criminal acts. The problem lies in disentangling the real effect on behaviour of the pornographic material. Is it the case that perfectly normal people, usually young people, are turned into savage marauders by viewing a film or playing a computer game? The answer, of course, is no: if films had that that much power they would be banned! This not to say that elements from a filmed material are not sometimes copied when a crime is committed, but the causes of crime are infinitely more complex than playing *Grand Theft Auto*.

Crime prevention through socio-legal change can also extend to more offender-focussed risk factors: in the topics discussed below the individual offender is at the centre of concern although there are wider social issues implicated in prevention.

Victim to offender

That idea that crime begets crime suggests a cycle of events that begins with an individual victim and ends with that person as an offender (Jennings, Piquero, & Reingle, 2012). The most obvious example of this cycle is the transition from abused child to adolescent delinquent to adult offender (Draucker & Martsolf, 2010; McGrath, Nilsen, & Kerley, 2011; Stewart, Livingston, & Dennison, 2007). In an investigation of the influence of the type of analysis used in studies of the offender-victim relationship, Deadman and MacDonald (2004) suggest that the extant research tends to underestimate the strength of the association. It is not just the physical experience of abuse that is associated with later criminal behaviour, being in an environment where violence is present, say in the form of partner violence or witnessing attacks on a caregiver or a sibling, can also have an adverse effect on the developing child (Finkelhor, Turner, Ormrod, & Hamby, 2009). It is known that victimisation in childhood has long-term consequences for the child's physical and mental health (Amstadter et al., 2011) and that these consequences increase the child's vulnerability to further victimization (Cuevas, Finkelhor, Clifford, Ormrod, & Turner, 2010). One way to bringing these various strands together to form a cogent picture is through application of the concept of trauma.

Trauma

Pearlman and Saakvitne (1995: 60) refer to trauma as an 'event or condition where the individual's ability to understand, process and cope with an emotional experience is overwhelmed as the individual experiences a threat to life, bodily integrity, or sanity'. Trauma may result from many types of experience, such as being in a natural disaster or combat in war, and is recognised by the two major diagnostic systems, International Classification of Diseases (ICD-10) and the *Diagnostic and Statistical Manual of Mental Disorders* (DSM-IV), as a form of mental distress. A growing body of evidence has shown how the effects of abuse – particularly multiple instances of abuse of different types including physical abuse, sexual abuse, and neglect – may mediate between victimisation and criminal behaviour, particularly violence (e.g., Falshaw, Browne, & Hollin, 1996; Maschi, Bradley, & Morgen, 2008; Widom, 1989). It is also the case that being a perpetrator of a violent act can be a traumatic experience for the aggressor (Welfare & Hollin, 2012). Given its association with violence, symptoms of trauma are at high levels among incarcerated offenders (Goff, Rose, Rose, & Purves, 2007), and are associated with suicide in prison (Mandelli et al., 2011). Yet further, trauma is often co-morbid with substance use (Barrett, Mills, & Teesson, 2011), which is itself a risk factor for offending. However, it is not just physical involvement in traumatic events that is associated with later criminal behaviour: the witnessing of violent acts such as domestic violence (Renner, 2012) and police arrests (Phillips & Zhao, 2010) may be traumatic experiences for the young child.

The level of assessment and treatment of traumatised offenders, particularly young offenders, is negligible within the criminal justice system. This is a major omission for several reasons: first, the effects of trauma can be highly distressing for the offender as, for example, they experience flashbacks to traumatic events in the form of intrusive memories, sometimes with strong olfactory and audial as well as visual qualities (Evans, Ehlers, Mezey, & Clark, 2007); second, the traumatised young offender will not find it easy to progress through a custodial sentence, particularly a long sentence for a violent crime such as murder, and may be a danger to other prisoners and to staff; third, the traumatised offender may be at an elevated risk of further offending (Heide & Solomon, 2006).

There are a range treatments available for those who have experienced childhood abuse (e.g., Taylor & Harvey, 2010; Trask, Walsh, & DiLillo, 2011) but these are not part of the standard interventions, such as offending behaviour programmes, used in prison and probation. It is appreciated that treatment of trauma and the associated issues raises complex professional concerns (see LaLiberte, Bills, Shin, & Edleson, 2010) but not to intervene is to fail to address a potentially significant risk factor for further violent conduct.

Finally, while there are effective treatments for the abused child and the traumatised offender these necessarily take place *after* the event. A coordinated societal response to prevent abuse *before* its harmful consequences for the individual and their victims is clearly desirable.

Gender

As discussed previously, there are similarities in the development of offending and in patterns of offending for males and females but there are also some gender differences. Thus, for example, a report on women in the criminal justice system by Hunter, Hearnden, and Gyateng (2009) noted that as young offenders from 10 years of age, the genders are equally represented in terms of contact with the system but the prison population, which is mainly adults, is 94 per cent male. Hunter et al. (2009: viii) note: 'The overall picture to emerge from the various recent statistics and surveys on offending is that there is a degree of convergence between the sexes in less serious offending, but that males remain disproportionately involved in more serious crime'. Rennison (2009) used large-scale American survey data to investigate the issue of the 'gender gap' in rates of offending. The results showed that, when controlling for age and race, the pattern of violent offending by gender remained stable over time, with considerably more violent offending carried out by males. Rennison (2009: 184) concludes that the findings 'clearly demonstrate that the growing concern over an epidemic about increasingly violent females is not supported. Violent offending among females continues to be low'.

A study by van Mastrigt and Farrington (2009) showed that as young offenders females are more likely to commit offences with other offenders rather than individually. In an American study of gender differences in referrals to juvenile court, prospective longitudinal data was gathered on 808 young people (Farrington et al., 2010). Thus, annual data were collected with regard to referrals to court and self-reported offending while the cohort were aged between 11 and 17 years. It was found that the boys were more likely than girls to be referred to juvenile court and that boys self-reported more offending. The probability of a self-reported offense leading to a court referral was similar for boys and girls: the greater rate of referrals to court for males was most likely a function of their higher rate of offending.

Does the gender gap in offending have any implications for crime prevention strategies? To ask this question is to open up a spirited debate within the literature, which hinges on the issue of whether the predictors of criminal behaviour for women can be generalised from the research that has predominately been conducted with male offenders. There are two strands to the literature to note: first, are the developmental factors leading to criminal behaviour similar for men and women?; second, are the risk factors (i.e., criminogenic needs) for offending the same for men and women?

With respect to the first strand, it is known that the shape of the age-crime curve is similar for males and females, although with a lower frequency of crime for females (Farrington, 1986). However, this does not mean that the nature of the factors involved in the development of anti-social and criminal behaviour are the same for males and females. It is evident that across most, if not all, societies there are gender differences in upbringing, expectations, and opportunity both generally and specifically with regard to criminal conduct (Heidensohn, 1996).

In an American study of 313 women on probation, Salisbury and Van Voorhis (2009) used both interviews and survey data to investigate the women's pathways into crime. They described three pathways that led the women to eventual incarceration: (1) a pathway starting with victimisation in childhood leading to a lifetime experience of mental illness and substance abuse; (2) a pathway through which dysfunctional intimate relationships bring about victimisation as an adult, thereby negatively affecting psychological factors such as self-efficacy and leading to mental illness and substance abuse; and (3) a 'social and human capital pathway' by which difficulties in education, family support, relationships, and psychological function create employment and financial problems that may lead to poverty. Javdani, Sadeh and Verona (in press) also suggest that a similar mixture of individual, relationship, and social factors is involved in the development of criminal behaviour by women during adolescence and into adulthood. The question that follows this research is whether there are gender specific criminogenic needs and, if so, how should they inform crime prevention strategies?

There are several studies comparing the criminogenic needs of men and women using standard assessments such as the LSI-R. Palmer and Hollin (2007) compared the LSI-R scores of male and female prisoners: they found that 'Females had higher levels of need than males in the areas of family and marital relationships, accommodation, comparisons, alcohol and drug problems, and emotional and personal issues' (2007: 977). Further, Palmer and Hollin also considered the predictive validity of the LSI-R with respect to reconviction. They reported that the reconvicted women had high LSI-R scores and were classified as being in the higher security bands. A multivariate analysis showed that both reconviction and time to reconviction were predicted by the LSI-R total score, security band, and high scores on the Companions subscale. However, there is some debate as to the utility of assessments such as the LSI-R with women given the doubts as to their gender neutrality (Coid et al., 2009; Reisig, Holtfreter, & Morash, 2006; Van Voorhis, Wright, Salisbury, & Bauman, 2010). Thus, the LSI-R may misclassify some women as high risk for recidivism because of their social and economic poverty, a risk that does not materialise in real-life (Holtfreter, Reisig, & Morash, 2004).

It may be the case that there are some criminogenic needs that are gender-neutral, in that they are equally applicable to predicting the offending of males and females, while others are much more gender-specific (Hollin & Palmer, 2006). Thus, for women offenders, criminogenic needs such as parental responsibility and stress, a history of physical and sexual abuse, and mental health difficulties including self-harm may be important risk factors but are not considered by standardised assessments. However, Rettinger and Andrews' (2010) analysis suggests that, with the exception of financial problems, highly female-specific factors such as a history of abuse do not add to the predictive equation regarding reoffending. This is not to dismiss the importance of these factors, Rettinger and Andrews suggest that they may be specific responsivity factors that are of critical importance for those working with women offenders. They state, for example, that 'Gender-responsive programming advocates propose that girls and women particularly will benefit from interventions that are relationship based, that is, where there is a strong therapeutic alliance between the counselor and the female client' (Rettinger & Andrews, 2010: 44).

One conclusion to draw from this debate is that it cannot be assumed that the interventions intended to reduce recidivism used with male offenders cannot simply be applied to women offenders.

Gender sensitive intervention

Blanchette and Brown (2006) make the case for an integrated approach to working with women offenders. Such an approach would draw on theory and supporting evidence related to offending by women, leading to gender-sensitive interventions both in terms of their content and delivery. In this light, the analysis offered by Van Voorhis et al. (2010) is to the point: they focus on high-risk women as those most likely to engage with the criminal justice system and so receive custodial sentences. If what constitutes 'high risk' is unpacked, then there will be a group of women who fall into that category (hence are highly prevalent in the prison population) because of mental illness, multiple instances of victimisation and economic disadvantage. Van Voorhis et al. (2010: 283) conclude: 'The more ideal approach would find policy makers and practitioners reconceptualising their notions of high risk. If high-risk women are actually women with multiple serious needs, shifting policy implications regarding 'high-risk' women from a punishment model to the rehabilitation model makes good sense'. However, as noted by Zahn, Day, Mihalic, and Tichavsky (2009: 288) in their review of programmes for girls in the criminal justice system, while a great deal has been learned about effective interventions, 'gender-specific programming has only recently garnered attention from scholars, practitioners, and policy makers'. It may be that this situation will change in the future although, as discussed in the following example, careful evaluation is required if the evidence-base is to be enhanced.

The Together Women Project (TWP), conducted in England, provides an example of a service intended to address the needs of women at risk of offending. TWP, described in Box 12.3, is discussed in several publications (Hedderman, Gunby, & Shelton, 2011; Hedderman, Palmer, & Hollin, 2008; Jolliffe, Hedderman, Palmer, & Hollin, 2011).

It may be thought that the problems noted in Box 12.3 in attempting to coordinate an evaluation of a complex project such as TWP are insurmountable. However, the Citizenship programme devised by Durham Probation Service is, like TWP, a large-scale community based project, for male and female offenders on probation, but which grappled much more successfully with the issues that beset the TWP evaluation. As described by Bruce and Hollin (2009),

Box 12.3   The Together Women Project (TWP)

TWP started between late 2006 and early 2007 at five centres in the north west and Yorkshire and Humberside with the aims of reducing reoffending and diverting women at risk of offending from prosecution and custody. As may be expected, the nature of support offered to women varied somewhat across the five centres in response to local demand and the availability and types of community partnerships. However, the TWP centres typically offered training and support on issues such as parenting, mental health needs, life skills, thinking skills, and addressing offending behaviour. The centres also arranged for various local service providers to offer surgeries to address matters such as benefit rights and accommodation. In addition, each centre acts as a 'drop-in' where women can freely gain access to activities such as reading groups and complementary therapies. Thus, if there is a local provision, Together Women attempts to form links; if there is nothing available it may commission another provider or deliver in-house. In practice, an assessment of need and a consequent support plan informs the level and range of services with which a woman engages. The women are fully involved in the formulation and review of their plan which is seen as an important step in enabling them to take control of their lives.

The 12-month evaluation found that the centres had been quickly and efficiently set up and had recruited enthusiastic, staff. Arrangements had been set up with local service providers and, in some cases, with local courts and probation services. The challenges lay in determining how best to engage the women using the centres, how to persuade the courts to use Together Women rather than custody, and in designing and implementing data gathering systems for generating throughput statistics, the types of need assessed, and measuring change. As the centres were funded through money from central government as a 'national demonstration project', the evaluation is particularly important in supporting the case for further funding and refining practice.

The second stage of the evaluation, published 3 years after the initial evaluation, reported mixed outcomes. In terms of practice, the centres had opened their doors to more than 3,500 women with many completed assessments and action plans. It was estimated that overall in excess of 1,000 women had received some support. About half of the women came to TWP either by referral from a criminal justice agency or another agency such as health or housing; the other half were self-referrals. However, the long-term evaluation hit difficulties that, in truth, should have been sorted out at the beginning of the project. These difficulties included the absence of an agreed protocol for assessment, so that 'at risk' remained undefined and open to different interpretations across the five centres; there was no standard system of information collection across centres, so that while some centres collected some information it was impossible to aggregate effects across centres; without a standardised measure of needs the level of change following contact with the centres was impossible to measure; the rather haphazard collection of information posed problems in formally identifying women in order to look at their criminal behaviour after contact with TWP. On the basis of the available data, Jolliffe et al. (2011) cautiously concluded that contact with TWP, while personally valued by the women, had no significant effect on rates of offending. Jolliffe et al. also emphasised that a major learning point for those commissioning the research was that 'In future projects it is essential that greater forethought is put into developing a shared understanding of project objectives and measurement for assessing outcomes. Trained evaluators should be involved at the initial planning stages to assist in developing the measurement tools and specifying the data monitoring requirements' (2011: 28).

Citizenship uses standardised data, drawn from the OASys system, to identify criminogenic need for offenders on probation. Using a modular system, assessed needs are addressed through a mixture of in-house individual work with offenders carried out by trained probation staff and through liaison with specialist service providers in the community. The quality of the data collected allowed, as planned from the onset, a rigorous evaluation to be conducted which showed that the programme was effective in significantly reducing reoffending and it was also financially cost effective (Pearson, McDougall, Kanaan, Bowles, & Torgerson, 2011).

Crime prevention: situational change

When using the word 'situation' in the context of situational crime prevention it is generally taken to refer to the features of the immediate environment preceding a crime. It may rightly be argued that, say, economic factors as reflected in rates of employment are part of the environment and are associated with crime (Tripodi, Kim, & Bender, 2010), however, in this approach they are considered as background factors that influence the immediate setting in which the crime occurs.

From a theoretical perspective, situational crime prevention is most closely associated with a rational-choice view of crime. This view holds that a crime can be understood as an individual's chosen response when in a situation which offers the opportunity for successful offending (Cornish & Clarke, 1986). The situational approach to crime prevention places an emphasis not on changing the individual offender but on changing the environment. There are two broad methods by which the environment may be modified in order to bring about situational change: first, reduce the opportunity to commit crime; second, increase the risk of detection should a crime be attempted.

Reducing opportunity

There are several ways in which the opportunity to commit crime can be reduced.

Hardening the target

If the target for a crime is made physically 'harder' so the opportunity to commit a crime involving that target is correspondingly diminished. The most obvious examples of this approach lie in the use of alarms, locks, and bars to obstruct and deny access to the potential offender. In the 1980s, theft of money from telephone kiosks was tackled by replacing the aluminium coin boxes with steel boxes, similarly in 1971 steering column locks on cars were introduced to prevent car theft. The success of these two initiatives illustrates two side effects of target hardening.

First, as suggested by Mayhew, Clarke, and Hough (1980), cars without the security afforded by steering column locks are made more vulnerable and more likely to be stolen, with the net result that they attract higher insurance premiums. Thus, consumer behaviour changed with a demand for 'hardened' vehicles so that car design changes to incorporate steering column locks as standard in all vehicles. Thus, all cars now have steering column locks as standard, along with various other security devices such as alarms, immobilisers, etching of the vehicle details on the windows (making it more difficult to change the vehicle's identity), electronic ignition keys and, as the technology develops, vehicle tracking devices. In addition, parts of the vehicle may be protected by, for example, wheel-locking devices and car radios that require a reactivation code if removed.

The second consequence of 'hardened vehicles' is that the behaviour of car thieves is modified. Offenders may become more sophisticated at disarming the security devices or switch from stealing the car to stealing unsecured parts from cars such as sound systems (it is not impossible to find the electronic code) or alloy wheels, which can be sold on for cash.

The principle of target hardening applies to other types of crime: for example, many properties have burglar alarms, and some women carry rape alarms. Another target hardening strategy is for householders to use 'invisible ink' marker pens to write identifying information, such as their post code, on property such as bicycles, televisions, and so on. If the property is stolen and later recovered then it can be identified, using a light that highlights the markings, by the police and returned to the owner.

There are other target hardening strategies such as entry phones to blocks of flats, security guards at clubs and building sites, and physical barriers such as fences and gates. There are security measures in many buildings to prevent free movement from location to location. For example, at my university I must always have hanging around my neck a piece of plastic the size of a credit card that shows my name, photograph, and department, which I must show to reception staff in order to gain entry to some university buildings, including my own department. This card also has a bar code that is programmed to act as a key to control my access to university buildings and car parks.

Removing the target

As well as hardening the target, crime can be prevented by removing the target from the environment. As time has moved on so theft from coin boxes in telephone kiosks has become something of an anachronism with the advent of 'phone cards and the ubiquitous mobile telephone. Similarly, there are now very few coin boxes in gas and electricity meters in residential properties as many people receive quarterly bills and pay through their bank. The technology that enables the of transfers of money between banks means that many peoples' wages are paid in this way, thereby removing the need physically to transport large amounts of cash and so eliminating the opportunity for wage snatches. There are other examples of target removal, such as parking your car in a garage at night rather than on the street.

People can also be removed from environments in which they are potential targets. Thus, the provision of transport for those working at night, such as hospital staff, or for people socialising at night removes the target from a setting in which they might be vulnerable to attack. Those universities where the halls of residence are some distance from the buildings where entertainment is on offer may have buses to take students home at the end of the evening thereby reducing the chances of assault and sexual attack.

Increasing the risk of detection

Would you commit a crime if you thought there was a high probability of being caught? Most people would pass up such an opportunity if they perceived that the risk of apprehension was too high. There are two main ways, both involving surveillance, in which the individual's perception of the risk of detection can be increased.

Formal surveillance

Formal surveillance refers to the monitoring of a given setting by people with the authority to intervene should it be necessary. The police are the most obvious group in this respect: a large police presence at, say, a football match or a political demonstration is a visible signal that there is an increased likelihood of detection of criminal behaviour. Of course, it is impossible to have large numbers of police present at every potential criminal situation and so police surveillance is particularly focussed on specific situations such as derby matches between rival football teams and political demonstrations involving diametrically opposed groups.

As well as the police, other figures may be involved in formal surveillance. The presence of someone in a position of authority, such as a bus conductor, a car park attendant, a steward at a sporting event, or a shop assistant may have the effect of reducing levels of crime. We stand patiently (or not) at airports to have our passports inspected and our baggage screened lest there is more to one of our fellow travellers than there appears to be.

Does formal surveillance reduce crime? As is often the case in applied research, this is not an easy question to answer. The simple evaluative design is to look at crime rates before and after the introduction of the surveillance, the drawback, however, is that it assumes that everything else remains constant over the time spanned by the study. In practice, it is often the case the several interventions are implemented simultaneously or sequentially over a period of time: in the car park example below, the introduction of security guards was accompanied by other measures such as placing fencing around the car park site and public awareness campaigns. The next best research design is to have a control condition and, best of all, randomisation of preventative measure to condition. Welsh, Farrington, and O'Dell (2010) reported a systematic review of studies of security guards, concentrating on those studies, of which there were five, with a strong design. All five studies – two were carried out in the USA, and one in each of Canada, the Netherlands, and the UK – concerned the effect of a security guard on car theft in car parks that were experiencing a high level of crime. The Canadian and UK schemes both significantly reduced vehicle thefts, the introduction of security guards in Rotterdam, the Netherlands, did not bring about any change in thefts from vehicles.

The security guards in two American schemes, one in New York the other in San Diego, were the volunteer group called Guardian Angels. The Guardian Angels began in New York in 1979 when a small group of New Yorkers began travelling on the city subway in order both to deter crime and to make citizen arrests when crime took place (Kenney, 1986). Welsh, Farrington, and O'Dell note that the evaluation of the Guardian Angels in New York did not show any effect of their presence, however in San Diego the Guardian Angels patrols in a downtown redevelopment area did reduced property crime but not violent crime.

Closed circuit television

The rapid pace of advances in technology allows formal surveillance to be carried out by means other than personal observation: there are cameras that check the speed at which you drive, cameras that monitor the speed at which you drive between two points, cameras that are used to monitor your behaviour in shops, petrol stations, and banks, cameras that allow you to be observed while using public transport, and cameras that watch you walking down the street. The use of closed circuit television (CCTV) has become so commonplace that we barely notice it unless there are large signs to advise us that we are being watched. Given the rapid expansion in the use of CCTV cameras, we might ask what purpose they serve.

There are two main uses to which CCTV is put with respect to crime: first, it allows formal surveillance of a part of a city, town, retail premises, or residential building to detect a crime and aid police investigation; second, it acts as a crime prevention measure by increasing the risk of detection. It is undoubtedly true that CCTV is an aid to crime detection: there are many instances of crimes recorded on CCTV being shown on national television and leading to the apprehension of the offender. Some of the most chilling pictures shown on television date from 1993 and show the 2-year-old James Bulger being led by the hand through a shopping centre by one of the boys who would later kill him.

The number of crimes solved through use of CCTV is impossible to know: a police investigation will draw on many sources of information and evidence so that it is not possible to isolate the effects of CCTV. However, the same is not the case for the preventative effects of CCTV where there is now a substantial body of research. Welsh and Farrington (2009) reported a systematic literature review and meta-analysis of 44 high quality studies of the preventative effects of CCTV. They report that across a range of settings, CCTV was associated with a significant 16 per cent decrease in crime when experimental areas were compared with control areas. However, Welsh and Farrington note that this overall result was mainly due to the 51 per cent decrease in crime associated with CCTV schemes in car parks, as opposed to town centres, public transport, and public housing.

Informal surveillance

As members of the public, we have a vested interest in the area where we live: we will act to protect our personal property and to defend our immediate environment. The notion of *defensible space* refers to the geographical area which an individual is able to survey and define as their territory and for which they are prepared to take responsibility (Newman, 1972). We are quite particular in what we are prepared to count as our defensible space: for example, in apartment blocks and high-rise flats there are 'semi-public' areas, such as the internal and external access and circulation routes, lifts, and stairways, which do not belong to any individual resident and so are not anyone's defensible space. It is these impersonal areas that are particularly prone to vandalism and so eventually become areas to avoid. So, is it possible to capitalise on our natural surveillance of defensible space in order to reduce crime?

One way to use defensible space is to bring targets for crime into environments where informal surveillance takes place. Clark (1982) notes that when public telephones are situated in public houses and launderettes or overlooked by residential buildings then they attract lower levels of vandalism than when on the street. Another means of using informal surveillance lies in organising people to take responsibility for looking out for themselves and those who live close by. The Neighbourhood Watch scheme is one means by which public willingness to report crimes has been encouraged.

Neighbourhood Watch

The idea of Neighbourhood Watch – also variously known as Home Watch, Block Watch, Community Alert, and Citizen Alert – is generally seen as beginning as a response to burglary which widened in scope. The premise unpinning Neighbourhood Watch is straightforward: through close relations between local residents and police, residents in a given area keep an open eye for suspicious activity and if any is seen they report it promptly to the local police. There are various other actions members of Neighbourhood Watch can take to encourage crime prevention among local residents, such as promoting property marking, informing parents if their children are misbehaving, and collecting milk and tidying away dustbins so that a property does not look empty when the owners are away.

When they function effectively, Neighbourhood Watch schemes can increase community cohesion and may reduce fear of crime. As ever, the acid test is whether they are effective in reducing crime. Bennett, Holloway, and Farrington (2006) reported a systematic review of 36 studies evaluative studies of Neighbourhood Watch and meta-analysis of 18 of these studies (those that provided the necessary statistical information for the further analysis). They found that the larger scale review suggested that about half of the evaluations were positive in that they led to a reduction in crime. The meta-analysis revealed that the scheme was associated with a 16 per cent reduction in crime. The evidence therefore suggests that this form of informal surveillance has the intended effect.

Street lighting

Most forms of surveillance, human or camera, rely on light levels that enable vision, infrared cameras can be used for security purposes but these are the exception rather than the rule. The elimination of darkness as a measure of crime prevention goes beyond simply increasing the risk of detection, darkness may also increase feelings of anonymity and so disinhibit our behavioural controls leading to acts of dishonesty (Zhong, Bohns, & Gino, 2010). As noted by Clark (2008), the process of eliminating darkness by improved street lighting is not straightforward as it may appear, as it must take into account the design of the street lights for maximum efficiency as well deciding which areas of a city to improve and balancing the costs involved.

Farrington and Welsh (2007) and Welsh and Farrington (2008) conducted systematic reviews of the evidence relating to the crime prevention effects of improved street lighting. They concluded that the weight of evidence across the 13 studies included in the review, eight from America and five from the UK, was positive overall and as well as reducing crime, 'Street lighting benefits the whole neighborhood rather than particular individuals or households. It is not a physical barrier to crime, it has no adverse civil liberties implications, and it can increase public safety and effective use of neighborhood streets at night. In short, improved street lighting has few negative effects and clear benefits for law-abiding citizens' (Welsh & Farrington, 2007: 28). However, Marchant (2010) offers the alternative view that these reviews contain flaws that could overestimate the crime reduction effects of improved street lighting.

Repeat victimisation

The phenomenon of repeat victimisation refers to the heightened probability of being a victim of crime after an initial victimisation. The repeat victimisation is likely to be close, hours and days not weeks and months, to the original event. Pease (1998) offers the following succinct description:

> Important conclusions justified by the research to date are that victimisation is the best single predictor of victimisation; that when victimisation recurs it tends to do so quickly; that high crime rates and hot spots are as they are substantially because of rates of repeat victimisation; that a major reason for repetition is that offenders take later advantage of opportunities which the first offence throws up; and that those who repeatedly victimise the same target tend to be more established in crime careers than those who do not.
>
> (Pease, 1998: v)

Repeat victimisation is not the province of a small number of crimes: there are recorded instances of repeated victimisation with, for example, bullying, burglary, car crime, credit card fraud, domestic violence, racial attacks, and shoplifting. Repeat victimisation helps explain findings, such as those from the British Crime Survey, which show that about

5 per cent of victims experience a disproportionately large 40 per cent of crime. As Farrell's (1995) analysis of the survey figures demonstrates, the exact figures regarding repeat victimisation vary across surveys. However, there is no doubt that many victims of crime are repeat victims, sometimes four, five, or more times.

Given that repeat victimisation occurs, how might it be prevented? Farrell and Pease (1993) have no doubt in stating that a 'quick and transient' response is essential, so that preventative measures are put in place immediately after a crime has taken place. In order to test these ideas, several demonstration projects were put into place in the 1990s.

Laycock (2001) describes the development of these demonstration projects – one to reduce domestic burglary on the Kirkholt Estate in Rochdale (Forrester, Chatterton, Pease, & Brown, 1990; Forrester, Frenz, O'Connell, & Pease, 1990), the other in a London housing estate (Sampson & Farrell, 1990) – and the influence their success had on later research and practice in crime prevention. In particular, Laycock notes how police data recording was central to the whole enterprise. Without accurate data recording within a very short space of time, it is impossible to pinpoint where immediate preventative resources should be directed. Of course, without this knowledge the whole scheme fails instantly. Further, Laycock discusses how the enterprise relies on a coordinated effort across several groups including the police, the researchers, policy-makers who commit funding to the project, citizen groups, and the victims themselves. The maintenance of productive working associations between these groups and keeping them on task is not straightforward!

Crime-focussed prevention

The rigour of the data collection and analysis informing the development of preventative measures has become increasingly sophisticated with time. Shaw and Pease (2000) looked at repeat victimisation across Scotland by analysis of police data, victim accounts, and offender accounts. They were able to build a comprehensive national picture to enable the police to become even more effective in implementing crime prevention strategies.

The application of crime prevention measures, influenced by the pioneering research in the 1990s, has become increasingly specialised in the sense of targeting a range of specific types of offence. Canter and Almond (2002) conducted a review of research and associated strategies for reducing arson. Alongside interventions directed at the offender, they note the possibilities of building design and a rapid police response to targets for arson such as abandoned vehicles. Similar arson prevention projects, sometimes dealing with phenomena such a bushfires, have been developed in several countries including Australia (Christensen, 2007/8) and America (Washington State, no date).

Violent crime is a perennial concern and several strategies have been implemented to attempt to prevent violence. One of the consequences of high levels of serious violence in schools in America was the introduction of a range of preventative measures. As noted by Time and Payne (2008: 301), these measures encompassed 'Metal detectors, spiked fences, electrical controlled gates, emergency alert systems, blast-proof doors and windows, open floor-plan in schools with staff and administrators' offices at the center built with glass walls, are among some of the structural changes suggested to minimize school violence'. Not surprisingly, critics argue that an environment reminiscent of a maximum security prison is perhaps not the right one to encourage learning.

The availability of firearms is linked with violence: in some countries the availability of guns is much more pronounced than in others. Sherman (2001) considers what is known to be effective in reducing gun violence. Sherman notes that the crime statistics reveal that most gun-related violence occurs in the poorest parts of the largest American cities. Two successful preventative strategies that can be applied in this context are gun patrols and background checks. The first is relies on formal surveillance in which 'gun patrols' involve the police in actively targeting city districts with high levels of gun ownership looking for guns that are being carried illegally. Sherman suggests, not unreasonably, that 'As people carry fewer guns, we expect fewer gun arrests, as well as fewer homicides' (2001: 17). The use of background checks, another type of formal surveillance, ensures that guns are not sold to those people, such as known criminals and those with certain mental disorders, who are legally barred from gun ownership.

There are other approaches to controlling gun ownership which have had rather less success. Barnes, Kurlychek, Miller, Miller, and Kaminski. (2010: 5) describe the CeaseFire programme, which '[s]eeks to increase perceptions of certainty and severity of punishment among a high-risk population. Certainty of punishment is increased through offender notification of the laws and consequences of gun possession during intake processes … aim to increase the severity of punishment by referring all violators to federal court for prosecution'. Barnes et al. found that this deterrence-based programme might have led to an *increase* in firearms-related incidents. This rise may have been a result of changes in police behaviour that led to a greater level of detection of illegal ownership and use of firearms.

There have been attempts to reduce other forms of violence through the application of preventative strategies. The provision of alternative accommodation in the form of shelters or safe housing is a preventative measure that can be used to attempt to reduce partner violence, including homicide (Wells, Ren, & DeLeon-Granados, 2010). In terms of sexual violence, there are various preventative strategies that can be applied: for example, educating children in strategies they can use to prevent sexual abuse is a form of target hardening (Hebenton, 2011).

In summary, the use of crime prevention measures based on situational crime prevention have become commonplace. As is generally the case, there is no gain without pain and there are a number of objections levelled at this approach.

Objections

Completeness

The first objection, which stems perhaps more from a theoretical than an applied stance (see Hayward, 2007), is that situational crime prevention ignores the person side of the person and environment interaction. If the person is ignored and if we concentrate on the physical rather than the social environment then our understanding of crime will never be complete. Without a full picture of crime, progress in the design of preventative measures will always be hindered.

Displacement

The second objection lies in the notion of displacement: the criminal, frustrated by situational measures, changes the time, place, method, or form of the crime in order to get what they want (Reppetto, 1976). As shown in Box 12.4, there are five different forms of displacement commonly referred to in the literature: these are (1) temporal, (2) tactical, (3) target, (4) territorial or spatial, and (5) offence.

Box 12.4   Types of displacement

Temporal. Criminals change the time at which they offend, say in order to avoid a police patrol.
Tactical. Criminals change the methods used to carry out crime, as in car thieves adapting in the ways they overcome security devices.
Target. Criminals change from one type of target to another, as in from stealing from machines to stealing from vulnerable people.
Territorial (or Spatial). Criminals switch from targets in one location to similar targets in another location (see Burrows' study of the London Underground).
Offence. Criminals switch from one type of crime to another, as in credit card scams rather than theft from the person for financial gain.

A good example of displacement is furnished by Burrows' (1980) study of the use of CCTV to prevent robbery and theft on the London Underground. The CCTV cameras were installed at four Underground stations, positioned to give a view of the platforms, ticket halls, and elevators, which are the high-risk parts of the station. In the four stations with CCTV, there were 252 reported offences in the 12 months prior to the installation of the CCTV: in the 12 months after the installation there were 75 reported offences, a 70 per cent fall in crime. Over the 12 months there was a fall of just over 25 per cent in 15 Underground stations geographically close to the four stations with CCTV; while for the 238 stations over the whole of the Underground the fall was 38 per cent. Thus, while reported crime was falling across the Underground, the decline was greatest where the CCTV was in operation. However, for the 15 stations closest to the CCTV protected stations, the fall in was less than across the rest of the system, suggesting that the thieves deterred by the CCTV had displaced their activities to the nearby stations.

Guerette and Bowers (2009) review of the findings of 102 studies reporting evaluations of situational crime prevention. An examination of the findings of these studies, some evaluating more than one prevention strategy, allowed Guerette and Bowers to reach the conclusion that displacement took place in about one-quarter of cases. Guerette and Bowers also looked at the *diffusion of benefit* where prevention measures were successful. Diffusion may be thought of as the opposite of displacement as Guerette and Bowers explain:

> Diffusion occurs when reductions of crime (or other improvements) are achieved in areas that are close to crime-prevention interventions, even though those areas were not actually targeted by the intervention itself ... This feature of crime-prevention activity has been referred to in a variety of ways, which include the 'bonus effect,' the 'halo effect,' the 'freerider effect,' and the 'multiplier effect'.
>
> (Guerette & Bowers, 2009: 1334)

They found that, like displacement, diffusion of benefit from situational crime prevention measures was found in about one-quarter of cases.

Civil liberties

A second objection to situational crime prevention lies in the domain of civil liberties. Clark (1982: 227) anticipated this issue in stating that '[a] certain level of crime may be the inevitable consequence of practices and institutions we cherish or find convenient and the costs of reducing crime below this level may be unacceptable'. Thus, at one level we may have aesthetic objections to living in an environment in which car alarms provide an incessant background, our neighbours' burglar alarm wakes us at night, we have a myriad of PIN numbers and passwords to remember, and in some public places we are endlessly reminded not to leave our bags unattended. These intrusive features of our environment may or may not be tiresome but they do not have the sinister aspect sometimes associated with surveillance.

Surveillance is the systematic investigation or monitoring of an individual or individuals, including their movements, who they meet, and their communications by letter, telephone, or email. The purpose of the surveillance, which may be in some cases be undertaken legally, is usually to gather information about the individuals concerned, their activities, and their friends and associates. On some occasions, such as political rallies or demonstrations, there may be *mass surveillance* of groups of people for the purpose of intelligence gathering and identifying people who belong to certain groups or organisations of interest to those undertaking the surveillance. The surveillance may be covert so those being observed are unaware they are being monitored, or overt so that it is plain to all exactly what is happening.

The practice of surveillance may take several forms, each heavily reliant on advances in technology to improve their range and effectiveness. Thus, *physical and communications surveillance* relies on observing and listening and can be technologically enhanced by the use of image-amplification instruments such as infrared binoculars, light and sound amplifiers, satellite cameras, image and sound-recording cameras, audio bugs and telephone taps, email interception, recording patterns of internet usage, and so on. This direct surveillance may be added to by gathering information from other people such as local neighbours or employers and workmates.

It is clear that a great deal of information about an individual can be collected relatively quickly. This collection and collation of information, sometimes called *personal data systems*, itself becomes an important source of information. Thus, *data surveillance* is the systematic use of such personal data systems to examine the behaviour and communications of an individual or a group. There are several advantages to this form of surveillance, as the data are already gathered so there are fewer costs involved and as it is in electronic form even very large searches can be carried out automatically.

Do we really want to live, as Lyon (1994) puts it, in a surveillance society with all the Orwellian overtones that phase commands? One counterargument is that if you are not doing anything wrong then you have no reason to be concerned about surveillance. On the other hand, we value our privacy both individually and as socially: we take it to be our right in a democratic country, with respect to the law and socially accepted values, to behave and to associate with others as we wish without the omnipresent threat of observation. There are no easy answers to this issue: there will be those who press for greater surveillance and those who resist what is seen as an intrusion into our lives.

The importance of evidence

In the closing section to this book, I want briefly to look at evidence and why it is critically important in advancing practice.

The phrase 'evidence-based policy' is one that is much used in discussions of the development of measures intended to reduce crime. It is doubtful that many would argue against the formulation and evaluation of policy and implementation of practice on grounds other than on the basis of supportive evidence (although there are numerous examples to be found, such as the *short, sharp shock* prison regime for young offenders, in the literature). However, as Mair (2005) discusses, what exactly is meant by 'evidence-based' is an interesting point. The term *evidence* is one that we perhaps associate with scientific evidence but this does not have to be the case and evidence comes in many forms. There is 'common sense' evidence that, of course, is what we all agree and know to be true; there is evidence that is based on personal experience; there is evidence in the daily newspaper of what people think should happen to criminals; there are surveys and internet-based straw polls; there are public documents and briefing notes written by lobby groups, professional groups, and political groups; and there are 'evidence-free' advocates of their own view of the world and its remedies.

The first point to make is that the way the evidence is gathered will be related to the question being asked. If you wish to know whether people in England and Wales support the return of capital punishment then a large scale survey, even a referendum, is required. If you want to know whether a crime prevention programme has reduced crime in a given area then some type of experimental design is called for. If we concentrate on experimental evaluation, which is what psychologists are trained to undertake, then we know that not all designs are of equal utility. There is a scale, called the Maryland Scale, which gauges the strength of a range of research designs used in criminological research, from simple correlations, through quasi-experimental designs, to fully randomised designs, in terms of their internal validity (Farrington, Gottfredson, Sherman, & Welsh, 2002). It is important to appreciate the value of the type of experimental design used in any research, although other considerations such as external validity must also be taken into account when looking at the evidence (see Hollin, 2011).

The second, related, point is that the debate about the strength of the evidence is not merely a pastime for academics. If the amount of crime in society and the associated damage is to be reduced, with all the attendant savings in human and financial costs, then it is a necessity, not a luxury, that the strangest possible evidence is gathered to inform understanding of what is and what is not effective.

Chapter summary

- There are two broad strategies which can be applied to prevent crime: (1) the use of social controls (including legal sanctions); (2) changing some aspect of the situation in which the crime takes place.
- The use of social sanctions is seen, for example, in laws restricting the sale and possession of certain types of drug. Social regulation is evident in film classification and censorship and restrictions on what may be shown on television: these restrictions invariably centre on sexual and violent material.
- Situational crime prevention relies on making it harder for the criminal to access targets and on increasing the likelihood of detection when committing a crime.
- There is a concern that situational crime prevention can lead to displacement such that rather than stopping crimes, the criminal acts shift to more vulnerable targets or to different geographical locations.
- Some aspects of situational crime prevention have raised concerns about infringement of our civil liberties: the term 'surveillance society' has been used to describe our world, which bristles with security cameras, speed cameras, CCTV, and so on.

Points for discussion

- Will tighter controls over the availability of pornography reduce the numbers of sexual crimes?

- Is there a point at which we say 'enough is enough' with regard to public surveillance or should it be the more the better?
- If we had a complete theoretical understanding of crime, what types of crime prevention measure might evolve from that understanding?

Essential reading

Diamond, M. (2009). Pornography, public acceptance and sex related crime: A review. *International Journal of Law and Psychiatry, 32*, 304–314.
An excellent overview of the issues surrounding pornography:

Ferguson, C. J. & Hartley, R. D. (2009). The pleasure is momentary ... the expense damnable? The influence of pornography on rape and sexual assault. *Aggression and Violent Behavior, 14*, 323–329.
This paper takes a critical view of the research 'proving' a link between media violence and criminal behaviour.

Hayward, K. (2007). Situational crime prevention and its discontents: Rational choice theory versus the 'culture of now'. *Social Policy and Administration, 41*, 232–250.
A considered view of the disquiet associated with situational crime prevention is to be found in this paper.

Useful websites

The British Board of Film Classification (BBFC) is the independent regulator of media content. The ratings you see before a film, DVD or computer game (U, PG, 12, etc.) are decided by the BBFC and are intended protect us, particularly children, from content which may be harmful. The BBFC website gives information into how decisions are made that determine who is legally allowed to see certain types of material, www.bbfc.co.uk.

The open-access journal *Surveillance and Society* makes available a wealth of material, www.surveillance-and-society.org.

Neighbourhood Watch signs are to be found in many cities, towns, and villages. The Neighbourhood Watch website provides a lot of information about just how they operate, www.ourwatch.org.uk.

I found this final website just by browsing: Roger Clarke is a consultant specialist in data surveillance and privacy working in Australia. The website gives an insight into the real world of surveillance with lots of links to other sites, www.rogerclarke.com.

References

Adachi, P. J. C. & Willoughby, T. (2011). The effect of violent video games on aggression: Is it more than just the violence? *Aggression and Violent Behavior, 16*, 55–62.

Amstadter, A. B., Elwood, L. S., Begle, A. M., Gudmundsdottir, B, Smith, D. W., Resnick, H. S., Hanson, R. F., Saunders, B. E., & Kilpatrick, D. G. (2011). Predictors of physical assault victimization: Findings from the National Survey of Adolescents. *Addictive Behaviors, 36*, 814–820.

Anderson, C. A., Berkowitz, L., Donnerstein, E., Huesmann, L. R., Johnson, J. D., & Wartella, E. (2003). The influence of media violence on youth. *Psychological Science in the Public Interest, 4*, 81–110.

Anderson, C. A., Shibuya, A., Ihori, N., Swing, E. L., Bushman, B. J., & Saleem, M. (2010). Violent video game effects on aggression, empathy, and prosocial behavior in eastern and western countries: A meta-analytic review. *Psychological Bulletin, 136*, 151–173.

Barnes, J. C., Kurlychek, M. C., Miller, H. V., Miller, J. M., & Kaminski, R. J. (2010). A partial assessment of South Carolina's Project Safe Neighborhoods strategy: Evidence from a sample of supervised offenders. *Journal of Criminal Justice, 38*, 383–389.

Barrett, E. L., Mills, K. L., & Teesson, M. (2011). Hurt people who hurt people: Violence amongst individuals with comorbid substance use disorder and post traumatic stress disorder. *Addictive Behaviors, 36*, 721–728.

Beauregard, E., Lussier, P. & Proulx (2004). An exploration of developmental factors related to deviant sexual references among adult rapists. *Sexual Abuse: A Journal of Research and Treatment, 16*, 151–161.

Bennett, T. & Holloway, K. (2009). The causal connection between drug misuse and crime. *British Journal of Criminology, 49*, 513–531.

Bennett, T., Holloway, K., & Farrington, D. P. (2006). Does neighbourhood watch reduce crime? A systematic review and meta-analysis. *Journal of Experimental Criminology, 2*, 437–458.

—— (2008). The statistical association between drug misuse and crime: A meta-analysis. *Aggression and Violent Behavior, 13*, 107–118.

Bhati, A. S. & Roman, J. K. (2010). Simulated evidence on the prospects of treating more drug-involved offenders. *Journal of Experimental Criminology, 6*, 1–33.

Blanchette, K. & Brown, S. L. (2006). *The Assessment and Treatment of Women Offenders: An Integrative Perspective.* Chichester, Sussex: John Wiley & Sons.

Boles, S. M. & Miotto, K. (2003). Substance abuse and violence: A review of the literature. *Aggression and Violent Behavior, 8*, 155–174.

Bruce, R. & Hollin, C. R. (2009). Developing citizenship. *EuroVista: Probation and Community Justice, 1*, 24–31.

Burrows, J. (1980). Closed circuit television and crime on the London Underground. In R. V. G. Clarke & P. Mayhew (Eds.), *Designing out Crime* (pp. 75–83). London: HM50.

Canter, D. & Almond, L. (2002). *The Burning Issue: Research and Strategies for Reducing Arson.* London: Arson Control Forum, Office of the Deputy Prime Minister.

Charbol, H., Rodgers, R. F., Sobolewski, G., & van Leeuwen, N. (2010). Cannabis use and delinquent behaviors in a non-clinical sample of adolescents. *Addictive Behaviors, 35*, 263–265.

Christensen, W. (2007/8). The prevention of bushfire arson through target hardening. *Flinders Journal of Law Reform, 10*, 693–713.

Clark, R. V. G. (1982). Crime prevention through environmental management and design. In J. Gunn & D. P. Farrington (Eds.), *Abnormal Offenders, Delinquency, and the Criminal Justice System* (pp. 213–230). Chichester, Sussex: John Wiley & Sons.

—— (2008). *Improving Street Lighting to Reduce Crime in Residential Areas.* Problem-Oriented Guides for Police, Response Guides Series, Guide No. 8. The Office of Community Oriented Policing Services, Washington, DC, US Department of Justice.

Coid, J., Ullrich, S., Zhang, T., Sizmur, S., Roberts, C., Farrington, D. P., & Rogers, R. D. (2009). Gender differences in structured risk assessment: Comparing the accuracy of five instruments. *Journal of Consulting and Clinical Psychology, 77*, 337–348.

Cornish, D. B. & Clarke, R. V. G. (Eds.) (1986). *The Reasoning Criminal: Rational Choice Perspectives on Offending.* New York, NY: Springer-Verlag.

Cramer, E., McFarlane, J., Parker, B., Soeken, K., Silva, C., & Reel, S. (1998). Violent pornography and abuse of women: Theory to practice. *Violence and Victims, 13*, 319–332.

Cuevasa, C. A., Finkelhor, D., Clifford, C., Ormrod, R. K., & Turner, H. A. (2010). Psychological distress as a risk factor for re-victimization in children. *Child Abuse & Neglect, 34*, 235–243.

Das, E., Bushman, B. J., Bezemer, M. D., Kerkhof, P., & Vermeulen, I. E. (2009). How terrorism news reports increase prejudice against outgroups: A terror management account. *Journal of Experimental Social Psychology, 45*, 453–459.

Deadman, D. & MacDonald, Z. (2004). Offenders as victims of crime? An investigation into the relationship between criminal behaviour and victimization. *Journal of the Royal Statistical Society, Series A, 167*, 53–67.

Department for Transport (2008). *Road Casualties Great Britain: 2007. Annual Report.* London: Department for Transport.

Diamond, M. (2009). Pornography, public acceptance and sex related crime: A review. *International Journal of Law and Psychiatry, 32*, 304–314.

Donnerstein, E. & Berkowitz, L. (1981). Victim reactions in aggressive erotic films as a factor in violence against women. *Journal of Personality and Social Psychology, 41*, 710–724.

Draucker, C. & Martsolf, D. (2010). Life-course typology of adults who experienced sexual violence. *Journal of Interpersonal Violence, 25*, 1155–1182.

Endrass, J., Urbaniok, F., Hammermeister, L. C., Benz, C., Elbert, T., Laubacher, A., & Rossegger, A. (2009). The consumption of internet child pornography and violent and sex offending. *BMC Psychiatry, 9*, 43.

Evans, C., Ehlers, A., Mezey, G., & Clark, D. M. (2007). Intrusive memories in perpetrators of violent crime: Emotions and cognitions. *Journal of Consulting and Clinical Psychology, 75*, 134–144.

Falshaw, L., Browne, K. D., & Hollin, C. R. (1996). Victim to offender: A review. *Aggression and Violent Behavior, 1*, 389–404.

Farrell, G. (1995). Preventing repeat victimisation. In M. Tonry & D. P. Farrington (Eds.), *Building a Safer Society: Strategic Approaches to Crime Prevention* (pp. 469–534). Chicago, IL: University of Chicago Press.

Farrell, G. & Pease, K. (1993). *Once Bitten, Twice Bitten: Repeat Victimisation and its Implications for Crime Prevention*. Police Research Group Crime Prevention Unit Series Paper No. 46. London: Home Office.

Farrington, D. P. (1986). Age and crime. *Crime and Justice, 7*, 189–250.

Farrington, D. P., Gottfredson, D. C., Sherman, L. W., & Welsh, B. C. (2002). The Maryland Scientific Methods Scale. In L. W. Sherman, D. P. Farrington, B. C. Welsh, & D. L. MacKenzie (Eds.), *Evidence-Based Crime Prevention* (pp. 13–21). London: Routledge.

Farrington, D. P., Jolliffe, D., Hawkins, J. D., Catalano, R. F., Hill, K. G., & Kosterman, R. (2010). Why are boys more likely to be referred to juvenile court? Gender differences in official and self-reported delinquency. *Victims and Offenders, 5*, 25–44.

Farrington, D. P. & Welsh, B. C. (2007). *Improved Street Lighting and Crime Prevention: A Systematic Review*. Stockholm: National Council for Crime Prevention.

Ferguson, C. J. (2010). Blazing angels or resident evil? Can violent video games be a force for good? *Review of General Psychology, 14*, 68–81.

Ferguson, C. J., Cruz, A. M., Martinez, D., Rueda, S, M., & Ferguson, D. E. (2010). Violence and sex as advertising strategies in television commercials. *European Psychologist, 15*, 304–311.

Ferguson, C. J. & Hartley, R. D. (2009). The pleasure is momentary … the expense damnable? The influence of pornography on rape and sexual assault. *Aggression and Violent Behavior, 14*, 323–329.

Ferguson, C. J. & Kilburn, J. (2009). The public health risks of media violence: A meta-analytic review. *Journal of Pediatrics, 154*, 759–763.

—— (2010). Much ado about nothing: The misestimation and overinterpretation of violent video game effects in Eastern and Western nations: comment on Anderson et al. (2010). *Psychological Bulletin, 136*, 174–178.

Feshbach, S. & Tangney, J. (2008). Television viewing and aggression: Some alternative perspectives. *Perspectives on Psychological Science, 3*, 387–389.

Finkelhor, D., Turner, H., Ormrod, R., & Hamby, S. L. (2009). Violence, abuse and crime exposure in a national sample of children and youth. *Pediatrics, 124*, 1411–1423.

Forrester, M., Chatterton, M., Pease, K., & Brown, R. (1990). *The Kirkholt Burglary Prevention Project, Rochdale*. Crime Prevention Unit Paper 13. London: Home Office.

Forrester, M., Frenz, S., O'Connell, M., & Pease, K. (1990). *The Kirkholt Burglary Prevention Project: Phase II*. Crime Prevention Unit Paper 23. London: Home Office.

Frasca, G. (2003). Sim Sin City: Some thoughts about Grand Theft Auto 3. *Game Studies: The International Journal of Computer Game Research, 3*, retrieved May 2012 from www.gamestudies.org.

Goff, A., Rose, E., Rose, S., & Purves, D. (2007). Does PTSD occur in sentenced prison populations? A systematic literature review. *Criminal Behaviour and Mental Health, 17*, 152–162.

Greer, C. & Reiner, R. (2012). Mediated mayhem: Media, crime, criminal justice. In M. Maguire, R. Morgan, & R. Reiner (Eds.), *The Oxford Handbook of Criminology* (pp. 245–278). Oxford: Oxford University Press.

Greitemeyer, T., Osswald, S., & Brauer, M. (2010). Playing prosocial video games increases empathy and decreases schadenfreude. *Emotion, 10*, 796–802.

Guerette, R. T. & Bowers, K. J. (2009). Assessing the extent of crime displacement and diffusion of benefits: A review of situational crime prevention evaluations. *Criminology, 47*, 1331–1368.

Hayward, K. (2007). Situational crime prevention and its discontents: rational choice theory versus the "culture of now". *Social Policy and Administration, 41*, 232–250.

Hebenton, B. (2011). From offender to situation: The "cold" approach to sexual violence prevention? *International Journal of Law and Psychiatry, 34*, 141–148.

Hedderman, C., Gunby, C., & Shelton, N. (2011). What women want: The importance of qualitative approaches in evaluating work with women offenders. *Criminology and Criminal Justice, 11*, 3–19.

Hedderman C., Palmer E., & Hollin, C. (2008). *Implementing Services for Women Offenders and Those 'At Risk' of Offending: Action Research with Together Women*. Ministry of Justice Research Series 12/08. London: Ministry of Justice.

Heide, K. M. & Solomon, E. P. (2006). Biology, childhood trauma, and murder: Rethinking justice. *International Journal of Law and Psychiatry, 29*, 220–233.

Heidensohn, F. (1996). *Women and Crime*. Basingstoke, Hants: Macmillan.

Hollin, C. R. (2011). Strengths and weaknesses of randomised control trials. In K. Sheldon, J. Davies, & K. Howells (Eds.), *Research in Practice for Forensic Professionals* (pp. 235–248). Cullompton, Devon: Willan Publishing.

Hollin, C. R. & Palmer, E. J. (2006). Criminogenic need and women offenders: A critique of the literature. *Legal and Criminological Psychology, 11*, 179–195.

Holtfreter, K., Reisig, M. D., & Morash, M. (2004). Poverty, state capital, and recidivism among women offenders. *Criminology and Public Policy, 3*, 185–208.

Huesmann, L. R. (2007). The impact of electronic media violence: Scientific theory and research. *Journal of Adolescent Health, 41*, S6–S13.

—— (2010). Nailing the coffin shut on doubts that violent video games stimulate aggression: Comment on Anderson et al. (2010). *Psychological Bulletin, 136*, 179–181.

Hunter, G., Hearnden, I., & Gyateng, T. (2009). *Statistics on Women and the Criminal Justice System. A Ministry of Justice Publication under Section 95 of the Criminal Justice Act 1991*. London: Ministry of Justice.

Itzin, C., Taket, A., & Kelly, L. (2007). *The Evidence of Harm to Adults Relating to Exposure to Extreme Pornographic Material: A Rapid Evidence Assessment (REA)*. Ministry of Justice Research Series 11/07. London: Ministry of Justice.

Javdani, S., Sadeh, N., & Verona, E. (in press). Expanding our lens: Female pathways to antisocial behavior in adolescence and adulthood. Clinical Psychology Review, doi: 10.1016/j. cpr.2011.09.002.

Jennings, W. G., Piquero, A. R., & Reingle, J. M. (2012). On the overlap between victimization and offending: A review of the literature. *Aggression and Violent Behavior, 17*, 16–26.

Jolliffe, D., Hedderman, C., Palmer, E., & Hollin, C. (2011). *Re-offending Analysis of Women Offenders Referred to Together Women (TW) and the Scope to Divert from Custody*. Ministry of Justice Research Series 11/11. London: Ministry of Justice.

Kenney, D. J. (1986). Crime on the subways: Measuring the effectiveness of the Guardian Angels. *Justice Quarterly, 3*, 481–496.

Kingston, D. A., Fedoroff, P., Firestone, P., Curry, S., & Bradford, J. M. (2008). Pornography use and sexual aggression: The impact of frequency and type of pornography use on recidivism among sexual offenders. *Aggressive Behavior, 34*, 341–351.

Krämer, P. (2011). Movies that make people sick: Audience responses to Stanley Kubrick's *A Clockwork Orange* in 1971/72. *Participations: Journal of Audience and Reception Studies, 8,* 416–430.

Kunich, J. C. (2000). Natural born copycat killers and the law of shock torts. *Washington University Law Quarterly, 78,* 1157–1270.

LaLiberte, T., Bills, J., Shin, N., & Edleson, J. L. (2010). Child welfare professionals' responses to domestic violence exposure among children. *Children and Youth Services Review, 32,* 1640–1647.

Laycock, G. (2001). Hypothesis-based research: The repeat victimization story. *Criminology and Criminal Justice, 1,* 59–82.

Lyon, D. (1994). *The Electronic Eye: The Rise of the Surveillance Society.* Minneapolis, MN: University of Minnesota Press.

Mair, G. (2005). Electronic monitoring in England and Wales: Evidence-based or not? *Criminal Justice, 5,* 257–277.

Malamuth, N. M. & Check, J. V. P. (1981). The effects of mass media exposure on acceptance of violence against women: A field experiment. *Journal of Research in Personality, 15,* 436–446.

Mancini, C., Reckdenwald, A., & Beauregard, E. (2012). Pornographic exposure over the life course and the severity of sexual offenses: Imitation and cathartic effects. *Journal of Criminal Justice, 40,* 21–30.

Mandelli, L., Carli, V., Roy, A., Serretti, A., & Sarchiapone, M. (2011). The influence of childhood trauma on the onset and repetition of suicidal behavior: An investigation in a high risk sample of male prisoners. *Journal of Psychiatric Research, 45,* 742–747.

Marchant, P. (2010). What is the contribution of street lighting to keeping us safe? An investigation into a policy. *Radical Statistics, 102,* 32–42.

Markey, P. M. & Markey, C. N. (2010). Vulnerability to violent video games: A review and integration of personality research. *Review of General Psychology, 14,* 82–91.

Maschi, T., Bradley, C. A., & Morgen, K. (2008). Unraveling the link between trauma and delinquency: The mediating role of negative affect and delinquent peer exposure. *Youth Violence and Juvenile Justice, 6,* 136–157.

Mayhew, P., Clarke, R. V. G., & Hough, J. M. (1980). Steering column locks and car theft. In R. V. G. Clarke & P. Mayhew (Eds.), *Designing Out Crime* (pp. 19–38). London: HMSO.

McGrath, S. A., Nilsen, A. A., & Kerley, K. R. (2011). Sexual victimization in childhood and the propensity for juvenile delinquency and adult criminal behavior: A systematic review. *Aggression and Violent Behavior, 16,* 485–492.

Ministry of Justice (2008). *Motoring Offences and Breath Test Statistics England and Wales 2006.* London: Ministry of Justice.

Newman, O. (1972). *Defensible Space: Crime Prevention Through Urban Design.* New York, NY: Macmillan.

Odgers, C. L., Caspi, A., Nagin, D. S., Piquero, A. R., Slutske, W. S., & Moffitt, T. E. (2008). Is it important to prevent early exposure to drugs and alcohol among adolescents? *Psychological Science, 19,* 1037–1044.

Paik, H. & Comstock, G. (1994). The effects of television violence on antisocial behavior: A meta-analysis. *Communication Research, 21,* 516–546.

Palmer, E. J., Hatcher, R. M., McGuire, J., Bilby, C. A. L., & Hollin, C. R. (2012). The effect on reconviction of an intervention for drink-driving offenders in the community. *International Journal of Offender Therapy and Comparative Criminology, 56,* 525–538.

Palmer, E. J. & Hollin, C. R. (2007). The Level of Service Inventory-Revised with English women prisoners: A needs and reconviction analysis. *Criminal Justice and Behavior, 34,* 971–984.

Pearson, D. A. S., McDougall, C., Kanaan, M., Bowles, R. A., & Torgerson, D. J. (2011). Reducing criminal recidivism: Evaluation of citizenship, an evidence-based probation supervision process. *Journal of Experimental Criminology, 7,* 73–102.

Pearlman, L. A. & Saakvitne, K. W. (1995). *Trauma and the Therapist.* New York, NY: Norton.

Pease, K. (1998). *Repeat Victimisation: Taking Stock.* Crime Detection and Prevention Series, Paper 90. London: Home Office.

Phillips, S. D. & Zhao, J. (2010). The relationship between witnessing arrests and elevated symptoms of posttraumatic stress: Findings from a national study of children involved in the child welfare system. *Children and Youth Services Review, 32*, 1246–1254.

Reisig, M. D., Holtfreter, K., & Morash, M. (2006). Assessing recidivism risk across female pathways to crime. *Justice Quarterly, 23*, 384–405.

Renner, L. M. (2012). Intrafamilial physical victimization and externalizing behavior problems: Who remain the "forgotten" children? *Aggression and Violent Behavior, 17*, 158–170.

Rennison, C. M. (2009). A new look at the gender gap in offending. *Women & Criminal Justice, 19*, 171–190.

Reppetto, T. A. (1976). Crime prevention and the displacement phenomenon. *Crime & Delinquency, 22*, 166–177.

Rettinger, L. J. & Andrews, D. A. (2010). General risk and need, gender specificity, and the recidivism of female offenders. *Criminal Justice and Behavior, 37*, 29–46.

Salisbury, E. J. & Van Voorhis, P. (2009). Gendered pathways: A quantitative investigation of women probationers' paths to incarceration. *Criminal Justice and Behavior, 36*, 541–566.

Sampson, A. & Farrell, G. (1990). *Victim Support and Crime Prevention in an Inner-City Setting.* Crime Prevention Unit Paper 21. London: Home Office.

Savage, J. & Yancey, C. (2008). The effects of media violence exposure on criminal aggression: A meta-analysis. *Criminal Justice and Behavior, 35*, 772–791.

Shaw, M. & Pease, K. (2000). *Research on Repeat Victimisation in Scotland: Final Report.* Edinburgh: The Scottish Executive Central Research Unit.

Sherman, L. W. (2001). Reducing gun violence: What works, what doesn't, what's promising. *Criminology and Criminal Justice, 1*, 11–25.

Stein, L. A. R., Colby, S. M., Barnett, N. P., Monti, P. M., Golembeske, C., & Lebeau-Craven, R. (2006). Effects of motivational interviewing for incarcerated adolescents on driving under the influence after release. *American Journal on Addictions, 15*, 50–57.

Stewart, A., Livingston, M., & Dennison, S. (2008). Transitions and turning points: Examining the links between child maltreatment and juvenile offending. *Child Abuse & Neglect, 32*, 51–66.

Taylor, J. E. & Harvey, S. T. (2010). A meta-analysis of the effects of psychotherapy with adults sexually abused in childhood. *Clinical Psychology Review, 30*, 749–767.

Time, V. & Payne, B. K. (2008). School violence prevention measures: School officials' attitudes about various strategies. *Journal of Criminal Justice, 36*, 301–306.

Trask, E. V., Walsh, K., & DiLillo, D. (2011). Treatment effects for common outcomes of child sexual abuse: A current meta-analysis. *Aggression and Violent Behavior, 16*, 6–19.

Trend, D. (2007). *The Myth of Media Violence: A Critical Introduction.* Oxford: Blackwell.

Tripodi, S. J. & Bender, K. (2011). Substance abuse treatment for juvenile offenders: A review of quasi-experimental and experimental research. *Journal of Criminal Justice, 39*, 246–252.

Tripodi, S. J., Kim, J. S., & Bender, K. (2010). Is employment associated with reduced recidivism? The complex relationship between employment and crime. *International Journal of Offender Therapy and Comparative Criminology, 54*, 706–720.

United Nations Office on Drugs and Crime (2009). *Annual Report 2009.* Vienna: United Nations Office on Drugs and Crime.

Van Voorhis, P., Wright, E. M., Salisbury, E., & Bauman, A. (2010). Women's risk factors and their contributions to existing risk/needs assessment: The current status of a gender-responsive supplement. *Criminal Justice and Behavior, 37*, 261–288.

van Mastrigt, S. B. & Farrington, D. P. (2009). Co-offending, age, gender and crime type: Implications for criminal justice policy. *British Journal of Criminology, 49*, 552–573.

Washington State (no date). *Fire-setting and Arson: Education and Prevention. Staff Training Manual.* Department of Social and Health Service, Washington State.

Welfare, H. & Hollin, C. R. (2012). Involvement in extreme violence and violence-related trauma: A review with relevance to young people in custody. *Legal and Criminological Psychology, 12*, 89–104.

Wells, W., Ren, L., & DeLeon-Granados, W. (2010). Reducing intimate partner homicides: The effects of federally-funded shelter service availability in California. *Journal of Criminal Justice, 38*, 512–519.

Welsh, B. P. & Farrington, D. P. (2008). *Effects of improved street lighting on crime. Campbell Systematic Reviews, 13.*

—— (2009). Public area CCTV and crime prevention: An updated systematic review and meta-analysis. *Justice Quarterly, 26*, 716–745.

Welsh, B. C., Farrington, D. P., & O'Dell, S. J. (2010). *Effectiveness of Public Area Surveillance for Crime Prevention: Security Guards, Place Managers and Defensible Space.* Stockholm: Swedish National Council for Crime Prevention.

Widom, C. S. (1989). Child abuse, neglect, and violent criminal behavior. *Criminology, 27*, 251–272.

Zahn, M. A., Day, J. C., Mihalic, S. F., & Tichavsky, L. (2009). Determining what works for girls in the juvenile justice system: A summary of evaluation evidence. *Crime & Delinquency, 55*, 266–293.

Zhong, C., Bohns, V. K., & Gino, F. (2010). Good lamps are the best police: Darkness increases dishonesty and self-interested behavior. *Psychological Science, 21*, 311–314.

Glossary

Actus Reus: In *common law, actus reus* is the 'guilty act' that together with *mens rea* must be proved beyond reasonable doubt to create criminal liability.

Adolescent-Limited Offenders: Those young people for whom, in contrast to **life-course persistent offenders**, offending begins and ends during childhood and adolescence (generally taken to be 8–17 years of age).

Adoption Study: A research design used in studies concerned with hereditary and environment: the basis of the design is that adoption involves two sets of parents, biological, and environmental, that in varying degrees may account for the behaviour.

Behaviourism: A philosophical position within psychology, often associated with learning theory, which holds that everything an organism does, be it an action, thought, or feeling, is a behaviour that is acquired and maintained through patterns of environmental reinforcement.

Boot Camp: A type of penal regime for young offenders, originating in the USA, typically characterised by a harsh military style environment that is intended to shock the offender and so reduce the likelihood of their further offending.

Capital Punishment: Also known as the death penalty, this punishment takes place in those jurisdictions where the legislation allows the state to execute a convicted criminal. The term is derived from *capitalis*, a Latin reference to 'the head', indicating execution by beheading.

Common Law: Common law, also known as case law or precedent, is a system of law which is developed by judges through court decisions to ensure that similar cases are treated in a similar on different occasions.

Constitutional Theory: This theory which posits a relationship between body build and personality and hence behaviour. The technique of somatotyping allows the individual's body build to be classified as either one of (or a mixture of) three basic types: *endomorphs* are sociable, *ectomorphs* are introverted, and *mesomorphs* are aggressive and most likely to be found in criminal populations.

Corporal Punishment: Corporal punishment is the deliberate and lawful infliction of pain by a person in a position of authority on a subordinate. It is usually justified in terms of retribution for an offence or as a means of teaching discipline.

Cost-Benefit Analysis: In financial terms, a comparison of the ratio of cost to output for two interventions intended to achieve the same benefit: for example, the ratio of cost to reduced reoffending for prison compared to probation.

Cost Effectiveness: In financial terms, the ratio of cost to outcome for a specific intervention: for example, the cost of probation services for the number of criminals on probation who do not reoffend. Unlike **cost-benefit analysis** there is no comparison with another approach.

Civil Law: This branch of law is concerned with disputes between individuals or organisations and the amount, if any, of compensation to be awarded.

Criminal Law: This branch of law concerns the rules for a given jurisdiction that specify both the conduct that is forbidden because of the harm it brings to citizens and the penalties to be imposed on those who break the rules.

Criminogenic Need: The attributes or circumstances of the individual (e.g., emotional problems, drug use, or homelessness), which are directly associated with their offending and so (unlike a **non-criminogenic need**) constitute a risk factor for their offending).

Criminological Psychology: Specialist area of mainstream psychology concerned with the study of crime and criminal behaviour.

Cross-over Sex Offender: A small group of sex offenders who 'cross-over' between types of sex offences, such as offending against both children and adult women.

Crown Court: Along with the High Court of Justice and the Court of Appeal, the Crown Court of England and Wales forms the Senior Courts of England and Wales. Crown Court is the higher court of first instance in criminal cases: i.e., the initial trial court where an action is brought.

Dark Figure: The term used for the numbers of crimes that are unreported or undiscovered and so do not appear in the official crime statistics.

Deterrence: The use or threat of punishment to deter people from offending.

DSPD: A dangerous and severe personality disorder is said to be, somewhat controversially, the distinguishing feature of a section of the criminal population.

DSM: The *Diagnostic and Statistical Manual of Mental Disorders* is published by the American Psychiatric Association and presents the standard criteria by which to classify mental disorders: the current version is DSM-IV-TR (4th edition, text revision) with DSM-V scheduled to appear in 2013. As with **ICD**, DSM is widely used internationally.

Differential Association Theory: A theory of the acquisition of criminal behaviour that suggests it is through association with others who favour criminal behaviour (including but not restricted to criminals) that the individual learns attitudes conducive to offending.

Differential Reinforcement Theory: A theory that holds it is the individual's learning history, in terms of patterns of reward and punishment, which accounts for the acquisition and maintenance of their criminal behaviour.

Dynamic Risk Factor: A risk factor for offending such as drug use or relationship problems which, unlike a **static risk factor**, is amenable to change.

EEG: Electroencephalography is the recording, through sensors attached to the scalp, of the brain's electrical activity.

Electronic Monitoring: A method of monitoring an offender's whereabouts (also known as **tagging**) through the use of either radio frequencies or global positioning systems (GPS).

Expert Witness: An individual with particular knowledge or skills relevant to a topic being examined by the court and who has been called, by either the prosecution or defence, to testify for the benefit of the court. An expert's testimony may be challenged either by cross-examination or by evidence from another expert.

False Confession: A false confession occurs when an individual says untruthfully that they committed a crime. A false confession may be given voluntarily or it may be coerced during the process of interrogation.

Firesetting: The act of setting illegal fires by young children is often referred to as firesetting, in those over the age of criminal responsibility the offence is one of arson.

Forensic Psychology: According to the *Oxford Dictionary* the word forensic means 'of or used in courts of law', so forensic psychology is the application of psychological knowledge to the courts. (This correct usage has been ignored in some quarters of psychology where the term forensic is used to refer to anything vaguely connected with crime.)

General Deterrence: The effect of sanctions, such as the use of imprisonment, in deterring criminal behaviour across the whole population (as distinct from **special deterrence**).

Genotype: This is the full hereditary information, carried by all living organisms, which is the 'blueprint' for building and maintaining a living creature. The information, found in most cells, is written in genetic code and is associated with the **phenotype**. The genotype is copied at the point of reproduction and so passed from one generation to the next.

Home Office: The Home Office is a department of the UK government with responsibility for immigration, security, and social order. The Home Office oversees the police, the Security Service (MI5). and the UK Border Agency. It was responsible for the Prison Service and Probation Service but in 2007 these were transferred to the newly created **Ministry of Justice**.

Hostile Violence: In contrast to **instrumental violence**, this term is used to describe violence, which may be carried out by an individual in an emotionally aroused state and where the intention is physically to hurt another person. It is also known as angry violence or hot violence.

ICD: As with **DSM**, The International Classification of Diseases (ICD) is a diagnostic system, developed by the World Health Organization (WHO), for the classification of diseases and other health problems, including mental health. ICD-10 came into use in WHO member states from 1994, the 11th revision is underway and is due to be completed in 2015.

Incidence: In contrast to **prevalence**, incidence refers to the number of crimes experienced by, say, an individual or members of a household.

Indictable Offence: This type of offence, as opposed to a **summary offence**, is one where an indictment is issued by the public prosecutor (in England and Wales this may be the Crown Prosecution Service acting on behalf of the Crown) and where the trial takes place in **Crown Court** with a jury determining the verdict and, when guilty, the presiding judge sets the sentence.

Instrumental Violence: This form of violence, unlike **hostile violence**, is premeditated and directed towards achieving an end such as financial gain or revenge. It is sometimes called *cold violence*.

Latent Delinquency: An idea formulated from Freudian theory: it holds that children become socialised as their basic drives are civilised through experience; if the process of socialisation is disturbed the child becomes a 'latent delinquent' and their delinquency will later become explicit through, say, provocation.

Life-course Persistent Offenders: Those offenders who, in contrast to **adolescent-limited offenders**, continue to commit offences after their adolescence.

Legal Psychology: A specialist area of mainstream psychology concerned with the study of law and the legal system.

Longitudinal Study: A research design that involves repeated observations of a group of people, known as a cohort, over long periods of time, typically decades, while monitoring changes in a set of variables. This type of study allows developmental patterns across the life span to emerge and identification of risk factors for different outcomes.

Magistrates' Court: In England and Wales, as in other **common law** jurisdictions, a Magistrates' Court is the lowest level of court. This type of court is presided over by a tribunal composed of three justices of the peace (magistrates) or by a district judge. Magistrates' Courts deal primarily with minor offences, which may be punished with fines up to £5,000 or a 6-month prison sentence.

Mala in se: An act, such as murder, that is universally seen to be wrong *or evil in itself.*

Malum prohibitum: This refers refer to those acts, such as drinking underage, which are deemed to be criminal for the greater good of society.

Mens Rea: In **common law**, *mens rea* is the 'guilty mind' (or intent) which together with *actus reus* must be proved beyond reasonable doubt in order to create criminal liability.

Mental Health Law: As an individual who is insane and commits an offence cannot tried under criminal law as their mental condition precludes *mens rea*. Mental Health Law is the legislation that allows those people diagnosed with a mental disorder and who commit offences to be detained in conditions of varying security for treatment of their disorder.

Meta-analysis: A statistical method used to combine and analyse evidence from individual primary studies on a particular topic in order to search for relationships within the findings. The statistical output of a meta-analysis is an effect size that gives an indication of the strength of any relationships between variables across studies. A meta-analyses may be carried out in conjunction with a **systematic review**.

Ministry of Justice: The Ministry of Justice is a department of the UK government, created in 2007, which holds responsibility for policy and practice in criminal law within the jurisdiction of England and Wales (formerly the duty of the **Home Office**). The Ministry of Justice has responsibility for all suspected offenders from the point of arrest to completion of sentence. Thus, through the **National Offender Management Service**, the Ministry of Justice commissions both prison and probation services and through the **Youth Justice Board** services for young offenders, alongside responsibility for patients detained under the **Mental Health Law**. The Ministry of Justice has various other responsibilities including coroners, criminal injuries compensation, family justice, legal aid, and victim support.

Narrative Review: A review of the literature that summaries current knowledge in a field, usually including the main findings alongside theoretical and methodological issues. This type of review can be expansive as it does not have the exclusionary rigour of a **systematic review**.

Nature-Nurture: The deliberations about the relative effects of heredity and environment on some aspect of functioning such as criminal behaviour.

National Offender Management Service (NOMS): NOMS is an executive agency of the **Ministry of Justice** responsible in England and Wales for commissioning and delivering adult offender management services from the Probation Service and HM Prison Service.

Non-criminogenic Need: As aspect of an offender's function that may be problematic and require attention, such as toothache, but is not a risk factor for offending.

Offending Behaviour Programme: An often manualised intervention, such as Reasoning and Rehabilitation, which is designed to reduce reoffending: it will have a clear structure, prearranged targets for change, and a prescribed method of delivery.

Offender Profiling: A somewhat controversial technique, sometimes called criminal profiling, by which an unknown offender's characteristics are deduced from aspects of the crime scene(s).

Operant Learning: A type of learning in which behaviour is reinforced or punished through its environmental consequences: this type of learning is the basis of **Differential Reinforcement Theory**.

Phenotype: The phenotype, associated with the **genotype**, is the observed properties of an organism, such as its biological form and structure, its development, and its behaviour.

Police Personality: There are two aspects to the notion of a police personality: first that the nature of police work is attractive to certain personality types, second that the police culture engenders a characteristic personality.

Penile Plethysmography (PPG):   PPG, sometimes called phallometry, is the measurement of blood flow to the penis and is used in the assessment of sex offenders.

Prevalence: In contrast to **incidence**, prevalence refers to the proportion of a specified population who were victims of an offence regardless of the number of times in a specified period.

Protective Factors: The factors that appear to protect the child and adolescent from developing criminal behaviour despite the presence of one or more risk factors.

Psychopath: An individual characterised by high levels of anti-social behaviour alongside a charming and manipulative personality.

Pyromania: A rare mental disorder involving deliberately setting fires.

Recidivism: Repeated instances of offending that may remain undetected or be detected and so become recorded crimes, as distinct from **reconviction** and **reoffending**.

Reconviction: Any subsequent court conviction following a first offence.

Recorded Crime: Those crimes that appear in official statistics.

Regulatory Offence: An offence, as associated for example with licensing, pollution, health and safety, and some driving offences, which is created by statute and not **common law**. These offences have a lower threshold for proving culpability as *mens rea* is not required and the aim is to deter potential offenders from dangerous behaviour rather than deliver retribution for moral trespass.

Reoffending: A generic term used to describe any further instances of offending after the initial offence.

Repeat Victimisation: The sequence of events after an initial victimisation through which the victim is at increased risk, diminishing over time, of another attack.

Responsivity: Qualities of an intervention that make it appropriate for use with a particular group of offenders.

Restorative Justice: A fluid approach to tackling crime with an emphasis on the needs of victims and involving offenders and victims, the community, and the statutory agencies.

Retribution: Recompense for wrongs done, one of the aims of sentencing.

Risk of Reoffending: The likelihood, sometimes expressed in numerical terms, of a criminal committing further crimes.

Risk Assessment: The process by which the **risk of reoffending** is estimated.

Risk Needs Responsivity (RNR):   A model informing practice intended to reduce criminal behaviour based on the criminal's level of risk, their **criminogenic needs**, and the style of intervention to which they would be **responsive**.

Sentencing Council: The remit of the Sentencing Council for England and Wales is to make sure that there is a consistent and generally understandable approach to sentencing and to develop sentencing guidelines and monitor their use. It is composed of members of the judiciary and non-judicial members with expert knowledge of the criminal justice system.

Serial Offenders: Those offenders who commit the same crime, usually a serious offence such as arson or murder, over a period of years rather than over a relatively short period as with **spree offenders**.

Sexual Murder: There is not a crime called 'sexual murder' but the term is used to denote those cases in which a sexual motive or sexual behaviour is attached to the killing.

Situational Crime Prevention: An approach to crime reduction that concentrates on the qualities of the environment, such as ease of access to the target or likelihood of detection, rather than the characteristics of the offender.

Social Learning Theory: The theory that emerged from the development of operant learning to include more explicitly internal states, such as thoughts and emotions, and learning through observation as well as by reinforcement.

Special Deterrence: The effect of sanctions, such as the use of imprisonment, in deterring the individual experiencing the sanction from further criminal behaviour (as distinct from **general deterrence**).

Special Hospital: A high security hospital, of which there are four in the UK, for mentally disordered offenders (known as State Hospitals in the USA).

Spree Offenders: This type of offender commits a large number of crimes, usually involving serious violence, over a few hours rather than the protracted time period characteristic of the serial offender. A spree sometimes ends with the offender's death either by suicide or in a confrontation with armed police.

Static Risk Factor: A risk factor for offending such as a history of offending or experience of abuse in childhood which, unlike a **dynamic risk factor**, cannot be changed.

Status Offence: A status offence is one that applies only to certain people, as with age-related offences such as underage drinking or school truancy. In the USA, this term is used in connection with offences such as traffic violations where the driver's motives are not taken into account in determining guilt (in Europe this type of offence may be termed a **regulatory offence**).

Summary Offence: This type of offence, as opposed to a more serious **indictable offence**, is one is heard and decided upon in the Magistrates' Court.

Supermax Prison: Super-maximum security or 'control-unit' prisons (or units within a prison), provide the highest level of custodial security for the prisoners with the highest security risk.

Surveillance Society: This term is used to describe a society characterised by high levels of electronic observation of its citizens, often in the name of **situational crime prevention**.

Systematic Review: Systematic reviews offer an alternative to the traditional **narrative review** in summarising a body of research. A systematic review, often conducted in conjunction with a **meta-analysis**, is based on a peer-reviewed protocol to facilitate replication and seeks to identify and impartially review all the evidence, published and unpublished, that meets the pre-set inclusion criteria.

Tagging: Another term for **electronic monitoring**.

Therapeutic Community (TC): An approach to treatment based on the healing properties of a community environment and which avoids authoritarian psychiatric practices by giving each member responsibility for their own treatment and that of other members of the community. TCs are residential with the clients and therapists sharing the treatment environment (or therapeuitic milieu). They have mainly been used to treat presenting problems such as long-term mental illness, personality disorders, and drug addiction; there are some instances of TCs running within prisons and addressing either or both of drug use and criminal behaviour.

Twin Study: Twin studies, like **adoption studies**, are concerned with the effects of hereditary and environment on behaviour. This type of study is based on a comparison of identical, or monozygotic (MZ), twins with fraternal, or dizygotic (DZ) twins. MZ twin pairs are siblings whose genotypes are duplicates, DZ twins share half their genes with each other. If biology has a greater effect on behaviour than the environment, then it is follows that MZ twins should behave with a higher degree of similarly than DZ twins.

Youth Justice Board (YJB):   The YJB for England and Wales is a non-departmental public body, sponsored by the **Ministry of Justice** with additional funding from the **Home Office** and the Department for Education, with responsibility for the youth justice system for England and Wales which consists of youth offending teams (which work through Local Authorities), staff working within security, and voluntary bodies.

Author index

Subject index